Quantitative Techniques

T. LUCEY M.Soc.Sc., F.C.M.A., F.C.C.A., J.Dip.M.A.

Terry Lucey *has been an accountant and consultant in industry and has had over twenty years examining and teaching experience at all levels of professional studies and for diploma and degree courses in business studies. He was previously Head of Department of Business Studies at the Polytechnic, Wolverhampton and is now a consultant and publisher.*

Amongst his other published works are:
Investment Appraisal: evaluating risk and uncertainty, Accounting and Computer Systems (co-author), Management Information Systems, Costing and Management Accounting.

3rd Edition

DP PUBLICATIONS LTD
Grand Union Industrial Estate – Unit 6
Abbey Road
London NW10 7UL

1988

Acknowledgements

The author would like to express thanks to the following for permission to reproduce past examination questions:

Chartered Association of Certified Accountants (ACCA)
Chartered Institute of Management Accountants (CIMA)
Chartered Institute of Public Finance and Accountancy (CIPFA)
Institute of Chartered Accountants (ICA)

A CIP catalogue record for this book is available from the British Library.

ISBN 0 905435 82 6

First Edition	***1979***
Reprinted	*1980*
Second Edition	***1982***
Reprinted	*1982*
Reprinted	*1983*
Reprinted	*1984*
Reprinted	*1985*
Third Edition	***1988***

Printed by Guernsey Press Company Ltd
Braye Road, Vale,
Guernsey, Channel Islands.

Preface

AIMS OF THE MANUAL

1. This manual is designed to provide a sound understanding of Quantitative Techniques and is particularly relevant for:

a. Students preparing themselves for professional examinations of the following bodies:

   Chartered Association of Certified Accountants
   Chartered Institute of Management Accountants
   Chartered Institute of Public Finance and Accountancy
   Institute of Chartered Accountants
   Institute of Chartered Secretaries and Administrators
   Institute of Data Processing Management

b. Students on B/TEC Higher Level Courses and undergraduates reading Business Studies, Accounting and any course including Quantitative Techniques.

c. Managers and others in industry, commerce, and local authorities who wish to obtain a working knowledge of quantitative techniques to aid them in their own work and to facilitate communication with accountants and operational research specialists.

TEACHING APPROACH

2. The manual has been written in a standardised format with numbered paragraphs, end of chapter summaries, with review questions and examination questions at the end of each chapter. This approach has been tested and found effective by thousands of students and the manual can be used for independent study or in conjunction with tuition at a college.

HOW TO USE THE MANUAL EFFECTIVELY

3. For ease of study the manual is divided into self contained chapters with numbered paragraphs. Each chapter is followed by *self review* questions, cross referenced to appropriate paragraph(s). You should attempt to answer the self review questions *unaided* then check your answer with the text.

In addition each chapter contains a number of test exercises and examination questions *with* suggested solutions. The test exercises are usually shorter and simpler than the examination questions and will be found useful for practice and consolidation. The examination questions have mostly been drawn from past professional examinations and have been selected not merely to repeat the material in the chapters but to extend knowledge and understanding. They should be considered an integral part of the manual. *Always* make some attempt at the question before reading the solution. It will be noted that some chapters have many more examination questions than others. This reflects the weighting given to the particular topic by the various professional bodies in their examinations.

Also at the end of each chapter there are a further selection of test exercises and examination questions, *without answers*. These can be used by lectures for classwork and assignments when the manual is being used as a course text or as extra practice when the manual is used for independent study.

A separate answer guide is available free to lecturers who adopt the manual as a course text. The answer guide contains full answers to all the exercises and examination questions.

SEQUENCE OF STUDY

4. The manual should be studied in the sequence of the chapters. The sequence has been arranged so that there is a progressive accumulation of knowledge and any given chapter either includes all the principles necessary or draws upon a previous chapter(s).

NOTES TO THE 3RD EDITION

The response to previous editions of this manual have been extremely gratifying and I would like to express my appreciation of the constructive feedback from lecturers and students.

Particular features of the 3rd Edition are:

a. Test exercises have been introduced at the end of chapters. There are over 140 exercises, approximately half with answers in the manual.
b. At numerous points in the text there have been revisions and extensions of coverage; examples include; probability, statistics, correlation, regression, confidence limits, multiple correlation, partial differentiation, simulation and sensitivity analysis.
c. Many more questions from recent Professional Examinations have been included. There are now over 200 questions, well over half of which have answers in the manual.
d. Many facets of quantitative techniques are now dealt with by using computers and computer packages. Examples of the use of computers and packages for solving statistical and quantitative problems are given in an Appendix.
e. A separate answer guide is available free to lecturers who adopt the manual as a course text. The guide contains answers to all end of chapter exercises and questions.

T. LUCEY 1988

Contents

1 Introduction to Quantitative Techniques

INTRODUCTION

1. This Chapter serves as an introduction to the whole book. It provides some basic definitions and clarifies some of the terminology used. The stages in an Operational Research study are explained and some of the problems in applying OR techniques are discussed.

DIFFERENCES IN TERMINOLOGY

2. The title used for this book is Quantitative Techniques. However, many other terms are also used for the concepts and techniques described in the book. These include - Management Mathematics - Operational Research or O.R. - Analytical Techniques - Quantitative Analysis - Business Mathematics and Management Science. Regardless of the name used it is important to realise that the same group of techniques are being described and, more importantly, the same approach is employed. This approach is brought out by the following British Standard definition of Operational Research.

OPERATIONAL RESEARCH DEFINITION

3. "The attack of modern science on complex problems arising in the direction and management of large systems of men, machines, materials and money, in industry, business, government and defence. The distinctive approach is to develop a scientific model of the system incorporating measurements of factors such as change and risk, with which to predict and compare the outcome of alternative decisions, strategies or controls. The purpose is to help management determine its policy and action scientifically."

ESSENTIAL FEATURES OF THE O.R. APPROACH

4. The above formal definition contains several essential features and these are:

a. Application of a model-based scientific approach,

b. Systems approach to organisations,

c. The recognition of risk and uncertainty,

d. Assistance to management decision making and control

APPLICATION OF A MODEL-BASED SCIENTIFIC APPROACH

5. The basis of the O.R. approach is that of constructing models of problems in an objective, factual manner and experimenting with these models to show the results of various possible courses of action. A model is any representation of reality and may be in graphical, physical or mathematical terms. The type of model most frequently used in O.R. is a mathematical model, ie one which tries to show the workings of the real world by means of mathematical symbols, equations and formulae. An example of a very simple mathematical model familiar to accountants could be the following equation to estimate the total overheads for a period. Assume that total overheads comprise fixed overheads and variable overheads which are directly related to the units produced, then the equation:-

$$y = a + bx$$

is a model of the relationship of total overheads to the number of units produced where

y = Total overheads

a = Fixed overheads per period

b = Variable overheads per unit (assumed to be constant)

x = Number of units produced

The above model is obviously very simple and most practical models are of necessity much more complex. It is important to realise that however complex looking is the model and however many variables it contains, it still involves considerable simplification of reality and any results or predictions obtained from the model must therefore be used with caution and judgement.

Although mathematical or symbolic models are the more usual, other types of models e.g. Iconic, Analogue, Simulation and Heuristic sometimes have applicability.

Iconic models are visual models of the real object(s) they represent. They may be larger or smaller than reality. For example, a model steam engine is much smaller than the real thing whilst the familiar coloured plastic models of molecular structures are much larger. Both of these are iconic models and so are pictures, maps and diagrams although these latter are in a different form to the reality they represent. These models are often difficult to manipulate experimentally (but not always, e.g. a wind tunnel model for aircraft) so are not used greatly in OR.

Analogue models use one set of physical movements or properties to represent another set. For example, the movement of a piece of metal under stress can be represented in a more observable form by the movement of a gauge finger. Fathom lines on charts and lines on graphs are also analogues of the reality they represent.

Although analogue models are more versatile than iconic models they generally lack the flexibility of mathematical models.

Simulation models represent the behaviour of a real system. Perhaps the best known example is the flight simulator used in the training of Pilots. Simulation models are used where there is no suitable mathematical model, where the mathematical model is too complex, or where it is not possible to experiment upon a working system without causing serious disruption - as in the case of the training of Pilots! One application of simulation models in the management context, is the study of the behaviour of people and objects in queues. Further with the development of relatively inexpensive computing facilities many business games are based on the simulation of the operation of the complete business. This area is dealt with more fully later in the manual.

Heuristic Models are models which use a set of intuitive rules which managers hope will produce at least a workable solution, and hopefully a better solution than that which is currently being practised. For example, a deliver van driver may be instructed to plan the day's deliveries using the following rule "After each call delivery to the nearest customer whom you have not yet visited." This will certainly give a "good" solution early in the day, but it can lead to some long distances being travelled at the end of the day back to the depot. The driver has no way of knowing whether the route gives optimum time and distances, and any improvements can come only through testing other heuristic approaches.

Models may be further classified into **normative and descriptive**. Normative models are concerned with finding the best, optimum or ideal solution to a problem. Many mathematical models fall into this classification. Descriptive models, as their name implies, describe the behaviour of a system without attempting to find the best solution to any problem. For example, simulation tends to fall within this category.

Perhaps the most important point to appreciate is not so much what a model is called, but what it does in helping managers to attain the goals that they have set.

SYSTEMS APPROACH TO ORGANISATION

6. The primary aim of O.R. is to attempt to identify the best way of conducting the affairs of the organisation ie the optimum. In studying problems the O.R. practitioner tries to optimise the operation of the organisation as a whole rather than narrow aspects of the business such as a single department or section. This is easier said than done and because of the practical necessity of dealing with manageable areas of work and thereby producing simplified and incomplete models of operations there may be a tendency to produce sub-optimal solutions, ie a solution which is optimal for a small section of the firm, but not

optimal for the firm as a whole. This is another point which should be watched when considering the results of an O.R. investigation.

RECOGNITION OF RISK AND UNCERTAINTY

7. All business planning and decision making involves forecasting future activities. This cannot be done with any certainty and so to provide the maximum possible assistance to planners and decision makers a systematic analysis of the possible extent of the risks and uncertainties involved is a vital part of any O.R. study. O.R.techniques do not of themselves remove the risks and uncertaintities, but they are able to highlight their effects on the firm's operations. An important method to help with this process is what is termed sensitivity analysis. When a solution has been obtained using one of the OR techniques (such as linear programming, inventory control, investment appraisal) alterations are made to the factors of the problem, such as, sales, costs, amount of materials, to see what effect there is on the original solution. If the value of the original solution alters considerably with minor changes in the factor values it is said to be sensitive. In such circumstances the whole problem will need much deeper analysis and a particularly sensitive outcome solution may cause decisions to be altered.

ASSISTANCE TO MANAGEMENT DECISION-MAKING AND CONTROL

8. In general O.R. practicioners do not make the business decisions. Their role is the provision of information to assist the planners and decision makers. The skill, experience and judgement of managers cannot be replaced by formal decision making techniques. The results of an O.R. investigation are but one input of information into the decision making process. There is a strong parallel between the O.R. practitioner supplying information for management decision making and that of other information specialists such as accountants. This is why a knowledge of O.R. for the accountant (and accountancy for the O.R. practitioner) can be very useful and can improve the quality of the information provided. There are strong reasons why the most effective O.R. teams contain people drawn from various backgrounds - economists, accountants, mathematicians, engineers, psychologists etc. In this way there is more chance that the numerous facets of business problems can be recognised and analysed.

QUANTIFICATION OF FACTORS

9. Not all the factors involved in a decision making or planning situation can be quantified, but the most readily usable O.R. techniques are those based on quantifiable factors such as costs, revenues, number of units etc. These techniques are the ones most commonly included in examinations and form the basis of the syllabuses of the major professional bodies. Hence the contents and title of this book.

STAGES IN O.R. STUDY

10. An O.R. study can be separated into seven steps

a. Problem recognition and definition

b. Model building

c. Data collection

d. Problem solution

e. Interpretation of solution

f. Implementation of final solution

g. Review and maintain

PROBLEM RECOGNITION AND DEFINITION

11. No technique can be applied or analysis undertaken until the problem has been recognised and carefully defined. Vague descriptions of problems are insufficient. What is required is a clear, detailed statement of what the problem really is. This is a difficult stage and thorough investigation is necessary. A superficial study may not identify the real problem. Close and friendly liaison with the people involved in the area will provide the best results.

MODEL BUILDING

12. Having defined the problem, a model must be developed which, hopefully, can be solved by an appropriate technique such as the ones described in this book. Care must be taken not to apply a standard O.R. technique tto a non-standard situation. One must ensure that the model incorporates the essential features of the problem being studied.

DATA COLLECTION

13. Data will be collected at the two previous stages, but to solve the problem much more data will be required. This data will include costs, revenues, production and stock data, etc and will be gained from past records and from estimates of the future. The data required will also include the quantification of factors not always quantified, such as risk and uncertainity.

PROBLEM SOLUTION.

14. For many problems, particularly those encountered in examinations, a solution can usually be obtained by standary mathematical means using a recognised O.R. technique. This does not, unfortunately, apply to all problems encountered in practice which may require the use of advanced mathematical analysis and nonstandard techniques. Even where a solution can be obtained by the use of a basic model, practical problems invariably involve large amounts of data necessitating repreated calculations making the use of computers an economic proposition.

INTERPRETATION OF SOLUTION

15. Although many O.R. techniques produce optimal solutions, it must be realised that the model does not provide a solution to the actual real life problem, but to a simplified version of the problem represented by the model. Accordingly results must be treated with caution and there must be due regard to the problems involved in all O.R. studies which include such factors as:-

i. The appropriateness of the model to the real problem
ii. The accuracy of the data used and assumptions made
iii. The dangers of sub-optimisation

Sub-optimisation is where the objectives of the sub-system (e.g. a department) are pursued to the detriment of the overall organisational goals which must be paramount.

IMPLEMENTATION OF FINAL SOLUTION

16. After careful interpretation of the results of the O.R. study and modification where appropriate, the resulting solution would normally be implemented. Sometimes the solution may not be implemented because, although technically valid, management may consider that its implementation would not be cost effective or that it might cause too much disruption to operations and/or employees, customers, suppliers and the general public.

REVIEW AND MAINTAIN

17. After implementation the performance of the model should be carefully monitored to ensure that it actually does work and fulfills its objectives. The review process should be at regular intervals so that appropriate adjustments can be made to meet minor changes in conditions or to recognise promptly when major changes have occurred, which render the implemented solution inappropriate. This is, of course, a form of audit procedure familiar to accountants.

All organisations are dynamic, open systems where change is endemic. In such circumstances no solution remains optimal for ever and changes in the system or in the environment of the system makes it essential continually to review the models used and the existing solutions to see if adjustments are required.

FOUNDATION MATHEMATICS AND STATISTICS

18. The syllabuses at which this book is aimed assume a basic knowledge of mathematics and statistics which would normally be gained in Foundation Level studies. Accordingly this book does not cover foundation level mathematics and statistics, but because of the step-by-step teaching approach used and the inclusion of some revision material (eg probability concepts) it should be readily comprehensible to all students, including those whose basic mathematics and statistics are a little rusty.

SUMMARY.

19.

a. Numerious names exist for the concepts and techniques covered in this book. More imporant than the name is the common approach adopted.

b. This approach is characterised by a scientific, model based approach to solving problems.

c. Whatever the problem, there are common stages in all O.R. studies. These are problem recognition, Model building, Data Collection, Solution, Interpretation and Implementation.

d. This book covers the full range of Quantitative Techniques normally encountered in professional examinations and assumes a knowledge of foundation level mathematics and statistics.

POINTS TO NOTE.

20.

a. O.R. should not be regarded as a compartmentalised area of study. The basic approach is applicable in virtually any situation, particularly those related to planning, control and decision making.

b. Formal mathematical notation is reduced to the absolute mainimum in this book and formal proofs are not given. This is in line with the philosophy adopted by the major professional bodies for their examinations which concentrate on the application of O.R. techniques in practical situations.

SELF REVIEW QUESTIONS

1. *Define OR in your own words. Compare your definition with the B.S. definition (2)*
2. *What are the essential features of the O.R. approach? (4)*
3. *How does O.R. assist management decision making? (8)*
4. *What are the stages in an O.R. study? (10)*
5. *Give reasons why the results of an O.R. study may not be implemented. (16)*

EXAMINATION QUESTIONS WITH ANSWERS COMMENCING PAGE 488

A1. What do you understand by the 'systems approach' in operational research? A more pragmatic approach, often used by operational researchers to model a complex problem area, is to build a series of smaller models relating to separate parts of the problem. As these submodels are often only loosely connected with each other they are usually solved separately or in a given sequence. How does this approach conflict with the systems approach?

(ACCA, Management Mathematics)

A2. The various quantitative techniques used in Operational Research and elsewhere are often classified as being either deterministic or probabilistic in nature. In reality this is not a useful distinction because, in the final analysis, all management problems involve uncertainty and are, therefore, by definition, probabilistic.

Required:

(a) Discuss the above statement.

(b) In the light of the above statement, explain how a basic cost-volume-profit analysis may be modified to take account of the element of uncertainty.

(ACCA Quantitative Analysis)

A3. 'There are......feelings in many senior managers' minds that some of the much heralded benefits from the new technology are proving to be rather elusive in practice'

J.W. Sellen, Management Accounting, January 1982, p33.

You are required to:

(a) explain how 'quantitative techniques' are expected to contribute to the benefits anticipated;

(b) explain why the anticipated benefits from the use of these techniques may not always be achieved;

(c) describe the procedures which should ensure that they will be achieved in the future.

(CIMA QUANTITATIVE TECHNIQUES)

A4. Should the operational researcher attempt initially to develop an elaborate model which represents the real world as accurately as possible or should he start off with a simpler but more manageable model and gradually attempt to refine it? Give reasons for your answer indicating the benefits and limitations of each approach.

(ACCA, Management Mathematics)

EXAMINATION QUESTIONS WITHOUT ANSWERS

B1. Most operational research applications possess certain distinguishing characteristics. These could be identified as follows:

a. A primary focus on decision making;

b. An investigation based on some measurable criteria;

c. The use of a formal mathematical model;

d. Dependence upon computing facilities.

Required: Explain each of the above characteristics.

(ACCA, Management Mathematics)

B2. . Discuss the methodology of operational research and describe the main stages in carrying out an operational research project.

(CIMA Quantitative Techniques)

B3. a. 'Searching for optimality in a rapidly changing world is like chasing a shadow - the optimum changes as our perception changes.'

b. The Operational Research Society's definition of Operational Research does not mention optimisation yet most Operational Research techniques assume it.

Required: 'Comment on the above statements giving examples where it might not be appropriate to seek an optimal solution, but, instead, to accept a sub-optimal solution.

(ACCA Management Mathematics).

2 Probability and Decision Making

INTRODUCTION

1. The laws of probability form the basis of most statistical theory and probability concepts are used in helping to solve many decision making problems. This chapter briefly reviews the basic rules of probability and shows how appropriate probability concepts can be used in helping to solve business problems. Various decision rules are explained including; expected value, maximin, minimax regret, maximax, and the use of opportunity losses.

PROBABILITY DEFINITION

2. For our purposes probability can be defined as the quantification of uncertainty. Uncertainty may also be expressed as 'likelihood', 'chance' or 'risk'. Probability is represented by p, and can only take values ranging from O, ie impossibility, to 1, ie certainty.

For example, it is impossible to fly to the moon unaided and it is certain that one day we will die. This is expressed as

$$\begin{aligned} \text{p(flying to the moon unaided)} &= 0 \\ \text{and p(Dying)} &= 1 \end{aligned}$$

OBJECTIVE AND SUBJECTIVE PROBABILITY

3. Where the probability of an event is based on past data and the circumstances are repeatable by test, the probability is known as statistical or objective probability. For example, the probability of tossing a coin and a head showing is 50% or $\frac{1}{2}$ or .5. This value can be shown to be correct by repeated trials. In most circumstances objective probabilities are not available in business situations, so that subjective probabilities must be used. These are quantifications of personal judgement, experience and expertise. For example, the Sales Manager considers that there is a 40% chance (ie $p = .4$) of obtaining the order for which the firm has just quoted. Clearly this value cannot be tested by repeated trials. In spite of the undoubted shortcomings of subjective probabilities they are all that is normally available and so they are used to help in the decision making process. It should be emphasised that the use of probabilities does not of itself make the decision. It merely provides more information on which a more informed decision can be taken.

BASIC RULES OF PROBABILITY

4. Whether the probabilities are objective or subjective, once they are established they are used in the same way according to the following rules. These rules are appropriate to statistically independent events, ie the occurrence of one event is completely independent of the occurrence of any other event, eg the outcome of a die throw is completely independent of the outcome of any previous throw.

a. MULTIPLICATION RULE (AND)

This rule is used when there is a string of independent events for which each individual probability is known and it is required to know the overall probability.

Example 1. What is the probability of throwing a 3 AND a 6 with two throws of a die?

$$\begin{aligned} \text{P(throwing a 3)} &= 1/6 \text{ and P(throwing a 6)} = 1/6 \\ \text{P(throwing a 3 } AND \text{ a 6)} &= 1/6 \times 1/6 \\ &= \mathbf{1/36} \end{aligned}$$

NOTE: The probability of 1/36 given above is the probability for throwing a 3 followed by a 6. If the order is unimportant ie if a 3 followed by a 6 or a 6 followed by a 3 is acceptable then the probability is doubled ie

$$\begin{aligned} \text{where P (3 and 6)} &= \text{P(3 followed by 6)} + \text{P (6 followed by 3)} \\ \text{then P(3 and 6)} &= 1/36 + 1/36 = 1/18 \end{aligned}$$

b. ADDITION RULE (OR)

This rule is used to calculate the probability of two or more mutually exclusive events. In such circumstances the probabilities of the separate events must be added.

Example 2. What is the probability of throwing a 3 OR a 6 with a throw of a die?

$$\begin{aligned} P(\text{throwing a 3}) &= 1/6 \text{ and P(throwing a 3)} = 1/6 \\ P(\text{throwing a 3 } OR \text{ a 6}) &= 1/6 + 1/6 = \mathbf{1/3} \end{aligned}$$

c. CONDITIONAL PROBABILITY

This is the probability associated with combinations of events but given that some prior result has already been achieved with one of them.

When the events are independent of one another, then the conditional probability is the same as the probability of the remaining event.

Example 3. The probability of throwing a total of 10 with 2 dice, before the events, is 1/12;

$$\begin{aligned} \text{i.e. } P(5 \textit{ and } 5) &= 1/6 \times 1/6 = 1/36 \\ P(6 \textit{ and } 4) &= 1/6 \times 1/6 = 1/36 \\ P(4 \textit{ and } 6) &= 1/6 \times 1/6 = 1/36 \\ &= 3/36 \\ &= \mathbf{1/12} \end{aligned}$$

but if one die has been thrown and shows a 4 then the conditional probability is the probability of throwing a 6 with the other die, which is a probability of 1/6.

Conditional probability is usually expressed in the form:

$P(x|y)$ which means

Probability of x *given* that y has occurred.

Example 4. From past experience it is known that a machine is set up correctly on 90% of occasions. If the machine is set up correctly then 95% of good parts are expected but if the machine is not set up correctly then the probability of a good part is only 30%.

On a particular day the machine is set up and the first component produced and found to be good. What is probability that the machine is set up correctly?

Solution.

This is displayed in the form of a PROBABILITY TREE or DIAGRAM as follows:

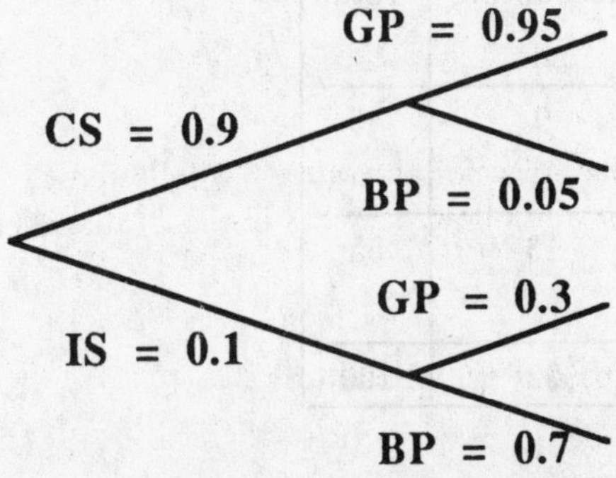

$$\therefore \quad CSGP = 0.9 \times 0.95 = 0.855$$
$$CSBP = 0.9 \times 0.05 = 0.045$$
$$ISGP = 0.1 \times 0.3 = 0.03$$
$$ISBP = 0.1 \times 0.7 = \underline{0.07}$$
$$\underline{\underline{1.00}}$$

CS = Correct set up

IS = Incorrect set up

GP = Good Part

BP = Bad Part

$\therefore$ Probability of getting a good part
$= CSGP + ISGP = 0.855 + 0.03 = 0.885$

$\therefore$ Probability that machine is correctly set up after getting good part is

$$\frac{\text{CSGP}}{\text{CSGP + ISGP}} = \frac{.855}{.885} = 0.966$$

Notes. 1. Good parts may be produced when the machine is correctly set up and also when it is incorrectly set up. In 1000 trials there will be 855 occasions when it is correctly set up and good parts are produced (shown as CSGP above) and 30 occasions when it is incorrectly set up yet good parts are produced (shown as ISGP above). Thus if a good part is produced we can state that there are 855 occasions out of 885 when the good part is from a correctly set up machine.

2. CSGP, CSBP, ISGP, and ISBP may also be written
CS & GP, CS & BP, IS & GP and IS & BP

FURTHER APPLICATIONS OF PROBABILITY

5. The concepts described so far may be conveniently summarised and developed using examples

Example 5.

There are 100 students in a first year college intake. 36 are male and are studying accounting, 9 are male and not studying accounting, 42 are female and studying accounting, 13 are female and are not studying accounting.

Use these data to deduce probabilities concerning a student drawn at random.

Solution

The most effective way to handle these data is to draw up a table

	Accounting A A	Not Accounting $\bar{A}$	Total
MALE M	36	9	45
FEMALE F	42	13	55
TOTAL	78	22	100

1. $P(M) = \frac{45}{100} = 0.45$
2. $P(F) = \frac{55}{100} = 0.55$
3. $P(A) = \frac{78}{100} = 0.78$
4. $P(\bar{A}) = \frac{22}{100} = 0.22$
5. $P(M \text{ and } A) = \frac{36}{100} = 0.36 = P(A \text{ and } M)$

This is so because the same cells in the table are involved.

6. $P(M \text{ and } \bar{A}) = \frac{9}{100} = 0.09$
7. $P(F \text{ and } A) = \frac{42}{100} = 0.42$
8. $P(F \text{ and } \bar{A}) = \frac{13}{100} = 0.13$

The probabilities 1 to 4 may be expressed in terms of probabilities 5 to 8.

9. $P(M) = P(M \text{ and } A) + P(M \text{ and } \bar{A})$
$= 0.36 + 0.09$
$= 0.45$

10. $P(F) = P(F \text{ and } A) + P(F \text{ and } \bar{A})$
$= 0.42 + 0.13$
$= 0.55$

11. $P(A) = P(A \text{ and } M) + P(A \text{ and } F)$
$= 0.36 + 0.42$
$= 0.78$

12. $P(\bar{A}) = P(\bar{A} \text{ and } M) + P(\bar{A} \text{ and } F)$
$= 0.09 + 0.13$
$= 0.22$

Now let the student be a male. This changes the situation because the female section of the table disappears.

Calculate the probability that the student is studying accounting.

P(A) is now no longer appropriate, for the required probability is $P(A|M)$ isthe probability that the student is studying accounting GIVEN he is male.

$$P(A|M) = \frac{36}{45} = 0.80$$
$$= \frac{P(A \text{ and } M)}{P(M)}$$

$$\therefore \quad P(\text{A and M}) = \text{P(M)} \times \text{P(A|M)}$$
$$\therefore \quad P(\text{A and M}) = 0.45 \times 0.80$$
$$= \mathbf{0.36}$$

Now let the student be studying accounting. Calculate the probability that the student is male. The required probability is P(M|A).

$$\text{P(M|A)} = \frac{.36}{.78} = \mathbf{0.462}$$
$$= \frac{\text{P(A and M)}}{\text{P(A)}}$$
$$\therefore \quad \text{P(A and M)} = \text{P(A)} \times \text{P(M|A)}$$

Note that P(A|M) ≠ P(M|A), but that there is a relation between the two through P(A and M) or P(M and A).

$$\text{P(M)} \times \text{P(A|M)} = \text{P(A and M)} = \text{P(A)} \times \text{P(M|A)}$$
$$\text{P(M)} \times \text{P(A|M)} = \text{P(A)} \times \text{P(M|A)}$$

thus

$$\text{P(A|M)} = \frac{\text{P(A)} \times \text{P(M|A)}}{\text{P(M)}}$$

and

$$\text{P(M|A)} = \frac{\text{P(M)} \times \text{P(A|M)}}{\text{P(A)}}$$

Example 6. A company has three production sections S_1, S_2, and S_3 which contribute 40%, 35% and 25% respectively to total output. The following percentages of faulty units have been observed:

S_1 2% (0.02)
S_2 3% (0.03)
S_3 4% (0.04)

There is a final check before output is despatched. Calculate the probability that a unit found faulty at this check has come from Section 1 (S_1)

Solution

Let F represent a unit which has been found to be faulty.
Let P(S_1) = probability that a unit chosen at random comes from S_1
Let P(S_2) = probability that a unit chosen at random comes from S_2
Let P(S_3) = probability that a unit chosen at random comes from S_3

$$\text{P}(S_1) = 0.40$$
$$\text{P}(S_2) = 0.35$$
$$\text{P}(S_3) = \underline{0.25}$$
$$1.00$$

The percentages of faulty units are as follows:

$$\text{P}(\text{F}|S_1) = 0.02$$
$$\text{P}(\text{F}|S_2) = 0.03$$
$$\text{P}(\text{F}|S_3) = 0.04$$

The required probability may be expressed as

$$P(S_1|F)$$

The unknown probability is P(F) to be slotted into the formula

$$P(S_1|F) = \frac{P(S_1) \times P(F|S_1)}{P(F)}$$

Note that .

$$P(S_2|F) = \frac{P(S_2) \times P(F|S_2)}{P(F)}$$

$$P(S_3|F) = \frac{P(S_3) \times P(F|S_3)}{P(F)}$$

The faulty part can only have come from S_1 or S_2 or S_3 and so

$$P(S_1|F) + P(S_2|F) + P(S_3|F) = 1.0$$

Since P(F) is a denominator and the sum equals unity then the expression

$$P(S_1) \times P(F|S_1) + P(S_2) \times P(F|S_2) + P(S_3) \times P(F|S_3)$$

must be equal to P(F)

$$\begin{aligned} \text{Thus}\quad P(F) &= (0.4 \times 0.02) + (0.35 \times 0.03) + (0.25 \times 0.04) \\ &= 0.0080 + 0.0105 + 0.0100 \\ &= 0.0285 \end{aligned}$$

Substitution into $P(S_1|F) = \frac{P(S_1) \times P(F|S_1)}{P(F)}$

$$\begin{aligned} \text{gives}\quad P(S_1|F) &= \frac{0.4 \times 0.02}{0.0285} \\ &= \frac{0.008}{0.0285} \\ &= \mathbf{0.2807} \\ \text{Also}\quad P(S_2|F) &= \frac{0.35 \times 0.03}{0.0285} \\ &= \frac{0.0105}{0.0285} \\ &= \mathbf{0.3684} \\ \text{and}\quad P(S_3|F) &= \frac{0.25 \times 0.04}{0.0285} \\ &= \frac{0.0100}{0.0285} \\ &= 0.3509 \end{aligned}$$

NB 0.2807 + 0.3684 + 0.3509 = 1.000

Thus if a faulty unit is chosen at random then the probability that it has come from S_1 is 0.2807.

BAYES RULE

6. The concept behind the above result is known as BAYES' RULE and it is interesting to note that the process involves working backwards from effect to cause. In this case a faulty item or unit **was** found and it was possible to work out the probability that it **had** come from S1

Bayes' Rule is frequently involved in the analysis of decisions using decision trees (see Chapter 3) where information is given in the form of conditional probabilities and the reverse of these probabilities must be found.

The general form of Bayes' Rule or theorem is:

$$P(A|B) = \frac{P(A).P(B|A)}{P(B)}$$

PERMUTATIONS

7. A permutation is an ordered arrangement of items. Thus AB is a different permutation to BA even though the individual two items A and B are the same, they are in a different order. Frequently an analyst has to work out the number of ways that an event can occur in order to calculate a required probability. If each possibility has to be listed this can be time consuming and error prone. Formulae can be used to make the task quick and easy.

Example 7

A restaurant offers a choice of 3 starters, 4 main courses and 3 sweets. How many different meals are available?

The solution is:

$3 \times 4 \times 3 = 36$ different meals.

This basic idea may be developed further

Example 8

A transport manager has to plan routes for his drivers. There are 3 deliveries to be made to customers; X, Y, and Z. How many routes can be followed?

In this case the routes can be listed:

ROUTE	1	*X*	*Y*	*Z*
— — —	2	*X*	*Z*	*Y*
— — —	3	*Y*	*X*	*Z*
— — —	4	*Y*	*Z*	*X*
— — —	5	*Z*	*X*	*Y*
— — —	6	*Z*	*Y*	*X*

This covers all possibilities and so the number of routes is 6. Note if there were 6 customers the number of routes "explodes" to 720. The question is how to work out the number of routes without listing them.

The first delivery may be chosen in 3 ways (X, Y, or Z). Let it be X. The second delivery may be made in two ways (Y or Z). Let it be Y. The third delivery can be made in only one way! The total number of routes is thus

$3 \times 2 \times 1 = 6$ ways.

If there are 6 customers then the number of routes is:

$$6 \times 5 \times 4 \times 3 \times 2 \times 1 = 720$$

These arrangements are known as PERMUTATIONS.

Note: $3 \times 2 \times 1$ is more usually written as 3!, pronounced 'three factorial'.

In general a permutation of n objects is written as:

$$n! = n(n-1)(n-2)(n-3)\dots(3)(2)(1)$$

Note that by definition $1! = 1$ and $0! = 1$

PERMUTATIONS OF GROUPS

8. The analyst may not wish to arrange all the items, but groups of items from within a list.

Example 9

A company has four training officers A, B, C, D, and two training sections. In how many different ways may the four officers be assigned to the two sections, X and Y?

The assignments are:

	X	Y
1	A	B
2	A	C
3	A	D
4	B	A
5	B	C
6	B	D
7	C	A
8	C	B
9	C	D
10	D	A
11	D	B
12	D	C

The first assignment may be made in 4 ways. For the second assignment there are only 3 officers left. There are no more assignments and so the number of permutations is:

$$4 \times 3\dagger = 12$$

Now let there be 6 officers and 3 sections
1st assignment = 6 ways 2nd assignment = 5 ways 3rd assignment = 4 ways
The number of permutations is:

$$6 \times 5 \times 4\dagger = 120$$

†Note the last figure in each case. Both are obtained in the same way.

Officers	Sections			
n	r			
4	-2	$+1$	=	3
6	-3	$+1$	=	4
$(n$	$-r$	$+1)$		

A convenient way to work out the number of permutations of n items r at a time is to use the following formula

$$n(n-1)(n-2)\ldots(n-r+1)$$

Note that there is an alternative calculation:

$$\frac{n!}{(n-r)!}$$

For the case with 4 officers and 2 sections

$$\frac{4!}{(4-2)!} = \frac{4 \times 3 \times 2 \times 1}{2 \times 1} = 12 \text{ ways}$$

PERMUTATIONS WITH SIMILAR ITEMS

9. There will be occasions when the items to be arranged will not all be different. If this is the case then the number of permutations will be reduced.

Example 10

If there are 3 items x, y, z then there are
$3 \times 2 \times 1 = 6$ permutations and these are

xyz yxz zxy

xzy yzx zyx

If however x = y = p the arrangement becomes

ppz	ppz	zpp
pzp	pzp	zpp

The number of permutations is reduced to 3. The version of the permutation formula which will accommodate this case is

$$\frac{n!}{n_1! \times n_2! \times n_3! \ldots n_x!}$$

where n_1 of the items are of one kind and n_2 of the items are of another type and so on up to x types. In the present case

$n_1 = 2$ and $n_2 = 1$ giving

$$\frac{3!}{2! \times 1!} = \frac{3 \times 2 \times 1}{2 \times 1 \times 1} = 3 \text{ ways}$$

Occasionally it is necessary to work out how many ways a group of people can be arranged around a table.

Example 11

A, B, C & D are to sit around a conference table: in how many ways may this be arranged?

Solution

Fix A in one place: This leaves three who may be placed using 3! as below:

A	*A*	*A*
B *D*	*B* *C*	*C* *D*
C	*D*	*B*
A	*A*	*A*
C *B*	*D* *B*	*D* *C*
D	*C*	*B*

There are thus 6 ways. Note that the 6 ways comes from 3! and 3! = (4-1)! and 4 is the number of people to arrange. Thus 7 people around a table can be arranged in 6! ways.

$6! = 6 \times 5 \times 4 \times 3 \times 2 \times 1 = 720$ ways

COMBINATIONS

10. There will be occasions when selections will be made where the order does not matter meaning that the arrangement a, b will be same as b, a. This is known as a combination.

Example 12

6 apprentices, A, B, C, D, E, F have to be paired into two's for an exercise. In how many ways may this be done? (A, B is the same as B, A etc.)

AB BC CD DE EF

AC BD CE DF

AD BE CF

AE BF

AF

There are 15 ways.

It is not necessary to list all the ways. The following formula can be used for combinations.

$$\frac{n!}{r!(n-r)!}$$

where n is the total number of items and r is the number of items per arrangement, the above Example works out as follows:

$$\frac{6!}{2!(6-2)!} = \frac{6 \times 5 \times 4 \times 3 \times 2 \times 1}{2 \times 1 \times 4 \times 3 \times 2 \times 1} = 15 \text{ ways}$$

This type of arrangement is known as a **combination** of n items r at a time and is denoted ^nC_r or $\binom{n}{r}$

This formula will be encountered again in Chapter 4 when dealing with the Binomial Distribution.
Note: A combination is a selection of items where the **order of sequence does not matter**.
i.e. AB = BA (because the same two items are selected)
A **permutation** is a selection where the order does matter.
i.e. $AB \neq BA$ (Although the same two items are present they are in a different sequence)

EXPECTED VALUE

11. The basic rules of probability so far outlined help to quantify the options open to management and thereby may help in coming to a decision. Where the options have values (so much profit, contribution etc) as well as probabilities, the concept of expected value is often used. The expected value of an event is its probability times the outcome or value of the event over a series of trials.

Example 13. Two projects are being considered and it is required to calculate the expected value of each project. The project data have been estimated as follows:-

	PROJECT A			PROJECT B		
	£	p	EV	£	p	EV
Optimistic Outcome	6000 ×	.2 =	1200	6500 ×	.1 =	650
Most likely Outcome	3500 ×	.5 =	1750	4000 ×	.6 =	2400
Pessimistic Outcome	2500 ×	.3 =	750	1000 ×	.3 =	300
PROJECT EV			£3700			£3350

EV = Expected Value
On the basis of Expected Value, Project A would be preferred as it has the higher value.
Notes

a. Although the EV of A is £3700, strictly this value would only be achieved in the long run over many similar decisions - extremely unlikely circumstances!
b. If the project was implemented, any of the three outcomes could occur, with the values stated.

EXPECTED VALUE-ADVANTAGES AND DISADVANTAGES.

12. Expected Value is a useful summarising technique, but suffers from similar advantages and disadvantages to all averaging methods.

Advantages:

a. Simple to understand and calculate
b. Represents whole distribution by a single figure
c. Arithmetically takes account of the expected variabilities of all outcomes.

Disadvantages:

a. By representing the whole distribution by a single figure it ignores the other characteristics of the distribution, eg the range and skewness.
b. Makes the assumption that the decision maker is risk neutral, ie he would rank equally the following two distributions:

		£	p	
	Pessimistic Outcome	18000	.25	
	Most likely Outcome	20000	.5	EV = £20000
	Optimistic Outcome	22000	.25	
and	Pessimistic Outcome	6000	.2	
	Most likely Outcome	18000	.6	EV = £20000
	Optimistic Outcome	40000	.2	

It is of course unlikely that any decision maker would rank them equally due to his personal attitude to risk.

Although it appears to be widely used for the purpose, the concept of expected value is not particularly well suited to one-off decisions. Expected value can strictly only be interpreted as the value that would be obtained if a large number of similar decisions were taken with the same ranges of outcome and associated probabilities. Hardly a typical business situation!

OPTIMISATION OF LEVELS OF ACTIVITY UNDER CONDITIONS OF UNCERTAINTY.

13. Expected Value concepts can be used to calculate the maximum stock or profit level when demand is subject to random variations over a period.

Example 14. A distributor buys perishable articles for £2 per items and sells them at £5. Demand per day is uncertain and items unsold at the end of the day represent a write off because of perishability. If he understocks he loses profit he could have made.

A 300 day record of past activity is as follows:

Daily Demand (Units)	No. of Days	p
10	30	.1
11	60	.2
12	120	.4
13	90	.3
	300	1.0

What level of stock should he hold from day to day to maximise profit?

Solution

It is necessary to calculate the *Conditional Profit* (CP) and *Expected Profit* (EP). CP = profit that could be made at any particular conjunction of stock and demand situation, eg if 13 articles were bought and demand was 10 then:

CP = (10 x 5) - (13 x 2) = £24.

EP = CP x probability of the demand

e.g. the CP above is £24 and p (demand = 10) = .1

EP = £24 x .1 = **£2.4**

CONDITIONAL AND EXPECTED PROFIT TABLE

Stock Options

Demand	p	10		11		12		13	
		CP £	EP £	CP £	EP £	CP £	EP £	CP £	EP £
10	.1	30	3	28	2.8	26	2.6	24	2.4
11	.2	30	6	33	6.6	31	6.2	29	5.8
12	.4	30	12	33	13.2	36	14.4	34	13.6
13	.3	30	9	33	9.9	36	10.8	39	11.7
	1.0		30		32.5		*34.0		33.5

* Optimum

Table 1.

The optimum stock position, given the pattern of demand, is to stock 12 units per day.

SOLUTION BY MARGINAL PROBABILITY FORMULA

14. An alternative approach to solving problems such as Example 14 above is to work out the marginal profit, MP, ie the profit from selling one more unit, and the marginal loss, ML, ie the loss from not selling the marginal unit and to calculate the relationship between MP and ML in terms of probability.

Example 15 Using the same data as in Example 14

Solve by using marginal profitability and marginal loss relationships.

From Example 14

MP = £3 and ML = £2

It follows that additional items will be stocked whilst the following relationship holds:

p(making additional sale). MP > p(not making additional sale). ML

If P denotes the probability of making the additional sale then (1-P) = probability of NOT making the sale.

$$\text{at breakeven point } P(MP) = (1 - P)(ML)$$
$$P(MP) + P(ML) = ML$$
$$P(MP + ML) = ML$$
$$P = \frac{ML}{MP + ML}$$

Inserting the data from Example 6 we obtain

$$P = \frac{2}{3+2}$$
$$= .4 \text{ ie. the probability at Break Even Point}$$

This probability is compared with the probability of demand at the various levels, the optimum position being the highest demand with a probability greater than P, ie.

Demand	**Probability**	
Greater than 10 units	1.00	
Greater than 11 units	.9	
Greater than 12 units	.7	Break Even probability = **.4**
Greater than 13 units	.3	

12 items is the most profitable stock level

VALUE OF PERFECT INFORMATION

15. Assume that the distributor in Example 14 could buy market research information which was perfect, ie it would enable him to forecast the exact demand on any day so that he could stock up accordingly. How much would the distributor be prepared to pay for such information? To solve this type of problem, the profit with perfect information is compared with the optimum EP from Table 1.

Profit with perfect information

					£
When demand is 10, stock 10	Profit	=	(10 x £3) x .1	=	3.0
When demand is 11, stock 11	Profit	=	(11 x £3) x .2	=	6.6
When demand is 12, stock 12	Profit	=	(12 x £3) x .4	=	14.4
When demand is 13, stock 13	profit	=	(13 x £3) x .3	=	11.7
					£35.7

As the EP from Table 1 was £34, the distributor could pay up to £1.70 (£35.7 - 34) for the information.

The above illustrates the general rule for calculating the value of perfect information. First, calculate the value of the outcome using expected value and then the value assuming perfect knowledge and deduct the one from the other.

In practice of course information is not perfect, yet may still be valuable. Organisations pay large sums for information which is reasonably accurate and which will enable them to improve their decision making. Market research opinion surveys, test marketing and so on produce imperfect information i.e. it is not perfectly accurate, yet it is still accurate enough to be relied upon. Under certain conditions it is possible to estimate the value of imperfect information.

VALUING IMPERFECT INFORMATION

16. Providing that there is some indication of how accurate the information is likely to be, it is possible to calculate the worth of imperfect information. For example if a firm had used a market research agency on numerous occasions it would be able to make an assessment of the acuracy of their information.

The method used to value imperfect information uses posterior probabilities based on Bayes Theorem and is demonstrated by the following example.

Example 15

Theta Limited are considering the launch of a new product, the Gamma.

Various prior estimates of outcomes have been made as follows and the expected values calculated.

MARKET STATE	PROBABILITY	PROFIT (LOSS)	EXPECTED VALUE
GOOD	0.2	£60,000	£12,000
AVERAGE	0.6	40,000	24,000
BAD	0.2	(40,000)	(8,000)
			EV = £28,000

In order to have more information on which to base their decision the management are considering whether to commission a market research survey at a cost of £1,000. The agency concerned produce reasonably accurate, but not perfect, information and Theta's Trade Association provided the following information about the Agency's performance

LIKELY ACTUAL MARKET STATE	MARKET RESEARCH AGENCY SURVEY FINDINGS:		
	GOOD	**AVERAGE**	**BAD**
GOOD	60%	30%	—
AVERAGE	40%	50%	10%
BAD	—	20%	90%

Solution

The first stage is to calculate the posterior probabilities i.e. the probability of the market state being good, average or bad **after** the market research survey results have become available.

CALCULATION OF POSTERIOR PROBABILITIES

PRIOR PROBABILITY	MARKET STATE	MARKET RESEARCH RESULTS		POSTERIOR
		STATE	PROBABILITY	PROBABILITY
0.2	GOOD	GOOD	0.6	GG = 0.12 †
		AVERAGE	0.4	GA = 0.08
0.6	AVERAGE	GOOD	0.3	AG = 0.18
		AVERAGE	0.5	AA = 0.30
		BAD	0.2	AB = 0.12
0.2	BAD	AVERAGE	0.1	BA = 0.02
		BAD	0.9	BB = 0.18
				1.00

†GG = 0.12 means that the probability of the market being **good** and the survey predicting a **good** state is 0.2 x 0.6 = 0.12.

From the table survey probabilities can be summarised thus:

P (SURVEY WILL SHOW 'GOOD')

$$= GG + AG = 0.12 + 0.18 = \mathbf{0.3}$$

P (SURVEY WILL SHOW 'AVERAGE')

$$= GA + AA + BA = 0.08 + 0.30 + 0.02 = \mathbf{0.4}$$

P (SURVEY WILL SHOW 'BAD')

$$= AB + BB = 0.12 + 0.18 = \mathbf{0.3}$$

Assuming that the product will be launched if the survey predicts a GOOD or AVERAGE market and **not** launched if the BAD state is predicted the following table can be prepared:

SURVEY RESULTS	DECISION	ACTUAL MARKET	POSTERIOR PROBABILITIES	PROFIT (LOSS) £	EV OF PROFITS (LOSSES) £
GOOD	LAUNCH	GOOD	0.12	60,000	7,200
		AVERAGE	0.18	40,000	7,200
AVERAGE	LAUNCH	GOOD	0.08	60,000	4,800
		AVERAGE	0.30	40,000	12,000
		BAD	0.02	(40,000)	(800)
BAD	DO NOT LAUNCH		0.3	—	—
			1.00		**£30,400**

∴ Value of imperfect information is
£30,400 - £28,000 = **£2,400**

As the survey cost is £1000 it would appear to be worthwhile. However, there is only a relatively small gain (£2,400) from having more information and because of estimation problems it is feasible that management would decide not to commission the survey.

ALTERNATIVE DECISION RULES

17. The rule so far covered in this chapter is to choose the alternative which maximises the expected value. This is the most commonly encountered decision rule and is the one which should be used unless there are clear instructions to the contrary. However alternative rules do exist and these include

the MAXIMIN rule
the MAXIMAX rule
the MINIMAX REGRET rule

These rules are illustrated using the following payoff table showing potential profits and losses which are expected to arise from launching various products in three market conditions thus.

Pay off table in £'000s

	BOOM CONDITIONS	STEADY STATE	RECESSION
Product A	+8	1	-10
Product B	-2	+6	+12
Product C	+16	0	-26

PAY OFF TABLE. Table 2.

The probabilities are, Boom 0.6, Steady State 0.3 and Recession 0.1 so that the expected values are

Product A = $(0.6 \times 8) + (0.3 \times 1) + (0.1 \times -10) = 4.1$
Product B = $(0.6 \times -2) + (0.3 \times 6) + (0.1 \times 12) = 1.8$
Product C = $(0.6 \times 16) + (0.3 \times 0) + (0.1 \times -26) = 7$

So using the expected value rule the ranking would be C, A, B.
What are the rankings using the alternatives?
MAXIMIN the 'best of the worst'
This is a cautious decision rule based on maximising the minimum loss that can occur. The worst losses

are:-

A −10

B −2

C −26

∴ Ranking using the MAXIMIN rule i.e. B A C
MAXIMAX the 'best of the best'
This is an optimistic rule and maximises the maximum that can be gained.
The maximum gains are:-

A + 8

B + 12

C + 16

Ranking using the MAXIMAX rule is C B A.

MINIMAX REGRET

18. This decision rules seeks to 'minimise the maximum regret' that there would be from choosing a particular strategy. To see this clearly it is necessary to construct a regret table based on the payoff table, Table 2. The regret is the opportunity loss from taking one decision given that a certain contingency occurs; in our Example whether there is boom, steady state, or recession.

Regret table in £'000s

	BOOM	STEADY STATE	RECESSION
Product A	8	5	22
Product B	18	0	0
Product C	0	6	38

TABLE 3

Note:

The above opportunity losses are calculated by setting the best position under any state to zero and than calculating the amount of shortfall there is by not being at that position. For example, if there is a recesion Product B gains + 12 but if Product A had been chosen there is a loss of - 10 making a total shortfall, as compared with B, of 22, which is the opportunity loss.

The maximum 'regrets are:-

A 22

B 18

C 38

∴ the ranking using the MINIMAX REGRET rule is B A C.

OPPORTUNITY LOSS AND EXPECTED VALUE

19. As a loss is the negative aspect of gain it is to be expected that opportunity loss and expected value are related. This is indeed so and the opportunity losses multipled by the probabilities i.e. the expected opportunity loss (EOL) can be used to arrive at the same ranking as the expected value (EV) rule except that where the maximum EV is chosen, the minimum EOL is required.

∴ MINIMISING EOL gives the same decision as MAXIMISING EV.

For example the EOL'S of Table 3 are:-

A $(0.6 \times 8) + (0.3 \times 5) + (0.1 \times 22) = 8.5$

B $(0.6 \times 18) + (0.3 \times 0) + (0.1 \times 0) = 10.8$

C $(0.6 \times 0) + (0.3 \times 6) + (0.1 \times 38) = 5.6$

∴ ranking in order of minimum EOL gives C A B which is identical to the ranking given by the expected value method.

SUMMARY

20.

a. Objective probabilities are rarely available in business decision making situations so that subjective probabilities, i.e. the quantification of judgement, are used.

b. The two basic rules of probability are the multiplication rule (AND) and the addition rule (OR)

c. Bayes Rule finds a conditional probability $(A|B)$ given its inverse $(B|A)$

d. The general form of Bayes Rule is

$$P(A|B) = \frac{P(A).\ P(B|A)}{P(B)}$$

e. A permutation is an ordered arrangement.

f. The number of permutations is written as ^nP_r and is calculated thus:

$$^nP_r = \frac{n!}{(n-r)!}$$

g. A combination is an arrangement without regard to order.

h. The number of combinations is written as ^nC_r and is calculated thus:

$$^nC_r = \frac{n!}{r!(n-r)!}$$

i. Expected Value (EV) has many uses in decision making situations and is calculated by multiplying the value of the outcome(s) by the probability. In general the option with the highest EV would be chosen.

j. Although useful, EV ignores the range and skewness of distributions, so that it needs to be used with judgement.

k. The value of perfect information is the difference between the profits obtainable from having perfect knowledge and the expected value of outcomes without perfect knowledge.

l. Alternative decision rules are MAXIMIN, MAXIMAX, and MINIMAX REGRET.

m. Opportunity loss is the shortfall between the best possible value in the state and the actual result.

n. Using the minimum expected opportunity loss as the decision criterion gives the same ranking as expected value.

POINTS TO NOTE.

21.

a. The use of probability concepts and expected value is widespread in professional examinations so that this chapter should be studied carefully.

b. Questions involving probability may appear in any part of the syllabus (inventory control, investment appraisal, network analysis etc).

c. The nature of probability is essentially that of assuming repetitive trials or occurrences. Accordingly the use of probability concepts in one-off decisions needs to be carefully considered.

d. The type of organisation, its objectives, style and ethos, are all involved in considering the appropriate decision criteria to use. A Public Sector organisation may be precluded from speculative investments and may have to fulfill Statutory Obligations at minimum cost. In such quite typical circumstances the use of the minimax criterion is likely to be appropriate whilst other types of organisations may tend to adopt a maximax rule.

SELF REVIEW QUESTIONS.

1. *Distinguish between objective and subjective probabilities. (3)*

2. *Define the multiplication and Addition rules of Probability .(4)*
3. *What is the basic concept behind BAYES RULE? (6)*
4. *Distinguish between a PERMUTATION and a COMBINATION (7 - 10)*
5. *How is Expected Value calculated. (11)*
6. *What are the advantages and disadvantages of using Expected Value as a decision criterion. (12).*
7. *Assuming that data on past demand and probabilities are available how might a value be imputed for receiving perfect information (14) imperfect information? (16).*
8. *Define the minimax and maximax decision rules (17)*
9. *How is the regret table calculated (18).*
10. *How are opportunity loss and expected value related? (19)*

EXERCISES WITH ANSWERS COMMENCING PAGE 488

A1. A card is drawn from a shuffled pack of 52 cards. What is probability of drawing a king or a heart?

A2. Records of service requests at a garage and their probabilities are as follows:

Daily demand	*Probability*
5	0.3
6	0.7

Daily demand is independent

What is probability that over a two day period the number of requests will be:

(a) 10 requests

(b) 11 requests

(c) 12 requests

A3. Analysis of questionnaire completed by holiday makers showed that 0.75 classified their holiday as **good** *at Costa Lotta. The probability of* **hot** *weather in the resort is 0.6. If the probability of regarding the holiday as* **good** *given* **hot** *weather is 0.9, what is the probability that there was hot weather if a holiday maker considers his holiday good?*

EXAMINATION QUESTIONS WITH ANSWERS COMMENCING PAGE 488

A4. A large restaurant purchases cakes daily from a local bakery. The cakes cost 10 pence each and sell at 15 pence each in the restaurant, but any which have not been sold there at the end of each day are sold through another outlet for 8 pence each. The relative frequency distribution of restaurant sales (Obtained from an analysis of past sales data) is given below:

Daily restaurant sales of cakes Dozens (1 dozen = 12 cakes)	*Relative frequency*
30	0.01
31	0.09
32	0.16
33	0.25
34	0.30
35	0.11
36	0.08

You are required to state:

a. The optimum quantity which the buyer should purchase in order to maximise expected profitsl;

b. how much the buyer could afford to pay for perfectly correct information about daily sales.

(CIMA. Quantitative Techniques)

A5. Every Friday morning Minos Security Limited delivers wages from a local bank to each of five firms in a certain area. Having collected the necessary money from the bank, a security van visits the five firms in turn but, as a precaution against robbery, the same route is not used on each occasion. Immediately prior to each Friday's delivery, the van driver chooses at random, according to a procedure established by the operations manager, the order in which the five firms will be visited.

Required:

(a) (i) What is the probability of the van following a particular route (i.e. visiting the firms in a particular order) on any specific occasions?

(ii) What is the probability of the van following a different route on each of four consecutive weeks?

(iii) What is the probability of two particular firms, A and B, being visited consecutively?

(b) In order to reduce the delivery time, the operations' manager has decided to modify the routing procedure. Firms A, B and C are close together, and so are firms D and E. Accordingly the van visits the first three firms in a randomly chosen order,a nd then visits the other two firms, again in random order. How does this modify each of the three probabilities in (a)?

(c) As an additional precaution to the procedure in (b), the van driver is instructed never to follow the same route on two successive weeks. What now is the probability of the van following a different route on each of four consecutive weeks?

(ACCA, Quantitative Analysis)

A6. firm is currently considering the purchase of new equipment to manufacture parts required by the north sea oil development programme. There are three types of equipment which could be purchased:

i. conventional - manual operation (Conv);

ii. numerically controlled (NC);

iii. computer numerically controlled (CNC)

The capital cost of the equipment rises from (i) through to (iii). The profit resulting from whichever course of action is finally taken depends on the size of the market to be supplied; at present this is uncertain. The market has been classified into three broad categories, poor, fair and good, and the profits (losses are given a negative sign) are shown for each market size/machine tool type in the table below:

	Profit (£million)		
	Market		
	Poor	*Fair*	*Good*
Conv	*0.5*	*1.0*	*1.5*
NC	*0*	*1.5*	*2.5*
CNC	*-1.5*	*0.5*	*3.5*

The chances of the market being poor, fair or good are assessed at 30%, 50% and 20% respectively by the firm's management.

A market research group could be employed to provide information on which market will be realised. Past experience with work from this group shows its information cannot be relied on to be absolutely accurate and management assesses the following chances of it indicating a poor (1), fair (11) and good (111) market when these are the actual states of the market to be as follows:

Indicated state	*1*	*11*	*111*
Actual state			
Poor ..	*0.7*	*0.2*	*0.1*
Fair ..	*0.2*	*0.7*	*0.1*
Good ..	*0*	*0.2*	*0.8*

You are required to:

a. prepare the conditional expected loss table based on the market assessment made by the firm;

b. calculate the expected value of perfect information;

c. prepare the conditional expected loss table based on the information which might be available from the market research; and

d. state the maximum amount it would be worthwhile for the firm to pay for the market research.

(CIMA, Quantitative Techniques)

A7. Many products, such as fresh vegetables, flowers, pastries etc, have a very short shelf life. A retailer of one of these has obtained the following estimates of daily demand during a year in which there are 250 working days:

Demand (units)	*Frequency, per year*
10	*60 times*
20	*70 times*
30	*80 times*
40	*40 times*

There is no indication of a seasonal pattern, and daily sales will be either 10, 20, 30 or 40 units exactly.

The product costs £4.00 per unit and may be sold to the public for £6.00 on the day of delivery. If it is not sold that day to the public, it is sold to the staff at the end of the day for £1.00.

Orders can be placed for either 10, 20, 30 or 40 units but the same quantity must be ordered and will be delivered each working day throughout the year.

You are required to:

(a) calculate the quantity that should be ordered and the profit that will be earned. (your answer should include conditional and expected profit tables);

(b) calculate and comment upon the effect of being able to store the product so that all purchases could be sold to the public at £6.00. (Your answer should include a calculation of the maximum amount it would be worth paying for this storage facility.)

(CIMA QUANTITATIVE TECHNIQUES)

EXERCISES WITHOUT ANSWERS

B1. The probability of snow in any hour is 0.3. A road lining firm has a contract to paint 5000 metres of white line. They normally paint 30 metres per hour unless it snows when their work rate is cut by 70%. What is the expected number of working hours to complete the contract?

B2. A committee of 4 must be chosen from 3 women and 4 men. Calculate;

(a) in how many ways the Committee can be chosen.

(b) the probability the Committee consists of 2 men and 2 women.

(c) the probability there are at least 2 women.

B3. Computer analysis of satellite data has correctly forecast locations of economic oil deposits 80% of the time. The last 24 oil wells drilled produced only 8 wells that were economic. The latest analysis indicates economic quantities at a particular location. What is the probability that the well will produce economic quantities of oil?

EXAMINATION QUESTIONS WITHOUT ANSWERS

B4. A centralised kitchen provides food for various canteens throughout an organisation. Any food prepared but not required is used for pig food at a net value of 1p per portion.

A particular dish, D, is sold to the canteens for £1.00 and costs 20p to prepare.

B ased on past demand, it is expected that during the 250-day working year the canteens will require the following quantities:

On 100 days	*40*
On 75 days	*50*
On 50 days	*60*
On 25 days	*70*

The kitchen prepares the dish in batches of 10 and has to decide how many it will make during the next year.

You are required to:

(a) Calculate the highest expected profit for the year that would be earned if the same quantity of D were made each day;

(b) calculate the maximum amount that could be paid for perfect information of the demand (either 40, 50, 60 or 70) if this meant that the exact quantity could be made each day.

(CIMA Quantitative Techniques)

3 Decision Trees

INTRODUCTION

1. This chapter developes the use of probability in decision making and cover the method of depicting a series of decisions and outcomes by decision trees.

DECISION TREES – DEFINITION

2. A pictorial method of showing a sequence of inter-related decisions and outcomes. They assist in the clarification of complex decisionmaking situations. Where probabilities and values of outcomes are known or are estimated, they assist in the quantification of the situation(s) so as to provide a better basis for rational decision making.

STRUCTURE OF DECISION TREES.

3. The structure and typical components of a decision tree are shown in the following illustration:

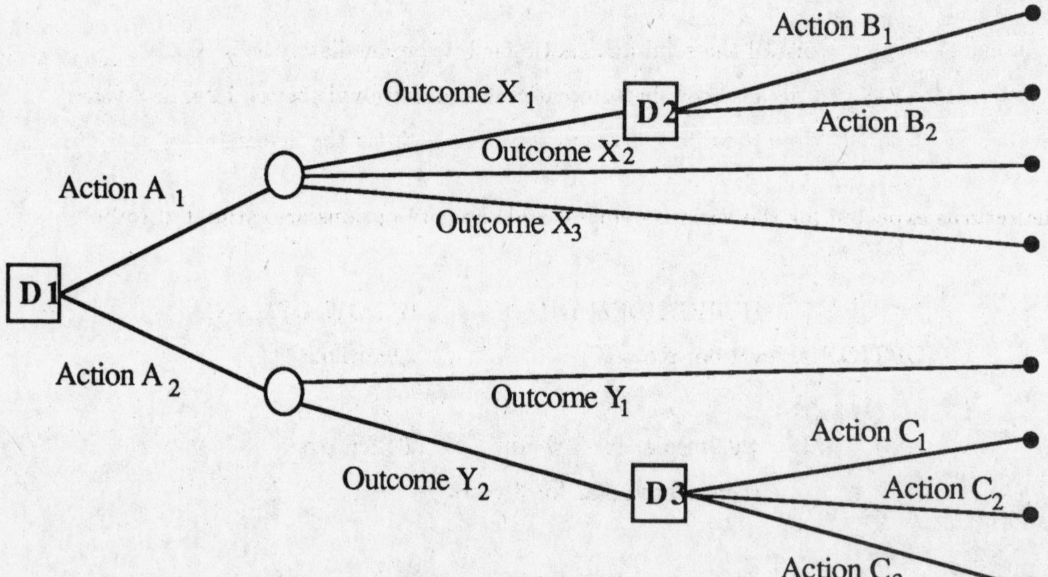

Figure 1

Notes:

a. It will be seen there are two types of nodes, Decision nodes depicted by squares and Outcome nodes depicted by circles.

b. The Decision nodes are points where a choice exists between alternatives and a managerial decision is made based on estimates and calculations of the returns expected.

c. The Outcome nodes are points where the events depend on probabilities, eg assume that Action A1 in Figure 1 was - Build branch factory - then outcomes X_1, X_2, and X_3 could represent various possible sales; high, medium, and low, each with an estimated probability.

DRAWING DECISION TREES

4. The procedure for drawing decision trees and evaluating the returns expected will be illustrated by using the following example:

Example 1.

A firm making widgets have been considering the likely demand for widgets over the next 6 years and think that the demand pattern will be as follows:

High demand for 6 years p	=	.5
Low demand for 6 years p	=	.3
High demand for 3 years followed by Low demand for 3 years p	=	.2

(No possibility is envisaged of Low demand followed by High demand).

Englargement of capacity is required and the following options are available:

Option A	Install fully automatic facilities immediately at a cost of £5.4m
B	Install semi-automatic facilities immediately at a cost of £4m.
C	Install the semi-automatic facilities immediately as in B and upgrade to fully automatic at an additional cost of £2m in 3 years time providing demand has been high for the 3 years.

The returns expected for the various demand and capacity options are estimated to be

	IF HIGH DEMAND	IF LOW DEMAND
OPTION A	£1.6m p.a.	£0.6m p.a.
B	£0.9m p.a. for 3 years then £0.5m p.a. for 3 years	£0.8m p.a.
C	£0.9m p.a. for 3 years then £1.1m for 3 years	£0.8m p.a. for 3 years then £0.3m p.a. for 3 years.

What decision(s) should the firm take?

Solution:

The decision tree is developed in two stages, the FORWARD PASS and the BACK-WARD PASS.

FORWARD PASS.

5. Draw the decision tree starting from the left showing the two Decision points and the various demand options. This is shown in Figure 2.

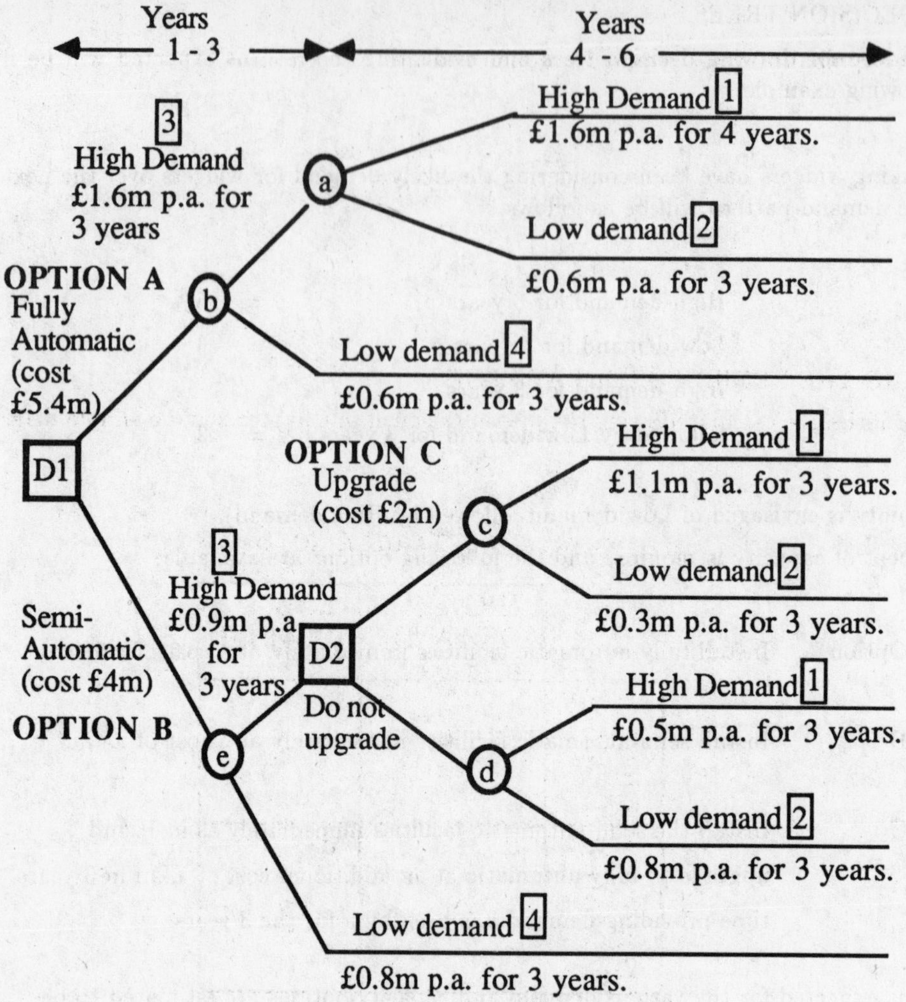

Figure 2 DECISION TREE FOR EXAMPLE 1

DEFINING THE REQUIRED PROBABILITIES

6. Once the decision tree is drawn, then the probabilities that are required for its evaluation must be deduced. This has been done for the problem and the required probabilities are shown as [1], [2], [3], [4]. Note that often these are NOT the probabilities as given in the problem originally but have to be derived from the figures provided.

Probability [1] is expressed as "High Demand in years 4–6, Given that there was actually High Demand in years 1–3" $(HD_{46}|HD_{13})$. This is a conditional outcome.

Probability [2] is expressed as "Low Demand in years 4–6, Given that there was actually High Demand in years 1–3" (LD_{46}/HD_{13}). This again is a conditional outcome.

Probability [3] is expressed as "High Demand in years 1–3" (HD_{13}).

Probability [4] is more involved than it looks for it is expressed as "Low Demand in years 1–3 followed by Low Demand in years 4–6" $(LD_{13}\&LD_{46})$. This is a joint outcome of two independent events.

Note that the probabilities as given are not single outcomes, but joint outcomes of independent events.

"High demand for 6 years" = "High demand in years 1–3 followed by High demand in years 4-6". $(HD_{13}\&HD_{46})$.

"Low demand for 6 years" = " Low demand in years 1–3 followed by Low demand in years 4–6 $(LD_{13}\&LD_{46})$. Note that because there is no possibility invisaged of low demand being followed by High demand, "Low Demand for 6 years will be numerically identical to Low Demand years 1–3.

"High demand for 3 years followed by Low demand for 3 years may be expressed as the joint outcome

$HD_{13}\&LD_{46}$.

Summarised symbolically the required probabilities are:

[1] $P(HD_{46}|HD_{13})$
[2] $P(LD_{46}|HD_{13})$
[3] $P(HD_{13})$
[4] $P(LD_{13})$

CALCULATING THE REQUIRED PROBABILITIES

7. The probabilities are calculated using the ideas developed in Chapter 2 and a simple diagram is shown below:

Years 4 to 6

Years 1 - 3	HIGH DEMAND	LOW DEMAND
HIGH DEMAND	a .5	b .2
LOW DEMAND	c 0	d .3

Box a: $P(HD_{13}\&HD_{46}) = 0.5$

Box b: $P(HD_{13}\&LD_{46}) = 0.2$

Box c: $P(LD_{13}\&HD_{46}) = 0$

Box d: $P(LD_{13}\&LD_{46}) = 0.3$

HD_{13} may be deduced from the sum of Boxes a and b.

$$\begin{aligned} P(HD_{13}) &= P(HD_{13}\&HD_{46}) + P(HD_{13}\&LD_{46}) \\ &= 0.5 + 0.2 \\ &= \mathbf{0.7}\ \boxed{3} \end{aligned}$$

ALSO

$$\begin{aligned} P(LD13) &= P(LD_{13}\&HD_{46}) + P(LD_{13}\&LD_{46}) \\ &= 0 + 0.3 \\ &= \mathbf{0.3}\ \boxed{4} \end{aligned}$$

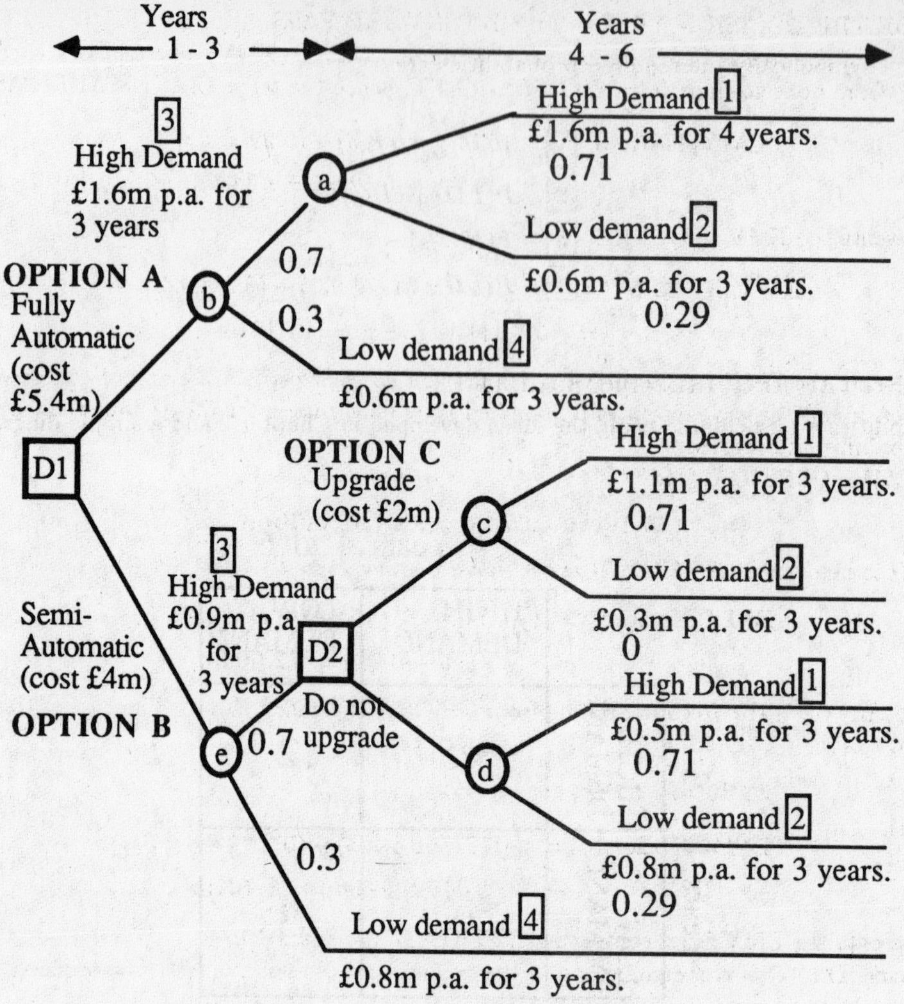

Figure 3 DECISION TREE WITH PROBABILITIES

Note $P(HD_{13}) + P(LD_{46}) = 1.0$

$0.7 + 0.3 = 1.0$

$$P(HD_{46}|HD_{13}) = \frac{P(HD_{13}\&HD_{46})}{P(HD_{13})}$$

$$= \frac{0.5}{0.7}$$

$= \mathbf{0.71}$ to 2 dp. 1

(See chapter 2 Example 5 for principle)

$$P(LD_{46}|HD_{13} = \frac{P(HD_{13}\&LD_{46})}{P(HD_{13})}$$

$= \frac{0.2}{0.7}$

$= \mathbf{0.29}$ to 2 dp. 2

These results may now be entered on the decision tree, Figure 3.

ANALYSIS OF THE DECISION TREE – THE BACKWARD PASS

8. The analysis of the tree is based on Expected Monetary Values (EMV) The analysis is carried out by "rolling back" from node to node from RIGHT to LEFT, hence the term "BACKWARD PASS"

$$\textbf{EMV Node a} = (0.71 \times 1.6 \times 3) + (0.29 \times .6 \times 3)$$
$$= £3.408 + 0.522\text{m} = £3.93\text{m}$$

This represents the EMV of OPTION A for years 4–6.

$$\textbf{EMV Node b} = (0.7((1.6 \times 3) + 3.93)) + (0.3 \times 0.6 \times 6)$$
$$= £6.111 + 1.08 \text{ m} = £7.191\text{m}$$

This represents the EMV for OPTION A for the full six year project horizon. Note how the £3.93m was brought back and the probability of 0.7 applied to it. The reason for this is that the result at Node a has a 0.7 probability of occurring.

The net EMV of OPTION A is

$$£7.191 \text{ m} - £5.4\text{m} = \mathbf{£1.791 \text{ million.}}$$

This result is held until OPTIONS B and C have been evaluated.

$$\textbf{EMV Node c} = (0.71 \times 1.1. \times 3) + (0.29 \times 0.3 \times 3)$$
$$= £2.343 + 0.261 = \mathbf{£2.604m}$$

This represents the EMV from upgrading from OPTION B to OPTION C. The cost of this is £2m and so the net EMV is

$$£2.604\text{m} - £2\text{m} = £0.604\text{m}$$

$$\textbf{EMV Node d} = (0.71 \times 0.5 \times 3) + (0.29 \times 0.8 \times 3)$$
$$= £1.065 + 0.696 = \mathbf{£1.761m}$$

This represents the EMV from continuing OPTION B into years 4 to 6.

EMV Node D2. This is a comparison of the results from Nodes c and D. The decision rule is to opt for that result which gives the greater EMV

EMV c : £0.604m

EMV d : £1.761m

Since 1.761 > 0.604 then the decision at Node D2 will be not to upgrade from OPTION B to OPTION C. This result is carried back to Node e.

$$\textbf{EMV node e} = (0.7((0.9 \times 3) + 1.761) + (0.3 \times 0.8 \times 6)$$
$$= £3.1227 + 1.44 = \mathbf{£4.5627m}$$

This represents the EMV from OPTION B. From this must be deducted the cost of OPTION B. Thus the net EMV of OPTION B IS

$$£4.5627\text{M} - £4\text{M} = \mathbf{£0.5627m}$$

EMV Node D1. This is a comparison of the results from Nodes b and e, and again the decision rule is to opt for that results which gives the greater EMV.

EMV b : £1.791m OPTION A

EMV e : £0.5627m OPTION B

Since £1.791m > £0.5627m, then the decision at Node D1 will be to opt for OPTION A that is to install the fully automatic machinery at the outset.

In practice, the conditional probabilities [1] & [2] and the initial probabilities [3] and [4] will not have to be deduced. The analyst will in fact ask the Manager what he believes these probabilities to be!

ALTERNATIVE METHOD OF SOLUTION FOR EXAMPLE 1.

9. There is an alternative method of solution for this problem whereby Option A is analysed and presented in a different way. Using this approach Nodes (a) and (b) are merged in one node (a). This is shown in Figure 4.

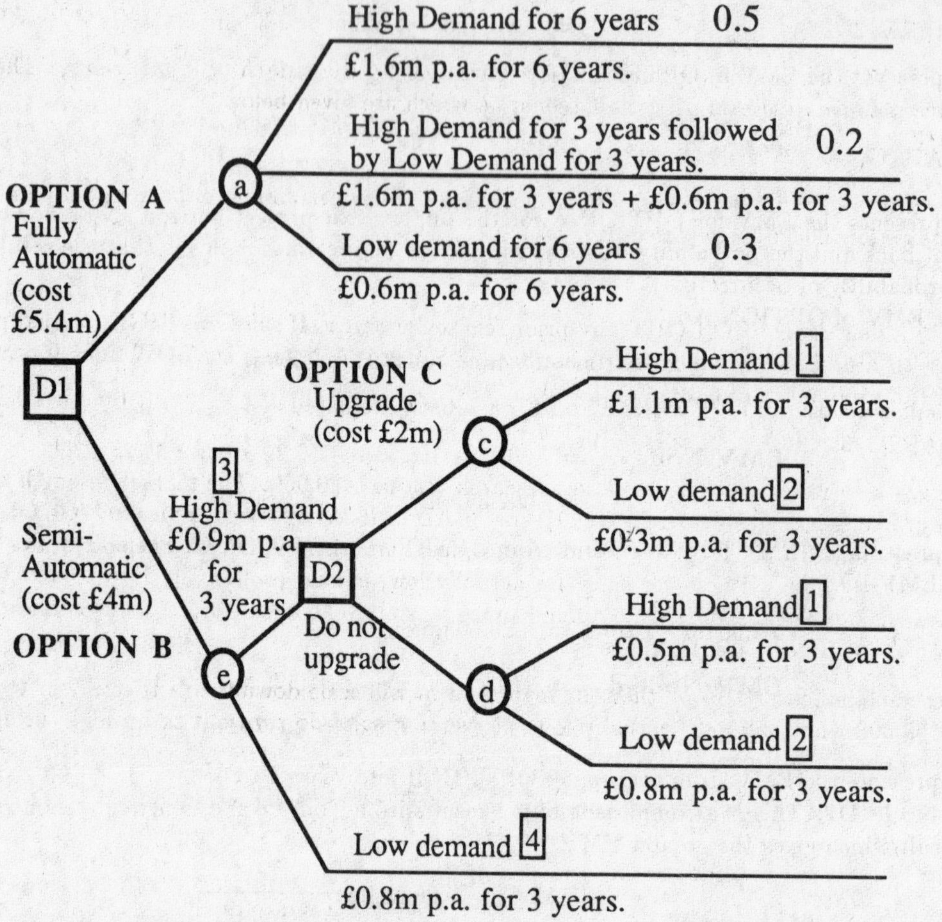

FIGURE 4 DECISION TREE DEPICTING ALTERNATIVE SOLUTION FOR EXAMPLE 1

Using this approach, the EMV Node a may be evaluated as follows:

$$(0.5 \times 1.6 \times 6) + (0.2((1.6 \times 3) + (0.6 \times 3))) + (0.3 \times 0.6 \times 6)$$
$$= 4.8 + 1.32 + 1.08 = \pounds\mathbf{7.2m}$$

It will be noted that the EMV for Node b was £7.191m. This is not a co-incidence since the £7.191m only occurred because of rounding, 0.71 actually being 0.7142857 and 0.29 actually being 0.2857142

Had Node (a) been evaluated as follows:

$$\left(\frac{5}{7} \times 1.6 \times 3\right) + \left(\frac{2}{7} \times 6 \times 3\right)$$
$$= \frac{24}{7} + \frac{3.6}{7}$$
$$= \frac{27.6}{7} = 3.9428571$$

and Node b as

$$(0.7((1.6 \times 3) + 3.942857)) + (0.3 \times 0.6 \times 6)$$
$$= 6.12 + 1.08 = \pounds\mathbf{7.20m} \text{ as above.}$$

the two results would be identical.

BAYES' THEOREM AND DECISION TREE ANALYSIS

The ideas developed in CHAPTER 2 on Bayes' Theorem may be applied to the analysis of decision trees. Consider the following example.

EXAMPLE 2

A company with an ageing product range is investigating the launch of a new range. Their business analysts have mapped out several possible scenarios which are given below.

SCENARIO 1

Continue with old range producing profits declining at 10% per annum on a compounding basis. Last year's profits were £60000 from this range.

SCENARIO 2

Introduce a new range WITHOUT any prior market research. If sales are HIGH, annual profit is put at £90000 with a probability which from past data is put at 0.7. If sales are LOW annual profit is put at £30,000 with a probability of 0.3.

SCENARIO 3

Introduce a new range with prior market research costing £30,000. The market research will indicate whether future sales are likely to be "GOOD' or "BAD". If the research indicates "GOOD", then the management will spend £35,000 more on capital equipment and this will increase annual profits to £100,000 if sales are actually high. If however sales are actually low, annual profits will drop to £25,000. Should market research indicate "GOOD" and should management NOT spend more on promotion then profit levels will be as for **SCENARIO 2.**

If the research indicates "BAD" then the management will scale down their expectations to give annual profits of £50,000 when sales are actually low. However if sales do turn out to be high, profits can only rise to £70,000 because of capacity constraints.

Past history of the market research company indicates the following results.

		ACTUAL SALES	
		High	Low
PREDICTED SALES LEVELS	GOOD	* .8	.1
	BAD	.2	.9

*When Actual Sales were **HIGH** the market research company **HAD** predicted **GOOD** sales levels 80% of the time and so on.

Use a Time Horizon of 6 years to indicate to the management of the company:-

1. Whether the market research is worth undertaking at £30,000.

2. Whether it is worthwhile to spend the extra £35,000 on capital equipment.

IGNORE THE TIME VALUE OF MONEY

DRAWING THE DECISION TREE

10. As always the first step is to draw the decision tree working from LEFT to RIGHT. The tree is shown in Figure 5.

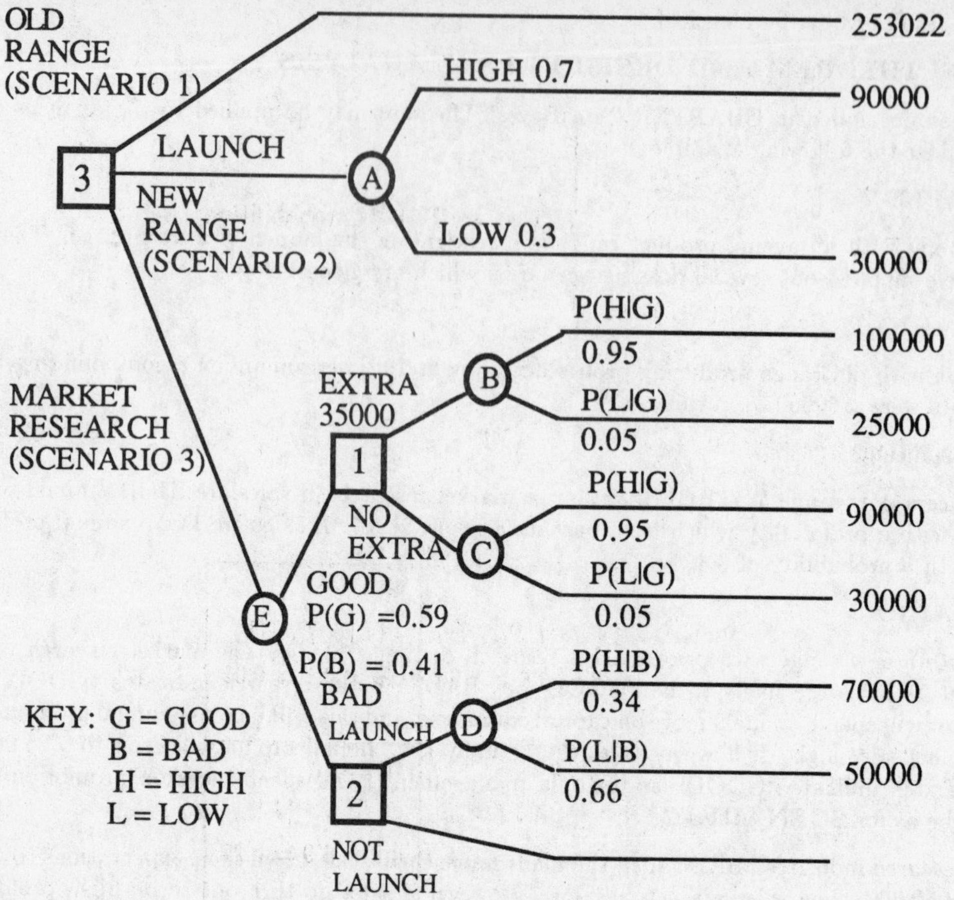

Figure 5 DECISION TREE EXAMPLE 2

NOTE: The various probabilities for Scenario 3 are calculated in Para 12 below.

CALCULATING THE PROBABILITIES

11. The decision tree reveals that the following probabilities must be calculated.

$$\left.\begin{array}{l} P(G) \\ P(B) \end{array}\right\} \text{for market research}$$

$$\left.\begin{array}{l} P(H|G) \\ P(L|G) \\ \\ P(H|B) \\ P(L|B) \end{array}\right\} \text{for sales outcomes}$$

From the data supplied the following probabilities are available.

$$\left.\begin{array}{ll} P(G|H) & 0.8 \\ P(B|H) & 0.2 \\ & \\ P(G|L) & 0.1 \\ P(B|L) & 0.9 \end{array}\right\} \text{These are PRIOR probabilities.}$$

The calculations are shown below:

	HIGH .7	LOW .3
GOOD	G & H = $P(H) \times P(G|H)$ $0.7 \times 0.8 = 0.56$	G & L = $P(L) \times P(G|L)$ $0.3 \times 0.1 = 0.03$
BAD	B & H = $P(H) \times P(B|H)$ $0.7 \times 0.2 = 0.4$	B & L $P(L) \times P(B|L)$ $0.3 \times 0.9 = 0.27$

$$\begin{aligned} P(G) &= P(H) \times P(G|H) + P(L) \times P(G|L) \\ &= P(G\&H) + P(G\&L) \\ &= 0.56 + 0.03 \\ &= \mathbf{0.59} \end{aligned}$$

$$\begin{aligned} P(B) &= P(H) \times P(B|H) + P(L) \times P(B|L) \\ &= P(B\&H) + P(B\&L) \\ &= 0.14 + 0.27 \\ &= \mathbf{0.41} \end{aligned}$$

NB P(G) + P(B) = 0.59 + 041 = 1.00

From Bayes' Rule.

$$P(H|G) = \frac{P(G|H) \times P(H)}{P(G)} = \frac{0.56}{0.59} = 0.95$$

$$P(L|G) = \frac{P(G|L) \times P(L)}{P(G)} = \frac{0.03}{0.59} = \mathbf{0.05}$$

$$P(H|B) = \frac{P(B|H) \times P(H)}{P(B)} = \frac{0.14}{0.41} = \mathbf{0.34}$$

$$P(L|B) = \frac{P(B|L) \times P(L)}{P(B)} = \frac{0.27}{0.41} = \mathbf{0.66}$$

These may be entered on the decision tree (See figure 5)

EVALUATING THE FINANCIAL OUTCOMES.

12. It is now possible to evaluate the financial outcomes of the three scenarios using the information given in the question and the probabilities calculated above.

SCENARIO 1.

Last year £60,000 profits.

Year	1	60000×0.9	=	54000
	2	60000×0.9^2	=	48600
	3	60000×0.9^3	=	43740
	4	60000×0.9^4	=	39366
	5	60000×0.9^5	=	35429.5
	6	60000×0.9^6	=	31886.5
				£253022.0

NOTE:

This calculation may also be carried out using geometric progressions. It is the sum of a geometric progression to 7 terms with the first term then deducted.

$$a = 60000$$
$$r = 0.9$$
$$n = 7$$

$$S_n = \frac{a(l - r^n)}{l - r} = \frac{60000(1 - 0.9^7)}{1 - 0.9} = \frac{60000(0.521703)}{0.1} = £313021.8$$

Deduct the first term 60000

= £313021.8 - 60,000
= £253021.8
£253022 as above

SCENARIO 2

Expected value of Direct Launch.

Node (A): $0.7(90000 \times 6) + 0.3(30000 \times 6)$

= £378000 + 54000 = **£432,000**

SCENARIO 3

Expected Value of Market Research

Node (B): $0.95(100000 \times 6) + 0.05(25000 \times 6)$

= £570000 + 7500 = **£577,500**

Deduct £35,000 for extensions

= **£542500**

Node (C): $0.95(90000 \times 6) + 0.05(30000 \times 6)$

= £513000 + 9000 = **£522,000**

Node [1] : Compare £542500 and £522000

∴ It is worth spending more.

Carrying £542500 back to (E).

Node (D):$0.34(70000 \times 6) + 0.66(50000 \times 6)$

£142800 + 198000 = £340,800

Node [2] : £340800 or £0 from no Launch.

Node (E): $0.59 \times 542500 + 0.41 \times 340800$

£320075 + 139728 = **£459,803**

Deduct Market Research Expenditure.

£459,803 - 30,000 = **£429,803**

Node [3] : Final Decision

Scenario 1 EMV = £253022

Scenario 2 EMV = £432000

Scenario 3 EMV = £429803

∴ Choose Scenario 2 as this gives the greatest expected monetary value. However Scenario 3 is close. Had the cash flows been discounted, the situation may be different.

POINTS TO NOTE.
13.

a. Decision trees do not show any more information than could be shown in a tabular form, but they may enable a clearer overview to be obtained.
b. Invariably decision tree problems involve investment situations spread over a number of years.
c. Because decision trees use expected values as the decision criterion they suffer from the same disadvantages as expected value which are given in Chapter 2.

SELF REVIEW QUESTIONS.

1. What are Decision Trees? (2)

2. Distinguish between the types of nodes found in Decision Trees (3)

3. What is the Forward Pass? (5)

4. What is the Backward Pass? (8).

EXERCISES WITH ANSWERS COMMENCING PAGE 488

A1. .A firm has developed a new product X. They can either test the market or abondon the project. The details are set out below.

Test market cost £50,000; likely outcomes are favourable (P = 0.7) or failure (P = 0.3)

If favourable they could either abandon or produce it when demand is anticipated to be

Low	*P=0.25*	*Loss*	*£100,000*
Medium	*P=0.6*	*Profit*	*£150,000*
High	*P=0.15*	*Profit*	*£450,000*

If the test market indicates failure the project would be abandoned. Abandonement at any stage results in a gain of £30,000 from the special machinery used.

Draw the decision tree showing the nodes and probabilities.

A2. Evaluate the decision tree in A1.

EXAMINATION QUESTIONS WITH ANSWERS COMMENCING PAGE 488

A3. company is considering whether to lease a large factory, with capactiy of 100,000 units p.a., or a smaller factory, with capactiy of 70,000 units p.a. for the manufacture of a new product, which is expected to have a life of 8 years. The company believes that there is a 40% chance that the demand will be 100,000 units p.a. during the first two years, and a 60% chance that it will be 70,000 units p.a. during this time. Demand for the subsequent six years is estimated as follows:-

Annual demand for the first 2 years	*100,000*			*70,000*		
Annual demand for the next 6 years	*100,000*	*70,000*	*50,000*	*100,000*	*70,0000*	*50,000*
Probability	*.3*	*.5*	*.2*	*.2*	*.6*	*.2*

The fixed costs of operation are estimated as £50,000 p.a. for the large factory and £40,00 p.a. for the smaller factory. Contribution per unit is expected to be £1 with the large factory and £0.9 with the smaller.

The company proposes to review the situation after two years, and would consider the following possible changes:-

a.the enlargement of the smaller factory to a capacity of 100,000 units p.a. if demand during the first two years is 100,000 units p.a. This would add

£12,000 p.a. to fixed costs, but would not affect contributions per unit.

b.the reduction of the large factory to a capacity of 70,000 units p.a. if demand during the first two years is 70,000 units p.a. This would save £8,000 p.a. on fixed costs, but would not affect contribution per unit.

By constructing and analysing a decision tree representing this situation, advise the company what course of action to pursue.

(Note: the use of discounted cash flows is not required).

A4. A company has the opportunity of marketing a new package of computer games. It has two possible courses of action: to test market on a limited scale or to give up the project completely. A test market would cost £160,000 and current evidence suggest that consumer reaction is equally likely to be 'positive' or 'negative'. If the reaction to the test marketing were to be 'positive' the company could either market the computer games nationally or still give up the project completely. Research suggests that a national launch might result in the following sales:

Sales	Contribution £million	Probability
High	1.2	0.25
Average	0.3	0.5
Low	-0.24	0.25

If the test marketing were to yield 'negative' results the company would give up the project. Giving up the project at any point would result in a contribution of £60,000 from the sale of copyright etc to another manufacturer. All contributions have been discounted to present values.

You are required to:

(a) draw a decision tree to represent this situation, including all relevant probabilities and financial values;

(b) recommend a course of action for the company on the basis of expected values;

(c) explain any limitations of this method of analysis.

(CIMA Quantitative Methods)

A5. The Cacus Chemical Company has recently developed a new product for which a substantial market is likely to exist in 1 year's time. Due to the highly unstable nature of this product, a new production process must be set up at a cost of £2.5 million to cope with the anticipated high temperature reactions. This process will take 1 year to develop, but it is estimated that there is only a 0.55 probability that it will provide adequate standards of safety.

In the light of this, the company are considering the additional development of a computerised control system (CCS) which will detect and warn against dangerous reaction conditions. Research on the CCS will take one year and cost £1 million and Cacus estimate that there is a 0.75 probability that the CCS can be developed successfully.

Development of the CCS can either begin immediately or be postponed for 1 year until the safety of the new process is known. If the CCS is developed immediately and the new process proves to have an adequate standard of safety, then the CCS will be unnecessary and the £1 million expenditure will have been wasted. On the other hand, if the CCS is postponed and the new process turns out to be unsafe, a subsequently successful development of the CCS will have delayed the product by 1 year. If neither the new process nor the CCS are successful, there is no way in which the product can be safely manufactured, and the project will have to be abandoned.

If sales of the new product can commence in 1 year's time, it has been estimated that the discounted profit would amount to a total of £10 million before any allowance is made for depreciation on the new process or the CCS. If the launch of the product is delayed by 1 year, however, the total returns is expected to fall to £8.5 million due to the possibility of other manufacturers entering the market. For simplicity, you may ignore the effects of discounting on the expenditure on the CCS.

Required:

(a) Draw a decision tree to represent the various courses of action open to the company.

(b) Which course of action would you recommend to the management of Cacus?

(c) By how much would the probability of a successful new process of development (currently estimated to be 0.55) have to change before you would alter your recommendation in (b)? Does the decision in question appear particularly sensitive to the value of this probability?

(ACCA Quantitative Analysis)

A6. a. Outline three different criteria for choosing between various alternative strategies in decision theory. Comment upon the strengths and weaknesses of each criterion.

b. An oil company is prospecting in a certain area in the North Sea for which it has already obtained a licence. For each potentially promising site they either drill directly in the hope of finding oil or they can carry out a survey first and then drill if the survey proves positive. If the survey does prove positive they know from experience that there is a 70% chance of striking oil in workable quantities. There is still a 10% chance even if the survey does prove negative. They have also found that in this area 20% of surveys prove positive.

You are required to:

i. Construct a decision tree for the problem.

ii. Calculate the probability of there being oil in workable quantities on a particular site.

iii. Apply one of the criteria outlined in (a) to determine what the company's policy should be in your opinion.

You are given the following additional information:

Cost of survey=£200,000

Cost of drilling per site=£3 million

Revenue from oil (if found in workable quantities) expected per site=£30 million

(CIPFA Analytical Techniques)

EXAMINATION QUESTIONS WITHOUT ANSWERS.

B1. An oil company has recently acquired rights in a certain area to conduct surveys and test drillings to lead to lifting oil where it is found in commercially exploitable quantities.

The area is already considered to have good potential for finding oil in commercial quantities. At the outset the company has the choice to conduct further geological tests or to carry out a drilling programme immediately. On the known conditions, the company estimates that there is a 70:30 chance of further tests showing a 'success'.

Whether the tests show the possibility of ultimate success or not or even if no tests are undertaken at all, the company could still pursue its drilling programme or alternatively consider selling its rights to drill in the area. Thereafter, however, if it carries out the drilling programme, the likelihood of final success or failure is considered dependent on the foregoing stages. Thus:

- *If 'successful' tests have been carried out, the expectation of success in drilling is given as 80:20;*
- *If the tests indicate 'failure', then the expectation of success in drilling is given as 20:80;*
- *If no tests have been carried out at all the expectation of success in drilling is given as 55:45.*

Costs and revenues have been estimated for all possible outcomes and the net present value of each is given below:

Outcome	*Net present value*
	£m
Success:	
With prior tests	*100*
Without prior tests	*120*
Failure:	
With prior tests	*-50*
Without prior tests	*-40*
Sale of exploitation rights:	
Prior tests show 'success'	*65*
Prior tests show 'failure'	*15*
Without prior tests	*45*

You are required to:

a. *draw up a decision (probability) tree diagram to represent the above information;*

b. *evaluate the tree in order to advise the management of the company on its best course of action;*

c. ***discuss the value of decision trees in providing management with guidance for decision making. Give examples of any situation where you consider their use would be of benefit.***

(CIMA QUANTITATIVE TECHNIQUES)

4 Statistics – Introduction

INTRODUCTION

1. The syllabuses at which this manual is aimed include selected aspects of statistical theory mainly concerning applications in significance testing, sampling and the determination of confidence limits. Before these applications can be studied in detail some preliminary knowledge is required regarding particular statistical concepts such as means, variance and standard deviation and of the general nature and characteristics of frequency distributions.

In addition some knowledge is required of the characteristics, properties and relationships of particular distributions namely the Normal, Binomial and Poisson Distributions.

Accordingly this background material is covered in this chapter. The treatment is relatively brief since for most students this will be by way of revision.

STATISTICAL ANALYSIS

2. Statistical Analysis or, more simply, Statistics deals with quantitative data. Statistical Analysis is a scientific method of analysing masses of numerical data so as to summarise the essential features and relationships of the data in order to generalise from the analysis to determine patterns of behaviour, particular outcomes or future tendencies. Statistics can be applied in any field in which there is extensive numerical data, not only in accounting and business but in medicine, engineering, the sciences, public administration and many other areas.

Statistical theory is based on the mathematics of probability which provides the basis for determining not only the general characteristics of data but also the reliability of each generalisation. From a business viewpoint the basic steps in statistical analysis include:

a. Collecting the data from records or other sources or from sample surveys.

b. Analysing and interpreting the figures by means of statistical techniques.

c. Using the calculated results together with probabilities, costs and revenues ot make more rational decision.

FREQUENCY DISTRIBUTIONS

3. Before data can be effectively used or analysed it is normal to group or arrange the raw data into a manageable form. An important form which is the basis of most of the applications described in this manual is the *frequency distribution.*

This shows the variable values and the number of occurrences (i.e the frequency) of each value, or more commonly, of each class of values, in which case it is known as a *grouped* frequency distribution.

For example, the outputs of 50 operators were recorded during a shift as follows

1286	1329	1410	1340	1277
1419	1103	1383	1401	1343
1509	1292	1227	1288	1596
1322	1457	1184	1359	1461
1128	1339	1429	1540	1235
1384	1485	1498	1322	1520
1505	1572	1517	1417	1485
1401	1292	1255	1132	1336
1362	1305	1262	1396	1426

Table 1

These data could be rearranged in ascending (or descending) order and would then be termed an *array*, or they could be listed in order but with each output listed only once and the frequency (usually denoted by f) written alongside. More simply the values would be grouped into classes and the frequency of the class entered.

Such an arrangement would be as follows.

OUTPUT	FREQUENCY (f)
1100 to under 1200	5
1200 to under 1300	9
1300 to under 1400	14
1400 to under 1500	15
1500 to under 1600	7
	50 $= \Sigma f$

GROUPED FREQUENCY DISTRIBUTION. Table 2

Where Σf is the total of the frequencies

Notes.

a. Such a table is a convenient and informative method of summarising the original raw data albeit with some loss of accuracy.

b. The above table uses equal class intervals. On occasions unequal or open ended class intervals are used.

c. It will be seen that $\Sigma f = 50$ i.e. the number of recording in the original data.

DISCRETE OR CONTINUOUS DATA

4. Discrete data have distinct values with no intermediate points. Thus the number of employees in a department may be 0, 1, 2, 3, 4 etc. but not 2.7 or 4.35. Continuous data can have any values over a range either a whole number or any fraction. Thus, if weights were recorded they might be any value e.g. 10.68 kg, 14.753 kg, 16 kg, 21.005 kg. If continuous data were formed into a frequency distribution it would be a *continuous frequency distribution*. Continuous frequency distributions are much more amenable to statistical analysis and most of the statistical tables are based on continuous values.

Because of this, where the statistical population is large, continuity of values is often assumed even though strictly the data are discrete.

For simplicity the same assumption is often made in examination questions.

Note:

The term population is used in the statistical sense meaning *all* possible observations of a given quantity in which one is interested. An alternative term is *universe*.

CHARTING FREQUENCY DISTRIBUTIONS

5. The most common method of charting a grouped frequency distribution is by a *histogram.* A histogram is a set of vertical bars or columns whose *areas* are proportional to the frequencies represented. Frequencies are plotted on the vertical axis and the class intervals of the values on the horizontal axis. Figure 1 shows the histogram of the distribution given in Table 2.

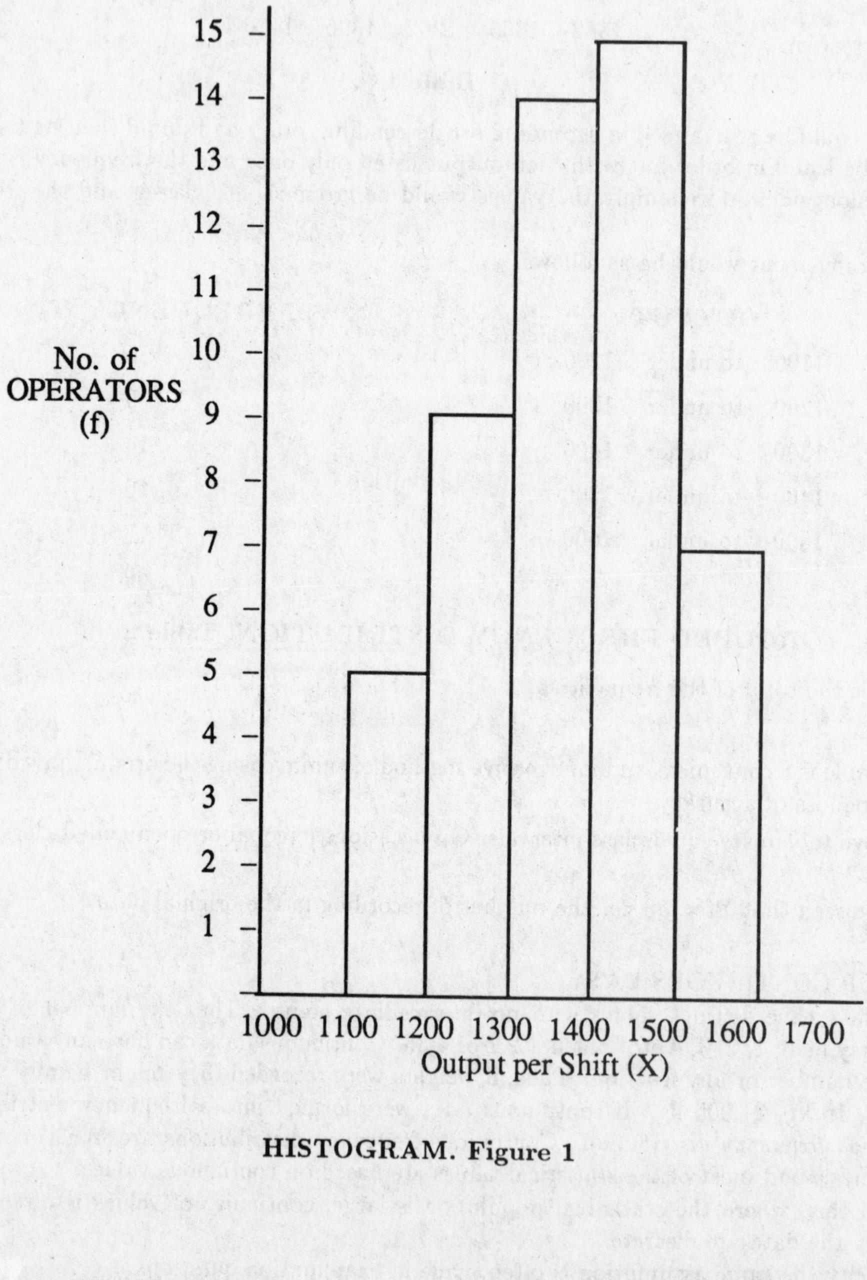

HISTOGRAM. Figure 1

An alternative to the histogram, based on the same scales, is the *frequency polygon* in which straight lines join the mid points of the class intervals. The area covered by the polygon is the same as the histogram. The data in Table 2 are shown as a frequency polygon in Figure 2.

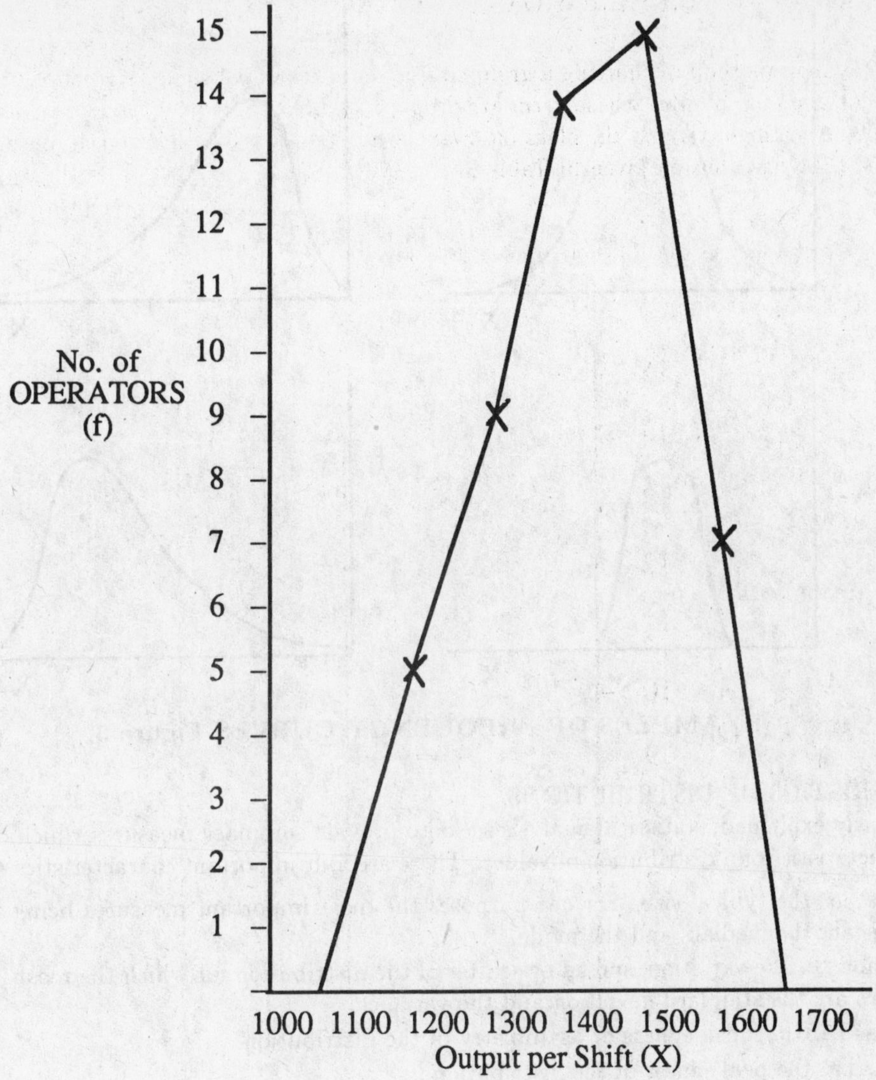

FREQUENCY POLYGON. Figure 2.

FREQUENCY CURVES

6. A smooth curve can be drawn to depict the frequency distributions of a population of continuous data. This is the limiting form of the histogram or frequency polygon as the number of classes becomes infinitely large and the class intervals become infinitely small. Some types of frequency curves are shown in Figure 3.

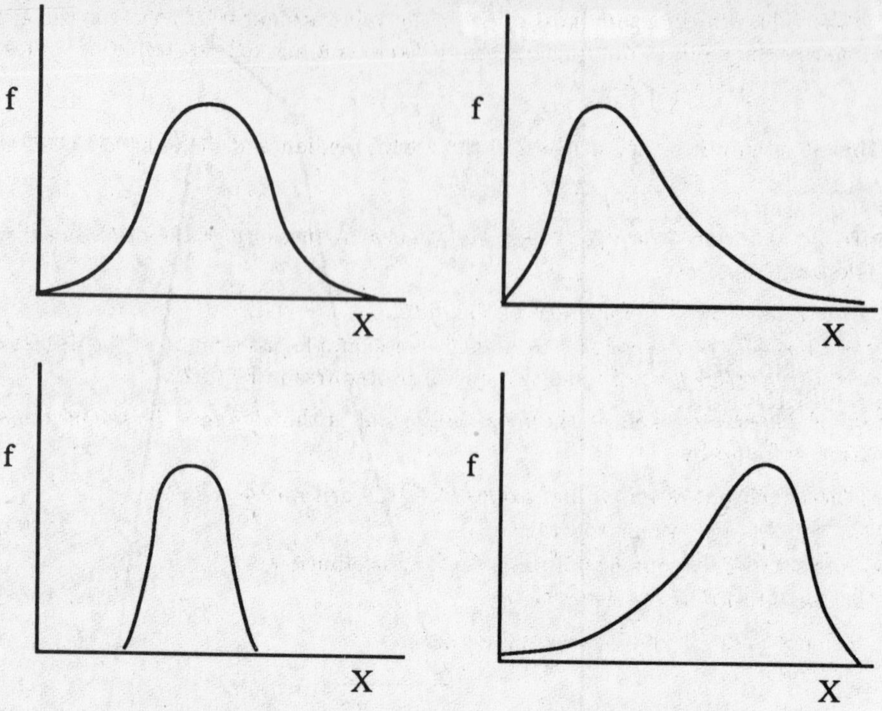

EXAMPLES OF FREQUENCY CURVES Figure 3.

CHARACTERISTICS OF DISTRIBUTIONS

7. As previously explained, statistical analysis seeks to provide summary measures which describe the important characteristics of a distribution of values. There are four important characteristics of distributions:

a. Average i.e. the typical size. For our purposes the most important measures being the arithmetic mean, the median, and the mode.
b. Dispersion i.e. the variation, spread or scatter of the distribution for which the most important measures are the standard deviation and the variance.
c. Skewness i.e. the lopsidedness or asymmetry of the distribution.
d. Kurtosis i.e. the peakedness of the distribution.

AVERAGE

8. By far the most important measure of central tendency is the arithmetic mean, usually denoted by $\overline{x}$. The arithmetic mean, or simply the mean, is calculated by the following formula.

$$\overline{x} = \frac{\Sigma x}{n}$$

where n is the number of values.

When the data are arranged in a grouped frequency distribution the formula is

$$\overline{x} = \frac{\Sigma f x}{\Sigma f}$$

where f is the number of values in an interval and x is the midpoint of the class interval.

The mean lends itself to subsequent analysis because it includes the values of all items. However it may not coincide with any actual value and may, in some circumstances, be unrepresentative because of the effect of extreme values.

The *median* of any set of data is the middle value in order of size if n is odd, or the mean of the two middle items if n is even. Where the data contain a few very large or small values the median value is often considered to be a more representative value than the mean although it cannot be used for subsequent calculations as is possible with the mean.

The *mode* is the value which occurs most often or the value around which there is the greatest degree of clustering. Ordinarily the mode is only meaningful if there is a marked clustering of values round a single point.

Note.

It follows that in a symmetrical distribution the mean, median and mode have the same value.

DISPERSION

9. Dispersion is the variation or scatter of a set of values. A measure of the degree of dispersion of data is needed for two basic purposes.

a. To assess the reliability of the average of the data.

b. To serve as a basis for control of the variability. For example, assessment of the degree of quality variation is an essential part of Quality Control procedures in factories.

The measure of dispersion which is the most important is the *standard deviation*, denoted by σ. The standard deviation is found by:

a. Squaring the deviations of individual values from the arithmetic mean.

b. Adding the squared deviations together.

c. Dividing this sum by the number of items in the distribution.

d. Taking the square root of the value in (c).

This basic formula is as follows for ungrouped data.

$$\sigma = \sqrt{\frac{\Sigma(x-\mu)^2}{N}}$$

where μ = population mean and N = population size

Note.

The above formula is the appropriate one where all the details are known of the whole population. Since in many circumstances the whole population is not known and a sample is taken in order to estimate the population characteristics the formula which provides the best estimate of the population standard deviation, based on the sample data, is:

$$s = \sqrt{\frac{\Sigma(x-\overline{x})^2}{n-1}}$$

where s is the estimate of σ, the population standard deviation.

The standard deviation is in the same units as the variable measured. For example, if the mean and standard deviation of the ages of a group of people were calculated the answers might be as follows

mean	$= \overline{x} =$	43.5 years
Standard deviation	$= \sigma =$	6.9 years.

The **variance** is the square of the standard deviation i.e.

$$\text{variance} = \sigma^2$$

Where the data are arranged in a grouped frequency distribution, the formulae are as follows:

For a population

$$\sigma = \sqrt{\frac{\Sigma f(x-\mu)^2}{\Sigma f}}$$

where $\Sigma f = N$ = population size

For a sample

$$s = \sqrt{\frac{\Sigma f(x-\overline{x})^2}{\Sigma f - 1}}$$

where $\Sigma f - 1 = n - 1$, and n is the sample size.

The above formulae are in a basic form and alternatives, which may reduce computation, are available. For example, the formula for the standard deviation of a sample

$$s = \sqrt{\frac{\Sigma(x - \overline{x})^2}{n - 1}}$$

can be re-arranged to produce an alternative formulation thus:

$$s = \sqrt{\frac{\Sigma x^2 - \frac{(\Sigma x)^2}{n}}{n - 1}}$$

Unlike standard deviations, variances can be added together. This is a useful property when two distributions have to be combined i.e. if two distributions A and B had variances of σ_A^2 and σ_B^2 then the variance of the combined distributions is $\sigma_A^2 + \sigma_B^2$.

The following example demonstrates the measures covered in paragraph 8 and 9.

Example 1.

Calculate the mean, standard deviation and variance of the following data.

5, 8, 15, 29, 47, 47, 64, 71, 74

SOLUTION. As there are 9 values, $n = 9$.

x	$x - \overline{x}$	$(x - \overline{x})^2$
5	−35	1225
8	−32	1024
15	−25	625
29	−11	121
47	+ 7	49
47	+ 7	49
64	+24	576
71	+31	961
74	+34	1156
$\Sigma x = 360$		5786

$\therefore\ \overline{x} = \frac{360}{9} = 40$

$\therefore$ variance $= \sigma^2 = \frac{5786}{9} = \underline{\underline{642.88}}$ Standard deviation $= \sigma = \sqrt{642.88} = \underline{\underline{25.355}}$

Note.

The median of the above data is the middle value i.e. the 5th, which is 47. The mode is the value which occurs most frequently which is also 47 as it occurs twice.

Example 2 mean and standard deviation - Grouped Data

Calculate the mean and standard deviation for the sample data in Table 2.

Class interval	mid-point x	f	fx	$f(x - \overline{x})^2$
1100 – 1200	1150	5	5750	242000
1200 – 1300	1250	9	11250	129600
1300 – 1400	1350	14	18900	5600
1400 – 1500	1450	15	21750	96000
1500 – 1600	1550	7	10850	226800
		50	68500	700000

Table 2

$$\overline{x} = \frac{\Sigma fx}{\Sigma f} = \frac{68500}{50} = 1370 \text{ units}$$

Since Table 2 represents sample data the standard deviation is calculated as below:

$$\begin{aligned} s &= \sqrt{\frac{\Sigma f(x-\overline{x})^2}{n-1}} \\ &= \sqrt{\frac{7000000}{49}} \\ &= \sqrt{14285.714} \\ &= \underline{\underline{119.52 \text{ units}}} \text{ to 2d.p.} \end{aligned}$$

RELATIVE AND ABSOLUTE DISPERSION

10. The standard deviation provides considerable information on the *absolute* dispersion of a given distribution, the higher the standard deviation the greater the amount of scatter.

On occasions it is useful to have a measure of the *relative dispersion* of a distribution, particularly if distributions are being compared. The measure which provides this relative view is the *coefficient of variation* or, as it is sometimes known, the *coefficient of dispersion.*

This is simply the ratio of the standard deviation of a distribution to the mean of the distribution, expressed as a percentage:

$$\text{Coefficient of variation } = \frac{\sigma}{\overline{x}} \times 100\%$$

For example, does distribution A vary relatively more than distribution B given that

$$\sigma_A = 5.5 \quad \overline{x}_A = 45$$

$$\sigma_B = 2.6 \quad \overline{x}_B = 18.5?$$

Coefficients of variation

$A = \frac{5.5}{45} \times 100 = 12.2\%$

$B = \frac{2.6}{18.5} \times 100 = 14.05\%$

$\therefore$ Distribution B is relatively more variable.

SKEWNESS

11. Where there is a lack of symmetry in a distribution, skewness exists. The effect of this is that the mode, mean, and median have differing values. Figure 4 illustrates *positive* and *negative* skewness and the position of the mean, mode and median.

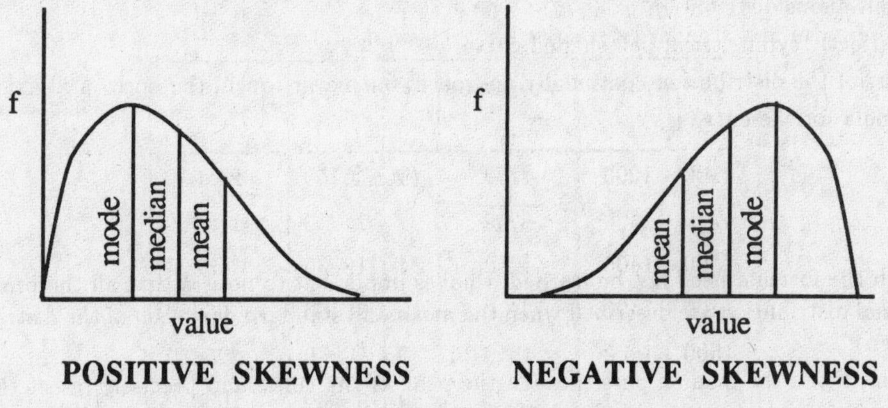

Figure 4

The accurate measure of skewness requires advanced techniques but an approximate measure of the amount and direction of skewness can be found by the *Pearson coefficient of skewness* thus

$$\text{Sk} = \frac{3\ (\text{Mean - Median})}{\sigma}$$

The formula has limited practical use and skewness is usually treated in descriptive terms rather than summarised by a single measure.

KURTOSIS

12. This relates to the peakedness of distributions. This can range from distributions which are *platykurtic* (flatter than normal) through *mesokurtic* (or normal peakedness to *leptokurtic* (more peaked than normal).

These are illustrated in Figure 5.

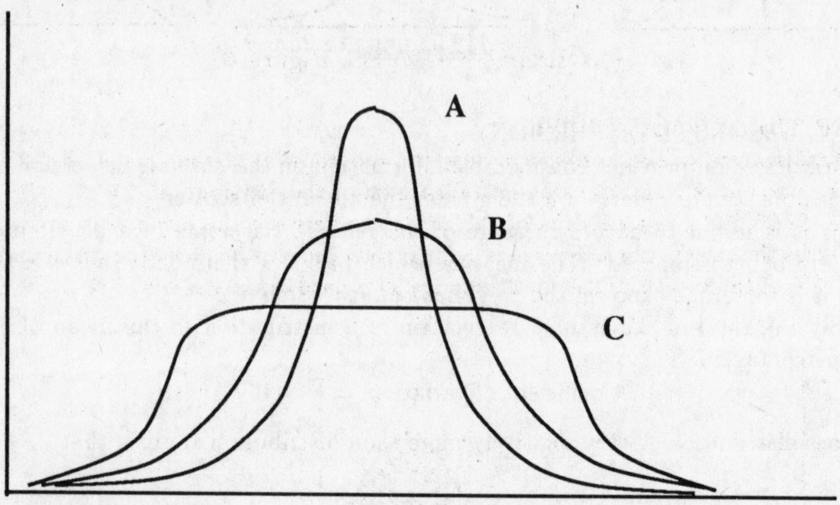

A – leptokurtic distribution
B – mesokurtic distribution
C – platykurtic distribution

Figure 5

THE NORMAL DISTRIBUTION

13. Having discussed the characteristics of distributions in general one particular distribution can now be examined in more detail. This is the *normal distribution* or *normal curve.* The normal distribution is the most important in statistics. It occurs frequently when describing natural occurrences and is of particular importance in sampling theory and statistical inference which are dealt with later in the manual.

The main features of the Normal Distribution are:

a. It is a continuous distribution.

b. It is a perfectly symmetrical bell shaped curve.

c. The 'tails' of the distribution continually approach, but never touch, the horizontal axis.

d. The formula for the curve is

$$y = \frac{1}{\sigma\sqrt{2\pi}}\, e^{-\frac{1}{2}\left(\frac{x-\bar{x}}{\sigma}\right)^2}$$

(although the formula need not be learned, what is important to note is that all the properties of a normal distribution are described when the mean and standard deviation of the distribution are known).

e. The mean, mode the median pass through the peak of the curve and precisely bisect the area under the curve into two equal halves.

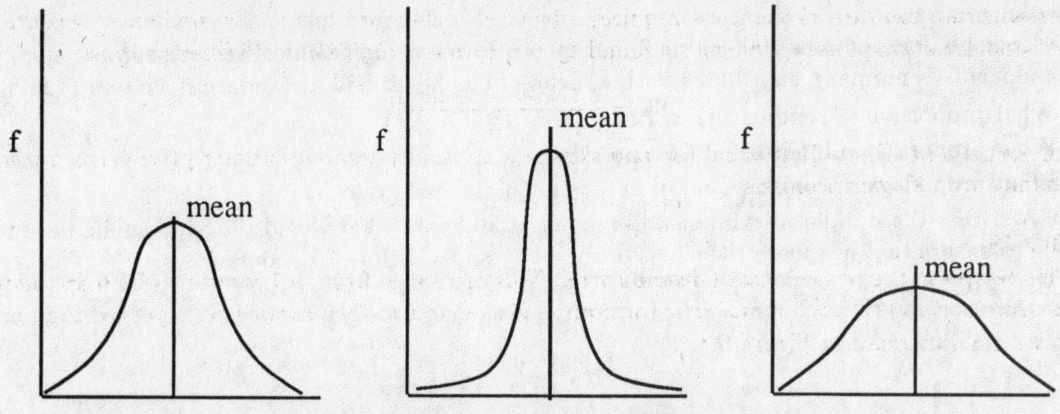

NORMAL CURVES. Figure 6.

AREAS UNDER THE NORMAL CURVE.

14. An important feature of the normal curve is the relationship of the area under the curve (i.e. the percentage of the population) and the standard deviation of the distribution.

For example, 68.25% of the total area of the curve lies between the mean plus and minus 1 standard deviation. It follows that as the normal curve is symmetrical the area between the mean and plus 1 standard deviation is 34.13% of the total and the mean minus 1 standard deviation is also 34.13%. This is shown in Figure 7.

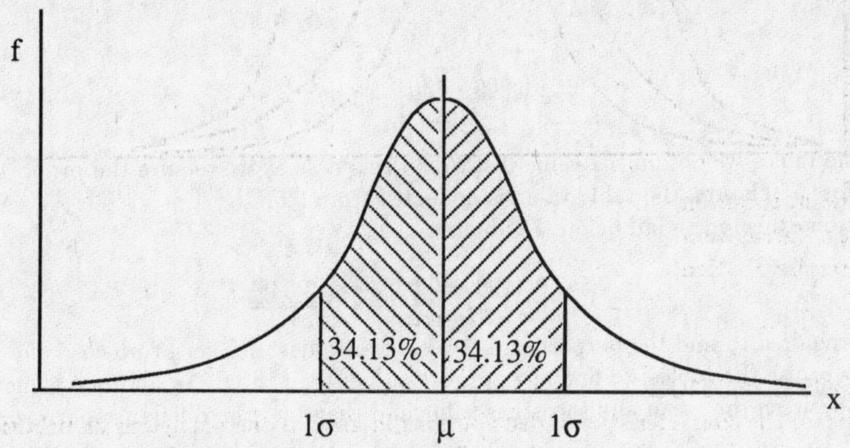

where μ (mu) is the population mean.

Figure 7.

The area between *any* two perpendicular, lines can be found from Table (1) 'Areas under the Normal Curve' but students will find that three particular values occur frequently in problems so that these should be learned.

mean $\pm 1\sigma$ includes 68.26% of the area.
mean$\pm 2\sigma$ includes 95.44% of the area.
mean $\pm 3\sigma$ includes 99.74% of the area.

It will be seen that virtually all of the distribution lies within between the mean minus 3σ and the mean plus 3σ i.e. a range of 6σ

USING THE NORMAL AREA TABLE (Table 1)

15. Normal area tables show the area under the normal curve between the mean and any given number of standard deviations (including fractional values). To use the tables it is necessary to calculate the ***standardised variate*** (often called the 'Z' score') which is simply the number of standard deviations that the required value is away from the mean.

Example.

An assembly line contains 2000 of a component which has a limited life. Records show that the life of the components is normally distributed with a mean of 900 hours and a standard deviation of 80 hours.

a. What proportion of components will fail before 1000 hours?
b. What proportion will fail before 750 hours?
c. What proportion of components fail between 850 and 880 hours?
d. Given that the standard deviation will remain at 80 hours what would the average life have to be to ensure that not more than 10% of components fail before 900 hours?

SOLUTION

a.

$$z = \left|\frac{1000 - 900}{80}\right| = \underline{1.25}$$

(i.e. this means that the value being investigated, 1000 hrs, is 1.25 standard deviations away from the mean of 900 hours).

If Table 1 is examined it will be seen that the value for a z score of 1.25 is 0.3944. As one half of the distribution is less than 900, the proportion which fail before 1000 hours is 0.5 + 0.3944 = $\underline{\underline{89.44\%}}$.

If required this could be expressed as the number of components which are expected to fail, thus

$$2000 \times .8944 = 1788.8 \text{ which would be rounded to } \underline{\underline{1789}}$$

b.

$$z = \left|\frac{900 - 750}{80}\right| = 1.875$$

and from the tables we obtain the value 0.4696. In this case as we require the proportion that will fail before 750 hours, the table value is deducted from 0.5.

∴ Proportion expected to fail before 750 hours.

$$= 0.5 - 0.4696 = \underline{0.0304} \text{ i.e. } \underline{\underline{3.04\%}}$$

c. When it is required to find the porportion between two values, neither of which is the mean, it is necessary to use the tables, to find the porportion between the mean and one value and the proportion between the mean and the other value and then find the difference between the two proportions.

$$z = \left|\frac{900 - 850}{80}\right| = 0.625 \text{ which gives a proportion of } \underline{\underline{0.2340}}$$

Similarly $z = \left|\frac{900 - 880}{80}\right| = 0.25$ which gives a proportion of $\underline{0.0987}$

∴ Proportion between 850 and 880 is

$$0.2340 - 0.0987 = \underline{0.1353} \text{ i.e. } \underline{\underline{13.53\%}}$$

Note.

This part of the example illustrates the proportion between two values on the *same side* of the mean. If the two values are on opposite sides of the mean, the calculated proportions would be *added*.

d. This problem is the reverse of the earlier questions although based on the same principles. The earlier problems started with the mean and standard deviation, found the z score and thence the proportion from the tables. We now *start* with the proportion and work back, through the tables, to find a new mean value.

If not more than 10% should be under 900 it follows that 90% of the area of the curve must be greater than 900 i.e. as shown in Figure 8.

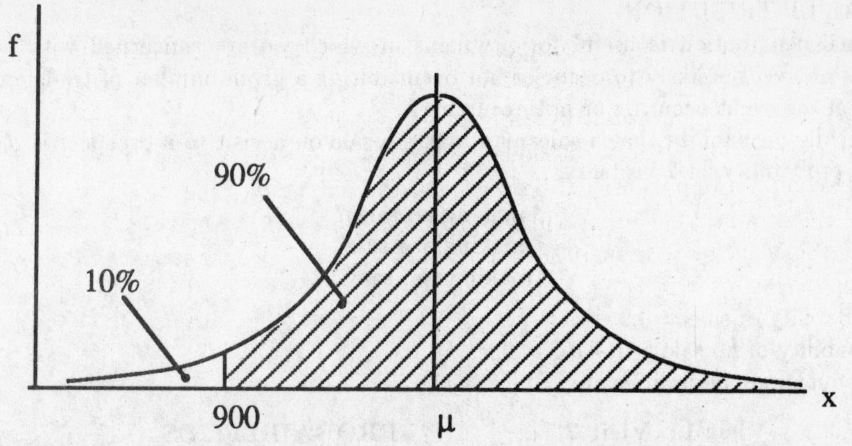

Figure 8

Bearing in mind that the tables only show values for half the distribution (because both halves are identical) we have to look in the tables for a value close to 0.4 (ie. 0.9 - 0.5).

It will be seen that there is a value in the body of the table of 0.3997 i.e. virtually 0.4. This value has a z score of 1.28.

$$\text{Thus } 1.28 = \left|\frac{\text{mean - 900}}{80}\right|$$

$$\therefore \ 102.4 = \text{mean - 900}$$

$$\therefore \ \text{mean} = \underline{1002.4 \text{ hours.}}$$

Thus if the mean life of the components is 1002.4 hours with a standard deviation of 80 hours, less than 10% of the components will fail before 900 hours.

SEE THE APPENDIX FOR A COMMENT ON NORMAL DISTRIBUTION TABLES.

OTHER PROBABILITY DISTRIBUTIONS

16. The binomial and Poisson distributions are probability distributions i.e. they directly depict the probability of the required frequency of an event occurring. The binomial and Poisson distributions describe the behaviour of *attributes* e.g. , success or failure, good or bad, black or white, whilst the Normal Distribution describes the behaviour of variables or measurements e.g. height, weight, length of life. The binomial and Poisson distributions are *discrete* distributions compared with the Normal Distribution which is continuous.

THE BINOMIAL DISTRIBUTION

17. The binomal distribution is useful for problems in which we are concerned with determining the number of times an event is likely to occur or not occur during a given number of trials and consequently the probability of the event occuring or not occurring.

For example, the probability that a salesman makes a sale on a visit to a prospect is *0.2*.
What is the probability, in 2 visits, of:

making no sales?
making one sale?
making two sales?

Let p = probability of sale = 0.2
let q = probability of no sale = 1 – 0.2 = 0.8
The various outcome possibilities are

Visit 1	**Visit 2**				**PROBABILITIES**		
Sale	Sale	i.e.	$p \times p$	=	$p^2 = 0.2^2$	=	0.04
Sale	No sale	i.e.	$p \times q$	=	0.02×0.8	=	0.16
No sale	Sale	i.e.	$q \times p$	=	0.8×0.2	=	0.16
No sale	No sale	i.e.	$q \times q$	=	$q^2 = 0.8^2$	=	0.64
							1.00

Thus P (no sales) = 0.64
P (one sale) = 0.32
P (two sales) = 0.04

In this simple example it is easy to show the whole process but this becomes lengthy and cumbersome where the number of trials (visits, in the above example) becomes larger.

Fortunately there is a simpler approach which is by the expansion of the binomial expression. The general form of the binomial expression is

$$(p+q)^n$$

where p = probability of an event occuring
q = probability of an event not occuring
and n = number of trials

In the above example p = probability of a sale i.e. 0.2, q = probability of no sale i.e. 0.8 and n = number of visits i.e. .2.

$$\therefore (p+q)^2 = p^2 + 2pq + q^2$$
$$= 0.2^2 + 2(0.2 \times 0.8) + 0.8^2$$
$$= 0.04 + 0.32 + 0.64 \text{ i.e. the values previously obtained.}$$

Where n becomes larger it is necessary to be able to calculate the coefficients of each part of the expansion in a direct manner rather than writing out the whole expansion.

THE BINOMIAL COEFFICIENTS

18. Tables are not always available in examinations and it is therefore necessary to be able to solve a binomial problem from first principles.

Assume that the full expansion is required of the binomial formula $(p+q)^5$.
The first step is to write down the successive terms within the brackets i.e.

$$(p^5) + (p^4q) + (p^3q^2) + (p^2q^3) + (pq^4) + (q^5)$$

It will be noted that

— the number of terms (i.e. 6 in this case) is one more than the power of n (i.e. 5 in this case).

— the power of p starts with the n'th power (i.e. 5 in this case) and decreases from term to term whilst conversely the power of q increases from term to term.

— the powers of p and q in every expression total n (i.e. 5 in this case).

The next step is to calculate the coefficient of each term i.e. the value in front of each bracket. This can be done by using either *Pascal's Triangle* or by the *combination formula.*

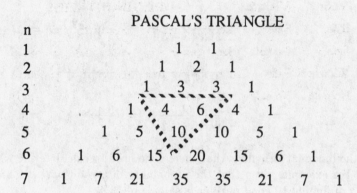

PASCAL'S TRIANGLE

n	
1	1 1
2	1 2 1
3	1 3 3 1
4	1 4 6 4 1
5	1 5 10 10 5 1
6	1 6 15 20 15 6 1
7	1 7 21 35 35 21 7 1

and so on for higher values of n.

The values in any line are derived by adding adjacent figures in the line above as shown by the dotted triangle. It will be noted that the values are symmetrical on each line and that there is one more number on each line than the value of n. The coefficients in the expansion can be read directly from the triangle against the value of n. Where n is 5, as in our example, the coefficients are

1 5 10 10 5 1

Thus the expansion of $(p+q)^5$ is

$$p^5 + 5(p^4q) + 10(p^3q^2) + 10(p^2q^3) + 5(pq^4) + q^5$$

COMBINATION FORMULA

19. Although useful for small values of n, Pascal's triangle becomes unwieldy for larger values but the combination formula can be used for any value of n with equal facility.

The general form of the combination formula dealt with in Chapter 2 enables us to find the number of combinations of r that are possible given that there is a total of n.

Using the combination formula to find the coefficients of our example, (p + q)5, we obtain the following:

								BINOMIAL COEFFICIENT
$\binom{5}{0}$	or $^5C_0$	=	$\frac{5!}{0! \times (5-0)!}$	=	$\frac{5.4.3.2.1}{5.4.3.2.1}$	=		1
		(note: 0! = 1)						
$\binom{5}{1}$	or $^5C_1$	=	$\frac{5!}{1! \times (5-1)!}$	=	$\frac{5.4.3.2.1}{4.3.2.1}$	=		5
$\binom{5}{2}$	or $^5C_2$	=	$\frac{5!}{2! \times (5-2)!}$	=	$\frac{5.4.3.2.1}{2.1 \times 3.2.1}$	=		10
$\binom{5}{3}$	or $^5C_3$	=	$\frac{5!}{3! \times (5-3)!}$	=	$\frac{5.4.3.2.1}{3.2.1 \times 2.1}$	=		10
$\binom{5}{4}$	or $^5C_4$	=	$\frac{5!}{4! \times (5-4)!}$	=	$\frac{5.4.3.2.1}{4.3.2.1 \times 1}$	=		5
$\binom{5}{5}$	or $^5C_5$	=	$\frac{5!}{5! \times (5-5)!}$	=	$\frac{5.4.3.2.1}{5.4.3.2.1}$	=		1

The advantage of the binomial formula is that there is no need to calculate the whole expansion if only one value is required. For example, given that the probability of a good part is 0.8 and a bad part is 0.2 what is the probability of finding 10 good parts in a sample of 12?

This means calculating the probability of one particular term in the binomial expansion i.e.

$$x(p^{10}q^2)$$

where x is the appropriate binomial coefficient and p is the probability of a good part and q the probability of a bad part.

To calculate the required coefficient:

$$^{12}C_{10} = \frac{12!}{10! \times (12-10)!} = \frac{12 \times 11}{2} = 66$$

$$\therefore\ 66(0.8^{10} \times 0.2^2) = \underline{\underline{0.2834}} \text{ i.e. } \underline{\underline{28.34\%}}$$

MEAN AND STANDARD DEVIATION OF THE BINOMIAL DISTRIBUTION

20. The mean of a binomial distribution is found by multiplying the probability of the event in which we are interested by n, the number of trials:

$$\text{Mean} = np$$

This value is the same as the *expected value* previously discussed in Chapter 2.

The variance of a binomial distribution is calculated as:

$$\text{variance} = npq \text{ so that the standard deviation is}$$
$$\sigma = \sqrt{npq}$$

Example.

Assuming the same data as in Paragraph 19 i.e. sample of 12 with the probability of a good part being 0.8, what is the expected number of good parts in a sample of 12 and what is the standard deviation?

Expected number of good parts $= np = 12 \times 0.8 = \underline{\underline{9.6}}$

Standard deviation $= \sqrt{npq} = \sqrt{12 \times 0.8 \times 0.2} = \underline{\underline{1.386}}$

CHARACTERISTICS OF THE BINOMIAL DISTRIBUTION

21.

a. It is a discrete distribution of the occurences of an event with two outcomes — success or failure, good or bad.

b. The trials must be independent of one another. This assumption implies sampling from an infinite population. Sampling *with* replacement fulfils this requirement but where sampling without replacement is used the binomial distribution is still useful provided that the sample size is less than 20

c. As the number of trials grows and if $p \simeq 0.5$ then the binomial distributions approaches the Normal Distribution. For the Normal Distribution to be an appropriate approximation, np should be > 5.

d. The main parameters of the binomial distribution are

$$\mu = np$$
$$\sigma = \sqrt{npq}$$
$$\text{Standardised skewness} = \frac{q-p}{\sqrt{npq}}$$

A PRACTICAL EXAMPLE USING THE BINOMIAL DISTRIBUTION

22. Components are placed into bins containing 100. After inspection of a large number of bins the average number of defective parts was found to be 10 with a standard deviation of 3.

Assuming that the same production conditions continue, except that bins containing 300 were used:

a. What would the average number of defective components per larger bin?

b. What would be standard deviation of the number of defective per larger bin?

c. How many components must each bin hold so that the standard deviation of the number of defective components is equal to 1% of the total number of components in the bin?

Solution

Proportion defective = $\frac{10}{100} = \underline{0.1}$

Proportion good = 1 - 0.1 = $\underline{0.9}$

Mean = np = 100 × 0.1 = 10 components defective on average.

Standard deviation = npq = 100 × 0.1 × 0.9 = $\underline{\underline{3}}$

thus confirming the values given in the example.

a. Larger bins of 300

$\therefore\ n = 300$

$\therefore$ Average number of defectives = 300 × 0.1 = $\underline{\underline{30}}$

b. Standard deviation becomes

$$\sqrt{npq} = \sqrt{300 \times 0.1 \times 0.9} = 5.2$$

c. Standard deviation to be 1% of total

$$\therefore \sqrt{npq} = \frac{n}{100}$$
$$\therefore \sqrt{n \times 0.1 \times 0.9} = \frac{n}{100}$$
$$\therefore n \times 0.1 \times 0.9 = \frac{n^2}{10,000}$$
$$900n = n^2$$
$$900 = \frac{n^2}{n} = n$$

$\therefore$ Bins must hold 900 components

NORMAL APPROXIMATION TO THE BINOMIAL

23. As a broad generalisation it is safe to use the Normal approximation to the binomial in the following circumstances:

$$\text{if } np > 5 \text{ when } p < 0.5$$

$$\text{if } nq > 5 \text{ when } p > 0.5$$

When ***proportions*** are being used instead of absolute numbers the formulae given previously do not apply and following relationships hold.

$$\text{population mean} = \mu = p$$
$$\text{standard deviation} = \sigma = \sqrt{\frac{pq}{n}}$$

Example.

Records show that 60% of students pass their examinations at the first attempt. Using the normal approximation to the binomial, calculate the probability that at least 65% of a group of 200 students will pass at the first attempt.

Solution

$$p = 0.6 \quad q = 1 - p \quad = 1 - 0.6 \quad = 0.4$$

$$\sigma = \sqrt{\frac{pq}{n}} \quad = \sqrt{\frac{0.6 \times 0.4}{200}} \quad = 0.035$$

$$z = \frac{0.65 - 0.60}{0.035} = 1.43 \text{ which gives } 0.4236\ (42.36\%)$$

from Table 1. This means that there is a (0.5 - 0.4236) 0.0764 (7.64%) chance of 65 or greater passing at the first attempt. This is shown graphically below.

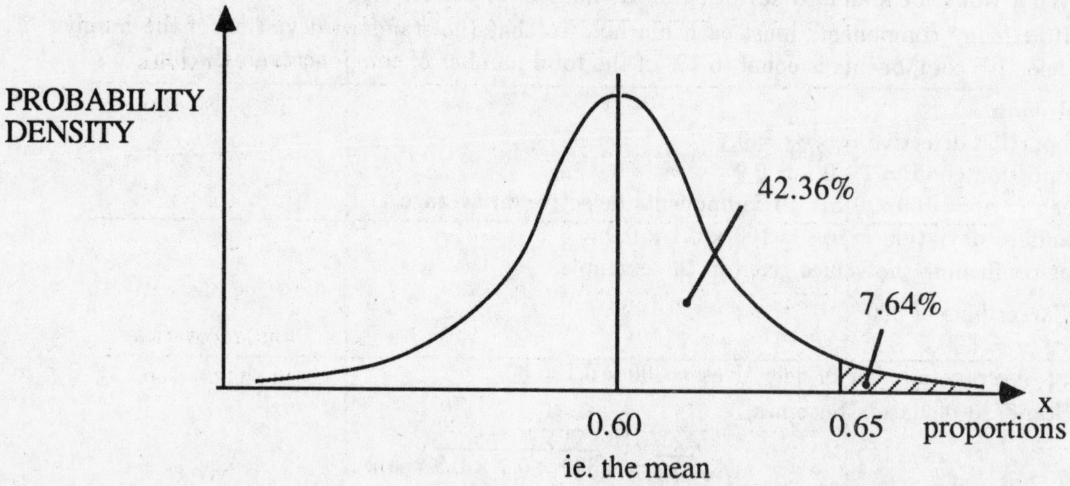

POISSON DISTRIBUTION

24. There are occasions when the binomial distribution cannot be used to find the probability that an event will occur 0, 1, 2, 3 etc. times within a number of trials because the values of 'n' and 'p' are not known. For example, we may know that on a given stretch of motorway 6 accidents happened in a year. However, we are unable to express the number 6 as a probability because we do not know the value of n, the total number of accident possibilities. Furthermore the term q i.e. the probability that an accident will not occur, has no meaning.

All we can say is that 'n', the number of opportunities for accidents, is infinitely large and that the number of accidents that actually happen is relatively small, hence 'p', the probability of an accident occuring is small.

In such circumstances i.e when n is infinitely large and p is small the Poisson distribution can be used. The Poisson distribution is a discrete distribution derived from the binomial distribution. The Poisson distribution can be used without knowing the value of n or p, being based on the *mean value* of the distribution. Thus, if we know the average number of times than an event occurred over a period then the probability that an event will occur 0, 1, 2, 3 etc. times is given by the successive terms of the expansion:

$$\frac{e^{-m}}{0!} + \frac{me^{-m}}{1!} + \frac{m^2e^{-m}}{2!} + \frac{m^3e^{-m}}{3!} \ldots\ldots$$

where e is the constant 2.718 and m is the mean occurrences in the period.

For example, in a transport fleet there is one breakdown a week on average which requires the vehicle to be recovered.

What is the expected pattern of recoveries in a 100 week period?

m = mean breakdowns per week = 1

Number of Recoveries	Probability	Recovery Pattern for 100 weeks
0	$\frac{e^{-m}}{0!} = \frac{2.718}{1} = \frac{1}{2.718} = 0.3679$	0.3679 × 100 = 37 weeks with no recoveries
1	$\frac{me^{-m}}{1!} = \frac{1 \times 2.718^{-1}}{1} = \frac{1}{2.718} = 0.3679$	0.36789 × 100 = 37 weeks with one recovery
2	$\frac{m^2e^{-m}}{2!} = \frac{1^2 \times 2.718^{-1}}{2 \times 1} = \frac{1}{5.436} = 0.1840$	0.184 × 100 = 18 weeks with two recoveries
3	$\frac{m^3e^{-m}}{3!} = \frac{1^3 \times 2.718^{-1}}{3 \times 2 \times 1} = 0.0613$	0.0613 × 100 = 6 weeks with three recoveries
4	$\frac{m^4e^{-m}}{4} = \frac{1^4 \times 2.718^{-1}}{4 \times 3 \times 2 \times 1} = 0.0153$	0.0153 × 100 ≃ 2 weeks with four recoveries
5	$\frac{m^5e^{-m}}{5!} = \frac{1^5 \times 2.718^{-1}}{5 \times 4 \times 3 \times 2 \times 1} = 0.0036$	0.0036 × 100 NIL
	Total Probability = 1.00	Total weeks = 100

It will be seen that the calculated probability of each successive term becomes smaller and smaller continually approaching, but never reaching zero.

These calculations are tedious and tables are available showing Poisson probabilities for any value of m. The tables can show individual or cumulative probabilities and Table VI shows an extract from each type of table.

STANDARD DEVIATION OF A POISSON DISTRIBUTION

25. For once, this is simplicity itself.

The variance of a Poisson distribution equals the mean and the standard deviation is the square root of the variance i.e.

$$\text{variance} = m$$
$$\text{Standard deviation} = \sqrt{m}$$

where m is the mean of the Poisson Distribution

CHARACTERISTICS OF POISSON DISTRIBUTION.

26.

a. It is a discrete distribution and is a limiting form of the binomial distribution when n is large and p or q is small.

b. Mean and variance are equal

c. Is usually definitely positively skewed but cannot be negatively skewed

d. The standardised skewness is found by $\frac{1}{\sqrt{m}}$ where m is the mean.

e. As n becomes very large the Poisson distribution approximates to the Normal Distribution.

f. The mean $= np$

APPLICATIONS OF POISSON DISTRIBUTION

27. The Poisson distribution is similar to the Binomial but is used when n, the number of items or events, is large or unknown and p, the probability of an occurrence, is very small relative to q, the probability of non-occurrence. A rule of thumb is that the Poisson distribution may be used when n is greater than 50 and np, the mean, is less than 5. Some examples follow but it is important to realise that the Poisson distribution only applies when the events occur randomly i.e. they are independent of one another.

EXAMPLE

Customers arrive randomly at a service point at an average rate of 30 per hour. Assuming a Poisson distribution calculate the probability that:

a. No customer arrives in any particular minute.

b. exactly one customer arrives in any particular minute.

c. two or more customers arrive in any particular minute.

d. three or fewer customers arrive in any particular minute.

SOLUTION

The time interval to be used is one minute with a mean of $\frac{30}{60} = 0.5$

a. P(no customer) = 0.6065 from Table VI(a)

b. P(1 customer) = 0.3033 from Table VI(a)

c. P(2 or more) = 1 - 0.9098
= <u>0.0902</u>
The value of 0.9098 is the cummulative probability of 1 or fewer customers arriving in a particular minute from Table VI(b). As the sum of the probability of every possible number of arrivals equals 1, the probability of 2 or more = 1 - P(1 or fewer).

d. P(3 or fewer) = 0.9982 from Table VI(b)

EXAMPLE

A firm buys springs in very large quantities and from past records it is known that 0.2% are defective. The inspection department sample the springs in batches of 500. It is required to set a standard for the inspectors so that if more than the standard number of defectives is found in a batch the consignment can be rejected with at least 90% confidence that the supply is truly defective.

How many defectives per batch should be set as the standard?

SOLUTION

With 0.2% defective and a sample size of 500 $m = 500 \times 0.2 = 1$.

To find the probability of 0, 1, 2, 3, etc or more defectives the probabilities from Table VI(b) are deducted from 1 as follows:

P(0 or more defectives) = certainty = 1

P(1 or more defectives) = 1 - 0.3679 = 0.6321

P(2 or more defectives) = 1 - 0.7358 = 0.2642

P(3 or more defectives) = 1 - 0.9197 = 0.0803

P(4 or more defectives) = 1 - 0.9810 = 0.0190

These probabilities mean, for example, that there is a 26.42% chance that 2 or more defectives will occur at random in a batch of 500 with a 0.2% defect rate. If batches with 2 or more were rejected then there can be 73.58% (1 - 0.2642) confidence that the supply is defective.

As the firm wishes to be at least 90% confident, the standard should be set at 3 or more defectives per batch. This level could only occur at random in 8.03% of occasions so that the firm can be 91.97% confident that the supply is truly defective.

SUMMARY

28.

a. Statistical analysis is the process of analysing data to obtain useful information.
b. A frequency distribution shows the number of occurrences of each variable value.
c. Discrete data have distinct values with no intermediate points whereas continuous data may have any value.
d. The major summary measures of distributions are — Average — Dispersion — Skewness — Kurtosis.
e. The most useful average is the Arithmetic Mean and the most useful measure of dispersion is the standard deviation. The coefficient of variation links these two measures and gives a measure of relative dispersion.
f. The Normal Curve is a continuous distribution which is bell shaped and perfectly symmetrical. It is completely described when its mean and standard deviation are known.
g. Table 1, Areas under the Normal Curve gives the percentage of the area under the curve according to the number of standard deviations a point is away from the mean. The number of standard deviations away from the mean is the standardised variate or z score.
h. The Binomial and Poisson Distributions are discrete probability distributions which describe the behaviour of attributes e.g. good or bad, black or white.
i. The general binomial formula is $(p+q)^n$ and the expansion of this formula, using Pascals Triangle or the combination formula, provides the probability of any combination of p and q.
j. The mean and standard deviation of a Binomial Distribution are given by np and $\sqrt{npq}$ respectively.
k. It is safe to use the Normal approximation to the Binomial if $np > 5$ when $p < 0.5$ or if $nq > 5$ when $p > 0.5$.
l. When n is infinitely large and p is small the Poisson distribution can be used. It can be used without knowing n or p, being based on the mean value.
m. The variance of a Poisson equals the mean i.e. Variance = m and standard deviation = $\sqrt{m}$, where m is the mean of the Poisson Distribution. Where n becomes very large the Poisson Distribution approximates to the Normal Distribution.

POINTS TO NOTE

29.

a. The points which are $+1\sigma$ and -1σ away from the mean of a Normal Curve are the inflexion points on the curve.
b. The grouping of data, as in a grouped frequency distribution, entails some loss of accuracy although obviously easing calculations.

c. Although the standard deviation is by far the most useful measure of dispersion, on occasions the range (difference between the highest and lowest values) and the average deviation are of some value.

SELF REVIEW QUESTIONS

1 What is statistical analysis? (2)

2 Describe a grouped frequency distribution. (3)

3. Distinguish between discrete and continuous data. (4)

4. What is a frequency polygon? (5)

5. What are the four important characteristics of distributions? (7)

6. What is the most important measure of central tendency? (8)

7. What is dispersion and what is the formula for the standard deviation? (9)

8. What is the measure of relative dispersion? (10)

9. Draw diagrams showing positive and negative skewness (11)

10. What is a platykurtic distribution? (12)

11. What are the main features of the Normal Distribution? (13)

12. What percentage of the area of a Normal Curve is between the mean $\pm 1\sigma$ *? (14)*

13. Define a probability distribution. (16)

14. What is the general form of the binomial expression? (17)

15. What are the alternative ways of establishing the binomial coefficients? (18)

16. What is the formula for the mean of a binomial distribution?, the standard deviation? (21)

17. When is it safe to use the Normal approximation to the binomial? (23)

18. Describe the Poisson distribution. (24)

19. What are the characteristics of the Poisson distribution? (26)

APPENDIX

The reader should note that there is more than one way to compile Normal Distribution Tables. Table 1 shows the area under the curve from 0 to Z as follows:

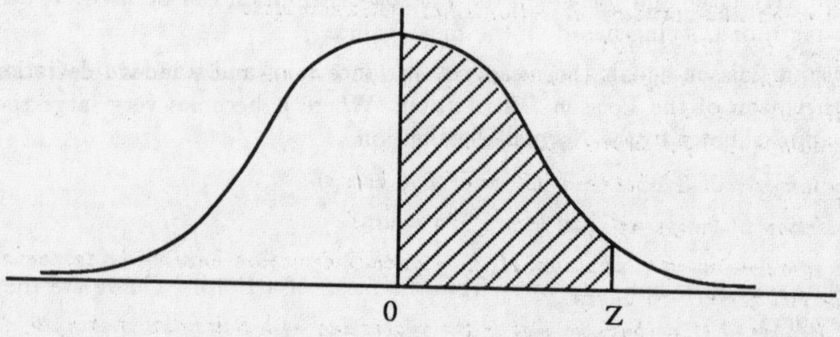

The alternative Table 11 is compiled such that the area from Z to ∞ is shown.

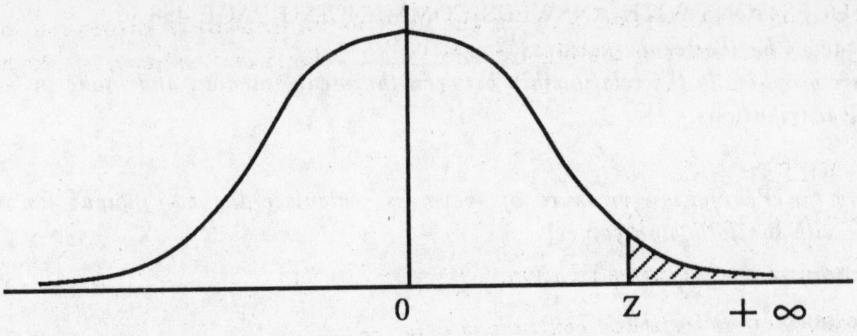

Clearly any answer to a problem will not differ because of this but the reader should be able to handle whichever form of the table is encountered.

For example in the diagram below the probability that x lies between A and B has to be calculated.

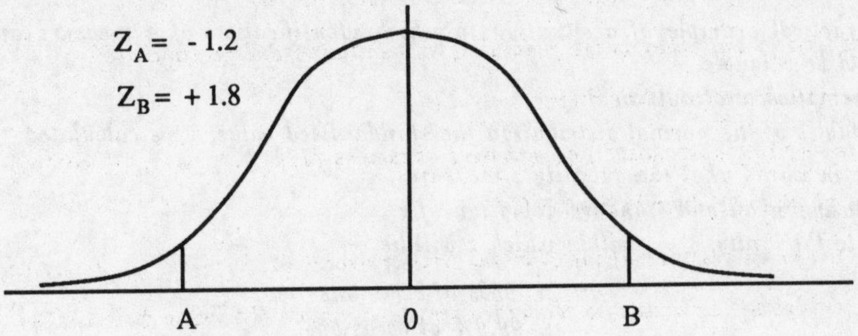

From Table I

$Z_A = -1.2$: Area 0 → A = 0.3849

$Z_B = +1.8$: Area 0 → B = 0.4641

Thus P(A < x < B) = 0.3849 + 0.4641

= <u>0.849</u>

From Table II

$Z_A = -1.2$: Area A → $-\infty$ = 0.115

$Z_B = +1.8$: Area B → $+\infty$ = 0.0036

Thus P(A < x < B) = 1.000 - (0.115 + 0.036)

= <u>0.849</u>

EXERCISES WITH ANSWERS COMMENCING PAGE 488

A1. Calculate the mean and standard deviation of the following data

12, 15, 19, 34, 46, 65, 79, 94, 108

A2. A batch of 5000 electric lamps have a mean life of 1,000 hours and a standard deviation of 75 hours. Assume a Normal Distribution.

(a) How many lamps will fail before 900 hours?

(b) How many lamps will fail between 950 and 1000 hours?

(c) What proportion of lamps will fail before 925 hours?

(d) Given the same mean life, what would the standard deviation have to be to ensure that not more than 20% of lamps fail before 916 hours?

A3. Assuming a Binomial Distribution what is the probability of a Salesman making 0, 1, 2, 3, 4, 5 or 6 sales in 6 visits if the probability of making a sale on a visit is 0.3?

(Do not use Tables)

EXAMINATION QUESTIONS WITH ANSWERS COMMENCING PAGE 488

A4. a. What is meant by the term 'skewness'?

b. Demonstrate graphically the relationship between the mean, median and mode in both positively and negatively skewed distributions.

c.

i. Using the Pearsonian measure of skewness, calculate the co-efficient for a frequency distribution with the following values:

mean	*15*
median	*16*
standard deviation ..	*6*

ii. What conclusion do you reach about this frequency distribution?

iii Using your own figures or adding to the figures given in (c) (i), calculate another measure of skewness.

d. Give a practical example of a situation in which identification of a measure of skewness of the distribution would be valuable.

(CIMA Mathematics and Statistics)

A5. . In using tables of the normal distribution the standardised value, z, is calculated.

i. State in words what the quantity z measures.

ii. State the mean and standard deviation of z.

iii. State the limits, ± A, within which z will lie on

i. 95% of occasions.

ii. 99.9% of occasions.

b. Find the value of z in each of the following cases. Give your answer correct to 1 decimal place.

i..

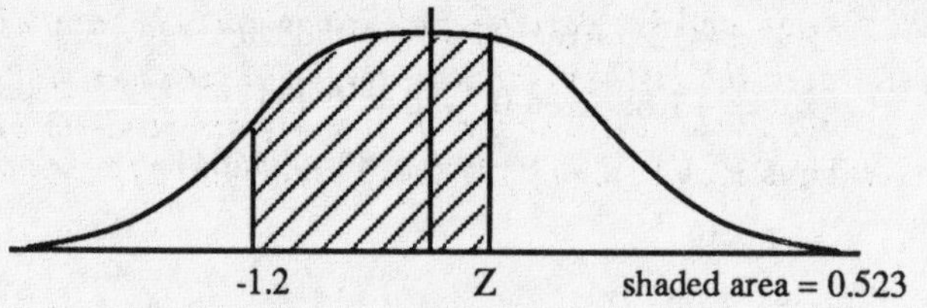

ii.

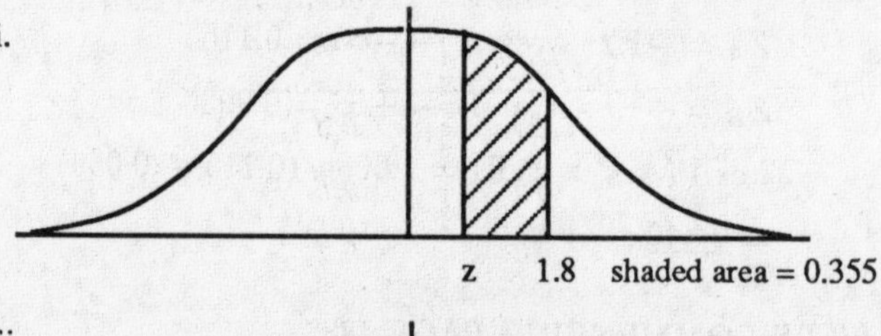

iii.

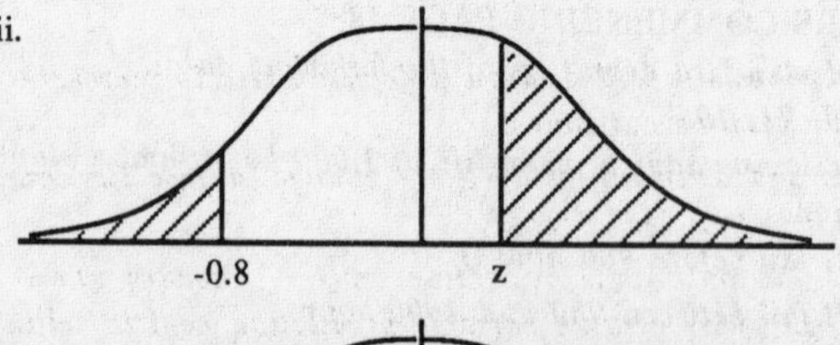

iv.

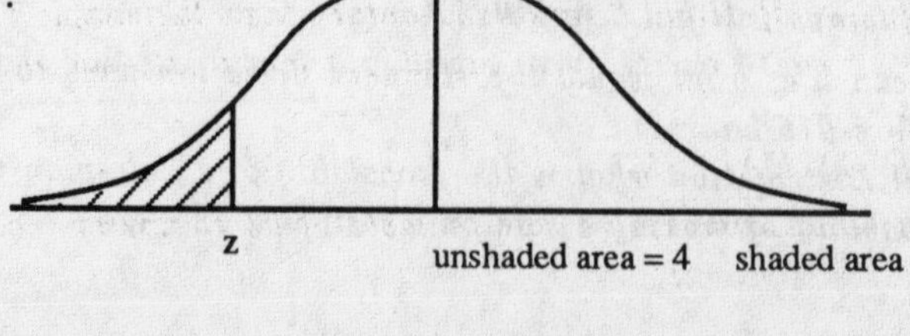

(ACCA Statistics)

A6. The life of a television (TV) tube, measured in hours of use, is approximately normally distributed with a mean of 5,000 hours and a standard deviaion of 1,000 hours.

Required:

a. Calculate the probability that a TV tube will last for

i. between 5,500 and 6,500 hours;

ii. less than the expected life of a tube.

b. Calculate the probability that, for someone using a TV for 1,500 hours per year the tube will last for less than five years.

c. Suppose that the company offers a guarantee to customers, at an additional charge of £25. Under the guarantee, the TV tube will be replaced free of charge if it fails within three years of purchase and will be replaced at a cost of £40 to the customer if it fails between the end of the third year and the end of the fifth year.

The cost of a TV tube to the company is £80.

Assuming that a TV is used for 1,500 hours per year, calculate the expected cost to the company through offering a guarantee on a tube.

(ACCA Statistics)

A7. Hetros Limited is a small specialist chemical company whose major product is Hetrozone, an expensive industrial solvent. Because Hetrozone deteriorates rapidly, production can only be scheduled on a monthly basis and stocks of Hetrozone cannot be kept from one month to the next. At the start of each month, a production figure for that month is decided upon and the necessary raw materials are obtained. Unfortunately, demand for Hetrozone varies randomly from month to month and, if demand exceeds the monthly production figure, sales are lost because demand must be satisfied more or less immediately. If, on the other hand, production exceeds demand in any month, the surplus is wasted and has no value. The selling price (p) of Hetrozone is £2,400 per ton and the variable production costs (v) amount to £1,500 per ton.

In an analysis of demand over the last few months, the sales manager finds that the monthly demand for Hetrozone is between 10 and 20 tons. In order to simplify his analysis of the demand situation, he decides to assume three levels of demand, 'Low' (10 tons), 'Medium' (15 tons) and 'High' (20 tons), with the following probabilities:

Demand (Tons)	*Probability*
10	*0.3*
15	*0.6*
20	*0.1*

Required:

(a) In terms of the demand levels specified, draw a decision tree to represent the production alternatives open to the company and their various outcomes.

(b) Assuming that the demand distribution does not change, advise the company on a production level that will maximise contribution in the long term.

(c) It may be shown that the optimum production level, Q, occurs where the probability of demand exceeding Q is equal to v/p (the ratio of unit variable production cost to selling price). Assuming, more realistically, that the distribution of demand is Normal rather than the simple distribution used in (a) and (b), estimate the mean and standard deviation of monthly demand and find the optimum production level Q.

(ACCA, QUANTITATIVE ANALYSIS)

A8. A mail-order company is analysing a random sample of its computer records of customers. Among the results are the following distributions:

Size of order	Number of customers	
£	*April*	*September*
Less than 1	8	4
1 and less than 5	19	18
5 and less than 10	38	39
10 and less than 15	40	69
15 and less than 20	22	41
20 and less than 30	13	20
30 and over	4	5
Total	144	196

You are required to:

(a) calculate the arithmetic mean and standard deviation order size for the April sample;

(b) find 95% confidence limits for the overall mean order size for the April customers and explain their meaning;

(c) compare the two distributions, given that the arithmetic mean and standard deviation for the September sample were £13.28 and £7.05 respectively.

(CIMA Quantitative Methods)

A9. The chief accountant of the Hyperion Hotels Group is analysing the profitability of the group's largest hotel, the Unicorn. The Unicorn has 120 bedrooms, each of which can be let as either a single or a double room. The price of a single room is £45 per night whereas for a double room it is £35 per person per night.

The hotel's other main source of revenue is the restaurant where the average price of an evening meal is £9. A proportion of residents can be expected to have an evening meal in the restaurant, and experience has shown that for the Unicorn this proportion is usually about 60%.

Required:

(a) Develop an expression for the average daily revenue (R) from residents at the hotel, including both the letting of rooms and evening meals in the restaurant.

Assume that

(i) the overall proportion of rooms occupied is p, and

(ii) a proportion q of the rooms that are occupied are let as single rooms.

(b) The proportion (q) of rooms which are let as single rooms is usually between 10% and 30%, and it can be assumed that this is independent of the overall proportion of rooms occupied (p).

Determine the average daily revenue (R) in terms of the parameter p for values of q of 10%, 20% and 30% and plot these three functions on a graph. What is the lowest percentage occupancy (p) which will yield an average daily revenue of £8,000, and for which of the given values of q does this occur?

(c) What is the overall relationship between R and p if the percentage of rooms let as single rooms is given by the following probability distribution?

q	*Probability*
10%	*0.3*
20%	*0.5*
30%	*0.2*

(d) Alternatively, if q has a normal distribution with a mean of 19% and a standard deviation of 7%, determine a 95% confidence interval for R in terms of the parameter p. (For the purposes of this calculation, you may ignore any variability in the proportion of residents who take an evening meal in the restaurant.)

(ACCA Quantitative Analysis).

A10. As a result of a recent analysis of labour costs throughout all the branches of the Olympus Assurance Company, it has been decided that the total number of employees should be reduced by 3%. The usual retirement age in the company is 65 and it is estimated that the desired reduction can be achieved by offering early retirement to all employees aged 62 and above. For this purpose, an early retirement scheme has been drawn up, based on negotiations with the unions concerned and the informal reactions of employees. It has been estimated that the probability of employees accepting the scheme depends on their age as follows:

Age	*Probability of Accepting Early Retirement*
62	*0.6*
63	*0.7*
64	*0.8*

In one particular branch of the company, there are 10 employees aged 62 and above as detailed in the following table.

Age	*62*	*63*	*64*
Number	*5*	*3*	*2*

Required:

(a) What is the expected number of employees accepting early retirement at this branch? What is the probability of early retirement being accepted by all 10 employees?

(b) What is the probability of exactly 9 employees accepting early retirement? Hint: The one person who does not accept early retirement can be age 62, 63, or 64. These three cases must be considered individually.

(c) Given that the variance of a Binomial distribution is np(1 - p), determine the variance of the total number of employees accepting early retirement from this branch. Using a Normal distribution approximation, estimate the probability of at least 8 employees accepting the scheme.

(ACCA Quantitative Analysis)

EXERCISES WITHOUT ANSWERS

B1. Given the probability of a good part is 0.9 and a bad part is 0.1 what is the probability of finding 15 good parts in a sample of 20?

(Do not use tables, use combination formula and appropriate term of binomial expansion).

B2. An X-ray machine tests for flaws in the welding of a pipe. On average there is 1 flaw per 20 metre length.

What is the probability that

(a) there are no flaws in a 10 metre length.

(b) there is more than 1 flaw in a 10 metre length.

(c) there are more than two flaws in a 20 metre length.

B3. Shoddy Airlines p.l.c. regularly overbook their flights because they know only 90% of pasengers who book actually turn up for the flight. The airline takes 145 bookings for the 138 seats available in their aircraft. Assuming that arrivals are normally distributed calculate the probability that there will be dissatisfied customers.

B4. a. A product is made by an automatic machine and contains 1000 identical components. The average number of defective components per product is known to be 25.

The products are inspected and faulty components are corrected manually. If products requiring more than 35 corrections are scrapped, what proportion of the products will be scrapped?

b. A cleaning contractor uses floor scouring machines and analysis of demand shows that the daily demand for these machines follows a Poisson distribution with a mean of 3. He can obtain the machines on long term hire at £20 per day to use as and when he requires or he can hire them on the day required at £60 per day.

How many machines, if any, should he have on long term hire in order to minimise costs?

An extract from Cumulative Poisson Probability Tables when the mean is 3 is given below.

Probability of 0 or more events	*1.00*
Probability of 1 or more events	*0.9502*
Probability of 2 or more events	*0.8009*
Probability of 3 or more events	*0.5768*
Probability of 4 or more events	*0.3528*
Probability of 5 or more events	*0.1847*

B5. ***The Vulcan Van Rental Company Limited has four Type C vans which are available for hire on a daily basis at a rate of £35 per day. Experience has shown that the daily demand for vans of this type has a Poisson distribution with a mean of 2. Vulcan have also estimated that the total cost of providing each van amounts to £3,250 per year (which consists of 300 working days).***

Required:

(a) What is the probability that, on any one day, all four vans will be out on hire?

(b) What proportion of the total demand for Type C vans will be unsatisfied because all four vans have already been hired by other customers?

(c) As a result of reviewing the profitability of the business, the general manager has suggested that it might be more economical to reduce the number of Type C vans for hire. Assuming that the demand pattern does not change, what would be your advice in this regard?

(ACCA, Quantitative Analysis)

5 Statistics – Statistical Inference

INTRODUCTION

1. This chapter introduces the concept of statistical inference i.e. inferring information about the population from samples. Estimation of population means and the properties of the standard error of the mean are explained together with the calculation and meaning of confidence limits. The uses of the finite population correction factor and of the students t distribution for small samples are discussed and exemplified.

STATISTICAL INFERENCE DEFINED.

2. Statistical inference can be defined as the process by which conclusions are drawn about some measures or attribute of a *population* (e.g. the mean or standard deviation) based upon analysis of *sample* data. This is a large and important area of the application of statistical theory and is the basis of many examination questions.

There are numerous reasons why samples are taken and analysed in order to draw conclusions about the whole population. For example, if it was desired to calculate the average weight of the adult population of Britain it would be impractical (except at enormous cost) to weigh each individual and calculate the average weight. More simply a sample would be taken and the population average deduced from the sample measurements. Alternatively, the measurement or testing process may be destructive so that sampling is the only feasible method. There would, for example, be little point in an electric bulb manufacturer testing *all* bulbs to destruction to discover the average life of his bulbs.

Sampling is cheaper, quicker and is often the only feasible method of finding information about the population. The type of sampling with which we are concerned is *random sampling* (sometimes known as *probability sampling*).In this type of sampling each item in the population has an equal probability of being chosen.

Random does not mean haphazard. Random Selection is determined objectively, usually by means of *random number tables* or by computer generated random numbers. Although simple random sampling is rarely used alone in business applications it is important because it is a basic part of more sophisticated sampling systems and because it illustrates the fundamental principles of sampling.

An outline of the more important sampling systems is given below:

SAMPLING

3. Sampling is the process of examining a representative number of items (people or things) out of the whole population or universe. The purpose is to gain an understanding about some feature or attribute of the whole population, based on the characteristics of the sample. We may wish to make an estimate of the mean or standard deviation of the population or to discover the type of distribution (eg Poisson, Normal and so on) which the population most resembles. A sample only provides an estimate of a population characteristic and the accuracy of the estimate will depend on:

a. the size of the sample-in general the larger the sample the greater the probability that the sample is truly representative of the population.

b. how the sample is selected

c. the extent of variability in the population.

In practice the design and operation of sampling investigations is a complex and technical matter but the overall objective is to select as representative sample as possible, without bias, at a realistic cost.

Pure random sampling ie where every item in the population has an equal chance of being chosen, is the best theoretical sampling method but it does require a *sampling frame.* A sampling frame is a list of every item or member of the population. Thus if it was required to select a random sample of rate payers in a district, the sampling frame would be the Register of Rate Payers maintained by the Local Authority. In practice a complete sampling frame is difficult, if not impossible, to obtain. This is because:

a. Even where lists are available they are often inaccurate or out of date.
b. There are many circumstances where a full sampling frame is not feasible. For example, a brewer wishes to sample lager drinkers. How could a sampling frame be constructed in these circumstances? The answer is that it could not be done.
c. The population may be continually growing and changing.
d. The costs of constructing a sample frame may be prohibitve and greater than the benefits of increased confidence in the accuracy of sample estimates.

Care is necessary where partial sample frames exist. For example, if it was wished to sample motorists', opinions and AA and RAC membership lists were used as a sampling frame then this would not be a random sample. This is because many motorists are not members of either organisation and would thus be excluded from the sample.

Because of the many practical problems various quasi-random sampling methods have been designed and are widely used.

QUASI-RANDOM SAMPLING

4. The various methods to be described in this paragraphs all seek to provide representative samples without undue bias whilst having due regard to cost and practicability. The methods are:

Systematic sampling

Stratified sampling

Multi-stage sampling

Cluster sampling

Quota sampling

SYSTEMATIC SAMPLING

This method is frequently used in production and quality control sampling. After a randomly selected start point(s) a sample item would be selected every n'th item. Assume that it was decided to sample every 100th item and a start point of 67 was chosen randomly, the sample would be the following items:

67th, 167th, 267th, 367th and so on

The gap between selections is known as the sampling interval and is itself often randomly selected.

Care is needed with this sytem to ensure that there is no regular pattern which by coinciding, or not coinciding, with the sampling interval, causes bias.

STRATIFIED SAMPLING

This is a commonly used method where the population can be divided into groups or strata.

Random samples are taken from within each group in the proportions that each group bears to the population as a whole. For example, assume it was required to sample 100 staff at a group of hospitals whose staff could be stratified as follows:

		Proportion
Doctors	200	10%
Nurses	600	30%
Ancilliary workers	800	40%
Administrators	400	20%
	2000	100%

With a sample of 100 these proportions would result in the following numbers being selected

Doctors	10
Nurses	30
Ancilliary workers	40
Administrators	20
	100

MULTI-STAGE SAMPLING

This is a practical system widely used to reduce the travelling time for interviewers and the subsequent costs. Multi-stage sampling is similar to stratified sampling except that the groups and sub-groups are selected on a geographical/location basis rather than some social characteristic. A country could be divided in areas (say counties) and a random choice of say 5 areas made. From each of these selected areas would be drawn a random sample of, say, 6 towns from each of which would be drawn a random sample of people to interview. The process of stratification might continue below the level of a town and would depend on the homogeneity of the population.

CLUSTER SAMPLING

This is a useful system for reducing sampling costs and dealing with the lack of a satisfactory sampling frame. A few geographical areas (perhaps a village or a street in a town) are selected at random and every single household is interviewed in the selected area.

QUOTA SAMPLING

This type of sample is not preselected but is chosen by interviewer on the spot up to the level of a quota. To avoid undue bias the quota is sub-divided into various categories eg male/female, old/young, working/unemployed and so on. The interviewer is given quotas for each category and uses discretion to select the interviewees. If done badly, substantial bias can be introduced with this system so close control and checks are employed. The method is cheap and reasonably effective and in consequence is widely used.

The above notes provide a brief outline of common sampling designs. In most examinations where some statistical analysis has to be carried out on the results of a sample, the statement is made that the results were obtained from a random sample. In such circumstances it can be assumed that the sample is truly representative and is without bias.

TYPES OF INFERENCE

5. Statistical inference can conveniently be divided into two types -*estimation* and *hypothesis testing.* Estimation deals with the estimation of population characteristics (such as the population mean and standard deviation) from sample characteristics (such as the sample mean and standard deviation). The population characteristics are known as population *parameters* whilst the sample characteristics are known as sample *statistics.* Estimation is dealt with in this chapter whilst hypothesis testing – i.e. the process of setting up a theory or hypothesis about some characteristic of the population and then sampling to see if the hypothesis is supported or not – is dealt with in the next chapter.

Initially it will be assumed that all the samples with which we are dealing are *large* samples (above, say, 30) drawn from an infinitely large population or that the sampling is carried out with replacement, which amounts to the same thing. Small samples and finite populations require somewhat different treatments which are dealt with subsequently.

PROPERTIES OF GOOD ESTIMATORS

6. There are four properties of a good estimator.

a. Unbiased. An estimator is said to be unbiased if the mean of the sample means $\overline{x}$ of all possible random samples of size n, drawn from a population of size N, equals the population parameter (μ). Thus the mean of the distribution of sample means would equal the population mean.

b. Consistency. An estimator is said to be consistent if, as the sample size increases, the precision of the estimate of the population parameter also increases.

c. Efficiency. An estimator is said to be more efficient than another if, in repeated sampling, its variance is smaller.

d. Sufficiency. An estimator is said to be sufficient it if uses all the information in the sample in estimating the required population parameter.

Rarely, in practical situations, do we have all the population values so that we are able to calculate the population parameters. Invariably, we sample in order to estimate the population parameters. Because of this, it is necessary to distinguish between the symbols used for sample statistics and population parameters as follows:

	SAMPLE STATISTIC	POPULATION PARAMETER
Arithmetic Mean	$\overline{x}$	μ
Standard Deviation	s	σ
Number of items	n	N

ESTIMATION OF THE POPULATION MEAN

7. The use of the sample mean $\overline{x}$, to make inferences about the population mean is a common procedure in statistics.

If a series of samples of size n ($n \geq 30$) is taken from a population it will be found that:

a. Each of the sample means is approximately equal to the population mean. (It would be pure coincidence if a sample mean was exactly equal to the population mean).

b. The sample means cluster much more closely around the population mean than the original individual values.

c. The larger the samples the more closely would their means cluster round the population mean.

d. The distribution of sample means follows a normal curve.

The latter point is one aspect of what is called the *central limit theorem.* This has been called the most important single theorem in statistics. This, in essence, states that the means of samples (and the median and the standard deviation) tend to be normally distributed as n increases in size *almost regardless of the shape of the original population.*

The central limit theorem gives the normal distribution its central place in the theory of sampling.

Because the distribution of the sample means is normal, or nearly so, it can be completely described by its mean and its standard deviation. The distribution of all possible sample means is known as the *sampling distribution of the mean* and its standard deviation is given the special name of *standard error.* This is convenient because whenever 'standard error' is used we know at once that a sampling distribution is referred to.

$$\text{Standard error of the mean } = s_{\overline{x}} = \frac{s}{\sqrt{n}}$$

Note that this formula is satisfactory when we have a large sample and a large population i.e. $n > 30$ and $n < 5\%$ of N.

The smaller the standard error the greater the precision of the sample value. The word 'error' is used in place of 'deviation' to emphasize that variation among sample means is due to sampling errors.

AN EXAMPLE OF THE MEAN AND STANDARD ERROR OF THE MEAN

8. A firm purchases a very large quantity of metal offcuts and wishes to know the average weight of an offcut.

A random sample of 625 offcuts is weighed and it is found that the mean sample weight is 150 grams with a sample standard deviation of 30 grams.

What is the estimate of the population mean and what is the standard error of the mean?

What would be the standard error if the sample size was 1225?

SOLUTION

The sample mean is 150 grams so that the estimate of the population mean is 150 grams.

i.e. $\bar{x} = 150$ grams $= \hat{\mu} = 150$ grams

where ^ means 'best estimate of'.

When $n = 625$

$$\text{Standard error of the mean} = \frac{s}{\sqrt{n}} = \frac{30}{\sqrt{625}} = \underline{\underline{1.2 \text{ grams}}}$$

When $n = 1225$

$$s_{\bar{x}} = \frac{30}{\sqrt{1225}} = \underline{\underline{0.857 \text{ grams}}}$$

It will be seen that increasing the sample size reduces the standard error. This accords with common-sense; we would expect a larger sample to be better than a smaller one.

The estimate obtained of the population mean, 150 grams, is what is known as a *point estimate*.

This estimate was easily made but so far we have ignored the all important question - how good an estimate is it? This is established by using what are known as confidence limits.

CONFIDENCE LIMITS.

9. Confidence limits are the outer limits to a confidence zone or interval. This is a zone of values within which we may be confident that the true population mean (or the parameter being considered) does lie. Confidence limits, for population means, are based on the sample mean, the standard error of the mean and on the known characteristics of Normal Distribution.

It is known that a Normal Distribution has the following characteristics.

mean $\pm 1.96\sigma$ includes 95% of the population.
mean $\pm 2.58\sigma$ includes 99% of the population.

These characteristics can be used to calculate confidence limits for the population mean when we have established the sample mean and the standard error.

For example, what are the 95% confidence limits for the estimate of the population mean given the data from the example in Paragraph 8 i.e.

$$\bar{x} = 150 \text{ grams and } s_{\bar{x}} = 1.2 \text{ grams}$$

∴ At the 95% confidence level

$$\mu = \bar{x} \pm 1.96 s_{\bar{x}}$$
$$= 150 \pm 1.96(1.2) \text{ grams}$$
$$= 150 \pm 2.35 \text{ grams}$$

This means that we are 95% confident that the population mean lies within the confidence zone i.e. somewhere between 147.65 grams and 152.35 grams.

At the 99% confidence level the limits are

$$\mu = 150 \pm 2.58(1.2) \text{ grams}$$

i.e. a range from 146.9 to 153.1 grams

Notes.

a. Raising the confidence factor from 95% to 99% increases the assurance that the confidence zone contains the population mean but it makes the estimate less precise.

b. ***Any*** confidence level could be chosen and the appropriate number of standard errors found from Normal Area Tables. However, the 95% and 99% values of 1.96σ and 2.58σ are widely used and should be remembered.

The principles involved in setting confidence limits can be used to determine what sample size should be taken, if we wish to achieve a given level of precision.

For example what sample size would be required in the example in Paragraph 8 if we wished to be 95% confident that the population mean is within ± 2 grams of the sample mean?

Because the confidence level is given, the only way that the precision can be increased is by ***reducing the standard error*** which can be done by ***increasing the sample size.***

To obtain 95% limits of ± 2 grams would require a standard error of 1.02 grams (i.e. $\frac{2 \text{ grams}}{1.96}$)

$$\therefore \text{ as } s_{\bar{x}} = \frac{s}{\sqrt{n}} \quad \text{then } 1.02 = \frac{30}{\sqrt{n}}$$

$$\therefore \quad \sqrt{n} = \frac{30}{1.20}$$

$$n = \underline{865}$$

The principles of confidence limits have been illustrated in connection with means but their use is not limited solely to the estimation of population means from a sample. The concept is applied across a broad range of statistical applications.

FINITE POPULATION CORRECTION FACTOR

10. Large samples drawn from infinitely large populations increase the accuracy of the sample standard deviation as an estimate of the population standard deviation, reduce the standard error and therefore increase the reliability of the sample mean as an estimate of the population mean.

Obviously not all populations are of infinite size or effectively so and a given population may be relatively small. In these circumstances the proportion of the population included in the sample may be relatively high. Where the sample contains in excess of 5% of the population, the standard error should be adjusted by multiplying it by the finite population correction factor i.e.

$$\text{Finite Population Correction Factor} = \sqrt{\frac{N-n}{N-1}}$$

where N is the population size and n is the sample size.

With this correction the standard error becomes:

Standard error (when sample size is > 5% of the population)

$$s_{\bar{x}} = \frac{\sigma}{\sqrt{n}}\sqrt{\frac{N-n}{N-1}}$$

Alternatively where the population, although small, is greater than 100 an approximation of the correction factor can be used.

$$s_{\bar{x}} = \frac{\sigma}{\sqrt{n}}\sqrt{1-\frac{n}{N}}$$

The use of the finite population correction factor always *reduces* the standard error.

Example

A sample of 80 is drawn at random from a population of 800. The samples standard deviation was found to be 6 grams.

What is the finite population correction factor?

What is the approximation of the correction factor?
What is the standard error of the mean?
Correction Factor

$$= \sqrt{\frac{N-n}{N-1}} = \sqrt{\frac{800-80}{800-1}} = \underline{\underline{0.9493}}$$

Approximation to Correction Factor

$$= \sqrt{1-\frac{n}{N}} = \sqrt{1-\frac{80}{800}} = \underline{\underline{0.9486}}$$

It will be seen that to 3 significant figures, accurate enough for all practical purposes, the two formulae give the same result i.e. 0.949.

Standard Error of the mean

$$s_{\bar{x}} = \frac{\sigma}{\sqrt{n}}\sqrt{\frac{N-n}{N-1}}$$
$$= \frac{6}{\sqrt{80}} \times 0.949$$
$$= \underline{\underline{0.637 \text{ grams}}}$$

Note. The standard error without correction is,

$$\frac{6}{\sqrt{80}} = \underline{\underline{0.671 \text{ grams.}}}$$

Thus the precision of the sample estimate, measured by the standard error, is determined not only be the absolute size of the sample but also to some extent by the proportion of the population sampled.

ESTIMATION OF POPULATION PROPORTIONS.

11. So far the process of statistical inference has been applied to the arithmetic mean. A similar process can be used for other types of statistical measures - medians, standard deviations, proportions and so on. In each case the analysis includes three essential elements:

a. The required measure as found from the sample.
b. The standard error of the measure involved.
c. The sampling distribution of the measure.

As explained in the previous chapter, a proportion represents an *attribute* of a population rather than the value of a variable. The proportion may represent the ratio of defective to good production, the proportion of consumers who plan to buy a given product or some similar piece of information.

Estimating population proportions from sample statistics follows the same pattern as outlined for means. The major difference being that the Binomial Distribution is involved. Statistical inference based on the Binomial Distribution involves complex technical difficulties caused by the discreteness of the distribution and the asymmetry of confidence intervals.

Fortunately when 'n' is large and np and nq are over 5 then the Binomial Distribution can be approximated by a Normal Distribution. This greatly simplifies the analysis and the concepts outlined for the mean can be applied directly to the proportion.

The relevant formula for the standard error of a sample proportion is

$$s_{ps} = \sqrt{\frac{pq}{n}}$$

Using this value we are able to set confidence limits for the estimate of the *population* proportion based on the *sample* proportion in exactly the same manner as outlined previously for the mean.

Example

A random sample of 400 rail passengers is taken and 55% are in favour of proposed new timetables. With 95% confidence what proportion of all rail passengers are in favour of the timetables?

Solution

$$n = 400 \quad p = 0.55 \text{ and} \quad q = 1 - 0.55 = 0.45$$

as $np = 220$ i.e. well over 5, the normal approximation can be used.

$$s_{ps} = \sqrt{\frac{pq}{n}} = \sqrt{\frac{0.55 \times 0.45}{400}} = 0.025$$

∴ We are 95% confident that the population proportion is

$$\begin{aligned} & p_s \pm 1.96 s_{ps} \\ = \; & 0.55 \pm 1.96(0.025) = 0.55 \pm 0.049 \\ = \; & \underline{\underline{0.501 \text{ to } 0.599}} \end{aligned}$$

ESTIMATION FROM SMALL SAMPLES

12. So far it has been assumed that all the samples have been large ($n > 30$) In such circumstances s, the sample standard deviation, is used as an estimate of σ, the population standard deviation. Further, it is known that the distribution of sample means is approximately normal so that the proporties of the Normal Distribution can be used to calculate confidence limits using the standard error of the mean.

However, the properties and relationships summarised above are not true if the sample size is small ($n <$ 30), because the arithmetic means of small samples are not normally distributed. In such circumstances *Student's t distribution* must be used.

To use this distribution all that is necessary is to substitute a given value of 't' (from Table III) for the value of z obtained from Table I, Areas under the Normal curve, thus;

Large sample

$$\mu = \overline{x} \pm z s_{\overline{x}}$$

At the 95% confidence level z = 1.96

At the 99% confidence level z = 2.58

(the values of z from Normal Area Tables)

Small sample

$$\mu = \overline{x} \pm t s_{\overline{x}}$$

Where the value of t is obtained from Table III for the required confidence level.

It will be seen that the processes are very similar with the exception that the Students distribution is used when the sample is small.

THE t DISTRIBUTION

13. This distribution is used when there are small samples and when it is necessary to make an estimate of σ, the population standard deviation, based on s, the sample standard deviation.

The statistic, t, is as follows:

$$t = \frac{\overline{x} - \mu}{\frac{s}{\sqrt{n}}} \quad \text{where } s \text{ is an estimate of } \sigma$$

$$s = \sqrt{\frac{\Sigma(x - \overline{x})^2}{n - 1}} \quad \text{as previously defined.}$$

The characteristics of the distribution are:

a. It is an exact distribution which is unimodal and symmetric about 0.
b. It is flatter than the Normal Distribution i.e. the areas near the tails are greater than the Normal Distribution.
c. As the sample size becomes larger the t distribution approaches the Normal Distribution.

To use the t distribution tables (Table III) it is necessary to find the *degrees of freedom* usually denoted by ν, thus

$\nu = n - 1$ where n is the number of items in the sample. For example, what is the t value, for a 95% confidence level, for a sample size of 10.

$\nu = 10 - 1 = 9$ and from the column in Table III headed .05 we find the value 2.262.

Example

A random sample of 10 items is taken and is found to have a mean weight of 60 grams and a standard deviation of 12 grams.

What is the mean weight of the population.

a. With 95% confidence?
b. With 99% confidence?

Solution

$\bar{x} = 60$ grams $s = 12$ $\nu = 10 - 1 = 9$ degrees of freedom

$$\mu = \bar{x} \pm t\frac{s}{\sqrt{n}}$$

At 95% confidence

$$\mu = 60\text{grams} \pm 2.262 \left(\frac{12}{\sqrt{10}}\right)$$

$$= 60 \pm 8.58 \text{ grams}$$

∴ We can state with 95% confidence that the population mean is between 51.42 and 68.58 grams.

At 99% confidence

$$\mu = 60\text{grams} \pm 3.250 \left(\frac{12}{\sqrt{10}}\right)$$

$$= 60 \pm 12.33 \text{ grams}$$

∴ We can state with 99% confidence that the population mean is between 57.67 and 72.33 grams.

SUMMARY

14.

a. Statistical inference is the process of drawing conclusions about the population from samples.
b. Random sampling means that every item in the population has an equal chance of being chosen and that there is no bias.
c. Estimation is concerned with estimating population parameters from sample statistics.
d. The distribution of sample means follows a normal curve.
e. The Central Limit Theorem states that the means of samples (and the medians and standard deviations) tend to be normally distributed almost regardless of the shape of the original population.
f. The standard deviation of the distribution of means is called the standard error of the mean i.e.

$$s_{\bar{x}} = \frac{s}{\sqrt{n}}$$

g. Confidence limits provide the limits to a confidence interval or zone in which we may be confident, at a given level, that the true population parameter lies.
h. The most commonly used confidence limits are the 95% level ($\pm 1.96\sigma$) and the 99% level ($\pm 2.58\sigma$).

i. Where the sample contains in excess of 5% of the population, the Finite Population Correction Factor ($\sqrt{\frac{N-n}{N-1}}$) needs to be applied.

j. Finding population proportions from sample information follows the usual estimation process provided that np and nq are over 5 so that the Normal approximation can be used.

k. Where $n < 30$ the sample is small, the Students t distribution must be used instead of the Normal Distribution.

POINTS TO NOTE

15.

a. The standard error of the mean, $\sigma_{\bar{x}}$ is always smaller than σ, the standard deviation of the values.

b. An alternative view of, say a 95% confidence level, is that there is a 5% or 1 in 20 chance of the population parameter being *outside* the confidence interval.

c. The Central Limit Theorem is valid for sampling from Normal and non Normal Distributions as in all cases the distribution of the means of samples tends towards a Normal Distribution.

d. The t distribution used for small samples also has important applications in hypothesis testing dealt with in the next chapter.

SELF REVIEW QUESTIONS

1. *What is statistical inference? (2)*
2. *What is the main feature of random sampling? (2)*
3. *What is the purpose of estimation? (5)*
4. *What are the properties of good estimators? (6)*
5. *What is the main feature of the Central Limit Theorem and why is it so important? (7)*
6. *What is the standard error of the mean? (7)*
7. *What are confidence limits? (9)*
8. *When is the Finite Population Correction Factor used? What is the formula? (10)*
9. *How are population proportions estimated? (11)*
10. *What adjustments are required when small samples are used? (12)*
11. *What are the characteristics of the t distribution? (13)*
12. *How are the number of degrees of freedom calculated? (13)*

EXERCISES WITH ANSWERS COMMENCING PAGE 488

A1. From a random sample of 529 televisions off the production line it was found that there were 8 faults on average with a standard deviation of 3.45 faults.

What are the confidence limits for the production as a whole: at the 99% level, at the 95% level.

A2. An inspection department is trying to determine the appropriate sample size to use. They wish to be within 1% of the true proportion with 99% confidence. Past records indicate that the proportion defective is 3 in a 100.

What sample size should they use?

A3. A random sample of 12 packets was taken and found to have a mean weight of 50 grams and a standard deviation of 9 grams.

What is the mean weight of the population.

(a) with 95% confidence.

(b) with 99% confidence?

EXAMINATION QUESTIONS WITH ANSWERS COMMENCING PAGE 488

A4. Your company manufactures goods for a market in which the technology of the products is changing rapidly. The research and development department has produced a new product which appears to have potential for commercial exploitation. A further £60,000 is required for development testing.

The company has 100 customers and each customer might purchase, at the most one unit of the product. Market research suggests a selling price of £6,000 for each unit with total variable costs of manufacture and selling estimated at £2,000 for each unit.

As a result of previous experience of this type of market, it has been possible to derive a probability distribution relating to the proportions of customers who will buy the product, as follows:

Proportion of customers	*Probability*
0.04	*0.1*
0.08	*0.1*
0.12	*0.2*
0.16	*0.4*
0.20	*0.2*

You are required to:

a. determine the expected opportunity losses, given no other information than that stated above, and to state whether, or not, the company should develop the product.

b. Calculate the probability that it would be wrong to go ahead with development if a random sample of 20 of the 100 customers is taken and three or more were to say they would purchase the product.

Table of Cumulative Binomial Probabilities

p = *probability of success in a sample trial;*

n = *number of trials. Table gives probability of r or more successes in n independent trials.*

r	n=20											r
	p = .01	.02	.03	.04	.05	.06	.07	.08	.09	.10	= (1 − p)	
1	1821	3324	4562	5580	6415	7099	7658	8113	8484	8784		19
2	0169	0599	1198	1897	2642	3395	4131	4831	5484	6081		18
3	0010	0071	0210	0439	0755	1150	1610	2121	2666	3231		17
4		0006	0027	0074	0159	0290	0471	0706	0993	1330		16
5			0003	0010	0026	0056	0107	0183	0290	0432		15
6				0001	0003	0009	0019	0038	0068	0113		14
7						0001	0003	0006	0013	0024		13
8								0001	0002	004		12
9										0001		11
	p = .11	.12	.13	.14	.15	.16	.17	.18	.19	.20	= (1 − p)	
1	9028	9224	9383	9510	9612	9694	9759	9811	9852	9885		19
2	6624	7109	7539	7916	8244	8529	8773	8982	9159	9308		18
3	3802	4369	4920	5450	5951	6420	6854	7252	7614	7939		17
4	1710	2127	2573	3041	3523	4010	4496	4974	5439	5886		16
5	0610	0827	1083	1375	1702	2059	2443	2849	3271	3704		15
6	0175	0260	0370	0507	0673	0870	1098	1356	1643	1958		14
7	0041	0067	0103	0153	0219	0304	0409	0537	0689	0867		13
8	0008	0014	0024	0038	0059	0088	0127	0177	0241	0321		12
9	0001	0002	0005	0008	0013	0021	0033	0049	0071	0100		11
10			0001	0001	0002	0004	0007	0011	0017	0026		10
11						0001	0001	0002	0004	0006		9
12									0001	0001		8

(CIMA Quantitative Techniques)

A5. Company keeps details of all purchases on magnetic tape. A computer run, for audit purposes, shows that there are 395 purchases of items under £500, and that these have a total value (T) of £76,859.45.

A simple random sample of 60 invoices is taken for audit checking. One of the validity checks on the sample is that it should correctly estimate T within the limits of sampling error.

The sample invoices have been summarised as follows:

Value of Purchase £	*Number of Purchase*
20-60	*4*
60-120	*9*
120-180	*12*
180-240	*16*
240-300	*11*
300-360	*6*
360-420	*2*
	60

Required:

a. Show that the two-sided 95% confidence interval for T based upon the above sample does include its known value.

b. If the value of T had not been £76,859.45, but had been some value outside the confidence interval that you have calculated, what interpretation would you put on this situation?

(ACCA Quantitative Analysis)

A6. Statistical sampling techniques are widely used for the collection of data in industry and business. Explain four of the following, illustrating your answer with examples:

(a) sampling frame;

(b) simple random sampling

(c) multi-stage sampling

(d) stratification;

(e) quota sampling;

(f) sampling with probability proportional to size.

(CIMA Quantitative Methods)

EXERCISES WITHOUT ANSWERS

B1. With a sample size of 400 the calculated standard error is 2 with a mean of 120.

(a) What is the sample standard deviation?

(b) What are the 95% confidence limits for the population mean.

(c) what sample size would be required so that we could be 95% confident that the population mean is within ±3.5 of the sample mean?

B2. A random sample of 16 people is taken and 12 were in favour of liberalising licensing laws. With 99% confidence what proportion of all people are in favour?

EXAMINATION QUESTION WITHOUT ANSWER

B3. The London Midland and Scottish Bank is at present reviewing its policy regarding the issue of statements to current account holders. Under the present system all customers receive a statement each quarter (i.e. every three months) as well as having the option of requesting a statement at any other time. It has been proposed, however, that all current account customers should be allowed to specify how frequently they wish to receive a statement by choosing one of the following 4 options:

(i) No regular statement.

(ii) Every month

(iii) Every 3 months.

(iv) Every 6 months.

In addition, customers would still have the freedom to request a statement at any other time to avoid having to wait for the arrival of their next regular statement. It has been estimated that there would be at most 600,000 irregular statement requests per year, which should occur more or less evenly throughout the year. At the present time, the bank has approximately 1.2 million current accounts.

To assess the acceptability of the new scheme, a random sample of 150 current account customers was selected and their preferences as regards the four statement options have been ascertained. The results are as follows:

Preferred Frequency	*No Statement*	*Every 1 month*	*Every 3 Months*	*Every 6 Months*
Number of Customers	*11*	*65*	*61*	*13*

Required:

(a) Construct a frequency distribution of the number of regular statements received per year for the sample of 150 customers and determine the mean and standard deviation of your distribution.

(b) Determine a 95% confidence interval for the true mean number of regular statements per customer per year and explain carefully the meaning of this interval.

(c) All statements are despatched daily from the bank's computer centre. Under present conditions, there is capacity for 33,000 statements to be issued each day. Assuming that the computer centre works for 300 days a year, comment on whether there will be sufficient capacity to cope with the likely number of statements which will have to be issued.

Your anaswer should incorporate an appropriate test of significance and any assumptions that you make should be clearly stated.

(ACCA Quantitative Analysis)

Study CHAPTER 6 before attempting part (c)

6 Statistics – Hypothesis Testing

INTRODUCTION

1. This chapter explains the procedures necessary to carry out hypothesis or significance testing. The distinction between Type I and Type II errors is explained together with the difference between one and two tailed tests. Hypothesis testing applied to means, proportions, and the differences between means and proportions is explained and exemplified. The use of the 't' and χ^2 distributions is outlined together with an introduction to the use of the f distribution in significance testing and in analysis of variance tests.

HYPOTHESIS TESTING DEFINED.

2. Hypothesis testing, alternatively called *significance testing,* is in many ways similar to the processes of Estimation dealt with in the last chapter. Random sampling is involved and the properties of the distribution of sample means and proportions are still used.

A hypothesis is some testable belief or opinion, and hypothesis testing is the process by which the belief is tested by statistical means.

For example, from a large batch of components a random sample may be taken to test the belief (i.e. the hypothesis) 'That the mean diameter of the population of components is 50 mm'. Based on the results obtained from the sample the hypothesis would either be accepted or rejected.

RESULTS OF HYPOTHESIS TESTING

3. There are only four possible results when we test a given hypothesis.

a. We *accept* a *true* hypothesis — a CORRECT decision.

b. We *reject* a *false* hypothesis — a CORRECT decision

c. We *reject* a *true* hypothesis — an INCORRECT decision. This is known an a TYPE I error.

d. We *accept* a *false* hypothesis — an INCORRECT decision. This is known as a Type II error.

TYPE I and TYPE II ERRORS

4. Obviously, efforts are made to avoid any type of error but as it is not possible to make a correct decision with 100% certainty when a hypothesis is tested by sampling, there is always a possibility of either a Type I or Type II error.

The errors are mutually exclusive; an error can be Type I or Type II but not both. The errors are split into two types because there are situations where it is much more important to avoid one type of error rather than the other.

For example, if we have the hypothesis, 'The Water is Shallow', the consequences of a Type II error could be fatal for a non-swimmer.

Although we shall not be showing the methods in this manual it is possible to calculate the probabilities of Type I and Type II errors occurring. These are usually denoted by α (alpha) and β (beta) respectively i.e.

$$P\ (\text{Type I error}) = \alpha$$

$$P\ (\text{Type II error}) = \beta$$

SIGNIFICANCE LEVELS

5. When a sample is taken to test some hypothesis it is likely that the information gleaned from the sample data (e.g. the sample mean or standard deviation) does not completely support the hypothesis. The difference could be due to *either* the original hypothesis being wrong or the sample being slightly unrepresentative, which virtually all samples will be to a greater or lesser extent.

It is clearly of importance to be able to test which of the two possibilities is the more likely and this is the main objective of hypothesis testing. The tests will show whether any differences can be attributed to ordinary random factors or not. If the difference is probably *not* due to chance factors the difference is said to be *statistically significant.*

Because we are dealing with samples and random factors, we cannot say with 100% certainty that a difference is significant. Accordingly, various levels of significance are chosen, most commonly 5% or 1% , and thus the result of a particular test might be expressed as follows:

'The difference between the sample mean and the hypothetical population mean is significant at the 5% level'.

Significance levels and confidence limits, used in the last chapter for Estimation, are complementary and are based on the similar principles.

Notes.

a. As with confidence limits, *any* level of significance could be used but 5% and 1% are the most common.

b. The phrase used above, 'The difference between the sample mean and the population mean is significant at the 5% level' could alternatively be stated as:
'There is 95% confidence that the difference between the sample mean and the population mean is not due to chance factors'.

c. It is because the significance level must be chosen before the test is carried out and because it is a critical factor in deciding whether to accept or reject a hypothesis that the term 'significance testing' is commonly used instead of hypothesis testing.

AN EXAMPLE OF HYPOTHESIS TESTING

6. A machine fills packets with spice which are supposed to have a mean weight of 40 grams. A random sample of 36 packets is taken and the mean weight is found to be 42.4 grams with a standard deviation of 6 grams. it is required to conduct a significance test at the 5% level.

To do this we set up the following hypothesis.

'The population mean weight, μ, is 40 grams'.

This hypothesis is known as the *Null Hypothesis*, designated H_0 , and means that we are assuming that there is no contradiction between the supposed mean and the sample mean and that any difference can be ascribed solely to random factors.

The *alternative hypothesis*, designated H_1 , is that

'the population mean does not equal 40 grams'.

More simply these hypotheses can be shown thus

$$H_0 : \mu = 40 \text{ grams}$$

$$H_1 : \mu \neq 40 \text{ grams}$$

The null hypothesis is the one which is tested. If it is found to be true, H_1 is rejected whilst if H_0 is found to be false, H_1 is accepted.

Based on similar principles to those covered in the previous chapter, we know that the 95% confidence limits (i.e. equivalent to the 5% level of significance) the sample mean must be within ±1.96 standard errors so that if H_0 is true, 95% of the means of all samples must be within the range.

$$\mu - 1.96s_{\bar{x}} \text{ to } \mu + 1.96s_{\bar{x}}$$

The standard error in this example is

$$s_{\bar{x}} = \frac{6}{\sqrt{36}} = 1$$

so this gives the range

$$40 \pm 1.96\ (1)\ \text{grams i.e.}$$
$$38.04\ \text{to}\ 41.96\ \text{grams}$$

This is shown diagrammatically in Figure 1.

DISTRIBUTION OF SAMPLE MEANS. Figure 1

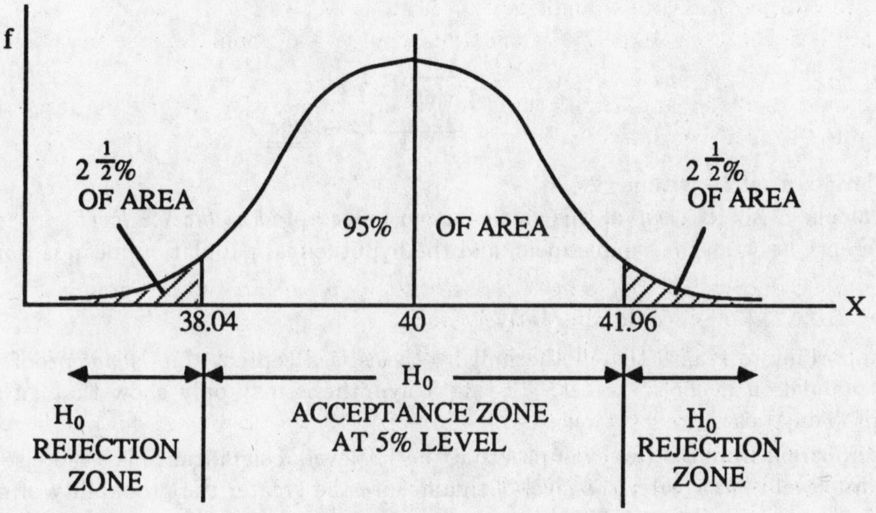

As the sample mean, 42.4 grams, is outside the acceptance zone we reject the H_0 hypothesis and accept the H_1 hypothesis i.e. $\mu \neq 40$ grams i.e. the difference between $\bar{x}$ and μ is *significant at the 5% level.*

As we have been concerned with *both* tails of the distribution this is known as a *two tail* test of significance. Some significance tests are *one tail* tests i.e. we are only concerned about differences in one direction. Examples of these are given later in the chapter.

A SIMPLER APPROACH TO HYPOTHESIS TESTING.

7. The preceding paragraph showed a particular method of solution mainly to illustrate the rationale of significance testing and the idea of a two tail test. There is, however, a simpler approach to the same conclusion and this is the approach recommended, provided that the underlying principles of testing a hypothesis are understood.

Example 1 will be reworked using the recommended approach i.e.

$$\begin{aligned}
H_0 : \mu &= 40\ \text{grams} \\
H_1 : \mu &\neq 40\ \text{grams (a two tail test)} \\
\bar{x} &= 42.4\ \text{grams (given)} \\
s &= 6\ \text{grams (given)} \\
n &= 36\ \text{grams (given)} \\
\text{Standard error} &= s_{\bar{x}} = \frac{6}{\sqrt{36}} = 1
\end{aligned}$$

$$\therefore z = \frac{\bar{x} - \mu}{s_{\bar{x}}} = \frac{42.4 - 40}{1} = \underline{\underline{2.24}}$$

At the 5% significance level the z value must be within ±1.96

∴ As the calculated score (2.24) is outside this value, H_0 is rejected.

This then is the usual method of testing a hypothesis; calculate the z score and compare the calculated value with the appropriate value for the required level of significance e.g. 1.96 for 5% , 2.58 for 1% (for two tail tests).

This approach can be used for the next example.

Example 2

Rework Example 1 using a 1% level of significance

$$\begin{aligned} H_0 : \mu &= 40 \text{ grams} \\ H_1 : \mu &\neq 40 \text{ grams} \\ \overline{x} &= 42.4 \text{ grams} \\ s &= 6 \text{ grams} \\ n &= 36 \\ \therefore s_{\bar{x}} &= \frac{6}{\sqrt{36}} = 1 \\ \therefore z &= \frac{42.4 - 40}{1} = \underline{\underline{2.24}} \end{aligned}$$

At the 1% level z must be within ±2.58.

∴ as the calculated score is *within* this value H_0 can be accepted *at the 1% level.*

i.e. the difference between the sample mean and the hypothetical population mean is ***not significant*** at the 1% level.

Notes

a. It is is important to realise that if the null hyothesis is accepted, this is ***not*** proof that the assumed population mean is correct. Testing a hypothesis may only show that an assumed value is probably false.

b. It will be apparent from the two examples that the 1% level of significance is a more severe test than the 5% level. The greater the level of significance the greater the probability of making a Type I error.

ONE TAILED TESTS

8. These are tests which can be simply defined as those tests in which the alternative hypothesis is concerned with only one of the tails of the distributions. For example, if the breaking strain of lifting cables was being studied there would only be concern if they were too weak. If the cables were designed to have a mean breaking point of 50 tonnes we would not be interested in the hypothesis that the true population mean was 50 tonnes *or more* but only if it was *less.*

The procedures for one-tailed tests are very similar to those previously described for two-tailed tests except for one important difference.

This is, that the number of standard errors for a given level of significance is different for one-tailed compared to two tailed tests. The values for the most common levels, 1% and 5% are shown below:

	Number of Standard Errors	
	Two-Tailed Tests	One-Tailed Tests
5% level of significance	1.96	1.65
1% level of significance	2.58	2.33

The reason for this is simply that when we are concerned with both tails of the distribution, the 5% (or 1% as the case may be) is shared between *both* tails as depicted in Figure 1, whereas in a one tailed test the 5% or 1% is only in the single tail. Values for any other required significance level can be obtained from Table1, Areas under the Normal Curve.

An example of a one-tailed test follows:

Example 3

Assume the same data as in Example 1 except that we require to test whether the population mean is *greater* than the assumed value of 40 grams, using a 5% level of significance.

$$\text{i.e.} H_0 : \mu = 40 \text{ grams}$$

$$H_1 : \mu > 40 \text{ grams}$$

This is a one tailed test as we are only interested in the right hand tail of the distribution.

As previously, the z score is 2.24 and for a one tailed test the z score should be within 1.65.

∴ as the calculated z score is outside the 5% value we reject the null hypothesis.

We can state:

'At the 5% level, H_1 , is accepted, the population mean is greater than 40 grams'.

Note

It is vital to ascertain whether a one tailed or two-tailed test is required so that the correct number of standard errors for the chosen significance level is used.

HYPOTHESIS TESTING OF PROPORTIONS

9. This follows a broadly similar approach to that outlined for means except that the standard error used is the standard error of a proportion i.e.

$$s_p = \sqrt{\frac{pq}{n}}$$

The z score is calculated as follows

$$z = \frac{p - \pi}{s_p}$$

where

p = proportion found in the sample.

π = the hypothetical proportion.

Example 4

It is required to test the hypothesis that 50% of households have a freezer. A random sample of 400 households found that 54% of the sample had freezers. The significance level is 5% .

Note

This is a two-tailed test because we wish to test the hypothesis as it is and not against a specific alternative hypothesis that the real proportion is either larger or smaller.

$$\text{i.e. } H_0 : \pi = 50\% \text{ of all households}$$

$$H_1 : \pi \neq 50\% \text{ of all households}$$

$$s_p = \sqrt{\frac{pq}{n}} = \sqrt{\frac{0.5 \times 0.5}{400}} = \underline{\underline{0.025}}$$

$$z = \frac{0.54 - 0.50}{0.025} = \underline{\underline{1.6}}$$

At the 5% level of significance for a two-tailed test the appropriate value is 1.96.

∴ as the calculated z score is 1.6 we can say that the difference is *not significant* and that H_0 should not be rejected.

HYPOTHESIS TESTING OF THE DIFFERENCE BETWEEN TWO MEANS

10. Where two random samples are taken, frequently it is required to know if there is significant difference *between* the two means. This hypothesis test follows the general pattern except that, once again, the standard error calculation differs.

The distribution of sample mean differences is normally distributed and remains normally distributed whatever the distribution of the population from which the samples are drawn. Where $n > 30$, i.e. large samples, the Normal Area tables are used, and when $n < 30$ the t distribution applies.

The standard errors of the difference of means $= s_{(\bar{x}_A - \bar{x}_B)} = \sqrt{\frac{s_A^2}{n_A} + \frac{s_B^2}{n_B}}$

where s_A = standard deviation of sample A, size n_A

where s_B = standard deviation of sample B, size n_B
and the z score is calculated thus

$$z = \frac{\bar{x}_A - \bar{x}_B}{s_{(\bar{x}_A - \bar{x}_B)}}$$

Example 5

Machine A and machine B produce identical components and it is required to test if the mean diameter of the components is the same. A random sample of 144 from machine A had a mean of 36.40 mm and a standard deviation of 3.6 mm; whilst a random sample of 225 from machine B had a mean of 36.90 mm and a standard deviation of 2.9 mm.

Are the means significantly different at the 5% level?

Solution

$$H_0 : \text{mean of A} = \text{mean of B}$$
$$H_1 : \text{mean of A} \neq \text{mean of B}$$

i.e. as we are not concerned with the direction of the variation this is a *two-tail test.*

$$s_{(\bar{x}_A - \bar{x}_B)} = \sqrt{\frac{3.6^2}{144} + \frac{2.9^2}{225}} = \underline{\underline{0.357}}$$

$$z = \frac{36.40 - 36.90}{0.357} = \underline{\underline{-1.4}}$$

The score for a two tailed test at the 5% level is ± 1.96.

∴ as the calculated z score of 1.4 is within this value there is nothing to suggest that there is any difference between the two means, i.e. H_0 would be accepted.

HYPOTHESIS TESTING OF THE DIFFERENCE BETWEEN PROPORTIONS

11. In a similar manner it may be required to test the differences between the proportions of a given attribute found in two random samples.

The following notation will be used:

	Sample 1	Sample 2
Sample size	n_1	n_2
Sample proportion of successes	p_1	p_2
Population proportion of successes	π_1	π_2

The Null Hypothesis will be $\pi_1 = \pi_2 (= \pi$, say) i.e. that the two samples are from the *same* population. This being so the best estimate of the standard error of the difference of p_1 and p_2 is given by pooling the samples and finding the pooled sample proportion thus

$$p = \frac{p_1 n_1 + p_2 n_2}{n_1 + n_2} \quad \text{and the}$$

Standard error is:

$$s_{(p_1 - p_2)} = \sqrt{\frac{pq}{n_1} + \frac{pq}{n_2}}$$

and

$$z = \frac{(p_1 - p_2) - (\pi_1 - \pi_2)}{s_{(\pi_1 - \pi_2)}}$$

but where the Null Hypothesis is $\pi_1 = \pi_2$ the second part of the numerator disappears.

Example 6 A ONE TAIL TEST

A market research agency take a sample of 1000 people and finds that 200 know of Brand X. After an advertising campaign a further sample of 1091 people is taken and it is found that 240 know of Brand X.

It is required to know if there has been an increase in the number of people having an awareness of Brand X at the 5% level.

Solution

$H_0 : \pi_2 = \pi_1$
$H_1 : \pi_2 \neq \pi_1$ (one tail test)

$$p_1 = \frac{200}{1000} = 0.2 \quad p_2 = \frac{240}{1091} = 0.22$$

$$\text{pooled sample proportion } p = \frac{200 + 240}{1000 + 1091} = 0.21$$

$$\text{and } q = 1 - p = 1 - 0.21 = 0.79$$

$$\therefore \; s_{(p_1 - p_2)} = \sqrt{\frac{0.21 \times 0.79}{1000} + \frac{0.21 \times 0.79}{1091}} = 0.0178$$

$$\therefore \; z = \frac{0.20 - 0.22}{0.0178} = -1.12$$

The critical value for a one-tailed test at the 5% level is -1.64 so that as the calculated value is within this value we conclude there is insufficient evidence to reject the null hypothesis.

Example 7 A TWO TAIL TEST

A survey was conducted in Birmingham and London to ascertain viewers habits regarding Channel 4 television. In Birmingham 1000 people were interviewed and 680 said they viewed Channel 4. In London 600 people were interviewed and 432 said they viewed Channel 4.

Is there a significant difference between the viewing habits in Birmingham and London at the 5% level? at the 1% level?

Solution

$$\text{In Birmingham } p = \frac{680}{1000} = 0.68 \text{ and } q = 0.32$$

$$\text{In London } p = \frac{444}{600} = 0.74 \text{ and } q = 0.26$$

$$\text{Pooled sample proportion} = \frac{680 + 444}{1000 + 600} = \underline{0.7025}$$

$$\therefore q = 1 - p = 1 - 0.7025 = 0.2975$$

$$\text{Standard Error} = \sqrt{\frac{0.7025 \times 0.2975}{1000} + \frac{0.7025 \times 0.2975}{600}} = \underline{0.0236}$$

$$z = \frac{0.74 - 0.68}{0.0236} = 2.54 \text{ standard errors}$$

At the 5% level for a two tail test $z = \pm 1.96$ and the calculated value is outside this.

$\therefore$ There is a significant difference at 5% .

At the 1% level $z = \pm 2.58$ and the calculated value is within this.

$\therefore$ There is not a significant difference in the viewing habits at the 1% level.

DISTRIBUTIONS OTHER THAN NORMAL

12. So far the discussion of statistical inference and hypothesis testing has been based on large samples resulting in a sampling distribution for the sample mean or proportion that is approximately normal. However, many sampling situations are not covered by this assumption. For example — it may be possible to use only a small sample — we may have an attribute that is classified into more than two categories — there may be samples from two or more populations to evaluate simultaneously — these and other special circumstances require distributions and other than the Normal.

Accordingly the previous material is extended to cover three more distributions; the t distribution, the χ^2 (chi-square) distribution and the f distribution.

HYPOTHESIS TESTING USING THE t DISTRIBUTION

13. There are many occasions where it is only feasible to use small samples, which is usually taken to be when $n < 30$. The means of small samples are distributed around the population mean in a manner similar to, but not exactly a normal distribution. The probability distribution of small sample means is known as a t distribution or students t distribution. When the t distribution applies, the value from the Normal Area Tables used so far in this chapter (eg 1.96 at the 95% level of confidence) is replaced by the t value from Table III. This value varies with ν, the degrees of freedom.

For a single sample this is $n - 1$, where two samples are being compared the degrees of freedom are $n_1 + n_2 - 2$

Apart from these differences the general procedures for hypothesis testing using the distribution follow the pattern previously described.

Example 8.

A firm ordered sacks of chemicals with a nominal weight of 50 kg. A random sample of 8 sacks was taken and it was found that the sample mean was 49.2 kg with a standard deviation of 1.6 kg. The firm wish to test whether the mean weight of the sample of sacks is significantly less than the nominal weight, using a 5% level of significance.

Solution

This is a one-tail test as we are only interested in whether the mean weight is *less* than the nominal.

$$\text{Ho : mean} = 50 \text{ kg}$$
$$\text{H1 : mean} < 50 \text{ kg}$$

Degrees of freedom $= n - 1 = 8 - 1 = \underline{7}$

Standard error of the mean $= \frac{s}{\sqrt{n}} = \frac{1.6}{\sqrt{8}} = \underline{0.566}$

$$\therefore t = \frac{\bar{x} - \mu}{s_{\bar{x}}} = \left| \frac{49.2 - 50}{0.566} \right| = \underline{1.413}$$

In order to find a one tailed 5% probability point we look up the .10 (two-tailed) point in Table III for 7 degrees of freedom. This value is 1.895.

Thus as the calculated t score, 1.413, is less than 1.895 we can accept the null hypothesis and reject the alternative hypothesis at the 5% level.

Note

The 10% probability point in Table III is spread between *both* tails, i.e. 5% in each tail.

t DISTRIBUTION TESTS OF THE DIFFERENCE BETWEEN MEANS

14. Previously this test was carried out using large samples. If the samples are small, the t distribution be used to test for differences in population means. In such circumstances two additional assumptions are necessary.

a. That the two sampled populations are normally or near normally distributed.
b. That the two standard deviations are equal or at any rate not significantly different. The best estimate of the population standard deviation is obtained by pooling the two sample standard deviations as shown below.

Given that two samples are taken and that n_1, x_1, s_1 and n_2, x_2, s_2 are the sample sizes, means and standard deviations respectively then the common or pooled estimate of the standard deviation for *both* populations (i.e. s_p) can be found as follows:

$$s_p = \sqrt{\frac{(n_1 - 1)s_1^2 + (n_2 - 1)s_2^2}{n_1 + n_2 - 2}}$$

s_p is then the best estimate of the standard deviation in each population.

The standard error for each sample mean can be calculated thus:

$$s_{\bar{x}_1} = \frac{s_p}{\sqrt{n_1}} \text{ and } s_{\bar{x}_2} = \frac{s_p}{\sqrt{n_2}}$$

and the sampling error of the distribution of differences in sample means is

$$s_{(\bar{x}_1 - \bar{x}_2)} = \sqrt{s_{\bar{x}_1}^2 + s_{\bar{x}_2}^2}$$

The value can be used to find the t score in the normal manner:

$$t = \frac{\overline{x}_1 - \overline{x}_2}{s_{(\overline{x}_1 - \overline{x}_2)}} \text{ with } n_1 + n_2 - 2 \text{ degrees of freedom.}$$

Example 9

The monthly incomes of two groups of salesmen are being investigated to see if there is a difference in the average income received. Random samples of 12 and 9 are taken from the two groups and it can be assumed that the incomes in both groups are approximately normally distributed and that the standard deviations are about the same. A 5% level of significance is to be used.

The sample results were

$$\begin{aligned} n_1 &= 12 & n_2 &= 9 \\ \overline{x}_1 &= £1060 & \overline{x}_2 &= £970 \\ s_1 &= £63 & s_2 &= £76 \end{aligned}$$

Solution

$$\begin{aligned} H_0 &: \mu_1 - \mu_2 = 0 \\ H_1 &: \mu_1 - \mu_2 \neq 0 \end{aligned}$$

It will be seen that this is a *two-tailed* test.

The common standard deviation is calculated first.

$$\begin{aligned} s_p &= \sqrt{\frac{(n_1 - 1)s_1^2 + (n_2 - 1)s_2^2}{n_1 + n_2 - 2}} \\ &= \sqrt{\frac{(12 - 1)63^2 + (9 - 1)76^2}{12 + 9 - 2}} \\ &= \underline{\underline{68.77}} \end{aligned}$$

$$\therefore s_{\overline{x}_1} = \frac{s_p}{\sqrt{n_1}} = \frac{68.77}{\sqrt{12}} = \underline{\underline{19.85}}$$

$$s_{\overline{x}_2} = \frac{s_p}{\sqrt{n_2}} = \frac{68.77}{\sqrt{9}} = \underline{\underline{22.92}}$$

$$\therefore s_{(\overline{x}_1 - \overline{x}_2)} = \sqrt{s_{\overline{x}_1}^2 + s_{\overline{x}_2}^2} = \underline{\underline{30.32}}$$

and, finally, the t score can be calculated

$$t = \frac{\overline{x}_1 - \overline{x}_2}{s_{(\overline{x}_1 - \overline{x}_2)}} = \frac{1060 - 970}{30.32} = \underline{\underline{2.97}}$$

From Table III the 5% value, with $(n_1 + n_2 - 2) = (12 + 9 - 2) = 19$ degrees of freedom is 2.093.

Since the calculated value is greater than this, the null hypothesis can be rejected at the 5% level i.e. we conclude that ***there is a significant difference*** between the mean monthly incomes.

THE CHI-SQUARE (χ^2) DISTRIBUTION

15. The χ^2 test is an important extension of hypothesis testing and is used when it is wished to compare an actual, observed distribution with a hypothesised, or expected distribution. If is often referred to as a 'goodness of fit' test.

The formula for the calculation of χ^2 is as follows:

$$\chi^2 = \sum \frac{(O - E)^2}{E}$$

where

O = the observed frequency of any value.

E = the expected frequency of any value.

The χ^2 value obtained from the formula is compared with the value from Table IV of χ^2 for a given significance level and the nu mber of degrees of freedom, i.e. the usual hypothesis testing procedures.

Table IV, the Distribution of χ^2, shows for the various degrees of freedom (ν) the cut off values at the two most common significance level, 5% and 1% .

The use of χ^2 will be explained using the following simple example.

A random sample of 400 householders is classified by two characteristics:

Whether they own a colour television and by what type of householder (i.e. owner-occupier, private tenant, council tenant). The results of this investigation are given below:

ACTUAL FREQUENCIES

	OWNER OCCUPIER	COUNCIL TENANT	PRIVATE TENANT	TOTAL
Colour TV	150	60	20	230
No colour TV	45	68	57	170
	195	128	77	400

Table 1

It is required to test at the 5% level, the following hypothesis.

H_0 : The two classifications are independent. (i.e. no relation between classes of householder and colour TV ownership).

H_1 : The classifications are NOT independent.

The first stage in the solution is to calculate the *expected frequencies* for each category which will then be compared with the *actual frequencies* shown above.

To find the expected frequencies.

These are found by making what is essentially the null hypothesis i.e. there is no differnce in the proportion of TV owners in each of the groups. The expected frequency in each cell in the table is found by apportioning the total of the type of householder in the ratio of colour TV ; No colour TV i.e. 230 : 170.

Thus, the 195 owner occupiers are split in the 230 : 170 proportion i.e. 112 : 83. The tenants are split in a similar fashion resulting in the following tables.

EXPECTED FREQUENCIES

	OWNER OCCUPIER	COUNCIL TENANT	PRIVATE TENANT	TOTAL
Colour TV	112	74	44	230
No colour TV	83	54	33	170
	195	128	77	400

Table 2

The χ^2 calculation can now be made.

OBSERVED FREQUENCIES (O)	EXPECTED FREQUENCIES (E)	(O - E)	$(O - E)^2$	$\frac{(O - E)^2}{E}$
150	112	+38	1444	12.89
45	83	-38	1444	17.40
60	74	-14	196	2.65
68	54	14	196	3.63
20	44	-24	576	13.09
57	33	+24	576	17.45
			χ^2	= 67.11

It is now necessary to find the appropriate χ^2 value from Table IV. This is done by establishing ν, the degrees of freedom. This is found by multiplying the number of rows in the table less one, by the number of columns less one, i.e.

ν = (Rows - 1) (Columns - 1), in this case

= (2 - 1) (3 - 1)

= 2 degrees of freedom

The value of the cut-off point of χ^2 for 2 degrees of freedom from Table IV is 5.991.

As the calculated value (67.11) is greater than the table value we reject the null hypothesis and accept that there is a connection between the type of householder and colour TV ownership.

Notes.

a. Table 1 and 2 illustrated in the example for the observed and expected frequencies are known as *contingency tables* or *two way classification tables.*

b. In calculating the number of degrees of freedom by the (Rows - 1) (Columns - 1) formula the row and column total cells are ignored.

c. If, when calculating the expected cell values, the expected frequency is less than 5, the χ^2 test becomes inaccurate. In such circumstances the cell which is less than 5 is merged with an adjoining cell so that the expected frequencies in all resulting cells are ≥ 5.

d. The larger the value of χ^2 the bigger the differences between actual and expected. If actual results were exactly as expected then (O-E) would equal zero and χ^2 would be zero.

ADDITIVE QUALITIES OF χ^2

16. χ^2 has the property (like variances) of being additive to other χ^2 values. If the results of a number of samples yield χ^2 values of χ_1^2, χ_2^2, χ_3^2 etc with ν_1, ν_2, ν_3, etc. degrees of freedom then the result of all the samples can be summarised with a single χ^2 value given by $\chi_1^2+\chi_2^2+\chi_3^2+$.....with $\nu_1+\nu_2+\nu_3+$ ....degrees of freedom.

'GOODNESS OF FIT' TESTS.

17. In addition to the use of χ^2 for comparing observed and expected frequencies in contingency tables as already explained, the χ^2 test can be used to determine how well empirical distributions i.e. those obtained from sample data, fit theoretical distributions such as the Normal, Poisson and Binomial. The procedure is similar to that previously described where the observed frequencies are compared with the expected frequencies. The expected frequencies are calculated in accordance with the assumed distribution characteristics based on the appropriate tables (Normal, Poisson etc.) and χ^2 calculated in the manner previously described. The procedure is demonstrated by the following examples.

EXAMPLE 10.

Torch bulbs are packed in boxes of 5 and 100 boxes are selected randomly to test for the number of defectives. The results were as follows:

NUMBER OF DEFECTIVES	NUMBER OF BOXES	TOTAL DEFECTIVES
0	40	0
1	37	37
2	17	34
3	5	15
4	1	4
5	0	0
	100	90

The probability of any individual bulb being a reject is

$\frac{90}{100 \times 5} = 0.18$ and it is required to test at the 5% level whether the frequency of rejects conforms to a binomial distribution.

SOLUTION

The observed frequencies are already given so it is only necessary to calculate the frequencies expected from a binomial distribution to the power 5 i.e. $(p+q)^5$, where $p = 0.18$ and $q = 1 - 0.18 = 0.82$.

The probabilities of the various values of p and q can be found from binomial probability tables if available. Alternatively they can be calculated from the binomial expansion as explained in Chapter 4 i.e.

$$p^5 + 5(p^4 + q) + 10(p^3 + q^2) + 10(p^2 + q^3) + 5(p + q^4) + q^5$$

This shows the probabilities for 5, 4, 3, 2, 1 and 0 defectives and when $p = 0.18$ (the probability of a bulb being defective) and $q = 0.82$ (probability of not being defective) the probabilities range from 0.0002 (ie 0.18^5) for five defectives to 0.3711 (ie 0.82^5) for no defectives. When the probabilities are known they are multiplied by 100 boxes to find the expected frequencies which are used in the normal χ^2 procedures.

The table below summarises the calculations:

DEFECTIVES	NO. OF BOXES OBSERVED	BINOMIAL PROBABILITIES	EXPECTED FREQUENCY	$(O - E)^2$	$\frac{(O - E)^2}{E}$
0	40	0.3711	37.11	8.35	0.22
1	37	0.4069	40.69	13.62	0.33
2	17	0.1786	17.86	0.74	0.04
3	5 }	0.0392	3.92 }		
4	1 }	0.0040	0.4 }	2.76	0.64
5	0 }	0.0002	0.02 }		
				χ^2	= 1.23

Note: Because of the very small values of the expected frequencies for 3, 4 and 5 defectives they have been combined into one but it makes little difference to the result if they are not combined.

The calculated χ^2 value is compared with a χ^2 value for the appropriate degrees of freedom. In this case the number is 2 which is arrived at by the following reasoning.

After combining the last three classes there are four classes in total. One degree of freedom has been used to make the totals agree (i.e. 100 boxes) and another to make the mean proportion of defectives (i.e. 0.18) agree. Thus the degrees of freedom is 4 - 2 = 2. If the classes had not been combined there would have been 6 - 2 = 4 degrees of freedom.

The χ^2 value for 2 degrees of freedom is 5.991 and as the calculated value is 1.23 is well below this we conclude that the observed values fit a binomial distribution of $(0.18 + 0.82)^5$ excellently.

EXAMPLE 11

An area of a city is divided into 600 squares and the frequency of burglaries noted in each square. The data were as follows:

Number of Burglaries	Number of Squares	Total Burglaries
0	279	0
1	200	200
2	90	180
3	25	75
4	5	20
5	1	5
	600	480

Average number of burglaries $= \frac{480}{600} = \underline{\underline{0.8}}$

Test the fit of the observed distribution to a Poisson distribution with a mean of 0.8, at the 5% level.

SOLUTION

This follows a similar pattern to the previous example except that Poisson probabilities are used (Table VI)

The summary table is thus.

NUMBER OF BURGLARIES	OBSERVED NO OF SQUARES	POISSON PROBABILITES	EXPECTED FREQUENCY (P × 600)	$(O - E)^2$	$\frac{(O - E)^2}{E}$
0	279	0.4493	269.58	88.73	0.33
1	200	0.3593	215.7	246.49	1.14
2	90	0.1438	86.28	13.83	0.16
3	25	0.0383	22.98	4.08	0.18
4	5 }	0.0077	4.62 }	0.44	0.08
5	1 }	0.0012	0.72 }		
				χ^2	$= \underline{\underline{1.89}}$

There are 5 (O-E) classes so the degrees of freedom are 5-2 = 3 and the χ^2 value for 3 degrees of freedom is 7.815 (Table IV). As the calculated value is less than this we conclude that the observed values fit a Poisson distribution well.

Note. A similar procedure would be used for testing the goodness of fit of an observed distribution to a Normal Distribution except, of course, the probabilities and frequencies appropriate to a Normal Distribution would be used. Also, we would use up three degrees of freedom fitting a Normal distribution to an observed distribution; as the distributions must have the same mean, total and standard deviation. This means that the χ^2 value would be for $n - 3$ degrees of freedom, where n is the number of classes of expected frequencies.

THE F DISTRIBUTION

18. The F distribution has many uses, particularly in advanced statistics, but for our purposes two important applications are

a. where the variability of samples have to be compared, and,

b. where the means of several populations have to be compared.

The F distribution is formed from the ratio

$$F = \frac{y_1/\nu_1}{y_2/\nu_2}$$

Where y_1 and y_2 are two independent random variables, each having χ^2 probability distribution with ν_1 and ν_2 degrees of freedom respectively. The F distribution has two parameters ν_1, and ν_2, the degrees of freedom in the numerator and denominator respectively.

The F variable has an expected or mean value of approximately 1, except when there are very small sample sizes in the denominator. As there is a different F distribution for each value of ν_1, and ν_2, full tables would be very lengthy. Accordingly Table V Percentage Points of the F Distribution, shows only a selection of F values. The table shows 0.05 and 0.01 (in brackets) values for ν_1, and ν_2 up to 12.

COMPARING SAMPLE VARIABILITIES USING THE F DISTRIBUTION

19. This particular test is important in some quality control applications where consistency of output is important.

Example 12

In a manufacturing process a sample of 10 items is found to have a standard deviation of 5 mm. The same items are produced by a different process and a sample of 12 items is found to have a standard deviation of 4.2 mm.

Is the new process more consistent than the old at the 5% level?

Solution

The sample details are

Sample 1	Sample 2
$s_1 = 5$	$s_2 = 4.2$
$s_1^2 = 25$	$s_2^2 = 17.64$
$n_1 = 10$	$n_2 = 12$
∴ degrees of freedom = 10 - 1 = 9	degrees of freedom = 12 - 1 = 11

Null Hypothesis:

There is no difference betwen the population variabilities i.e.

$$H_0 : \sigma_1^2 = \sigma_2^2$$

Alternative hypothesis: That the new processis more consistent than the old.

$$H_1 : \sigma_1^2 < \sigma_2^2 \text{ (one tail test)}$$

$$\text{F score} = \frac{s_1^2}{s_2^2} = \frac{25}{17.64} = \underline{\underline{1.42}}$$

The F score from Table V where $\nu_1 = 9$ and $\nu_2 = 11$, at the 5% level, is 2.90.

∴ The Null hypothesis cannot be rejected. Based on the sample results there is no significant difference between the two processes.

ANALYSIS OF VARIANCE (ANOVA) TESTS)

20. Tests of the difference between *two* sample means have already been explained earlier in the chapter.

However, it is sometimes necessary to test the hypothesis that the means of *several* sampled populations are equal. These types of tests use the F distribution and are known as analysis of variance or ANOVA tests. These tests are complex with many intermediate calculations and it is considered unlikely that a student would be asked to carry out a full ANOVA test under examination conditions. However, a broad understanding of the objectives of the tests and sufficient knowledge to interpret the results of such tests are likely requirements.

For example a firm wishes to analyse the effectiveness of advertising with 3 different style advertisements; block, classified and display. Each is tried in a sample of 4 publications of equal circulation and the resulting enquiries are shown in the following table.

	STYLE OF ADVERTISEMENT		
	BLOCK	CLASSIFIED	DISPLAY
NUMBER	8	5	21
OF	4	10	18
ENQUIRIES	7	12	14
FROM	5	5	11
PUBLICATIONS			
GROUP AVERAGE	$\bar{x}_1 = 6$	$\bar{x}_2 = 8$	$\bar{x}_3 = 16$

Table 3

The overall average is 10. The firm wishes to know if the observed difference are significant or if they could be attributable to chance variations.

Before this can be tested two assumptions are necessary.

a. Enquiries within each style of advertisement are normally distributed.
b. The variances within each group (i.e. style of advertisement) are the same.

The Null hypothesis is that there is no difference in the population means i.e.

$$\mu_1 = \mu_2 = \mu_3 = \mu$$

This hypothesis is tested by breaking the total variation of all observations about the overall mean (10 in our example) into two parts.

a. The within-group variations i.e. the variations of the individual values about the group means, and
b. The between-group variations i.e. the variations of the group means about the overall mean.

These types of variations have, in our example,. 9 and 2 degrees of freedom respectively i.e.

$$\text{— within group } = \nu_1 + \nu_2 + \nu_3 = 3 + 3 + 3 = 9$$

where ν_1, ν_2, ν_3 are the degrees of freedom in each group (4 - 1)

$$\text{— between group } = \text{Number of groups } - 1 = 3 - 1 = 2$$

The analysis of these variations (not dealt with in this manual) eventually produces two estimates of σ i.e. the common variance within each group. From these estimates the F ratio is prepared.

Assume that the results of analysing our example are as follows:

SOURCE OF VARIATION	DEGREES OF FREEDOM	ESTIMATE OF σ^2
BETWEEN GROUPS	2	95
WITHIN GROUPS	9	12

$$\therefore \text{ F ratio} = \frac{\text{Estimate of } \sigma^2 \text{ from between groups}}{\text{Estimate of } \sigma^2 \text{ from within groups}} = \frac{95}{12} = \underline{7.92}$$

Looking up the F score from Table V at the 5% level for 2 and 9 degrees of freedom we find 4.26. Since the calculated value is greater than this the null hypothesis can be rejected i.e. the variation between group means is significant and is too large to be attributable to chance.

Note.

Where the calculated F ratio is less than 1 it can be assumed that the variations are NOT significant. There is no need for comparison with the Table V value.

TWO WAY ANALYSIS OF VARIANCE

21. The process described above could be extended to test another factor in addition to the previous classifications. For example, the firm in the example might wish to test the type of publication as well as the advertisement style i.e.

		ADVERTISEMENT STYLE		
		BLOCK	CLASSIFIED	DISPLAY
TYPE	DAILY	××	××	××
OF	WEEKLY	××	××	××
PUBLICATION	MONTHLY	××	××	××

Table 4

The overall objective of such two way ANOVA tests is the same, i.e. to find estimate of σ^2 for each group but naturally there are more sources of variation. These are as follows:

a. **Row Effects:** These are the effects of the type of publication. They are measured as differences from the overall mean.

b. **Column Effects:** These are the effects of the advertisement styles. They also are measured as differences from the overall mean.

c. **Interaction Effects:** The effect of any cell in the table is assumed to be a sum of the row and column effects. Sometimes, however, there is an interaction effect in which the effect in a given cell is greater (or less) than the combined row and column effects. In our example this might mean that classified advertisments were effective in *daily* publications but not in monthly.

d. **Residual Effects:** This is the within-group variation previously described.

Assume that the two way ANOVA test has been carried out on the data in Table 4. The results might be as follows:

ASSUMED RESULTS OF TWO-WAY ANOVA TEST ON TABLE 4

SOURCE OF VARIATION	DEGREES OF FREEDOM	ESTIMATE OF σ^2	F RATIO
ROWS	2	6.2	0.488
COLUMNS	2	137.8	10.85
INTERACTIONS	4	3.2	0.25
RESIDUAL (WITHIN-GROUP)	9	12.7	

Table 5

Notes

a. The F ratios are the ratios of the various σ^2 estimates to the residual estimate of σ^2. e.g. Row-F ratio is $\frac{6.2}{12.7} = 0.488$

b. The calculated values are compared with the F scores from Table V for the appropriate degrees of freedom as follows:

	Value from Table V	Calculated Value from above	Significant?
ROW	F(2,9) = 4.26	0.488	No (less than 1)
COLUMN	F(2,0) = 4.26	10.85	Yes
INTERACTION	F(4,9) = 3.63	0.25	No (less than 1)

c. As the column effects are significant it means that the different advertisement styles differ significantly in their effectiveness but the types of publication did not, nor were the interactions between advertisement style and publication type significant.

d. Although the actual values of σ^2 have been assumed in Table 5 the number of degrees of freedom for each source of variation is correct and so are the F ratios (based on the assumed σ^2 values.)

SUMMARY

22.

a. Hypothesis or significant testing is testing a belief or opinion by statistical methods.

b. A Type I error is rejecting a true hypothesis and a Type II error is accepting a false hypothesis.

c. Significance levels are complementary concepts to confidence limits. 1% and 5% are the most usual levels.

d. The Null hypothesis (H_0) usually assumes there is no difference between the observed and believed values.

e. A one-tail test is concerned with only one tail of the distribution i.e. a difference in one direction only.

f. Hypothesis testing is commonly used for testing sample means and proportions.

g. The difference between the means and proportions of two samples are also used in significance testing.
The standard error of the distribution of means is:

$$s_{(\bar{x}_A - \bar{x}_b)} = \sqrt{\frac{s_A^2}{n_A} + \frac{s_B^2}{n_B}}$$

The standard error of the difference between proportions is

$$s_{(p_1 - p_2)} = \sqrt{\frac{p_1 q_1}{n_1} + \frac{p_2 q_2}{n_2}}$$

h. The 't' distribution is used for significance testing when the sample size is less than 30. The number of degrees of freedom, ν, is $n - 1$ or, for two samples $n_1 + n_2 - 2$. However, if the ***population*** standard deviation is known then the Normal distribution can be used. The t distribution is required when we have to estimate σ from s.

i. The chi-square (χ^2) distribution is used for comparing an actual distribution with an expected distribution. The formula is

$$\chi^2 = \sum \frac{(O - E)^2}{E}$$

j. χ^2 values, like variances, can be added.

k. The F distribution is used where the variability of samples has to be compared. The F value is a ratio and degrees of freedom for both the numerator and denominator are required i.e. ν_1 and ν_2.

l. The F distribution is also used in 'Analysis of Variance' (ANOVA) tests which may be one way or two way analyses.

POINTS TO NOTE

23.

a. A significant difference is one which is unlikely to have arisen by chance.

b. A shorthand way of expressing the level of significance for a test is $\chi^2_{.05}$, i.e. a χ^2 test using a 5% level of significance, $t_{0.1}$ i.e. a t test using a 1% level of significance and so on.

c. The statistical tests described generally require assumptions regarding the underlying distribution from which the sample is taken e.g. the t tests and F tests assume Normality. There are tests which do not require such assumptions; they are called ***non parametric*** or ***distribution free*** tests.

SELF REVIEW QUESTIONS

1. What is hypothesis testing? (2)

2. Define Type I and Type II errors. (4)

3. What is a significance level? (5)

4 What is the difference that is statistically significant? (5)

5. What is the Null Hypothesis? - the Alternative Hypothesis? (6)

6. What is the two tail test? (6)

7. What are the appropriate number of Standard Errors to use in a one-tailed test at the 5% level?, at the 1% level? (8)

8. What is the standard error of a proportion? (9)

9. How is the standard error of the distribution of means calculated? (10)

10. When is the t distribution used? (12)

11. What is the best estimate of the population standard deviation when two samples are taken? (14)

12. What is the χ^2 formula? (15)

13. How are the 'expected frequencies' calculated for use in the χ^2 formula? (15)

15. What is a 'goodness of fit' test? (17)

16. What are two important applications of the F distribution? (18)

17. What is an ANOVA test? (20)

18. What are the four sources of variation in two way ANOVA tests? (21)

EXERCISES WITH ANSWERS COMMENCING PAGE 488

A1. The output of two workers was compared over a number of days with the following results.

	Average Output per day	Standard Deviation	Number of Days Observed
Man A	30	6	50
Man B	32	5	60

Is there a significant difference in output at the 95% level?

A2. Express Packets guarantee 90% of their deliveries are on time. In a recent week 80 deliveries were made and 6 were late and the Managing Director says that, at the 95% level, there has been a significant improvement in deliveries.

(a) Can the M.D's statement be supported?

(b) If not, at what level of confidence could it be supported?

A3. Ten electronic weighing machines have been tested and their errors noted as follows:

Meter	Errors(gms)
1	4.6
2	8.2
3	2.1
4	6.3
5	5.0
6	3.6
7	1.4
8	4.1
9	7.0
10	4.5

The Purchasing manager has previously accepted machines with a mean error of 3.8 gms and asserts that these 10 meters are below standard.

Test the assertion at the 5% level.

EXAMINATION QUESTIONS WITH ANSWERS COMMENCING PAGE 488

A4. An investigation is being carried out into delays in the payment of invoices by customers of your company. Details of the present position are given in the following table; the figures in the table represent the number of customers.

	Class of customer company		
	Private limited companies		Public
Status as a payer	Capitalised at < £1 million	Capitalised at > £1 million	limited companies
Very slow (> 4 months)	20	10	10
Slow (3 and 4 months)	16	14	12
Average (1 and < 3 months)	22	12	10
Prompt (< 1 month)	8	8	8

You are required to prepare a statistical analysis to determine whether there is any relationship between the class of company and its status as a payer. Use the 5% level of significance and show clearly all your workings.

(CIMA, Quantitative Techniques)

A5. a. The label on a container of a liquid chemical sold at 10 pence per litre states the contents to be 10 litres. However, the filling equipment cannot fill each container with exactly the same volume of liquid: the volumes are normally distributed with a standard deviation of 0.2 litre. The latter may be treated as a constant, but the mean fill (at present 10 litres) can be adjusted. Regulations require that no more than one in a hundred containers should contain less than 10 litres.

A company has designed a modification which can be fitted to the filling equipment and would reduce the standard deviation to 0.15 litres. It would cost £5,000 for the modification which would need to be replaced after 100,000 containers had been filled.

You are required to:

i. State the level at which the mean fill should be set in order to meet the regulations, without using the modifications;

ii. Advise management if the modification is a worthwhile purchase.

b. 'The variance of the distribution of the difference between sample means is calculated by adding together the variances obtained from two samples'.

i. State if the above statement is correct or not, giving reasons for your answer;

ii. Explain your answer in statistical terms.

(CIMA Quantitative Techniques)

A6. The Arcas Appliance Company is currently considering various changes to its pension scheme. In particular, male employees' contributions are to be increased from 5% to 7% of the basic wage, in return for which there will be enhanced pension provision for wives and children in the event of the employee dying before reaching retirement age. It is envisaged that all future employees will be obliged to join the new scheme, but existing employees will be allowed to choose whether or not they will change from the old scheme to the new one. To assess the likely level of acceptance of the new scheme among existing employees, a survey was conducted at one of the company's factories, producing the following results according to age and marital status.

Do you intend to change to new scheme?	Age 30 or Under		Age over 30	
	Married	Single	Married	Single
Yes	109	153	362	52
No	43	124	207	67
Don't Know	27	102	46	3

Required:

(a) Describe in general terms the main features which seem to be indicated by the data.

(b) Assuming that the results obtained may be regarded as a random sample of the company's employees, test whether there is evidence of a different attitude to the new scheme depending upon the

(i) age of the employee (ignoring marital status)

(ii) marital status of the employee (ignoring age)

(c) Discuss briefly various ways in which 'Don't Knows' could be dealt with in an analysis of this type and justify the approach that you have adopted.

(ACCA Quantitative Analysis)

A7. As part of an annual company audit, the 12,143 sales invoices issued by Ixion plc during the last year have been sampled and checked for accuracy. The required sample of 200 invoices was drawn randomly and the results were classified according to the number of items that each invoice contains, giving rise to the following data.

Items per Invoice	Number Sampled	Number of Invoices with 0 errors	1 error	2 errors
1 - 5	64	60	2	2
6 - 10	90	74	8	8
10+	46	32	8	6
	200			

Required:

(a) Estimate the proportion of all invoices which contain at least one error, complete with a 95% confidence interval.

(b) Is there any statistical evidence of an association between the number of errors observed per invoice and the size of the invoice?

(c) Calculate the total number of errors observed for each different size of invoice, and compare these with the number that would be expected if errors have been equally likely to occur on invoices of any size. Is the difference significant?

(ACCA Quantitative Analysis)

A8. The reported unpaid debts to sales percentages of the Newtown and Leftwich branches of Modern Clothing (Wholesale) p.l.c. are quoted below.

Month	1	2	3	4	5	6	7	8	9	10	11	12
Newtown	5.0	5.5	6.0	4.0	4.0	6.0	6.0	6.0	6.0	3.5	5.5	5.0
Leftwich	4.0	4.0	6.5	7.0	5.0	5.5	5.5	4.5	5.0	6.0	4.0	4.5

Assume both sets of ratios to be Normally distributed and their variances to be equal.

	Mean	Variance
Newtown	5.2083	0.8390
Leftwich	5.1250	1.0057

The management of Modern Clothing wishes to know whether there is a statistically significant difference in debtor control in the two branches.

You are required to:

(a) carry out a test on the difference between the two sample means at the 5% level of significance.

(b) explain your conclusions.

(CIMA Quantitative Techniques)

A9. Croesus Construction Ltd has recently been analysing the unit cost associated with different types of building. It has obtained the following data relating to a random sample of 7 schools and 5 office blocks that were completed during the period 1971 to 1980. The data show the cost per square metre of floor area (in terms of 1982 prices) for each building involved.

Cost per Square Metre

Schools	Offices
28	37
31	42
26	34
27	37
23	35
38	
37	

Required:

(a) Do the data support the hypothesis that during the period in question the cost per square metre for the office blocks was greater than that for schools?

(b) If it were known that, during the period 1971-80, the company had completed 24 school buildings and 27 office blocks, would this cause you to alter the conclusion that you have reached in (a) and, if so, how?

(c) Briefly discuss some of the limitations to the analysis you have performed and suggest two other factors that you might take into account in a more detailed comparison of unit costs.

(ACCA Quantitative Analysis)

A10. A survey of the principal methods used by a sample of U.K. and U.S. companies to evaluate capital expenditure proposals produced the following results.

Principal evaluation method	Number of companies U.K.	U.S	Total
Discounted cash flow (either IRR or NPV)	100	170	270
Payback period (undiscounted)	130	90	220
Return on capital employed	80	50	130
Non-financial criteria	80	40	120

You are required to:

(a) use the χ_2 test to determine whether there is a significant difference in the approaches to capital expenditure evaluation adopted by the U.K. and U.S. companies included in the survey, stating clearly the hypothesis to be tested and the conclusions that may be drawn from the results of the test;

(b) discuss briefly the conditions under which this test would be valid.

(CIMA QUANTITATIVE TECHNIQUES)

EXERCISES WITHOUT ANSWERS

B1. The mean life of neon tubes is expected to be 2000 hours. To test this a sample of 12 was taken which showed a mean life of 1880 hours with a standard deviation of 120 hours. Test the hypothesis at the 95% and 99% levels that the mean lifetime of the tubes has not changed.

B2. In district A out of a sample of 400, 285 people owned a car. In district B out of 500, 335 owned a car. Is there any difference between the proportion owning cars?

B3. A sample of 500 households is classified by 2 characteristics; whether they own a pet or not and what type of household it is, thus:

	SINGLE PERSON HOUSEHOLD	MARRIED HOUSEHOLD	MARRIED WITH CHILDREN HOUSEHOLD	TOTALS
OWN PET	50	32	120	202
NO PET	100	58	140	298
	150	90	260	500

Is there a connection between Pet ownership and type of household?

EXAMINATION QUESTIONS WITHOUT ANSWERS.

B4. The Alpha Group has two factories in different parts of the country. Their resources, including the labour force skills are regarded as identical and both factors were built at the same time.

A random sample of output data during a given period has been taken from each factory and converted to standard hours of output per employee. The data are given below:

Factory 1: 142, 150, 143, 139, 141, 149, 152, 141, 146, 148

Factory 2: 139, 145, 136, 142, 152, 137, 143, 141, 140, 139

Total standard hours for Factory 1 = 1,451

Total standard hours for Factory 2 = 1,414
You are given:
Factory 1: Mean = 145.1; Variance = 20.1
Factory 2: Mean = 141.4; Variance = 21.16

You are required to:

(a) determine whether there is a statistically significant difference in the mean standard hours per employee between the two factories.

(b) comment briefly on the conditions of the test and interpret the outcome.

(CIMA Quantitative Techniques)

B5. A small office equipment leasing company employs two engineers carrying out repair work in the Midlands district. Over a given period of time, the recorded work sheet times show the following distribution of repair times.

Repair time (minutes)	Observed frequency
Less than 5	0
5 to less than 15	24
15 to less than 25	98
25 to less than 35	56
35 to less than 45	36
45 to less than 55	18
55 to less than 65	8
65 and above	0

As part of a study to plan its capacity to repair equipment, the company has calculated an expected frequency distribution, based on a service pattern exhibiting the characteristics of a negative exponential distribution.

Observed frequency	Expected Frequency
0	39
24	60
98	42
56	30
36	21
18	14
8	10
0	24

The formula for the negative exponential distributionis given as:

$$f(x) = (\frac{1}{m})^x e^{-x/m}, x \geq 0$$

where x is the service time and m is the average service time.

Expected frequencies can be derived from the cumulative distribution:

$$F(x) = 1 - e^{-x/m}, x \geq 0$$

You are required to:

(a) show how the first term only of the expected frequency distribution has been obtained.

***(b)** carry out a χ^2 test to determine whether the observed and expected distributions are significantly different.*

(CIMA Quantitative Techniques)

7 Correlation and Regression

INTRODUCTION

1. This chapter considers the problems of analysing the relationship between variables. Different types of scatter diagrams are depicted and the method of calculating r, the correlation coefficient, is explained. Straight line equations are described and the method of calculating the least squares regression line is described in detail. The uses and method of calculating the coefficient of determination are described and the development of confidence limits for the regression line is explained in detail. The chapter concludes with an explanation of the Rank Correlation coefficient.

RELATIONSHIPS BETWEEN VARIABLES

2. There are, frequently occasions in business when changes in one factor appear to be related in some way to movements in one or several other factors. For example, a marketing manager may observe that sales increase when there has been a change in advertising expenditure. The transport manager may notice that as vans and lorries cover more miles then the need for maintenance becomes more frequent.

Certain questions may arise in the mind of the manager or analyst. These may be summarised as follows:

a. Are the movements in the same or in opposite directions?
b. Could changes in one phenomenon or variable be causing or be caused by movements in the other variable? (This is an important relationship known as a CAUSAL RELATIONSHIP).
c. Could apparently related movements come about purely by chance?
d. Could movements in one factor or variable be as a result of combined movements in several other factors or variables?
e. Could movements in two phenomena be related, not directly, but through movements in a third variable hitherto unnoticed?
f. What is the use of this knowledge anyway?

Very frequently, the manager or analyst is interested in prediction of some kind. For example, the quality control manager may want to know what might be the effect on the number of faulty parts discovered if the amount of expenditure on inspection were increased. The Sales Manager may wish to predict sales levels if advertising were increased by say 20% . Here there is clearly some kind of causal model in the minds of the two managers.

METHODOLOGY

3. Suppose that a manager has sensed that two variables or phenomena are behaving in some "related" way, how might that manager proceed to investigate the matter further? A possible methodology might be as follows.

a. Observe and note what is happening in systematic way.
b. Form some kind of theory about the observed facts.
c. Draw a graph or diagram of what is being observed.
d. Measure what is happening.
e. Use the results.

This methodology is develped throughout this Chapter and the various stages are illustrated using the problem shown in Example 1.

EXAMPLE 1

The managers of a company with ten operating plants of similar size producing small components have observed the following pattern of expenditure on inspection and defective parts delivered to the customer:

Observation Number	Inspection Expenditure per 1000 units pence	Defective Parts per 1000 units Delivered
1	25	50
2	30	35
3	15	60
4	75	15
5	40	46
6	65	20
7	45	28
8	24	45
9	35	42
10	70	22

They are wondering how strong the relationship is between inspection expenditure and the numberof faulty items delivered and to what extent they may predict the number of faulty parts delivered from a knowledge of expenditure on inspection.

DRAWING A DIAGRAM FOR EXAMPLE 1

4. Clearly in this problem the managers have already noted and recorded what is happening in a systematic manner. They would also reasonably deduce that there is likely to be a causal relationship between the expenditure on inspection and the number of defectives parts delivered to the customer; the *higher* the expenditure, the *fewer* defective parts are delivered. Based on this assumption - which is a form of hypothesis - the data can be graphed using the accepted convention that the horizontal or x axis is used for the independent or causing variable in this case, expenditure. The y or vertical axis is used for the dependent variable, in this case, defective parts delivered. This type of diagram is known as a scatter diagram.

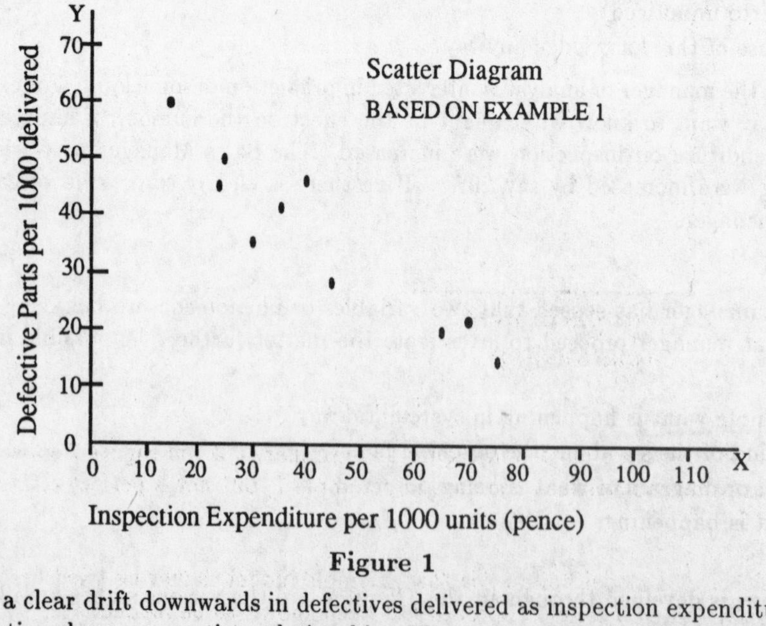

Figure 1

Figure 1 shows a clear drift downwards in defectives delivered as inspection expenditure increases. This is known as a negative slope or negative relationship. The next paragraph deals with other relationships that may be found in different circumstances.

DIFFERENT RELATIONSHIPS BETWEEN VARIABLES.

5. Figure 1 was based on the data from Example 1. In other situations numerous other possibilities exist ranging from a perfect negative or perfect positive relationship to no discernible relationship at. A perfect relationship is one where a single straightline can be drawn through all the points, for example 2.1 and 2.2. in Figure 2.

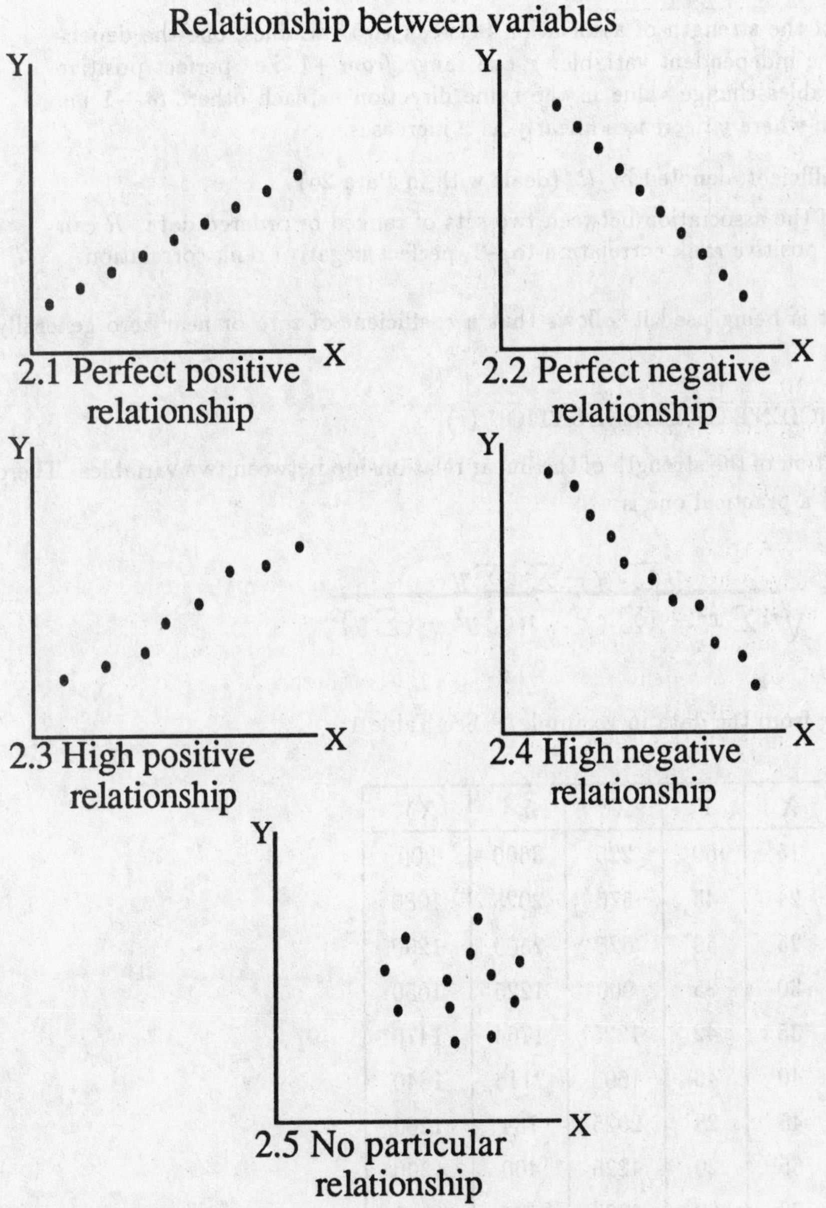

Figure 2

It will be seen that the points plotted in Figure 1 are similar to 2.4 in Figure 2 so we can conclude there is a high negative relationship between the data in Example 1, but not a perfect relationship.

CORRELATION

6. An important feature of model building is that a simple model should be tried first and more complex models being used only when a simple approach has been shown to be inadequate.

The problem posed in Example 1 is no exception. The simplest model that can be used is known as a two variable linear model where y is thought to move in an approximately linear relationship to changes in x.

In statistics, a measure of the strength of a linear relationship between two sets of numbers i.e. if a change in one number is accompanied by a change in the other, is known as correlation.

There are, in fact, two measures of correlation:

a. The Product moment Coefficient of Correlation, denoted by r.

   This provides a measure of the strength of association between two variables; one the dependent variable, the other the independent variable. r can range *from* +1, i.e. perfect positive correlation where the variables change value in the same direction as each other, *to* −1 i.e. perfect negative correlation where y decreases linearly as x increases.

b. The Rank Correlation Coefficient, denoted by R. (dealt with in Para 26)

   This provides a measure of the association between two sets of ranked or ordered data. R can also vary from +1, perfect positive rank correlation to −1, perfect negative rank correlation.

Whichever type of coefficient is being used it follows that a coefficient of zero or near zero generally indicates no correlation.

PRODUCT MOMENT COEFFICIENT OF CORRELATION (r)

7. This coeffcient gives an indication of the strength of the linear relationship between two variables. There are several possible formulae but a practical one is:

$$r = \frac{n\sum xy - \sum x \sum y}{\sqrt{n\sum x^2 - (\sum x)^2}.\sqrt{n\sum y^2 - (\sum y)^2}}$$

This formula is used to find r from the data in Example 1. See Table 1.

X	Y	X^2	Y^2	XY
15	60	225	3600	900
24	45	576	2025	1080
25	50	625	2500	1250
30	35	900	1225	1050
35	42	1225	1764	1470
40	46	1600	2116	1840
45	28	2025	784	1260
65	20	4225	400	1300
70	22	4900	484	1540
75	15	5625	225	1125
424	363	21926	15123	12815
$\sum X$	$\sum Y$	$\sum X^2$	$\sum Y^2$	$\sum XY$

Table 1

Using the formula above

$$r = \frac{10 \times 12815 - 424 \times 363}{\sqrt{10 \times 21926 - 424^2}.\sqrt{10 \times 15123 - 363^2}}$$
$$= \frac{128150 - 153912}{\sqrt{2109260 - 179776}.\sqrt{151230 - 131769}}$$
$$= \frac{-25762}{\sqrt{39484}\sqrt{19461}}$$
$$= \frac{-25762}{198.7058127 \times 139.5026881}$$
$$= \underline{\underline{-0.93}}$$

Thus the correlation coefficient is −0.93 which indicates a strong negative linear association between expenditure on inspection and defective parts delivered. It will be seen that the formula automatically produces the correct sign for the coefficient.

Note:

A strong correlation between two variables would produce an r value in excess of +0.9 or −0.9. If the value was less than, say 0.5 there would only be a very weak relationship between the variables.

INTERPRETATION OF THE VALUE OF r

8. Care is needed in the interpretation of the calculated value of r. A high value (above +0.9 or −0.9) only shows a strong association between the two variables if there is a *causal relationship* i.e. if a change in one variable *causes* changes in the other. It is possible to find two variables which produce a high calculated r value yet which have no casual relationship. This is known as *spurious* or *nonsense correlation.*

An example might be the wheat harvest in America and the number of deaths by drowning in Britain. There *might* be a high apparent correlation between these two variables but there clearly is no causal relationship.

A low correlation coefficient, somewhere near zero, does not always mean that there is no relationship between the variables. All it says is that there is no *linear* relationship between the variables - there may be a strong relationship but of a *non-linear* kind.

A further problem in interpretation arises from the fact that the Product Moment Coefficient of Correlation measures the relationship between a *single* independent variable and dependent variable, whereas a particular variable may be dependent on *several* independent variables in which case *multiple correlation* should have been calculated rather than the simple two-variable coefficient.

Note that in Figure 2

Diagram 2.1 $r = +1$
Diagram 2.2 $r = -1$
Diagram 2.3 r is close to +1
Diagram 2.4 r is close to −1
Diagram 2.5 r is close to ZERO

THE SIGNIFICANCE OF r

9. Frequently the set of X and Y observations is based upon a sample. Had a different sample been drawn then the value of r would be different, although the degree of correlation in the parent population would remain the same. In the same way that a knowledge of $\overline{x}$ enables an estimate to be made of μ, then the knowledge of r enables the analyst to make an estimate of ρ, the population co-efficient of correlation.

Generally in examination questions the sample size is limited to some figure that can be dealt with in the time allowed. It is questionable whether the sample size given in examinations gives enough data for a credible judgement to be formed about a possible relationship between the X and Y values. If r is high, does this mean that there **IS** really a close relationship between the X and Y values or is it just that the particular samples gives this impression?

Conversely, if r is low does it really imply a lack of a relationship? There may indeed be a close relationship but the data has not revealed it. Further, the relationship may exist, but it may not be linear or it may not be direct.

It is possible to test whether the value of ρ is sufficiently different from zero for the analyst to decide whether the X and Y values are correlated. The test may be stated in summary

$$H_0 : \rho = O$$
$$H_1 : \rho \neq O$$

It is a t test for which the test statistic is given by

$$|t| = \left| \frac{r - \rho}{1 - r^2} \times \sqrt{n-2} \right|$$

$$|t| = \left| \frac{-0.929365247}{\sqrt{1 - 0.8637196}} \times \sqrt{8} \right|$$

$$= 2.517502 \times 2.8284271$$

$$= 7.1205708 = \underline{\underline{7.12}}$$

The tabulated value for $n - 2$ or 8 degrees of freedom using a five percent level of significance is 2.306. Since 7.12 is greater than 2.306 the conclusion is that the numerical evidence is strong enough to reject the null hypothesis and conclude that the value of p is not zero. The trouble is that despite the test, a small sample can be associated with the rejection of Ho, when there has been seen to be no correlation in the parent population. Further, cases have occurred where low values of r have been observed and the evidence has not been strong enough to reject Ho. but where, in the parent population, there has been a high level of correlation.

USING THE RESULTS FOR PREDICTION

10. Given that the manager is satisfied with the value of r (-0.93 based on Example 1 data), it is possible that he would want to predict likely levels of faulty parts delivered for levels of inspection expenditure not yet recorded. For example, how many defective parts might be expected if 50p per 1000 units was spent on inspection?

Inspection of Figure 1 and the sample data shows that the is a general downwards drift of the scatter points. It will be seen that making predictions from say, two values of x would be inaccurate because they may not be representative of the general relationship betwen x and y. What is required is to be able to predict an expected or mean value of y (i.e. defective parts) for a given value of x (i.e. expenditure) using the whole, known relationship between x and y. The process by which this is calculated is known as REGRESSION ANALYSIS and is developed below using the properties of a straight line graph.

A STRAIGHT LINE GRAPH.

11. Straight line, or linear, relationships are commonly encountered in business and personal life. For example, many public utilities charge their customers on the basis of a fixed charge plus a charge per unit for gas, electricity, or telephone time units consumed. Suppose the charge for using the telephone is £15 per quarter plus 5p for each unit of time that the user is connected on a call. If the subscriber uses 50 units then the telephone bill for the quarter may be predicted thus:

TELEPHONE BILL $= £15.00 + 50 \times 0.05$

$= £15.00 + 2.50$

$= \underline{£17.50}$

Indeed a table of charges may be built up as follows

UNITS	RENTAL	CALL CHARGE	TOTAL
50	15.00	2.50	17.50
100	15.00	5.00	20.00
150	15.00	7.50	22.50
200	15.00	10.00	25.00

This table may be drawn as a graph, and the similarity to a scatter diagram cannot be ignored.

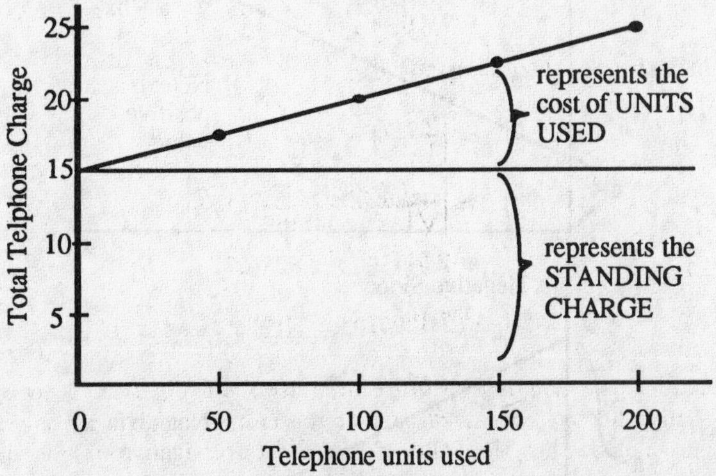

Figure 3

It is possible for a subscriber to read off from Figure 3 the total telephone charge. If say 130 units of telephone time were used the charge would be £21.50. The important point to note here is that it is possible to make a unique prediction of Y from a value of X.

THE EQUATION OF A STRAIGHT LINE

12. The total telephone charge graph may be made more general. Let the following symbols be used for actual values as follows:

£15 : a

£0.05 : b

The total charge may now be expressed as:

$$y = a + bx$$

Where x is the number of units of telephone time used 'a' is the constant factor and 'b' is the rate at which the charge rises per unit. This is the general form of the equation for ANY straight line.

'a' represents the fixed element

'b' represents the slope of the line equivalent to the variable element.

Figure 4 shows the graph of the two commonly encountered straight lines. One has a positive value of b and hence a positive slope (like the telephone charge example) and one has a negative value of b and hence a negative slope (like Example 1).

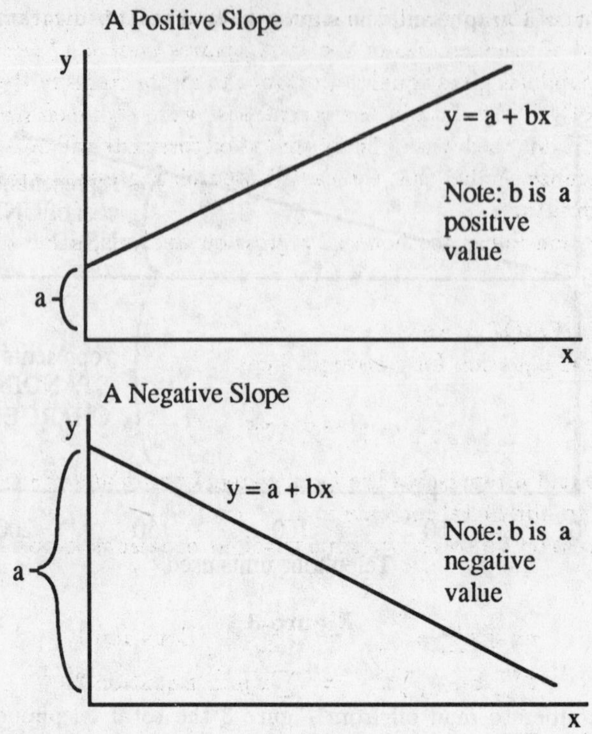

GRAPHS OF STRAIGHT LINES Figure 4

REGRESSION ANALYSIS OR CURVE FITTING

13. This is a statistical technique which can be used for medium term forecasting which seeks to establish the line of 'best fit' to the observed data. The data can be shown as a scatter diagram with lines of best fit drawn freehand, but naturally the lines drawn in this way would vary according to the judgement of individuals, for example: Figure 5 is a reproduction of Figure 1 with two of the many possible lines of best fit drawn. Although the freehand method is quick, no claims can be made for its accuracy and it is more normal to calculate the line of best fit mathematically using the method of least squares.

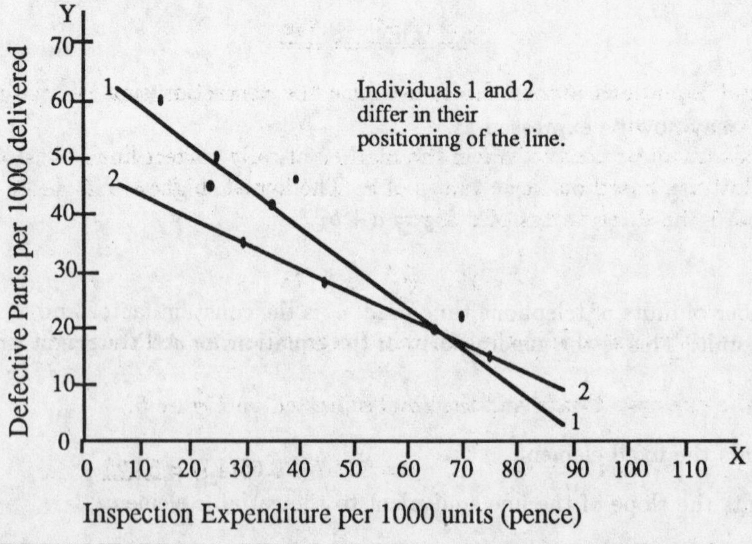

FREEHAND LINES OF BEST FIT FOR EXAMPLE 1 Figure 5

LEAST SQUARES

14. It has been found that to calculate the line of best fit mathematically it is necessary to calculate a

line which minimises the total of the squared deviations of the actual observations from the calculated line. This is known as the method of *least squares* or the *least squares method of linear regression.*

Least squares regression analysis gives equal importance to all the items in the time series, the older and the more recent. Consequently if the data in the recent past were obtained from conditions significantly different from long past conditions then it is unlikely that good forecasts will be achieved using least squares regression analysis. It is because of this that forecasts based on regression analysis should only be made for the near to medium term future.

Note: There are many non-linear methods of regression analysis, some of which are dealt with in Chapter 8.

CALCULATING THE VALUES OF a AND b

15. In the general form of the equation for a straight line

$$y = a + bx$$

where a and b are constants and a represents the fixed element and b and the slope of the line ie the ratio of the vertical increase in y to horizontal increase in x.

To find a and b it is necessary to solve two simultaneious equations known as the 'Normal Equations which are

$$an + b\sum x = \sum y \text{.... Equation 1}$$
$$a\sum x + b\sum x^2 = \sum xy \text{.... Equation 2}$$

where n = number of pairs of figures

Note. The slope of the line, b, is sometimes called the regression coefficient.

The use of these equations will be demonstrated using the Example 1 data contained in Table 1, para 7.

The equations became

$$10a + 424b = 363$$

$$424a + 21926b = 12815$$

Solving gives $a = 63.97$ and $b = -0.65$ to 2 decimal places

∴ The regression line for Example 1 is

$$\underline{\underline{y = 63.97 - 0.65x}}$$

Note that the Normal Equations automatically produce the correction sign (+ or -) for the regression coefficient b; in this case, minus.

The calculated values can be used to drawn the mathematically correct line of best fit on a graph. This is usually done by plottings based on three values of x. The lowest, highest and mean.

Based on Example 1 the three values of x are

$$15, \ \frac{424}{10} \text{ and } 75$$

Each of these values are substituted into the calculated regression line and the result values plotted on the graph.

This is done for the example 1 data and the results plotted on Figure 6.

When $x = 15$ $\quad y = 63.97 - 0.65(15) = \underline{54.22}$

When $x = 42.4$ $\quad y = 63.97 - 0.65(42.4) = \underline{36.41}$

When $x = 75$ $\quad y = 63.97 - 0.65(75) = \underline{15.22}$

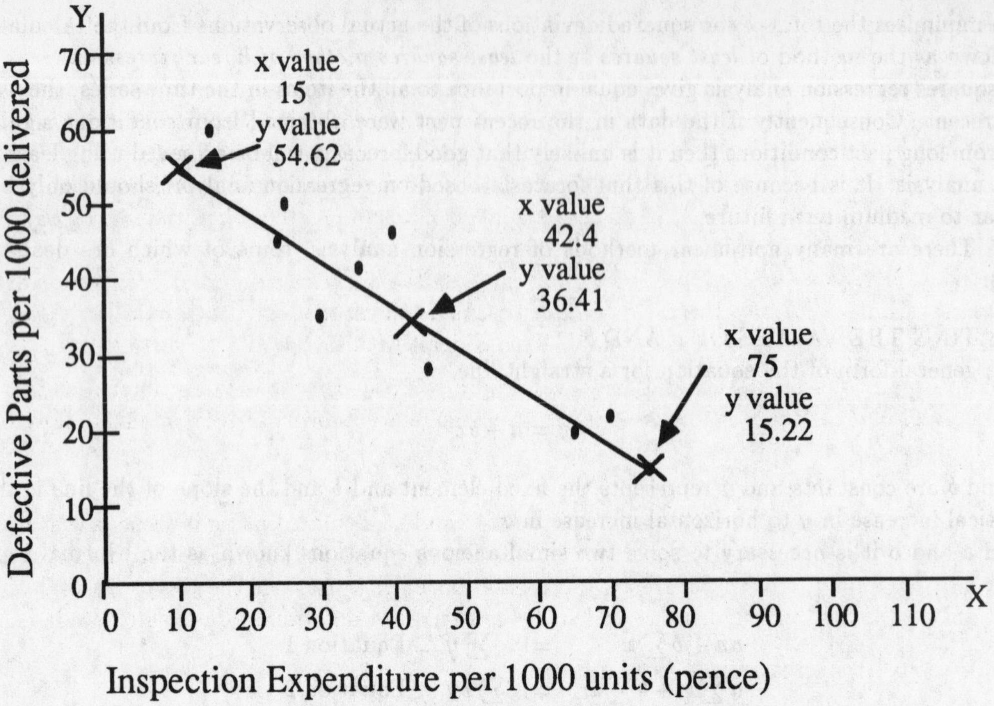

CALCULATED LINES OF BEST FIT Figure 6

Notes:

1. The values of a and b have been calculated in the example above by substituting in the Normal Equations. An alternative is to transpose the Normal Equations so as to be able to find a and b directively. The formulae are as follows:

$$a = \frac{\sum y}{n} - \frac{b\sum x}{n}$$

$$b = \frac{n\sum xy - \sum x \sum y}{n\sum x^2 - (\sum x)^2}$$

It is often more convenient to use this alternative form especially when using a calculator. Values for a and b are re-calculated using the transposed formulae and the Table 1 data.

$$b = \frac{10 \times 12815 - 424 \times 363}{10 \times 21916 - (424)^2}$$

$$= -0.652467 = \underline{-0.65} \text{ (2d)}$$

$$a = \frac{363}{10} - 0.652467 \times \frac{424}{10}$$

$$= \underline{63.97} \text{ (2d)}$$

USING THE RESULTS OF THE REGRESSION ANALYSIS

16. When the values have been calculated for a and b, predictions or forecasts can be made for values of x which have not yet occurred. The predictions can be read from the graph on which the line of best fit has been plotted, Figure 6, or the values inserted into the straight line formula.

Reverting to Example 1 it will be recalled that the manager wished to know the likely number of defects if 50p per 1000 was spent on inspection.

From Figure 6 it will be seen that the number of defects would be 31 per 1000. The formula can also be used, thus:

$$y = 63.97 - 0.65x$$

so when x is 50

$$y = 63.97 - 0.65(50) = \underline{31.47}$$

Thus the manager would conclude that, on average, 31.47 defects per 1000 would be found if 50p per 1000 was spent on inspection.

Great care must be taken with any form of prediction otherwise absurd results may be obtained. Whilst any value of x can be used mechanically to make a prediction this does not necessarily make a practical forecast. Based on Example 1 data, a forecast based on values of x outside the range 15 to 75 (the highest and lowest recorded values) implicitly assumes that the calculated relationships will continue to apply, which may or may not be true. Taking this to the extreme if $x = 98$p per 1000 then the formula and graph would 'predict' zero defects which is extremely unlikely.

It is important to realise that any prediction, for example the 31.47 calculated above, is no more than a single or point estimate and, like the use of sample means as an estimate of the population mean, needs to be qualified by the use of a confidence interval. This is dealt with in Para 20.

Note: Predictions *outside* the observed values (15 to 75 in Example 1) are known as EXTRAPOLATIONS. Predictions *within* the observed range are known as INTERPOLATIONS.

ACCURACY OF THE REGRESSION LINE.

17. However wide the scatter of the data, a line of best fit can be calculated using least squares. Although such a line can always be calculated, it does not follow that the 'best fit' line is likely to be much use for predictive purposes, unless it is an accurate prepresentation of any trend in the data. To find out how good the line of best fit really is, a measure called the coefficient of determination is calculated.

COEFFICIENT OF DETERMINATION

18. This measure denoted by r^2 (because it is the square of the correlation coefficient, r) calculates what proportion of the variation in the actual values of may be predicted by changes in the values of x

thus r^2

is the ratio $\dfrac{\text{Explained Variation}}{\text{Total variation}} = \dfrac{\sum(YE - \bar{Y})^2}{\sum(y - \bar{Y})^2}$

where YE = estimate of y given by the regression equation for each value of x

$\bar{Y}$ = mean of actual values of y

y = individual actual values of y

r^2 will be calculated for the data in example 1 for which it will be recalled that the regression line was

$$y = 63.97 - 0.65x$$

$$\bar{y} = \frac{363}{10} = 36.3$$

X	Y	YE	$YE - \bar{Y}$	$(YE - \bar{Y})^2$	$Y - \bar{Y}$	$(Y - \bar{Y})^2$
15	60	54.18	17.88	319.61	23.7	561.69
24	45	48.31	12.01	144.13	8.7	75.69
25	50	47.65	11.35	128.89	13.7	187.69
30	35	44.39	8.09	65.46	-1.3	1.69
35	42	41.13	4.83	23.31	5.7	32.49
40	46	37.87	1.57	2.45	9.7	94.09
45	28	34.60	-1.70	2.88	-8.3	68.89
65	20	21.55	-14.75	217.44	-16.3	265.69
70	22	18.29	-18.01	324.29	14.3	204.49
75	15	15.03	-21.27	452.43	21.3	453.69
	363			1680.89		1946.10

$$r^2 = \frac{1680.89}{1946.10}$$
$$= 0.8637223$$
$$= 0.86 \text{ to 2 dp}$$

$$\therefore 100r^2 = \underline{\underline{86.37\%}}$$

This result may be interpreted that in the problem 86.37% of the variation in actual faulty parts delivered may be predicted by change in the actual value of x amount spent on inspection. Factors other than changes in the value of x account for 13.63% of the variation in y.

The above can also be calculated using

$$r^2 = \frac{(n\sum xy - \sum X \sum Y)^2}{(n\sum X^2 - (\sum X)^2(n\sum Y^2 - (\sum Y)^2)}$$

Notes:

a. If the values obtained for a and b are based on a sample, then they are only estimates of the true values of the population regression coefficients usually denoted by α (alpha) and β(beta). This is only an extension of the principle covered in the previous chapters on statistics whereby the sample mean (or standard deviation or proportion) is used as an estimate of the true population value.

b. To keep the example small only 10 pairs of values were used. In practice many more are likely to be involved.

c. The regression analysis above is the regression line of y on x. The vertical axis represents y, the dependent variable and the horizontal axis represents x, the independent variable.

d. The 'y on x' regression analysis given is the most commonly used, but students should be aware that there exists the regression line of x on y, ie where x is the dependent variable.

e. If r^2 is low then the analyst should look for a non-linear relationship between x and y, or another or other causal factors.

STANDARD ERROR OF REGRESSION

19. As with means and proportions, dealt with in earlier chapters, we have to consider the sampling errors associated with the estimates a and b. The inferences about these estimates can be made, as previously, either as significance tests or more usefully in the case of regression analysis as confidence limits. In either case the standard error of regression must be calculated. There are several possible formulae but the one given below is a useful, practical example.

Standard error of regression $= S_e = \sqrt{\dfrac{\sum y^2 - a\sum y - b\sum xy}{n-2}}$

This formula does not provide an exact standard error because it involves the values of a and b which are themselves estimates.

This standard error, is also known as the 'residual standard deviation'.

The use of the formula is shown below again based on the Example data.

$$= \sqrt{\frac{15123 - 63.97 \times 363 - (-0.65) \times 12815}{10-2}}$$

$$= 5.76 \text{ defective parts}$$

This value is used below in setting confidence limits for the calculated regression line.

SETTING CONFIDENCE LIMITS

20. The standard error of regression calculated above can be used to establish the confidence limits for an individual prediction or to set confidence limits for the whole of the regression equation. Both are illustrated below. The line of best fit $= a + bx$ is an average line which passes through x and y and any estimate based upon this line must be a mean value or a point estimate. The confidence limits for the whole of the regression line are calculated by using a quantity known as the standard error of the average forecast which is given by

$$S_{ef} = S_e \sqrt{\frac{1}{n} + \frac{(X - \bar{X})^2}{\sum X^2 - \frac{(\sum X)^2}{n}}}$$

Although in a given problem S_e will be a constant amount, the expression

$$\sqrt{\frac{1}{n} + \frac{(X - \bar{X})^2}{\sum X^2 - \frac{(\sum X)^2}{n}}}$$

will vary according to the value of X. The calculation for $X = 15$ to $X = 75$ are given below. When the lines which represent the upper and lower confidence limits plotted they will be seen to be curved and the confidence interval is at a minimum value when $X = \bar{X}$. The expressions

$$\frac{1}{n} \text{ and } \sum X^2 - \frac{(\sum X)^2}{n}$$

are both constant for a given problem. It is

$$(X - \bar{X})^2$$

which will vary and must be calculated for each value of X.

For the present problem based on Example 1 data.

$$\frac{1}{n} = \frac{1}{10} = 0.1$$

$$\begin{aligned}\sum X^2 - \frac{(\sum X)^2}{n} &= 21926 - \frac{424^2}{10} \\ &= 21926 - 17977.6 \\ &= 3948.4 \\ \bar{X} &= \frac{424}{10} \\ &= 42.4\end{aligned}$$

The expression $(X - \bar{X})^2$ will vary as follows

$$\begin{array}{llcr} X = 15 & (15 - 42.4)^2 & = & 750.76 \\ X = 24 & (24 - 42.4)^2 & = & 338.56 \\ X = 25 & (25 - 42.4)^2 & = & 302.76 \\ X = 30 & (30 - 42.4)^2 & = & 153.76 \\ X = 35 & (35 - 42.4)^2 & = & 54.76 \\ X = 40 & (40 - 42.4)^2 & = & 5.76 \\ X = 45 & (45 - 42.4)^2 & = & 6.76 \\ X = 65 & (65 - 42.4)^2 & = & 510.76 \\ X = 70 & (70 - 42.4)^2 & = & 761.76 \\ X = 75 & (75 - 42.4)^2 & = & 1062.76 \end{array}$$

The expression $\sqrt{\frac{1}{n}+\frac{(X-\bar{X})^2}{\sum X^2-\frac{(\sum X)^2}{n}}}$

may now be evaluated:

when

$$x = 15: \quad \sqrt{\frac{1}{10}+\frac{750.76}{3948.4}}$$

$$= \sqrt{0.1+0.1901428}$$

$$= \sqrt{0.2901428}$$

$$= 0.538649$$

when

$$x = 24: \quad \sqrt{\frac{1}{10}+\frac{338.56}{3948.4}}$$

$$= \sqrt{0.1+0.0857461}$$

$$= 0.4309827$$

In a similar fashion the other values are calculated and the results tabulated:

when x is:	value of $\sqrt{\frac{1}{n}+\frac{(X-\bar{X})^2}{\sum X^2-\frac{(\sum X)^2}{n}}}$ is
15	0.538649
24	0.4309827
25	0.420332
30	0.3722774
35	0.3374446
40	0.318526
45	0.3189233
65	0.4789144
70	0.5412289
75	0.607581

*Table*2

These values are used in the calculation of the confidence intervals.

CONSTRUCTING THE CONFIDENCE INTERVAL

21. The actual confidence interval is constructed in exactly the same way as that for a mean or for a proportion. In this case since the number of observations is 10, then the t distribution is used with 10 - 2 = 8 degrees of freedom.

The interval is calculated by estimating the fitted value of y for each value of x in the original data using the equation $y = a + bx$. The interval then takes the form.

$$y \pm S_{ef} \times t$$

Given that (based on Example 1)

$$a = 63.97$$
$$b = -0.65$$
$$S_e = 5.76$$

$$S_{ef} = S_e\sqrt{\frac{1}{n} + \frac{(X - \bar{X})^2}{\sum X^2 - \frac{(\sum X)^2}{n}}}$$

$= 5.76 \times$ Value from Table 2 above

and t = 2.306 for 8 degrees of freedom and a 95% confidence interval.

The confidence intervals can be now calculated as follows:

When $x = 15$ $y = 63.97 - 0.65(15) = \underline{54.2}$

The limits round this estimate are

$$54.2 \pm 2.306 \times 5.76 \times 0.538649$$

$$= 54.2 \pm 7.15$$

This gives an upper limit of 61.35 and a lower limit of 47.05

When $x = 24$ $y = 63.97 - 0.65(24) = 48.37$

The limits round this estimate are

$$48.37 \pm 2.306 \times 5.76 \times 0.4309827$$

$= 48.37 \pm 5.72$ giving a 54.09 upper limit and a 42.65 lower limit.

This process is repeated for the other values of x resulting in the following summary table, Table 3. suitably rounded.

x	y	CONFIDENCE INTERVAL	
		LOWER LIMIT	UPPER LIMIT
15	54.2	47.05	61.35
24	48.37	42.65	54.09
25	47.72	42.14	53.57
30	44.47	39.53	49.41
35	41.22	36.74	45.7
40	37.97	33.74	42.2
45	34.72	30.48	38.96
65	21.72	15.36	28.08
70	18.47	11.28	25.66
75	15.22	7.15	23.29

TABLE 3

Together with the line of best fit these values are plotted on Figure 7 from which will be noted the curved shape of the confidence limits. The narrowest confidence interval corresponds to the mean of x ie 42.4 and it will be seen that three of the original observed values lie outside the confidence bands.

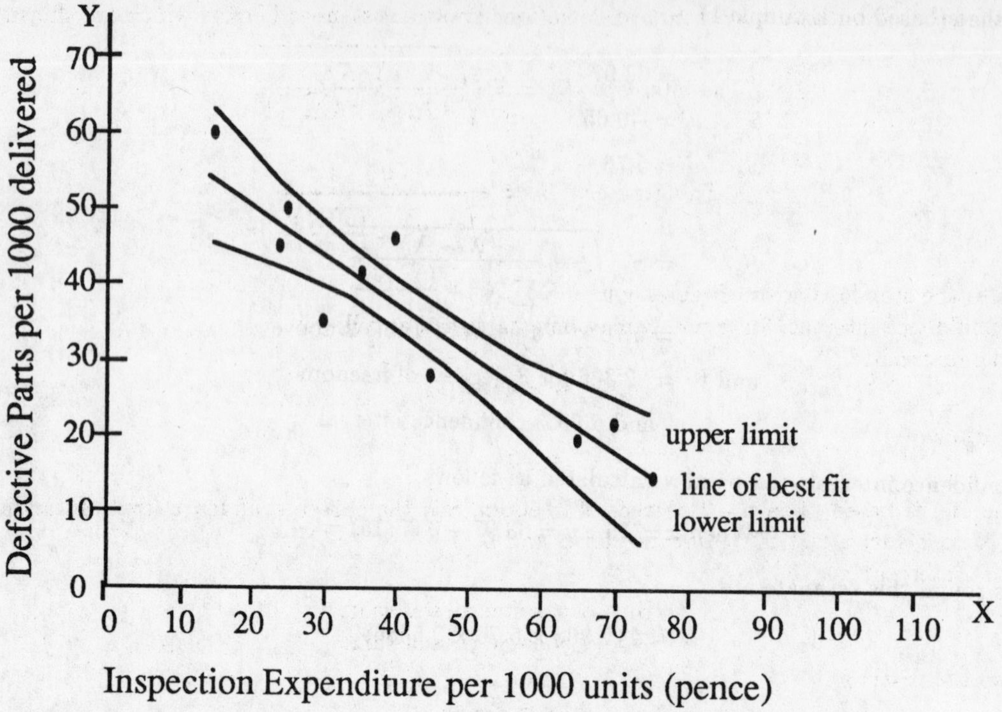

GRAPH SHOWING 95% CONFIDENCE LIMITS Figure 7

CONFIDENCE INTERVALS FOR INDIVIDUAL PREDICTIONS

22. When making an individual prediction for y for technical reasons it is necessary to amend the formula previously used to calculate the confidence interval. The amended formula calculates what is known as the *standard error of the individual forecast* and is shown below.

$$S_{ef_{(\text{individual})}} = S_e\sqrt{1+\frac{1}{n}+\frac{(x-\overline{x})^2}{\sum X^2 - \frac{(\sum X)^2}{n}}}$$

Once again using Example 1 data and a value of X of say 45 the use of the above formula can be demonstrated.

$$S_{ef_{(\text{individual})}} = 5.76\sqrt{1+\frac{1}{10}+\frac{(45-42.4)^2}{(21926-\frac{424^2}{10}}} = 6.04$$

When $x = 45$ $y = 34.72$ which has individual confidence intervals of

$$34.72 \pm 2.306 \times 6.04 \text{ giving}$$

a lower limit of 20.79 and an upper limit of 48.65.

These values should be contrasted with the values obtained for the general confidence intervals in Table 3 which, when $x = 45$ range from 30.48 to 38.96. Thus it will be seen that when an individual prediction of y is made the confidence intervals are much wider.

STANDARD ERRORS OF THE INTERCEPT (a) AND THE GRADIENT (b)

23. If a and b are calculated from a sample, then they may be looked upon as estimates of the population intercept and gradient, α and β. In a manner similar to the distribution of sample means a distribution of values of a and a distribution for values of b emerge from repeated sampling.

The mean value for a is expressed as α and is the population value for the intercept.

The mean value for b is expressed as β and is the population value for the gradient.

Both these distributions have standard deviations known as standard errors which are shown below:

$$\text{The intercept } S_a = S_e\sqrt{\frac{\sum X^2}{n\sum X^2 - (\sum X)^2}}$$

$$\text{The gradient } S_b = \frac{S_e}{\sqrt{\sum X^2 - \frac{(\sum X)^2}{n}}}$$

where S_e is the standard error of regression.

The confidence intervals for α and β may be established as follows:

For the intercept

$$\alpha = a \pm t \times s_a$$

For the Gradient

$$\beta = b \pm t \times s_b$$

The value of t is based upon n - 2 degrees of freedom, and the chosen confidence level. In addition, it is possible to construct a test of significance for α and β.

For the Intercept

$$H_0 : \alpha = \text{some chosen value}$$
$$H_1 : \alpha \neq \text{some chosen value}$$

The test statistic is

$$t = \frac{a - \alpha}{S_a}$$

For the Gradient

$$H_0 : \beta = 0$$
$$H_1 : \beta \neq 0$$

The test statistic is

$$t = \frac{b - \beta}{S_b}$$

in both cases, the calculated value of t is compared with the tabulated value for n-2 degrees of freedom at the chosen level of significance.

In the case of the gradient, $\beta = 0$ is generally used because if β is found not to be significantly different from 0 then $Y = a + bx$ collapses into $Y = a$ and since the line of best fit passes through X and Y it will be horizontal at the value of Y. Thus for all values of X the forecast of Y will be $\bar{Y}$. The significance test for β is probably the more important of the two for practical purposes.

USING THE FORMULAE

24. The above formulae may be illustrated using Example 1 data.

$$n = 10 \qquad a = 63.97$$
$$\sum X^2 = 21926 \qquad b = -0.65$$
$$\sum X = 424 \qquad t = 2.306$$
$$S_e = 5.76$$

The standard error of the intercept

$$S_a = 5.76\sqrt{\frac{21926}{39484}}$$
$$= \underline{4.29}$$

The 95% confidence interval of the intercept is,

$$\alpha = 63.97 \pm 2.306 \times 4.29$$
$$= 63.97 \pm 9.89$$

which gives an upper limit of 73.86 and a lower limit of 54.08.

Significance test for the intercept

$$H_0 \ \alpha = 0$$
$$H_1 \ \alpha \neq 0$$

$$t = \frac{a - \alpha}{S_a}$$
$$= \frac{63.97 - 0}{4.29} = \underline{14.91}$$

Since 14.91 is much greater than 2.306 (the value from t tables) H_0 can be rejected.

Standard error of the slope

$$S_b = \frac{5.76}{\sqrt{21926 - \frac{424^2}{10}}}$$
$$= \underline{0.092}$$

The 95% confidence interval for the slope is

$$\beta = -0.65 \pm 2.306 \times 0.092$$
$$= -0.65 \pm 0.212$$

giving an upper limit of -0.438 and a lower limit of -0.862.

Significance test for slope

$$H_0 \ \beta = 0$$
$$H_1 \ \beta \neq 0$$

$$t = \frac{b - \beta}{S_b} = \frac{-0.65 - 0}{0.092} = \underline{\underline{7.07}}$$

Since 7.07 > 2.306 H_0 can be rejected.

On the basis of this evidence the regression equation

$y = 63.97 - 0.65x$ could be used as a basis of prediction for Example 1.

CHARACTERISTICS OF LINEAR REGRESSION

25.

a. Useful means of forecasting when the data has a generally linear relationship. Over operational ranges linearity (or near linearity) is often assumed for such items as costs, contributions and sales.

b. A measure of the accuracy of fit (r^2) can be easily calculated for any linear regression line.

c. To have confidence in the regression relationship calculated it is preferable to have a large number of observations.

d. With further analysis confidence limits can be calculated for forecasts produced by the regression formula.

e. Any form of extrapolation, including that based on regression analysis, must be done with great care. Once outside the observed values relationships and conditions may change drastically.

f. Regression is not an adaptive forecasting system, ie it is not suitable for incorporation in, say a stock control system where the requirements would be for a forecasting system automatically producing forecasts which adapt to current conditions. These types of systems are covered in Chapter 9.

g. In many circumstances it is not sufficiently accurate to assume that y depends only on one independent variable as discussed above in simple linear regression. Frequently, a particular value depends on two or more factors in which case multiple regression analysis is employed. For example, analysis of a firm might produce the following multiple regression equation:

$$\begin{aligned} \text{Overheads} &= \pounds 10,500 + 6.8x + 9.2y + 2.7z \\ \text{where } x &= \text{labour hours worked} \\ y &= \text{machine hours} \\ z &= \text{tonnage produced} \end{aligned}$$

This concept is dealt with in Chapter 8.

THE RANK CORRELATION COEFFICIENT (R)

26. This coefficient is also known as the Spearman Rank Correlation Coefficient. Its purpose is to establish whether there is any form of association between two variables when the variables are arranged in a *ranked* form.

The formula is as follows:

$$R = 1 - \frac{6\sum d^2}{n(n^2-1)}$$

where d = difference between the pairs of ranked values
n = number of pairs of rankings.
This will be illustrated by the following example.

Example 2

A group of 8 accountancy students are tested in Quantiative Techniques and Management Accountancy. Their rankings in the two tests were:

STUDENT	Q.T. Ranking	M.A. Ranking	d	d^2
A	2	3	-1	1
B	7	6	+1	1
C	6	4	+2	4
D	1	2	-1	1
E	4	5	-1	1
F	3	1	+2	4
G	5	8	-3	9
H	8	7	+1	1
				$\sum d^2 = \underline{\underline{22}}$

Table 4

The 'd column' is obtained by QT ranking - MA ranking

$$\therefore R = 1 - \frac{6\sum d^2}{n(n^2-1)} = 1 - \frac{6 \times 22}{8(8^2-1)} = \underline{\underline{+0.74}}$$

As the Rank Correlation coefficient is +0.74 we are able to say that there is a reasonable agreement between the student's performances in the two types of tests.

Notes:

a. R can vary, like r, between +1 and -1 with similar meanings.
b. As with r, care should be taken in any interpretation of the value of R whether it is a particularly high or low value.
c. The values in Table 4 are the rankings of the students not the actual marks obtained in the tests.

TIED RANKINGS

27. A slight adjustment to the formula is necessary if some students obtain the same marks in a test and thus are given the same ranking.

The adjustment is

$$\frac{t^3 - t}{12}$$

where t is the number of tied rankings and the adjusted formula is

$$R = 1 - \frac{6\left(\sum d^2 + \frac{t^3 - t}{12}\right)}{n(n^2 - 1)}$$

For example assume that students E and F achieved equal marks in QT and were given joint third place. The revised data are

STUDENT	Q.T. Ranking	M.A. Ranking	d	d^2
A	2	3	-1	1
B	7	6	+1	1
C	6	4	+2	4
D	1	2	-1	2
E	$3\frac{1}{2}$	5	$-1\frac{1}{2}$	$2\frac{1}{4}$
F	$3\frac{1}{2}$	1	$+2\frac{1}{2}$	$6\frac{1}{4}$
G	5	8	-3	9
H	8	7	+1	1
			$\sum d^2 =$	$25\frac{1}{2}$

$$\therefore R = 1 - \frac{6\left(\sum d^2 + \frac{t^3 - t}{12}\right)}{n(n^2 - 1)} = 1 - \frac{6\left(25\frac{1}{2} + \frac{2^3 - 2}{12}\right)}{8(8^2 - 1)} = \underline{\underline{+0.69}}$$

As will be seen, the R value has moved also from +0.74 to 0.69

Note:

It is conventional to show the shared rankings as above i.e. the shared 3rd place takes up the 3rd and 4th rankings thus it is divided between the two as $3\frac{1}{2}$ each.

SUMMARY

a. Correlation measures the interdependence between two sets of numbers.

b. The two main measures of correlation are the Product moment coefficient of correlation (r) and the Spearman Rank Coefficient of Correlation (R).

c. The formula for r is

$$r = \frac{n\sum xy - \sum x \sum y}{\sqrt{n\sum x^2 - (\sum x)^2} \times \sqrt{n\sum y^2 - (\sum y)^2}}$$

d. There must be a causal connection between the variables otherwise spurious or nonsense correlation exists.

e. Care should be taken in interpreting both high and low values of the correlation coefficient. A low value indicates little linear relationship but a curvi-linear relationship may exist.

f. The Rank Coefficient of Correlation formula is:

$$R = 1 - \frac{6\sum d^2}{n(n^2 - 1)}$$

g. A common form of prediction is to calculate a linear regression line using the method of least squares and to use this line for extrapolation and interpolation.

h. The least squares method finds values for the coefficients a and b, in the equation for a straight line, ie $y = a + bx$

i. To assess the accuracy of the regression line the coefficient of determination is calculated.

j. Confidence limits based on the standard errors of the estimates and forecasts can be prepared for individual predictions or for the regression line as a whole.

POINTS TO NOTE

28.

a. The coefficient, r, measures only the strength of a linear relationship in two sets of data. It does not mean that, there is a cause-effect relationship.

b. The coefficient of determination,r^2, measures the extent to which movements in y are associated with movements in x. There is an implied causality from x to y.

c. r, a and b are sample statistics used to estimate ρ, α and β the population parameters.

SELF REVIEW QUESTIONS.

1. *What is a scatter diagram? (4)*
2. *What is meant by correlation? (6)*
3. *What is the Product Moment Coefficient of Correlation? (7)*
4. *What is a nonsense correlation? (8)*
5. *What is the general equation for a straight line? (12)*
6. *Distinguish between a positive slope and a negative slope. (12)*
7. *Define the Least Squares Method of Linear regression. (14)*
8. *What are the Normal Equations for calculating the constants a and b in the equation*

$$(y = a + bx \qquad ? \ (15)$$

9. *Why is the co-efficient of determination calculated? (17 & 18)*
10. *Why are confidence intervals calculated for the line of best fit? (20)*
11. *What value of x corresponds to the narrowest part of the confidence interval? (21)*
12. *What is the standard error of the individual forecast? (22)*
13. *What are the standard errors of a and b? (23)*
14. *What are the significance tests for the intercept and slope? (24)*
15. *Define R (26)*

EXERCISES WITH ANSWERS COMMENCING PAGE 488

A1. The following data have been collected regarding sales and advertising expenditure.

Sales	*Advertising Expenditure*
(£ms)	*(£'000s)*
8.5	*210*
9.2	*250*
7.9	*290*
8.6	*330*
9.4	*370*
10.1	*410*

Plot the above data on a scatter diagram and using judgement, decide whether there is a correlation between sales and advertising expenditure.

A2. Calculate r for the data in A1 and interpret.

A3. Calculate r^2 for the data in A1 and interpret.

EXAMINATION QUESTIONS WITH ANSWERS COMMENCING PAGE 488

A4. The Azund Electrical Co. Ltd. specialises in the batch productionof switches used in complex electronic equipment. It has been asked to tender for producing a switch for use in desk-top computers. An examination of its records shows that it has had 10 production runs on similar types of switches over the past two years. Using current cost data, the total cost of those 10 runs, when updated, are:

Switch Code No.	*Production X(100s)*	*Total Costs Y (£10)*
EW11	9	116
EW18	16	211
EW23	14	152
EW47	38	410
EW48	21	256
EW54	25	298
EW70	20	220
EW82	15	180
EW88	15	185
EW96	11	129

$$\Sigma X = 184 \quad \Sigma Y = 2157 \quad \Sigma XY = 47,667 \quad \Sigma X^2 = 4014 \quad \Sigma Y^2 = 535,187$$

Required:

a. Obtain the least squares straight line of best fit ($\hat{Y} = a + bX$) to the data.

b. Interpret your answer in terms of fixed and variable costs of production.

c. Given that $S_b = \sqrt{\frac{\Sigma(Y-\hat{Y})^2}{n-2}} \simeq 220$ (in £10 units)

provide a 95% confidence interval for the mean value of total costs when the batch size is 4000 switches.

(ACCA, Quantitative Analysis)

A5. A manufacturer wishes to establish a procedure to estimate direct labour costs for small batch production orders. He has obtained a random sample of recorded actual direct labour costs for a sample of ten batches as follows:

Batch size in units	Direct labour costs £
(x)	(y)
15	200
18	240
18	260
21	290
23	300
23	320
26	380
28	370
32	400
37	470
$\Sigma x = 241$	$\Sigma y = 3,230$

$$\Sigma xy = 82,780 \ \Sigma x^2 = 6,225 \ \Sigma y^2 = 1,103,900$$

You are required to:

a. calculate the least squares regression line relating labour costs to batch size;

b. provide the manufacturer with information on the range within which the estimates may be expected to lie by calculating the 95% confidence limits for the regression line and explain the meaning of the term 'confidence limits';

c. calculate a statistic which summarises how well the least squares regression line explains the variability in the original data;

d. provide the manufacturer with an estimate of direct labour cost for an order for a batch of 25 items;

e. plot on a graph the original data and the values given in the answers to sections (a) and (b).

(CIMA Quantitative Techniques)

A6. the London and South Eastern Bank charges its current account customers on a quarterly basis. If the balance of the account does not fall below £50 during the quarter, there are no account charges. If the balance does fall below £50 at any time, however, a fixed charge is incurred for each transaction made during the quarter. This is offset by a nominal interest paid to the customer on the daily balance whilst the account is in credit, otherwise overdraft charges are also incurred. The bank has recently been analysing its charging policy, and the following data have been collected from a random sample of ten current accounts for the previous quarter:

	X	Y
Account Number	*Average Balance (£)*	*Account Charge (£)*
1	83	5.42
2	26	14.27
3	54	7.83
4	104	2.62
5	43	8.64
6	156	0
7	187	0
8	65	4.20
9	38	10.01
10	142	0

Required:

(a) Represent the data graphically, and comment briefly on the form of your graph.

(b) By making appropriate use of the data, determine a least squares linear relationship between the average account balance and the charges paid. What is the minimum average balance which must be maintained if there are to be, on average, no account charges?

(c) Indicate two other factors which you think should be considered in a more comprehensive analysis of account charges. Give reasons for your choice.

(ACCA, Quantitative Analysis)

A7. The chief account of Orthus Limited is currently reviewing his company's vehicle replacement policy. The company's sales representatives are all provided with the same model of car, and their sales territories have been planned so that the distances travelled by each of them in the course of a week are more or less the same. Each car is given a routine maintenance service once every 3 months and, on examining the most recent service records, the following data are assembled for a random sample of 10 cars.

Car	Age of Car (months)	Service Cost (£)
1	3	51
2	12	69
3	18	81
4	30	112
5	15	70
6	18	89
7	24	104
8	12	82
9	9	55
10	21	102

The model of car currently being used by the representatives costs £4,200 and Orthus have negotiated an arrangement with the garage which supplied their vehicles whereby the "trade-in" value decreases by £225 per quarter (starting from a figure of £4,000) for cars up to three years old. This means that, for example, the trade in value of a one year old car would be £3,100.

Required:

(a) Using the method of least squares, estimate a relationship of the form

$$S = a + bx$$

between the quarterly service cost (S) and the age of the car (x)

(b) It is company policy to replace all company cars after either 1, 2 or 3 years. Show that, for this model of car, the policy which minimises the average quarterly capital and servicing costs is to replace every 2 years. (You may assume that all cars are serviced every quarter, including the one immediately before trade-in).

†Note for overseas candidates:

"Trade-in" is a system of purchasing a new car in which the seller of the new car agrees to buy back a used car from the purchaser; the price of the used car being offset against the price of the new car.

'Quarter' means three months, (quarter of a year).

(ACCA Quantitative Analysis)

A8. Seat bookings on First National's holiday package flight programme are thought to be related to the level of gross national product (GNP) in real terms. Data for seat bookings and GNP are given below:

Year	Seat bookings(000s) (Y)	GNP (£billion, real terms) (X)
1	100	250
2	115	255
3	120	258
4	130	267
5	145	270
6	152	272
7	155	273

$$(\Sigma X = 1,845;\ \Sigma Y = 917\ \Sigma XY = 242,804;\ \Sigma X^2 = 486,791;\ \Sigma Y^2 = 122,679)$$

Forecast GNPs for years 8 and 9 are given as £276 billion and £280 billion respectively.

You are required to;

(a) obtain the simple linear regression of Y on X using the least squares method;

(b) estimate the level of seat bookings for years 8 and 9 using the regression equation obtained from (a);

(c) test the significance of the slope coefficient at the 5% level;

(d) derive the 95% confidence interval for the regression line;

(e) discuss whether the relationship between seat bookings and GNP appears to be a sound one for purposes of prediction. Give reasons for your assessment and state two additional statistics which could be used to analyse further the relationship between the two sets of data.

Calculate to two decimal places.

(CIMA Quantitative Techniques)

EXERCISES WITHOUT ANSWERS

B1. Using the data in A1 calculate the regression line $y = a + bx$

B2. Use the values obtained in B1 to estimate the sales if advertising expenditure was:

(a) £450,000
(b) £310,000

and comment on the results

B3. Calculate the standard error of regression for the data in A1.

EXAMINATION QUESTIONS WITHOUT ANSWERS

B4. Unlisted p.l.c. hopes to achieve a Stock Market quotation for its shares. A profit forecast is necesary and, in order to obtain such a forecast, the company has experimented with a number of approaches.

The following are details from a linear regression on the last 11 years' profit figures:

$$X = \text{years (expressed 1 to 11)}$$
$$Y = \text{annual profit figures}$$
$$\Sigma X = 66$$
$$\Sigma Y = 212.10$$
$$\Sigma X^2 = 506$$
$$\Sigma XY = 1,406.70$$
$$\Sigma Y^2 = 4,254.08$$

$\Sigma(Y - \hat{Y})^2 = 0.916$ *where* $\hat{Y}$ *represents profit values estimated by the regression line.*
The following formulae are given:

Standard error of the regression line $\sigma_R = \sqrt{\frac{\Sigma(Y-\hat{Y})^2}{d.f.}}$

Coefficient of correlation $(r) = \sqrt{\frac{\text{Explained variation}}{\text{Total variation}}}$

You are required:

(a) to obtain the simple least squares regression line of Y on X;

(b) to use the line to estimate profit in each of the next two years;

(c) to calculate the coefficient of determination for the line and to explain its meaning.

(d) to calculate the standard error of the regression line and to use this to obtain the 95% confidence interval for the line;

(e) on the basis of the information given on your answer (a) to (d) to determine whether it is likely that the regression line will be a good estimator of profit.

(CIMA QUANTITATIVE TECHNIQUES)

B5. The following data have been collected relating to the returns which would have been earned from an investment of an equal sum of money in the shares of E.T. p.l.c. and a group of market shares:

Year	*Returns on E.T. p.l.c shares (y) (£)*	*Returns on group of market shares (x) (£)*
1	7.8	11.1
2	11.0	12.3
3	15.2	18.5
4	23.1	25.4
5	29.7	28.7
6	37.4	33.8
7	44.6	37.7
8	52.8	39.6
9	60.2	44.7
10	63.9	45.5

$$\Sigma y = 345.7;\ \Sigma X = 297.3;\ \Sigma y^2 = 15,711.59;\ \Sigma x^2 = 10,285.83;\ \Sigma xy = 12,577.02$$

The standard error of the regression coefficient is:

$$\frac{\text{Standard error of the regression line}}{\sqrt{\Sigma X_i^2 - n\overline{x}^2)}}$$

and where the standard error iof the regression line is:

$$\sqrt{[\frac{\Sigma(y_i - \hat{y})^2}{n-2}]}$$

You are required to:

(a) plot the original data on a graph, calculate the least squares regression of y on x and draw the regression line on the graph;

(b) test the significance of the slope of the line at the 5% level;

(c) discuss the outcomes of (a) and (b) in the context of a comparison of the two investments as alternatives.

(CIMA QUANTITATIVE TECHNIQUES)

B6. An accountant has derived the following data on production costs (£Y) and units of output for the last twelve months:

Y:	*150*	*63*	*65*	*165*	*126*	*120*	*91*	*60*	*100*	*90*	*90*	*120*
X:	*30*	*3*	*6*	*34*	*27*	*21*	*15*	*12*	*20*	*13*	*10*	*16*

$$\Sigma X = 207,\ \Sigma Y = 1,240,\ \Sigma X^2 = 4,565,\ \Sigma Y^2 = 140,676,\ \Sigma XY = 24,686$$

You are required:

(a) to plot a scatter diagram of Y against X;

(b) to find the least squares regression of production costs on output, and plot the line on the diagram.

(c) without performing any further calculations, to estimate the approximate value of the correlation coefficient between X and Y.

(d) to predict production costs for next month if it is planned to produce 20 units of output, and discuss the likely reliability of this prediction.

(CIMA Quantitative Methods)

8 Multiple and Non-linear Regression

INTRODUCTION

1. The chapter shows the development of a multiple regression model and how the closeness of fit is measured by the coefficient of multiple determination. Various non-linear models such as the exponential, logarithmic and hyperbolic functions are explained and exemplified and the chapter concludes with an analysis of learning curves.

ALTERNATIVES TO A SIMPLE LINEAR FUNCTION

2. There will be occasions when the value of r^2 in the simple linear model, $y = a + bx$, will not be considered satisfactory. This means that the simple linear model will not be a good enough predictor. In such circumstances there are two possible courses of action.

a. To investigate the possibility that movements in y, the dependent variable, are caused by several independent factors and not just one as in the basic model. For example, changes in demand for a product may depend on

— the price of the product

— the price of substitutes

— the level of incomes

— consumer tastes and so on

If linearity can be assumed then a linear multiple regression model can be used. These models are dealt with in the first part of the chapter.

b. Alternatively a non-linear model may be considered more appropriate and several of the more important non-linear functions are dealt with later in the chapter.

MULTIPLE REGRESSION-MODEL DEVELOPMENT

3. A model which incorporates several independent variables is known as a multiple regression model. Because of the lengthy nature of the calculations it would be unlikely that a detailed question on multiple regression would appear in the examinations for which this manual is intended. Familiarity with the processes involved and the structure of the model is, however, necessary. The development of the model is shown below:

The basic two variable model (one dependent and one independent variable) is:

$$y = a + bx$$

which can be solved using the Normal Equations thus:

$$\sum y = an + b\sum x$$

$$\sum xy = a\sum x + b\sum x^2$$

From this can be developed models with more than 2 variables and this is illustrated below using a 3 variable model (one dependent and two independent variables; y, x_1, and x_2)

$$y = a + b_1 x_1 + b_2 x_2$$

which can be solved by the Normal Equations for a three variable model, as follows:

$$\sum y = an + b_1 \sum x_1 + b_2 \sum x_2$$

$$\sum x_1 y = a \sum x_1 + b_1 \sum x_1^2 + b_2 \sum x_1 x_2$$

$$\sum x_2 y = a \sum x_2 + b_1 \sum x_1 x_2 + b_2 \sum x_2^2$$

The *line* of best fit gives way to a *plane* of best fit. b_1 is the slope of the plane along the x_1 axis, b_2 is the slope along the x_2 axis, and the plane cuts the y axis at 'a'

The aim of adding to the simple two variable model is to improve the fit of the data. The closeness of fit is measured by the co-efficient of multiple determination R^2 for which the genral formula and a useful computational formula are given below:

$$R^2 = \frac{\text{Explained Variation}}{\text{Total variation}}$$

$$= \frac{\sum(YE - \overline{Y})^2}{\sum(Y - \overline{Y})^2}$$

where YE now equals the estimate of Y for each value of x_1 and x_2.

$$R^2 = \frac{a\sum y + b_1 \sum x_1 y + b_2 \sum x_2 y - \frac{(\sum y)^2}{n}}{\sum y^2 - \frac{(\sum y)^2}{n}}$$

It is not necessarily the case that the value of the co-efficient of determination will improve with the addition of extra variables.

The above models are illustrated by the following examples.

EXAMPLE OF MULTIPLE REGRESSION

Example 1

4. The Association of Accountants is investigating the relationship between performance in Quantitative Methods and hours studied per week and the general level of intelligence of candidates. The Association has data on ten students which are:

STUDENT	HOURS STUDIED	I.Q.	EXAMINATION GRADE
	x_1	x_2	y
1	9	99	56
2	6	100	45
3	12	119	80
4	14	95	73
5	11	110	71
6	6	117	55
7	19	98	95
8	16	101	86
9	3	100	34
10	9	115	66

It is required to calculate the separate regressions, the multiple regression and the coefficients of determination.

SOLUTION

PART A- CALCULATION OF SEPARATE REGRESSIONS

	y	y^2	x_1	x_1^2	x_2	x_2^2	x_1y	x_2y	x_1x_2
1	56	3136	9	81	99	9801	504	5544	891
2	45	2025	6	36	100	10000	270	4500	600
3	80	6400	12	144	119	14161	960	9520	1428
4	73	5329	14	196	95	9025	1022	6935	1330
5	71	5041	11	121	110	12100	781	7810	1210
6	55	3025	6	36	117	13689	330	6435	702
7	95	9025	19	361	98	9604	1805	9310	1862
8	86	7396	16	256	101	10201	1376	8686	1616
9	34	1156	3	9	100	10000	102	3400	300
10	66	4356	9	81	115	13225	594	7590	1035
	661	46899	105	1321	1054	111806	7744	69730	10974

TABLE 1

For Regression y on x_1 (Exam. Scores: hours studied)

$$b_{x_1} = \frac{n\sum x_1y - \sum x_1 \sum y}{n\sum x_1^2 - (\sum x_1)^2}$$

$$\frac{10 \times\ 7744 - 105 \times\ 661}{10 \times\ 1321 - 105^2}$$

$$b_{x_1} = 3.68$$

$$a_{x_1} = \frac{\sum Y}{n} - \frac{bx_1 \sum x_1}{n}$$

$$= \frac{661}{10} - \frac{3.67734 \times\ 105}{10}$$

$$a_{x_1} = 27.59$$

The regression equation for the relationship of hours studed and examination result is

$$y_{x_1} = a_{x_1} + b_{x_1} x_1$$

$$= 27.59 + 3.68$$

The co-efficient of correlation for this relationship is

$$r_{x_1} = \frac{n\sum x_1y - \sum x_1 \sum y}{\sqrt{n\sum x_1^2 - (\sum x_1)^2} \times \sqrt{n\sum y^2 - (\sum y)^2}}$$

NB This formula is a direct equivalent of that given in CHAPTER 7 but is easier to work with since all except

$n\sum y^2 - (\sum y)^2$ is already known.

$$n\sum y^2 - (\sum y)^2 = 10 \times \ 46889 - 661^2$$

$$= 468890 - 436921 = 31969$$

$$r_{x_1} = \frac{8035}{\sqrt{2185}\sqrt{31969}}$$

$$r_{x_1} = 0.9613$$

$\therefore r_{x_1}^2 = \underline{0.9243}$ i.e. coefficient of determination for $y : x_1$.
In a similar manner the regression y on x_2 (exam.scores: IQ scores) is calculated resulting in

$$y_{x_2} = a_{x_2} + b_{x_2}x_2$$

$$= 57.16 + 0.085x_2$$

$$\text{and } r_{x_2}^2 = 0.001608$$

The scatter diagrams for the two independent variables with the least squares lines of best fit are shown in Figures 1 and 2

SCATTER DIAGRAM OF EXAMINATION SCORES AND HOURS STUDIED ($y : x_1$)

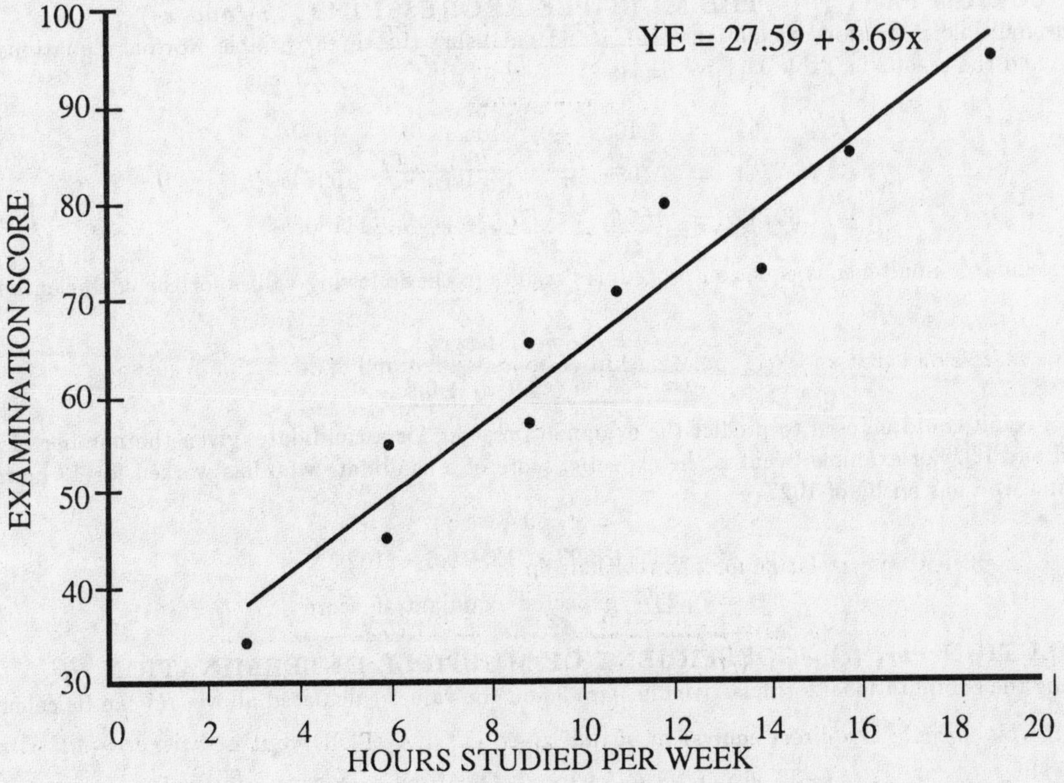

Figure 1

SCATTER DIAGRAM OF EXAMINATION SCORES IQ SCORES ($y : x_2$)

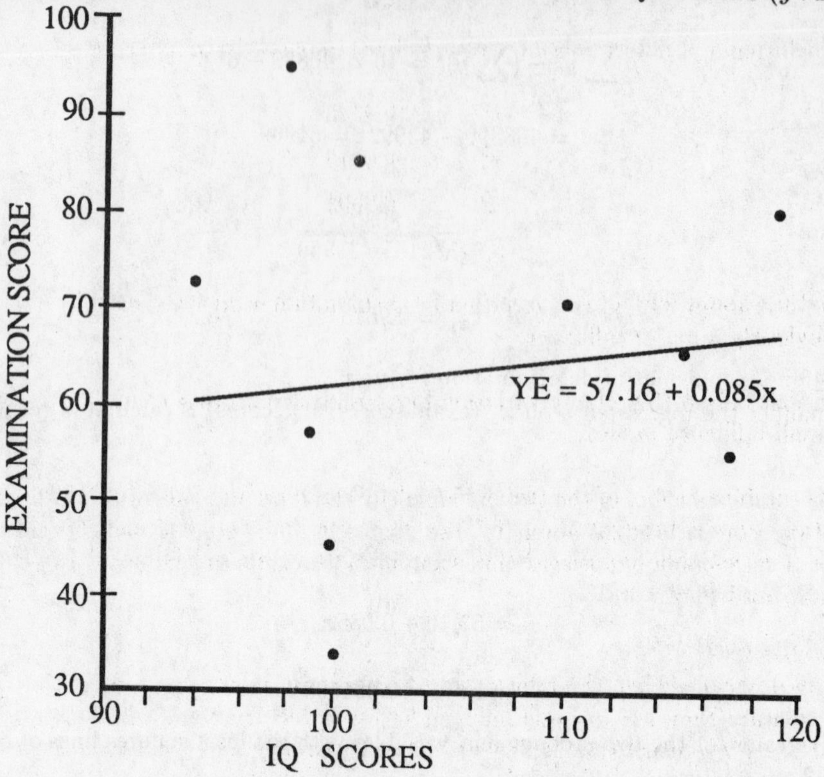

Figure 2

SOLUTION PART (b) - THE MULTIPLE REGRESSION ($y : x_1$ and x_2)

The multiple regression calculations are carried out using the three variable Normal Equations from Para 3 and the results in Table 1 above, thus:

$$\begin{aligned} 661 &= 10a + 105b_1 + 1054b_2 \\ 7744 &= 105a + 1321b_1 + 10974b_2 \\ 69730 &= 1054a + 10974b_1 + 111806b_2 \end{aligned}$$

Using standard simultaneous equation procedures results in the following values for the coefficients in the equation

$$y = a + b_1x_1 + b_2x_2$$

$$\underline{y = -38.06 + 3.93x_1 + 0.6x_2}$$

This result could be used to predict the examination score for a candidate, given the number of hours worked and IQ. For example, what is the expected score of a candidate who has worked for 13 hours per week and who has an IQ of 102?

$$\begin{aligned} y &= -38.06 + 3.93 \times 13 + 0.6 \times 102 \\ &= \underline{74.23\%} \text{ expected examination score} \end{aligned}$$

SOLUTION Part (c) - COEFFICIENT OF MULTIPLE DETERMINATION, R^2.

Using the computational formula given in Para 3 and the values calculated above, R^2 can be calculated thus:

$$R^2 = \frac{(-38.66 \times 661) + (3.93 \times 7744) + (0.6 \times 69730) - \frac{661^2}{10}}{46889 - \frac{661^2}{10}}$$

$= \underline{0.9995}$

The various coefficients of determination can now be summarised and interpreted

$$r^2_{x_1} = 0.9243$$
$$r^2_{x_2} = 0.0016$$
$$R^2 = 0.9995$$

$r^2_{x_1}$

This indicates that about 92% of the variation in examination scores is caused by variation in hours of study, which is obviously a major influence.

$r^2_{x_2}$

This indicates that only 0.16% of any variation in examination score is caused by variation in IQ score which is a very small influence indeed.

R^2

This shows the combined effect of the two independent variables and indicates that 99.95% of the movement in examination score is brought about by movements in hours studied and IQ score. This, however, assumes that it is a reasonable hypothesis that examination results are influenced by the intelligence of candidates and how hard they work!

NON-LINEAR MODELS

5. There are many occasions when the relationship between variables cannot be adequately described by linear functions, whether they use a single independent variable or several. In such circumstances some form of non-linear or curvi-linear model is likely to be more suitable and the following paragraphs describe some commonly encountered non-linear models.

EXPONENTIAL GROWTH

6. A linear trend line as previously described is suited to data which are expected to increase by the same ABSOLUTE amount in each period. Where this relationship does not apply some form of non-linear regression must be used and an important non-linear function relates to what is known as exponential growth, ie where the data is expected to grow by the same PROPORTION or PERCENTAGE in each period.

A typical example of exponential growth was world fertiliser usage between 1938 and 1968 as shown in Figure 3.

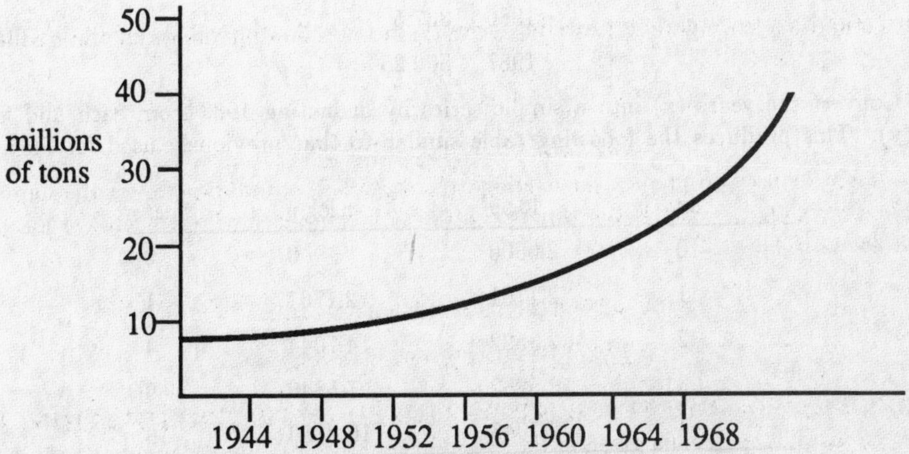

WORLD FERTILISER CONSUMPTION 1938 - 1968

Figure 3

The shape of this graph, a typical exponential growth curve, should be compared with the typical linear trend line shown in Figure 1.

THE EXPONENTIAL FUNCTION.

7. The exponential function takes the form

$$y = ab^x$$

where y is the variable to be predicted. (millions of tons in Figure 3)
a and b are constants
and x denotes the number of the period (shown on the time axis in Figure 3)

It follows that y takes the value of 'a' at time 0 and is multiplied by a factor of b^x in each period. If 'b' exceeds 1 there is exponential growth, if 'b' is less than 1 there is exponential decay. The variable 'y' is said to be an expondential function of x.

LINEAR FORM OF THE EXPONENTIAL FUNCTION

8. The exponential function can be reduced to linear form by taking the logarithm of the function thus

$$\log y = \log a + x \log b$$

or

$$\log y = A + Bx \quad \text{where} \quad A = \log a, \quad B = \log b$$

The similarity of this expression and the linear regression line previously discussed will be apparent. An interesting feature of the log form of the exponential function is that it is equivalent to fitting a straight line to a graph drawn on semi-logarithmic scale graph paper (ie a logarithmic scale on the vertical axis and an ordinary arithmetic scale on the horizontal axis).

CALCULATION OF THE EXPONENTIAL FUNCTION

9. The calculation will be illustrated by using the following data.

Year	Sales £'m's
1983	100
1984	150
1985	225
1986	337.5
1987	506.25

Step 1. Convert the years (x) into a simple series by deducting 1983 from each and find the logs of the sales (y). This produces the following table similar to that previously used for linear regression calculations.

x	$\log y$	$x \log y$	x^2
0	2.0000	0	0
1	2.1761	2.1761	1
2	2.3522	4.7044	4
3	2.5282	7.5846	9
4	2.7045	10.8180	16
$\sum x = 10$	$\sum y = 11.7610$	$\sum xy = 25.2831$	$\sum x^2 = 30$

These values can then be substituted into the formulae for a and b given in Chapter 7.

$$A = \frac{\sum y}{n} - \frac{b \sum x}{n}$$

$$B = \frac{n\sum xy - \sum x \sum y}{n\sum x^2 - (\sum x)^2}$$

ie

$$\log b = \frac{5 \times 25.2831 - 10 \times 11.7610}{5 \times 30 - 100} = \frac{8.8055}{50} = 0.17611$$

(The antilog of 0.17611 is 1.5, but as the expression for '*a*' utilises log *b*, the log, 0.17611 is used directly)

$$\log a = \frac{11.7610}{5} - \frac{0.17611 \times 10}{5} = 2.3522 - 0.3522 = 2.000$$

$$\log a = 2.000 = 100 \text{ actual value}$$

$$\log b = 0.17611 = 1.5 \text{ actual value}$$

The exponential function obtained is

$$y = ab^x$$

$$= \underline{\underline{100.1.5^x}}$$

Thus when $x = 0$

$$y = 100.1.5^0 = 100.1 = \underline{\underline{100}}$$

when $x = 1$

$$y = 100.1.5^1 = 100.1.5 = \mathbf{150}$$

and so on

Note: In this artificial example the data were a perfect exponential function, therefore the values of a and b obtained fit perfectly. This is, of course, unlikely to happen in practice.

LOGARITHMIC FUNCTIONS

10. An alternative non-linear function is what is known as a logarithmic function which has the form of

$$y = ax^b$$

where y denotes variable to be predicted, a and b are constants and x denotes the time periods.

As with the exponential function, this function can be expressed in a linear form using logarithms thus

$$\log y = \log a + b \log x$$

In this function y is said to be a logarithmic function of x.

This function is equivalent to fitting a straight line to a graph drawn on log-log paper (ie both horizontal and vertical scales being logarithmic)

CALCULATION OF THE LOGARITHMIC FUNCTION.

11. The calculations will be illustrated using the following data

Period	Sales £m's
1	50
2	200
3	450
4	800
5	1250

As for the exponential function the linear logarithmic form will be used, ie

$$\log y = \log a + b \log x$$

It will be noted that logs of both the periods (x) and of the sales (y), are required whereas in the exponential calculations only $\log y$ was necessary.

$logx$	$logy$	$logx^2$	$logx.logy$
0	1.6990	0	0
0.3010	2.3010	0.0906	0.6926
0.4771	2.6532	0.2276	1.2658
0.6021	2.9031	0.3625	1.7479
0.6990	3.0969	0.4886	2.1647
$\sum x = 2.0792$	$\sum y = 12.6532$	$\sum x^2 = 1.1693$	$\sum xy = 5.8710$

$$b = \frac{5 \times 5.8710 - 2.0792 \times 12.6532}{5 \times 1.1693 - 2.0792^2} = \frac{3.0465}{1.5234} = \underline{\underline{2.00}}$$

$$\log a = \frac{12.6532}{5} - \frac{2 \times 2.0792}{5} = 1.6989 \text{ the antilog of which is } \underline{\underline{50}}$$

$\therefore$ the values of the logarithmic function are

$$\begin{aligned} y &= ax^b \\ &= \underline{\underline{\mathbf{50.x^2}}} \end{aligned}$$

$$\begin{aligned} \text{Thus when } x &= 1 \\ y &= 50.1^2 = 50.1 = 50 \\ \text{when } x &= 2 \\ y &= 50.2^2 = 50.4 = 200 \\ \text{when } x &= 3 \\ y &= 50.3^2 = 50.9 = 450 \end{aligned}$$

and so on

Note:

Once again to illustrate the function caculations simply, a perfect set of data has been used which is unlikely to be met in practice.

THE HYPERBOLIC CURVE

12. This is another type of non-linear curve and takes the form

$$y = a + \frac{b}{x}$$

The values of a and b are calculated by reference to amended formulae:

$$b = \frac{n\sum(\frac{1}{x})y - \sum(\frac{1}{x})\sum y}{n\sum(\frac{1}{x})^2 - (\sum \frac{1}{x})^2}$$

$$a = \frac{\sum y}{n} - \frac{b\sum(\frac{1}{x})}{n}$$

Figure 4 shows typical hyperbolic curves for plots of y against x and y against $\frac{1}{x}$.

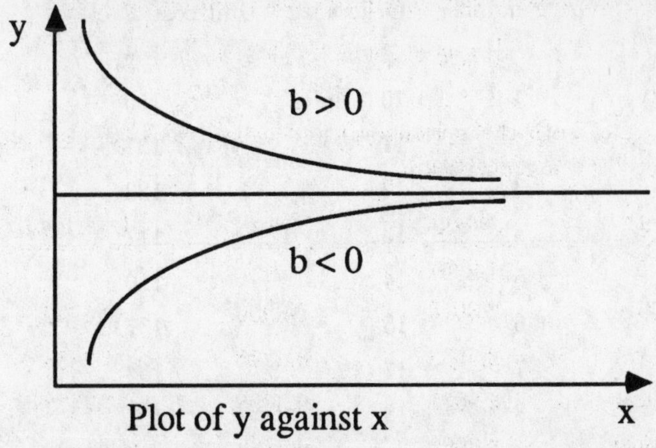

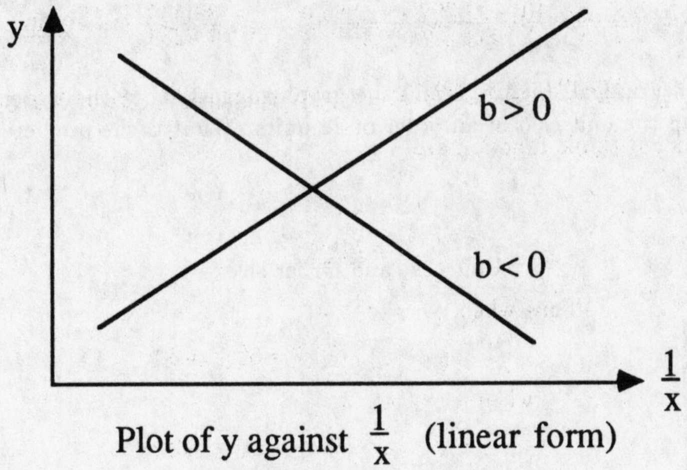

HYPERBOLIC CURVES

Figure 4

The use of the formulae are illustrated in the following example.

HYPERBOLIC CURVE EXAMPLE

13. Data have been kept for 10 orders showing the variation in unit cost against order size, as follows.

Order number	Order size x		Unit cost £ y
1	10	units	150
2	11		127
3	12		123
4	13		117
5	14		110
6	15		107
7	17		104
8	18		101
9	19		97
10	20		95

These data have been graphed, Figure 5, and the graph suggests that the hyperbolic curve might be appropriate for predicting the unit cost of an order of 22 units. What is the predicted cost?

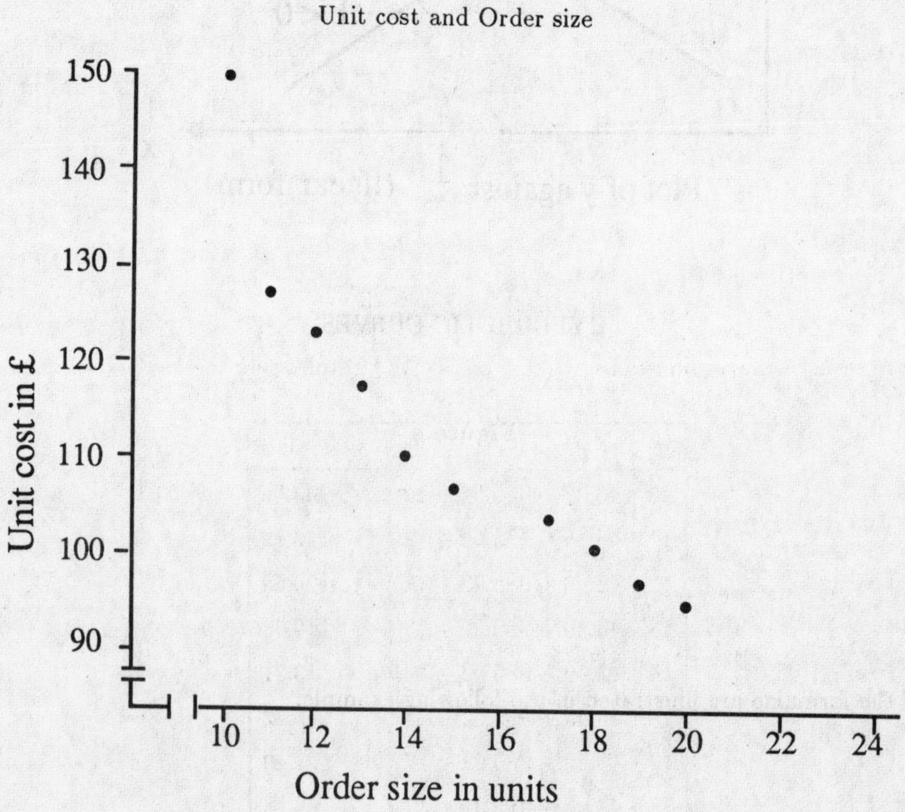

Figure 5

SOLUTION

The calculations for the least squares line of best fit are shown in Table 2

Table 2

	$\frac{1}{x}$	y	$(\frac{1}{x})^2$	$(\frac{1}{x})y$
1	0.100	150	0.0100	15.000
2	0.090	127	0.0083	11.545
3	0.083	123	0.0069	10.250
4	0.077	117	0.0059	9.000
5	0.071	110	0.0051	7.857
6	0.067	107	0.0044	7.133
7	0.059	104	0.0035	6.118
8	0.056	101	0.0031	5.611
9	0.053	97	0.0027	5.105
10	0.050	95	0.0025	4.750
$\sum$	0.706	1131	0.0524	82.369

These values are then used in the formula given in Para 12

$$b = \frac{10 \times 82.369 - 0.706 \times 1131}{10 \times 0.0524 - (0.706)^2}$$

$$b = \underline{985.92}$$

$$a = \frac{1131}{10} - 985.92 \times \frac{0.706}{10}$$

$$= \underline{43.49}$$

Thus the hyperbolic function is

$$y = 43.49 + \frac{985.92}{x}$$

The calculated least squares line can now be fitted on the graph using the calculated values in Table 3

Table 3

x	$a + \frac{b}{x}$	value of y
10	$43.49 + 985.92 \div 10$	142.08
11	$43.49 + 985.92 \div 11$	133.12
12	$43.49 + 985.92 \div 12$	125.65
13	$43.49 + 985.92 \div 13$	119.33
14	$43.49 + 985.92 \div 14$	113.91
15	$43.49 + 985.92 \div 15$	109.22
17	$43.49 + 985.92 \div 17$	101.49
18	$43.49 + 985.92 \div 18$	98.26
19	$43.49 + 985.92 \div 19$	95.38
20	$43.49 + 985.92 \div 20$	92.79

These values are plotted on Figure 6

SCATTER DIAGRAM WITH FITTED HYPERBOLIC CURVE

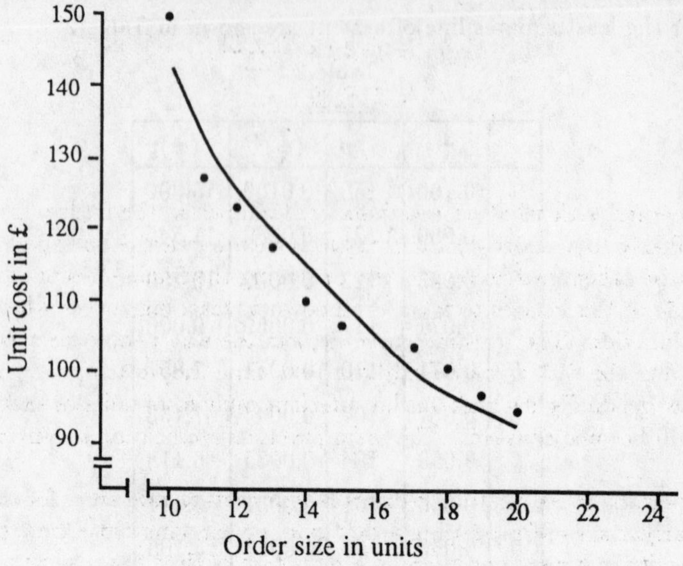

Figure 6

The same information can be reproduced in a linear form where the x axis is defined as $\frac{1}{x}$. This is shown in Figure 7.

LINEAR FORM OF HYPERBOLIC FUNCTION

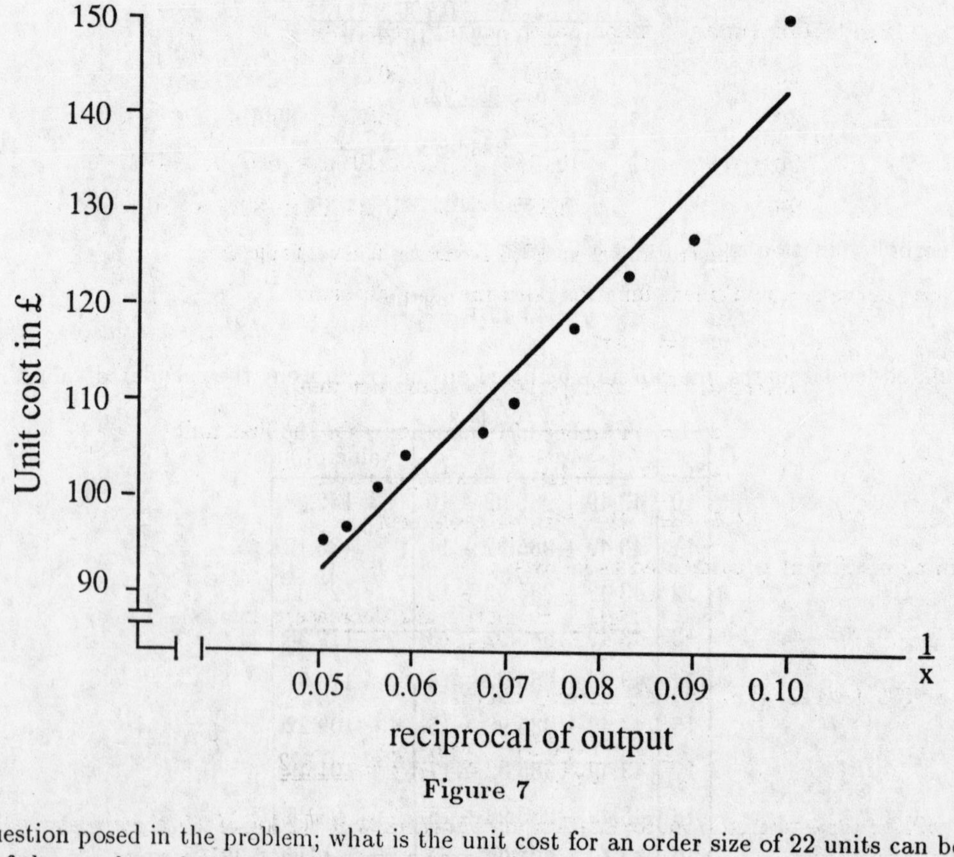

Figure 7

The question posed in the problem; what is the unit cost for an order size of 22 units can be answered from one of the graphs or by direct calculation.

On the assumption that the known relationship between x and y continues beyond the observed range then the unit cost for an order size of 22 is

$$\begin{aligned} y &= 43.49 + \frac{985.92}{22} \\ &= \underline{\underline{£88.30}} \end{aligned}$$

LEARNING CURVES

14. Forecasting is concerned with what we anticipate will happen in the future. Unthinking extrapolation of past conditions is unlikely to produce good forecasts. If we are aware of an expected change in conditions in the future this must be taken into account when preparing the finalised forecast.

A particular example of this relates to what are known as learning curves which are a practical application of a non-linear function. The learning curve depicts the way people learn by doing a task and are therefore able to complete the task more quickly the next time they attempt it. Learning is rapid in the early stages and the rate gradually declines until a sufficient number of units or tasks have been completed, when the time taken will become constant. The main practical application is concerned with direct labour times and costs.

Cost predictions especially those relating to direct labour costs should allow for the effects of the learning process. During the early stages of producing a new part or carrying out a new process, experience and skill is gained, productivity increases and there is a reduction of time taken per unit.

Studies have shown that there is a tendency for the time per unit to reduce at some constant rate as production mounts. For example, an 80% learning curve means that as cumulative production quantities double the average time per unit falls by 20% .

This is shown in Table 4

Cumulative Production (units)	Cumulative Time Taken (mins)	Average Time Per Unit
20	400	20
40	640	16(20 × 80%)
80	1024	12.8(20 × 80% × 80%)
160	1638.4	10.24(20 × 80% × 80 80%)

Illustration of an 80% Learning Curve Table 4

The learning curve is a non-linear function with the general form:

$$y = ax^b$$

where y = average labour hours per unit

a = number of labour hours for the first unit

x = cumulative number of units

b = the learning coefficient

The learning coefficient is calculated as follows:

$$b = \frac{\log(1 - \text{Proportionate decrease})}{\log 2}$$

thus for a 20% decrease (i.e. an 80% learning curve)

$$b = \frac{\log(1 - 0.2)}{\log 2} = \frac{\bar{1}.90309}{0.30103} = \underline{\underline{-0.322}}$$

Note: It will be remembered from foundation mathematics that the log of 0.8 is conventionally written as $\bar{1}.90309$ but is actually $-1 + 0.90309$ i.e. -0.09691 which, divided by 0.30103, gives -0.322.

Having established the values for the funciton it can be used to find the expected labour time per unit. For example, with an 80% learning curve and a time of 10 minuts for the first unit, what is the expected time per unit when cumulative production is 20 units?

$$y = ax^b = 10 \times 20^{-0.322} = \underline{\underline{3.812 \text{ mins.}}}$$

Note.

a. whilst it is clear that learning does take place and that average times are likely to reduce, in practice it is highly unlikely that there will be a regular consistent rate of decrease as exemplified above. Accordingly, any cost predictions based on conventional learning curves should be viewed with caution (as should any form of prediction!)

LINEAR TRANSFORMATION OF LEARNING CURVE

15. An alternative method of calculating the learning curve coefficient uses the linear transformation formed by taking the logarithm of the function thus

$$\log y = \log(ax^b)$$

$$\log y = \log a + b \log x$$

This will be recognised as a transformation to the general linear form

$$y = a + bx$$

If

X stands for $\log x$ and
Y stands for $\log y$

then the standard formulae for a and b become

$$b = \frac{n\sum XY - \sum X \sum Y}{n\sum X^2 - (\sum X)^2}$$

$$\log a = \frac{\sum Y}{n} - b\frac{\sum X}{n}$$

The above formulae are illustrated using the data in the previous paragraph thus

CUMULATIVE PRODUCTION	CUMULATIVE TIME	AVERAGE TIME
x		y
20	400	20
40	640	16
80	1024	12.8
160	1638.4	10.24

The logarithms of the cumulative production, x, and the average time, y, are used to find the values for the formulae above and are shown in Table 5.

X ie $\log x$	Y $\log y$	X^2 $(\log x)^2$	XY $\log x . \log y$
1.30103	1.30103	1.69268	1.69268
1.60206	1.20412	2.56659	1.92907
1.90309	1.10721	3.62175	2.10712
2.20412	1.010303	4.85815	2.22682
$\sum X =$ 7.01030	$\sum Y =$ 4.62266	$\sum X^2 =$ 12.73917	$\sum XY =$ 7.95569

Table 5

These values are inserted into the formula

$$b = \frac{4 \times 7.95569 - 7.01030 \times 4.62266}{4 \times 12.73917 - 7.01030^2} = \underline{-0.3223}$$

This will be seen to be the same value as calculated in Para 14 above. The learning curve thus has the form

$$y = ax^{-0.3223}$$

For completeness the value of a is calculated. This represents the number of labour hours for the first unit. This was not one of the observed values, which started at 20 units, so the value represents the theoretical time for the first unit; given the relationships found for the observed range of 20 to 160 units.

Using the formula given above

$$\log a = \frac{4.62266}{4} - (-0.3223)\frac{7.01030}{4}$$

$\log a = 1.72052$, and finding the antilog gives $a = 52.546$. The full learning curve formula is thus:

$$\underline{\underline{y = 52.546x^{-0.3223}}}$$

The value of 52.546 hours for the first unit can be proved by inserting one of the observed values, say 20 units, and checking that the calculated time agrees with the observed time of 20 minutes.

To find the value of $y = 52.46 \times 20^{-0.3223}$

Number	log	
20	1.30103	
1.30103 × 0.3223	0.41932	
0 - 0.41932	$\bar{1}.58068$	(this represents $20^{-0.3223}$)
52.546	$\underline{1.72052^{+}}$	
	$\underline{1.30120}$	the anti-log

of which is almost exactly 20 thus proving the values of the coefficient a and b.

SUMMARY

16.

a. If a linear two variable model is deemed inappropriate then multiple linear regression models or non-linear regression models can be tried.

b. The *line* of best fit for the two variable model becomes a *plane* of best fit in a three variable model.

c. Multiple regression uses R^2, the coefficient of multiple determination to assess the improvement in the fit of the model on the introduction of one or more additional causal variables.

d. The exponential growth model deals with situations where the y variable is expected to grow by a constant proportion for a given change in the x value.

e. There are occasions where a non-linear relationship may be converted to a linear relationship by the use of logarithms. This is known as a logarithmic function and takes the form $y = ax^b$.

f. The hyperbolic curve uses the reciprocal of x rather than x itself. It takes the form

$$y = a + \frac{b}{x}$$

g. The learning curve is an important application of a non-linear function and takes the form

$$y = ax^{-b}$$

POINTS TO NOTE

17.

a. The process of plotting the calculated values for a non-linear function onto a scatter diagram is known as curve fitting.

b. Although it is unlikely that full analysis of multiple regression would be required in a time constrained examination understanding of the method is necessary.

SELF REVIEW QUESTION

1. *What is multiple regression? (3)*
2. *Define R^2 and explain its purpose? (3)*
3. *How does exponential growth differ from linear growth? (6)*
4. *What is exponential decay? (7)*
5. *What is the linear form of the exponential function? (8)*
6. *What is a logarithmic function? (10)*
7. *What is the form of a hyperbolic curve? (12)*
8. *What is a learning curve? (14)*
9. *How is the learning coefficient calculated? (14 & 15)*

EXERCISES WITH ANSWERS COMMENCING PAGE 488

A1. Analysis of representatives' car expenses shows that the expenses are dependent on the miles travelled (x_1) and the type of journey (x_2). The general form is:

$$y = a + b_1x_1 + b_2x_2$$

Calculations have produced the following values (where y is expenses per month)

$$\begin{aligned} y &= £86 + 0.37x_1 + 0.08x_2 \\ r^2x_1 &= 0.78 \\ r^2x_2 &= 0.16 \\ R^2 &= 0.88 \end{aligned}$$

Interpret these values

A2. For a given operation a 10% learning curve operates. Assuming that the first unit takes 30 minutes, how long does the 20th unit take?

A3. Assume the same problem as A2 but with a 30% learning curve.

EXAMINATION QUESTIONS WITH ANSWERS COMMENCING PAGE 488

A4. Growell Wholesale Seed Merchants Limited has asked its sales manager to provide a forecast of sales for the next year as a basis for its budget.

Data relating to the volume of sales over the past five years are available:

Year	Packets of seeds (millions)
1971	1.5
1972	1.6
1973	1.8
1974	2.2
1975	2.7

The sales manager has fitted two trend curves to this data:

i. a straight line ($y = a + bx$)

ii. a logarithmic (geometric) curve ($y = ax^b$)

and proposes to use one of these to extrapolate a forecast for 1977.

You are required to:

a. plot the original data and trend curves on a graph;

b. state the forecast sales figures for 1977 which would be given by each trend curve;

c. determine, on the basis of the data available, which would be the better curve to use;

d. comment on the results obtained from working through steps a. to c. above;

e. comment on the advantages and disadvantages of these types of functions in forecasting.

(CIMA, Quantitative Techniques)

A5. Odin Chemicals Limited is aware that its power costs are a semi-variable cost and over the last six months these costs have shown the following relationship with a standard measure of output.

Month	Output (Standard Units)	Total Power Costs (£'000s)
1	12	6.2
2	18	8.0
3	19	8.6
4	20	10.4
5	24	10.2
6	30	12.4

Required:

(a) Using the method of least squares, determine an appropriate linear relationship between total power costs and output.

(b) If total power costs are related to both output and time (as measured by the number of the month) the following least squares regression equation is obtained

$$Power\ Costs = 4.42 + 0.82 \times Output + 0.10 \times Month$$

where the regression coefficients (i.e. 0.82 and 0.10) have t values of 2.64 and 0.60 respectively, and the coefficient of multiple correlation amounts to 0.976.

Compare the relative merits of this fitted relationship with the one you determined in (a). Explain (without doing any further analysis) how you might use the data to forecast total power costs in month 7.

(ACCA, Quantitative Analysis)

A6. A motor manufacturer produces a particular type of small 25 seater motor coach which is built to order. Due principally to economies of scale obtained in the purchasing of certain key components, the manufacturer is aware that his unit total costs are not constant, but decrease with increasing order size. On analysing the last 6 orders that he has fulfilled, the following data on unit total costs (in terms of 1982 prices) are obtained.

Size of Order (No. of Coaches) x	*Unit Total Cost (£ per coach)* y
5	27.5
2	29.2
10	26.7
8	26.8
1	33.2
3	28.5

Required:

(a) By plotting a graph of y *against* $1/x$ *show that a relationship of the form*

$$y = a + \frac{b}{x}$$

fits the above data reasonably well.

(b) By means of a process of least squares linear regression, estimate the coefficients a and b. what do you estimate would be the total cost of an order for 6 coaches?

(c) In the context of this example, how would you interpret the coefficients a and b?

(ACCA, Quantitative Analysis)

A7. (a) The Far Flung Toy Company Ltd. manufactures plastic toys. A new toy has been created with an estimated product life of twelve months. There are two alternative marketing strategies for which the forecast sales volume and advertising expenditures are given below:

1985/1986

	Feb	Mar	Apl	May	June	July	Aug	Sept	Oct	Total for 9 mths to Oct	Nov	Dec	Jan	Total for the year
Strategy I														
Sales Volume ('000)	10	15	20	30	30	30	10	10	20	175	50	50	25	300
Advertising (£'000)	10	20	20	20	20	20	–	20	50	180	50	50	5	285
Strategy II														
Sales Volume ('000)	–	–	–	–	–	10	10	30	30	80	80	30	30	270
Advertising (£'000)	–	–	–	–	–	10	20	25	25	80	55	55	20	210

Strategy 1 requires the immediate start of production and sales of the toy in February 1985. Far Flung would sell the toy for £3.25, (recommended retail price £4.50). Then at the beginning of November 1985 the recommended retail price would be reduced to £3.50, with Far Flung receiving £2.50. A big increase in advertising would be undertaken, aimed at the Christmas market.

Strategy II delays taking the product to the market until July 1985 and then builds up steadily towards Christmas. The recommended retail price of £4.00 would be unchanged throughout with Far Flung receiving £3.00 per toy.

Labour is the major cost element. There is a learning curve effect on the labour costs. From past experience, when the volume is doubled the new average cost is 80% of that at the previous volume. The formula for the learning curve effect is:

$$y = ax^{-b}$$

where:

y is the average number of hours per batch of 10 toys

a is 52 hours – the time taken for the first batch of 10 toys

x is the cumulative number of batches of 10 toys, and

b is the index of learning to be calculated from the 80 per cent learning curve. The labour rate per hour is £6.00

Other costs not affected by the learning curve are, per batch of 10 toys, materials £3.00 and variable overheads £1.10, with separable fixed overheads of £4,500 per month. However, if strategy II is undertaken separable fixed overheads will be £1,500 per month for the first five months of the year and £4,500 per month for the remaining seven months. The tooling costs of the project are £40,000. Net cash inflows are usually 90% of accrued profit at any intermediate date during a project. There is another project requiring £50,000 outlay on 1st November 1985 and it is hoped that cash from the toy project will contribute to this outlay. Assume all toys made are sold.

You are required to compute and show the profit statements for the two alternative strategies under consideration making use of the learning curve and the information given above. Present sufficient information to enable management to consider the effects of the strategies bearing in mind the corporate cash needs. State with reasons, your recommendations for the strategy to be selected.

NOTE: Ignore taxation

(b) A competitor has learnt of Far Flung's intent to market this particular toy and is considering the manufacture and marketing of a cheaper version of poorer quality in direct competiion. If the competitor does enter the market then Far Flung's forecasts under its two strategies would be revised as shown in the following table, which also gives forecasts of the competitor's likely sales volumes.

1985/1986

	Feb	Mar	Apl	May	June	July	Aug	Sept	Oct	Total for 9 mths to Oct	Nov	Dec	Jan	Total for the year
Strategy I														
Competitor's														
Sales Volume ('000)	–	–	–	16	16	20	10	10	20	92	30	30	10	162
Far Flung														
Sales Volume ('000)	10	15	20	25	24	24	8	8	16	150	35	35	10	230
Advertising (£'000)	10	20	10	15	15	15	–	–	25	110	40	40	–	190
Strategy II														
Competitor's														
Sales Volume ('000)	–	–	–	–	–	8	15	22	25	70	50	55	5	180
Far Flung														
Sales Volume ('000)	–	–	–	–	–	8	15	20	20	63	55	60	12	190
Advertising (£'000)	–	–	–	–	–	5	15	20	20	60	50	50	–	160

The labour costs using the learning curve have been calculated for the following volumes:

Volume ('000)	Labour Cost (£)
63	117,622
150	211,817
190	248,644
230	283,036

The other costs will be incurred on the same basis as in section (a) except for the advertising budget revised above. For the competitor the net profits for the two strategies are estimated at £26,000 and £15,000 for I and II respectively. The competitor's choice of strategy is not known.

You are required to:

(i) set out for Far Flung's management, with appropriate financial information, recommendations as to which strategy to adopt. Remember there is no certainty that the competitor will enter the market but that these are the only two possible strategy combinations and

(ii) prepare a minimax regret table and select the appropriate strategy for Far Flung. Use the information in sections (a) and (b) and assume that there are only two market states, either the competitor does not enter the market, or if it does, it then follows the same strategy as Far Flung.

NOTE: Ignore taxation

(ICA MANAGEMENT ACCOUNTING)

A8. The following data relate to a regression model of the sales of a particular product (Y) and three independent variables thought to have an effect in determining the sales of Y.

The model is of form:

$$Y = a + b_1x_1 + b_2x_2 + b_3x_3$$

where x_1 etc. represent the independent variables.

The regression equation is given as:

$$Y = 0.07 + 0.34x_1 + 0.31x_2 = 0.07x_3$$

Further analysis of the data gives the following information:

Variable	Standard error (b_i)	't'-statistic value
x_1	0.36	0.947
x_2	0.06	5.04
x_3	0.23	0.31

Multiple Correlation Coefficient (R)

Multiple R	R^2
0.951	0.904

Analysis of Variance:

Source	Sum of Squares	Degrees of freedom	Mean	'F'-statistic
Regression	3.341	3	1.114	22.05
Residuals	0.354	7	0.051	
Total	3.695	10		

You are required:

(a) using the above data to illustrate your answer where appropriate, to explain the meaning of the terms:

(i) standard error (b_i);
(ii) the 't' statistics;
(iii) the multiple correlation coefficient; and
(iv) all the terms of the analysis of variance;
(b) to test the significance of the 't' and 'F' values at the 0.05 level of significance and explain the meaning of your answer;
(c) assuming the variables x_1, x_2, x_3 could be used in practice to predict the value of sales Y, to make a critical assessment of the use of this particular regression formulation for this purpose and give reasons for your comments relating to the assessments;
(d) to give one other piece of statistical information which apart from known the nature of the variables, could be of value in assessing the equation.
(CIMA QUANTITATIVE TECHNIQUES.)

EXERCISES WITHOUT ANSWERS

B1. Using the following values calculate a, b_1, b_2 in the equation.

$$y = a + b_1x_1 + b_2x_2$$

$$\begin{array}{lcllcllcl} \Sigma y &=& 800 & n &=& 12 & \Sigma x_1 &=& 135 \\ \Sigma x_2 &=& 1300 & \Sigma x_1 y &=& 8300 \\ \Sigma x_1^2 &=& 1450 & \Sigma x_1 x_2 &=& 11,600 \\ \Sigma x_2 y &=& 73,000 & \Sigma x_2^2 &=& 115,000 \end{array}$$

B2. Given a 80% learning curve the time for the 50th component was 10 minutes. How long did the first component take?

EXAMINATION QUESTIONS WITHOUT ANSWERS

B3. Abourne Ltd. manufactures a micro-computer for the home use market. The management accountant is considering using regression analysis in the annual estimate of total costs. The following information has been produced for the twelve months ended 31st December, 1983.

			Direct Labour	
Month	*Total Cost*	*Output*	*Number of Employees*	*Hours Worked*
	(Y)	(X_1)	(X_2)	(X_3)
	(£)	*(Numbers)*	*(Numbers)*	*(Hours)*
1	38,200	300	28	4,480
2	40,480	320	30	4,700
3	41,400	350	30	4,800
4	51,000	500	32	5,120
5	52,980	530	32	5,150
6	60,380	640	35	5,700
7	70,440	790	41	7,210
8	32,720	250	41	3,200
9	75,800	820	41	7,300
10	71,920	780	39	7,200
11	68,380	750	38	6,400
12	33,500	270	33	3,960
	$\Sigma Y =$ 637,200	$\Sigma X_1 =$ 6,300	$\Sigma X_2 =$ 420	$\Sigma X_3 =$ 65,220

Additionally:

$$\Sigma Y^2 = 36,614.05 \times 10^6 \quad \Sigma X_1^2 = 3.8582 \times 10^6 \quad \Sigma X_2^2 = 14,954 \quad \Sigma X_3^2 = 374.423 \times 10^6$$

$$\Sigma X_1 Y = 373.5374 \times 10^6 \quad \Sigma X_2 Y = 22.81284 \times 10^6 \quad \Sigma X_3 Y = 3692.2774 \times 10^6$$

The management accountant wants to select the best independent variable (X_1, X_2, or X_3) to help in future forecasts of total production costs cusing an ordinary least squares regression equation. He is also considering the alternatives of using the Hi-Lo and multiple regression equations as the basis for future forecasts.

You are required to:

(a) identify which one of the three independent variables (X_1, X_2, X_3) given above is likely to be the least good estimator of total costs (Y). Give your reasons, but do not submit any calculations .

(b) compute separately, for the remaining two independent variables, the values of the two parameters α and β for each regression line. Calculate the coefficient of determination (R^2) for each relationship.

(c) state, with reasons, which one of these independent variables should be used to estimate total costs in the future given the results of (b) above .

(d) devise the two equations which could be used, using the Hi-Lo technique, instead of the two regression lines computed in (b) above and comment on the differences found between the two sets of equations, and

(e) comment critically on the use of Hi-Lo and ordinary least squares regression as forecasting and estimating aids using the above results as a basis for discussions. In addition, comment on the advantages and problems of using multiple regression for forecasting and estimating; and state whether, in your opinion, the management accountant should consider using it in the present circumstances.

NOTE: Formulae you may require are to be found in the box.

$$\beta = \frac{\Sigma xy - n\bar{x}\bar{y}}{\Sigma x^2 - n\bar{x}^2} \qquad \alpha = \bar{y} - \beta\bar{x}$$

$$R^2 = \frac{\alpha\Sigma y + \beta\Sigma xy - n\bar{y}^2}{\Sigma y^2 - n\bar{y}^2}$$

$$S_e = \sqrt{\frac{\Sigma y^2 - \alpha\Sigma y - \beta\Sigma xy}{n-2}} \qquad S_\beta = \frac{S_e}{\sqrt{\Sigma x^2 - n\bar{x}^2}}$$

(ICA Management Accounting)

B4. The following data were collected from the industrial Products Manufacturing Company Limited.

Month	*Total Overhead*	*Direct Labour hours (DLH)*	*Plant hours (PH)*
	y	x	
January	*15,000*	*736*	*184*
February	*14,500*	*800*	*160*
March	*15,750*	*1,008*	*168*
April	*15,250*	*880*	*176*
May	*16,250*	*1,056*	*176*
June	*15,000*	*840*	*168*
	$\Sigma y = 91,750$	$\Sigma x = 5,320$	
	$y = 15,291.7$	$x = 886.7$	

You are required to:

a. compute a least squares cost equation based on direct labour hours;

b. compute the coefficient of determination (r^2) for (a);
c. compare and discuss the relationship of your solution in (a) to the equation of:

$$Total\ overhead = 5,758 + 4.7\ DLH + 31PH$$

(where, DLH = Direct labour hours, PH - plant hours)
obtained by a regression using DLH and PH as variables and coefficient of determination $R^2 = 0.9873$;
d. estimate the total overhead for a month with 1,000 DLH and 168 PH, using the equation in (c).
(CIMA Quantitative Techniques)

9 Forecasting – Time Series Analysis

INTRODUCTION

1. The two previous chapters have considered the relationship between sets of observations and the idea of using movements in one (or more) variables to predict or forecast movements in another variable. This chapter deals with the more familiar interpretation of forecasting which deals with time and the process of looking into the future in an attempt to ascertain what might happen. Qualitative forecasting methods are considered including the Delphi System and historical analogy. Time series analysis by moving averages and exponential smoothing is explained and the decomposition of times series is described and illustrated. The measurement of forecast errors is discussed and the chapter concludes with an illustration of longer term forecasting using regression analysis.

FORECASTING – DEFINITION

2. For our purposes forecasting can be defined as attempting to predict the future by using qualitative or quantitative means. In an informal way, forecasting is an integral part of all human activity, but from the business point of view increasing attention is being given to formal forecasting systems which are continually being refined. Some forecasting systems involve very advanced statistical techniques beyond the scope of this book, so are not included.

All forecasting methodologies can be divided into three broad headings i.e. forecasts based on:-

What people have DONE	**What people SAY**	**What people DO**
examples:	examples:	examples:
Time Series Analysis	Surveys	Testing Marketing
Regression Analysis	Questionnaires	Reaction tests

The data from past activities are cheapest to collect but may be outdated and past behaviour is not necessarily indicative of future behaviour.

Data derived from surveys are more expensive to obtain and needs critical appraisal - intentions as expressed in surveys and questionnaires are not always translated into action.

Finally, the data derived from recording what people actually do are the most reliable but also the most expensive and occasionally it is not feasible for the data to be obtained.

FORECASTING – APPLICATION

3. Virtually every form of decision making and planning activity in business involves forecasting. Typical applications include:

production planning

inventory control

investment cash flows

cost projections

demand forecasts

advertising planning

corporate planning

budgeting

QUALITATIVE AND QUANTITATIVE TECHNIQUES

4. A convenient classification of forecasting techniques is between that are broadly qualitative and those that are broadly quantitative. These classifications are by no means rigid or exclusive but serve as a means of identification.

QUANTITATIVE TECHNIQUES

5. These are techniques or varying levels of statistical complexity which are based on analysing past data of the item to be forecast eg sales figures, stores issues, costs incurred. However sophisticated the technique used, there is the underlying assumption that past patterns will provide some guidance to the future. Clearly for many operational items (material usage, sales of existing products, costs) the past does serve as a guide to the future, but there are circumstances for which no data are available eg the launching of a completely new product, where other, more qualitative techniques are required. These techniques are dealt with briefly first and then the detailed quantitative material follows.

QUALITATIVE TECHNIQUES

6. These are techniques which are used when data are scarce, eg the first introduction of a new product. The techniques use human judgement and experience to turn qualitative information into quantitative estimates. Although qualitative techniques are used for both short and long term purposes, their use becomes of increasing importance as the time scale of the forecast lengthens. Even when past data are available, so that standard quantitative techniques can be used, longer term forecasts require judgement, intuition, experience, flair etc, that is, qualitative factors, to make them more useful. As the time scale lengthens, past patterns become less and less meaningful. The qualitative methods briefly dealt with in this manual are the DELPHI METHOD, MARKET RESEARCH, and HISTORICAL ANALOGY.

DELPHI METHOD

7. This is a technique mainly used for longer term forecasting, designed to obtain expert consensus for a particular forecast, without the problem of submitting to pressure to conform to a majority view. The procedure is that a panel of experts independently answer a sequence of questionnaires in which the responses to one questionnaire are used to produce the next questionnaire. Thus any information available to some experts and not others is passed on to all, so that their subsequent judgements are refined as more information and experience become available.

MARKET RESEARCH

8. Widely used procedures involving opinion surveys, analyses of market data, questionnaires designed to gauge the reaction of the market to a particular product, design, price etc. Market research is often very accurate for the relatively short term, but longer term forecasts based purely on surveys are likely to be suspect because peoples' attitudes and intentions change.

HISTORICAL ANALOGY

9. Where past data on a particular item are not available, eg. for a new product, data on similar products are analysed to establish the life cycle and expected sales of the new product. Clearly, considerable care is needed in using analogies which relate to different products in different time periods, but such techniques may be useful in forming a broad impression in the medium to long term.

Note on qualitative methods:

a. When past quantitative data are unavailable for the item to be forecast, then inevitably much more judgement is involved in making forecasts.

b. Some of the qualitative techniques mentioned above use advanced statistical techniques, eg some of the sampling methods used in Market Research. Nevertheless, any such method may prove to be a relatively poor forecaster, purely due to the lack of appropriate quantitative data relating to the factor being forecast.

QUANTITATIVE FORECASTING.

10. A prerequisite to the use of the technique to be described is data on past usage or demand. The longer a period covered by the data, the more likely that the patterns in the data will be representative of the future. This is the main assumption behind the use of statistical forecasting techniques. Nevertheless, however long a period is covered by past data, any extrapolations or forecasts produced from that data *by whatever technique* should be treated with caution. Conditions can, and do, change quite rapidly. Judgement, experience and a wide knowledge of the market place always play a part in establishing a reliable forecast.

TIME SERIES ANALYSIS.

11. As the name suggests, time series analysis uses some form of mathematical or statistical analysis on past data arranged in a time series, eg sales by month for the last ten years. Time series analyses have the advantage of relative simplicity, but certain factors need to be considered.

a. Are the past data representative? For example, do they contain the results of a recession/boom, a major shift of taste, etc, etc.

b. On the whole, time series methods are more appropriate where short term forecasts are required. Over the longer term external pressures, internal policy changes make historical data less appropriate.

c. Time series methods are best suited to relatively stable situations. Where substantial fluctuations are common and/or conditions are expected to change, then time series methods may give relatively poor results.

TIME SERIES ANALYSIS – MOVING AVERAGE.

12. If the forecast for next month's sales, say December, was the actual sales for November, then the forecasts obtained would fluctuate up and down with every random fluctuation. If the forecast for the next month's sales was an average of sales for several preceding months then, hopefully, random fluctuations would cancel each other out, ie would be smoothed away. This is the simple principle of the moving average method which is one of the smoothing techniques. The method is illustrated by the following example.

Example 1

PAST SALES DATA OF WIDGETS		FORECASTS PRODUCED BY		
Month	Actual Sales (Units)	3 monthly moving average	6 monthly moving average	12 monthly moving average
January	450			
February	440			
March	460			
April	410	450		
May	380	437		
June	400	417		
July	370	397	423	
August	360	383	410	
September	410	377	397	
October	450	380	388	
November	470	407	395	
December	490	443	410	
January	460	470	425	424

Table 1

Any month's forecast is the average of the proceding n months' actual sales. For example, the 3 monthly moving average forecasts were prepared as follows:

$$\text{APRIL'S FORECAST} = \frac{\text{Jan. Sales} + \text{Feb. Sales} + \text{Mar. Sales}}{3}$$

$$= \frac{450 + 440 + 460}{3} = \underline{\underline{450}}$$

$$\text{MAY'S FORECAST} = \frac{\text{Feb.Sales} + \text{March Sales} + \text{April Sales}}{3}$$

$$= \frac{440 + 460 + 410}{3} = \underline{\underline{437}}$$

Similar logic applies for the 6 and 12 monthly moving averages.

Note:

A moving average can be used as a forecast as shown above but when graphing moving averages it is important to realise, that being averages, they must be plotted at the mid point of the period to which they relate.

CHARACTERISTICS OF MOVING AVERAGES.

13.

a. The different moving averages produce different forecasts.

b. The greater the number of periods in the moving average, the greater the smoothing effect.

c. If the underlying trend of the past data is thought to be fairly constant with susbtantial randomness, then a greater number of periods should be chosen.

d. Alternatively, if there is thought to be some change in the underlying state of the data, more responsiveness is needed, therefore fewer periods should be included in the moving average.

LIMITATIONS OF MOVING AVERAGES.

14.

a. Equal weighting is given to each of the values used in the moving average calculation, whereas it is reasonable to suppose that the most recent data is more relevant to current condtions.

b. An n period moving average requires the storage of $n - 1$ values to which is added the latest observation. This may not seem much of a limitation when only a few items are considered, but it becomes a significant factor when, for example, a company carries 25,000 stock items each of which requires a moving average calculation involving say 6 months usage data to be recorded.

c. The moving average calculation takes no account of data outside the period of average, so full use is not made of all the data available.

d. The use of the unadjusted moving average as a forecast can cause misleading results when there is an underlying seasonal variation.

EXPONENTIAL SMOOTHING

15. This is a frequently encountered forecasting technique which largely overcomes the limitations of moving averages. The method involves the automatic weighting of past data with weights that decrease exponentially with time, ie the most current values receive the greatest weighting and the older observations receive a decreasing weighting. The exponential smoothing technique is a weighted moving average system and the underlying principle is that the

New Forecast = Old Forecast + a proportion of the forecast error

The simplest formula is

New forecast = Old forecast + α(Latest Observation - Old Forecast)

where α (alpha) is the smoothing constant.

THE SMOOTHING CONSTANT

16. The value of α can be between 0 and 1. The higher value of α (ie the nearer to 1), the more sensitive the forecast becomes to current conditions, whereas the lower the value, the more stable the forecast will be, ie it will react less sensitively to current conditions. An approximate equivalent of α values to the number of periods' moving average is given below:

α Value	Approximate Periods in equivalent moving average
.1	19
.25	7
.33	5
.5	3

The total of the weights of observations contributing to the new forecast is 1 and the weight reduces exponentially progressively from the α value for the latest observation to smaller values for the older observations. For example, if the α value was .3 and June's sales were being forecast, then June's forecast is produced from averaging past sales weighted as follows.

.3 (May's Sales) + .21 (April's Sales) + 0.147 (March's Sales)
+ 0.1029 (February Sales) + 0.072 (January Sales)
+ 0.050 (December Sales), etc.

From this it will be noted that the weightings calculated approach a total of 1. It should be emphasised that the application of the formula given in Para 15 automatically gives these weightings; further calculations are not required.

EXPONENTIAL SMOOTHING ILLUSTRATION.

17. The data in Table 1 are reproduced below and forecasts have been prepared using α values of .2 and .8.

MONTH	ACTUAL SALES (UNITS)	EXPONENTIAL FORECASTS α Values 0.2	α Value 0.8
January	450		
February	440	450	450
March	460	448	442
April	410	450.4	456.4
May	380	442.32	419.28
June	400	429.86	387.86
July	370	423.89	397.57
August	360	413.11	375.51
September	410	402.49	363.102
October	450	403.99	400.62
November	470	413.19	440.12
December	490	424.55	464.02
January	460	437.64	484.80

Table 2

Notes:

a. Because in this example no previous forecast was available, January sales were used as February's forecast.

b. Thereafter the normal formula was used, for example, when $\alpha = 0.2$

MARCH FORECAST = February Forecast + .2(Feb Sales - February Forecast)

MARCH FORECAST = 450 + .2(440 - 450)

MARCH FORECAST = **448**

and similarly for all other forecasts.

c. In practice the forecasts would be rounded to the nearest unit. They have been left as calculated so that students may check and compare some of their own calculations.

d. It will be apparent that the higher α value, 0.8, produces a forecast which adjusts more readily to the most recent sales.

EXTENSIONS OF EXPONENTIAL SMOOTHING.

18. The basic principle of exponential smoothing has been outlined above, but to cope with various problems such as seasonal factors, strongly rising or falling demand, etc many developments to the basic model have been made. These include double and triple exponential smoothing and correction for trend and delay factors, etc. These are outside the scope of the present manual, so are not covered.

CHARACTERISTICS OF EXPONENTIAL SMOOTHING

19.

a. Greater weight is given to more recent data

b. All past data are incorporated there is no cut-off point as with moving averages.

c. Less data needs to be stored than with the longer period moving averages.

d. Like moving averages it is an adaptive forecasting system. That is, it adapts continually as new data becomes available and so it is frequently incorporated as an integral part of stock control and production control systems.

e. To cope with various problems (trend, seasonal factors, etc) the basic model needs to be modified.

f. Whatever form of exponential smoothing is adopted, changes to the model to suit changing conditions can simply be made by altering the alpha value.

TIME SERIES ANALYSIS – DECOMPOSITION

20. With some types of time series to provide a reasonably accurate forecast it is necessary to separate out the various features which together make up the overall pattern. These features are as follows:

a. Seasonal variation, eg. a periodic rise and fall in sales that tends to repeat itself annually. Numerous industries are affected in this way, eg heating fuel usage, sales of sporting goods, greeting cards, etc.

b. The trend; the long term tendency of the whole series to rise or fall.

c. The cyclical factor; the periodic rise and fall of the whole series over a number of years.

d. Random or residual variations. The remaining variations in the data which cannot be attributed to a., b., or c.

Time series decomposition (sometimes called simply time series analysis), seeks to separate each of these elements, quantify its value and prepare a forecast combining all the elements. Of the various elements the most important are the first two, ie the trend and seasonal variation, so this manual concentrates upon these two.

ILLUSTRATION OF TIME SERIES DECOMPOSITION

21. The following data will be used to illustrate how the trend and seasonal variation is calculated.

SALES OF WIDGETS IN '000s

	Quarter 1	Quarter 2	Quarter 3	Quarter 4
Year 19-1	20	32	62	29
19-2	21	42	75	31
19-3	23	39	77	48
19-4	27	39	92	53

It will be apparent that there is a strong seasonal element in the above data (low in Quarter 1 and high in Quarter 3) and that there is a generally upward trend.

The steps in analysing the data are:

Step 1: Calculate the trend in the data using the least squares method.

Step 2: Estimate the sales for each quarter using the regression formula established in step 1.

Step 3: Calculate the percentage variation of each quarter's actual sales from the estimates obtained in Step 2.

Step 4. Average the percentage variations from Step 3. This establishes the average seasonal variations.

Step 5. Prepare forecast based on trend ± percentage seasonal variations.

Step 1.

Calculate the trend in the data by calculating the least squares linear regression line

$$y = a + bx$$

by the procedure explained in Chapter 7

x (quarters)	y (sales)	xy	x^2
1	20	20	1
2	32	64	4
3	62	186	9
4	29	116	16
5	21	105	25
6	42	252	36
7	75	525	49
8	31	248	64
9	23	207	81
10	39	390	100
11	77	847	121
12	48	576	144
13	27	351	169
14	39	546	196
15	92	1380	225
16	53	848	256
$\sum x = 136$	$\sum y = 710$	$\sum xy = 6661$	$\sum x^2 = 1496$

Table 3

Least squares equations

$$
\begin{aligned}
\sum y &= an + b\sum x \\
\sum xy &= a\sum x + b\sum x^2 \\
710 &= 16a + 136b \\
6661 &= 136a + 1496b \\
\therefore 626 &= 340b \\
b &= 1.84 \text{ and substituting we obtain} \\
a &= 28.74 \\
\text{Trendline} = \quad y &= 28.74 + 1.84x
\end{aligned}
$$

Steps 2 and 3

Using the trend line to calculate the sales for each quarter i.e. the estimate of $y = Ye$. Using this figure calculate the percentage variation of the difference between actual sales (y) and the trend estimate (Ye) to the trend estimate (Ye).

This is shown on the following table:

x	y	Ye	Percentage Variation $\frac{(y - Ye)}{(Ye)}100$(to nearest %)
1	20	30.58	-35
2	32	32.42	-1
3	62	34.26	+81
4	29	36.10	-20
5	21	37.94	-45
6	42	39.78	+6
7	75	41.62	+80
8	31	43.46	-29
9	23	45.30	-49
10	39	47.14	-18
11	77	48.98	+57
12	48	50.82	-6
13	27	52.66	-49
14	39	54.50	-29
15	92	56.34	+63
16	53	58.18	-8

Table 4

Trend Estimates and Percentage Variations

Step 4.

Average the percentage variations to find the average seasonal variations.

	Q_1	Q_2	Q_3	Q_4
	-35	-1	+81	-20
	-45	+6	+80	-29
	-49	-18	+57	-6
	-49	-29	+63	-8
	-178	-42	+281	-63
$\div 4 =$	**-45%**	**-11%**	**+70%**	**-16%**

Table 5

Step 5.

Prepare final forecast based on the trend estimate and the percentage variation found. Note that the percentage variation is the amount that the actual sales were above or below the trend line expressed as a percentage of the trend. The seasonally adjusted forecast is given in the following table:

x	y	Seasonally adjusted Forecast
1	20	16.82
2	32	28.85
3	62	58.24
4	29	30.32
5	21	20.87
6	42	35.40
7	75	70.75
8	31	36.51
9	23	24.92
10	39	41.95
11	77	83.27
12	48	42.69
13	27	28.96
14	39	48.50
15	92	95.78
16	53	48.87

Table 6

Seasonally adjusted Forecasts

Note:

Each of the forecasts is produced by adjusting the trend value (Ye) by the appropriate seasonal adjustment.

eg for Q_1 Ye = 30.58 (Table 4) and seasonal adjustment
= -45% (Table 5)

Seasonally adjusted forecast

$$= 30.58(1 - .45)$$

$$= \underline{\underline{16.82}}$$

Extrapolation using the trend and seasonal factors.

Once the formulae above have been calculated, they can be used to forecast (extrapolate) future sales. If it is required to estimate the sales for the next year (ie Quarters 17, 18, 19 and 20 in our series) this is done as follows:

Quarter 17.

$$\text{Basic Trend} = 28.74 + 1.84(17)$$

$$= 60.02$$

Seasonal adjustment for a first quarter = -45%

$$\text{Adjusted Forecast} = 60.02(1 - .45)$$

$$= \underline{\underline{33.01}}$$

A similar process produces the following figures.

Adjusted forecasts

Quarter 18	=	55.06
19	=	108.30
20	=	55.05

Notes:

a. Time series decomposition is not an adaptive forecasting system like moving averages and exponential smoothing.

b. Forecasts produced by such an analysis should always be treated with caution. Changing conditions and changing seasonal factors make long term forecasting a difficult task.

MEASURING FORECAST ERRORS.

22. Errors in forecasts may arise from many causes, for example, the choice of the incorrect forecasting system or the choice of the incorrect α value in exponential smoothing or a substantial change in usage or sales patterns. Whatever the cause, management wish to know the extent of the forecast errors and various methods exist to calculate these errors. A commonly used technique, appropriate to time series, is to calculate the ***mean squared error of the deviations between forecast and actual*** and choose the forecasting system and/or parameters which gives the lowest value of mean squared errors, ie akin to the 'least squares' method of establishing a regression line.

ILLUSTRATION OF MEAN SQUARED ERROR CALCULATION

23. The forecasts produced for July to January by the 3 monthly and 6 monthly moving average calculations in Table 1 will be used as a basis for an illustrative calculation.

Extract from Table 1

	Actual Sales (units)	3 monthly moving Average	Forecast Error	Squared Error	6 monthly moving Average	Forecast Error	Squared Error
July	370	397	+27	729	423	+53	2809
Aug.	360	383	+23	529	410	+50	2500
Sept.	410	377	-33	1089	397	-13	169
Oct.	450	380	-70	4900	388	-62	3844
Nov.	470	407	-63	3969	395	-75	5625
Dec.	490	443	-47	2209	410	-80	6400
Jan	460	470	+10	100	425	-35	1225
				13525			22572

Table 7

Mean Squared Errors are

$$\text{3 monthly M.A.} = \frac{13525}{7-1} = \underline{2254}$$

$$\text{and 6 monthly M.A.} = \frac{22572}{7-1} = \underline{3762}$$

On the basis of the few readings available the 3 monthly moving average would be preferred to the 6 monthly.

Note: The denominator of the above calculations will be recognised as the degrees of freedom i.e. $n-1$.

LONGER TERM FORECASTING

24. Moving averages, exponential smoothing and decomposition methods tend to be used for short to medium term forecasting. Longer term forecasting is usually less detailed and is normally concerned with forecasting the main trends on a year by year basis. Any of the techniques of regression analysis described in the preceding chapters could be used depending on the assumptions about linearity or non-linearity, the number of independent variables and so on. The least squares regression approach is often used for trend forecasting and is illustrated below.

FORECASTING USING LEAST SQUARES

EXAMPLE 2

25. Data have been kept of sales over the last seven years.

YEAR	1	2	3	4	5	6	7
SALES	14	17	15	23	18	22	27

(in '000 Units)

It is required to forecast the sales for year 8 and to calculate the coefficient of determination, the confidence intervals for the regression line and for the individual forecast.

SOLUTION

The data are drawn on a time series graph where x_1, the independent variable representing time is represented on the horizontal axis of Figure 1. Note that unlike a scatterdiagram, the points are joined. The least squares line of best fit will become the linear trend when plotted on the graph.

TIME SERIES GRAPH — SALES in 000's
EXAMPLE 2

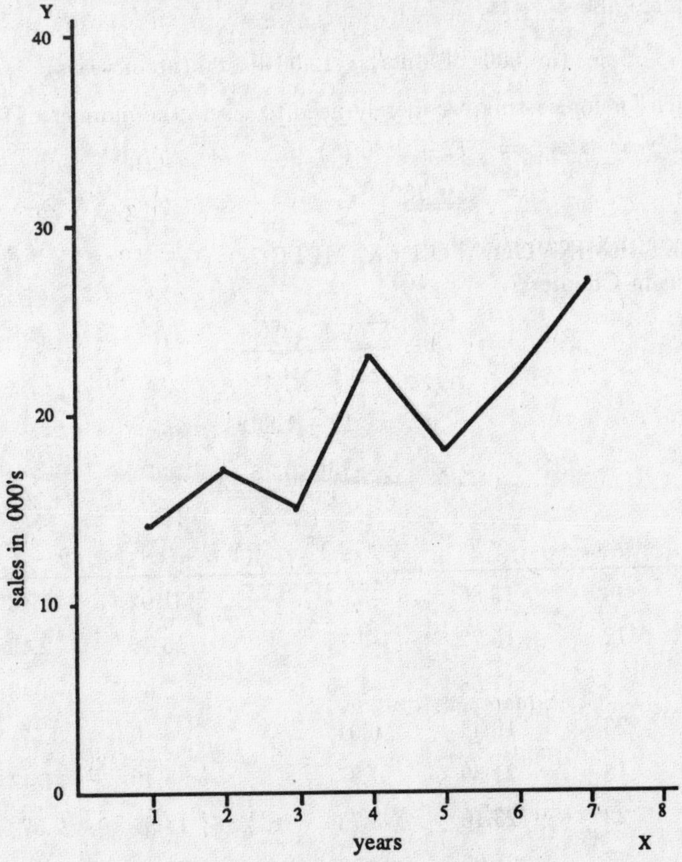

Figure 1

The calculations for the regression line are given below and follow the principles already explained in Chapter 7.

Example 2.

As there are 7 pairs of readings n = 7 the data are set out as follows:

Years(x)	Sales (y)	xy	x^2
1	14	14	1
2	17	34	4
3	15	45	9
4	23	92	16
5	18	90	25
7	27	189	49
$\sum x = 28$	$\sum y = 136$	$\sum xy = 596$	$\sum x^2 = 140$

(All calculations to two decimal places).

$$136 = 7a + 28b$$
$$596 = 28a + 140b$$
$$52 = 28b$$
$$b = \underline{1.86}$$ and substituting in one of the equations we obtain

$$\underline{a = 12}$$

$\therefore$ Regression line = $y = 12 + 1.86x$ or
in terms of the problem above

Sales (in '000s of units) = 12.00 + 1.86 (no of years)

To use this expression for forecasting, we merely need to insert the number of the year required.

For example, 8th year sales = 12 + 1.86 (8)

= $\underline{26.88}$

COEFFICIENT OF DETERMINATION FOR EXAMPLE 2

26. This is calculated as in Chapter 7.

$$r^2 = \frac{\sum(YE - \overline{Y})^2}{\sum(Y - \overline{Y})^2}$$

$$y = 12 + 1.86x$$

$$\therefore \overline{Y} = \frac{136}{7} = \underline{19.43}$$

$x(years)$	$y(sales)$	YE	$YE - \overline{Y}$	$(YE - \overline{Y})^2$	$y - \overline{Y}$	$(y - \overline{Y})^2$
1	14	13.86	−5.57	31.02	−5.43	29.48
2	17	15.72	−3.71	13.76	−2.43	5.90
3	15	17.58	−1.85	3.42	−4.43	19.62
4	23	19.44	0.01	0	3.57	12.74
5	18	21.30	1.87	3.49	−1.43	2.04
6	22	23.16	3.73	13.91	2.57	6.60
7	<u>27</u>	25.02	5.59	<u>31.24</u>	7.57	<u>57.30</u>
	$\sum y = 136$		$\sum(YE - \overline{Y})^2$	= 96.84	$\sum(y - \overline{Y})^2$	= 133.68

Table 2

$$r^2 = \frac{\sum(YE - \overline{Y})^2}{\sum(y - \overline{Y})^2} = \frac{96.84}{133.68} = \underline{\underline{72.44\%}} = \underline{\underline{72\%}}$$

This can be interpreted that in the example given 72% of the variations of the actual values of y (sales) may be predicted by changes in the actual values of x (years). In other words, factors other than changes in the value of x influence y to the extent of (100 – 72)% ie 28% .

THE STANDARD ERROR OF REGRESSION

Again this is calculated as

$$S_e = \sqrt{\frac{\sum y^2 - a\sum y - b\sum xy}{n-2}} = \sqrt{\frac{2776 - 12 \times 136 - 1.86 \times 596}{7-2}}$$
$$= \underline{\underline{2.66}} \text{ (Sales in '000's of units)}$$

ESTABLISHMENT OF CONFIDENCE INTERVALS FOR EXAMPLE 2

27. There is no difference in approach in setting confidence interval for time series forecasting compared with the techniques shown in chapter 7. The confidence intervals will be calculated without detailed explanation.

$$S_{ef} = Se\sqrt{\frac{1}{n} + \frac{(x - \overline{x})2}{\sum x^2 - \frac{(\sum x)^2}{n}}}$$

$$\overline{x} = 4$$

$(x - \overline{x})^2$ varies as follows

$$X = 1 \quad (1-4)^2 = 9$$
$$X = 2 \quad (2-4)^2 = 4$$
$$X = 3 \quad (3-4)^2 = 1$$
$$X = 4 \quad (4-4)^2 = 0$$
$$X = 5 \quad (5-4)^2 = 1$$
$$X = 6 \quad (6-4)^2 = 4$$
$$X = 7 \quad (7-4)^2 = 9$$

$$\sum X^2 - \frac{(\sum X)^2}{n} = 140 - 112 = 28$$

The expression $\sqrt{\frac{1}{n} + \frac{(X - \overline{X})^2}{\sum X^2 - \frac{(\sum X)^2}{n}}}$

will vary as below:

$X = 1:$ gives 0.6813851

$X = 2:$ gives 0.5345224

$X = 3:$ gives 0.4225771

$X = 4:$ gives 0.3779644

$X = 5:$ gives 0.4225771

$X = 6:$ gives 0.5345224

$X = 7:$ gives 0.6813851

For each value of X, the fitted values are as follows:

$X = 1 \quad Y = 13.86$

$X = 2 \quad Y = 15.72$

$X = 3 \quad Y = 17.58$

$X = 4 \quad Y = 19.44$

$X = 5 \quad Y = 21.30$

$X = 6 \quad Y = 23.16$

$X = 7 \quad Y = 25.02$

The 95% confidence intervals are summarised (assuming $7 - 2 = 5$ d. of f. and t score of 2.571)

X	Lower Limit	Upper Limit
1	9.36	18.51
2	12.09	19.35
3	14.71	20.45
4	16.84	22.04
5	18.43	24.17
6	19.53	26.79
7	20.37	29.67

These values are plotted on Figure 2

LINE OF BEST FIT AND CONFIDENCE INTERVALS

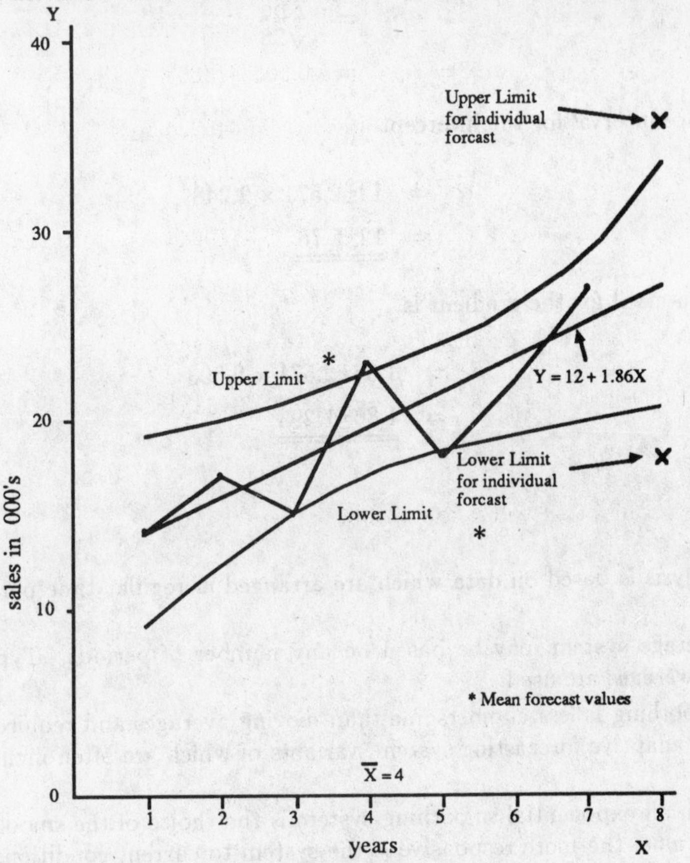

Figure 2

Using similar principles to those previously explained the 95% confidence intervals for the individual forecast for the 8th year can be calculated and at the 95% level, are as follows:

$$\text{Sales in year 8} = 26.88 \pm 2.571\ (3.48)$$
$$= 26.88 \pm 8.95$$

Thus it is possible to say that, assuming past conditions apply in the future, there is a 95% probability that sales in year 8 will lie between 17,930 units and 35,830 units.

These limits have also been plotted in Figure 2.

CONFIDENCE INTERVALS FOR PARAMETERS

28. Although not requested in Example 2 it is also possible to calculate the confidence intervals for the intercept and slope of the line. This is done below using the data from the problem.

$$a = 12 \qquad \sum x^2 = 140$$
$$b = 1.86 \qquad \sum x = 28$$
$$n = 7 \qquad Se = 2.66$$
$$\sum x^2 - \frac{\sum x^2}{n} = 28$$

Standard Error of the Intercept

$$S_a = 2.66 \times \sqrt{\frac{140}{7 \times 28}}$$
$$= 2.248$$

The standard error of the Gradient

$$S_b = \frac{2.66}{\sqrt{28}}$$
$$= 0.503$$

The 95% confidence interval for the intercept

$$\alpha = 12 \pm 2.571 \times 2.248$$
$$= \underline{\underline{12 \pm 5.78}}$$

The 95% confidence interval for the gradient is

$$\beta = 1.86 \pm 2.571 \times 0.503$$
$$= \underline{\underline{1.86 \pm 1.293}}$$

SUMMARY

29.

a. Time series analysis is based on data which are arranged in regular time periods, eg sales per month.

b. The moving average system may be based on any number of periods. Typically 3, 6 or 12 month moving averages are used.

c. Exponential smoothing is less cumbersome than moving averages and requires much less data storage. It is an adaptive forecasting system, variants of which are often included in inventory control systems.

d. The key factor in an exponential smoothing system is the choice of the smoothing constant, α The higher the value, the more responsive is the system to current conditions. Typical values are from 0.3 to 0.5.

e. Time series decomposition, or time series analysis, separates out from the data, the trend, seasonal factors and the cyclical movement.

f. To enable the best forecasting system to be chosen, it is necessary to calculate the forecast errors. A common method is to calculate the mean squared error of the deviations.

g. The techniques of least squares regression are frequently used for time series analysis.

POINTS TO NOTE.

30.

a. The basic forecasting methods and principles have been described in the last three chapters, but many hybrid systems exist in practice.

b. Questions involving forecasting could occur in virtually any syllabus, perhaps on their own or as part of some other topic.

c. For short term forecasting single and double exponential smoothing systems are the most commonly used and most computer based stock control and forecasting systems incorporate these methods. For longer term forecasting the use of trend curves developed by mathematical regression, are the most useful in terms of reliability.

SELF REVIEW QUESTIONS.

1. *What is meant by forecasting? (2)*
2. *Distinguish between quanlitalive and qualitative forecasting techniques (5, 6, 7)*
3. *What is the Delphi Technique? (7)*
4. *What is Time Series Analysis? (11)*
5. *What is the Moving Averages system of forecasting? (12)*

6. What are the limitations of the basic moving averages system and how does exponential smoothing overcome these? (14 and 15)

7. What are the main characteristics of exponential smoothing? (15 and 16)

8. Into what factors can a Time Series be separated? (20)

9. What are the steps in Time Series Decomposition? (21)

10.How can forecast errors be caculated? (22)

11.How may correlation and regression techniques be applied to time series forecasting? (24)

EXERCISES WITH ANSWERS COMMENCING PAGE 488

A1. Calculate the 3 and 6 monthly averages of the following data.

	Sales
January	*1200*
February	*1280*
March	*1310*
April	*1270*
May	*1190*
June	*1290*
July	*1410*
August	*1360*
September	*1430*
October	*1280*
November	*1410*
December	*1390*

A2. Using the January sales as the old forecast and a smoothing constant of 0.3 (α value) calculate the forecast for February onwards using Exponential smoothing.

A3. Calculate the forecast errors for the 3 and 6 monthly moving averages calculated in A1.

EXAMINATION QUESTIONS WITH ANSWERS COMMENCING PAGE 488

A4. In March and April 1983, 'Management Accounting' included two articles concerning the use of forecasts and forecasting techniques by management. The following questions should be answered within the context of the use and value of forecasting techniques to the management of economic entities.

You are required to:

(a) list two basic forecasting techniques within each of the following categories.

(i) subjective

(ii) purely statistical;

(iii) causal model-building;

(b) list eight significantly different factors which it is considered limit the accuracy of forecasts and discuss briefly four of them;

(c) describe briefly a technique which could provide accurate short-term cash flow forecasts.

(CIMA QUANTITATIVE TECHNQUES)

EXERCISES WITHOUT ANSWERS COMMENCING PAGE

B1. The following data have been recorded for sales over the last four years.

Sales in '000s

Year 1	70	32	55	60
2	65	29	50	58
3	76	43	58	62
4	83	54	65	71

Calculate the trend in the data using the least squares method.

B2. Use the trend line in B! to calculate the estimated sales for each quarter and the percentage variation.

B3. Find the average seasonal variation in B2 and prepare the final forecast based on the trend in B1 and the average seasonal variations.

EXAMINATION QUESTION WITHOUT ANSWERS

B4. A hop growers association is analysisng demand for its hops and has collected the following data:

Year to December	Bushels of hops purchased (000 bushels)	Average price per bushel £
1972	500	9.00
1973	530	8.60
1974	510	11.60
1975	580	9.50
1976	600	9.30
1977	600	13.00
1978	630	11.50

Theassociation's statistician has calculated the following equations and test statistics in relation to the above information:

i. *Quantity purchased (y) in relation to time(x):*

$$y = 4.75.7 + 22.14x$$

R^2 *(unadjusted)* $= .8931$; *F ratio* $= 41.78$;
Regression coefficient t value $= 6.464$

ii. *Quantity purchased (y) in relation to price (x):*

$$y = 410.7 + 14.96x$$

R^2 *(unadjusted)* $= .22.46$; *F ratio* $= 1.45$;
Regression coefficient t value $= 1.204$

iii. *Deviation of quantity purchased from trend (y) (as expected in (i) above) in relation to price (x):*

$$y = 611.2 - .59x$$

R^2 *(unadjusted)* $= ..3300$; *F ratio* $= 2.46$;
Regression coefficient t value $= 1.569$

You are required to:

a. describe the information given by the R^2 *F and t statistics, using the information in the sections (i) to (iii) above to illustrate your answer;*

b. examine each question in turn and discuss its suitability for use as a predictor of the demand for hops;

c. give two other factors which could be present in the situation and exerting an influence on the demand for hpops.

(CIMA Quantitative Techniques)

10 Calculus

INTRODUCTION

1. Calculus does not appear directly in all syllabuses but questions in other areas often require a working knowledge of the results of calculus. Thus this chapter has been included covering elementary calculus.

Calculus is a large and complex area of mathematics with applications in many different fields. This manual does not purport to cover the whole range of calculus and concentrates only upon applications in accounting and business which are likely to be relevant for the intended readership.

Emphasis is given to the *use* of calculus and not to formal mathematical proofs. Differential calculus is given more attention because of its use in finding critical values such as marginal revenue and points of maximum profit or minimum cost.

The rules and procedures given are operating rules only and exceptions can occur in particular circumstances but it is felt that these should not occur in the examinations at which this manual is aimed.

WHY IS CALCULUS USED?

2. Frequently it is possible to represent relationships by simple linear functions.

For example, a simple linear function for total cost might have the form:

$$y = a + bx$$

where

y = total cost, the dependent variable.

x = output or activity, the independent variable and a and b are constants.

representing fixed cost and variable (or marginal) cost respectively.

Such a function is shown in Figure 1

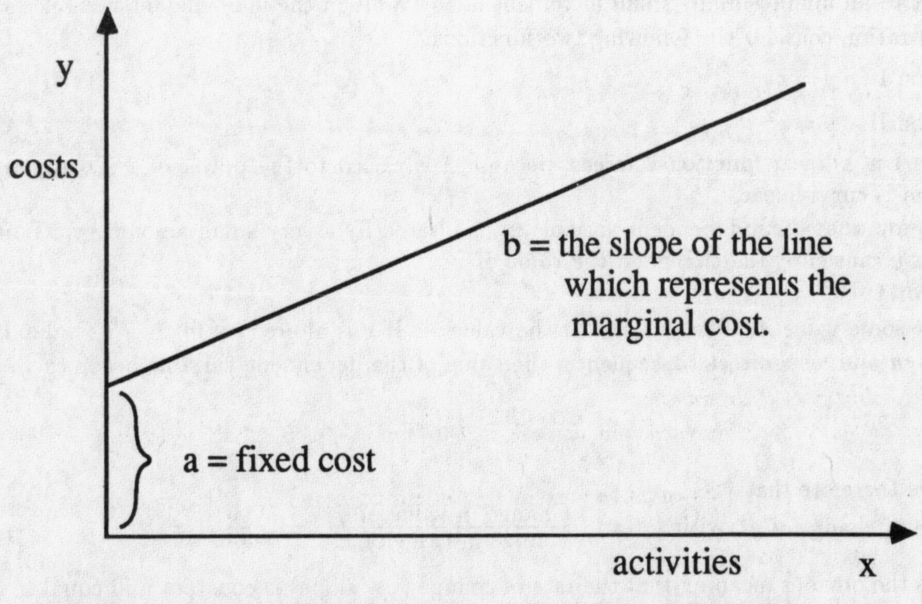

GRAPH OF A SIMPLE LINEAR COST FUNCTION. Figure 1

In such a function the rate of change of cost (represented by "b", the gradient of the line) is constant at all levels of activity and will not increase or decrease at any level of activity. This is, of couse what is meant by a linear function. The value of b can be easily found by simple arithmetic without recourse to more sophisticated techniques.

However, there are many occasions when a linear function is not an accurate representation of reality and some form of curvi-linear function is required. Some examples are given in Figure 2.

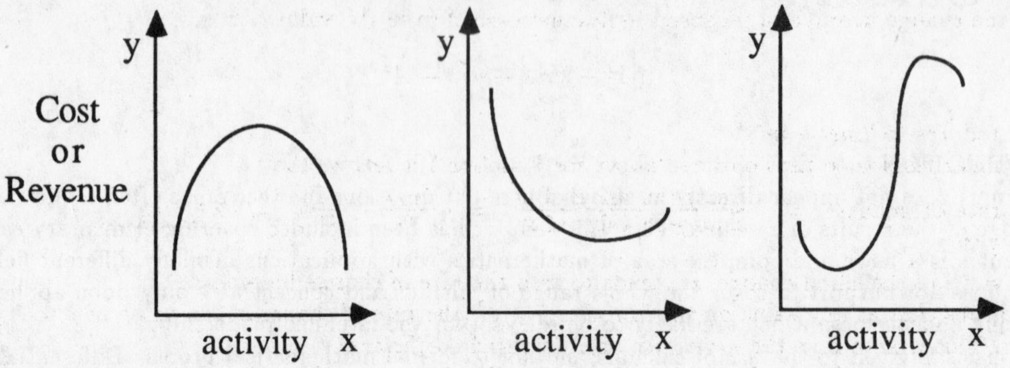

EXAMPLES OF CURVI-LINEAR FUNCTIONS. Figure 2.

Examination of curvilinear functions shows that the slope or gradient changes at various activity levels and that at some maximum or minimum value - or both - there is a turning point. For many business applications it is essential to know the *rate of change* of a function (representing say, marginal cost or marginal revenue) and also the point of zero gradient, the *turning point* (representing, say, maximum revenue or minimum cost). The process of *differentiation* provides a ready means of finding the rates of change of curvi-linear functions and of their turning points and it can thus be used as a simple means of optimising.

In addition, it is sometimes necessary to be able to calculate the total amount of revenue or cost between two activity levels on a curvi-linear function. This is done by the process of *integration* which provides the means of summation for such functions.

DIFFERENTIATION.

3. The process of differentiation establishes the slope of the graph of a function at a particular point. Alternatively this can be described as establishing the rate of change of the dependent variable (say, cost) with respect to an infinitesimally small increment in the value of the independent variable (say, activity).

For illustration consider the following two functions:

Function I $\quad y = x$

Function II $\quad y = x^2$

Function I is a linear function whereas, because x is raised to the power of 2 (i.e.x^2) in Function II, that function is curvi-linear.

Assume now that the independent variable, x, is altered by a very small amount, m. What is the rate of change in y caused by the change in the value of x?

Function I

If x is at some value A, then y is also at the value A. If x is altered by m then its value becomes $x = A + m$ and, as a direct consequence, the value of the dependent variable becomes

$$y = A + m.$$

It follows therefore that:-

The rate of change of y with x $= \dfrac{\text{Change in value of } y}{\text{change in value of } x} = \dfrac{m}{m} = 1$

This has the obvious meaning that the rate of change (i.e. slope) is constant and equal to one so that y changes by exactly the same amount as x, regardless of the level of activity or the amount of the change.

Function II

What is the consequence of x change from $x = A$ to $x = A + m$, along the function $y = x^2$?

$$\begin{aligned} &\text{When } x = A & y &= A^2 \\ &\text{When } x = A + m & y &= (A+m)^2 = A^2 + 2mA + m^2 \end{aligned}$$

Thus the change in value of y caused by the increase of m in the value of x is

$$(A^2 + 2mA + m^2) - A^2$$

which reduces to $2mA + m^2$

In a similar fashion to that outlined above for Function I it follows that:

$$\text{The rate of change of y with x} = \frac{\text{change in value of } y}{\text{change in value of } x} = \frac{2mA}{m} + \frac{m^2}{m} = \underline{\underline{2A + m}}$$

If the value of the small change, m, tends to zero the rate of change becomes $2A$.

This means that at any value on the function $y = x^2$, the rate of change in the value of y with respect ot x is $2x$. This is known as the *derivative* or *differential coefficient*.

Thus the derivative for the function $y = x^2$ is $2x$. The following tables gives some numerical examples for this function.

Value of x (independent variable)	Value of y (dependent variable) $y = x^2$	Rate of Change of y i.e. the value of the derivative, $2x$.
1	1	1
2	4	4
3	9	6
4	16	8
5	25	10
6	36	12
7	49	14

Notes

a. The small change in value denoted above as m, is conventionally known as Δx (delta x). As this value tends towards zero i.e. $\Delta x \to 0$, the comparison of the changes in value becomes:

$$\text{Limit}_{\Delta x \to 0} \frac{\Delta y}{\Delta x}$$

generally written as $\frac{dy}{dx}$, which means the derivative of a function when Δx tends towards zero.

$$\begin{aligned} \text{Thus, Original function:} \quad y &= x^2 \\ \text{Derivative:} \quad \frac{dy}{dx} &= 2x \end{aligned}$$

b. The derivative of a function gives the *exact* rate of change at a *point* and only gives an approximate result when used over a finite range. An example of the effect of this is where differentiation is used to obtain the marginal cost from a curvi-linear cost function. Accountants frequently define marginal cost as the increase in total cost due to an increase in output of one unit. A whole unit is a finite range as far as differentiation is concerned and consequently the marginal cost obtained from the derivative is only an approximation. This is a technical point which is considered not to be of great practical significance.

RULES FOR FINDING DERIVATIVES

4. In a similar fashion to that outlined above the derivative of any type of function could be found from first principles. However, this would be a tedious, lengthy process and, once the general ideas of differentiation is understood, it is much simpler to follow a few simple rules which are shown in the following paragraphs.

DERIVATIVES - THE BASIC RULE

5. Where the function is $y = x_n$

$$\text{The derivative } \frac{dy}{dy} = nx^{n-1}$$

Examples

Function	Derivative
$y = x^2$	$\frac{dy}{dx} = 2x$
$y = x^{10}$	$\frac{dy}{dx} = 10x^9$
$y = -x^2$	$\frac{dy}{dx} = -2x$
$y = \sqrt{x}($ i.e. $x^{\frac{1}{2}})$	$\frac{dy}{dx} = \frac{1}{2}x^{-\frac{1}{2}}$ or $\frac{1}{2\sqrt{x}}$

Note: All the other rules are merely extensions of the basic method so it must be understood at this stage. All that is necessary is to multiply x by its original index and to realise that the new index of x is one less than the original value.

DERIVATES – WHERE THE FUNCTION HAS A COEFFICIENT

6. Where $y = kx^n$ (k is the coefficient)

$$\frac{dy}{dx} = nkx^{n-1}$$

Examples

Function	*Derivative*
$y = 3x^2$	$\frac{dy}{dx} = 6x$
$y = 8x^4$	$\frac{dy}{dx} = 32x^3$
$y = -7x^5$	$\frac{dy}{dx} = -35x^4$
$y = \frac{1}{2}x^9$	$\frac{dy}{dx} = 4.5x^8$
$y = 3x$	$\frac{dy}{dx} = 3$

DERIVATIVES-WHERE THE FUNCTION CONTAINS A CONSTANT

7. Where $y = x^n + c$ (c is the constant)

$$\frac{dy}{dx} = nx^{n-1}$$

Examples

Function	Derivative
$y = x^3 + 8$	$\frac{dy}{dx} = 3x^2$
$y = 6x^4 + 27$	$\frac{dy}{dx} = 24x^3$
$y = \frac{1}{3}x^3 - 15$	$\frac{dy}{dx} = x^2$

Note: On differentiation the constant disppears. This is to be expected because the derivative measures the rate of change and a constant (e.g. fixed cost) by definition does not change.

DERIVATIVES – WHERE THE FUNCTION IS A SUM

8. Where $y = x^n + x^m$

$$\frac{dy}{dx} = nx^{n-1} + mx^{m-1}$$

Examples

Function	Derivative
$y = x^2 + 6x^4$	$\frac{dy}{dx} = 2x + 24x^3$
$y = \frac{1}{6}x^2 - 12x^5$	$\frac{dy}{dx} = \frac{1}{3}x - 60x^4$
$y = 3x^4 + 10x^2 + 9x^3$	$\frac{dy}{dx} = 12x^3 + 20x + 27x^2$

DERIVATIVES – WHERE THE FUNCTION IS A PRODUCT

9. Let m and n represent function of x and $y = mn$ then

$$\frac{d}{dx}(mn) = m\frac{dn}{dx} + n\frac{dm}{dx}$$

To illustrate this consider the function

$$y = (8x + 4)(2x^3 + 6)$$

$(8x + 4)$ represents m and

$(2x^3 + 6)$ represents n

$$\therefore \quad \frac{dm}{dx} = 8$$

$$\frac{dn}{dx} = 6x^2$$

$$\therefore \quad \frac{dy}{dx} = (8x + 4)6x^2 + (2x^3 + 6)8$$

$$= 48x^3 + 24x^2 + 16x^3 + 48$$

$$= 64x^3 + 24x^2 + 48$$

Examples

Function	Derivative
$y = (10x^2 + 5)(3x^3 + 2)$	$(10x^2 + 5).9x^2 + (3x^3 + 2).20x$
$y = (x^2 + 4)(6x^{\frac{1}{2}} + 3)$	$(x^2 + 4).3x^{-\frac{1}{2}} + (6x^{\frac{1}{2}} + 3).2x$

DERIVATIVES-WHERE THE FUNCTION IS A QUOTIENT

10. Let m represent the function of x which is the numerator and n represents the function which is the denominator, then:

$$y = \frac{m}{n} \text{ and } \frac{dy}{dx} = \frac{n\frac{dm}{dx} - m\frac{dn}{dx}}{n^2}, n \neq 0$$

As an illustration consider the function

$$y = \frac{4x^3 + 2}{x^6} \quad \text{so} \quad \frac{dm}{dx} = 12x^2$$

$$\text{and} \quad \frac{dn}{dx} = 6x^5$$

$$\therefore \frac{dy}{dx} = \frac{x^6.12x^2 - (4x^3+2)6x^6}{(x^6)^2}$$
$$= \frac{12x^8 - 24x^8 - 12x^5}{x^{12}}$$
$$= -(\frac{12x^5 + 12x^8}{x^{12}})$$
$$= -(\frac{12+12x^3}{x^7})$$

Examples

Function	Derivative
$y = \frac{3-2x}{3+2x}$	$\frac{dy}{dx} = \frac{-12}{(3+2x)^2}$
$y = \frac{x}{1-4x^2}$	$\frac{dy}{dx} = \frac{1+4x^2}{(1-4x^2)^2}$

DERIVATIVES – FUNCTIONS OF A FUNCTION

11. Where $y = (2x+6)^3$ and the expression in the brackets is a differentiable function say, m, i.e. $m = 2x+6$, the whole expression can be written as $y = m^3$.

In such cases the rule for differentiation is $\frac{dy}{dx} = \frac{dy}{dm} \times \frac{dm}{dx}$ which is known as the *chain rule.*

Thus to differentiate $y = (2x+6)^3$

let $m = 2x+6$ then $y = m^3$

and $\frac{dy}{dm} = 3m^2$ and $\frac{dm}{dx} = 2$

$$\therefore \frac{dy}{dx} = 3(2x+6)^2.2$$
$$= \underline{\underline{6(2x+6)^2}}$$

Examples

Functions	Derivatives
$y = (1-6x)^6$	$\frac{dy}{dx} = -36(1-6x)^5$
$y = (8+4x-x^2)^{\frac{1}{2}}$	$\frac{dy}{dx} = (2-x)(8+4x-x^2)^{-\frac{1}{2}}$
	or $\frac{2-x}{y}$

Note: The derivative $\frac{dy}{dx}$ is the inverse of the derivative $\frac{dx}{dy}$ i.e.

$$\frac{dy}{dx} = \frac{1}{(\frac{dx}{dy})}$$

A PRACTICAL EXAMPLE OF DIFFERENTIATION.

12. Now that the idea of differentiation has been explained and the rules given for differentiating common functions, a practical example can be considered.

A firm has analysed their operating conditions, prices and costs and have developed the following functions.

Revenue $£(R) = 400Q - 4Q^2$ and Cost $£(C) = Q^2 + 10Q + 30$ where Q is the number of units sold
The firm wishes to maximise profit and wishes to know

a. What quantity should be sold?
b. At what price?
c. What will be the amount of profit?

Note: Previous examples have used y and x which results in the derivative $\frac{dy}{dx}$.
This example uses R, C and Q and results in the derivatives $\frac{dR}{dQ}$ and $\frac{dC}{dQ}$

Solution.
From basic economic theory it will be recalled that profit is maximised when Marginal Cost = Marginal Revenue and, as explained in this chapter, differentiating a function gives the rate of change of that function which is equivalent to the marginal cost or revenue.

$$£R = 400Q - 4Q^2 \text{ and } \frac{dR}{dQ} = 400 - 8Q = \text{Marginal Revenue}$$

$$\text{and } £C = Q^2 + 10Q + 30 \text{ and } \frac{dC}{dQ} = 2Q + 10 = \text{Marginal Cost}$$

Point of profit maximisation is when

$$MR = MC \text{ or } \frac{dR}{dQ} = \frac{dC}{dQ}$$

i.e. $400 - 8Q = 2Q + 10$

$\therefore$ Q = 39 answer (a)

Total Revenue = 400(39) – 4(39²)

= £9516 and as 39 will be sold

the price will be $\frac{9516}{39}$ = £244 each answer (b)

Total Profit = Revenue - Cost

Revenue = £9516 from above and

Cost = $(39)^2 + 10(39) + 30$ = 1941

$\therefore$ Profit = £7575 answer (c)

TURNING POINTS

13. Some functions have turning points i.e. points of local minima or maxima and these points are of particular interest in many business applications because they represent points of minimum cost or maximum profit or revenue.

Figure 3 shows two such turning points

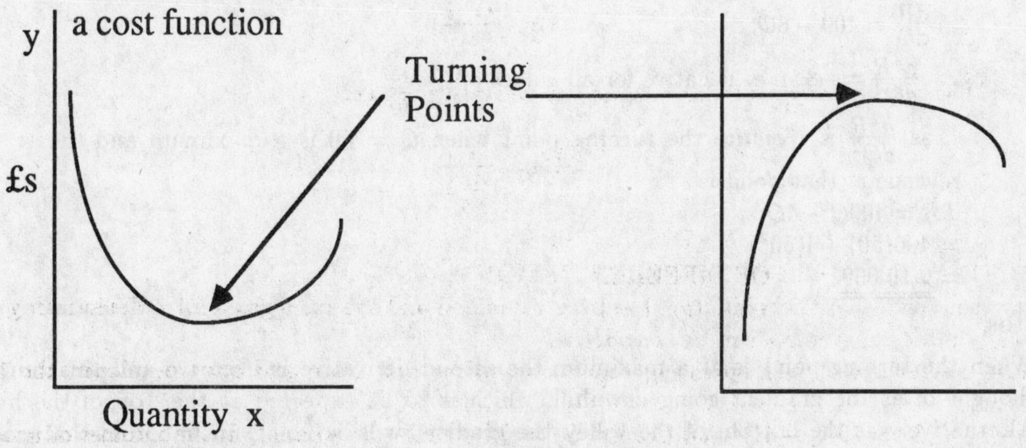

Figure 3.

These points are points of zero slope or gradient and can be likened to the exact top of a hill. One climbs up to the summit and once it has been passed one starts to go down. On the exact top-most point (or bottom-most point) one is not going up or down so there is zero gradient. At that point, if a tangent is drawn it will be parallel to the x axis i.e. horizontal.

USING DIFFERENTIATION THE FIND TURNING POINTS

14. The derivative of a function shows the slope or rate of change of the function. If the derivative is calculated and equated to zero this will show the turning point of the function.

For many functions this turning point will be the required maximum or minimum point. However, there are certain functions which have two (or indeed more than two) turning points so that it is necessary to test whether the calculated turning point is at a maximum or minimum value.

This is done by calculating the *second derivative*, designated as $\frac{d^2y}{dx^2}$ (d two y, dx squared).

The second derivative is found by differentiating the first derivative, i.e. $\frac{dy}{dx}$ using the normal rules of differentiation. If the second derivative is *negative* the turning point is a *maximum*, if the second derivative is *positive* the turning point is a minimum.

This procedure is summarised in the following table.

TO FIND THE MAXIMUM OR MINIMUM VALUE OF A FUNCTION

Step 1 Find first derivative of the function

i.e. $\frac{dy}{dx}$

Step 2 Set $\frac{dy}{dx}$ to zero and calculate the turning point where, say x = a

Step 3 Find the second derivative i.e. $\frac{d^2y}{dx^2}$, by differentiating the first derivative.

Step 4 If $\frac{d^2y}{dx^2}$ is NEGATIVE at the point $x = a$ the turning point is a MAXIMUM

If $\frac{d^2y}{dx^2}$ is POSITIVE at the point $x = a$ the turning point is a MINIMUM

Example

Find the point of maximum value of the Revenue function in Paragraph 12.

i.e. $R = 400Q - 4Q^2$

Step 1 $\frac{dr}{dQ} = 400 - 8Q$

Step 2 At the turning point $\frac{dy}{dx} = 0$

$\therefore\ 400 - 8Q = 0$

$\therefore\ Q = \underline{50}$

Step 3 $\frac{dR}{dQ} = 400 - 8Q$

$\therefore\ \frac{d^2R}{dQ^2} = -8$ i.e. negative for all values of Q.

Step 4 as $\frac{d^2R}{dQ^2}$ is *Negative* the turning point when $Q = 50$ is a maximum and the revenue at that point is

$£R = 400Q - 4Q^2$

$= 400(50) - 4(50^2)$

$= \underline{\underline{£10{,}000}}$

Notes

a. When the turning point is at a maximum the second derivative is negative and this can be thought of as the gradient going downhill, which is to be expected at the 'top of the hill'. Alternatively at the bottom of the valley the gradient will be going up hill from that point which is shown by the second derivative being positive.

b. On occasions the second derivative will be found to be zero. This denotes what is known as an *inflexional point*, which is a bend in the curve, and is not a true turning point.

c. The inverse relationship between $\frac{dy}{dx}$ and $\frac{dx}{dy}$ does NOT apply to the second derivatives i.e.

$$\frac{d^2y}{dx^2} \neq \frac{1}{(\frac{d^2x}{dy^2})}$$

d. Notes (a) and (b) above are generalisations which are broadly accurate but there are specialised circumstances in which they do not apply.

DERIVATIVES WITH MORE THAN ONE INDEPENDENT VARIABLE

15. So far in this chapter the functions have contained a single independent variable, for example:

$$y = x^2 + 6x^4, \quad \text{where } y \text{ is}$$

dependent upon the value of the independent variable, x. The rules of differentiation covered earlier provide a method of finding the rates of change (slopes of the curve) for any value of x, the single independent variable.

However there are occasions where the functions contains two or more independent variables as, for example, when the cost function of a firm depends on both labour hours and machine hours. If it is required to find the rates of change in these circumstances a process known as *partial differentiation* is used.

PARTIAL DIFFERENTIATION

16. Assume that a cost function is as follows:

$$y = 10x^2 + 5z^2 - 4xz + 12$$

where

y = total cost (the dependent variable)

x = labour hours (an independent variable)

z = machine hours (an independent variable)

With such a function there is a multi-dimensional cost surface with several slopes thus:

(a) the slope when x changes but z is held constant

(b) the slope when z changes but x is held constant

(c) the slope when both x and z are changing

Each of these slopes has a special derivative. (a) and (b) are known as *partial derivatives* and (c) is known as a *total derivative.*

Here we are concerned with the partial derivatives and these are written as follows:

Partial derivative (a) above.

i.e. when x changes and z is constant $= \frac{\partial y}{\partial x}$

(this is called 'the partial derivative of y with respect to x')

Partial derivative (b) above

i.e. when z changes and x is constant $= \frac{\partial y}{\partial z}$

(this is called 'the partial derivative of y with respect to z')

Note: Learn the difference between the symbol used for partial differentiation, ∂, and the symbol used previously, d.

The derivative $\frac{dy}{dx}$ calculated in the early part of this chapter is an example of a total derivative.

RULES FOR PARTIAL DERIVATIVES

17. Fortunately, the rules already given for ordinary derivatives also apply to partial derivatives. These are illustrated using the cost function given earlier thus:

$$y = 10x^2 + 5z^2 - 4xz + 12$$

The problem is to find the partial derivatives, $\frac{\partial y}{\partial x}$ and $\frac{\partial y}{\partial z}$.

This is done by differentiating in the normal way for one of the independent variables, say x, whilst at the same time treating the other variable (z in this case) as a constant, as follows:

$$\frac{\partial y}{\partial x} = 20x - 4z$$

Note: As explained in the early part of the chapter, any part of the expression which does not contain the variable being differentiated (x in this case) disappears. Thus $5z^2$ and 12 disappear. In the case of the mixed element ($-4xz$) this is treated as $(-4z)x$, which becomes $-4z$ when differentiated with respect to x.

In a similar manner the other partial derivative is derived thus:

$$\frac{\partial y}{\partial z} = 5z - 4x$$

PRACTICAL EXAMPLE OF PARTIAL DIFFERENTIATION

18. DIY Ltd supply tool kits for the home handyman. Each tool kit comprises a standard plastic box which contains a variable number of tools depending on the type of tools, the market, and the wholesalers requirements. The firm has derived a profit function which shows that their profits are dependent both on the number of tool kits supplied and the number of tools in each kit. The profit function is as follows:

$$P = 8k - 0.0001K^2 + 0.05KT - 77.5T^2 - 10,000$$

$$\begin{aligned} \text{where } P &= \text{Profit in £'s} \\ K &= \text{No. of kits} \\ T &= \text{No. of tools in each kit.} \end{aligned}$$

How many tool kits containing how many tools should be sold?

SOLUTION

$$\begin{aligned} \frac{\partial P}{\partial K} &= 8 - 0.0002K + 0.05T &&= 0 \text{ at maximum} \\ \frac{\partial P}{\partial T} &= 0.05K - 155T &&= 0 \text{ at maximum} \end{aligned}$$

(Note: The second derivatives of each are negative, -0.0002 and -155, respectively indicating maxima)

$\therefore$ solving for T and substituting gives

$$\begin{aligned} 0.05K &= 155T \\ \therefore T &= \frac{0.05K}{155} = 0.0003226k \end{aligned}$$

and substituting as follows:

$$\begin{aligned} 8 - 0.0002K + 0.05(0.0003226K) &= 0 \\ \therefore 8 - 0.0001839K &= 0 \\ \therefore K = \frac{8}{0.0001839} &= \underline{\underline{43,509}} \text{ tool kits.} \end{aligned}$$

This value can be substituted into the partial derivative $\frac{\partial P}{\partial T}$ thus:

$$0.05K - 155T = 0$$

$$0.05(43509) - 155T = 0$$

$$\therefore T = \frac{0.05(43509)}{155}$$

$$\simeq \underline{\textbf{14 TOOLS}}$$

Thus profit will be maximised by the sale of 43,509 kits each containing 14 tools. This gives a profit of **£63,735.**

INTEGRATION

19. For our purposes integration can be regarded as the reverse of differentiation.

Differentiation establishes the slope of the function at a point whereas integration can be defined as the procedure for finding the area under the curve of a function i.e. integration is a process of summation.

As integration is the reverse of differentiation it follows that:

ORIGINAL FUNCTION	DERIVATIVE	ORIGINAL FUNCTION	INTEGRAL
x^4	$4x^3$	$4x^3$	x^4

The integral can be written as

$$\int 4x^3\,dx = x^4$$

which can be described as

'the function which gives $4x^3$ when differentiated with respect to x is x^4

However the integral above is not complete because it will be recalled from paragraph 7 that $x^4 + 10$, or $x^4 + 50$, or $x^4 + c$, where c is any constant also have as their derivative $4x^3$ so that is is essential to recognise this possibility by writing

$$\int 4x^3\,dx = x^4 + c$$

The integral including the undetermined constant is known as the *indefinite integral.*

The value of the constant can, in some instances, be inferred to be zero or it may have a value when additional information known as an *initial condition* is supplied. Examples of both are given later in the chapter.

BASIC RULE FOR INTEGRATION.

20. As integration is the reverse of differentiation it follows that whereas differentiation reduced the index of x by 1 and used the old index as the coefficient of x, integration requires us to *increase* the index of x by 1 and then to divide through by the value of the new index.

i.e. where $y = kx^n$

$$\int y\,dx = \frac{kx^{n+1}}{n+1} + c \ (n \neq -1)$$

Examples

Functions	*Integral*	
$y = 10x^4$	$\int 10x^4\,dx = \frac{10x^5}{5} + c = 2x^5 + c$	
$y = 6x^3 + 2x + 3$	$\int(6x^3 + 2x + 3)\,dx$	$= \frac{6}{4}x^4 + \frac{2}{2}x^2 + 3x + c$
		$= 1.5x^4 + x^2 + 3x + c$

Notes

a. It will be seen that a constant is added to each integral.

b. Since differentiation is a more straight forward process is is useful to check the integral by differentiating it to see that it comes back to the original expression. For instance differentiating $2x^5 + c$ gives $10x^4$ which is the first example above.

THE VALUE OF THE INTEGRATION CONSTANT

21. Before numeric results can be obtained from the integral, which is the typical requirement in business applications, it is often necessary to establish the value of c, the constant. The value of c depends entirely on the particular situation in which the function is being used. Two examples are given below.

Example 1.

Assume that a marginal revenue function is

$$y = 3x + 10 \text{ where } x \text{ is sales in units.}$$

The integral is: $\int(3x + 10)\,dx = \frac{3}{2}x^2 + 10x + c$
which is the Total Revenue function. Now by inference when sales are zero (i.e. $x = 0$) revenue is zero.

$$\text{thus, when } x = 0$$

$$R = \tfrac{3}{2}x^2 + 10x + c = 0$$

$\therefore$ c must equal zero as this is the only value which satisfies this equation.

Example 2.

Assume that a marginal profit function is

$$y = 100 - 2x \text{ when } y \text{ is the £'s and } x \text{ is sales in units.}$$

You also establish that the company breaks even on sales of 5 units. (This is the additional information known as an initial condition). What are the fixed costs of the company?

Solution.

The first step is to find the Total Profit function which is found by integrating the marginal function thus

$$\int (100 - 2x)\,dx = 100x - x^2 + c$$

In addition we know that the company breaks even (i.e. total profits are zero) when x = 5

$$\therefore\ P = 100x - x^2 + c = 0 \text{ when } x = 5$$

$$\therefore\ 100(5) - 5^2 + c = 0$$

$$\therefore\ c = \underline{-475}$$

c represents the fixed costs of the company so the answer is **£475.**

(Alternatively this can be expressed as follows; What would be the value of the profit function at zero activity i.e. $x = 0$? This is a loss of £475 which represents the fixed costs of the organisation).

DEFINITE INTEGRALS

22. When we require a numeric result, say, the total revenue between two activity levels, the expression is termed a definite integral and is written thus.

$$\int_a^b y\,dx \text{ where } a \text{ is a definite value and } b \text{ is some larger definite value.}$$

For example, what is the increase in profit in moving from an activity level of 10 units to 15 units when the marginal profit function is as given in Example 2 above i.e. $y = 100 - 2x$.

The definite integral of this function is written thus

$$\begin{aligned}\int_{10}^{15} (100 - 2x)\,dx &= \left[100 - x^2\right]_{10}^{15} \\ &= [100(15) - 15^2] - [100(10) - 10^2] \\ &= \underline{£375}\end{aligned}$$

Note: It will be seen that the constant, c, has been omitted. This is because the value of c (in this case - 475) is the same at both the higher and lower limits and therefore it cancels out and is not a factor when we are seeking the increase in profit by moving from one activity level to another.

SUMMARY.

23.

a. Differential calculus is used to find rates of change and turning points of functions.

b. The differential coefficient or derivative is the rate of change of y (the dependent variable) with respect to an infinitesimally small change in x (the independent variable).

c. Where the function is $y = x^n$ the derivative is

$$\frac{dy}{dx} = nx^{n-1}$$

d. Differentiation rules exist where the function has a constant, is a sum, is a product, is a quotient, is a function of a function and for many other types of more complex functions.

e. Major practical application of differentiation include finding marginal revenue, marginal cost, marginal profit and thereby establishing output levels which maximise profit.

f. Some functions have turning points and these can represent points of maximum revenue or minimum cost.

g. By calculating the derivative of a function and setting this to zero the turning point can normally be found.

h. The turning point should always be tested to see if it is a maximum or minimum. This is done by finding the second erivative i.e.

$\frac{d^2y}{dx^2}$ If this is *negative* the turning point is a *maximum*, if *positive* it is a *minimum*.

i. Partial differentiation is used when there is more than one independent variable.

j. The normal rules for differentiation apply with one of the independent variables being treated as a constant whilst the other is differentiated.

k. integration is the reverse of differentiation is denoted thus

$$\int y\,dx$$

l. The basic integration rule is

$$\int kx^n\,dx = \frac{kx^{n+1}}{n+1} + c \quad (n \neq -1)$$

m. The value of the constant depends on circumstances and may be found by inference or by some additional information known as an *initial condition.*

n. When a numeric answer is required the expression becomes a definite integral.

POINTS TO NOTE

24.

a. Differentiation and integration presuppose continuous functions. Business functions may be stepped or discontinuous so it may not be possible to apply the techniques in every case.

b. Frequently the total cost or revenue functions are known. If so, total values or values between two activity levels can be found easily and directly without using integration.
Integration becomes necessary when *only* the marginal curves are known.

c. A word of caution. Calculus is a vast, complex subject which this chapter barely introduces. Many of the rules given are operational rules only and exceptions can occur in particular circumstances. Nevertheless the chapter provides sufficient material to cope with the examinations for which it is intended.

d. As explained in this chapter, calculus is frequently used to find information about economic and business models which, by their nature, are normally approximations so that any results obtained need to be used with caution.

SELF REVIEW QUESTIONS.

1. In what circumstances is calculus used? (2)

2. What is the objective of differentiation? (3)

3. What is the basic rule for finding derivatives? (4)

5. How can differentiation be used to find a turning point? (14)

6. What is the second derivative? (14)

7. What is a partial derivative? (16)

8. How is a partial derivative found? (17)

9. What is the relationship between integration and differentiation? (19)

10. What is the basic integration rule? (20)

11. Distinguish between a definite and indefinite integral (22)

EXERCISES WITH ANSWERS COMMENCING PAGE 488

A1. Find the derivative of

$$(a)\ y = 6x - x \qquad (b)\ y = \frac{1}{x^2}$$
$$(c)\ y = \sqrt{1+2x} \qquad (d)\ y = \frac{1}{\sqrt{x}}$$

A2. A cost function is

$$£(c) = Q^2 - 30Q + 200$$

where Q = quantity of units produced
Find the point of minimum cost

A3. A firm selling a Trade Directory has developed a profit function as follows:

$$P = 9D - 0.0005D^2 + 0.06DA - 80A^2 - 5000$$

where D = number of directories sold and
A = number of advertising pages.

How many directories containing how many advertising pages should be sold to maximise profits?

EXAMINATION QUESTIONS WITH ANSWERS COMMENCING PAGE 488

A4. M Limited, as a result of past experience and estimates for the future, has decided that the cost of production of their sole product, P, an advanced process machine, is:

$$C = 1064 + 5x + 0.04x^2$$

where C = *total cost in £000*

x = *quantity produced (and sold).*

The marketing department has estimated that the price of the product is related to the quantity produced and sold by the equation:

$$P = 157 - 3x$$

where P = *price per unit in £000*

x = *quantity sold*

The government has proposed a tax of £t'000 per unit on product P but it is not expected that this will have any effect on the costs incurred in making P or on the demand/price relationship.

You are required to calculate and state:

a. the price and quantity that will maximise profit when there was no tax;

b. the price and quantity that will maximise profit if the proposed tax is introduced;

c. how much of the tax t per unit is passed on to the customer;

d. the effect on the profit of the company if t was fixed at £4,000 per unit.

(CIMA, Quantitative Techniques)

A5. A company has the following demand and cost functions for a particular item

Demand function: $p = 600 - 2q^2$

Cost function: $C = 100 + 216q$

where p is the price of the item (£), q is the quantity produced and sold, and C is the total cost of producing the item (£).

Required.

i. Determine the price and quantity for maximum sales revenue and find the maximum revenue.

ii. Determine the price and quantity for maximum profit and find the maximum profit.

iii. Given that the point of elasticity of demand (E) is defined as

$E = \frac{p}{q}\frac{dq}{dp}$ *determine E at the point of maximum revenue and at the point of maximum profit. Comment on your results from an economist's point of view.*

iv. Assume that the demand situation has changed such that the point elasticity of demand is now given by the function:

$E = \frac{-p}{10q^2}$ *and that when the price is £256 the demand is 10, determine the new demand function and hence the new maximum profit.*

(ACCA, Management Mathematics)

A6. An accountant has estimated that the weekly costs of production, C, for a product are given by the equation:

$$C = 100 + 23x + \frac{1}{2}x^2,$$

where x is the number of tonnes produced. The weekly revenue equation, R, is given by

$$R = 100x - x^2 \quad (x < 100)$$

You are required to:

(a) find the production level(s) at which profit is maximised;

(b) find any break-even point(s);

(c) find the point at which revenue would be maximised;
(d) sketch a graph which describes approximately the cost/revenue situation;
(e) recommend a level of x which it would be rational to produce and justify your answer.
(CIMA QUANTITATIVE METHODS)

A7. Sid Fields wishes to have the grounds of his house landscaped. He considers two firms for the project.
Gracious Gardens Ltd. will take t days to do the job where the probability of completing the job in t days is derived from the function:

$$p(t) = \frac{1}{4,500}t(30 - t) \quad where \quad 0 \leq t \leq 30$$

Speedy Landscaping Ltd. will take t days to do the job where the probability of completing the job in t days is derived from the function:

$$p(t) = \frac{3}{40,000}t^2(20 - t) \text{ where } 0 \leq t \leq 20$$

The probability that ti is less than some value A is given by:

$$p(t \leq A) = \int_0^A p(t)dt$$

Required:
a. Find the expected time that it will take each company to complete the job, where the expected value of t is defined as $E(t) = \int tp(t)dt$.
b. Gracious Gardens Ltd. would be able to start work on the 1 July but Speedy Landscaping Ltd. would not be able to start until 5 days later - on the 6 July.
What is the probability, in each case, of the job remaining unfinished after the 15 July assuming that no rest days are to be taken?
c. Gracious Gardens Ltd. charge £20 per day plus a fixed cost for materials of £250. Speedy Landscaping charge £30 per day plus a fixed cost of £220.
Find the expected cost of the work for each company.
d. Which company would you recommend Sid Fields to use? Give your reasons.
(ACCA Management Mathematics)

EXERCISES WITHOUT ANSWERS

B1. Find the derivative of:

$$(a)\ y = 3 - 6x \qquad (b)\ y = \sqrt{x}$$

$$(c)\ y = \frac{(1 + 2x)}{(1 - 2x)}$$

B2. A revenue function is

$$£R = 1000Q - 8Q^2$$

(a) what is the marginal revenue when Q is 50
(b) What is the point of maximum revenue?

B3. A marginal profit function is

$$y = 200 - 3x \text{ where } y \text{ is in } £s$$

and x is sales in units: It is known that the company breaks even when 50 units are sold. What are the fixed costs of the company?

EXAMINATION QUESTIONS WITHOUT ANSWERS

B4. Regression analysis of the costs incurred in the manufacture and sale of product K has established the relationship:

$$C = 31,500 + 6x + 0.07x^2$$

where C = total cost of manufacture and sale

and x = quantity produced and sold per annum.

There appears to be an unlimited demand from long-established home customers for product K at a price of £300 per unit. The sales department has recently been approached by an overseas agent who has identified a potential market where the selling price per unit (S) is related to the quantity sold by the equation:

$$S = 441 - 0.8q$$

where q = quantity sold in this export market, per annum.

You are required:

(a) calculate the optimum annual profit that can be earned from the sale of product K in the overseas market, assuming nothing is sold to the long-established customers;

(b) calculate the optimum annual profit that can be earned from the sale of product K, assuming that sales are made to make the maximum profit from the overseas market with the remaining output sold to the long-established customers;

(c) calculate the optimum annual profit that can be earned by the sale of product K;

(d) state **four** *significantly different factors, apart from optimum short-term annual profit, which should be considered by the directors before they decide which sales policy to adopt.*

(CIMA Quantitative Techniques)

B5. A company making a single product has manufacturing and distribution divisions. Stocks of finished goods are not held, all products being to order.

The average net revenue per unit, allowing for quantity discounts, is £100 - £0.01Q where Q is the quantity sold.

The average variable costs per unit for the two divisions are:

Manufacturing	=	*£10 + £0.015Q*
Distribution	=	*£2 + £0.001Q*

The fixed costs per annum are:

Manufacturing	*£40,000*
Distribution	*£20,000*

You are required to calculate:

a. the optimum annual production quantity to maximise the profit of the company;

b. the profit of the company at the level of activity in (a) above;

c. the annual production quantity to maximise the manufacturing division's profit, if it has been instructed to transfer the product to the distribution division at £73 per unit;

d. the profit of the company, showing the results of the two divisions, at the level of activity in (c) above.

(CIMA Quantitative Techniques)

11 Inventory Control – Introduction and Terminology

INTRODUCTION

1. This chapter explains why stocks or inventories are held, gives the objectives of inventory control and the basic definitions used. It sets the framework for the subsequent three chapters which explain various detailed aspects of inventory control.

TYPES OF INVENTORY

2. A convenient classification of the types of inventory is as follows:

a. Raw materials - the materials, components, fuels etc. used in the manufacture of products.
b. Work-in-Progress – (W–I–P) – partly finished goods and materials, sub-assemblies etc. held between manufacturing stages.
c. Finished goods – completed products ready for sale or distribution.

The particular items included in each classification depend on the particular firm. What would be classified as a finished product for one company might be classified as raw materials for another. For example, steel bars would be classified as a finished product for a steel mill and as raw material for a nut and bolt manufacturer.

REASONS FOR HOLDING STOCKS

3. The main reasons for holding stocks can be summarised as follows:

a. to ensure that sufficient goods are available to meet anticipated demand;
b. to absorb variations in demand and production;
c. to provide a buffer between production processes. This is applicable to work-in-progress stocks which effectively decouple operations;
d. to take advantage of bulk purchasing discounts;
e. to meet possible shortages in the future;
f. to absorb seasonal fluctuations in usage or demand;
g. to enable production processes to flow smoothly and efficiently;
h. as a necessary part of the production process eg, the maturing of whiskey;
i. as deliberage investment policy particularly in times of inflation or possible shortage.

ALTERNATIVE REASONS FOR THE EXISTENCE OF STOCKS

4. The reasons given in Para. 3. above are the logical ones based on deliberate decision. However, stocks accumulate for other, less praiseworthy reasons, typical of which are the following:

a. Obsolete items are retained in stock.
b. Poor or non existent inventory control resulting in over-large orders, replenishment orders being out of phase with production, etc.
c. Inadequate or non-existent stock records.
d. Poor liaison between the Production Control, Purchasing and Marketing departments.

e. Sub-optimal decision making, eg the Production Department might increase W–I–P stocks unduly so as to ensure long production runs.

STOCK COSTS.

5. Whether as a result of deliberate policy or not, stock represents an investment by the organisation. As with any other investment, the costs of holding stock must be related to the benefits to be gained. To do this effectively, the costs must be identified and this can be done in three categories; costs of holding stock, costs of obtaining stock, and stockout costs.

COSTS OF HOLDING STOCK

6. These costs, also known as carrying costs, include the following;:

a. Interest on capital invested in the stock.
b. Storage charges (rent, lighting, heating, refrigeration, air conditioning, etc).
c. Stores staffing, equipment maintenance and running costs.
d. Handling costs.
e. Audit, stocktaking or perpetual inventory costs.
f. Insurance, security.
g. Deterioration and obsolescence.
h. Pilferage, vermin damage.

COSTS OF HOLDING STOCK

7. These costs, sometimes known as ordering costs, include the following

a. the clerical and administrative costs associated with the Purchasing, Accounting, and Goods Received departments.
b. Transport costs.
c. Where goods are manufactured internally the set up and tooling costs associated with each production run.

Note:

Some students consider ordering costs to include only those costs associated with ordering external to the firm. However, internal ordering (ie own manufacture) may involve high costs for production planning, set-up.

STOCKOUT COSTS

8. These are the costs associated with running out of stock. The avoidance of these costs is the basic reason why stocks are held in the first instance. These costs include the following:

a. Lost contribution through the lost sale caused by the stockout.
b. Loss of future sales because customers go elsewhere.
c. Loss of customer goodwill.
d. Cost of production stoppages caused by stockouts of W–I–P or raw materials.
e. Labour frustration over stoppages.
f. Extra costs associated with urgent, often small quantity, replenishment purchases.

Clearly many of these costs are difficult to quantify, but they are often significant.

OBJECTIVE OF INVENTORY CONTROL.

9. The overall objective of inventory control is to maintain stock levels so that the combined costs, detailed in Paras. 6, 7 and 8 above, are at a minimum. This is done by establishing two factors, when to order and how many to order. These factors are the subject of the following chapters, but before these factors can be explained in detail some basic terminology must be dealt with.

INVENTORY CONTROL TERMINOLOGY.

10. Brief definitions of common inventory control terms are given below and are illustrated in Para 11.

a. Lead or Procurement time. The period of time, expressed in days, weeks, months, etc between ordering (either externally or internally) and replenishment, ie when the goods are available for use.

b. Demand. The amount required by sales, production, etc. Usually expressed as a rate of demand per week, month, etc. Estimates of the rate of demand during the lead time are critical factors in inventory control systems. This is dealt with in more detail in Chapter 14.

c. Economic Ordering Quantity (EOQ) or Economic Batch Quantity (EBQ). This is a calculated ordering quantity which minimises the balance of costs between inventory holding costs and reorder costs. The rationale of EOQ and derivation of the EOQ formulae are dealt with in Chapter 13.

d. Physical stock. The number of items physically in stock at a given time.

e. Free stock. Physical stock *plus* outstanding replenishment orders *minus* unfulfilled requirements.

f. Buffer Stock or Minimum Stock or Safety Stock. A stock allowance to cover errors in forecasting the lead time or the demand during the lead time. Buffer stock is further explained in Chapter 14.

g. Maximum Stock. A stock level selected as the maximum desirable which is used as an indicator to show when stocks have risen too high.

h. Reorder level. The level of stock at which a further replenishment order should be placed. the reorder level is dependent upon the lead time and the demand during the lead time.

i. Reorder Quantity. The quantity of the replenishment order. In some types of inventory control systems this is the EOQ, but in some other systems a different value is used. This aspect is dealt with in detail in Chapter 14.

A SIMPLE STOCK SITUATION ILLUSTRATED.

11. The following diagram shows a stock situation simplified by the following assumptions: regular rates of demand, a fixed lead time, and replenishment in one batch.

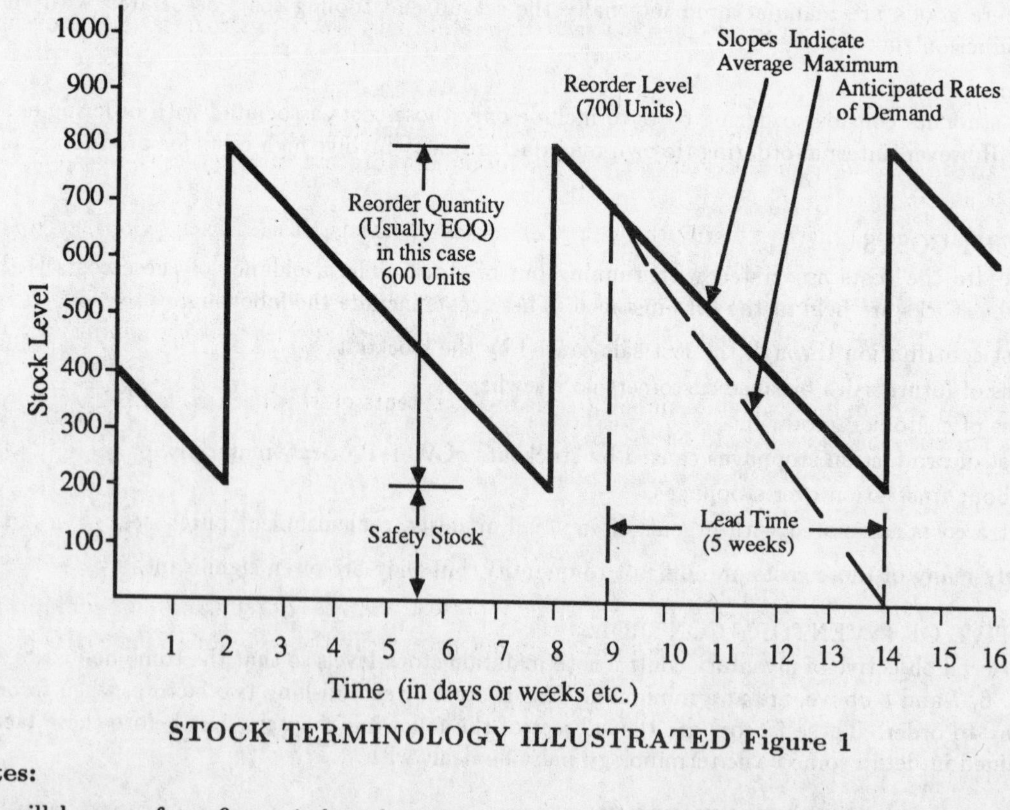

STOCK TERMINOLOGY ILLUSTRATED Figure 1

Notes:

a. It will be seen from figure 1 that the safety stock in this illustration is needed to cope with periods of maximum demand during the lead time.

b. The lead time as shown in 5 weeks, the safety stock 200 units, and the reorder quantity 600 units.

c. With constant rates of demand, as shown, the average stock is the safety stock *plus* $\frac{1}{2}$ Reorder quantity; for example, in figure 1 the average stock is

$$200 + \frac{1}{2}(600) = \underline{500 \text{ units.}}$$

PARETO ANALYSIS.

12. The whole process of detailed stock control uses time and resources and can cost a considerable amount of money. Because of this it is important that the effort is directed where it can be most cost effective – there is little point in elaborate and costly recording and control procedures for an item of insignificant value.

Because of this it is worthwhile carrying out a so called *Pareto* or *ABC analysis.* It is often found that a few items account for a large proportion of the value and accordingly should have the closest monitoring. A typical analysis of stock items could be as follows

CLASS A ITEMS	–	80% of value in 20% of items – Close day-to-day control
CLASS B ITEMS	–	15% of value in 30% of items – Regular review
CLASS C ITEMS	–	5% of value in 50% of items – Infrequent review.

Such a review can help to ensure that resources are used to maximum advantage.

Detailed, selective control will be more effective than a generalised approach which treats all items identically.

SUMMARY.

13.

a. Stocks may conveniently be classified into Raw Materials, Work-in-Progress, and Finished Goods.

b. The classification of an item depends upon the nature of the firm.

c. Stocks are held to satisfy demands quickly, to allow unimpeded production, to take advantage of bulk purchasing, as a necessary part of the production process, and to absorb seasonal and other fluctuations.

d. Stocks accumulate unnecessarily through poor control methods, obsolescence, poor liaison and sub-optimal decision making.

e. The costs associated with stock are: holding costs, costs of obtaining stock, and stockout costs.

f. The overall objective of inventory control is to maintain stock at a level which minimises total stock costs.

g. Inventory control has its own terminology, the basic contents of which are given in this chapter. The various definitions should be thoroughly learned.

POINTS TO NOTE.

14.

a. Inventory control is an important area of financial control which is often neglected.

b. A few per cent saving on inventory costs would represent millions of pounds on a national scale.

c. The stocks recorded by the official system are not necessarily the only stocks held. Unofficial stocks - often as unofficial WIP - often occur.

d. Pareto analysis is sometimes known as the 80:20 rule.

SELF REVIEW QUESTIONS.

1. How may inventories be classified? (2)

2. Why are stocks held? (3)

3. *What are the major categories of cost associated with stocks? (5 to 8)*
4. *What is the overall objective of stock control systems? (9)*
5. *Define at least six common terms used in Inventory Control. (10)*
6. *What is ABC analysis? (12)*

EXAMINATION QUESTIONS WITH ANSWERS COMMENCING PAGE 488

A1. *Control of inventory (stock) is an important aspect of management.*
You are required to discuss:
a. the purpose of inventory; and
b. methods to ensure that the optimum investment is made in this asset.
(CIMA, Quantitative Techniques)

12 Inventory Control – Types of Control System

INTRODUCTION

1. This chapter describes the two main inventory control systems, the Reorder Level and Periodic Review systems, gives an example of each and explains in what circumstances each system is likely to be more appropriate.

RE-ORDER LEVEL SYSTEM.

2. This system is also known as the two-bin system. Its characteristics are as follows:

a. A predetermined re-order level is set for each item.

b. When the stock level falls to the reorder level, a replenishment order is issued.

c. The replenishment order quantity is invariably the EOQ.

d. The name 'two-bin system' comes from the simplest method of operating the system whereby the stock is segregated into two bins. Stock is initially drawn from the first bin and a replenishment order issued when it becomes empty.

e. Most organisations operating the re-order level system maintain stock records with calculated re-order levels which trigger off the required replenishment order.

Note:

The illustration in Para. 11 of Chapter 11 as of a simple re-order level system. The re-order level system is widely used in practice and is the subject of frequent examination questions.

ILLUSTRATION OF A SIMPLE MANUAL RE-ORDER LEVEL SYSTEM.

3. The following data relate to a particular stock item.

Normal usage	110 per day
Minimum usage	50 per day
Maximum usage	140 per day
Lead Time	25–30 days
EOQ (Previously calculated)	5000

Using this data the various control levels can be calculated.

Re-order Level = Maximum Usage x Maximum Lead Time
= 140×30
= **4,200 units**

Minimum Level = Re-order Level – Average Usage for Average Lead Time
= $4,200 - (110 \times 27.5)$
= **1,175 units**

Maximum Level = Re-order Level + EOQ – Minimum Anticipated Usage in Lead Time
= $4,200 + 5,000 - (50 \times 25)$
= **7,950 units**

Notes:

a. The three levels would be entered on a Stock record card and comparisons made between the actual stock level and the control levels each time an entry was made on the card.
b. The re-order level is a definite action level, the minimum and maximum points are levels at which management would be warned that a potential danger may occur.
c. The re-order level is calculated so that if the worst anticipated situation occurs, stock would be replenished in time.
d. The minimum level is calculated so that management will be warned when demand is above average and accordingly buffer stock is being used. There may be no danger, but the situation needs watching.
e. Maximum level is calculated so that management will be warned when demand is the minimum anticipated and consequently the stock level is likely to rise above the maximum intended.
f. In a manual system if warnings about maximum or minimum level violations were received, then it is likely that the re-order level and/or EOQ would be recalculated and adjusted. In a computer based system such adjustments would take place automatically to reflect current and forecast future conditions.
g. A critical factor in establishing re-order levels and for calculating EOQs is the forecast of expected demand. Forecasting has been covered earlier in the manual.

PERIODIC REVIEW SYSTEM.

4. This system is sometimes called the constant cycle system. The system has the following characteristics:
   a. Stock levels for all parts are reviewed at fixed intervals e.g. every forthnight.
   b. Where necessary a replenishment order is issued.
   c. The quantity of the replenishment order is not a previously calculated EOQ, but is based upon; the likely demand until the next review, the present stock level and the lead time.
   d. The replenishment order quantity seeks to bring stocks up to a predetermined level.
   e. The effect of the system is to order *variable quantities* at *fixed intervals* as compared with the re-order level system, described in Para. 2, where *fixed quantities* are ordered at *variable intervals.*

ILLUSTRATION OF A SIMPLE MANUAL PERIODIC REVIEW SYSTEM.

5. A production control department maintains control of the 500 piece parts used in the assembly of the finished products by the periodic review system. The stock levels of all 500 parts are reviewed every 4 weeks and a replenishment order issued to bring the stock of each part up to a previously calculated level. This level is calculated at six-monthly intervals and is based on the anticipated demand for each part.

Based on the above system, the following graph shows the situation for one of the piece parts, part No.1101x, over a period of 16 weeks.

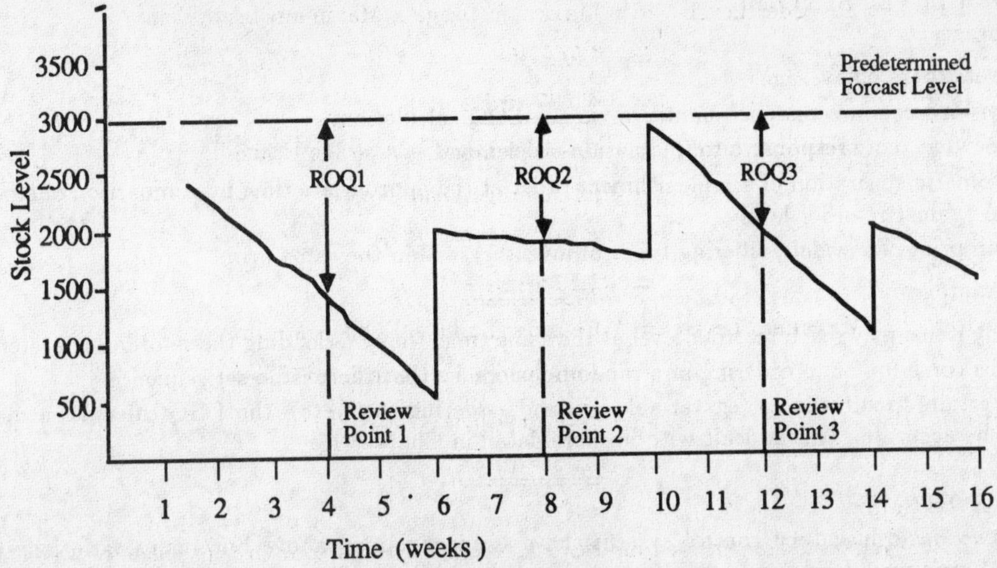

Figure 1

Stock Levels of Part No. 1101

ROQ = Reorder quantity

Notes:

a. The re-order quantities, based on the agreed system are 1500 units, 1000 units, and 1400 units.

b. It will be seen that the rates of usage are assumed to be variable and the lead time has been assumed to be 2 weeks.

c. The above illustration is merely one way of operating a periodic review system and many variants exist, particularly relating to the method of calculating the re-order quantities.

PERIODIC REVIEW SYSTEM.

6. Advantages:

a. All stock items are reviewed periodically so that there is more chance of obsolete items being eliminated.

b. Economies in placing orders may be gained by spreading the purchasing office load more evenly.

c. Larger quantity discounts may be obtained when a range of stock items are order at the same time from a supplier.

d. Because orders will always be in the same sequence, there may be production economies due to more efficient production planning being possible and lower set up costs. This is often a major advantage and results in the frequent use of some form of periodic review system in production control systems in firms where there is a preferred sequence of manufacture, so that full advantage can be gained from the predetermined sequence implied by the periodic review system.

Disadvantages:

a. In general larger stocks are required, as re-order quantities must take account of the period between reviews as well as lead times.

b. Re-order quantities are not at the optimum level of a correctly calculated EOQ.

c. Less responsive to changes in consumption. If the rate of usage change shortly after a review, a stockout may well occur before the next review.

d. Unless demands are reasonably consistent, it is difficult to set appropriate periods for review.

RE-ORDER LEVEL SYSTEM.

7. Advantages:

a. Lower stocks on average.
b. Items ordered in economic quantities via the EOQ calculation.
c. Somewhat more responsive to fluctuations in demand.
d. Automatic generation of a replenishment order at the appropriate time by comparison of stock level against re-order level.
e. Appropriate for widely differing types of inventory within the same firm.

Disadvantages:

a. Many items may reach re-order level at the same time, thus overloading the re-ordering system.
b. Items come up for re-ordering in a random fashion so that there is no set sequence.
c. In certain circumstances (eg variable demand, ordering costs etc), the EOQ calculation may not be accurate. This is dealt with in more detail in Chapter 16.

HYBRID SYSTEMS.

8. The two basic inventory control systems have been explained above but many variations exist in practice. A firm may develop a system to suit their organisation which contains elements of both systems. In stable conditions of constant demand, lead times, and costs, both basic approaches are likely to be equally effective.

SUMMARY.

9.

a. There are two basic inventory control systems, the re-order level or two-bin system and the periodic review system.
b. The re-order level system usually has three control levels; re-order level, maximum level and minimum level.
c. In the re-order level system the usual replenishment order quantity is the EOQ.
d. The re-order level system results in fixed quantities being ordered at variable intervals dependent upon demand.
e. The periodic review system means that all stocks are reviewed at fixed intervals and replenishment orders issued to bring stock back to predetermined level.
f. The replenishment order quantity is based upon estimates of the likely demand until the next review period.
g. The periodic review system results in variable quantities being ordered at fixed intervals.

POINTS TO NOTE.

10.

a. Many examination questions seem implicitly to assume that all inventory control systems are Re-order Level systems. This is not so.
b. The importance of forecasting in inventory control cannot be over emphasised. Adaptive forecasting systems, already described are frequently an integral part of inventory control systems, particularly those which are computer based.
c. There is a tendency for the stock level to increase in line with $\sqrt{n}$, where n is the number of items in stock. Accordingly, standardisation of products, parts and materials can help to reduce stock levels. However, gains from reduced stocks may be offset by loss of marketability so care needs to be taken with standardisation policies.

SELF REVIEW QUESTIONS.

1. *What are the characteristics of the Re-order Level System of Inventory Control? (2)*
2. *What are the three levels commonly calculated for use in re-order level systems? (3)*
3. *Define the Periodic Review system and explain how it differs from the Re-order Level system? (4)*

4. What are the major advantages and disadvantages of the Periodic Review system? (6)

5. What are the major advantages and disadvantages of the Re-order Level system? (7)

EXERCISES WITH ANSWERS COMMENCING PAGE 488

A1. The following data relate to a given stock item.

Normal usage	*1300 per day*
Minimum usage	*900 per day*
Maximum usage	*2000 per day*
Lead time	*15 – 20 days*
EOQ	*30,000*

Calculate the various controls levels.

EXAMINATION QUESTIONS WITH ANSWERS COMMENCING PAGE 488

A2.

a. You are required to state the advantages and disadvantages of the Periodic Review system of inventory control.

b. Best Value Supermarkets Limited buys an economy size instant coffee to market under its own brand name. The monthly sales in all its stores, assuming 25 days in a month are 50,000 units. The sales occur evenly throughout the month.

The company currently orders in lots of 50,000 at a time at a price of £0.25 per unit with a lead time of 15 days. A base inventory of 20,000 units is kept as a buffer stock.

You are required to calculate the re-order point.

c. The supplier has offered to reduce the price to £0.23 per unit if the order size is increased to 200,000 units for delivery within 30 days. If these terms were accepted the company would still keep a base inventory of 20,000 units but would have to rent additional storage space at a cost of £6,000 per annum. Carrying costs to the company, excluding additional storage space, are 20% per annum. Terms of settlement are the same under both current and proposed delivery patterns.

You are required to state, and support with calculation, whether or not the new terms be accepted. The only costs to be considred are those given above.

(CIMA QUANTITATIVE TECHNIQUES)

A3. a. How are the costs that are incurred in inventory control normally classified for use with O.R. models?

Give a detailed breakdown of the components of these costs and the assumptions adopted.

b. Describe the re-order level system of inventory control and explain the essential differences between it and the economic batch quantity system.

(ACCA Management Mathematics)

13 Inventory Control – Economic Order Quantity

INTRODUCTION

1. In chapter 11 the EOQ was defined. This chapter derives the EOQ formulae from first principles and shows how it is modified to deal with situations where replenishment is not instantaneous and where discounts can be gained by purchasing larger quantities.

EOQ ASSUMPTIONS.

2. The EOQ has been previously defined as the ordering quantity which minimises the balance of cost between inventory holding costs and re-order costs. To be able to calculate a basic EOQ certain assumptiosn are necessary.

a. That there is a known, constant stockholding cost,

b. That there is a known, constant ordering cost,

c. That rates of demand are known,

d. That there is a known, constant price per unit.

e. That replenishment is made instantaneously, ie the whole batch is delivered at once.

f. No stockouts allowed.

Notes:

a. It will be apparent that the above assumptions are somewhat sweeping and they are a good reason for treating any EOQ calculation with caution.

b. Some of the above assumptions are relaxed later in this chapter.

c. The rationale of EOQ ignores buffer stocks which are maintained to cater for variations in lead time and demand.

A GRAPHICAL EOQ EXAMPLE.

3. The following data will be used to develop a graphical solution to the EOQ problem.

Example 1.

A company uses 50,000 widgets per annum which are £10 each to purchase. The ordering and handling costs are £150 per order and carrying costs are 15% per annum, ie it costs £1.50 p.a. to carry a widget in stock (£10 × 15%).

To graph the various costs involved the following calculations are necessary:

Total Costs p.a. = Ordering Cost p.a. + Carrying Cost p.a.

where

Ordering Cost p.a. = No. of orders × £150 and

the No. of orders = $\frac{\text{Annual Demand}}{\text{Order Quantity}}$

(For example, if the order quantity was 5,000 widgets,

the no. of orders = $\frac{50{,}000}{5{,}000}$ = 10 and ordering cost p.a.

= 10 × £150 = £1,500)

and carrying cost p.a. = average stock level × £1.5

and the average stock = $\frac{\text{order quantity}}{2}$

(For example if the order quantity is 5,000, carrying costs p.a. are $\frac{5000}{2} \times £1.5 = £3,750$)

Based on the above principles, the following table gives the costs for various order quantities.

Column I	II	III	IV	V	VI
Order Quantity	Average No. of Orders p.a.	Annual Ordering Cost	Average Stock	Stock Holding Cost p.a.	Total Cost
	$\frac{50{,}000}{\text{Col.I}}$	Col.II × £150	$\frac{\text{Col.I}}{2}$	Col. IV × £1.5	Col.III + Col.V
		£		£	£
1000	50	7500	500	750	8250
2000	25	3750	1000	1500	5250
3000	$16\frac{2}{3}$	2500	1500	2250	4750
4000	$12\frac{1}{2}$	1875	2000	3000	4875
5000	10	1500	2500	3750	5250
6000	$8\frac{1}{3}$	1250	3000	4500	5750

Ordering and Stock Holding Costs for various Order Quantities Table 1

The costs in Table 1 can be plotted in a graph and the approximate EOQ ascertained.

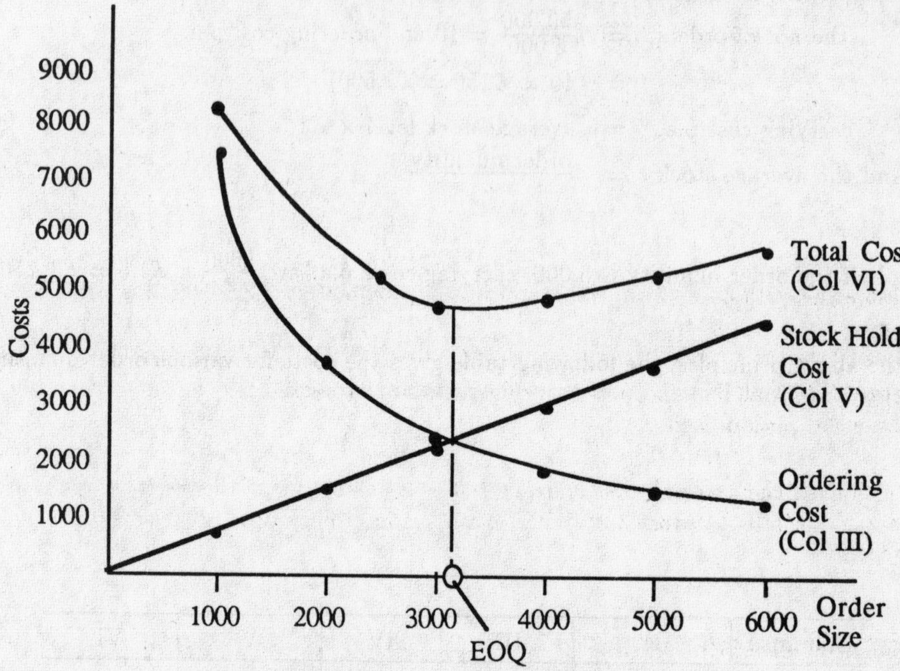

Graph of Data in Table 1 Figure 1

From the graph it will be seen that the EOQ is approximately 3,200 widgets, which means that an average of slightly under 16 orders will have to be placed a year.

Notes:

a. From a graph closer accuracy is not possible and is unnecessary anyway.

b. It will be seen from the graph that the bottom of the total cost curve is relatively flat, indicating that the exact value of the EOQ is not too critical. This is typical of most EOQ problems.

THE EOQ FORMULA.

4. It is possible, and more usual, to calculate the EOQ using a formula. The formula method gives an exact answer, but do not be misled into placing undue reliance upon the precise figure. The calculation is based on estimates of costs, demands, etc which are, of course, subject to error. The EOQ formula is given below and should be learned. The mathematical derivation is given in Appendix 1 of this chapter.

Basic EOQ formula

$$\text{EOQ} = \sqrt{\frac{2.\text{Co}.\text{D}.}{\text{Cc}}}$$

where Co = ordering cost per order

D = Demand per annum

Cc = Carrying cost per item per annum

Using the data from Example 1, the EOQ can be calculated:

$$Co = £150$$

$$D = 50{,}000 \text{ widgets}$$

$$Cc = £10 \times 15\% \text{ or } £1.5 \text{ per widget.}$$

$$EOQ = \sqrt{\frac{2.150.50{,}000}{1.5}}$$

$$= \sqrt{10{,}000{,}000}$$

$$= \underline{\underline{3162 \text{ widgets.}}}$$

Notes:

a. The closest value obtainable from the graph was approximately 3,200 which is very close to the exact figure.

b. Always take care that demand and carrying costs are expressed for the same time period. A year is the usual period used.

c. In some problems the carrying cost is expressed as a percentage of the value whereas in others it is expressed directly as a cost per item. Both ways have been used in this example to provide a comparison.

EOQ WITH GRADUAL REPLENISHMENT.

5. In example 1 above the assumption was that the widgets were ordered externally and that the order quantity was received as one batch, ie instantaneous replenishment as shown in the following diagram.

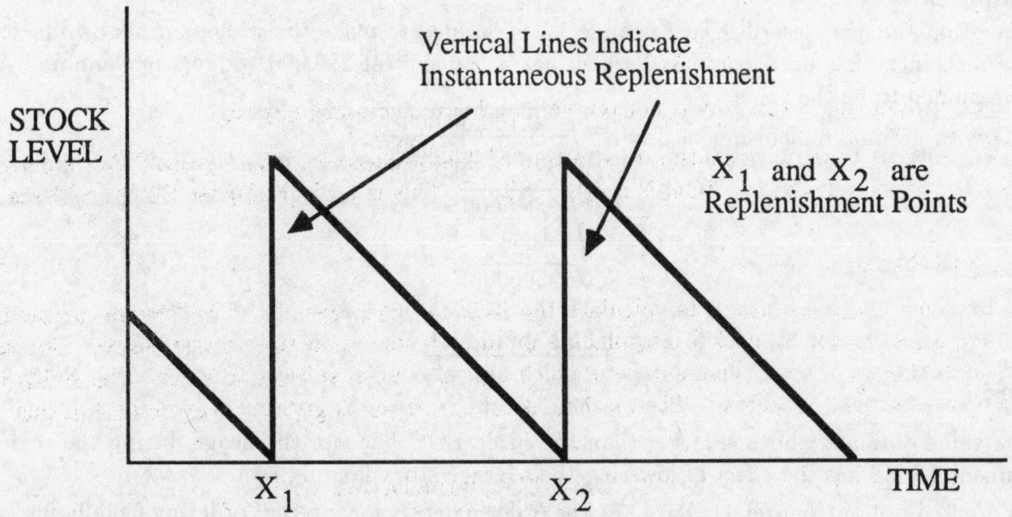

Stock Levels showing Instantaneous Replenishment Figure 2

If however, the widgets were manufactured internally, they would probably be placed into stock over a period of time resulting in the following pattern:

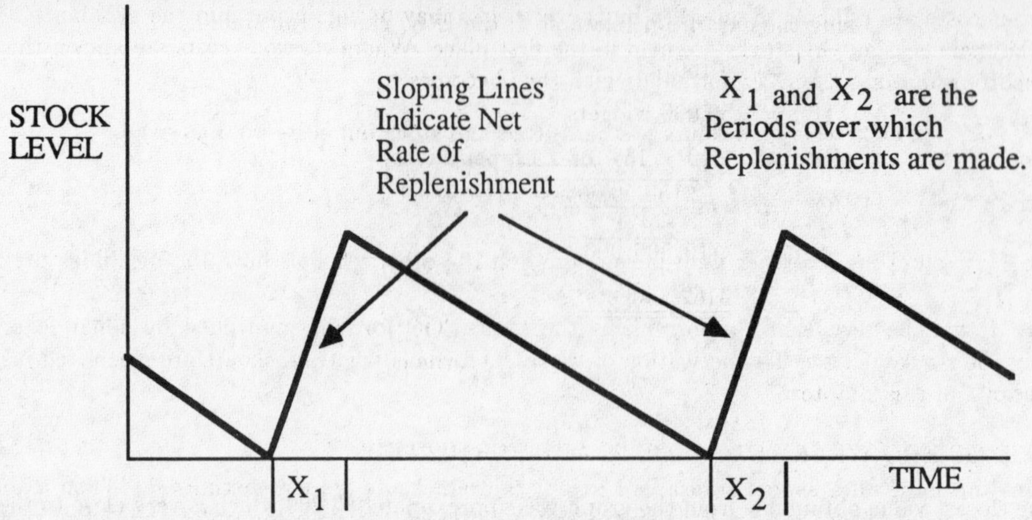

Stock Levels showing Non-instantaneous Replenishment. Figure 3

The net rate of replenishment is determined by the rate of replenishment and the rate of usage during the replenishment period. To cope with such situations, the basic EOQ formula needs modification thus:

$$\text{EOQ with gradual replenishment} = \sqrt{\frac{2.\text{Co}.\text{D}}{\text{Cc}(1 - \frac{\text{D}}{\text{R}})}}$$

where R = Production rate per annum, ie the quantity that would be produced if production of the item was carried on the whole year.

All other elements in the formula have meanings as previously defined in Para.4.

Note:

The derivation of the above formula is given in Appendix 2 of this chapter.

EXAMPLE OF EOQ WITH GRADUAL REPLENISHMENT.

6. **Example 2.**

Assume that the firm described in Example 1 has decided to make the widgets in its own factory. The necessary machinery has been purchased which has a capacity of 250,000 widgets per annum. All other data are assumed to be the same.

$$\text{EOQ with gradual replenishment} = \sqrt{\frac{2.150.50{,}000}{1.5\ (1 - \frac{50{,}000}{250{,}000})}}$$

$$= \sqrt{\frac{15000000}{1.5(.8)}}$$

$$= \sqrt{12500000}$$

$$= \underline{\textbf{3535 widgets}}$$

Notes:

a. The value obtained above is larger than the basic EOQ because the usage during the replenishment period has the effect of lowering the average stock holding cost.

b. As pointed out in Chapter 11, Para. 7., the ordering costs for internal ordering usually include set up and tooling costs as well as paper work and administration costs.

EOQ WHERE STOCKOUTS ARE PERMITTED.

7. It will be recalled that the overall objective of stock control is to minimise the balance of the three main areas of cost i.e. holding costs, ordering costs and stockout costs.

Stockout costs are difficult to quantify but nevertheless may be significant and the avoidance of these costs is the main reason why stocks are held in the first place. Where stockout costs are known then they can be incorporated into the EOQ formula which thus becomes

EOQ (where stockouts are permitted and stock out costs are known)

$$= \sqrt{\frac{2C_oD}{C_c}} . \sqrt{\frac{C_c + C_s}{C_s}}$$

where C_s = stockout costs per item per annum and the other symbols have the meanings previously given.

Note: It will be seen that the formula is the basic EOQ formula multiplied by a new expression containing the stockout cost. The derivation of the EOQ formula where stockouts are permitted ius given in Appendix 3 of this chapter.

EXAMPLE OF EOQ WHERE STOCKOUTS ARE PERMITTED.

8. Assume the same data as in Paragraph 4 except that stockouts are now permitted. When a stockout occurs and an order is received for widgets the firm has agreed to retain the order and, when replenishments are received, to use express courier service for the delivery at a cost of £0.75 per widget. Other administrative costs associated with stockouts are estimated at £0.25 per unit. What is the EOQ?

C_o = £150

D = 50,000

C_c = £1.5

C_s = £0.75 + £0.25 = £1

Thus EOQ (with stockouts)

$$= \sqrt{\frac{2.150.50000}{1.5}} \quad \sqrt{\frac{1.5 + 1}{1}}$$

= 3162 . 1.58

= <u>4996</u>

EOQ WITH DISCOUNTS.

9. A particularly unrealistic assumption with the basic EOQ calculation is that the price per item remains constant. Usually some form of discount can be obtained by ordering increased quantities. Such price discounts can be incorporated into the EOQ formula, but it becomes much more complicated. A simpler approach is to consider the costs associated with the normal EOQ and compare these costs with the costs at each succeeding discount point and so ascertain the best quantity to order.

FINANCIAL CONSEQUENCES OF DISCOUNTS.

10. Price discounts for quantity purchases have three financial effects, two of which are beneficial and one adverse.

Beneficial Effects: Savings come from

a. Lower price per item
b. The larger order quantity means that fewer orders need to be placed so that ordering costs

Adverse Effects:

a. Increased costs arise from the extra stockholding costs caused by the average stock level being higher due to the larger order quantity.

Example 3- Example of EOQ with Discounts.

A company uses a special bracket in the manufacture of its products which it orders from outside suppliers. The appropriate data are

Demand = 2000 per annum

Order cost = £20 per order

Carrying cost = 20% of item price

Basic item price = £10 per bracket

The company is offered the following discounts on the basic price:

For order quantities	400 - 799	less 2%
	800 - 1599	less 4%
	1600 and over	less 5%

It is required to establish the most economical quantity to order.

This problem can be answered using the following procedure:

A. Calculate the EOQ using the basic price.

B. Compare the savings from the lower price and ordering costs and the extra stockholding costs at each discount point (ie 400, 800 and 1600) with the costs associated with the basic EOQ, thus

$$\text{Basic EOQ} = \sqrt{\frac{2.2000.20}{10 \times .2}}$$

$$= \underline{200 \text{ brackets}}$$

Based on this EOQ the various costs and savings comparisons are given in the following table:

Order Quantity	200 (EOQ)	400	800	1600	Line No.
Discount	–	2%	4%	5%	1
Average No. of Orders p.a.	10	5	$2\frac{1}{2}$	$1\frac{1}{4}$	2
Average No. of Orders saved p.a.	–	5	$7\frac{1}{2}$	$8\frac{3}{4}$	3
Ordering cost Savings p.a.	–	(5 × 20) = £100	($7\frac{1}{2}$ × 20) £150	($8\frac{3}{4}$ × 20)= £175	4
Price saving per item	–	20p	40p	50p	5
per annum	–	(2000 × 20p) =400	(2000 × 40p) = 800	(2000 × 50p) = 1000	
TOTAL GAINS		£500	£950	£1175	6
Stockholding Cost p.a.	(100 × 10 × .2) = £200	(200 × 9.8 × .2) = £392	(400 × 9.6 × .2) = £768	(800 × 9.5 × .2) = £1520	7
Additional costs incurred by increased order	–	(£392 – £200) = £192	(£768 – £200) = £568	(£1520 – £200) = £1320	8
NET GAIN (LOSS)	–	£308	£382	(£145)	9

Cost/Savings Comparisons EOQ to Discount Points.

Table 2

From the above table it will be seen that the most economical order quantity is 800 brackets, thereby gaining the 4% discount.

Notes:

a. Line 2 is $\frac{\text{Demand of 2000}}{\text{Order quantity}}$

b. Line 7 is the cost of carrying the average stock, ie

$\frac{\text{order quantity}}{2}$ × Cost per item × carrying cost percentage.

c. Line 9 is Line 6 minus Line 8.

MARGINAL COSTS AND EOQ CALCULATIONS.

11. It cannot be emphasised too strongly that the costs to be used in EOQ calculations must be true marginal costs, ie the costs that alter as a result of a further order of carrying another item in stock. It follows therefore that fixed costs should not be used in the calculations. In the examples used in this chapter the costs have been clearly and simply stated. In examination questions this is not always the case and considerable care is necessary to ensure that the appropriate costs are used.

SUMMARY.

12.

a. The EOQ is the order quantity which minimises the total costs involved which include holding costs and order costs.

b. The basic EOQ calculation is based on constant ordering and holding costs, constant demand and instantaneous replenishment.

c. The basic EOQ formula is $\sqrt{\frac{2.Co.D}{Cc}}$

d. Where replenishment is not instantaneous, eg in own manufacture the formula becomes $\sqrt{\frac{2.Co.D}{Cc(1 - \frac{D}{R})}}$

e. Where replenishment is not instantaneous, the EOQ calculated is larger than the basic EOQ.

f. Where stockouts are permitted and stock-out costs are known, the formula becomes:

$$\sqrt{\frac{2.Co.D}{C_c}} \cdot \sqrt{\frac{C_c + C_s}{C_s}}$$

g. Where larger quantities are ordered to take advantage of price discounts stockholding costs increase, but savings are made in the price reductions and reduced ordering costs.

h. The costs to be used in EOQ calculations must be marginal costs. Fixed costs should not be included.

SELF REVIEW QUESTIONS.

1. *What are the assumptions usually made in EOQ calculations? (2)*
2. *What is the basic EOQ formula? (4)*
3. *How is the formula modified to take account of gradual replenishment? (5)*
4. *What is the formula when stockouts are permitted? (7)*
5. *What are the cost effects of buying larger quantities to obtain a quantity discount? (9)*
6. *What type of costs should be used in EOQ calculations? (11)*

APPENDIX 1.

Derivation of basic EOQ formula.

Let	D	=	annual demand
	O	=	order quantity
	Co	=	Cost of ordering for one order
	Cc	=	carrying cost for one item p.a.

$$\text{Average Stock} = \frac{Q}{2}$$

$$\text{Total annual stock holding cost} = \frac{QCc}{2}$$

$$\text{Number of orders per annum} = \frac{D}{Q}$$

$$\text{Annual ordering costs} = \frac{DCo}{Q}$$

$$\text{TOTAL COST} = \frac{QCc}{2} + \frac{D}{Q}\,Co$$

The order quantity which makes the total cost (Tc) at a minimum is obtained by differentiating with respect to Q and equating the derivative to zero.

$$\frac{dTc}{dQ} = \frac{Cc}{2} - \frac{DCo}{Q^2}$$

and when $\frac{dTC}{dQ} = 0$ costs are at a minimum,

$$\text{ie } 0 = \frac{Cc}{2} - \frac{DCo}{Q^2}$$

and to find Q,

$$\frac{DCo}{Q^2} = \frac{Cc}{2}$$

$$2DCo = Q^2Cc$$

$$\frac{2DCo}{Cc} = Q^2$$

$$Q \text{ (ie the EOQ)} = \sqrt{\frac{2.Co.D}{Cc}}$$

APPENDIX 2.

Derivation of EOQ with gradual replenishment

It will be recalled that gradual replenishment results in a stock level profile of the following shape where replenishment takes over time, t, at rate R.

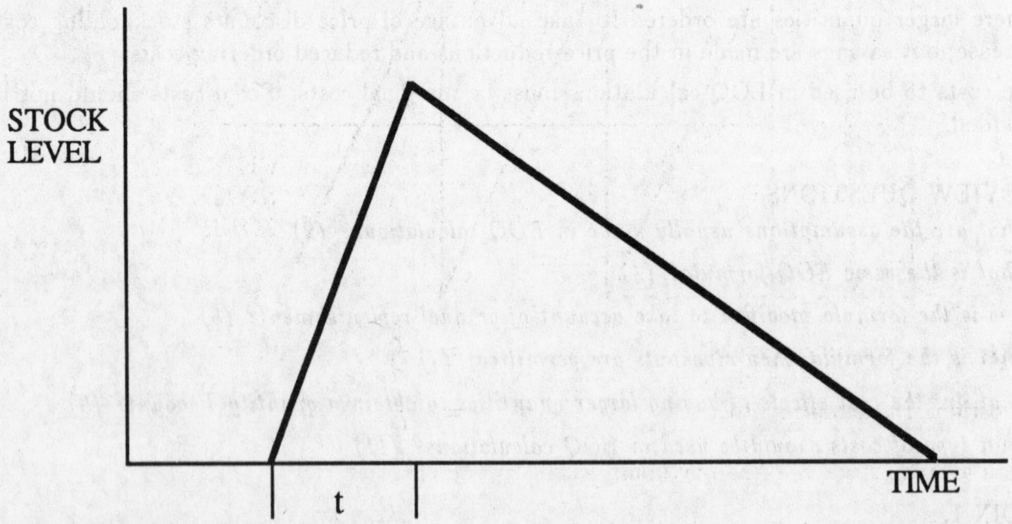

$$\text{as No. of batches} \times R \times t = D$$

$$\text{ie } \frac{D}{Q} \times R \times t = D$$

$$\therefore t = \frac{Q}{R}$$

The average stock is half the height of the triangle and the height is determined by the rate of replenishment less the demand over the replenishment time.

$$\text{Average stock} = \frac{t(R\text{-}D)}{2}$$

Substituting for t

$$\text{Average stock} = \frac{\frac{Q}{R}(R - D)}{2}$$

$$\text{or} \quad \frac{Q(1 - \frac{D}{R})}{2}$$

$$\text{Total annual stockholding cost} = \frac{Q(1 - \frac{D}{R})Cc}{2}$$

which expression can be substituted for the corresponding expression in Appendix 1, and the identical steps following resulting in a modified EOQ formula thus

$$\text{EOQ (with gradual replacement)} = \sqrt{\frac{2.Co.D}{Cc(1 - \frac{D}{R})}}$$

APPENDIX 3.

Derivation of EOQ where stockouts are permitted

Let all symbols have the meanings previously described.

Total cost = Ordering Cost + Carrying Cost + Stockout Cost

$$\text{where Annual ordering cost} = \frac{DC_0}{Q}$$

To find the carrying and stockout costs it is necessary to find how much of the time the firm carries stock or is out of stock thus.

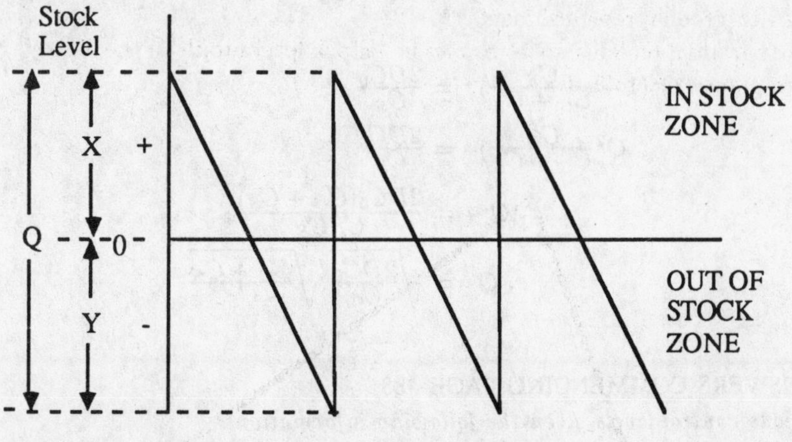

$\therefore$ Proportion of time in stock $= \frac{x}{Q}$

proportion of time out of stock $= \frac{y}{Q}$

and as average stock is $\frac{1}{2}$ the maximum level

Carrying Cost (i.e. relating to 'instock' zone) $= \frac{1}{2}xCc\frac{x}{Q}$

Out of stock cost (i.e. relating to 'stockout' zone) $= \frac{1}{2}yCs\frac{y}{Q}$

Thus Total Cost

$$= \frac{DC_0}{Q} + \frac{1}{2}xCc\frac{x}{Q} + \frac{1}{2}yCs\frac{y}{Q}$$

and substituting for y

$$= \frac{DC_0}{Q} + \frac{\frac{1}{2}x^2C_C}{Q} + \frac{\frac{1}{2}(Q-x)^2}{Q}C_S$$

This is the total cost function and, as usual, to find the minimum it is necessary to differentiate and set the result to zero.

However as there are two independent variables x and Q it is necessary to partially differentiate with respect to x and Q and set the results to zero.

$$\frac{\partial T}{\partial x} = \frac{xC_C}{Q} - \frac{(Q-x)C_S}{Q}$$

$$\frac{\partial TC}{\partial Q} = \frac{-DC_0}{Q^2} - \frac{\frac{1}{2}x^2C_C}{Q^2} + \frac{Q(Q-x)C_S - \frac{1}{2}(Q-x)^2}{Q^2}C_S$$

Setting to zero and solving

$$\frac{1}{Q^2}(xC_C - (Q-x)C_S) = 0$$

$$\therefore\ x = Q\frac{C_S}{C_C + C_S}$$

$$-\frac{1}{Q^2}(DC_0 + \tfrac{1}{2}x^2C_C - \tfrac{1}{2}(Q^2 - x^2)C_S) = 0$$

$$Q^2 = \frac{2DC_0}{C_S} + \frac{x^2C_C}{C_S} + x^2$$

$$= \frac{2DC_0}{C_S} + x^2\frac{(C_C + C_S)}{C_S}$$

and as $x = Q\frac{C_S}{C_C + C_S}$ this can be substituted as follows

$$Q^2 = \frac{2DC_0}{C_C} + \frac{Q^2C_S}{C_C + C_S}$$

$$\therefore\ Q^2(1 - \frac{C_S}{C_C + C_S}) = \frac{2DC_0}{C_S}$$

$$Q^2\frac{C_C}{C_C + C_S}) = \frac{2DC_0}{C_S}$$

$$\therefore\ Q^2 = \frac{2DC_0(C_C + C_S)}{C_CC_S}$$

$$\therefore\ Q = \sqrt{\frac{2DC_0}{C_C}}.\sqrt{\frac{C_C + C_S}{C_S}}$$

EXERCISES WITH ANSWERS COMMENCING PAGE 488

A1. Calculate the various control levels given the following information:

Normal usage	*560 per day*
Minimum usage	*240 per day*
Maximum usage	*710 per day*
Lead Time	*15-20 days*
EOQ	*10,000*

A2. (a) A company uses 100,000 units per year which cost £3 each. Carrying costs are 1% per month and ordering costs are £250 per order.

What is the EOQ?

(b) What would be the EOQ if the company made the items themselves on a machine with a potential capacity of 600,000 units per year?

A3. Demand is 5000 units per year. Ordering costs are £100 and the basic unit price is £5. Carrying costs are 20% p.a.

Discounts are available thus:

1200 – 1399	*less 10%*
1400 – 1499	*less 15%*
1500 and over	*less 20%*

What is the most economical quantity to order?

EXAMINATION QUESTIONS WITH ANSWERS COMMENCING PAGE 488

A4. You are determining the stock policy for Part K and have the following data:

Cost of placing an order and receiving delivery £50
Holding cost per unit of stock for one year £2.40
Annual demand, certain and regular 48,000 units
Estimated purchase cost per unit £1.00
Delivery time after placing the order 2 weeks

You are required to:

(a) calculate the total cost of placing orders and holding stock if 20, 40, 60, 80 or 100 orders are placed during the year.

(b) determine the minimum cost using a simple EBQ model of

$$q = \sqrt{\frac{2cd}{h}}$$

(c) calculate, and comment upon, the effect of a discount of 5% for orders in excess of 2,000 units.

(CIMA QUANTITATIVE TECHNIQUES)

A5. The purchasing manager of Elstore Limited, an electrical components retailer, holds a regular stock of, among other things, quasitrons. Over the past year he has sold, on average, 25 a week and he anticipates that this rate of sale will continue during the next year (which you may take to be 50 weeks). He buys quasitrons from his supplier at the rate of £5 for 10, and everytime he places an order it costs on average £10 bearing in mind the necessary secretarial expenses and the time involved in checking the order. As a guide to the stockholding costs involved, the company usually value their cost of capital at 20% and as the storage space required is negligible, he decides that this figure is appropriate in this case. Furthermore, the prices charged to customers are determined by taking the purchasing and stockholding costs and applying a standard mark up of 20% .

Required:

(a) Currently the manager is reviewing his ordering and pricing policies and needs to know how many quasitrons he should order each time and what price he should charge. What would be your advice? (State any assumptions that you make.)

(b) If he now finds out that he can get a discount of 5% for ordering in batches of 1,000, would you advise him to amend the ordering and pricing policy that you have suggested and, if so, to what?

(c) How large would the percentage holding cost have to be for the manager to be indifferent between taking advantage of the quantity discount and maintaining the original ordering policy that you have suggested? Comment on the value that you have obtained.

(ACCA, Quantitative Analysis)

A6. An electrical wholesaler sells, amongs other things, a certain model of refrigerator, for which he pays £100. To avoid paying the manufacturer's delivery charge he arranges collection of the refrigerators from the manufacturer's warehouse. This is done by a small local haulier who has available two sizes of van, the smaller holding up to 20 refrigerators and the larger being able to carry anything up to 30. The prices charged by the haulier depend upon which van is used (but not upon how many refrigerators are actually delivered in each van load). These prices are:

Small Van: £50 per delivery
Large Van: £70 per delivery

On analysing the demand pattern for this model of refrigerator, the wholesaler finds that he has sold, on average 240 a year over the last 3 years at an approximately constant rate throughout the year. He expects this demand pattern to continue for the foreseeable future. The annual stockholding cost is unknown but may be taken as a proportion i of the unit cost of a refrigerator.

Required:

(a) The wholesaler has to decide whether he should arrange delivery using the smaller van or the larger van. For what range of values of i would it be more economical for the wholesaler to make use of the smaller van?

(b) Having decided to use the smaller van, the wholesaler is now made an offer by the haulier whereby the small van could make two trips on each occasion and so delivery up to 40 refrigerators. The price of the total delivery would be only £75. For what range of values of i would it be more economical for the wholesaler to take advantage of the offer?

(c) Comment on the analysis that you have performed and advise the wholesaler on the course of action regarding the delivery of refrigerators.

(ACCA Quantitative Analysis)

A7. Raw material Z is used by your organisation at the rate of 200 kgs per week in a 50 week year. The cost of the purchasing office for the forthcoming year has been budgeted using the formula.

$$\textit{Total cost } (\pounds) = 10,000 + 15 \times \textit{number of orders.}$$

when the number of orders is between 1,000 and 1,500 per annum.

The cost of Z is expected to be stable throughout the year at £30 per kg.

There are no variable costs associated with receipt of the material as it is delivered by the suppliers directly into storage.

Stockholding costs have been estimated at 25% per annum,.

You are required to:

(a) calculate the economic order quantity using the basic model.

$$q* = \sqrt{\frac{2 \times \textit{annual demand} \times \textit{cost of order}}{\textit{cost of capital} \times \textit{unit price}}}$$

(b) describe briefly and calculate the effect on the economic order quantity of the following independent events:

(i) an increase in stockholding costs to 35%

(ii) a reduction in the price of Z to £20 per kg.

(ii) an increase to 250 kgs in the quantity used per week.

(c) comment on the sensitivity of the economic order quantity to changes in the variables as evaluated in (b)

(CIMA QUANTITATIVE TECHNIQUES)

A8. Your organisation uses 5,000 units of part F each year and 10,000 units of part G each year of 48 working weeks.

From the regular supplier, part F costs £25 per unit.

From a different regular supplier, parg G costs £32 per unit.

Because of the technical characteristics of the product the cost of order, receiving and testing each batch of either F or G has been estimated at the relatively high amount of £150.

A third suplier has recently offered to supply parts F and G on a regular monthly, i.e. twelve times per annum, basis. He quotes the same price per unit for both F and G, and your organisation has estimated the cost of ordering, receiving and testing of each monthly batch at £250 per month.

Whichever supplier is used, the storage costs are £2 per unit per annum based on the average annual stock.

Assume certainty of demand, lead time and costs.

You are required to:

(a) calculate and state the EOQ for part F and for part G from the present supplier.

(b) calculate and state the total minimum cost for part F and for part G for the year from the present supplier,

(c) calculate and state the price for part F and for part G if a change to the new supplier is to be worthwhile.

(CIMA QUANTITATIVE TECHNIQUES)

A9. The demand for a particular product is 12,000 units per year.

The costs associated with ordering include fixed salaries and costs of £4,000 per annum and variable costs of £30 per order. Storage costs consist of rent of £2,000 per annum and interest and variable costs at the rate of £25 per unit of product.

You are required to:

a. state five of the normal assumptions incorporated in the simple economic batch quantity (EBQ) ordering model sometimes presented as:

$$Q = \sqrt{\frac{2cd}{ip}}$$

b. extend the simple model to include the situation where the business is making the parts itself at a rate R per annum instead of ordering them from an outside supplier. Show clearly the derivation of this extension. Draw a diagram to show how stock levels will vary over time;

c. calculate the economic order quantity with replenishment taking place:

i. of the whole order at the same time;

ii. at the rate of 50,000 per annum;

d. comment on your answers to (c) (i) and (ii) above.

(CIMA Quantitative Techniques)

A10. A company works 50 weeks in a year. For a certain part, included in the assembly of several products, there is an annual demand of 10,000 units. The part may be obtained from either an outside supplier or a subsidiary company. The company's cost of capital is 20% per annum.

The following data relating to the part are given.

	From outside supplier	From subsidiary company
	£	£
Purchase price, per unit ...	12	13
Storage and all carrying costs, including capital costs per unit per annum	2	2
Cost of placing an order ...	10	10
Cost of receiving an order ...	20	15
	weeks	weeks
Delivery time, certain ...	10	5

You are required to:

a. calculate the minimum cost for a year using the outside supplier;

b. calculate the minimum cost for a year using the subsidiary company;

c. state, with reasons and numerical calculation, the difference it would make to these total costs if storage and carrying costs rose to £5 per unit per year.

(CIMA Quantitative Techniques)

EXERCISES WITHOUT ANSWERS

B1. A firm uses 20,000 units p.a., ordering costs are £500 and the unit price is £6. If carrying costs are 20% p.a. and the cost of a stockout is estimated at £3 per item what is the EOQ?

B2. A firm estimated demand at 10,000 units, at £5 each carrying cost with an order cost of £200 and calculated the EOQ accordingly which was used throughout the year when stocks were exhausted. In the event demand was 13,000 units. What was the cost or gain from the inaccurate demand forecasting?

B3. Assume the same data as Exercise A3 except discounts of 4% , 6% and 8% respectively. What is the most economical quantity to order?

EXAMINATION QUESTIONS WITHOUT ANSWERS.

B4. Electropoint Ltd. is concerned about the stock level of their positronic circuits which appears to be too low. They are currently ordering the circuits, which cost £4 each, in batches of 200 and demand for the circuits is fairly constant at 10 a day for each of the 250 working days in the year. The cost of ordering a batch of circuits is £25. The inventory carrying cost is estimated at 12 1/2% of the cost of a circuit.

Required:

a. Calculate the economic order quantity and the annual savings which would be made over the current policy of ordering in batches of 200.

b. The supplier of the positronic circuits has agreed to reduce the price of the circuits for larger orders. The negotiated price structure is:

Order Level	*Unit Cost (£)*
0–399	*4.00*
400–599	*3.90*
600+	*3.80*

How does this affect the optimal order quantity?

c. One of the major problems in inventory control is the estimation of the inventory carrying cost. In this problem we have assumed that the carrying cost is proportional to the cost of a unit, i.e. 12 1/2% . In practice, what approach might the accountant use when estimating the magnitude of such a cost?

(ACCA Management Mathematics)

B5. A company has estimated its requirements for a particular component over the next twelve months to be as follows:

Month	*Jan.*	*Feb.*	*Mar.*	*Apr.*	*May*	*June*
Demand (Units)	*2,000*	*2,025*	*1,950*	*2,000*	*2,100*	*2,050*
Month	*July*	*Aug.*	*Sept.*	*Oct.*	*Nov.*	*Dec.*
Demand (Units)	*2,000*	*1,975*	*1,900*	*2,000*	*1,900*	*2,100*

The components are purchased from an outside supplier for £2 each and the annual inventory holding costs are estimated to be 10% of the cost of the component. The order cost averages £150 per day.

Required:

i. As the above demand figures exhibit relatively little variability treat the problem as one of constant demand and determine the economic order quantity (EOQ). How frequently should orders be plaed and what would be the total annual inventory holding cost?

ii. It is now the 1 January and you have no stock on hand. You have just received your first order of components from the suppliers. Given that the demand pattern above actually occurs and that you use an economic order quantity policy as calculated in (i) determine for each month the starting and ending stock. Hence, calculate the actual annual inventory holding cost assuming that all demands are to be satisfied. If, in addition, there is a shortage cost of £4 per item per year, calculate the total annual shortage cost incurred.

iii. Comment on the difference between the two inventory holding costs calculated in (i) and (ii) and indicate the implications of this for the economic order quantity model.

(ACCA Management Mathematics.)

B6. Your organisation uses 1,000 packets of paper each year of 48 working weeks. The variable costs of placing an order, progressing delivery and payment have been estimated at £12 per order.

Storage and interest costs have been estimated at £0.50 per packet per annum based on the average annual stock.

The price from the usual supplier is £7.50 per packet for any quantity.

The usual supplier requires four weeks between order and delivery.

A potential supplier has offered the following schedule of prices and quantities.

£7.25 per packet for a minimum quantity of 500 at any one time.

£7.00 per packet for a minimum quantity of 750 at any one time.

£6.94 per packet for a minimum quantity of 1,000 at any one time.

If more than 450 packets are received at the same time an additional fixed storage cost of £250 will be payable for the use of additional space for the year.

Assume certainty of demand, lead time and costs.

You are required to:

(a) calculate and state the EOQ from the existing supplier.

(b) calculate and state the stock level at which the orders will be placed.

(c) calculate and state the total minimum cost for the year from the existing supplier.

(d) calculate and state the total minimum cost if you change to the new supplier.

(CIMA Quantitative Techniques)

14 Inventory Control – Safety Stocks and Reorder Levels

INTRODUCTION

1. This chapter shows how re-order levels and safety stocks are calculated so as to take account of the uncertainty inherent in demand and lead time estimates.

SETTING RE-ORDER LEVELS IN CONDITIONS OF CERTAINTY.

2. Where the rate of demand and the lead time is known with certainty, the reorder level is the rate of demand times the lead time. This means that, regardless of the length of the lead time or of the rate of demand, no buffer stock is necessary. This results in a situation as follows

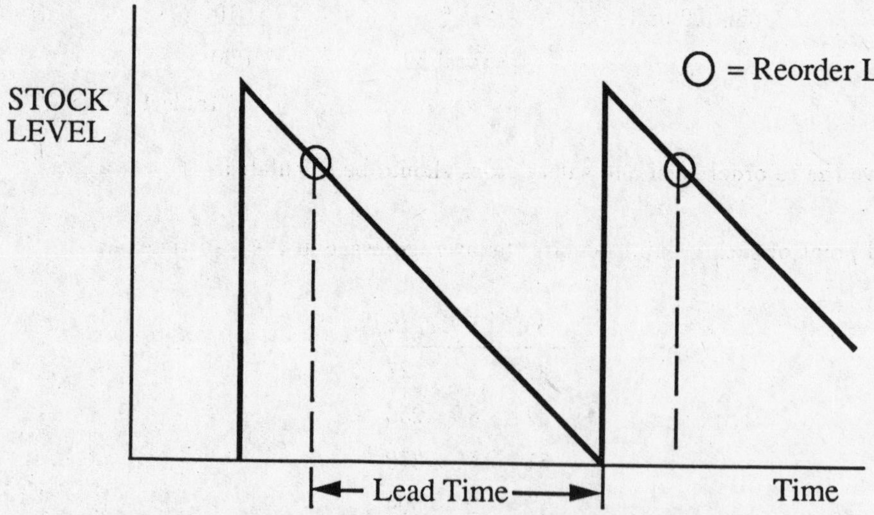

Re-order level in conditions of certainty. Figure 1

RE-ORDER LEVEL AND SAFETY STOCK RELATIONSHIP.

3. It will be seen from Figure 1 that, in conditions of certainty, the re-order level can be set so that stock just reaches zero and is then replenished. When demand and/or lead time vary, the re-order level must be set so that, on average, some safety stock is available to absorb variations in demand and/or lead time. In such circumstances the re-order level calculation can be conveniently considered in two parts.

a. the normal or average rate of usage *times* the normal or average lead time (ie as the re-order level calculation in conditions of certainty) PLUS
b. the safety stock

SAFETY STOCK CALCULATION BY COST TABULATION.

4. The amount of safety stock is the level where the total costs associated with safety stock are at a minimum. That is, where the safety stock holding cost plus the stock out cost is lowest. (it will be noted that this is a similar cost position to that described in the EOQ derivation described in chapter 13). The appropriate calculations are given below based on the following illustration.

that this is a similar cost position to that described in the EOQ derivation described in chapter 13). The appropriate calculations are given below based on the following illustration.

Example 1.

An electrical company uses a particular type of thermostat which costs £ 5. The demand averages 800 p.a. and the EOQ has been calculated at 200. Holding costs are 20% p.a. and stock out costs have been estimated at £ 2 per item that is unavailable. Demand and lead times vary, but fortunately the company has kept records of usage over 50 lead times as follows:

(a) Usage in Lead Time	(b) Number of times Recorded	(c) Probability ($\frac{b}{50}$)
25 – 29 units	1	.02
30 – 34 units	8	.16
35 – 39 units	10	.20
40 – 44 units	12	.24
45 – 49 units	9	.18
50 – 54 units	5	.10
55 – 59 units	5	.10
	Total 50	1.00

Table 1

From the above the re-order level and safety stock should be calculated.

Step 1.

Using the mid point of each group calculate the average usage in the lead time.

x	t	tx
27	1	27
32	8	256
37	10	370
42	12	504
47	9	423
52	5	260
57	5	285
	50	2125

Table 2

$$\text{Average usage} = \frac{2150}{50} = \underline{42.5}$$

Step 2.

Find the holding and stock out costs for various re-order levels.

A	B	C	D	E	F	G	H
Re-order Level	Safety Stock (A – 42.5)	Holding Cost (B × £1)	Possible Shortages (Mid-Points) Table 2 - A)	Probability (From Table 1)	No of Orders p.a. $(\frac{800}{200})$	Shortage Cost (D × E × F × £2)	Total Cost (C + G)
		£				£	£
45	2.5	2.5	2	.18	4	2.88	
			7	.10	4	5.6	
			12	.10	4	9.6	20.58
50	7.5	7.5	2	.10	4	1.6	
			7	.10	4	5.6	14.7
55	12.5	12.5	2	.10	4	1.6	14.1
60	17.5	17.5					17.5

Table 3

From Table 3 it will be seen that the most economical re-order level is *55 units.* This re-order level, with the average demand in the lead time of 42.5, gives a safety stock of 12.5, say 13 units.

SAFETY STOCK CALCULATION BY STATISTICAL METHODS.

5. The previous method of calculating Safety Stock was based on relative holding and stock out costs, but on occasions these costs, particularly the effects of stock outs, are not known. In such circumstances management may decided upon a particular risk level they are prepared to accept and the safety stock and re-order level are based upon this risk level. For example, management may decided that they are prepared to accept a 5% possibility of a stock out.

ILLUSTRATION OF A SAFETY STOCK CALCULATION BY STATISTICAL METHODS.

6. **Example 2.**

Using the data from Example 1, it was found that the average demand during the lead time was $42\frac{1}{2}$ units. The company has carried out further analysis and has found that this average lead time demand is made up of an average demand (D) of 3.162 units per day over an average lead time (L) of 13.44 days. Both demand and lead time may vary and the company has estimated that the standard deviation of demand (σ_D) is .4 units and the standard deviation of lead time (σ_L) is .75 days. The company are prepared to accept a 5% risk of a stock out and wish to know the safety stock required in the following three circumstances:

i. Where demand varies and lead time is constant
ii. Where the lead time varies and demand is constant
iii. Where both demand and lead time vary.

In each of these cases the ***average usage*** is $D \times L$ ie. $3.162 \times 13.44 = 42\frac{1}{2}$ units.

a. Safety stock given variable demand and constant lead time.

From normal area tables it will be found that 5% of the area lies above the mean $+1.64\sigma$.

$$\therefore \text{Safety stock} = 1.64 \times \text{standard deviation of demand for 13.44 days}$$
$$= 1.64 \times (0.4 \times \sqrt{13.44})$$
$$= \underline{\underline{2.40}}$$

Note: The standard deviation of *daily demand,* 0.4 is multiplied by $\sqrt{13.44}$ because standard deviations are not additive.

a. Safety Stock given variable lead time and constant demand.

$\therefore$ Safety stock = 1.64 × standard deviation of lead time for a demand of 3.162.

= 1.64 × (0.75)

= <u>1.23</u>

b. This is a combination of the two previous sections and is the sum of the separate safety stocks already calculated.

= 2.40 + 1.23

= <u>3.63</u>

Notes:

a. Safety stock calculations based on risk levels are commonly used.

b. In varying lead time/demand situations it can be very expensive to maintain sufficient safety stocks for very low stock out risks.

The above example uses the properties of the Normal Distribution and values obtained from Normal Area tables. It is but one further application of the statistical concepts covered earlier in the manual using continuous probability distributions. Discrete probabilities and expected values can also be used to incorporate variability.

SUMMARY.

7.

a. Safety stocks are necessary because of demand and/or lead time variations.

b. Re-order level is the average demand over the average lead time plus safety stock.

c. The safety stock level can be established by comparing the safety stock holding cost and the stock out cost at various re-order levels.

d. Where it is necessary to calculate the safety stock level to cater for a given risk of stock out, statistical methods, based on areas under the normal curve, can be used.

e. The means and standard deviations of demand and lead time must be calculated or estimated and the number of standard deviations appropriate to the risk level added to the average demand and/or lead time before multiplying together to establish the re-order level and thus the safety stock.

POINTS TO NOTE.

8.

a. This chapter concerns the effects of uncertainty (ie variability) on inventory control. It will be recalled from Chapter 1 that including risk and uncertainty is a necessary part of all OR studies.

b. Although some OR techniques have little practical application, this is definitely not true of inventory control.

SELF REVIEW QUESTIONS.

1. How is the re-order level set when demand and lead times are known with certainty? (2)

2. Why is the establishment of safety stocks essentially a cost balancing exercise? (4)

3. What are the appropriate costs to be considered in establishing an appropriate Safety Stock Level? (4)

4. How can safety stocks be estimated if all the relative costs are not known? (5 and 6)

EXERCISES WITH ANSWERS COMMENCING PAGE 488

A1. A company uses 2000 components per annum and the cost is £6 per component. Holding costs are £2 per component p.a. and stock out costs are £3 per component per item unavailable. The EOQ is 500 and demand is variable as follows:

Usage in lead time	Probability
80	0.2
90	0.5
100	0.3

What is the most economical re-order level 90, 95 or 100?

A2. The demand for an item is normally distributed with a mean of 50 per day and a standard deviation of 5 units. Given a lead time of 20 days what is the re-order level and safety stock to meet 90% of demands?

EXAMINATION QUESTIONS WITH ANSWERS COMMENCING PAGE 488

A3. Electropoint Ltd. has expanded the production of its domestic robots and now requires each year and at a constant rate, 200,000 positronic circuits which it obtains from an outside supplier. The cost of placing each order for the positronic circuits is £32 . For any circuit in stock it is estimated that the annual holding cost is equal to 10% of its cost. The circuits cost £8 each. No stock outs are permitted.

Required:

a. What is the optimal order size, and how many orders should be placed in a year?

b. What are the ordering and holding costs and hence what is the total relevant inventory cost per annum?

c. If the demand has been underestimated and the true demand is 242,000 circuits per annum, what would be the effect of keeping to the order quantity calculated in a. above and still meeting demand, rather than using the new optimal order level?

d. What does your answer to c tell you about the sensitivity of your model to changes in demand?

(ACCA Management Mathematics).

A4. Electra Limited is a small electronics company specialising in the assembly of a range of items from bought in components. The company is organised into a number of largely autonomous departments, each department dealing with one or two similar items. Department Q assembles just one item, a newly developed electronic appliance. The retail price of the appliance is £85 and it is assembled from five major components. The numbers of each component used in each appliance and their costs are as follows:

Componenet	Number per appliance	Unit cost (£)
A	2	7
B	2	4
C	5	2
D	1	10
E	5	1

The appliance is sold through just one major retail chain, and a contract has been signed for the supply of 5,000 appliances per year at a constant rate of 100 per week. In order to ensure continuous production adequate stocks of each component are kept as insurance against the suppliers' lead times, which are in some cases quite large. The stock control system devised for these five components operates as follows:

Component	Re-order Level	Re-order Quantity	Lead Time (Weeks)
A	500	1,000	2
B	1,000	2,000	4
C	2,000	5,000	3
D	300	500	2
E	5,000	10,000	8

As a guide to the stock costs involved, the element of the fixed overheads of the purchasing department which has been allocated to Department Q is £2,500 per year. Variable overheads amount to £25 per order placed plus £0.01 per item ordered. Likewise, the allocation of warehousing costs to Department Q amounts to a fixed, annual overhead of £4,000 plus 20% per annum of the value of the items in stock.

Required:

(a) Determine the total annual stockholding cost incurred by Department Q.

(b) Assuming that the given lead times are constant, determine the minimum cost stockholding system. What is the annual saving obtained by implementing this system?

(ACCA Quantitative Analysis)

A5. The following problem is concerned with inventory models in three particular circumstances: first, certain lead time and demand during the lead time; secondly, constant lead time but uncertain demand; and finally, uncertain lead time and uncertain demand.

The basic data have been determined as:

(i) an EOQ of 140 units (relevant to parts (a), (b) and (c);

(ii) orders placed every ten days (relevant to parts (a), (b) and (c); and

(iii) a seven-day lead time (relevant to parts (a) and (b)

(a) You are required to calculate and state the re-order point when lead time and demand are known with certainty.

(b) Analysis of past data, at a time which reflects environmental conditions which are expected to continue, provides the following probability distribution and cost data:

7 day lead time usage:	49 units	98 units	147 units
Probability	0.3	0.4	0.3

Cost per unit of overstock £1 each occurrence

Cost per unit of understock: £3 each occurrence

You are required to calculate and state the re-order point which, will on average, provide the lowest expected cost when there is an uncertain demand during the lead time.

(c) Consider finally a further element of uncertainty by assuming that the lead time previously taken to be 7 days certain, is now represented by a probability distribution:

Lead time	6 days	7 days	8 days
Probability	0.4	0.2	0.4

and that the probabilities are independent of the rate of demand during the lead time, which is also uncertain but with the following probability distribution for the daily rate of demand during the lead time:

Daily rate	7 units	21 units
Probability	0.5	0.5

The daily rate of demand during the lead time is either 7 units per day or 21 units per day of the lead time.

You are required to calculate and state the re-order point which will, on average, provide the lowest expected cost in the conditions of uncertain lead time and uncertain demand.

(CIMA Quantitative Techniques)

A6. One form of the economic order quantity (EOQ) model is

$$q* = \sqrt{\frac{2AC_0}{iC_S}}$$

where

$q*$ = *the optimal order quantity*

A = *the annual demand*

C_0 = *the cost associated with the placing of an order and subsequent receipt of the goods*

C_S = *the cost of the item*

i = *the opportunity cost of capital invested in stock*

Data that have been obtained from the records of the company include:

- estimated annual demand: 4,000 for a 50-week year
- cost of purchase order and specification sets: £6 each
- annual salary of purchase order clerk who prepares and processes 2,000 orders per year: £8,000
- goods received and inspection staff and associated expenses: estimated at £50 per order, of which £45 is fixed given the expected level of activity
- purchase price of the item: £1.10 per unit
- selling price: £1.50 per unit
- opportunity cost of capital for the next year. 20% per annum.

Analysis of demand during the average lead time of two weeks showed:

30 units in excess of average on	*15% of the occasions*
average on	*45% of the occasions*
15 units below average on	*40% of the occasions*

The cost of being out of stock of a unit when there was a demand for it has been estimated as merely the loss of profit which would have been earned if the unit had been available for sale.

You are required to:

(a) calculate the EOQ for this product;

(b) calculate the optimal reorder point;

(c) list and comment upon four *factors that would be relevant in determining the value of i;*

(d) comment upon the view sometimes expressed in the literature that EOQ models are too simple for practical purposes; in particular that they lead to overstock and waste.

(CIMA Quantitative Techniques)

EXERCISES WITHOUT ANSWERS

B1. The demand for an item is normally distributed with a mean of 200 units per day and a standard deviation of 18. The lead time is on average 30 days with a standard deviation of 5 days. What is the safety stock if the firm is prepared to accept a 10% risk of a stock out.

B2. Assume the data in B1 but calculate the safety stock if the firm is only prepared to accept a 1% risk of a stock out.

B3. Electropoint Ltd.has expanded the production of its domestic robots and now requires each year and at a constant rate, 200,000 positronic circuits which it obtains from an outside supplier. The cost of placing each order for the postronic circuits is £32. For any circuit in stock it is estimated that the annual holding cost is equal to 10% of its cost. The circuits cost £8 each. No stock outs are permitted:

Required:

a. What is the optimal order size, and how many orders should be placed a year?

b. What are the ordering and holding costs and hence what is the total relevant inventory cost per annum?

c. If the demand has been underestimated and the true demand is 242,000 circuits per annum, what would be the effect of keeping to the order quantity calculated in a. above and still meeting demand, rather than using the new optimal order level?

d. What does your answer to c. tell you about the sensitivity of your model to changes in demand?

(ACCA Management Mathematics)

B4. The usual inventory model $q = \sqrt{\frac{2C_0 D}{C_C}}$

where

q = *order quantity*
C_0 = *cost of placing an order*
D = *annual demand*
C_C = *cost per annum of carrying one unit*

includes amongst it assumptions that no stock-outs are permitted. In many situations it is possible to accumulate orders received, when there is no inventory to satisfy them, and deliver the accumulated ordrs immediately the product is received from the supplier. There may be a variety of costs associated with this situation and in the following calculations you should assume that these costs are equal to £2.

Other data, from which you should select those which are relevant includes: annual uniform demand 24,000 units per annum, the cost of placing an order is £20, of receiving, inspecting and checking a delivery is £70, the cost of carrying stock is £3 per unit per annum, lead time is 1/24th of a year, interest paid by the company, on average, for funds employed is 12% per annum, and the cost of extra storage facilities would be £500 per annum.

You are required to:

a. show that the economic batch quantity (EBQ) when stockouts are permitted is

$$q = \sqrt{\frac{2C_0D}{C_C}} \cdot \sqrt{\frac{C_0 + C_C}{C_S}}$$

where C_S is the stock-out cost;

b. calculate the EBQ and re-order point if no stock-outs are permitted:

c. calculate the EBQ and re-order point when stock-outs are permitted.

(CIMA, Quantitative Techniques)

15 Queueing

INTRODUCTION.

1. This chapter considers the application of queueing theory in a number of typical circumstances. Detailed derivation of the various formulae used is not given because the examinations for which most students are preparing concentrate on the practical use of the theory rather than on formal mathematical proofs.

QUEUE DEFINITION.

2. Queue. A queue, for queueing theory purposes, can be defined as an aggregation of items awaiting a service function. In our everyday lives we tend to think of queues as relating to people only. In dealing with queueing theory we must broaden our viewpoint considerably. Queues may consist of people, cars, components awaiting machining, telephone calls, aeroplanes, indeed any discrete items.

QUEUEING THEORY.

3. This can be defined as the construction of mathematical models of various types of queueing systems so that predictions may be made about how the system will cope with demands made upon it. Queueing theory is best suited to relatively simple queueing systems. More complex situations are normally dealt with by simulation techniques (to be dealt with later in the manual).

QUEUEING SITUATIONS.

4. In general, queues form when the rate of arrival of items requiring service is greater than the rate of service. This imbalance may only be temporary but during that temporary imbalance period a queue will form. Typical of the circumstance in which queueing theory might be applied are the following:

a. Shop counters. Customers arrive at varying intervals requiring service which takes a variable time. What is the number of assistants that will maximise profit, or provide the best service?
b. Telephone exchanges. The smaller the exchange the lower the cost but the greater the congestion. The larger the exchange the higher the costs but with reduced congestion.
c. Parts stores. Production workers waiting to draw out parts. What is appropriate number of service points and staff to produce lowest overall cost?
d. Airport runways. How many runways are needed to provide landing facilities after a reasonable queue (stack) time?

It will be seen from the representative examples given above that queueing theory may be applied in virtually any area where a bottleneck occurs.

ELEMENTS OF QUEUEING SYSTEMS.

5. A queue situation can be divided into four elements thus:

$$\underbrace{\text{ARRIVALS} \longrightarrow \text{QUEUE} \longrightarrow \text{SERVICE} \longrightarrow \text{OUTLET}}_{\text{SYSTEM}}$$

a. Arrivals. This is the element concerned with how items (people, components, cars etc) arrive in the system. Generally when dealing with queueing problems we are concerned with the rate of arrival or the time gap between arrivals, which amounts to the same thing. This chapter only deals with discrete item arrivals and does not consider continuous arrivals such as, for example, oil flow in a pipeline.

b. Queue. This element is concerned with what happens between the arrival of an item requiring service and the time when service is carried out. This is known as the QUEUE DISCIPLINE which is generally assumed to be First Come, First Served. Other disciplines are possible and these include, Last come First served, various priority methods based on urgency or importance, or priorities based on safety factors eg a large passenger aircraft might be allowed to land before a small one man plane which had been waiting longer.

c. Service. This element is concerned with the time taken to service a customer. The time may be constant (eg a machine process) or more likely, it will vary. Service times may be reduced by better training, more personnel, more or better equipment, all of which increase costs. Typically a queueing problem involves striking a balance between the cost of making reductions in service time and the benefits to be gained from such a reduction.

d. Outlet. The exist from the system. Generally this factor can be ignored but on occasions this may influence service and/or arrival times. For example, if there is only one door to the service point, through which people enter and leave after being serviced, it is possible that people leaving could affect the rate of arrival.

e. System. The whole situation being considered from arrival to exit. The time in the system is generally taken to be the queueing time plus the service time.

CLASSES OF QUEUEING SYSTEM.

6. Clearly there are inumerable classes of queueing systems in practice particularly if all the variations in queue discipline are considered, but the following four classes cover the simpler type of queueing systems likely to be met in examination questions.

a. single queue – single service point

b. multiple queues – multiple service points

c. single queue – multiple service points.

d. multiple queues – single service points

Problems which involve more complex patterns are normally best dealt with by simulation methods as previously mentioned.

ARRIVAL & SERVICE TIMING PATTERNS.

7. A better understanding of queueing theory and the various formulae will be gained if some consideration is given to the assumptions which are generally made regarding timing patterns.

Arrival patterns. The assumption in most queueing problems is that arrivals occur singly ie no simultaneous arrivals are possible. Arrivals may form a regular patterns by arriving at constant intervals, they may occur in groups, for example when a train arrives, or they may be at random intervals. Because arrival rates in most queueing situations are impossible to control, the random arrival pattern is most common. Study has indicated that in many circumstances the random arrival pattern can be approximated by a Poisson distribution.

Poisson distribution. It will be recalled that the poisson distribution is a special case of the binomial distribution. It is a discrete probability distribution (e.g. the number of arrivals in a minute may be 0, 1, 2, 3 etc, ie it must be an integer) which is related to a continuous probability distribution, i.e. the time interval between arrivals can be of any value (not just integers) and thus the distribution is continuous.

Service patterns. The time taken to service an item may be constant but, more likely, the time will vary. It may be possible to control the average service time (by training, better equipment) but the performance achieved for any given customer will almost certainly vary. To be able to tackle queueing systems mathematically the assumption often made is that service times form a negative exponential distribution.

Negative exponential distribution. This is a continuous probability distribution and provides the probability of the service being completed within a given period. With a negative exponential distribution the probability of a short service time is highest with reducing probabilities of longer service times. This can be depicted as follows:

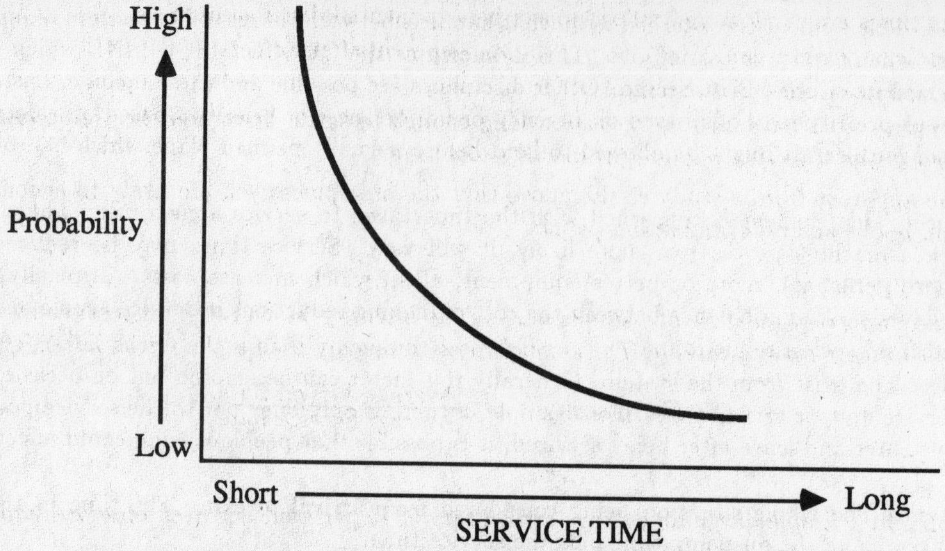

DISTRIBUTION OF SERVICE TIMES Figure 1

Clearly this is not realistic for many situations but the assumption of a more appropriate distribution, for example, a symmetrical normal distribution, makes mathematical analysis exceedingly complex and renders simulation necessary.

ARRIVAL AND SERVICE RATES.

8. As discussed above the two major factors in queueing problems are the arrival and service rates.

a. Arrival rate. The average rate of arrivals per unit of time. the symbol most commonly used is the Greek letter LAMBDA, λ

   Examples. Ten staff on average visit a stationery store each hour

$$\lambda = 10 \text{ (where time unit is an hour)}$$

   On average a plane arrives at an airport every 5 minutes.

$$\lambda = 12 \text{ (where time unit is an hour)}$$

b. Service rate. The average number of services completed in a unit of time. The symbol most commonly used is the Greek letter MU, μ.

   Examples. A cashier at a supermarket is able to deal with, on average, 480 customers per 8 hours shift.

$$\mu = 60 \quad \text{(where time unit is an hour)}$$

$$\text{or} \quad \mu = 480 \quad \text{(where time unit is an 8 hour shift)}$$

   In a given queueing problem it is, of course, necessary to express λ and μ in terms of the same unit. Invariably the unit chosen is an hour.

SIMPLE QUEUE CHARACTERISTICS.

9. The term 'simple queue' is a technical expression which should strictly be only applied to queuing problems with the following characteristics.

a. Single queue and a single service point.
b. The queue discipline is First come First served.
c. The queue has infinite capacity.
d. Arrivals are random and follow a Poisson distribution.
e. No simultaneous arrivals.

f. Service times are random and follow a negative exponential distributionm.
g. Discrete customers from an infinite population of potential customers.
h. Single, follow-on service discipline.
i. The system must have been in operation long enough to settle down and the traffic intensity (defined in the following paragraph) must be less than 1.

It will be apparent from a study of the above that the only places you are likely to encounter simple queues are in books and on examination papers.

TRAFFIC INTENSITY.

10. The most important measure of a simple queue is its intensity which is the ratio of the average arrival rate, λ to the average service rate, μ. The symbol most commonly used is the Greek letter RHO, ρ.

$$\text{Traffic Intensity} = \frac{\text{Average Arrival Rate}}{\text{Average Service Rate}}$$

$$\text{ie } \rho = \frac{\lambda}{\mu}$$

Example. In a simple queue an average arrival rate of 15 per hour has been observed and the service facility can on average deal with 20 items per hour.

$$\rho = \frac{\lambda}{\mu} = \frac{15}{20} = \underline{.75}$$

On occasions the arrival and service speeds are expressed differently. For example, the above situation could have been expressed as follows – The average time between arrivals is 4 minutes and the average service time is 3 minutes. In such cases

$$\text{Traffic intensity} = \frac{\text{average service time}}{\text{average inter-arrival time}}$$

$$\rho = \frac{3}{4} = \underline{.75}$$

Interpretation of traffic intensity. If there is no traffic in the system the traffic intensity is 0. If however the traffic intensity is 1 or more the queue will, theoretically, be of infinite length. In general the traffic intensity should not be greater than .8 because it can be shown that the average time in the system increases dramatically above this value. The only way that the traffic intensity can be kept at a reasonable figure is to provide adequate service facilities, assuming of course that the arrival rate cannot be controlled.

SIMPLE QUEUE FORMULAE.

11. Based on the arrival rate, the sevice rate, μ and the traffic intensity, ρ, formulae are available which enable predictions to be made about the systems behavour. There are three areas of importance to do with NUMBERS, TIMES and PROBABILITIES.

NUMBERS.

a. The average number of items in the queue including the times when there is no queue.

$$\frac{\rho^2}{1-\rho}$$

Example 1. (This example and the succeeding ones are based on the factors in Para. 10 ie $\lambda = 15$, $\mu = 20$ and $\rho = .75$)

$$\frac{.75^2}{1-.75} = \underline{\underline{2.25 \text{ items}}}$$

b. The average number of items in the queue when there is a queue

$$\frac{1}{1-\rho}$$

Example 2.

$$\frac{1}{1-.75} = \underline{\underline{4 \text{ items}}}$$

c. The average number of items in the system. The system includes items both in the queue and receiving service.

$$\frac{\rho}{1-\rho}$$

Example 3

$$\frac{.75}{1-.75} = \underline{\underline{\textbf{3 items}}}$$

Note that the average number in the queue is *NOT* 1 less than the average number in the system.

TIME.

d. The average time in the queue

$$\frac{\rho}{1-\rho} \times \frac{1}{\mu}$$

Example 4.

$$\frac{.75}{1-.75} \times \frac{1}{20} = \frac{3}{20} \text{ of an hour} = \underline{\underline{\textbf{9 MINS.}}}$$

e. The Average time in the system ie queue and service.

$$\frac{1}{1-\rho} \times \frac{1}{\mu}$$

Example 5.

$$\frac{1}{1-.75} \times \frac{1}{20} = \frac{1}{5} \text{ of an hour} = \underline{\underline{\textbf{12 MINS.}}}$$

Note. Average time in the system can also be found by finding the average time in the queue (ie. 9 MINS) and adding the average service time (ie 3 mins), making 12 mins in total.

PROBABILITIES.

f. The probability of queueing on arrival is equal to the traffic intensity,
Example 6.

$$\rho = \underline{\underline{\textbf{.75}}}$$

g. Probability of NOT queueing on arrival

$$1-\rho$$

Example 7.

$$1 - .75 = \underline{\underline{\textbf{.25}}}$$

h. Probability of there being any particular number, say n, in the system $= (1-\rho)\rho^n$.
Example 8. What is the probability of there being 2 items in the system?, 3 items?, 4 items?
2 items

$$(1-.75).75^2 = .141$$

There is a 14% chance (approx.) of there being 2 items in the system.
3 items

$$(1-.75).75^3 = .105$$

There is a 10% chance (approx.) of there being 3 items in the system.
4 items

$$(1-.75).75^4 = .079$$

There is an 8% chance (approx.) of there being 4 items in the system.

i. The probability of there being n or more items in the system $= \rho^n$

Example 9

What is the probability of there being 2 or more items in the system? 3 or more? 4 or more?

2 or more items

$$\rho^n = 0.75^2 = \underline{0.5625}$$

3 or more items

$$\rho^n = 0.75^3 = \underline{0.4219}$$

4 or more items

$$\rho^n = 0.75^4 = \underline{0.3164}$$

Note: Contrast these probabilities with those obtained in Example 8 for exactly 2, 3 and 4 items in the system.

Notes on formulae.

1. All of the formulae are useful at some time or other but the ones for the number and time in the queue and the number and time in the system are invariably required in examination questions.
2. Alternative forms of the formulae are possible but in order to avoid confusion these are not given.

USING QUEUEING THEORY.

12. Typically questions involve the cost of improving a service facility compared with the benefits to be gained from the improvement.

The cost factors generally involved include:

Service Costs.

a. The people required to provide or improve a service, eg packers are often provided by the side of supermarket cash desks to reduce service time.
b. The cost of better equipment or facilities, eg the provision of calculating display scales in some departmental stores or the provision of computer terminals in some travel agencies.
c. The provision of more service points.

Queueing Costs.

a. Lost costs of idle time due to waiting. Particularly important where the queue is formed by the firm's own employees, for example, fitters waiting at a Parts Store.
b. Lost sales due to customers going elsewhere upon seeing large queues.
c. Lost earning power when equipment has to wait some time to be repaired.

Cost balance. It must not be assumed that the best situation is to plan for no queues at all. The cost of providing and maintaining the service facilities must be compared with the cost of some queueing. The more service facilities that are provided inevitably means that they will be idle for some of the time. This may not seem too significant if a single clerk at an enquiry desk is considered but it would be an entirely different matter if the service facility was a large dry dock or an airport runway. The balance between service and queueing costs is often a matter of judgement. Queueing theory helps to provide some of the data on which to base that judgement.

Example 10.

In a large maintenance department, fitters draw parts from the Parts Store which is at present staffed by 1 storeman. The maintenance foreman is concerned about the time spent by fitters getting parts and wants to know if the employment of a stores labourer would be worthwhile. On investigation it is found

a. a simple queue exists
b. fitters cost £2.50 per hour
c. the storeman costs £2 per hour and can deal, on average, with 10 staff per hour
d. A stores labourer could be employed at £1.75 per hour and would increase the capacity of the stores to 12 per hour.

e. On average 8 fitters visit the store each hour.

There are two ways of tackling this problem.

Method 1.

Calculate the average number in the system before and after the introduction of the labourer, and compare the reduction in queueing costs thereby achieved with the extra service costs incurred. ie

CURRENT SYSTEM (ie 1 STOREMAN).

$$\rho = \frac{8}{10} = .8$$

Number in system

$$\frac{\rho}{1-\rho} = \frac{.8}{1-.8} = \underline{\mathbf{4Fitters}}$$

Costs/hour = 4 × £2.50 = **£10.00**

PROPOSED SYSTEM (ie STOREMAN + LABOURER).

$$\rho = \frac{8}{12} = .66$$

Number in system

$$\frac{\rho}{1-\rho} = \frac{.66}{1-.66} = \mathbf{2Fitters}$$

Costs.

Fitters Costs/hour = 2 × £2.50	=	£5.00
PLUS COST OF Labourer	=	£1.75
		£6.75

∴ Net saving of £3.25 so the employment of labourer would be recommended.

Method 2.

Calculate the average time in the system and multiply this by the number and cost of items requiring the service. This would be done for the current and proposed systems and the queueing savings achieved would be compared with the extra service costs incurred, ie.

CURRENT SYSTEM (ie 1 STOREMAN).

$$\rho = \frac{8}{10} = .8$$

Time in system

$$\frac{1}{1-\rho} \times \frac{1}{\mu} = \frac{1}{1-.8} \times \frac{1}{10} = \frac{1}{2} \text{ hour}$$

Fitters Costs/hour = $\frac{1}{2}$ × 8 × £2.50 = **£10.00**

PROPOSED SYSTEM (STOREMAN + LABOURER).

$$\rho = \frac{8}{12} = .66$$

Time in system

$$\frac{1}{1-.66} \times \frac{1}{12} = \frac{1}{4} \text{ hour}$$

Costs

Fitters costs/hour	=	$\frac{1}{4} \times 8 \times$ £2.50	= £5.00
PLUS COST of Labourer	=		£1.75
			£6.75

Results and recommendation identical to method 1.

Notes on example.

a. As example 10 illustrates there is usually more than one way to solve queueing problems.

b. The Storeman's cost of £2 per hour is common to both the current and proposed systems therefore it does not influence the result. This illustrates the general rule that it is the marginal increase/decrease in costs compared with the marginal increase/decrease in benefits with which we are concerned.

MULTI CHANNEL SYSTEMS.

13. A multi channel system is one where there is more than one service point. Many possible combinations exist eg channels in series, channels in parallel or combinations of series and parallel. Most of the types mentioned are best solved by simulation techniques but one particular variant can be adequately solved by the appropriate formulae.

Parallel multi channel system. This is a system with parallel service points of equal capacity served by a single queue with all of the other simple queue requirements fulfilled. The formulae involved are lengthy and if they are required in an examination it would be reasonable to expect them to be provided.

Traffic intensity for a parallel multi-channel system. It will be recalled that the traffic intensity for a single channel system was

$$\rho = \frac{\lambda}{\mu}$$

For a multi-channel system the only modification required is to multiply the service rate by the number of channels thus

$$\rho = \frac{\lambda}{c\mu}$$

where c is the number of service channels.

Example 11. The WYLE-U-WATE heel bar employs 3 operatives who can on average each repair the heels of 5 pairs of shoes an hour. If the average number of customers requiring service is 10 per hour calculate the traffic intensity.

Note:- This is a multi channel system where $c = 3$.

$\therefore$ Traffic Intensity $= \rho = \frac{\lambda}{c\mu}$

$= \frac{10}{3 \times 5} = \underline{\underline{.66}}$

Other multi channel formulae. Naturally, because multi channels are involved, the various formulae are more complicated. In addition each of the formulae use the value of the probability of there being no units in the system (P_0). This value may be given in an examination question but where it is not available the following formula can be used.

$$P_0 = \frac{c!(1-\rho)}{(\rho c)^c + c!(1-\rho)\left[\sum_{n=0}^{n=c-1} \frac{1}{n!}(\rho c)^n\right]}$$

where c = number of channels

$!$ = Factorial (eg 4! is $4 \times 3 \times 2 \times 1$ ie 24)

ρ = traffic intensity ie $\frac{\lambda}{c\mu}$

n = Integers from 0 to one less than the number of channels eg if numbers of channels was 4, n would be 0, 1, 2 and 3.

Note: The summation expression in the denominator in square brackets may look fearsome but it simplifies dramatically for example

when $c = 1$ the expression in square brackets $= 1$

$c = 2$ the expression in square brackets $= 1 + 2\rho$

$c = 3$ the expression in square brackets $= 1 + 3\rho + \frac{1}{2}(3\rho)^2$

and so on

EXAMPLE 12

Find the value of P_0 with the following values.

Let $\lambda = 12$, $\mu = 5$, $c = 3$

then $\rho = \frac{12}{3 \times 5} = \underline{0.8}$

$$\therefore P_0 = \frac{3!(1-0.8)}{(0.8 \times 3)^3 + 3!(1-0.8)\left[\frac{1}{0!}(0.8 \times 3)^0 + \frac{1}{1!}(0.8 \times 3)^1 + \frac{1}{2!}(0.8 \times 3)^2\right]}$$

$$= \frac{6 \times 0.2}{2.4^3 + 6 \times 0.2[1 + 3 \times 0.8 + \frac{1}{2}(3 \times 0.8)^2]}$$

$$= \frac{1.2}{13.824 + 1.2[1 + 2.4 + 2.88]}$$

$$= \frac{1.2}{21.36}$$

$$= \underline{\underline{\mathbf{0.056}}}$$

MULTI- CHANNEL FORMULAE.

14. The most important formulae are:

a. those concerned with TIME

Average time a customer is in the system (ie queueing and service)

$$= \frac{(\rho c)^2}{c!(1-\rho)^2 c\mu} P_0 + \frac{1}{\mu}$$

Average time a customer is in the queue (including times there is no queue)

$$= \frac{(\rho c)^c}{c!(1-\rho)^2 c\mu} P_0$$

b. those concerned with NUMBERS

Average number of customers in the system

$$= \frac{\rho(\rho c)^c}{c!(1-\rho)^2} P_0 + \rho c$$

Average number of customer in the queue

$$= \frac{\rho(\rho c)^c}{c!(1-\rho)^2} P_0$$

c. those concerned with PROBABILITY

Probability of queueing on arrival

$$= \frac{(\rho c)^c}{c!(1-\rho)} P_0$$

Probability of NOT queueing on arrival

$$= 1 - \frac{(\rho c)^c}{c!(1-\rho)} P_0$$

Probability of there being no units in the system

ie P_0 (formula given above)

Example 13
It will be recalled from the above that where $\lambda = 12$, $\mu = 5$ and $c = 3$

$$\rho = .8 P_0 = .056$$

Using this data calculate

i. The average time a customer is in the system.
ii. The average number of customers in the system.
iii. Whether any time would be saved for customers if the three channel system with a service rate of 5 per hour was replaced by a single channel system with an average service rate of 15 per hour.

i. Average time in system

$$= \frac{(\rho c)^c}{c!(1-\rho)^2 c\mu} P_0 + \frac{1}{\mu}$$

$$= \frac{(0.8 \times 3)^3}{3!(1-0.8)^2 3 \times 5} \times 0.056 + \tfrac{1}{5}$$

$$= \frac{(2.4)^3 0.056}{6(0.2)^2 15} + 0.2$$

$$= .415 \ hour$$

$$= \underline{25 \ MINS}$$

ii. Average number in the system

$$\frac{\rho(\rho c)^c}{c!(1-\rho)^2} P_0 + \rho c$$

$$= \frac{0.8(0.8 \times 3)^3}{3!(1-0.8)^2} \times 0.056 + (0.8 \times 3)$$

$$= 2.58 + 2.4$$

$$= \underline{\underline{\mathbf{4.98}}}$$

iii. Average time in 3 channel system (from a. above) = 25 mins.
Average time in a single channel system where $\lambda = 12$, $\mu = 15$, $\rho = 0.8$ is

$$\frac{1}{1-\rho} \times \frac{1}{\mu} \text{ (from Para 11e)}$$

$$= \frac{1}{1-0.8} \times \frac{1}{15} = .33 \text{ hr} = 20 \text{ MINS}$$

∴ There would be on average a 5 minutes savings for each customer by having a single channel fast service rather than having multiple channels each with a slow rate of service even though the multi channel system has a shorter queue time. In general queue time will always be less in a multi channel system which has the same value of p as a single channel system.

SUMMARY.

15.

a. Queues may consist of any discrete item eg cars, people, components.

b. Queues occur when service rates are out of balance with arrival rates albeit temporarily.

c. A queueing system includes the queue and the service point.

d. Arrivals are generally assumed, fairly realistically, to follow a Poisson distribution.

e. Service times are generally assumed, somewhat unrealistically, to follow a negative exponential distribution.

f. A simple queue is a queueing situation which fulfils a number of statistical requirements.

g. The traffic intensity of a system is the ratio of arrival rate to service rate and is generally known as RHO, ρ.

h. Numerous formulae exist to provide information about simple queueing systems. The more important ones being; average, number and time in the queue, and average, number and time in the system.

i. Typical simple queueing applications involve balancing the costs of reducing service times against the advantages to be gained by the reduction.

j. The multi channel systems covered in this chapter are those in which all simple queue requirements are covered except that more than one service point exists.

k. Typically when more complex queueing systems are being considered analytical methods ie those utilising queueing theory formulae, are usually too complex and simulation methods would be used.

POINTS TO NOTE.

16.

a. Many factors to do with real life queueing systems are not considred in this chapter eg the tendency for service rates to speed up during rush hours, bulk service situations eg. at a coach station.

b. If all service and arrival rates were constant queues would be non existent. It is the variability of these factors which is of importance.

c. Where the traffic intensity is say .5 or below, congestion is very slight and changes in traffic intensity do not make much difference. When ρ approaches unity small changes make substantial differences to congestion.

d. When multi channel systems are being considered it seems common practice for the formulae to be given in the examination paper.

e. A standardised notation for describing queues has been devised. This can be written as

(a/b/c)

a = arrival distribution

b = departure or service distribution

c = number of parallel servers

Thus a (M/M/3) queue may be described as one where the arrival distribution is poisson or Markovian, the service distribution is exponential, and there are three parallel service points.

This is known as the Kendall Notation and was devised in 1953.

The letter M appears because of the fact that queueing theory is related to a branch of quantitative analysis known as Markovian Decision Processes.

SELF REVEIW QUESTIONS.

1. Define a Queue (2)

2. What are the elements of a queueing system? (5)

3. What is the usual assumption regarding arrival rates? (7)

4. What are the symbols most commonly used for arrival rates and service rates? (8)

5. Define a simple queue (9)

6. What is the traffic intensity and how is it calculated? (10)

7. What are the simple queue formulae for:
the average number of items in the system,
the average time in the system, and
the probability of n items being in the system? (11)

8. What is a multi channel system? (13)

EXERCISES WITH ANSWERS COMMENCING PAGE 488

A1. A team of 10 unloaders is employed in the goods reception bay of a large warehouse. During an 8 hour day 40 lorries arrive and it takes the team 10 minutes to unload each lorry. Each team member is paid £3 per hour and it costs £10 per hour to keep lorries waiting. Studies show that increasing the team to 14 men would reduce the unloading time to 7 minutes.

Would it be worthwhile increasing the team to 14?

A2. A stores has an average arrival rate of 30 per hour. The management are seeking to assess whether there should be a two service point system each being capable of dealing with 18 per hour or a three service point system each dealing with up to 14 per hour. The two point system costs £80 per hour total and the three point system, £100 per hour in total. Customers waiting time is assessed at £6 per hour.

Calculate Po for the two and three service point systems.

A3. Which system in A2 is cheaper?

EXAMINATION QUESTIONS WITH ANSWERS COMMENCING PAGE 488

A4. It has been estimated that 20 people per hour will arrive for service. On average servicing will take two minutes. The cost of providing this service has two components: a fixed cost of £100 per hour for each service point and a variable cost of £20 per service.

You are required:

(a) to list three *of the significantly different basic assumptions on which simple queueing theory is based;*

(b) to calculate and state in the simple system described above;

(i) the traffic intensity and average time in the system;

(ii) the cost of providing the system;

(c) assuming that the one-channel system is modified at an extra cost of £20 per hour and £5 per service to provide a service time of one and a half minutes, to calculate and state:

(i) the traffic intensity and average time in the system;

(ii) the cost of providing the system.

(CIMA Quantitative Techniques)

A5. a. Describe, with the aid of realistic examples, the basic features of a 'queuing problem'. Your answer should indicate what information we need for analysing:

i. the input process;

ii. the service mechanism;

iii. the queue discipline.

You should also comment on the major assumptions implicit in the queuing model.

b. Discuss in general the major limitations of queuing theory and indicate ways in which these limitations might be overcome.

(ACCA Management Mathematics)

A6. Carnucopia is a large motor dealer with 12 showrooms in the South of England. In recent months problems have arisen with the supply of new cars to customers as unanticipated delays have been occurring in the pre-delivery inspection stage. The system operated by Carnucopia is that all stocks of new cars are held in a central compound and, when a sale is made at any one of the showrooms, the order is telephoned through to the compound and the car in question is taken from stock and submitted to pre-delivery inspection at the company's main workshop. After the car has been inspected and any faults repaired, the car is delivered to the appropriate showroom for collection by the customer.

In recent months, the company has been selling new cars at a rate of about 38 per week with no significant seasonable variation. Furthermore it seems reasonable to assume that sales are occurring randomly throughout the week as no regular patterns are discernible. Pre-delivery inspection is carried out on a "first-come-first-served" basis and taken on average about 2 hours for all models. The workshop has two inspection bays and the engineers who carry out the pre-delivery inspections work a 40 hour week. when the inspection is completed, delivery to the showroom usually takes one working day. You may assume that inspection engineers work a 5 day week and you should ignore the effects of weekends.

Required:

(a) State the two main conditions which must be satisfied by the pre-delivery inspection stage if it is to be regarded as a multiple server (M/M/c) queueing situation.

(b) Show that Po (the proportion of time that the workshop is idle) is 0.0256 and determine the average time which elapses between an order being placed and the car being delivered to the showroom.

(c) In view of the delays which have been occurring, the company accountant has been asked to advise whether it would be worthwhile employing two extra engineers in the workshop at a total cost of £220 per week. It has been estimated that this would reduce the average inspection time to $1\frac{1}{2}$ hours and the resulting earlier delivery would produce a saving of £2 per day for an average car as a result of earlier payment by the customer.

Would you recommend that the two extra engineers should be employed?

You are reminded that, with an arrival rate of λ and a service rate of μ in each of c channels.

$$\text{Average time in queue} = \frac{(\rho c)^c P_0}{c!(1-\rho)^2 c\mu}$$

$$\text{Average time in system} = \frac{(\rho c)^c P_0}{c!(1-\rho)^2 c\mu} + \frac{1}{\mu}$$

$$\text{where } P_0 = \left\{\sum_{i=0}^{c-1} \frac{(\rho c)^i}{i!} + \frac{(\rho c)^c}{c!(1-\rho)}\right\}^{-1} \quad \text{and } \rho = \frac{\lambda}{c\mu}$$

(ACCA Quantitative Analysis)

EXERCISES WITHOUT ANSWERS

B1. Calculate P_0 for a multi-channel system having 2 channels each capable of dealing with 20 arrivals per hour and where the average number of customers is 45 per hour.

B2. What is the average number of customers in the queue in the system depicted in B1?

B3. What is the average time a customer is in the system depicted in B1?

EXAMINATION QUESTIONS WITHOUT ANSWERS.

B4. Your company is considering changing the present system of serving customers who arrive in person and wait for service. The existing single service channel can service ten people an hour at a variable cost of £8 per person. The service facilities have a fixed cost of £50 per hour. The demand for these services has increased from four persons per hour when first offered, to the current eight per hour and is expected to increase to 15 per hour next year.

Alternative service patterns have been considered. Either a larger single service channel that would be able to service 20 people an hour at a variable cost of £7 per person and fixed costs of £120 per hour, or the addition of another single service channel which would still have a variable cost of £8 per person but additional fixed costs of £60 per hour. Customer time has been estimated to have a value of £25 per hour.

You are reminded that:

- *for a single system:*

$$\text{Average time a customer is in the system} = \frac{1}{1-\rho} \times \frac{1}{\mu}$$

$$\text{Average time a customer is in the queue} = \frac{\rho}{1-\rho} \times \frac{1}{\mu}$$

- *for a multiple system:*

$$\text{Average time a customer is in the system} = \frac{(\rho c)^c}{c!(1-\rho)^2 c\mu} P_0 + \frac{1}{\mu}$$

$$\text{Average time a customer is in the queue} = \frac{(\rho c)^c}{c!(1-\rho)^2 c\mu} P_0$$

and that: $$P_0 = \frac{c!(1-\rho)}{(\rho c)^c + c!(1-\rho)\left\{\sum_{n=0}^{c-1} \frac{1}{n!}(\rho c)^n\right\}}$$

You are required to:

a. calculate the cost to the company of the optimum service system, ignoring customers' time, currently and next year;

b. calculate the cost in each system to the customer next year;

c. state which system the company should choose next year if it takes into account half the value of customers' time.

(CIMA Quantitative Techniques)

16 Simulation

INTRODUCTION

1. This chapter defines models and simulation and shows how simulation can be used in a variety of business planning and decision making circumstances. Simulations involving random factors (so called Monte Carlo simulations) are explained and also the widespread use of computers for simulation purposes.

SIMULATION DEFINITION.

2. Simulation is the process of experimenting or using a model and noting the results which occur. In a business context the process of experimenting with a model usually consists of inserting different input values and observing the resulting output values. For example, in a simulation of a queueing situation the input values might be the number of arrivals and/or service points and the output values might be the numbers and/or times in the queue.

WHY IS SIMULATION USED?

3. Simulation is used where analytical techniques are not available or would be overly complex. Typical business examples are: most queueing systems other than the very simplest, inventory control situations, production planning problems, corporate planning etc, etc. Simulation often provides an insight into a problem which would be unobtainable by other means. By means of simulation the behaviour of a ystem can be observed over time and, because only a model of the system is used the actual time span can be compressed.

Thus for example, the simulation of an 'inventory systems' performance over 30 months could be carried out using a computer in as many minutes. In addition, the analyst can manipulate or experiment with the system at will. He could for example, alter the frequencies of receipts and issues, the decision rules governing re-order levels and re-order quantities and so on to observe the effects of these changes on the system being simulated or imitated. Fundamental to simulation is the concept of a model.

BUSINESS MODELS.

4. A model is any representation (physical or abstract) or a real thing, event or circumstances. Physical models, such as aircraft models for wind tunnel testing, models of space capsule controls, architectural layout models, are well known, but for business planning and decision making purposes are rarely appropriate. Instead, symbolic models are generally used. These are models which represent reality in numeric, algebraic or graphical form. The most useful models for business simulation are discrete models. These are models which enable the system being simulated to be observed or sampled at selected time intervals. Thus an inventory simulation might show stock levels on a daily basis. Alternatively a queuing simulation for supermarket checkouts might use a five minute interval to assess performance. The interval chosen should be that appropriate to the operational reality of the system being simulated.

MODEL CONSTRUCTION.

5. The success of a simulation exercise is related to the predictive quality of the underlying model, so that considerable care should be taken with model construction. Important factors in model development are:

a. Objective oriented. The model should be constructed with some definite purpose and the model results must be directly related to this purpose.

b. Critical variables and relationships. Model buildings is an iterative, creative process with the aim of identifying those variables and relationships which must be included in the model. It is not essential or indeed desirable to include all variables in the model.

c. Simplicity. The best model is the simplest that has adequate predictive qualities.

d. Management involvement. To construct good models there must be a thorough understandingof actual operations. Only management have this knowledge, so they must be involved. If model building is left entirely to OR or computer specialists , over-elaborate and sophisticated models may result which do not accurately represent reality.

e. Model development. If a model is to be used more than once, eg a corporate planning model used each quarter, care must be taken to modify and refine the model characteristics so that it continues to represent reality.

Figure 1 provides an overview of model development and use.

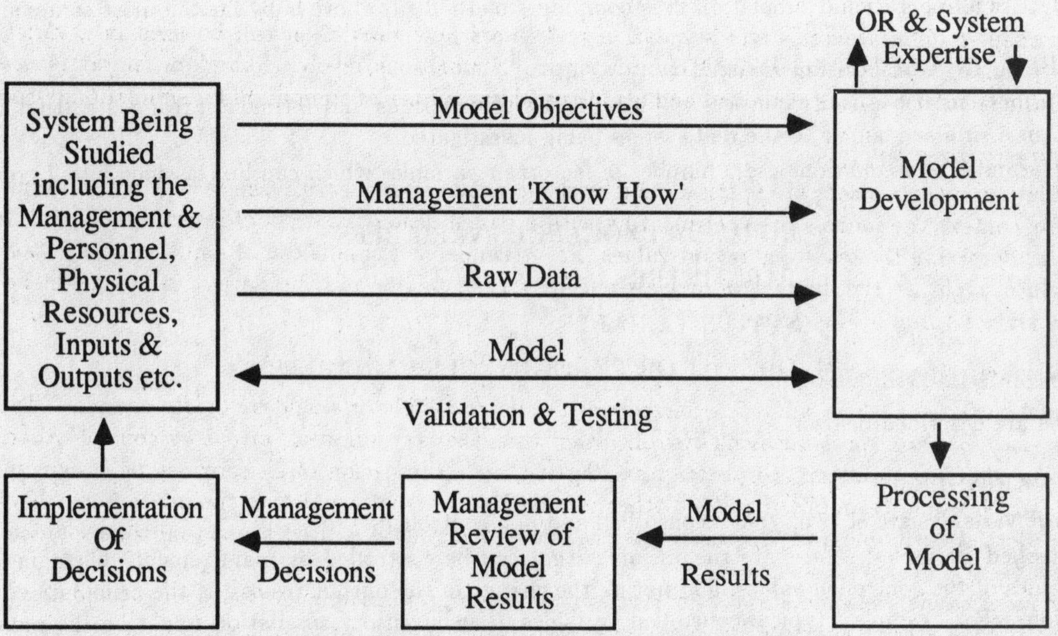

MODEL DEVELOPMENT AND USE Figure 1

ASSESSING A MODEL'S SUITABILITY.

6. Models are intelligent simplications of reality and there is no way of proving that a model gives adequate prediction in unknown circumstances. However, many models are developed to help forecast what might happen when an existing operation is enlarged or has extra demands made upon it. In such circumstances, when the model is constructed, values are input that correspond to current operational levels and the output values calculated. If these values correspond to the present situation, then there are reasonable grounds for believing that the model is a fair representation of reality.

MONTE CARLO SIMULATION.

7. Any realistic business situation involves probabilistic or random features, eg arrivals at a store may average 80 per day, but the actual arrival pattern is likely to be highly variable; in a corporate planning exercise forecasts of the likely sales will obviously vary according to different circumstances etc. Because models must behave like the system under observation, the model must contain these probabilistic elements. Simulations involving such random elements are sometimes termed Monte Carlo simulations.

RANDOM SELECTION.

8. To carry out a realistic simulation involving probabilistic elements, it is necessary to avoid bias in the selection of the values which vary. This is done by selecting randomly (using the term in its statistical sense) using one of the following methods:

a. Random number generation by computer.

b. Random number tables. These consist of a table of randomly selected numbers in which bias does not exist.

c. Lottery slection; eg put all the numbers in a bag, shake well, draw out a number.

d. Roulette wheel. The wheel is spun and a ball dropped in to select a number (hence the name 'Monte Carlo simulation').

e. Dice or cards. These can also be used, although with cards the card drawn should be replaced and the pack reshuffled before another card is selected.

The repeated random selection of input values and the logging of the resultant outputs is the very essence of simulation. In this way an understanding is gained of the likely pattern of results so that a more informed decision can be taken.

Note: As all operational simulation uses computers method (a) above is by far the most common.

VARIABLES IN A SIMULATION MODEL.

9. A business model ususally consists of linked series of equations and formulae arranged so that they 'behave' in a similar manner to the real system being investigated.

The formulae and equations use a number of factors or variables which can be classified into 4 groups.

a. INPUT OR EXOGENOUS VARIABLES

b. PARAMETERS

c. STATUS VARIABLES

d. OUTPUT OR ENDOGENEOUS VARIABLES

These are described below.

INPUT VARIABLES.

10. These variables are of two types - controlled and non-controlled.

Controlled Variables: These are the variables that can be controlled by management. Changing the input values of the controlled values, and noting the change in the output results, is the prime activity of simulation . For example , typical controlled variables in an inventory simulation might be the re-order level and re-order quantity. These could be altered and the effect on the system outputs noted.

Non-controlled variables: These are input variables which are not under management control. Typically these are probabilistic or stochastic variables ie they vary but in some uncontrollable, probabilistic fashion.

For example, in a production simulation the number of breakdowns would be deemed to vary in accordance with a probability distribution derived from records of past breakdown frequencies. In an inventory simulation, demand and lead time would also be generally classed as non-controllled, probabilistic variables.

PARAMETERS.

11. These are also input variables which, for a given simulation have a constant value. Parameters are factors which help to specify the relationships between other types of variables. For example in a production simulation a parameter (or constant) might be the time taken for routine maintenance; in an inventory simulation a parameter might be the cost of a stock-out.

STATUS VARIABLES.

12. In some types of simulation the behaviour of the system (rates, usages, speeds, demand and so on) varies not only according to individual characteristics but also according to the general state of the system at various times or seasons. As an example, in a simulation of supermarket demand and checkout queueing, demand will be probabilistic and variable on any given day but the general level of demand will be greatly influenced by the day of the week and the season of the year. Status variables would be required to specify the day(s) and season(s) to be used in a simulation.

Note: On occasions, status variables and parameters would both be termed just parameters, although strictly there is a difference between the two concepts.

OUTPUT VARIABLES.

13. These are the results of the simulation. They arise from the calculations and tests performed in the model, the input values of the controlled values, the values derived for the probabilistic elements and the specified parameters and status values. The output variables must be carefully chosen to reflect the factors which are critical to the real system being simulated and they must relate to the objectives of the real system. For example, output variables for an inventory simulation would typically include:

- cost of stock holding
- number of stockouts
- number of unsatisfied orders.
- number of replenishment orders
- cost of the re-ordering and so on

CONSTRUCTING A SIMULATION MODEL.

14. Some broad guidelines for constructing a simulation model are given below. These will be found useful for dealing with examination questions but in this area especially, practice is vital.

STEP 1.

Identify the objective(s) of the simulation

A detailed listing of the results expected from the simulation will help to clarify step 5 - the output variables.

STEP 2

Identify the input variables.

Distinguish between controlled and non-controlled variables.

STEP 3

Where necessary determine the probability distribution for the non-controlled variables.

STEP 4

Identify any parameters and status variables.

STEP 5

Identify the output variables.

STEP 6

Determine the logic of the model.

This is the heart of the simulation construction. The key questions are: how are the input variables changed into output results? what formulae/decision rules are required? how will the probabilistic elements be dealt with? how should the results be presented?

To illustrate these steps a simple problem follows together with a solution using the six step approach given above.

A SIMPLE INVENTORY SIMULATION.

15. EXAMPLE 1

A wholesaler stocks an item for which demand is uncertain. He wishes to assess two re-ordering policies ie order 10 units at a reorder level of 10, or order 15 units at a reorder level of 15 units, to see which is most economical over a 10 day period.

The following information is available:

Demand per day (units)	Probability
4	0.10
5	0.15
6	0.25
7	0.30
8	0.20

Carrying costs £15 per unit per day. Ordering costs £50 per order. Loss of goodwill for each Unit out of stock £30. Lead time 3 days. Opening Stock 17 units.

The probability distribution is to be based on the following random numbers

41	92	05	44	66	07	00	00	14	62
20	07	95	05	79	95	64	26	06	48

Note: The reorder level is physical stock plus any replenishment orders outstanding.

SOLUTION.

STEP 1 Objectives of simulation.

To simulate the behaviour of two ordering policies - order 15 at reorder level of 15 and order 10 at reorder level of 10 - to establish the cheaper policy.

STEP 2 Identify the input variables.

Controlled variables:

Order quantity

Reorder level

Non-Controlled variable:

Probabilistic demand

STEP 3 Determine probability distribution.

The random numbers are allocated to the demand as follows

Demand	Probability	Cumulative Probability	Random Numbers
4	10%	10%	00 — 09
5	15%	25%	10 — 24
6	25%	50%	25 — 49
7	30%	80%	50 — 79
8	20%	100%	80 — 99

The two random number sequences supplied can then be used for the two runs of the simulation with each pair of digits used to select a demand. For example, for the 15 order quantity simulation, the first two digits, 41, give a Day 1 demand of 6 units. The next two digits, 92, give a Day 2 demand of 8 units and so on.

STEP 4 Identify Parameters and Status Variables

Parameters

Opening Stock	17 units
Carrying costs	£15 per unit per day
Ordering costs	£50 per order
Loss of goodwill	£30
Lead time	3 days

There are no status variables in this simple example.

STEP 5 Identify the output variables

The main output variable is Total Cost. However ancillary output variables which arise from the simulation include:

- No of orders placed
- No of stockouts
- Cost of stockouts
- Total carrying cost
- Total order cost

STEP 6 Determine model logic.

In this simple example the logic and rules required are nothing more than the basics of inventory control thus:

Reorder level	=	Physical stock + Replenishment Orders outstanding
Closing stock	=	Opening stock - Demand
Carrying cost per day	=	Stock × £15 per unit
Goodwill costs	=	Stock shortfall × £30 per unit
Total cost	=	Goodwill costs + carrying costs + ordering costs.

The information, values and rules are then used to simulate the two ordering policies. The results of these simulations are shown in the schedules in Figure 2 and 3 from which it will be seen that the simulation shows that the 'order 15' policy is more economical over the 10 days simulated.

It must be emphasised that in practice the simulations would be carried out over many more cycles than 10 days in order to obtain a truly representative picture.

RESULTS OF SIMULATION USING ORDER QUANTITY AND REORDER LEVEL OF 15 UNITS

DAY	OPENING STOCK	DEMAND	CLOSING STOCK	ORDER COSTS	CARRYING COSTS	STOCK OUT COSTS	TOTAL COST
1	17	6	11	£50	£165		£215
2	11	8	3		£45		45
3	3	4	–		–	£30	30
4	+ 15	6	9	£50	£135		185
5	9	7	2		£30		30
6	2	4	–		–	£60	60
7	+ 15	4	11	£50	£165		215
8	11	4	7		£105		105
9	7	5	2		£30		30
10	+15+2	7	10	£50	£150		200
				£200	£825	£90	£1115

Figure 2

RESULTS OF SIMULATION USING ORDER QUANTITY AND RE-ORDER LEVEL OF 10 UNITS

DAY	OPENING STOCK	DEMAND	CLOSING STOCK	ORDER COSTS	CARRYING COSTS	STOCK OUT COSTS	TOTAL COST
1	17	5	12		£180		£180
2	12	4	8	£50	120		170
3	8	8	–		–	–	–
4	–	5	–		–	£150	150
5	+10	7	3	50	45		95
6	3	8	–		–	150	150
7	–	7	–		–	210	210
8	+10	6	4	50	60		110
9	4	4	–		–		–
10	–	6	–		–	180	180
				£150	£405	£690	£1245

Figure 3

FURTHER EXAMPLE OF SIMULATION.

16 A common application of simulation is to examine the behaviour of queues in circumstances where the use of queueing formulae is not possible. The following example is typical.

EXAMPLE 2.

A filling station is being planned and it is required to know how many attendants will be needed to maximise earnings. From traffic studies it has been forecast that customers will arrive in accordance with the following table:

Probability of 0 customers arriving in any minute .72
Probability of 1 customer arriving in any minute .24
Probability of 2 customer arriving in any minute .03
Probability of 3 customer arriving in any minute .01

From past experience it has been estimated that service times vary according to the following table

Service Time in minutes	1	2	3	4	5	6	7	8	9	10	11	12
Probability	.16	.13	.12	.10	.09	.08	.07	.06	.05	.05	.05	.04

If there are more than two customers waiting, in addition to those being serviced, new arrivals drive on and the sale is lost.

A petrol pump attendant is paid £20 per 8 hour day, and the average contribution per customer is estimated to be £2.

How many attendants are needed?

SOLUTION.

STEP 1: Objectives of simulation

To find the number of attendants to maximise earnings

STEP 2: Input variables

Controlled - Number of attendants

Non-Controlled - Customer arrival rate
Service time

STEP 3: Probability distribution

As previously a random number table is used and an extract is given below

5053225496	9565241457	7354776952	2149630416	5579018342
7245174840	2275698645	8416549348	4676463101	2229367983
6749420382	4832530032	5670984959	5432114610	2966095680
7164238934	7666237259	5263097712	9999089966	7544056852
4192054466	0700014629	5169439659	8408705169	1074373131
9697426117	6488888550	4031652526	8123543276	0927534537
2007950579	9564268448	3457415998	1531027886	7016633739
4584768758	2389278610	3859431781	3643768456	4141314518
3840145867	9120831830	7228567652	1267173884	4020651657

Table 1

The arrival pattern estimated is reproduced below with random numbers assigned.

			Random Nos. assigned
Probability of 0 customers arriving in any minute	=	.72	01 – 72
Probability of 1 customer arriving in any minute	=	.24	73 – 96
Probability of 2 customer arriving in any minute	=	.03	97 – 99
Probability of 3 customer arriving in any minute	=	.01	00

Similarly for the service pattern we assign the random numbers in a similar fashion thus:

Service time minutes	1	2	3	4	5	6	7	8	9	10	11	12
Likelihood	.16	.13	.12	.10	.09	.08	.08	.06	.05	.05	.05	.04
Random Numbers Assigned	01-16	17-29	30-41	42-51	52-60	61-68	69-75	76-81	82-86	87-91	92-96	97-00

The random number table is read in any direction in groups of two digits and, according to the digits, the appropriate arrival pattern or service time is selected.

For example, assume that for the arrival pattern the table is read from left to right starting from the first row.

Minute No.	Random Digits from table	No of arrivals
1	50	0
2	53	0
3	22	0
4	54	0
5	96	1
6	95	1
7	65	0
8	24	0
9	14	0
10	57	0
11	73	1
12	54	0
13	77	1
14	69	0
15	52	0
16	21	0
17	49	0
etc		

Table 2

Selecting on this basis over say, a week's operations, will result in a random selection reflecting the estimated probabilities.

STEP 4: Parameters

Attendant cost £20 per day

Average contribution per customer £2

STEP 5: Output variables

Average contributions per day

Attendant costs per day

No. of unsatisfied customers

STEP 6: Logic of simulation

In this case the logic is shown using a flowchart Figure 4 and the results of the simulation would be entered on a simple worksheet, figure 5.

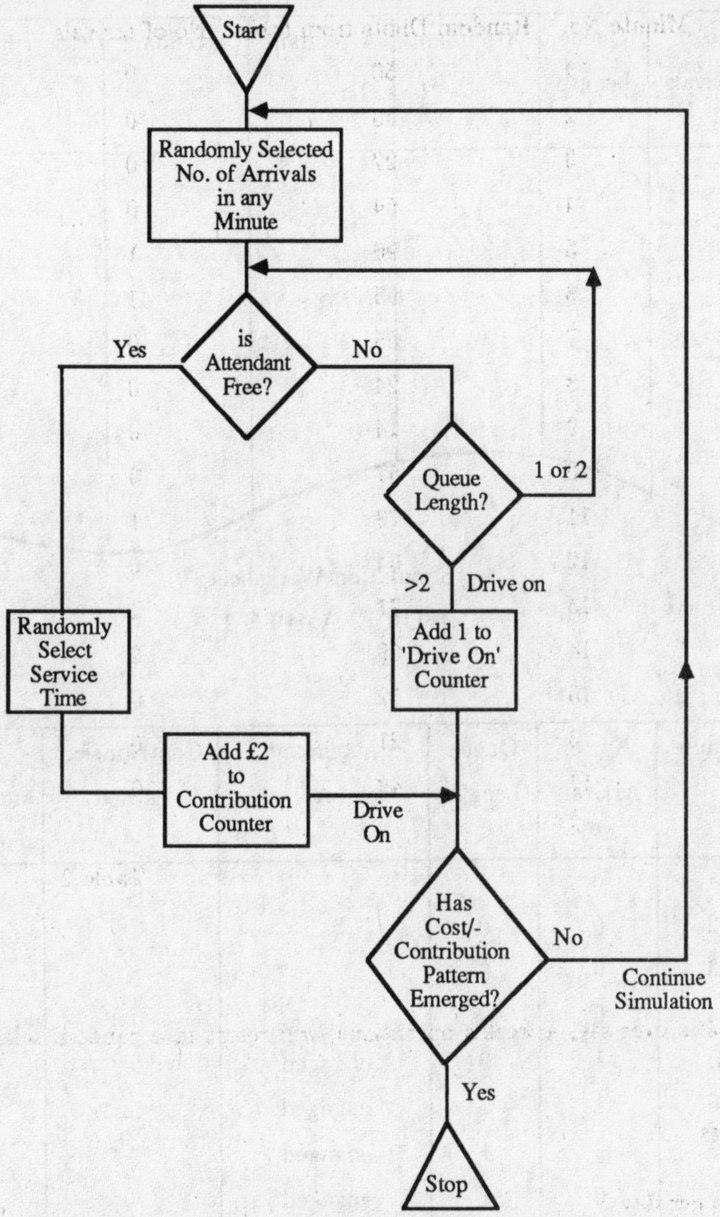

SIMULATION LOGIC – EXAMPLE 2 Figure 4

The results of such a simulation could be entered on a simple worksheet as follows:

Minute	No.of Arrivals	Queue Length	Attendant	Attendant	Attendant	Contribution earned	No . of Unsatisfied customers
1							
2							
3							
4							
5							
6							
7							
8							
etc							

Simulation Worksheet
FOR EXAMPLE 2

Figure 5

Minute	No. of Arrivals	Queue Length	Attendant A	Contribution earned	No. of unsatisfied customers
1	0	0			
2	0	0			
3	0	0			
4	0	0			
5	1	0	engaged		
6	1	1	engaged		
7	0	1	engaged		
8	0	1	engaged		
9	0	1	engaged		
10	0	1	engaged		
11	1	2	engaged		
12	0	2	engaged		
13	1	2	engaged		1
14	0	2	engaged	£2	
15	0	1	engaged (and another random time selection made)		

Simulation Worksheet with one Attendant

Figure 6

CARRYING OUT THE SIMULATION.

16. Now that the objectives, variables, logic and so on have been established the simulation is carried out for a number of iterations each representing 1 minutes operations; first with 1 attendant, then 2 attendants, then 3 and so on until a cost/ contribution pattern emerges.

As the flowchart, Figure 4, is worked through every minute, the number of arrivals would be randomly selected as in Table 2. If an attendant was free, a random selection of service time would be made and the appropriate number of minutes logged against the attendant. For example, in Table 2 an arrival occurred in minute 5. If the random selection of service time was, say 10 minuts, and the simulation was dealing with one attendant then that attendant would be engaged from minute 5 to minute 14.

In such circumstances the worksheet would be as Figure 6.

It will be apparent that such a simulation is simple to set up and use but becomes very tedious indeed to repeat for hundreds of iterations.

RESULTS OF SIMULATION.

17. The above simulation has been worked through for several days' operation with 1,2,3 and 4 attendants and the results obtained are tabulated below.

No. of Attendants	Average Contribution per Day	Attendant(s) Cost per day	Average No. of Vehicles/Day driving on
	£	£	
1	156	20	81
2	260	40	29
3	288	60	16
4	300	80	2

Results of Simulation

Table 3

From the table it will be seen that there is little difference in net profit per day between 2, 3 and 4 attendants, although there is of course a substantial difference in the average number of vehicles driving on. The results of a simulation do not necessarily indicate an optimal solution but provide more information upon which a reasoned decision can be taken.

COMPUTERS AND SIMULATION.

18. To carrying out any sort of realistic simulation, the use of a computer becomes a necessity. This is not because of any great complexity, but merely because of the large number of times that one has to work through the model. In the above example a computer was used to establish the table of results, but it did nothing more than could have been achieved using the model flowchart and the worksheets and a lot of patience. Because of the importance of computers in simulation, special simulation languages have been developed to facilitate the program writing and the use of the model. The GPSS (General Purpose Systems Simulator) exists for most computer systems and the increasing availability of micro-computers and terminal access to larger machines renders manual simulation virtually obsolete.

ADVANTAGES OF SIMULATION.

19.

a. Can be applied in areas where analytical techniques are not available or would be too complex.
b. Constructing the model inevitably must involve management and this may enable a deeper insight to be obtained into a problem.
c. A well constructed model does enable the results of various policies and decisions to be examined without any irreversible commitments being made.
d. Simulation is cheaper and less risky than altering the real system.

DISADVANTAGES OF SIMULATION.

20.

a. Although all models are simplifications of reality, they may still be complex and require a substantial amount of managerial and technical time.

b. Practical simulation inevitably involves the use of computers which may be a handicap to firms without computer facilities or ready access to a computer.

c. Simulations do not produce optimal results. The manager makes the decision after testing a number of alternative policies. There is always the possibility that the optimum policy is not selected

SUMMARY.

21.

a. Simulation is the process by which a model is experimented upon and the results of various policies examined.

b. At the heart of simulation is the concept of a model. A model is any representation of reality and business models can take the forms of flowcharts, formulae, equations etc.

c. A model must reflect reality and reality inevitably involves variable or probabilistic elements. Practical simulations must include these variations and this is sometimes known as Monte Carlo simulation.

d. Because of the iterative nature of simulation the use of a computer is a necessity for all practical problems.

POINTS TO NOTE.

22.

a. Simulation has many potential business applications; these include:
queueing problems, capital rationing problems in investment analysis, corporate planning.

b. Because it is very time consuming to carry out a full simulation, it is thought unlikely that students would be required to do this. However, the model construction or some general question on the applicability of simulation is well within the scope of most syllabuses.

SELF REVIEW QUESTIONS.

1. *Why is the concept of a model basic to the technique of simulation? (2 to 4)*
2. *What are the major factors to be considered in constructing a model? (5)*
3. *What is the essential feature of Monte Carlow Simulations? (7)*
4. *What types of variables are found in simulation models? (9 to 13)*
5. *What are the steps in constructing a simulation model? (14)*
6. *What is the role of computers in carrying out simulations (19)*
7. *What are the advantages and disadvantages of simulation? (20 to 21)*

EXAMINATION QUESTIONS WITH ANSWERS COMMENCING PAGE 488

A1. For several years our local council's policy on housing has given widespread cause for concern. The main body of criticism has been levelled at the priority scheme operated by our council. This involves an allegedly crude classification of applicants as 'urgent' or 'non urgent'. Urgent cases move directly to the head of the housing list provided no other urgent case is already there. The destitute fall into this category but similar accelerated treatment of other needy groups, eg the disabled, is being pressed.

Applications for housing are received at the rate of two per week. The following table details the rates at which houses are found for those reaching the head of the list.

Case type	Percentage of applicants	Time in days to find acceptable accommodation
Urgent	10	2
Non-urgent a.	80	5
b.*	10	7

(Assume a 5-day working week)

**Applicants with 'special requirements', eg disabled applicants.*

Required:

a. Describe how you would carry out a simulation of the present policy clearly stating each logical step. Point out all the assumptions you make.

b. What further simulations would you want to carry out in order to advise the local council about extending its priority scheme?

c. How would you carry out the simulations to minimise the effect of chance creating differences between the existing scheme and any proposed new scheme?

(ACCA Management Mathematics).

A2. A cost clerk in the sales office of Jupiter Metals is responsible for preparing a sales invoice, following the receipt of an order from a customer. One invoice is required for each hour. Orders arrive in the office at an average rate of 5 per hour, and it takes the clerk, on average, 10 minutes to make out an invoice. The office is open for 7 hours a day: in the morning from half-past eight until midday, and in the afternoon from half-past one until five o'clock. The outgoing mail is collected from the office at 10 o'clock each morning and 2 o'clock each afternoon. In order that all sales invoices are despatched to customers as quickly as possible, the sales manager has indicated that efforts should be made to ensure that for each order received during the morning, an invoice is sent out that same afternoon, and that an invoice for each order received during the afternoon should be sent the following morning.

Required:

(a) If this situation is to be analysed by means of the basic single server queueing model, identify the components of the queueing system, indicate the assumptions which must be made, and comment on the appropriateness of the assumptions in this particular set of circumstances.

(b) Explain, in detail, how a simulation of the system might be carried out in order to estimate the proportion of invoices which fail to meet the despatch deadlines suggested by the sales manager.

A3. The Casualty Department of the Metropolitan Hospital is concerned that the control of medical supplies is unsatisfactory resulting in high carrying costs for some items and high stockout costs for others. It has been decided to conduct an investigation into the demand for the ordering of a number of items.

The past demand and order lead time patterns for one of the items are given below:

Daily demand units	Probability	Lead time* days	Probability
4	0.07	3	0.14
5	0.12	4	0.41
6	0.14	5	0.26
7	0.19	6	0.19
8	0.18		
9	0.13		
10	0.09		
11	0.05		
12	0.03		

**Note: A lead time of, e.g., 3 days, means the order is placed at the end of the day that stock runs out and is received after 3 full days.*

A proposal has been made that a policy of ordering a basic 38 units should be adopted whenever stock falls below 30 units. To the order of 38 units there should be added the number of units necessary to bring stock up to the re-order point of 30 units at the time the order is made.

A stock of 60 units is in hand. Ordering costs amount ot £10 per order, carrying costs are 50 pence per day and stock-out costs are £2 per unit. Stock-out costs are incurred automatically whenever there is no stock in store, since the stock has to be procured immediately from an outside source.

The hopsital administrators decided to carry out a Monte Carlo simulation of the demand for this item.

Random numbers for 24 days of the demand sequence are given below:

Demand: 03, 97, 16, 12, 55, 16, 84, 63, 33, 57, 18, 26, 23, 52, 37, 70, 56, 99, 16, 31, 68, 74, 27, 00.

Lead time: 47, 74, 76, 56, 59, 22, 42, 01, 21, 60.

You are required to:

(a) carry out the simulation of the 24 days' demand on stock levels;

(b) calculate the average daily stock cost;

(c) discuss the proposed ordering policy on the assumption that the simulation which has been carried out is considered to be sufficiently representative of demand;

(d) discuss the advantages and limitations of the use of simulation in circumstances of the kind described above.

CIMA Quantitative Techniques.

A4. As a result of a routine analysis of cash flows, the Chief Accountant of Odin Chemcials Limited considers that there are only three types of cash flow which are likely to vary significantly from month to month. These are:

Wages and salaries.
Raw materials purchases.
Sales revenue.

Using data that have been collected over the last two years, and taking into account likely changes in the level of operations during the next few months, the following distributions have been estimated for the monthly cash flow in each of these three categories.

Wage and Salaries (£'000)	*Probability*	*Raw Materials*	*Probability*
10–12	0.3	6–8	0.2
12–14	0.5	8–10	0.3
14–16	0.2	10–12	0.3
		12–14	0.2

Sales Revenue (£'000)	*Probability*
30–34	0.1
34–38	0.3
38–42	0.4
42–46	0.2

All other cash flows can be regarded as fixed, and amount to a net cash outflow of £14,000 per month. Currently Odin has cash assets of £50,000.

Required:

(a) Using the random numbers given at the end of the question, simulate 6 months' cash flows. You may assume that all cash flows are independent and take place at the end of the month. From your simulation, estimate the probability of a net cash outflow in any month, and the cash balance at the end of 6 month period.

(b) What is the expected cash balance at the end of the 6 month period?

Explain briefly why this value may be different from a corresponding value obtained from a simulation experiment.

(c) If a more comprehensive and realistic model is to be constructed, discuss carefully and concisely the points which must be considered when simulating cash flows over a period of time.

Random Numbers:

Wages and Salaries	*2 7 9 2 9 8*
Raw Materials	*4 4 1 0 3 4*
Sales Revenue	*0 6 6 8 0 2*

(ACCA, Quantitative Analysis)

A5. A retailer has placed an order for 40 units to be delivered daily. The estimated sales for each day are expected to follow the following probability distribution, to which random number digits have been allocated:

Demand	*Probability*	*Random number digits*
10	*0.06*	*00–15*
20	*0.10*	*06–15*
30	*0.15*	*16–30*
40	*0.40*	*31–70*
50	*0.16*	*71–86*
60	*0.13*	*87–99*

Units cost £20 each, are sold for £30 each and it has been estimated that if there is no stock to satisfy a particular customer the business will suffer a 'loss' of £6 for each unit of unsatisfied demand. The retailer has no storage facilities; any units no sold by the end of a day are thrown away.

Random number digits to be used for daily demand, starting with the first '93' are 93538193882322967906149467 35.

You are required to:

(a) simulate 10 days' demand;

(b) calculate, and state, the resulting profit or loss to the business;

(c) calculate, and state, the effect of increasing the daily order to 50 units, still with no storage facilities;

(d) calculate, and state, the effect of a daily order of 50 units if there were free, unlimited storage facilities;

(e) comment briefly on the use of simulation in decision making.

(CIMA Quantitative Techniques)

A6. The examination papers set by the Association typically consist of a fixed number of questions set on a published syllabus which usually covers several major areas, each with an appropriate weight. An illustration of the weights for one particular subject might be as follows:

Section	*A*	*B*	*C*	*D*
Weight	*35%*	*15%*	*20%*	*30%*

Required:

(a) Suppose that in any one examination paper for the subject illustrated above, seven questions were to be allocated randomly to the four sections of the syllabus. Explain in detail how this allocation might be done, bearing in mind the published weightings.

(b) One factor which must be borne in mind by the examiner is to ensure that the syllabus is adequately covered within a few consecutive examination papers. Describe briefly an alternative procedure to the one described in (a) which might be used to allocate the questions on any particular paper in order to achieve the required syllabus coverage within a few consecutive papers.

(c) Describe a method for checking that the six papers for the above subject set over a period of three years do not differ significantly from the published weightings. Illustrate your method using the following breakdown of the papers set in the period 1982-84.

Questions per Section	*June 1982*	*Dec. 1982*	*June 1983*	*Dec. 1983*	*June 1984*	*Dec. 1984*
A	3	3	3	3	2	3
B	0	1	1	1	1	1
C	1	2	1	0	2	1
D	3	1	2	3	2	2

(ACCA Quantitative Analysis)

EXAMINATION QUESTIONS WITHOUT ANSWERS.

B1. Waferthin p.l.c. supplies silicon chips to the computer information technology industry.

It is considering investing in the manufacture of a new propduct for installation in telephone circuits. Investment outlay costs for the new equipment are £150,000 and the cost of money is 10% .

Although operating costs can be estimated with reasonable accuracy, sales revenue, and hence net income, is subject to a considerable degree of uncertainty. The following estimates with respect to the likely range of outcomes are provided by the management.

Net Income £000	*Probability*
32	0.05
43	0.25
50	0.40
56	0.20
61	0.10

These figures are applicable over a five year period and it is assumed that outcomes from one year to the next are independent.

The following random number sequence is given:

53633563980264855834036208070172884596435022963178

You are required to:

(a) prepare a five-run simulation of the net outcomes for the project;

(b) calculate, using the results of the simulation, the expected net present value and standard deviation of the project;

(c) comment on the simulation you have carried out and the value of the results.

(CIMA Quantitative Techniques)

B2. Queueing theory is concerned with a very common and practical situation, yet practical solutions to most problems are not readily available.

You are required to:

(a) describe the important variables that are present in most practical queueing situations.

(b) state the conditions necessary for a stable system in a simple queue;

(c) explain two of the difficulties in the practical implementation of a theoretical solutions;

(d)

(i) discuss whether it would be practical to apply queueing theory to the analysis of the number of traffic toll booths needed to service a new motorway tunnel link;

(ii) describe how the process of simulation may be used to help provide an answer to this problem.

(CIMA Quantitative Techniques)

B3. Coltel Ltd is considering the introduction of a new product and has compiled the following information:

Variable	*Expected Value*	*Standard deviation*
Sales quantity	*5,000*	*400*
Selling price per unit (£)	*300*	*5*
Fixed costs (£)	*580,000*	*10,000*
Variable costs per unit (£)	*175*	*7.5*

(For simplicity assume that all the random variables are independent and that the probability distributions are normal).

Required:

a. Calculate, using breakeven analysis and expected values, the breakeven volume and the expected profit for the period.

b. Explain how you would carry out a simulation to arrive at an approximate distribution of profits. Illustrate your answer by using the cumulative normal distribution below and the following random numbers 20, 96, 68, 59 to obtain one simulated figure for profit.

c. What is the value to Coltel Ltd. of having carried out a simulation rather than simply estimating profit using expected values?

Cumulative Normal Distribution Table.

Random number	Number of deviations from mean	Random number	Number of deviations from mean	Random number	Number of deviations from mean
00	-2.5	22–24	-0.7	79–81	0.8
01	-2.3	25–27	-0.6	82–83	0.9
02	-2.0	28–31	-0.5	84–85	1.0
03	-1.9	32–34	-0.4	86–87	1.1
04	-1.8	35–38	-0.3	88–89	1.2
05	-1.7	39–42	-0.2	90–91	1.3
06	-1.6	43–46	-0.1	92	1.4
07	-1.5	47–53	0.0	93	1.5
08	-1.4	54–57	0.1	94	1.6
09–10	-1.3	58–61	0.2	95	1.7
11–12	-1.2	62–65	0.3	96	1.8
13–14	-1.1	66–68	0.4	97	1.9
15–16	-1.0	69–72	0.5	98	2.0
17–18	-0.9	73–75	0.6	99	2.3
19–21	-0.8	76–78	0.7		

(ACCA, Management Mathematics)

17 Linear Programming – Introduction

INTRODUCTION

1. This chapter introduces the important technique called Linear Programming (LP). The chapter explains in what circumstances LP can be used and how to formulate LP problems in a standardised manner.

LP AND ALLOCATION.

2. Allocation problems are concerned with the utilisation of limited resources to best advantage. It is clear that many management decisions are essentially resource allocation decisions and various techniques exist to help management in this area. LP is one technique and is closely related to Assignment and Transportation techniques covered in Chapters 21 and 22 which are also allocation techniques.

LP DEFINITION,

3. LP is a mathematical technique concerned with ther allocation of scarce resources. It is a procedure to optimise the value of some objective (for example, maximum profit or minimum cost) when the factors involved (for example, labour or machine hours) are subject to some constraints (for example, only 1000 labour hours are available in a week).

Thus LP can be used to solve problems which conform to the following.

a. The problem must be capable of being stated in numeric terms.

b. All factors involved in the problem must have linear relationships eg a doubling of output requires a doubling of labour hours; if one unit provides £10 contribution 10 units will produce £100 and so on.

c. The problem must permit a choice or choices between alternative courses of action.

d. There must be one or more restrictions on the factors involved. These may be restrictions on resources (labour hours, tons of material etc) but they may be on particular characteristics, for example, a fertiliser must contain a minimum of 15% phosphates and 30% nitrogen or a patent fuel must contain not more than 6% ash, 2% phosphorous and 1% sulphur.

Note:

The 'linear' part of the term LP is explained above. The 'programming' part refers to the derivation of the optimum schedule. This is invariably carried out by an iterative process whereby one moves from one solution to a better solution progressively on until a solution is reached which cannot be improved upon ie optimum. In this context therefore the term programming is not connected with computer programming.

LINEARITY REQUIREMENT.

4. A major factor in LP is the requirement that all relationships are linear. Obviously not all factors involved in business decisions are linear and indeed in some situations non-linear relationships are typical and desirable eg a production process could be increased in size so that economies of scale are realised and unit costs reduced. Fortunately it is found that many factors (eg labour hours, machine utilisation, contributions) are reasonably linear or can be linearly approximated over the operational range of the values being considered. It will be realised that this is a similar approach to that adopted by accountants when considering marginal costing and P/V analysis. If it is considered that the factor is definitely non-linear then LP cannot be used.

EXPRESSING LP PROBLEMS.

5. Before considering the detailed methods of solving LP problems it is necessary tobe able to express a problem in a standardised manner which not only facilitiates the calculations required for a solution but also ensures that no important element of the problem is overlooked. The two major factors are the

OBJECTIVES and the LIMITATIONS or CONSTRAINTS.

Objectives. The first step in LP is to decide what result is required ie. the objective. This may be to maximise profit or contribution, or minimise cost or time or some other appropriate measure. Having decided upon the objective it is now necessary to state mathematically the elements involved in achieving this. This is called the OBJECTIVE FUNCTION.

Example 1.

A factory can produce two products, A and B. The contribution that can be obtained from these products are,

A contributes £20 per unit B contributes £30 per unit

and it is required to maximise contribution

The objective function for this factory can be expressed as

MAXIMISE $20x_1 + 30x_2$

where x_1 = number of units of A produced

and x_2 = number of units of B produced

Notes.

This problem has 2 unknowns, x_1 and x_2. These are sometimes known as the DECISION VARIABLES. Only a single objective at the time (in this case, to maximise contribution) can be dealt with in an LP problem.

Example 2.

A farmer mixes three products to feed his pigs. Feedstuff M costs 20p per pound, feedstuff Y costs 40p per lb and feedstuff Z costs 55p per lb. Each feedstuff contributes some essential part of the pigs diet and the farmer wishes to feed the pigs as cheaply as possible.

The objective function is

MINIMISE $20x_1 + 40x_2 + 55x_3$

Where x_1 = Number of pounds of M

x_2 = Number of pounds of Y

x_3 = Number of pounds of Z

Alternatively, if the costs were required in £'s, the objective function could be expressed as follows,

MINIMISE $.2x_1 + .4x_2 + .55x_3$

Note.

This example has 3 decision variables. The number of decision variables can vary from 2 to many hundreds. For examination purposes 4 or 5 is the maximum that is likely to be encountered. Linearity has been assumed in both examples above and is assumed in all those that follow.

LIMITATIONS OR CONSTRAINTS.

6. Circumstances always exist which govern the achievement of the objective. These factors are known as LIMITATIONS or CONSTRAINTS. The limitations in any given problem must be clearly identified, quantified, and expressed mathematically. To be able to use LP they must, of course, be linear.

LIMITATION EXAMPLES.

7. **Example 3.**

A factory can produce four products and wishes to maximise contribution. It has an objective function as follows:

MAXIMISE $5.5x_1 + 2.7x_2 + 6.0x_3 + 4.1x_4$

where x_1 = number of units of A produced

x_2 = number of units of B produced

x_3 = number of units of C produced

x_4 = number of units of D produced

and the coefficients of the objective function (ie 5.5., 2.7, 6.0 and 4.1) are the contributions per unit of the products.

The factory employs 200 skilled workers and 150 unskilled workers and works a 40 hour week. The times to produce 1 unit of each product by the two types of labour are given below

	PRODUCTS			
	A	B	C	D
SKILLED HOURS	5	3	1	8
UNSKILLED HOURS	5	7	4	11

The limitations as regards to labour can be stated as follows

$$\text{SKILLED:} \quad 5x_1 + 3x_2 + x_3 + 8x_4 \leq 8000$$

$$\text{UNSKILLED:} \quad 5x_1 + 7x_2 + 4x_3 + 11x_4 \leq 6000$$

In addition a general limitation applicable to all maximising problems is that it is not possible to make negative quantities of a product, ie.

$$x_1 \geq 0, \quad x_2 \geq 0, \quad x_3 \geq 0, \quad x_4 \geq 0$$

Notes.

a. The resource limitations in this maximising problem follow a typical pattern being of the less than or equal to type ($\leq$)

b. The formal statement of the non-negativity constraints on the unknowns (x_1, x_2 etc) has to be made for computer solutions but is normally inferred when solving by manual means.

c. This above restriction applies to labour hours: Machine hour restrictions would be dealt with in a similar fashion.

Example 4.

A company produces four products P, Q, R, S, which are made from two basic materials, Sludge and Slurry. Only 1000 tons of Sludge and 800 tons of Slurry are available in a period. The usage of the materials in the products is as follows.

		PRODUCT				
		P	Q	R	S	
	SLUDGE	2.6	1	5	0	tons/unit
MATERIAL	SLURRY	3.3	4	0	6.2	tons/unit

$\therefore$ Limitations are as follows:

$$\text{Sludge restriction} \quad 2.6x_1 + x_2 + 5x_3 \leq 1000$$

$$\text{Slurry restriction} \quad 3.3x_1 + 4x_2 + 6.2x_4 \leq 800$$

$$x_1 \geq 0, \quad x_2 \geq 0, \quad x_3 \geq 0, \quad x_4 \geq 0$$

where x_1 = units of P

x_2 = units of Q

x_3 = units of R

x_4 = units of S

Example 5.

Sales limitations, because of quota and/or contract requirements, may be of the 'greater than or equal to' variety ($\geq$) or 'less than or equal to' ($\leq$)

A company is in a trading federation and has agreed to accept sales quotas on certain of its products. It has also contracted with some regular customers to supply minimum quantities of certain products. The details are as follows:

QUOTAS (as agreed with the Sales Federation)

	PRODUCT				
	A	B	C	D E	
MAXIMUM SALES	500	1000	No Limit	2000	Units/Period

CONTRACTS WITH REGULAR CUSTOMERS

Minimum Quantities that must be Supplied	–	300	400	–	Units/Period

∴ Limitations are as follows

Quota Constraints	x_1				≤ 500
Quota Constraints		x_2			≤ 1000
Quota Constraints				$x_4 + x_5$	≤ 2000
Contract Constraints		x_2			≥ 300
Contract Constraints			x_3		≥ 400

$$x_1 \geq 0, \quad x_4 \geq 0, \quad x_5 \geq 0.$$

where x_1 to x_5 are the quantities of A to E respectively to be produced.

Notes.

a. The usual non-negativity constraints are not required from x_2 and x_3 because the contract restrictions are of the greater than or equal to type.

b. Example 3, 4 and 5 above are maximising problems where the restrictions are generally (but not exclusively) or the 'less than or equal to' type.

MINIMISATION PROBLEMS.

8. Minimisation problems (ie as Example 2) are normally concerned with minimising the cost of fulfilling some objective, subject to limitations. The limitations are generally of the 'greater than or equal to' type ($\geq$) for the the logical reason that the best way to minimise costs would be to produce nothing, therefore the limitations must be set so as to produce the minimum possible that fullfills certain requirements.

Example 6.

A farmer feeds his pigs a mixture of swill, vitamins and a proprietary brand of feedmix. He owns 100 pigs who eat at least 20 kilogrammes of food per day each. He wishes to minimise the cost of feeding the pigs whilst at the same time ensuring that the animals receive a balanced diet. The following dietary and cost factors have been obtained.

	CALORIES	VITAMINS 1	2	3	
Minimum Daily Dietary Requirements/Pig	40	20	10	30	
CONTENTS OF FOODSTUFFS					COSTS
SWILL/KG	1.5	.5	–	–	5p/KG
FEEDMIX/KG	2.0	.5	–	1	10p/KG
VITAMINS/BOTTLE	–	.5	7	14	20p/ BOTTLE

The LP formulation can be stated as follows:

OBJECTIVE FUNCTION:

$$\text{Minimise}\quad 5x_1 + 10x_2 + 20x_3$$

CONSTRAINTS

Total Weights (ie 100 × 20)	x_1	+	x_2			≥ 2000
Calories (ie 100 × 40)	$1.5x_1$	+	$2x_2$			≥ 4000
Vitamin 1 (ie 100 × 20)	$.5x_1$	+	$.5x_2$	+	$5x_3$	≥ 2000
Vitamin 2 (ie 100 × 10)					$7x_3$	≥ 1000
Vitamin 3 (ie 100 × 30)			x_2	+	$14x_3$	≥ 3000

$x_1 \geq 0,\ x_2 \geq 0$

where x_1 = kilogrammes of swill

x_2 = kilogrammes of feedmix

x_3 = bottles of vitamins

Notes.

a. The restrictions are all of the 'greater than or equal' type ($\geq$) which is typical of minimisation problems.

b. In the total weight restriction the weight of the vitamins has been assumed to be negligible and has been ignored.

c. The non-negativity constraint for x_3 is not necessary in this problem because the Vitamin 2 constraint is for x_3 only and is of the 'greater than or equal to' type.

FIXED COSTS.

9. LP is concerned with *changes* in cost and revenues so it follows that a factor such as fixed costs which would be unchanged over the range of output being considered should not be included in the LP formulation. To eliminate the effect of fixed costs and to maintain linear relationships it is normal to use contribution (ie sales less marginal cost) rather than profit in the objective function.

SUMMARY.

10.

a. LP is a solution method to problems where an objective has to be optimised subject to constraints.

b. All factors concerned must be numeric and there must be linear relationships.

c. Before attempting to solve any LP) problem it should be formulated in a standardised manner. The steps in the process are:

   i. Decide upon the objective.

ii. Calculate the contribution per unit for maximising or the cost per unit for minimising (ignoring fixed costs in both circumstances).

iii. State the objective function noting how many unknowns, or decision variables, appear.

iv. Consider what factors limit or constrain the quantities to be produced or purchased.

v. State these factors mathematically taking care to ensure that the inequalities (ie $\geq$ or $\leq$) are of the correct type.

vi. Before attempting to solve the problem ensure that all the relationships established are linear or can be reasonably approximated by a linear function.

vii. Solve the problem by either drawing a graph dealt with in Chapter 18 or by the use of what is known as the simplex method (dealt with in Chapter 19).

POINTS TO NOTE.

11.

a. LP is an important practical technique with a wide variety of applications.

b. A substantial proportion of marks in examination questions is given for the formulation of the problem so this chapter will repay careful study.

c. In practice the *sensitivity* of a solution is a critical factor. An optimal solution may hold for only a very narrow range of constraint values and would thus be termed *sensitive,* alternatively it may hold good over a wide range of values and would thus be termed *robust.* The examination over which range of values the solution remains valid is termed sensitivity analysis. This is dealt with in later chapters.

SELF REVIEW QUESTIONS.

1. *What are the essential characteristics of problems than can be solved by LP methods? (3 and 4)*
2. *What is the 'objective function'? (5)*
3. *How many objectives can be dealt with at one time in an LP problem? (5)*
4. *What are limitations or constraints? (6)*
5. *Distinguish minimising from maximising problems. (8)*
6. *Why are fixed costs irrelevant to LP problems? (9)*

EXERCISES WITH ANSWERS COMMENCING PAGE 488

A1. A factory produces four products A, B, C and D which earn contributions of £20, £25, £12 and £30 per unit respectively. The factory employs 500 workers who work a 40 hour week. The hours required for each product and the material requirements are set out below:

	Products			
	A	*B*	*C*	*D*
Hours per unit	6	4	2	5
Kgs Material X per unit	2	8.3	5	9
Kgs Material Y per unit	10	4	8	2
Kgs Material Z per unit	1.5	-	2	8

The total availability of materials per week is:

X	*100,000 kgs*
Y	*65,000 kgs*
Z	*220,000 kgs*

The company wish to maximise contribution:

Formulate the LP problem in the standard manner.

A2. Green Bakeries Ltd. have received a rush order from Camfam for high protein biscuits for famine relief. Costs must be minimised and the mix must meet minimum nutrition requirements.

The order will require 1000 kgs of biscuits mix which is made from four ingredients R, S, T, U which cost £8, £2, £3 and £1 per kilogram respectively. The batch must contain a minimum of 400 kilos of protein, 250 kilos of fat, 300 kilos of carbohydrate and 50 kilos of sugar. The ingredients contain the following percentages by weight:

	PROTEIN	FAT	CARBOHYDRATE	SUGAR	FILLER
R	50%	30%	15%	5%	0
S	10%	15%	50%	15%	10%
T	30%	5%	30%	30%	5%
U	0	5%	5%	30%	60%

Only 150 kilos of S and 200 kilos of T are immediately available.

Formulate the LP problem in the standard manner.

EXAMINATION QUESTIONS WITH ANSWERS COMMENCING PAGE 488

A3. The use of statistical decision theory allows the manager to incorporate the effects of uncertainty regarding future results into his or her analysis.

Inventory control models provide more rational ways of evaluating inventory policy than do guesses and intuitive methods.

Linear programming is a useful tool when the manager must decide how best to use existing resources.'

As a company management accountant you not only supply information for these techniquest o be applied, but also assist in problem formulation and the interpretation of results to management.

You are required, for the three techniques mentioned in the above statement, to discuss the following issues:

(a) What are the objectives of each?

(b) What are the information requirements?

(c) What are their capabilities and limitations?

(CIMA Quantitative Techniques)

A4. The management accountant of Fenton Enterprises Ltd. has suggested that a linear programming model might be used for slecting the best mix of five possible products, A, B, C, D, E.

The following information is available:

	Per unit of product				
	A	B	C	D	E
	£	£	£	£	£
Selling price	48	42	38	31	27
Costs:					
Materials	15	14	16	15	16
Direct loabour	18	16	6	4	4
Fixed overheads*	9	8	3	2	2
Total cost	42	38	25	21	22
Net profit	6	4	13	10	5

** Based on 50% of direct labour cost*

b. Expected maximum unit demand per week for each product at the prices indicated:

A	B	C	D	E
1500	1200	900	600	600

c. Costs of materials includes a special component which is in short supply; it costs £3 a unit. Only 5,800 units will be available to the company during the week. The number of units of the special component needed for a unit of each product is:

A	B	C	D	E
1	1	3	4	5

d. Labour is paid at a rate of £1.50 per hour and only 20,000 hours will be available in a week.

e. The management of Fenton Enterprises Ltd. has rules that expenditure on materials must not exceed a sum of £30,000.

f. All other resources are freely available in sufficient quantities for planned needs.

Required:

a. Formulate a linear programming model stating clearly the criterion you use.
(You are not expected to produce a numerical solution to your model).

b. Describe the problems likely to be encountered in the application of linear programming to determine the 'best' product mix for Fenton Enterprises Ltd.

(ACCA Management Mathematics)

A5. On the 1 January 1982, the manager of a share portfolio finds that he has £100,000 to invest in government stocks. A preliminary analysis of his situation indicates five stocks in which he could invest. These stocks have the following characteristics:

	Stock	Nominal Yield (%)	Current Price (£)	Redemption Yield (%)
A	Treasury 1984	9	$94\frac{1}{2}$	13.5
B	Excheque 1988	12	$91\frac{1}{8}$	12.2
C	Treasury 1989	$11\frac{1}{2}$	$82\frac{3}{4}$	14.3
D	Treasury 1998	14	92	14.9
E	Treasury 1999	10	$78\frac{1}{4}$	15.1

His objective is to maximise the overall redemption yield from his investment but conditions dictate that he must have an overall interest-only running yield of at least 13%. Furthermore, at least £30,000 must be in short term stocks (up to five years to redemption) and no more than £40,000 should be in long term stocks (over fifteen years to redemption).

Note: The interest-only running yield is calculated as

$$\text{Nominal Yield} \times 100/\text{Current Price}$$

Required:

(a) Formulate a linear programming model for this investment problem, clearly indicating the objective function and all the relevant constraints.

(b) It may be shown that the optimum portfolio is to invest.

£30,000 in A
£30,000 in C
£35,350 in D
£4,650 in E

giving an overall redemption yield of 14.31%. If there were no restriction on the proportion which could be invested in long term stocks, determine by how much the overall redemption yield could be improved and what would be the new portfolio. (This new problem may be solved graphically if appropriate deductions and simplications are first made).

(ACCA Quantitative Analysis)

Note Ignore part (b) at this stage

EXERCISES WITHOUT ANSWERS

B1. A firm makes 2 products X and Y which are usually sold in sets having 3 times as many units of X as Y in a set. X makes £10 contribution and Y £8. The production data are as follows:

	PRODUCTS		
	X	Y	TOTAL AVAILABLE
Labour hours per unit	3	4	4000
Material Kgs per unit	2	1	1500
Machine hours per unit	4	6	12000

The firm wish to maximise contribution.

Formulate the LP problem

B2. A firm has an order to supply at least 500 units in total of products V and W with at least twice as many units of V as W. The production data are:

	V	W	TOTAL AVAILABLE
Labour hours per units	4	3	3500
Material Kgs per units	1	2	1800

Because of deterioration the firm wishes to ensure that all the material already available is used on the order although new material could be obtained at short notice if required.

The variable costs of V and W are £55 and £40 respectively and the firm wishes to meet the order at minimum cost.

Formulate the LP problem.

EXAMINATION QUESTIONS WITHOUT ANSWERS

B3. The Exbridge region of Barsands Bank is trying to determine its overall loan policy for the region for the coming month. Its customers can be classified into four groups: industrial, agricultural, personal - without solidarity, personal - with solidarity. The total amount available for loans in the coming month is estiamted at £50 million.

The interest rates charged and the percentage of bad debts are given in the following table:

Customer type	Interest rate charged per annum %	Risk level bad debts
Industrial	9	0.2
Agricultural	10	0.5
Personal-without solidarity	13	1.0
Personal-with solidarity	14	2.0

There are a number of restrictions on loan policy, which the region must observe, due to the regulations set by the Bank of England and the national policy of Barsands Bank. These can be summarised as follows:

i. Personal loans must not exceed 40% of the value of total loans.

ii. Personal-with solidarity loans must not exceed 20% of the total personal loans.

iii. Total agricultural loans must not exceed £10 million.

iv. Industrial loans should not be less than £20 million

v. The average risk factor must not exceed 0.8% .

Required:

a. Formulate a linear programming model of the bank's problem. Your model should be in a form suitable for solution by a linear programming computer package. State clearly in your answer how you derive your objective function and constraints.

b. If you were to solve this problem by the simplex method, explain (but do not solve) how you would deal with this situation where you have inequalities of both types (i.e. 'greater than' and 'less than')

c. If the bank were to reclassify the customer types to accord with the document 'classifications of advances' issued by the Bank of England, which gives a long list of groupings, then the LP model would tend to have more original variables than constraints. How would this affect the solution and what, in practice, would be the consequences for the bank? How might the Bank deal with this situation?

(ACCA Management Mathematics)

Note: Ignore parts (b) and (c) at this stage.

18 Linear Programming – Graphical Solutions

INTRODUCTION

1. This Chapter describes the graphical method of solving LP problems and shows in a step by step fashion how to solve maximising and minimising problems. The calculation of Shadow prices is described and their interpretation is discussed. The process of sensitivity analysis is explained and exemplified.

GRAPHICAL LP SOLUTION.

2. Graphical methods of solving LP problems can only be used for problems with *TWO* unknowns or decision variables. Problems with *THREE OR MORE* unknowns must be solved by techniques such as the simplex method (dealt with in Chapter 19). Graphical methods are the simplest to use and should be used wherever possible.

a. Limitations. Graphical methods can deal with any number of limitations but as each limitation is shown as a line on a graph a large number of lines may make the graph difficult to read. This is rarely a problem in examination questions.

b. Types of problems and limitations. Both maximisation and minimisation problems can be dealt with graphically and the method can also deal with limitations of the 'greater than or equal to' ($\geq$) type and the 'less than or equal to' ($\leq$) type.

c. Graphical example. The method of solving LP problems graphically will be described step by step using the following maximising example as a basis.

Example 1.

A manufacturer produces two products, Klunk and Klick. Klunk has a contribution of £3 per unit and Klick £4 per unit. The manufacturer wishes to establish the weekly production plan which maximises contribution.

Production data are as follows:

	PER UNIT		
	Machining (Hours)	Labour (Hours)	Material (lbs)
Klunk	4	4	1
Klick	2	6	1
Total Available per week	100	180	40

Because of a trade agreement, sales of Klunk are limited to a weekly maximum of 20 units and to honour an agreement with an old established customer at least 10 units of Klick must be sold per week.

STEP 1. Formulate the LP model in the standardised manner described in Chapter 17 thus:

$$\text{Maximise} \quad 3x_1 + 4x_2$$

SUBJECT TO CONSTRAINT	A.	$4x_1$	+	$2x_2$	$\leq$	100	(Machining hours constraint)
	B	$4x_1$	+	$6x_2$	$\leq$	180	(Labour hours constraint)
	C.	x_1	+	x_2	$\leq$	40	(Materials constraint)
	D	x_1			$\leq$	20	(Klunk sales constraint)
	E.			x_2	$\geq$	10	(Klick sales constraint)

$$x_1 \geq 0$$

where x_1 = number of units of Klunk

x_2 = number of units of Klink

Notes:

As it is impossible to make negative quantities of the products it is necessary formally to state the non-negativity constraint (ie $x_1 \geq 0$)

The resource and sales constraints include both types of restrictions (ie $\geq$ and $\leq$).

As this is a problem with only 2 unknowns (ie x_1 and x_2) it can be solved graphically. The number of limitations does not exclude a graphical solution.

STEP 2. Draw the axes of the graph which represent the unknowns, x_1 and x_2 thus

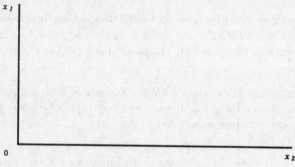

Figure 1

Note.

The scales of the axes are best determined when the lines for the limitations are drawn. Each axis must start at zero and the scale must be constant (ie linear) along the axis but it is not necessary for the scales on both axes to be the same.

STEP 3. Draw each limitation as a separate line on the graph.

Sales Limitations. These normally only affect one of the products at a time and in Example 1 the sales restrictions were

$$x_1 \leq 20 \quad \text{and} \quad x_2 \geq 10$$

These limitations are drawn on the graph as follows:-

The Klunk sales constraint ie $x_1 \leq 20$ CONSTRAINT D

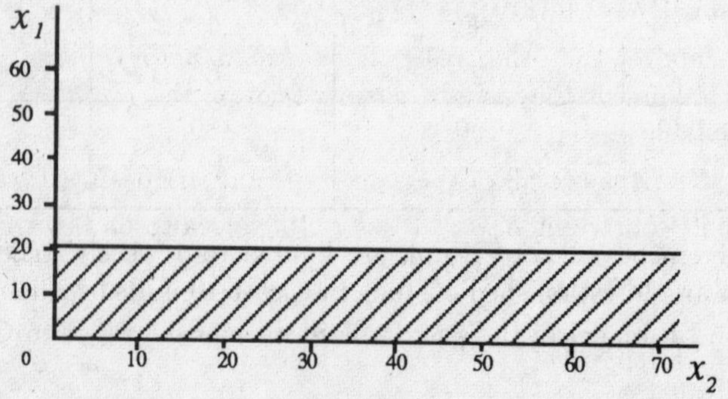

Figure 2

Note.

The horizontal line represents $x_1 = 20$ and the hatched area below the line represents the area containing all the values less than 20.

The Klick sales constraint (constraint E) ie $x_2 \geq 10$ is now entered thus:

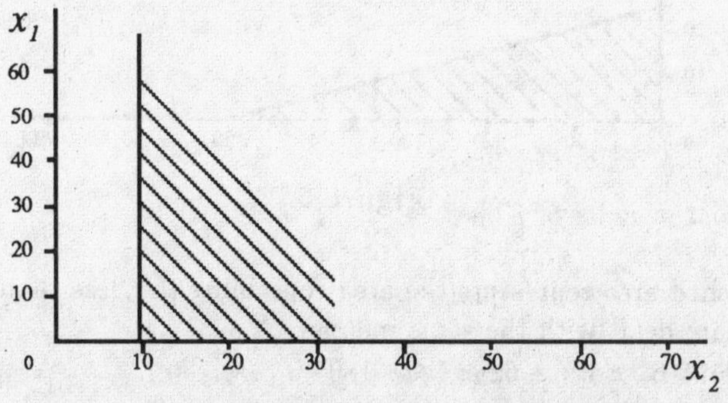

Figure 3

Note.

The vertical line represents $x_2 = 10$ and the hatched area to the right of the line represents the area containing all values greater than 10.

These two sales limitations can be shown on the same graph thus

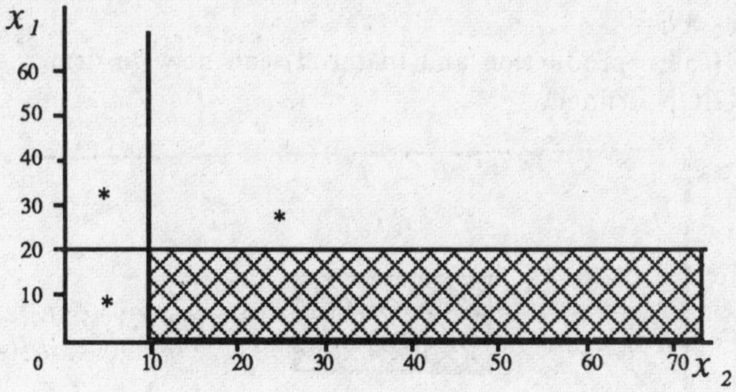

Figure 4

Notes.

The cross hatched area represents the area of possible production (ie which does not violate the constraints drawn) and is called the FEASIBLE REGION. The areas on the graph marked * violate one or both of the constraints.

PRODUCTION AND MATERIAL LIMITATIONS.

3. In a similar fashion to above, the other restrictions should be drawn on the graph. Because these restrictions involve BOTH unknowns they will be sloping lines on the graph and not horizontal or vertical lines like the sales restrictions.

The three remaining restrictions are all of the same type and are dealt with as follows:

The machining constraint, constraint A, $4x_1 + 2x_2 \leq 100$ is drawn on the graph as $4x_1 + 2x_2 = 100$.

Therefore when $x_1 = 0$, $x_2 = 50$ (ie $\frac{100}{2}$)

and when $x_2 = 0$, $x_1 = 25$ (ie $\frac{100}{4}$)

and so a line can be drawn from 25 on the x_1 axis to 50 on the x_2 axis thus

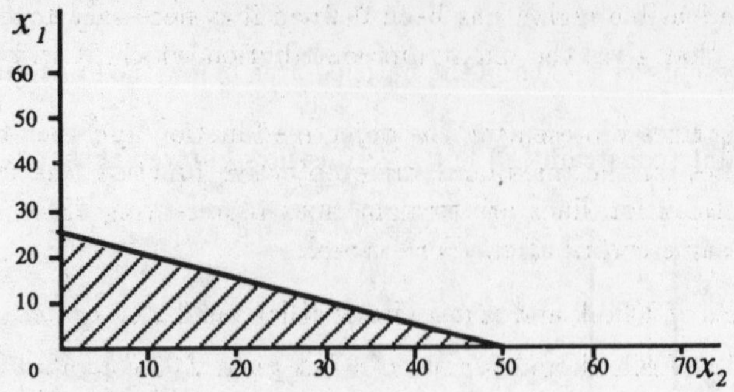

Figure 5

Note.

As previously, the hatched area represents the area containing the 'less than' values.

The other constraints are dealt with the same manner.

ie The labour constraint B, $4x_1 + 6x_2 \quad \leq \quad 180$

is drawn on the graph as $4x_1 + 6x_2 \quad = \quad 180$

Therefore when $x_1 = 0$, $x_2 = 30$ (ie. $\frac{180}{6}$)

and when $x_2 = 0$, $x_1 = 45$ (ie $\frac{180}{4}$)

and so a line can be drawn from 45 on the x_1 axis to 30 on the x_2 axis.

The materials constraint, (c), $x_1 + x_2 \leq 40$, is drawn on the graph as $x_1 + x_2 = 40$

Therefore when $x_1 = 0$, $x_2 = 40$ and when $x_2 = 0$, $x_2 = 40$ and so a line can be drawn from 40 on the x_1 axis to 40 on the x_2 axis.

All of the constraints (sales, production and material) can now be drawn on a single graph and the resulting FEASIBLE REGION defined.

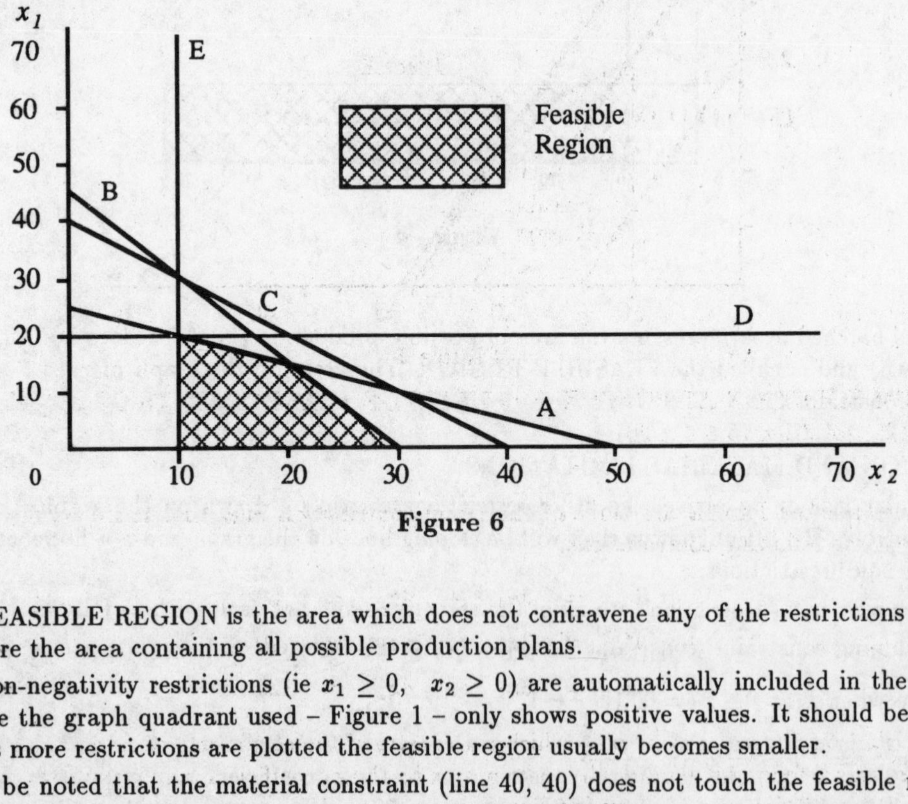

Figure 6

Notes.

a. The FEASIBLE REGION is the area which does not contravene any of the restrictions and is therefore the area containing all possible production plans.

b. The non-negativity restrictions (ie $x_1 \geq 0$, $x_2 \geq 0$) are automatically included in the graph because the graph quadrant used – Figure 1 – only shows positive values. It should be noted that as more restrictions are plotted the feasible region usually becomes smaller.

c. It will be noted that the material constraint (line 40, 40) does not touch the feasible region. This is an example of a *redundant* constraint ie it is non binding.

STEP 4. Now that the feasible region has been defined it is necessary to find the point in or on the edge of the feasible region that gives the maximum contribution which, it will be recalled, is the specific objective.

This is done by plotting lines representing the objective function and thereby identifying the point in the feasible region which lies on the maximum value objective function line that can be drawn. These objectives function on contribution lines are straight lines representing different combinations of Klunk and Klick which yield the same contribution. For example,

20 units of Klunk and zero units of Klick yield £60 contribution.

12 units of Klunk and 6 units of Klick yield £60 contribution.

8 units of Klunk and 9 units of Klick yield £60 contribution.

zero units of Klunk and 15 units of Klick yield £60 contribution.

etc.

Very many other contribution lines could be drawn and if a number of these lines were drawn on the graph it would be noticed that:

a. They are parallel to each other with the same slope, which is determined by the relative contribution of the products.
b. The further to the right they are drawn the higher value of contribution they represent.

It therefore follows that the contribution line furthest to the right but still touching the feasible region shows the optimum production plan to provide the maximum possible contribution, thus

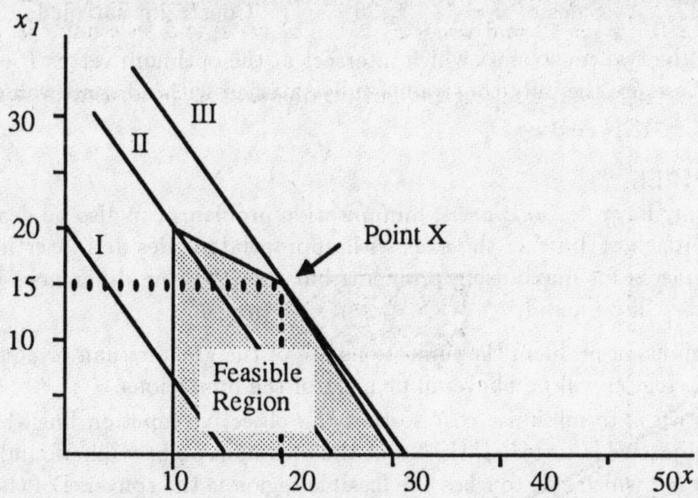

Figure 7

OPTIMUM SOLUTION AT POINT X ie 15 UNITS OF x_1 AND 20 UNITS OF x_2 yielding a contribution of £125. (ie £3 x 15 + 4 x 20)

Notes.

a. The lines marked I to III are three of the many contribution lines that could be drawn and represent the following contributions.

$$\text{I} = 3x_1 + 4x_2 = 60$$

$$\text{II} = 3x_1 + 4x_2 = 90$$

$$\text{III} = 3x_1 + 4x_2 = 125$$

The contribution line has a slope of $\frac{4}{3}$ which is the ratio of the coefficients of x_1 and x_2. The intercept on, say, the x_1 axis is found by dividing the contribution by the x_1 coefficient, and vica versa. The intercepts for line II in Figure 7, for example, are as follows:

$$\text{Intercept on } x_1 \text{ axis} = \frac{\text{contribution}}{x_1 \text{ coefficient}} = \frac{90}{3} = \underline{\underline{30}}$$

$$\text{Intercept on } x_2 \text{ axis} = \frac{90}{4} = \underline{\underline{22.5}}$$

a. Only parts of lines I, II and III are feasible but as we require to maximise contribution we are only interested in Point X where line III touches the feasible region.

b. Various contribution lines have been drawn on Figure 7 for instructional purposes. For examinations it is sufficient to draw only the contribution line representing the optimum position, ie in the example above, line III.

c. The contribution lines are sometimes termed ISO-PROFIT lines.

d. A simple way to check your answer is actually possible is to insert the values of the unknowns in the constraints and check whether the constriants are satisfied eg the optimum solution of Example 1 found from Figure 7 is,

$$x_1 = 15 \text{ units}$$
$$x_2 = 20 \text{ units}$$

these values can be inserted into the constraints thus,

CONSTRAINT A	$(4 \times 15) + (2 \times 20)$	= 100	Constraint satisfied, no spare
CONSTRAINT B	$(4 \times 15) + (6 \times 20)$	= 180	Constraint satisfied, no spare
CONSTRAINT C	$(1 \times 15) + (1 \times 20)$	= 35	Constraint satisfied, 5 below maximum
CONSTRAINT D	Sales of x_1	= 15	Constraint satisfied, 5 below maximum
CONSTRAINT E	Sales of x_2	= 20	Constraint satisfied, 10 above minimum

It will be noted that the two constraints which intersect at the optimum vertex (See Figures 6 & 7) are constraints A and B. These are the only constraints fully satisfied with no spare values. This is a general rule.

MINIMISATION EXAMPLE.

4. Provided that they only have *two unknowns,* minimisation problems can also be dealt with by graphical means. The general approach of drawing the axes with appropriate scales and inserting lines representing the limitations is the same as for maximising problems but the following differences between maximising and minimising problems will be found.

a. Normally in a minimising problem the limitations are of the greater than or equal to type ($\geq$) so that the feasible region will be above all or most of the limitations.

b. The normal objective is to minimise cost so that the objective function line(s) represent cost and because the objective is to MINIMISE cost the optimum point willbe found from the cost line *furthest to the left* which still touches the feasible region ie the converse of the method used for maximising problems.

Example 2.

A manufacturer is to market a new fertiliser which is to be a mixture of two ingredients A and B. The properties of the two ingredients are:

	INGREDIENT ANALYSIS				
	BONE MEAL	NITROGEN	LIME	PHOSPHATES	COST/LB
Ingredient A	20%	30%	40%	10%	1.2p
Ingredient B	40%	10%	45%	5%	0.8p

It has been decided that

a. the fertiliser will be sold in bags containing a minimum of 100 lbs.

b. it must contain at least 15% nitrogen

c. it must contain at least 8% phosphates

d. it must contain at least 25% Bone Meal

The manufacturer wishes to meet the above requirements at the minimum cost possible.

SOLUTION.

Because of the basic similarity between graphing minimising and maximising problems (except for the two differences mentioned above) the detailed intermediate steps given in Example 1 will not be repeated.

The problem in standardised format is as follows

OBJECTIVE FUNCTION.

MINIMISE $12x_1 + 8x_2$ (cost expressed in tenths of a penny)

subject to

CONSTRAINT A.	x_1	+	x_2	$\geq$	100	(Weight constraint)
B.	$3x_1$	+	$.1x_2$	$\geq$	15	(Nitrogen constraint)
C.	$.1x_1$	+	$.05x_2$	$\geq$	8	(Phosphates constraint)
D.	$.2x_1$	+	$.4x_2$	$\geq$	25	(Bone Meal constraint)

$x_1 \geq 0$ and $x_2 \geq 0$

where x_1 = lbs of ingredient A

x_2 = lbs of ingredient B

Notes on Figure 8.

OPTIMUM SOLUTION AT POINT X ie 60 lbs of x_1 and 40 lbs of x_2 GIVING A COST OF

$1.2 \times 60 + .8 \times 40 =$ £1.04 per 100 lb bag

Notes.

a. Only one cost line ($12x_1 + 8x_2 = 1040$ in tenths of a penny) has been drawn so as to show the optimum position.

b. Each restriction on the graph is labelled A, B, C, D and can be cross referenced to those stated in the standardised format above.

c. The optimum position in the feasible region is the furthest point *TO THE LEFT* touched by the cost line. This is because it is a MINIMISING problem.

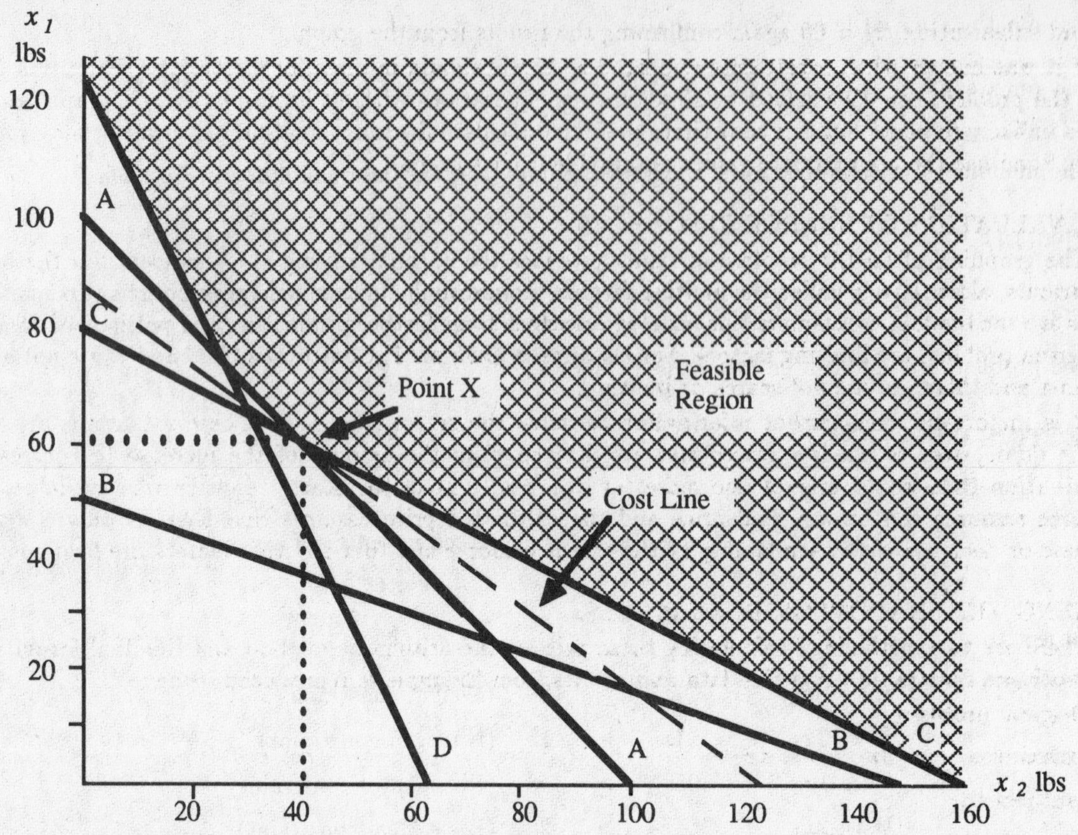

Figure 8

USING SIMULTANEOUS EQUATIONS.

5. An alternative method of finding the solution values of the constraints at any intersection of the graph, including the optimal vertex, is to solve the simultaneous equations of the relevant constraints. To illustrate this, the answers to the maximising problem in Example 1 and the minimising problem in Example 2 will be recalculated using simultaneous equations.

REWORKING OF EXAMPLE 1,

The two constraints which intersected at optimum were constraints A and B (See Figures 6 & 7) thus:

Constraint A $4x_1 + 2x_2 \;=\; 100$

Constraint B $4x_1 + 6x_2 \;=\; 180$

Solving, by deducting A from B gives

$$4x_2 = 80$$
$$\therefore\ x_2 = 20 \text{ and}$$
$$\text{substituting, } x_1 = 15, \text{ which}$$

confirms the answer found by reading off the intercepts of the graph.

REWORKING EXAMPLE 2.

The intersecting constraints were A and C (See Figure 8) thus

Constraint A $x_1 + x_2 = 100$

Constraint C $0.1x_1 + 0.05x_2 = 8$

$\therefore\ A - 10C = 0.5x_2 = 20$

$\therefore\ x_2 = \underline{40}$

and substituting, $x_1 = 60$ again confirming the results from the graph.

If it was known what constraints appeared at the optimum intersection before the graph was drawn, then the problem could be solved by simultaneous equatations without having to draw a graph. However this is unlikely to occur but it is sometimes useful to calculate the exact solution values using the equations, rather than use the approximate values obtainable from a graph.

THE VALUATION OF SCARCE RESOURCES.

6. The graphing of an LP problem not only provides the optimal answer but also identifies the binding constraints, alternatively called the limiting factors. For example, in example 1 machining hours and labour hours are the binding constraints, the shortage of which limit further production and profit. Not all factors in a given problem are limiting factors. For instance in example 1, Constraints C, D and E are not at their maxima and therefore are not scarce or limiting.

It is important management information to value the scarce resources. These valuations are known as the dual prices or shadow prices and are derived from the amount of the increase (or decrease) in contribution that would arise if one more (or one less) unit of the scarce resource was available. Only a scarce resource can have a dual price and the calculated price assumes that there is only a marginal increase or decrease in the availability of the scarce resource and that all other factors are held constant.

FINDING THE SHADOW OR DUAL PRICES.

7. There are two methods of calculating these prices - the arithmetic method and the dual formulation - and both are illustrated using the data and results from Example 1, reproduced below:

Original problem

maximise	$3x_1$	$+$	$4x_2$			
subject to						
Constraint A	$4x_1$	$+$	$2x_2$	$\leq$	100	machining hours
Constraint B	$4x_1$	$+$	$6x_2$	$\leq$	180	labour hours
Constraint C	x_1	$+$	x_2	$\leq$	40	materials
Constraint D	x_1			$\leq$	20	sales
Constraint E			x_2	$\geq$	10	sales

where x_1 = units of klunk

x_2 = units of klick

The solution was: Produce $15x_1$ and $20x_2$ giving a contribution of £125. Constraints A and B are binding.

The problem now is to find the shadow prices of the two binding constraints, machine hours and labour hours ie what is the valuation of one more (or less) machine hour and one more (or less) labour hour?

ARITHMETIC METHOD OF FINDING SHADOW PRICES.

8. Dealing first with machine hours, we assume that 1 more machine hour is available (but labour hours are constant at 180) and calculate the resulting difference in contribution, thus:

The binding constraints become

Machine hours $4x_1 + 2x_2 = 101$ (ie original 100 + 1)

Labour hours $4x_1 + 6x_2 = 180$ (unchanged)

Solving these simultaneous equations, new values for x_1 and x_2 are obtained:

$x_1 = 15.375$ and $x_2 = 19.75$ and substituting into the objective function gives a new contribution.

$3(15.375) + 4(19.75)$	=	£125.125
Original contribution	=	£125
Difference	=	£0.125

Thus 1 extra machine hour has resulted in an increase in contribution of £0.125 which is the *shadow price per machining hour.*

A similar process for labour hours is shown below:

New constraints with extra labour hour (but machine hours constant at 100).

$$\text{Machine hours:} \quad 4x_1 + 2x_2 = 100$$

$$\text{Labour hours} \quad 4x_1 + 6x_2 = 181$$

and solving gives, $x_1 = 14.875$ and $x_2 = 20.25$

$$\text{New contribution} = 3(14.875) + 4(20.25) = £125.625$$

$$\text{Original contribution} = \underline{£125}$$

$$\text{Difference} \quad \underline{£0.625}$$

$$\therefore \text{ shadow price per labour hour} = \underline{£0.625}$$

The two values obtained can be verified by showing that the quantities of the binding constraints at their shadow price valuations do produce the contribution of £125 shown in the optimum solution thus:

$$100(£0.125) + 180(£0.625) = \underline{\underline{£125}}$$

Notes.

a. Similar results would be obtained in each case if *1 less* hour had been used in the calculations. Verify this yourself.

b. The shadow prices calculated above only apply whilst the constraint is binding. If, for example, more and more machining hours became available there would eventually be so many machining hours that they would no longer be scarce and some other constraint would become binding. This point is developed further in Para 12.

DUAL FORMULATION METHOD FOR SHADOW PRICES.

9. Every LP problem has an *inverse* or *dual* formulation. If the original problem, known as the *primal problem*, is a maximising one then the dual formulation is a minimising one and vica versa. Thus, as the Example 1 primal formulation is a maximising problem, its dual is the minimising problem. Solving the dual problem gives the shadow prices of the binding constraints, hence the alternative term, dual prices.

The stages in finding and solving the dual for the solution to Example 1 are shown below:

The relevant parts of the original full formulation which appear in the solution are:

$$\text{Maximise} \quad 3x_1 + 4x_2 \qquad \text{(objective function)}$$

$$\text{subject to} \quad 4x_1 + 2x_2 \leq 100 \quad \text{(Machine hours)}$$

$$4x_1 + 6x_2 \leq 180 \quad \text{(labour hours)}$$

(Constraints C, D, E are non-binding so do not appear in the solution).

The minimising dual problem is formed by *inverting* the above formulation, ie making the columns into rows and the rows into columns thus:

Dual formulation.

$$\text{minimise} \quad 100M + 180L \qquad \text{(ie originally the constraint } \textit{column}\text{)}$$

$$\text{subject to} \quad 4M + 4L \geq 3 \quad \text{(originally the } x_1 \textit{ column}\text{)}$$

$$2M + 6L \geq 4 \quad \text{(originally the } x_2 \textit{ column}\text{)}$$

What are now the constraints can be solved by simultaneous equations:

$$4M + 4L = 3$$
$$2M + 6L = 4$$

Solving gives $M = 0.125$ and $L = 0.625$ which will be recognised as the valuations already calculated in para 8.

If these dual prices are inserted into the objective function of the dual, exactly the same value is obtained as in the primal problem.

$$\text{ie } 100(0.125) + 180(0.625) = \underline{\pounds 125}$$

This result is identical to the Primal problem and this will always be so.

Notes:

a. The dual formulation above is a contraction of the full dual formulation. This is possible here because the problem had already been solved and it was thus known that three of the constraints (C, D and E) were non-binding.

b. The dual formulation is developed further Chapter 20.

INTERPRETATION OF SHADOW PRICES.

10. The shadow price of a binding constraint provides valuable guidance because it indicates to management the extra contribution they would gain from increasing by one unit the amount of the scarce resource. As an example, the shadow price of labour hours calculated above is £0.625 per hour. This means that management would be prepared to pay up to £0.625 per hour extra in order to gain more labour hours. If the current labour cost was £4 per hour then management would be prepared to pay upto £4.625 per hour for extra labour hours; perhaps from overtime working.

It is important to realise that only binding constraints have shadow or dual prices. Those that are not binding have zero shadow prices. This accords with common sense for there would be little point in paying more to increase the supply of a resource of which you already have a surplus. In example 1, constraints C, D and E have zero shadow prices.

SENSITIVITY ANALYSIS.

11. This is the process of changing the values and relationships within the problem and observing the effect on the solution. The general aim is to discover how sensitive is the optimal solution to the changes made. With two variable problems ie those that can be solved graphically, sensitivity analysis can be visualised as the process of altering the angle, or distance from the origin, of the the lines on the graph.

As an example, it was mentioned earlier that if more and more machine hours became available there would come a point where machine hours would cease to be a restriction. This is, incidentally, the range over which the shadow price of £0.125 applies. Assume that management wish to know how many extra machine hours are necessary before machine hours cease to be a binding constraint and also the same information relating to labour hours.

NUMBER OF EXTRA MACHINE HOURS.

If figure 9 is examined it will be seen that the original solution to example 1 is reproduced together with new constraints labelled (A) and (B) shown by dotted lines.

Dealing first with A, the machine hour constraint, the dotted line is drawn parallel to the original constraint and up to the intersection of constraints B and D, where (A) ceases to be binding as it is on the edge of the new feasible area.

The BD intersection – Point M on the graph is then solved using simultaneous equations in the normal way.

$$4x_1 + 6x_2 = 180 \quad \text{(constraint B)}$$
$$x_1 = 20 \quad \text{(Constraint D)}$$

Solving gives $x_1 = 20$ and $x_2 = 16\frac{2}{3}$ which is the new production plan assuming that machine hours are increased. At this point $113\frac{1}{3}$ machine hours are required ie $4(20) + 2(16\frac{2}{3}) = 113\frac{1}{3}$

The original number of machine hours was 100 so that only $13\frac{1}{3}$ extra machine hours are necessary for the machine hour constraint to be non-binding. The $13\frac{1}{3}$ hours is also the range over which the calculated shadow price of £0.125 applies.

Number of extra labour hours.

This follows a similar pattern with the intersection being where constraint C joins the x_2 axis – Point L. Equations are not required here as the new optimum output is clearly 40 units of x_2 and nil x_1.

Substituting in the labour hour constraint gives

$$4(0) + 6(40) = 240$$

Thus the extra labour hours are 60 (ie $240 - 180$) and the shadow price of £0.625 would apply over the range from 180 hours to 240 hours.

Note: Although not shown on Figure 9 for clarity, changing the constraints as done above will cause the feasible region to change.

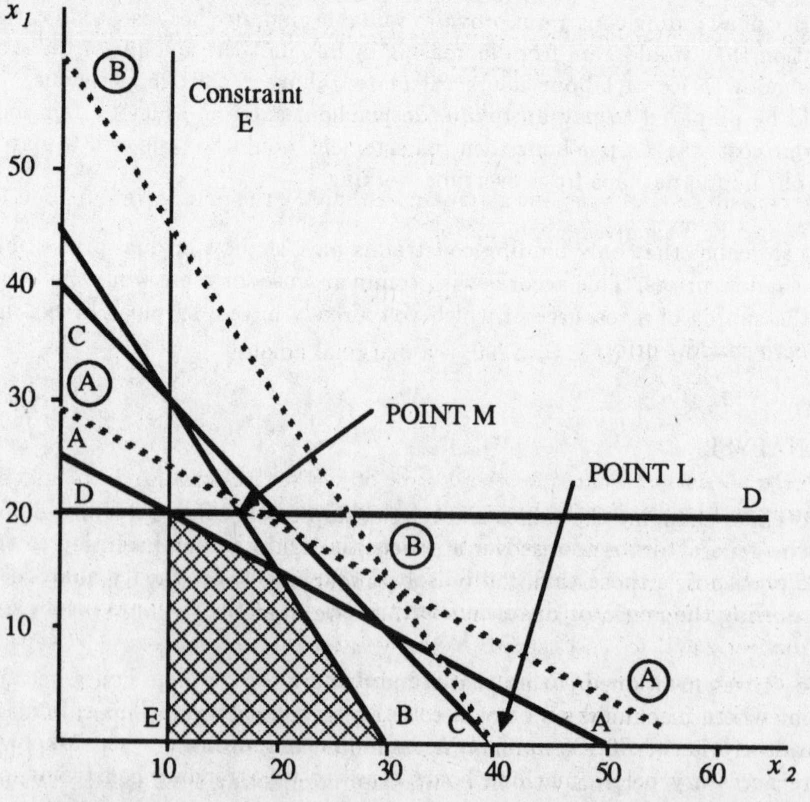

SENSITIVITY ANALYSIS ON EXAMPLE 1 Figure 9

FURTHER ASPECTS OF SENSITIVITY ANALYSIS.

12. If the *amount* of a constraint is altered, then the new line on the graph is parallel to the original constraint line – this is the case for the machine hours and labour hours constraints dealt with in Para 11.

On the other hand, if the *relationship changes* between the variables in the constraints or objective function, then the *slope* of the line changes.

For example, assume that management are able to adjust the contribution of x_1 in Example 1, with all other factors remaining the same. Management wish to know.

a. What would be new *reduced* contribution per unit of x_1 to cause the optimum solution to change from the existing one of 15 units x_1, and 20 units x_2?
b. Conversely, what would be *increased* unit contribution to cause a change?.

SOLUTION.

The original objective function, $3x_1 + 4x_2$, had a slope of

$$\frac{\text{coefficient of } x_2}{\text{coefficient of } x_1} \text{ ie } \frac{4}{3} \text{ or } \frac{1\frac{1}{3}}{1}.$$

This slope produced an optimum solution at the intersection of constraints A and B.

Reducing the coefficient (the contribution) of x_1 causes the slope of the objective function to steepen. At present the objective function has a less steep slope than constraint B, which has a $\frac{6}{4}$ or $\frac{1\frac{1}{2}}{1}$ slope. If follows, therefore that when the objective functions slope steepens to the slope of constraint B (in fact, just marginally steeper) the optimum solution will change.

Thus, the new objective function's minimum slope must be $\frac{x_2}{x_1} = \frac{1\frac{1}{2}}{1}$. As the coefficient of x_2 is unchanged at 4, x_1 can be deduced as $\frac{4}{1\frac{1}{2}} = \underline{\underline{2\frac{2}{3}}}$. At just marginally lower than this value the objective function shows that the optimum point is Point B on Figure 9. This gives a solution of

Nil units x_1, 30 units x_2

Contribution 30 × £4 = <u>£120</u>

Conversley when the contribution of x_1 *increases*, the slope of the objective function becomes *less steep*. The maximum slope it can be is that of Constraint A.

$$\therefore \text{ maximum slope} = \text{constraint A slope} = \frac{2}{4} = \frac{1}{2}$$

$$\therefore \text{ as } x_2 = 4 \text{ and } \frac{x_2}{x_1} = \frac{1}{2}, x_1 = \underline{8}$$

Thus, when the contribution of x_1 is marginally more than £8 the new optimum point is the intersection of constraints D, A and E. This gives a solution of

$$20x_1, 10x_2$$

Contribution: 20 (£8+) + 10 (£4) = £200 + a marginal amount.

SUMMARY.

13.

a. LP is a resource allocation technique where some objective, for example to maximise contribution, is required to be optimised subject to resource constraints.
b. All factors involved – objective, constraints – must have linear relationships.
c. LP problems should be expressed initially in a standardised format consisting of an objective function followed by the various constraints taking care to identify whether the constraints are of the 'less than or equal to' ($\leq$) type or of the 'greater than or equal to' ($\geq$) type.
d. LP problems can be maximising or minimising problems.
e. If an LP problem has 2 unknowns it may be solved by graphical means regardless of the number of constraints and whether it is a maximising or minimising problem.
f. To solve graphically it is necessary to draw two axes representing the 2 unknowns and then plot lines representing the constraints.

g. When the constraints have been drawn the feasible region can be identified. The feasible region is the area on the graph which does not contravene any of the constraints. Any point inside or on the edge of the feasible region is a possible solution although not necessarily the optimum solution.

h. To establish the optimal solution it is necessary to draw a line representing the objective function. For maximising problems typically this is a contribution line and for minimising problems a cost line.

i. In a maximising problem the optimum position in the feasible region is the furthest point *to the right* touched by the contribution line, conversely in a minimising problem it is the furthest point *to the left* touched by the cost line.

j. The exact values at any intersection can be found using simultaneous equations.

k. Shadow or dual prices are the valuations of scarce resources.

l. Shadow prices can be calculated arithmetically or by solving the dual.

m. Shadow prices show the *extra* contribution per unit of a binding constraint.

n. Sensitivity analysis changes values and relationships in the problem to see the effect on the original solution.

POINTS TO NOTE.

14. a In examination questions it is often difficult to formulate the LP problem in the standardised format. If you do have difficulty concentrate on these basic questions - What are the unknowns? What is the objective? - What factors govern the achievement of the objective?

a. As with all graphs, some trial and error is necessary to establish suitable scales for the axes. Remember they do not have to be the same scale on each axis but the chosen scale must, of course, be constant and continuous along each axis.

b. Although the examples used in this chapter have produced whole number solutions, fractional solutions are quite possible and often occur.

c. For simple LP problems the identification of the optimum point (ie Point X in Figures 7 and 8) is straightforward and can often be done without drawing the objective function line. However, this is not recommended and students should always draw the objective function line to identify the optimum point.

d. A simple way to check your answer is actually possible is to insert the values of the unknowns in the constraints and check whether the constraints are satisfied.

e. The solution is *always found at a vertex on the graph* ie the junction of two or more of the constraint lines. Having located the optimum vertex it is useful, on occasions, to evaluate the coordinates by solving simultaneous equations. This can be important when it is difficult to choose between two points, both sets of coordinates can be evaluated and the values of the resulting objective functions compared.

f. Every primal problem has a DUAL problem which is minimised if the primal is maximised or maximised if the primal is minimised.

SELF REVIEW QUESTIONS.

1. What types of LP problems can be solved by graphical methods? (2)

2. How many constraints can be handled by graphical methods? (2)

3. What is the feasible region? (3)

4. How is optimum point on the feasible region determined? (3)

5. What are the differences in dealing with minimising and maximising problems by graphical means? (4)

6. How can simultaneous equations be used in solving LP problems? (5)

7. What are shadow or dual prices? (6)

8. What methods can be used to calculate shadow prices? (7)

9. What is the primal problem and what is the dual problem? (9)

10. What do shadow prices tell management? (10)

11. What is sensitivity analysis and how is it carried out? (11 & 12)

EXERCISES WITH ANSWERS COMMENCING PAGE 488

A1. A firm produces two products, X and Y with a contribution of £8 and £10 per unit respectively. Production data are: (per unit)

	Labour hours	Material A	Material B
X	3	4	6
Y	5	2	8
TOTAL AVAILABLE	500	350	800

Formulate the LP model in the standardised manner.

A2. Solve the model in A1 using the graphical method.

A3. Calculate the shadow prices of the binding constraints and interpret.

EXAMINATION QUESTIONS WITH ANSWERS COMMENCING PAGE 488

A4. A confectionery manufacturer makes two kinds of chocolate bar, A and B, each of which requires three stages of production: mixing, cooking and boxing. The number of minutes required to complete each process for a box of chocolate bars is as follows:

	Mixing	Cooking	Boxing
A	1.25	0.5	1.5
B	1.2	1.5	0.5

All the production equipment is available for eight hours each day. Accountants have calculated that the contribution on each box of A is £0.50 and on B is £1. The equipment may be used to produce A and B simultaneously. All production may be sold.

You are required to:

(a) state the objective function in mathematical terms, assuming the manufacturer wishes to maximise contributions;

(b) state all the constraints (equations/inequalities) which are relevant to this production problem;

(c) graph the constraints, shading any unwanted regions, and determine the optimum production position;

(d) find the contribution which is generated by this optimum position;

(e) comment on any assumptions and practical limitations of this method of analysis.

(CIMA quantitative methods)

A5. The board of Priam Properties plc is considering the company's planned workload for the next financial year. Priam undertakes both the construction of new houses and also the repair and renovation of old buildings, and it is important for the company's long term plans to obtain a suitable mix of new houses and repair work each year. For planning purposes, the profit on new houses is taken to be 20% of their total value whereas on repairs and renovations it is 25% .

To avoid the problems of having to acquire large amounts of land for the building of new houses, Priam always plans for at least £4 million of repair and renovation work each year but at the same time the company ensures that repairs and renovations do not account for more than half of their total workload. Furthermore, in costing all new and repair work, 5% of the total value of the work is included to cover fixed overheads. It is the board's wish that the total of these overhead charges does in fact cover the company's actual fixed overheads which have been estimated at £500,000 for the coming year.

The other major consideration is the amount of skilled labour (bricklaying, plastering, plumbing, carpentry and electrical work) which is available. It has been estimated that £1 million of new house building involves 12 man years of skilled labour, whereas £1 million of repair and renovation work requires 18 man years of skilled labour. The company currently employs 180 skilled workmen and it would be difficult to recruit more skilled labour in the short term.

Required:

(a) Develop a linear programming model of the planning problem facing Priam Properties.

(b) Using a graphical approach, or otherwise, determine the total value of both new building work and repair and renovation work that should be undertaken next year to maximise profit.

(c) What increase in profit (if any) would be achieved if the company were to remove the condition of having at least £4 million of repair and renovation work each year?

(ACCA Quantitative Analysis)

A6. The Milton Company has been manufacturing two ranges of carpet for many years, one range for commercial use, the other for private use. The main difference between the two ranges is in the mix of wool and nylon; with the commercial range having 80% wool and 20% nylon and the private range 20% wool and 80% nylon. The designs of each range are the same and each range can be made in 5 different colours. There are variations in the cost of the dyes used for the different colours in the range, but they are all within 5% of each other so the accountant takes an average cost of dyeing in her costing.

The Board has just decided to use up its remaining stocks of wool and nylon and transfer its production over to making acrylic carpets in three months' time. The company's objective is to maximise the contribution from the running down of the stocks of wool and nylon over that period subject to any operating constraints. Data concerning its present carpet range is given below. It is assumed that sufficient demand exists to ensure all production can be sold at the stated price.

	Per Roll	
	Private use	*Commercial use*
	£	*£*
Selling price	*2,400*	*3,200*
Manufacturing costs		
Material–Wool	*140*	*700*
–Nylon	*320*	*100*
Direct Labour	*90*	*108*
Variable production costs...	*250*	*312*
Fixed production overheads based on 200% direct labour ...	*180*	*216*
Standard full cost	*980*	*1,436*
Production requirements		
Wool (lbs)	*40*	*200*
Nylon (lbs.)	*160*	*50*
Direct machine time (hours) ...	*30*	*56*

There are 24,000 lbs of wool and 25,000 lbs of nylon in the stores to be used up. At the end of the quarter, when it changes production to the new carpet, any wool or nylon left can be sold for £1 per lb. The production manager forecasts that the machines can operate for a total of 6,600 hours during the next quarter.

You are required to:

(a) formulate the above problem in a linear programming format. Solve the problem and provide the production manager with the required output mix of rolls of private and commercial carpets. State whether any of the raw material has to be sold off as scrap at the end and thus what the total contribution for the quarter's production should be.

(b) show whether or not it will be necessary to recompute the optimum solution if due to economic difficulties, the cost of the dyes for the carpets are to be increased by £110 and £40 per roll of private and commercial carpet respectively.

(c) describe what would happen in physical and financial terms if the availability of one of the fully utilised resources were to be increased by a small amount, and

(d) comment on the advisability of introducing the concept of opportunity costs into the budgetary control framework, by using the output from the linear programming solution to the optimum production mix .

(ICA Management Accounting)

A7. a. In relation to linear programming, explain the implications of the following assumptions of the model:

i. linearity of the objective function and constraints;
ii. continuous variables;
iii. certainty.

b. From the following information construct a graphical linear programme to maximise contribution and interpret the results:

A company manufactures two products, A and B.
Contributions per unit are: A, £4 and B, £3.
Total labour hours available are 110 hours
Labour required per unit is: A, 1 hour and B, 2 hours.
Production capacity limitations are: 70 units of A, 150 units of B.

c. Owing to uncertainty about aspects of the information in (b) above you are required to carry out a simple sensitivity test of the results obtained in (b) and to state your findings in each of the following cases:

i. a £1 decrease in the contribution per unit of B;
ii. a ten-hour increase in the total labour hours available;
iii. a 10% increase in the labour hours per unit of A.

Treat each case separately in relation to the solution you obtained in (b)

d. Following on from (b) above, assume that product B is required as a component input to product A. B can still be sold outside on the open market, but the demand made by the prodction of A has first priority. B is to be credited with the same unit contribution as in (b).

Show how you would incorporate the new requirement and produce a graphical solution to this situation.

(CIMA, Quantitative Techniques)

A8. Complete part (b) of A5 Chapter 17.

EXERCISES WITHOUT ANSWERS

B1. A firm makes a fertiliser from two ingredients V and W and wishes to minimise costs.

The properties and costs of the ingredients are as follows:

	Analysis			*Cost/Kg*
	Nitrogent	*Lime*	*Potash*	
V	*40*	*50*	*10*	*20p*
W	*20*	*40*	*40*	*10p*

The finished product must contain:

(a) at least 30% nitrogen
(b) at least 45% lime
(c) at least 25% potash

Formulate the problem in the standard manner.

B2. Solve the problem in B1 graphically.

EXAMINATION QUESTIONS WITHOUT ANSWERS

B3. The Superseal Company Ltd. manufactures amongst other products, two types of sealing ring (SRI and SRII) for airtight jars. These are sold to the trade in packs of 1,000. A number of processes are involved in the manufacture of both types of ring. These processes take place within three different departments and the times required in each department for each pack of rings are given in the following table:

Processing time per pack

(Hours)

	SRI	SRII
Department A	3	1
Department B	1	1
Department C	1	2

The departments have the following machine hours available for these products.

Department	A	B	C
Machine Hours	120	60	100

The contribution per pack is £50 for type SRI and £80 for the type SRII.

Required:

a. Formulate this linear programming problem and determine graphically the optimal solution.

b. If the number of machine hours available in Department B is increased to 61 hours, how does the optimal solution change? (State any assumptions made). How could this be determined from the optimal tableau?

c. If the cost of increasing the machine hours available in Department B is relatively small, by how many hours would you recommend that the number of hours available in Department B be increased?

(ACCA, Management Mathematics)

19 Linear Programming – Simplex Method for Maximisng

INTRODUCTION

1. This chapter describes the simplex method of solving LP maximising problems. The simplex method is suitable for solving problems with 2 or more unknowns and can be used for very large problems indeed involving thousands of unknowns and limitations. No advanced mathematics are required to use the simplex method. All that is required is simple arithmetic and the ability to follow a set of rules.

SIMPLEX METHOD DEFINITION.

2. A step by step arithmetic method of solving LP problems whereby one moves progressively from a position of, say, zero production, and therefore zero contribution, until no further contribution can be made. Each step produces a feasible solution and each step produces an answer better than the one before ie either greater contribution in maximising problems, or less cost in minimising problems. The mathematics behind the simplex method are complex and this chapter does not try to explain why the method works but it does describe how to use the technique.

FORMULATING THE SIMPLEX MODEL.

3. To use the simplex method it is first necessary to state the problem in the standardised manner previously described in Chapter 17. It will be recalled that this results in an objective function and a number of constraints which are inequalities either of the $\geq$ or $\leq$ type. Having stated the problem in the standardised format it is necessary to convert all the inqualities into equations. This is because it is not possible to perform arithmetic upon an inequality. For example, if a manufacturer made two products A and B, which took 3 and 5 hours respectively to machine on a drilling machine which was available for up to 320 hours per period the constraint would be written in the standardised format as follows:

$$3x_1 + 5x_2 \leq 320 \quad \text{where} \quad x_1 = \text{units of A}$$
$$x_2 = \text{units of B}$$

This is converted into an equation by adding an extra variable called a SLACK VARIABLE thus

$$3x_1 + 5x_2 + x_3 = 320$$

The slack variable, x_3 in this case, represents any unused capacity in the constraint and can thus take any value from

320 hours – ie the position of zero production and therefore maximum unused capacity, to

0 hours – ie the position of the machine being fully utilised and therefore zero unused capacity.

Notes.

a. Each constraint will have its own slack variable

b. Once the slack variable has been incorporated into the constraint the simplex method automatically assigns it an appropriate value at each iteration.

A SIMPLEX MAXIMISING EXAMPLE.

4. The following maximising example will be used to provide a step by step approach to the simplex method.

Example 1.

A company can produce three products, A, B and C. The products yield a contribution of £8, £5 and £10 respectively.

The products use a machine which has 400 hours capacity in the next period. Each unit of the products uses 2, 3 and 1 hour respectively of the machine's capactiy.

There are only 150 units available in the period of a special component which is used singly in products A and C.

200 kgs only of a special alloy is available in the period. Product A uses 2 kgs per unit and Product C uses 4 kgs per units.

There is an agreement with a trade association to produce no more than 50 units of Product B in the period.

The company wishes to find out the production plan which maximises contribution.

STEP 1. As in Chapter 17 express the problem in the standardised format thus:

Objective function:

$$\text{Maximise } 8x_1 + 5x_2 + 10x_3$$

Subject to:-

$$\begin{array}{rcrcrcrl}
2x_1 & + & 3x_2 & + & x_3 & \leq & 400 & \text{(Machine hours constraint)} \\
x_1 & & & + & x_3 & \leq & 150 & \text{(Component constraint)} \\
2x_1 & & & + & 4x_3 & \leq & 200 & \text{(Alloy constraint)} \\
 & & x_2 & & & \leq & 50 & \text{(Sales constraint)} \\
x_1 & \geq & 0, & & x_2 & \geq & 0, & x_3 \geq 0
\end{array}$$

$$\begin{array}{rcl}
\text{where } x_1 & = & \text{no. of units of Product A} \\
x_2 & = & \text{no. of units of Product B} \\
x_3 & = & \text{no. of units of Product C}
\end{array}$$

STEP 2. Make the inequalities in the constraints into equalities by adding a 'slack variable' in each constraint, thus:

$$\text{Maximise } 8x_1 + 5x_2 + 10x_3$$

Subject to:-

$$\begin{array}{rcrcrcrcr}
2x_1 & + & 3x_2 & + & x_3 & + & x_4 & = & 400 \\
x_1 & + & & & x_3 & + & x_5 & = & 150 \\
x_1 & & & & x_3 & + & x_6 & = & 200 \\
 & & x_2 & & & + & x_7 & = & 50
\end{array}$$

Note. x_4, x_5, x_6, x_7 are the slack variables and represent the spare capacity in the limitations.

STEP 3. Set up the initial Simplex Tableau by arranging the objective function and equalised constraints from Step 2 in the following form.

INITIAL SIMPLEX TABLEAU

SOLUTION VARIABLE	PRODUCTS x_1	x_2	x_3	SLACK VARIABLES x_4	x_5	x_6	x_7	SOLUTION QUANTITY
x_4	2	3	1	1	0	0	0	400
x_5	1	0	1	0	1	0	0	150
x_6	2	0	4	0	0	1	0	200
x_7	0	1	0	0	0	0	1	50
Z	8	5	10	0	0	0	0	0

Table 1

Notes.

a. It will be seen that the values in the body of the table are the values from the objective function and constraints in Step 2.

b. The variable 'Z' has been used for the objective function and represents total contribution.

c. The tableau shows that $x_4 = 400$, $x_5 = 150$, $x_6 = 200$, $x_7 = 50$ and $Z = 0$.

d. The tableau shows a feasible solution, that of nil production, nil contribution, and maximum unused capacity as represented by the values of the slack variables x_4, x_5, x_6 and x_7 .

e. Although feasible, this plan can obviously be improved and this is done as follows:

STEP 4. Improve the previous feasible solution by making as many as possible of the product with the most contribution, ie the highest figure in the Z row. The number than can be made will be limited by one or more of the constraints becoming operative thus:

Select highest contribution in Z row – ie 10 under x_3.

Divide the positive numbers in the x_3 column into the solution quantity column.

$$
\begin{aligned}
\text{ie } 400 &\div 1 = 400 \\
150 &\div 1 = 150 \\
200 &\div 4 = 50 \\
50 &\div 0 = \text{IGNORE}
\end{aligned}
$$

Select the row that gives the *LOWEST* answer (in this case the row identified x_6). Ring the element which appears in both the identified column (x_3) and the identified row (x_6), this element is known as the PIVOT ELEMENT, thus

INITIAL SIMPLEX TABLEAU REPRODUCED.

SOLUTION VARIABLE	PRODUCTS x_1	x_2	x_3	SLACK VARIABLES x_4	x_5	x_6	x_7	SOLUTION QUANTITY
x_4	2	3	1	1	0	0	0	400
x_5	1	0	1	0	1	0	0	150
$\longrightarrow x_6$	2	0	[4]	0	0	1	0	200
x_7	0	1	0	0	0	0	1	50
Z	8	5	10	0	0	0	0	0
			$\uparrow$					

Table 2

STEP 5. Divide all the elements in the identified row (x_6) by the value of the pivot element (4) and change the solution variable to the heading of the identified column (x_3) thus

OLD ROW

x_6	2	0	4	0	0	1	0	200

Divide by 4 and retitling the new row becomes

NEW ROW

x_3	$\frac{1}{2}$	0	1	0	0	$\frac{1}{4}$	0	50

Enter this row in a new tableau

SECOND SIMPLEX TABLE

ROW NO.	SOLUTION VARIABLE	PRODUCTS			SLACK VARIABLES				SOLUTION QUANTITY
		x_1	x_2	x_3	x_4	x_5	x_6	x_7	
1	x_4	2	3	1	1	0	0	0	400
2	x_5	1	0	1	0	1	0	0	150
3	x_3	$\frac{1}{2}$	0	1	0	0	$\frac{1}{4}$	0	50
4	x_7	0	1	0	0	0	0	1	50
5	Z	8	5	10	0	0	0	0	0

Table 3

Notes.

a. The row numbers have been included to aid the explanatory material which follows and form no part of the simplex tableaux.

b. It will be seen that this second tableau is identical to the first except for row 3 which was calculated above.

c. Row 3 means that 50 units of x_3 are to be produced.

STEP 6. As a consequence of producing 50 units of x_3 it is necessary to adjust the other row so as to take up the appropriate number of hours, components etc. used and to show the contribution produced for the 50 units of x_3. This is done by repetitive row by row operations using Row 3 which makes all the other elements in the pivot elements column into zeros. To maintain each row as an equality it is, of course, necessary to alter each element along the row on both sides of the equality sign. Using Row 1 in the Second Tableau as an example the process is as follows.

	ROW 1.	x_4	2	3	1	1	0	0	0	=	400
MINUS	ROW 3.	x_3	$\frac{1}{2}$	0	1	0	0	$\frac{1}{4}$	0	=	50
PRODUCES A											
NEW ROW		x_4	$1\frac{1}{2}$	3	0*	1	0	$-\frac{1}{4}$	0	=	350

Notes:

a. This new row will be inserted into a third tableau along with all the other altered rows and Row 3 from the second tableau.

b. The aim of this row operation was to produce the zero (marked *). In this case a simple substraction was all that was necessary but to make a zero in other cases may require further operations using Row 3 as a basis.

The other rows in the second tableau are operated on a similar fashion.

	ROW 2	x_5	1	0	1	0	1	0	0	=	150
MINUS	ROW 3	x_3	$\frac{1}{2}$	0	1	0	0	$\frac{1}{4}$	0	=	50
PRODUCES A											
NEW ROW		x_5	$\frac{1}{2}$	0	0*	0	1	$-\frac{1}{4}$	0	=	100

ROW 4 needs no operation because the element in column x_3 is already zero.

	ROW 5	Z	8	5	10	0	0	0	0	=	0
MINUS	10 TIMES										
	ROW 3	x_3	5	0	10	0	0	$2\frac{1}{2}$	0	=	500
PRODUCES A											
NEW ROW		Z	3	5	0*	0	0	$-2\frac{1}{2}$	0	=	-500

Notes.

a. To produce the required zero (0*) it was necessary to multiply the Row 3 by 10 and then subtract. from Row 5.

b. The '-500' at the end of the new Z row is the contribution earned by 50 units of x_3 at £10 ie £500. The negative sign is merely a result of the simplex method and the fact that the contribution is shown as a negative figure can be disregarded.

STEP 7. When all the row operations have been done a third tableau can be produced thus.

THIRD SIMPLEX TABLEAU

ROW NO.	SOLUTION VARIABLE	PRODUCTS			SLACK VARIABLES				SOLUTION QUANTITY
		x_1	x_2	x_3	x_4	x_5	x_6	x_7	
6 (Row 1-Row 3)	x_4	$1\frac{1}{2}$	3	0	1	0	$-\frac{1}{4}$	0	350
7 (Row 2-Row 3)	x_5	$\frac{1}{2}$	0	0	0	1	$-\frac{1}{4}$	0	100
8 (ie Row 3)	x_3	$\frac{1}{2}$	0	1	0	0	$\frac{1}{4}$	0	50
9 (as Row 4)	x_7	0	1	0	0	0	0	1	50
10 (Row 5 - 10 × Row 3)	Z	3	5	0	0	0	$-2\frac{1}{2}$	0	-500

Table 4

Notes.

a. All the new rows produced by the row operations in Step 6 have been inserted into the third tableau.

b. The rows have been consecutively numbered again and a summary of the operations carried out in Step 6 to produce the new lines has been given against the new row numbers.

eg Row 10 was produced by multiplying Row 3 by 10 and subtracting it from Row 5.

STEP 8. To produce subsequent tableaux and eventually an optimum solution, steps 4 to 7 are repeated until no positive numbers can be found in the A row.

From Row 10 it will be seen that the maximum contribution is 5.

∴ x_2 column is chosen.

The positive numbers in the x_2 column are divided into the solution quantities and the lowest result selected.

ie ROW 6	350	÷	3	=	$116\frac{2}{3}$
ROW 7	100	÷	0		ignore
ROW 8	50	÷	0		ignore
ROW 9	50	÷	1	=	50

∴ Row 9 is selected and the pivot element identified and the solution variable altered to x_2 thus

Row 9 $\quad x_2 \quad 0 \quad \boxed{1} \quad 0\ 0\ 0\ 0\ 1 \quad = \quad 50$

As the pivot element is already 1 no further action is necessary on it but the other elements in the pivot element column (x_2) must be made into zeros by using row operations based on Row 9 thus

ROW 6	x_4	$1\frac{1}{2}$	3	0	1	0	$-\frac{1}{4}$	0	=	350
MINUS 3 TIMES										
ROW 9	x_2	0	3	0	0	0	0	3	=	150
PRODUCES A NEW ROW	x_2	$1\frac{1}{2}$	0*	0	1	0	$-\frac{1}{4}$	−3	=	200

Note.

It was necessary to multiply Row 9 by 3 to produce the zero in column x_2 (0*)

Rows 7 and 8 need no operation because the elements in column x_2 are already zero

ROW 10	Z	3	5	0	0	0	$-2\frac{1}{2}$	0	=	−500
MINUS 5 TIMES										
ROW 9	x_2	0	5	0	0	0	0	5	=	250
PRODUCES A NEW ROW	Z	3	0*	0	0	0	$-2\frac{1}{2}$	−5	=	−750

The new row produced can now be entered into a fourth tableau as follows

FOURTH SIMPLEX TABLEAU

ROW NO.	SOLUTION VARIABLE	PRODUCTS x_1	x_2	x_3	SLACK VARIABLES x_4	x_5	x_6	x_7	SOLUTION QUANTITY
11 (Row 6 – 3 × 9)	x_4	$1\frac{1}{2}$	0	0	1	0	$-\frac{1}{4}$	−3	200
12 (as Row 7)	x_5	$\frac{1}{2}$	0	0	0	1	$-\frac{1}{4}$	0	100
13 (as Row 8)	x_3	$\frac{1}{2}$	0	1	0	0	$\frac{1}{4}$	0	50
14 (Pivot Row as Row 9)	x_2	0	1	0	0	0	0	1	50
15 (Row 10 – 5 × Row 9)	Z	3	0	0	0	0	$-2\frac{1}{2}$	−5	−750

Table 5

Notes.

a. The above tableau shows that 50 units of Products B and C could be made (x_2 and $x_3 = 50$).

b. As a result of this amount of production £750 contribution would be gained (Z = -750)

STEP 9. Because there is still a positive number in the Z row (3 under column x_1) the iterative process is repeated in precisely the same manner. Column x_1 is chosen and the positive numbers in the x_1 column are divided into the solution quantities and the lowest number selected.

Row 11	200	÷	$1\frac{1}{2}$	=	$133\frac{1}{3}$
Row 12	100	÷	$\frac{1}{2}$	=	200
Row 13	50	÷	$\frac{1}{2}$	=	100
Row 14	50	÷	0		ignore

∴ Row 13 is selected and the pivot element identified and the solution variable altered to x_1 thus

$$\text{Row 13} \quad x_1 \quad \boxed{\tfrac{1}{2}} \quad 0 \; 1 \; 0 \; 0 \; \frac{1}{4} \; 0 \; = \; 50$$

The pivot element must be made into a 1 so the whole row is multiplied by 2 thus

$$\text{Row 13} \quad x_1 \quad \boxed{1} \quad 0 \; 2 \; 0 \; 0 \; \frac{1}{2} \; 0 = \; 100$$

The rest of the elements in column x_1 must now be made into zeros by the usual row operations

	ROW 11	x_4	$1\frac{1}{2}$	0	0	1	0	$-\frac{1}{4}$	-3	=	200
MINUS $1\frac{1}{2}\times$											
	ROW 13	x_1	$1\frac{1}{2}$	0	3	0	0	$\frac{3}{4}$	0	=	150
PRODUCES A											
NEW ROW		x_4	0*	0	-3	1	0	-1	-3	=	50
	ROW 12	x_5	$\frac{1}{2}$	0	0	0	1	$-\frac{1}{4}$	0	=	100
MINUS $\frac{1}{2}\times$											
	ROW 13	x_1	$\frac{1}{2}$	0	1	0	0	$\frac{1}{4}$	0	=	50
PRODUCES A											
NEW ROW		x_5	0*	0	-1	0	1	$-\frac{1}{2}$	0	=	50

ROW 14 needs no operation because the element in column $x_1$is already zero

	ROW 15	Z	3	0	0	0	0	$-2\frac{1}{2}$	-5	=	-750
MINUS $3\times$											
	ROW 13	x_1	3	0	6	0	0	$1\frac{1}{2}$	0	=	300
PRODUCES A											
NEW ROW		Z	0*	0	-6	0	0	-4	-5	=	-1050

The new rows produced can now be entered into a fifth tableau thus

FIFTH SIMPLEX TABLEAU

ROW NO.	SOLUTION VARIABLE	PRODUCTS			SLACK VARIABLES				SOLUTION QUANTITY
		x_1	x_2	x_3	x_4	x_5	x_6	x_7	
16 (Row 11 – $1\frac{1}{2}$ × Row 18)	x_4	0	0	-3	1	0	-1	-3	50
17 (Row 12 – $\frac{1}{2}$ × 18)	x_5	0	0	-1	0	1	$-\frac{1}{2}$	0	50
18 (Pivot Row 2 × Row 13)	x_1	1	0	2	0	0	$\frac{1}{2}$	0	100
19 (as Row 14)	x_2	0	1	0	0	0	0	1	50
20	Z	0	0	-6	0	0	-4	-5	-1050

Table 6

As there are no positive values in the *Z* row the optimum solution has been reached.

STEP 10. All that remains is to obtain the maximum information from the fith tableau.
Optimum product mix

$x_1 = 100$ ie Produce 100 units of Product A

$x_2 = 50$ ie Produce 50 units of Product B

The valuation of the slack variables can be confirmed and the total contribution checked again by multiplying the slack variable valuations (£4 and £5) by the amount of the original constraints, thus

x_6	£4 ×	200	=	£800
x_7	£5 ×	50	=	250
				£1050

The valuation of the other two slack variables are

$$x_4 = 0 \text{ and } x_5 = 0$$

This means that there is *NO* value to be gained by altering the machine hours and the component constraints. This follows because there is spare capacity in both machining and components (50 in each). It is a general rule that constraints only have a valuation when they are fully utilised.

These valuations are known as the SHADOW PRICES or SHADOW COSTS or DUAL PRICES or SIMPLEX MULTIPLIERS. A constraint only has a shadow price when it is binding ie fully utilised, and the shadow price indicates the amount by which the objective function would be increased if the constraint was increased by 1 unit. In the example above, if an extra kg of alloy could be obtained it would result in an increase of £4 contribution.

When solving LP problems by graphical means the shadow prices have to be calculated separately. When using the simplex process they are an automatic by product.

Notes.

a. Each variable in the final solution variable column has a specific meaning which is detailed above.

b. Using step 10 as a guide interpret the meanings of the solution variables and the valuations in the Z row of the intermediate tableaux.

c. Take heart. To work through a normal Simplex problem with 3 unknowns is a very quick process once the foregoing steps are mastered.

MIXED LIMITATIONS.

5. The maximising example given above had constraints all of which were of the 'less than or equal to' type ($\leq$). This is a common situation but on occasions the constraints contain a mixture of $\leq$ and $\geq$ varieties. The usual cause of one or more 'greater than or equal to ($\geq$) constraints is the requirement to produce at least a given number of certain products. In such circumstances the simplest approach is to reduce the capacity of the other limitations by the amounts required to make the required number of the product(s) specified. Then maximise in the normal way and add back the quantities which were required to be produced, to the optimum solution found by the normal simplex method. The method is shown in the following example.

EXAMPLE CONTAINING MIXED CONSTRAINTS.

6. Assume that an LP problem had been set up in the usual standardised format as follows:

Example 2.

Objective Function.

Maximise		$5x_1$	+	$3x_2$	+	$4x_3$				
Subject to constraint	a.	$3x_1$	+	$12x_2$	+	$6x_3$	$\leq$	660	Machine hrs constraint
Subject to constraint	b.	$6x_1$	+	$6x_2$	+	$3x_3$	$\leq$	1230	Labour hrs constraints
Subject to constraint	c.	$6x_1$	+	$9x_2$	+	$9x_3$	$\leq$	990	Component constraint
Subject to constraint	d.					x_3	$\geq$	10	Sales constraint

where x_1, x_2 and x_3 represent units of Products A, B and C.

Only one of the constraints d. is of the $\geq$ variety so we decide to make the minimum quantity possible to satisfy constraint d. ie 10 units of x_3. The resource requirements for 10 units of x_3 must be subtracted from the total available in constraints a, b. and c thus

Constraint a.	$3x_1 + 12x_2 + 6x_3 \leq 660$	- (6 × 10)
b.	$6x_1 + 6x_2 + 3x_3 \leq 1230$	- (3 × 10)
c.	$6x_1 + 9x_2 + 9x_3 \leq 990$	- (9 × 10)

Notes.

a. In each case the expression in the bracket represents the coefficient of x_3 in each constraint multiplied by the 10 units being made.

b. An alternative way of dealing with the $\geq$ constraint is to multiply both sides by -1 and change the inequality sign

$$\text{ie } (x_3 \geq 10)x - 1$$

becomes

$$-x_3 \leq -10$$

This constraint can then be used in the normal manner.

Having eliminated constraint d. and made the appropriate reductions in the other constraints the initial simplex tableau can be set up.

INITIAL SIMPLEX TABLEAU EXAMPLE 2.

Modified Constraint	SOLUTION VARIABLE	PRODUCTS x_1	x_2	x_3	SLACK VARIABLES x_4	x_5	x_6	SOLUTION QUANTITY
a.	x_4	3	12	6	1	0	0	600
b.	x_5	6	6	3	0	1	0	1200
c.	x_6	6	9	9	0	0	1	900
	Z	5	3	4	0	0	0	0

Table 7

Note.

This is now a normal maximising simplex model with a slack variable for each constraint and is solved by exactly the same process covered in the earlier part of the chapter.

After carrying out the usual simplex procedure the final tableau becomes:

FINAL SIMPLEX TABLEAU EXAMPLE 2

SOLUTION VARIABLE	PRODUCTS x_1	x_2	x_3	SLACK VARIABLES x_4	x_5	x_6	SOLUTION QUANTITY
x_4	0	$7\frac{1}{2}$	$1\frac{1}{2}$	1	0	$-\frac{1}{2}$	150
x_5	0	−3	−6	0	1	−1	300
x_1	1	$1\frac{1}{2}$	$1\frac{1}{2}$	0	0	$\frac{1}{6}$	150
Z	0	$-4\frac{1}{2}$	$-3\frac{1}{2}$	0	0	$-\frac{5}{6}$	−750

Table 8

Solution from final tableau: – 150 units of x_1 producing £750 contribution.
PLUS PRODUCTION TO
SATISFY CONSTRAINT d. 20 units of x_3 producing £40 contribution.
∴ Total solution is 150 units of x_1 and 10 units of x_3 giving £790 contribution.
As previously described in Step 10 the tableau can be interpreted as follows:
Spare capacity

$x_4 \quad = \quad$ 150, means that there are 150 spare machining hours

$x_5 \quad = \quad$ 300, means that there are 300 spare labour hours

Products not being made.

From the final tableau Table it will be seen that x_2 and x_3 do not appear in the Simplex solution and they have valuations in the Z row of $-4\frac{1}{2}$ and $-3\frac{1}{2}$ respectively. We already know that 10 units of x_3 will be made and the tableau informs us that the 10 units of x_3 which we have had to make have cost £35 in reduced contribution. Any units of x_2 that were made would similarly reduce contribution by £4.50 per unit.

Valuation of Slack Variables.

Only one constraint (constraint c, components) is fully utilised and thus has a valuation. The tableau shows that for every extra component that could be obtained contribution would be increased by £5/6

An alternative method of dealing with mixed limitations uses what are termed ARTIFICIAL VARIABLES as well as slack variables. This method is outside the scope of this book.

COMPARING SIMPLEX AND GRAPHICAL SOLUTIONS.

7. The simplex method can be used for problems with any number of unknowns even those with only 2 unknowns which can also be solved graphically. To illustrate both solution methods Example 1 used and solved graphically in Chapter 18 is solved below using the simplex method.

EXAMPLE 1 reproduced from Chapter 18.

$$\begin{array}{llllllll}
\text{Maximise} & 3x_1 & + & 4x_2 & & & \\
\text{Subject to} & 4x_1 & + & 2x_2 & \leq & 100 & \text{A} \\
 & 4x_1 & + & 6x_2 & \leq & 180 & \text{B} \\
 & x_1 & + & x_2 & \leq & 40 & \text{C} \\
 & x_1 & & & \leq & 20 & \text{D} \\
 & & & x_2 & \geq & 10 & \text{E}
\end{array}$$

This problem is inserted into the initial tableau with a slack variable for each of the five constraints and with constraint E multiplied by -1 to reverse the inequality sign.

Initial Tableau Equivalent to Point 0, FIGURE 1

SOLUTION	PRODUCTS		SLACK VARIABLES					SOLUTION
VARIABLE	x_1	x_2	x_3	x_4	x_5	x_6	x_7	QUANTITY
x_3	4	2	1	0	0	0	0	100
x_4	4	6	0	1	0	0	0	180
x_5	1	1	0	0	1	0	0	40
x_6	1	0	0	0	0	1	0	20
x_7	0	−1	0	0	0	0	1	−10
Z	3	4	0	0	0	0	0	0

Table 9

The problem is then solved by the usual simplex iterations. Each iteration improves on the one before and the process continues until optimum is reached. The following tables show the position after each iteration and each one is cross referenced to Figure 1 which is a reproduction of the graphical solution.

FIRST ITERATION. EQUIVALENT TO POINT 1 ON FIGURE 1

SOLUTION VARIABLE	PRODUCTS x_1	x_2	SLACK VARIABLES x_3	x_4	x_5	$4x_6$	x_7	SOLUTION QUANTITY
x_2	0	1	0	0	0	0	−1	10
x_3	4	0	1	0	0	0	2	80
x_4	4	0	0	1	0	0	6	120
x_5	1	0	0	0	1	0	1	30
x_6	1	0	0	0	0	1	0	20
Z	3	0	0	0	0	0	4	−40

Table 10

This shows $10x_2$ being produced and £40 contribution. The first four constraints have surpluses of 80, 120, 30 and 20 respectively. NOT optimum, as there are still positive values in Z row.

SECOND ITERATION. EQUIVALENT TO POINT 2 ON FIG. 1

SOLUTION VARIABLE	PRODUCTS x_1	x_2	SLACK VARIABLES x_3	x_4	x_5	x_6	x_7	SOLUTION QUANTITY
x_2	0.667	1	0	0.167	0	0	0	30
x_3	2.667	0	1	−0.333	0	0	0	40
x_5	−0.333	0	0	−0.167	1	0	0	10
x_6	1	0	0	0	0	1	0	20
x_7	0.333	0	0	0.167	0	0	1	20
Z	0.333	0	0	−0.667	0	0	0	−120

Table 11

This shows $30x_2$ being produced and £120 contribution. All constraints have surpluses except labour hours. Not optimum as there is a positive value in Z row.

THIRD ITERATION. EQUIVALENT TO POINT 3 ON FIG.1

	PRODUCTS x_1	x_2	SLACK VARIABLES x_3	x_4	x_5	x_6	x_7	SOLUTION QUANTITY
x_1	1	0	0.375	0.125	0	0	0	15
x_2	0	1	−0.25	0.25	0	0	0	20
x_5	0	0	−0.125	−0.125	1	0	0	5
x_6	0	0	−0.375	0.125	0	1	0	5
x_7	0	0	−0.25	0.25	0	0	1	10
Z	0	0	−0.125	−0.625	0	0	0	−125

Table 12

This is the optimum and shows all the information obtained previously.

Solution $15x_1$ and $20x_2$ giving £125 contribution

shadow prices x_1 = £0.125 and

x_2 = £0.625

Non binding constraints C, D & E with 5, 5 and 10 spare respectively.

Note: By seeing how the simplex interations move from one vertex to an improved vertex on the feasible region it is possible to gain a better understanding of the process.

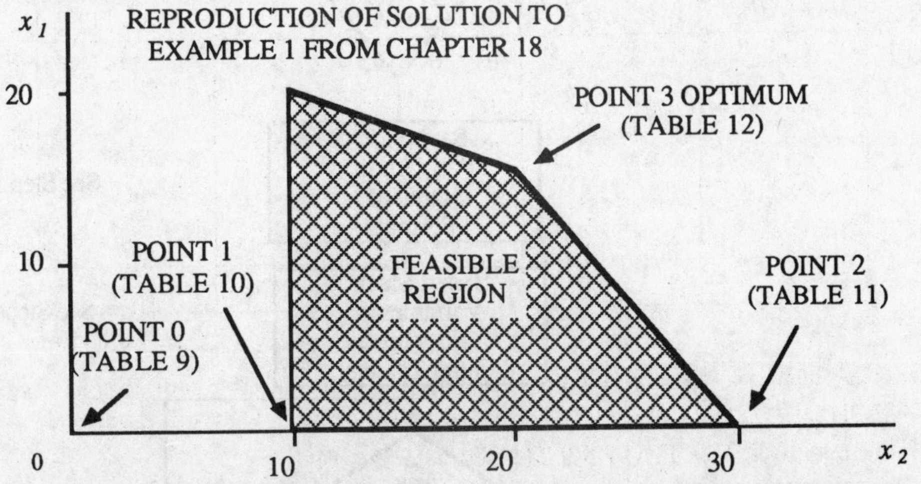

GRAPHICAL/SIMPLEX COMPARISON Figure 1

SUMMARY OF SIMPLEX METHOD

8. Flowchart 1 provides a concise summary of the Simplex method and is cross referenced to key points in the chapter.

SENSITIVITY ANALYSIS AND THE SIMPLEX.

9. In practice virtually all LP problems are solved by computer packages which incorporate numerous facilities to test the sensitivity of the solution to changes in the problem. Typically these facilities include showing the effects of changes in:

a. the amounts of the resources and constraints b. the coefficients of the objective function and the constraints.

Most of these forms of sensitivity analysis are outside the scope of the manual and the syllabuses at which it is aimed. One form of sensitivity analysis is however covered, as it is a typical examination topic. That is, the aspect concerned with variations in the total amount of the resources/constraints.

This is demonstrated by again using example 1 from Chapter 18 which was solved by the simplex method in Para 7 above.

The procedure is to use the *simplex multipliers* which are the + and - values found in the slack variable columns in the final tableau, Table 12. Multiplication of the variation in the constraint by the multipliers gives the change in the solution quantities.

Assume that it is required to calculate the effect on the solution of having 5 extra labour hours (represented by slack variable x_3).

Multipliers for x_3	×	Change in Constraint	=	Change in Solution	+	Original Solution	=	New Solution
0.375	×	5	=	1.875	+	15	=	16.875
−0.25	×	5	=	−1.25	+	20	=	18.75
−0.125	×	5	=	−0.625	+	5	=	4.375
−0.375	×	5	=	−1.875	+	5	=	3.125
−0.25	×	5	=	−1.25	+	10	=	8.75
−0.125	×	5	=	−0.625	+	(−125)	=	−125.625

Thus if 5 extra labour hours were available the solution is 16.875 units of x_1 , 18.75 units of x_2 giving a contribution of £125.625. the other values in the solution column are, as before, the unused amounts of constraints C, D and E represented by slack variables x_5, x_6 and x_7.

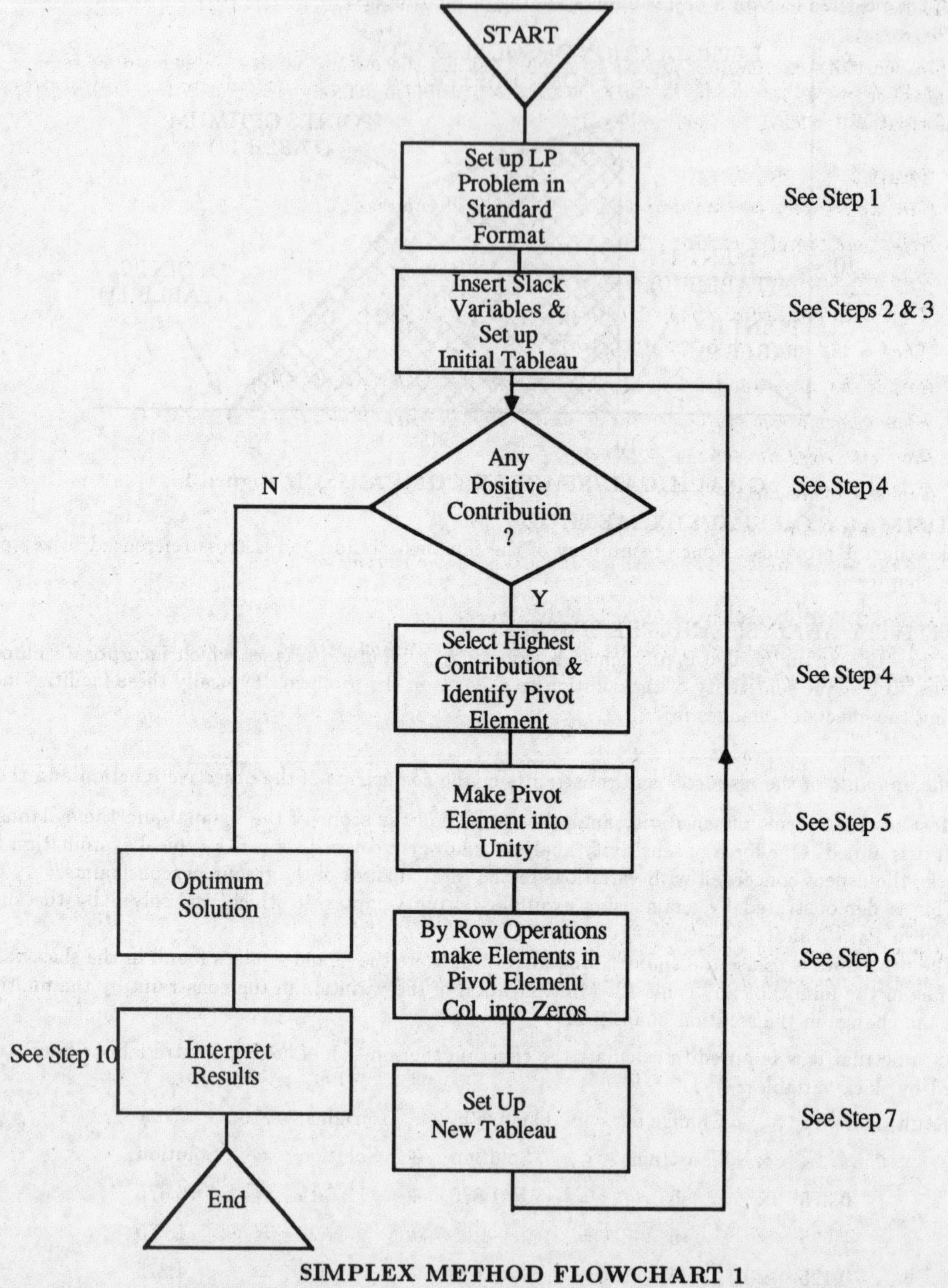

SIMPLEX METHOD FLOWCHART 1

POINTS TO NOTE.

10.

a. The simplex method is not only capable of dealing with more unknowns than the graphical method but more information is automatically produced.

b. In every tableau it will be noted that the solution variable column always contains a single 1 with the rest of the column elements being zeros.

c. The valuations of the Z row of the final tableau are known as shadow prices or shadow costs. These valuations can be of considerable value in valuing the contributions made by scarce resources.

d. On occasions examination questions merely ask for the initial Simplex Tableau to be set up. Make sure that you obtain as much practice as possible in defining problems in the standardised format and setting up the Simplex Tableau.

SELF REVIEW QUESTIONS.

1. Can the Simplex method deal with more than 2 unknowns? (1)

2. Define the Simplex method. (2)

3. Why are slack variables necessary? (3)

4. What does the Initial Simplex Tableau show? (4, Step 3)

5. What is the pivot element? (4, Step 4)

6. How is the optimum solution identified in simplex table? (Table 6)

7. What information can be derived from the final Simplex Tableau? (4, Step 10)

8. How are mixed limitations dealt with? (5)

9. Can you relate the various Simplex Tableau to vertices on a graph? (7)

9. What are the key steps in the Simplex method? (8)

10. What is one method of sensitivity analysis with the simplex method? (9)

EXERCISES WITH ANSWERS COMMENCING PAGE 488

A1. A firm produces three products X, Y, Z with a contribution of £20, £18 and £16 respectively. Production data are as follows:

	Machine Hours	*Labour Hours*	*Materials*
X	*5*	*2*	*8*
Y	*3*	*5*	*10*
Z	*6*	*3*	*3*
Availability	*3000*	*2500*	*10,000*

Set up the initial Simplex Tableau including the necessary slack variables.

A2. Carry out the first iteration of the tableau in A1.

A3. Interpret the final tableau of a simplex solution shown below:

	A	B	C	$S1$	$S2$	$S3$	$S4$	
$S2$	0	0	0	$1\frac{1}{4}$	1	2	−1.5	520
A	1	0	0	$\frac{3}{4}$	0	$1\frac{3}{4}$	3.0	276
B	0	1	0	0	0	3	1	68
C	0	0	1	−1.5	0	$-1\frac{1}{4}$	1.5	127
	0	0	0	−6	0	−12.5	−25	−48,600

A = Product A
B = Product B
C = Product C
S1 = Slack variable labour hours
S2 = Slack variable material
S3 = Slack variable machine hours
S4 = Slack variable sales restriction A.

EXAMINATION QUESTIONS WITH ANSWERS COMMENCING PAGE 488

A4. Calyce Checials Limited operates a small plant for the manufacture of three types of industrial solvent Aldex (A), Betdex (B) and Gamdex (C). These solvents each involve three basic chemicals (X, Y and Z) which are produced at the plant. As regards these three chemicals, the composition (by volume) of each solvent is as follows:

	Chemical		
	X	Y	Z
Aldex	20%	10%	5%
Betdex	10%	10%	10%
Gamdex	10%	20%	15%

The maximum output of each of the three chemicals (in litres per month) and their production costs are:

Chemical	Max. Output	Cost (£/litre)
X	1,500	3.50
Y	1,200	4.20
X	1,000	6.80

The current market prices of the three solvents are:

Aldex: £5.60 per litre
Betdex: £4.80 per litre
Gamdex: £8.70 per litre

Aldex and Betdex are general purpose solvents for which the market is in excess of the present production capactiy. Gamdex, however, is a specialist product with a limited market and it has been estimated that monthly sales are unlikely to exceed 1,200 litres.

Required:

(a) Formulate a linear programming model to determine production levels for the three solvents (A, B and C) to give maximum total contribution to profits.

(b) Write down the dual problem to the one you have formulated in (a)

(c) the final tableau of a Simplex solution to the primal problem in (a) is as follows:

A	B	C	X	Y	Z	S	P	
1	0	0	10	-10	0	1	0	4,200
0	1	0	-10	20	0	-3	0	5,400
0	0	0	0.5	-1.5	1	0.1	0	*
0	0	1	0	0	0	1	0	1,200
0	0	0	7.9	25.6	0	0.58	1	*

where A, B and C are the monthly production levels for the three solvents.

X, Y and Z are the amounts by which the usage of the three chemicals falls short of the maximum possible monthly output in each case.

S is the amount by which the production of Gamdex falls short of the estimated maximum monthly demand.

(i) What are the optimum production levels for the three solvents?

*(ii) Determine the two missing 'right hand side values' denoted by * in the final tableau.*

(iii) State the solution to the dual problem in (b) and explain briefly the inter- pretation of the values of the dual variables in the optimum solution.

(ACCA Quantitative Analysis)

A5. Ken Wong, the financial controller of Eastern Fruit Canners Limited, is planning production levels of pineapple products for the forthcoming period. The company has already agreed the purchase of 80,000 kg *of 'large' pineapples at \$ 0.21 per kg, and 120,000 kg of 'smalls' at \$ 0.16 per kg, in order to meet estimated demands for pineapple products during the coming period. The current prices and estimated demands are as follows:*

Product	*Demand*	*Price(\$)*
Pineapple juice	*17,000 litres*	*2.21/litre*
Pineapple Chunks	*60,000 cans*	*2.40/can*
Pineapple Slices	*50,000 cans*	*2.81/can*

Only large pineapples can be sold as 'slices' but both pineapple juice and chunks may be produced from large or small pineapples.

The variable costs associated with each product are as follows:

Variable Cost (\$)	*Juice (litre)*	*Chunks (can)*	*Slices (can)*
Direct Labour	*0.50*	*0.62*	*0.78*
Variable Overhead	*0.36*	*0.40*	*0.44*
Variable Selling	*0.15*	*0.12*	*0.12*
Canning	*0.20*	*0.22*	*0.22*
*Pineapples**	*0.51*	*0.24*	*0.36*

**These pineapple costs are allocated on the basis of an average purchasing cost of \$0.18 per kg.*

Under normal processing the following yields can be expected from 1,000 kg of pineapples:

350 litres of 'juice'
or 750 cans of 'chunks'
or 500 cans of 'slices'

Furthermore, in producing 750 cans of chunks, there is a by-product of 10 litres of juice whereas with 500 cans of slices, there is a by-product of 5 litres of juice. This by-product juice undergoes effectively the same processing as ordinary juice and so incurs the same variable costs.

Required:

(a) Explain why, when using a 'linear programming' approach, the cost of the pineapples is irrelevant to the product mix decision.

(b) Formulate a linear programming model to maximise contribution from pineapple products for the coming period. Your model should entail the following variables:

X_j - *The number of Kg of large pineapples used to produce juice*
Y_j - *The number of Kg of small pineapples used to produce juice*
X_c - *The number of Kg of large pineapples used to produce chunks*
Y_c - *The number of Kg of small pineapples used to produce chunks*
X_s - *The number of Kg of large pineapples used to produce slices.*

(c) The final tableau of a linear programming solution to the product mix problem is as follows:

X_j	Y_j	X_c	Y_c	X_s	S_1	S_2	S_3	S_4	S_5	P	
1	0	1	0	1	1	0	0	0	0	0	80,000
0	1	-1	0	0	0	1	0	-1.333	0	0	40,000
0.345	0	0.345	0	0	-0.005	-0.35	1	0.453	0	0	1,800
0	0	1	1	0	0	0	0	1.333	0	0	80,000
-0.5	0	-0.5	0	0	-0.5	0	0	0	1	0	10,000
0.28	0	0.28	0	0	0.63	0.35	0	0.587	0	1	127,000

where $S_1, S_2, \ldots, S_5$ denote slack variables introduced into the relevant constraints and P is the contribution function excluding pineapple costs.

What is the optimum product mix for the coming period and what is the total contribution from pineapple products?

(ACCA Quantitative Analysis)

A6. A chemical manufacturer is developing three fertiliser compounds for the agricultural industry. The product codes for the three products are X1, X2 and X3 and the relevant information is summarised below:

Chemical constituents: percentage make-up per tonne

	Nitrate	Phosphate	Potash	Filler
X1	10	10	20	60
X2	10	20	10	60
X3	20	10	10	60

Input prices per tonne

Nitrate	£150
Phosphate	£60
Potash	£120
Filler	£10

Maximum available input in tonnes per month

Nitrate	1,200
Phosphate	2,000
Potash	2,200
Filler	No limit

The fertilisers will be sold in bulk and managers have proposed the following prices per tonne:

X1	£83
X2	£81
X3	£81

The manufacturing costs of each type of fertiliser, excluding materials, are £11 per tonne.

You are required to:

(a) formulate the above data into a linear programming model so that the company may maximise contribution;

(b) construct the initial simplex tableau and state what is meant by 'slack variables' (Define X4, X5, X6 as the slack variables for X1, X2 and X3 respectively);

(c) indicate, with explanations, which will the 'entering variable' and 'leaving variable' in the first iteration;

You are not required to solve the model

(d) interpret the final matrix of the simplex solution given below:

Basic Variable	X1	X2	X3	X4	X5	X6	Solution
X1	1	0	3	20	-10	0	4,000
X2	0	1	-1	-10	10	0	8,000
X6	0	0	-0.4	-3	1	1	600
Z	0	0	22	170	40	0	284,000

(e) use the final matrix above to investigate:

(i) the effect of an increase in nitrate of 100 tonnes per month;

(ii) the effect of a minimum contract from an influential customer for 200 tonnes of X3 per month to be supplied.

(CIMA Management Accounting Techniques)

A7. In order to try to improve plant yields in a certain district of a developing country, the government is providing farmers in that area with a subsidy of £50 per acre (the sterling equivalent of the local currency) to purchase fertilisers. Two fertilisers are required: 'Super X' and 'Base Y'. They may be applied in various combinations to achieve different plant yields.

Basic data are as follows:

Fertiliser combination	*Quantity of 'Super X' per acre*	*Quantity of 'Base Y' per acre*	*Estimated plant yield per acre*
	Kgs	*Kgs*	*Kgs*
A	0	0	400
B	50	50	600
C	100	50	680
D	150	50	700
E	50	100	630
F	100	100	750
G	150	100	800
H	50	200	680
I	100	200	780
J	150	200	800

The cost of 'Super X' is 38 pence per kg and 'Base Y' costs 23 pence per kg. In addition there is a further cost of applying the fertiliser amount to 2 pence per kg. There are no other relevant costs.

The crop sells for 80 pence per kg.

The outcome of a linear programme set up to solve the problem of achieving the best return to the farmers is given below.

LP optimum found at step 3

Objective function value

1) 494,615387

Variable	Value	Reduced Cost
A	0.000000	40.000000
B	0.461538	0.000000
C	0.000000	9.846161
D	0.000000	67.692291
E	0.000000	22.153839
F	0.538462	0.000000
G	0.000000	33.846161
H	0.000000	74.461517
I	0.000000	68.307678
J	0.000000	126.153839

Row	Slack or surplus	Dual prices
2)	0.000000	2.692308
3)	0.000000	360.000000

Number of iterations 3

Ranges in which the basis is unchanged

Objective coefficient ranges

Variable	Current coefficient	Allowable increase	Allowable decrease
A	320.000000	40.000000	INFINITY
B	447.500000	55.000015	20.000000
C	491.500000	9.846161	INFINITY
D	487.500000	67.692291	INFINITY
E	459.000000	22.153839	INFINITY
F	535.000000	40.000000	16.00013
G	555.000000	33.846161	INFINITY
H	474.000000	74.461517	INFINITY
I	534.000000	68.307678	INFINITY
J	530.000000	126.153839	INFINITY

Righthand side ranges

Row	Current RHS	Allowable Increase	Allowable decrease
2	50.000000	15.000000	17.500000
3	1.000000	0.538462	0.230769

You are required to:

(a) formulate the original linear programme; (Arrange the tabulation so that the objective row is stated first, the subsidy constraint second and the acreage constraint third.)

(b) interpret the outcome as presented, explaining fully the meaning of all variables and values. (The outcome follows the formulation structure as in (a).

(CIMA Quantitative Techniques)

EXERCISES WITHOUT ANSWERS

B1. Set up the initial Simplex Tableau of A1, Chapter 17.

B2. Carry out the first iteration of the Tableau in B1.

EXAMINATION QUESTIONS WITHOUT ANSWERS

B3. Detterem Limited manufactures household chemical products. There are three products in its range and two manufacturing processes are required in the refining of the raw materials into the final products. The capacity of these processes together with certain legal and financial constraints are the limitations faced by the company when trying to organise production to obtain maximum contribution to profit. Details of these limitations are given below:

a. Production:

Details	*Process 1*	*Process 2*
Processing time per 1,000 gallons in hrs:		
Clean Drain	*8*	*4*
Sink Sparkle	*2*	*1*
Carpet Reviver	*4*	*2*
Total process hours available in period 1	*1,000*	*600*

b. Prices and costs.

		Product	
	Clean Drain	*Sink Sparkle*	*Carpet Reviver*
	£	*£*	*£*
Selling price per gallon	*11*	*2*	*6*
Variable production cost per gallon	*10*	*1*	*2*

c. Environmental restriction:

The company is restricted to a maximum production of 500,000 gallons of Sink Sparkle by government regulations due to environmental problems caused one of the product's constitutent chemicals.

d. Finance:

The company has a £1,200,000 bank loan and is required by the bank to maintain a minimum £300,000 cash cover against this loan. The company allows its customers credit for two periods but the variable costs are all cash expenses. The working capital position of the company at the beginning of the current period is:

	£000's	£000's
Current liabilities		
Bank loan		1,200
Current assets:		
Debtors		900
(payments due: period 1	400	
period 2	500)	
Stocks		–
Cash		300
		1,200

You are required to:

a. formulate the above information as a profit maximising linear programme for the first period;

b. solve the linear programme using the Simplex method;

c. interpret the result for management, drawing attention to major production and financial factors.

(CIMA Quantitative Techniques)

B4. a. The following details are taken from the forecasts for 1979 of XYZ Limited.

Sales demand:	*Thousands of units per annum, maximum*
Super de luxe model (x_1)	500
De luxe model (x_2)	750
Export model (x_3)	400

Production:

Two production facilities are required, machining and assembly, and these are common to each model. Capacity in each facility is limited by the number of direct labour hours available.

	Direct labour, total hours available in millions	*Direct labour hours, per unit for each model* x_1	x_2	x_3
Machining (x_4)	1.4	0.5	0.5	1.0
Assembly (x_5)	1.2	0.5	0.5	2.0

Contribution, estimated to be

Model	*Amount per thousand units in £*
x_1	1,500
x_2	1,300
x_3	2,500

You are required, using the above information, to set up the first tableau of a linear programme to determine the product mix which will maximise total contribution and then to complete the first iteration only.

b. Interpret the following tableau, given that it is the final solution to the above problem. The s variables (s_1, s_2, s_3, s_4, s_5) *relate to the constraints in the same sequence as presented in (a) above.*

x_1	x_2	x_3	s_1	s_2	s_3	s_4	s_5	b_{ij}
1	0	0	1	0	0	0	0	500
0	0	0	0.25	0.25	1	0	-0.5	112.5
0	0	1	-0.25	-0.25	0	0	0.5	287.5
0	0	0	-0.25	-0.25	0	1	-0.5	487.5
0	1	0	0	1	0	0	0	750
0	0	0	-875	-675	0	0	-1,250	-2,443,750

(CIMA) Quantitative Techniques)

B5. Mega Manufactures has three product lines: A, B and C. There are four constraints on its operations, indicated below. Management has set up the following linear programme to find the optimal production plan:

Maximise:	6.0A	+	12.0B	+	18.0C			
Subject to:	0.75A	+	1.5B	+	0.37C	$\leq$	1,500	*(skilled labour hours)*
	3.0A	+	0.3B	+	1.5C	$\leq$	8,500	*(machine hours)*
	4.5A	+	3.0B	+	1.1C	$\leq$	7,500	*(despatch handing units)*
	-	+	0.25B	+	2.0C	$\leq$	4,000	*(cubic foot storage capacity)*

[Note: Row 1 is the objective row.]
The solution to this problem is given as:
Objective function value: 42,080.0

Variable	Value	Reduced cost
A	1,013.33	0.00
B	0.00	1.88
C	2,000.00	0.00

Row	Slack or surplus	Dual prices
2	0.00	8.00
3	2,460.00	0.00
4	740.00	0.00
5	0.00	7.52

Ranges in which the basis is unchanged:

Variable	Current coefficient	Allowable increase	Allowable decrease
A	6.00	30.49	0.97
B	12.00	1.88	Infinity
C	18.00	Infinity	15.04

Right-hand-side ranges (RHS)

Row	Current RHS	Allowable increase	Allowable decrease
2	1,500.00	123.33	760.00
3	8,500.00	Infinity	2,460.00
4	7,500.00	Infinity	740.00
5	4,000.00	4,108.11	1,321.43

You are required, with suitable explanation, to state:

(a) the optimal production plan, the contribution margin it is expected to earn and the amounts of any unused resources:

(b) the effect on the contribution margin if Mega produces one unit of B;

(c) the effect on the contribution margin if Mega can obtain one more hour of skilled labour time at a premium of £1.00 per hour over existing rates;

(d) whether the company should acquire further storage space that can be obtained at a cost of £5.00 per unit;

(e) the effect on the contribution margin if Mega, due to site renovation, loses 1,000 units of its own storage capacity.

(f) what increase in despatch handling facilities there can be before the solution changes;

(g) how far despatch handling facilities may contract before the solution changes.

(h) the allowable range for products A's contribution margin such that the solution will not change and give conclusions about product A and its costing that you would draw from this;

(j) whether more than one question at a time can be investigated with respect to the initial solution; for example, the combined effect of changes in both skilled labour and machine hours.

(CIMA Quantitative Techniques)

B6. (a) Hitech, a division of Sunrise p.l.c., produces and sells three products.

HTO1, HTO2 and HTO3

The following details of prices and products costs have been extracted from Hitech's cost accounting records.

	Product		
	HTO1	HTO1	HTO3
Price per unit	£150	£200	£220
Costs per unit:			
Direct labour at £4/hr	£100	£120	£132
Direct material at £20/kg	£20	£40	£40

Direct labour is regarded as a variable product cost.

A regression analysis has been carried out in order to estimate the relationship between overhead costs and production of the three products. Expressed in weekly terms the results of the analysis show:

$$Y = 4,000 + 0.5x_1 + 0.7x_2 + 0.8x_3$$

where Y = *total overhead cost per week*

x_1 = *HTO1, weekly direct labour hours*

x_2 = *HTO2, weekly direct labour hours*

x_3 = *HTO3, weekly direct labour hours*

The company operates a 46-weekly year.

You are required to compute the total variable product costs for each of HTO1, HTO2 and HTO3.

(b) The material used by Hitech is also used in a wide variety of other applications and is in relatively limited supply. As business conditions improve in general, there will be pressure for the price of this material to rise, but strong competition in Hitech's sector of the market would make it unlikely that increased material

costs can be passed on to customers in higher product prices. The position on material supplies is that Hitech can obtain 20,000 kgs at current prices.

Further, reductions in the skilled labour force made during the recession mean that the number of available direct labour hours is estimated at nor more than 257, 600 hours for the next year.

Demand for each product over the year is forecast to be:

HTO1	*16,000 units*
HTO2	*10,000 units*
HTO3	*6,000 units*

You are required to formulate a linear programme from the above data in order to obtain the annual production/sales plan which will

(c) The following are the final tableau and its immediately preceding tableau, obtained as a result of running a linear programme.

Final Tableau

HT01	*HT02*	*HT03*	S_1	S_2	S_3	S_4	S_5	B_{ij}
0.0	0.0	1.0	0.0	0.0	0.0	0.0	1.0	6,000.0
1.0	1.2	1.3	0.0	0.0	0.0	0.0	0.0	10,304.0
0.0	-1.2	-1.3	-0.0	0.0	1.0	0.0	0.0	5,696.0
0.0	1.0	0.0	0.0	0.0	0.0	1.0	0.0	10,000.0
0.0	0.8	1.7	-0.0	1.0	0.0	0.0	0.0	9,696.0
0.0	2.0	1.5	0.7	0.0	0.0	0.0	0.0	180,320.0

Preceding Tableau

HT01	*HT02*	*HT03*	S_1	S_2	S_3	S_4	S_5	B_{ij}
0.0	-0.5	0.0	0.0	-0.6	0.0	0.0	1.0	228.6
1.0	0.6	0.0	0.1	-0.8	0.0	0.0	0.0	2,685.7
0.0	-0.6	0.0	-1.0	0.8	1.0	0.0	0.0	13,314.3
0.0	1.0	0.0	0.0	0.0	0.0	1.0	0.0	10,000.0
0.0	0.5	1.0	-0.0	0.6	0.0	0.0	0.0	5,771.4
0.0	1.3	0.0	0.7	-0.9	0.0	0.0	0.0	171,663.0

where S_1 – S_5 are the slack variables for labour, materials, HTO1, HTO2, AND HTO3 respectively.

You are required to:

(i) provide as complete an interpretation of the final tableau as you can; compare the outcome of the final with that of the preceding tableau and give an estimate of the final net profit figure;

(ii) state, if material prices were to rise, the order in which production of each of Hitech's products would cease to be worthwhile.

(CIMA Quantitative Techniques)

20 Linear Programming – Simplex Method for Minimising

INTRODUCTION

1. This chapter develops the preceding chapters on LP to deal with minimisation problems using the simplex method. The simplex method is equally suitable for solving minimisation problems, the only difference in approach being a change in the way the initial tableau is set up and some differences in interpretation of the final tableau.

MINIMISATION EXAMPLE.

2. The following simple example will be used as a basis for explaining the methods to be used.

Example 1.

A chemical manufacturer processes two chemicals, Arkon and Zenon, in varying proportions to produce three products, A, B and C. He wishes to produce at least 150 units of A, 200 units of B and 60 units of C. Each ton of Arkon yields 3 of A, 5 of B and 3 of C. Each ton of Zenon yields 5 of A, 5 of B and 1 of C.

If Arkon costs £340 per ton and Zenon £50 per ton advise the manufacturer how to minimise his cost.

STEP 1. In exactly the same manner as previously described formulate the problem in the standardised way, thus:

Objective function:

$$\text{Minimise } 40x_1 + 50x_2$$

Subject to:-

$$3x_1 + 5x_2 \geq 150 \quad \text{Product A constraint}$$
$$5x_1 + 5x_2 \geq 200 \quad \text{Product B constraint}$$
$$3x_1 + x_2 \geq 60 \quad \text{Product C constraint}$$
$$x_1 \geq 0, \quad x_2 \geq 0$$

where x_1 = number of tons of Arkon

x_2 = number of tons of Zenon

Note:

This will be seen as a simple minimisation problem with all constraints being of the $\geq$ type.

STEP 2. Formulate the INVERSE or DUAL of the formulation above. That is, make the formulation above into a maximising problem by making a *COLUMN* for each *LIMITATION* and a *CONSTRAINT ROW* for each *ELEMENT* in the objective function thus:

$$\text{Maximise } 150A + 200B + 60C$$

Subject to:

$$3A + 5B + 3C \leq 40$$
$$5A + 5B + C \leq 50$$

Notes.

a. In step 1 there were 2 columns (x_1 and x_2) and 3 constraints (Products A, B & C). There are now 3 columns (one for each of original constraints) and 2 constraint rows (one for each of the original objective function elements, x_1 and x_2).

b. There is a dual or inverse of every LP problem ie for every maximising problem there is an equal but opposite minimising problem, and for every minimising problem there is an equal but opposite maximising problem. Because solving simplex maximising problems is quite straightforward it is normal to convert minimising problems into maximising problems.

c. It will be noted that the original quantity column (150, 200 and 60) has become the objective function and the original costs (40 and 50) have become the amounts of the constraints.

d. What are now the constraints are of the $\leq$ type ie as a normal maximising problem.

e. The original problem is known as the PRIMAL and the inverse is known as the DUAL.

f. Maximise $C(x)$ is the same as Minimise $-C(x)$ thus Minimise $C(x)$ is the same as Maximise $-C(x)$ and constraint $F(x) \geq B$ is the same as $-F(x) \leq -B$.

STEP 3. Now that a standard maximising problem has been obtained, the initial simplex tableau, complete with slack variables, can be set up in the normal manner thus:

INITIAL SIMPLEX TABLEAU

ROW	A	B	C	SLACK VARIABLES x_1	x_2	COST
x_1	3	5	3	1	0	40
x_2	5	5	1	0	1	50
QUANTITY	150	200	60	0	0	0

Table 1

STEP 4. Proceed in the step by step manner previously described until the tableau is reached showing optimum ie when there are no positive values in the bottom row thus:

FINAL SIMPLEX TABLEAU

ROW	A	B	C	SLACK VARIABLES x_1	x_2	COST
B	0	1	6/5	-3/10	-3/10	5
A	1	0	-1	-1/2	+1/2	5
QUANTITY	0	0	-30	-25	-15	-1750

Table 2

STEP 5. The tableau above is the normal result of a simplex maximising routine. However, to obtain the solutions to the original minimising problem some differences in the usual interpretation are necessary as follows.

OPTIMUM SOLUTION.

Quantities to be purchased.

The figures under the slack variable columns represent the quantities to be purchased.

ie $x_1 = -25$ Purchase 25 tons of ARKON

$x_2 = -15$ Purchase 15 tons of ZENON

Total Cost.

The figure at the bottom of the cost column represents total cost.

ie -1750 represents a cost of £1750.

(25 × £40 + 15 × £50 = £1750).

Valuation of constraints.

Rows titled B and A indicate the cost of changing the limitation of 200 B and 150 A. If either of these limitations are changed by one unit the total cost will change by £5. ie these are the shadow prices.

Proof: $(200 \times 5 + 150 \times 5) =$ £1750 total cost.

Overproduction. The −30 under column C indicates an overproduction of 30 units.

proof:

	A	B	C
25 tons ARKON yields	$25 \times 3 = 75$	$25 \times 5 = 125$	$25 \times 3 = 75$
15 tons ZENON yields	$15 \times 5 = 75$	$15 \times 5 = 75$	$15 \times 1 = 15$
	150	200	90
	= MINIMUM REQUIRED	= MINIMUM REQUIRED	= OVER-PRODUCTION OF 30 UNITS

Notes.

a. Once the inversion process and the method of interpretation is understood, minimising problems are no more difficult to solve than maximising problems.

b. The particular example used here had only 2 unknowns (tons of Arkon and Zenon) so it could also have been solved by graphical means. The simplex method is, of course, equally suitable for any number of unknowns.

SUMMARY

3.

a. The simple transformation given above may be applied to all minimisation problems with all constraints of the greater than or equal type. The simplex method can be applied to all combinations but only a restricted range of problems is covered here.

b. After formulating the problem in the standardised manner, the formulation must be INVERTED, ie the columns made into rows and the constraint rows into columns. This converts it into a maximising problem.

c. The maximising problem is solved by the usual simplex steps.

d. Optimum is recognised in the usual manner ie no positive values in base row.

e. The solutions to the minising problem can be read directly from the final tableau. The quantities required are found at the bottom of the slack variable columns and the total cost at the bottom of the cost column.

POINTS TO NOTE.

4.

a. Most past examination questions appear to be maximising problems but students should be capable of dealing with minimising problems of the type covered in this chapter.

b. The non-negativity constraints which appeared in maximising problems are not necessary because the constraints are already of the $\geq$ variety.

c. If you have the option and there are only 2 unknowns solve minimising problems by the graphical method already described.

SELF REVIEW QUESTIONS.

1. *What is the dual of a minimising LP problem? (2, Step 2)*
2. *Why is it usual to convert a minimising problem into a maximising? (2)*
3. *How is the final Simplex Tableau interpreted? (2, Step 5).*

EXERCISES WITH ANSWERS COMMENCING PAGE 488

A1. Form the dual of the following problem

$$\begin{aligned} \text{Minimise} \quad & 30A + 60B + 20C \\ \text{subject to} \quad & 5A + 10B + 15C \geq 2000 \\ & 2A + 3B + 1C \geq 300 \\ & 8A + 6B + 4C \geq 650 \end{aligned}$$

A2. Form the dual of the following problem:

$$\begin{aligned} \text{Minimise} \quad & 200X + 250Y - 100Z + 50W \\ \text{Subject} \quad & 6X + 10Y - 3Z \geq 55 \\ & 9X + 7Y + 3W \geq 40 \end{aligned}$$

$X, Y, Z, W \geq 0$

EXAMINATION QUESTIONS WITH ANSWERS COMMENCING PAGE 488

A3. C Limited produces container cases for sale to toiletry producers. It has four product lines: cases for talcum power, shaving foams, hair spray and deodorant.

The following data are given:

	x_1 Talcum powder	x_2 Shaving foam	x_3 Hair spray	x_4 Deodorant	Total process hours available per week
Contribution per 1,000 cases (£)	80	70	95	90	
Process times for manufacture (hours per 1,000 cases)					
Production (x_5)	5.0	5.0	4.0	4.0	450
Finishing (x_6)	1.0	1.0	1.0	1.0	120
Printing (x_7)	2.0	2.5	3.5	3.5	280
Packaging (x_8)	0.5	0.5	0.5	0.5	80
Maximum expected weekly demand (1,000 cases) (x_9 to x_{12}	30	40	20	25	

You are required to:

a. formulate the above information to give either the initial equations or the first tableau of a linear programme to maximise the total contribution which may be earned. This is the primal problem.

b. reformulate (a) to obtain the dual of the primal problem and state the meaning of the dual formulation;

c. interpret the tableau given below which is the solution to the primal problem of (a).

x_1	x_2	x_3	x_4	x_5	x_6	x_7	x_8	x_9	x_{10}	x_{11}	x_{12}	b_{11}
0	1	0	0	.2	0	0	0	-1	0	-.8	-.8	24
0	0	0	0	-.2	1	0	0	0	0	-.2	2	21
0	0	0	0	-.5	0	1	0	.5	0	-1.5	-1.5	2.5
0	0	0	0	-.1	0	0	1	0	0	-.1	-.1	30.5
1	0	0	0	0	0	0	0	1	0	0	0	30
0	0	0	0	-.2	0	0	0	1	1	.8	.8	16
0	0	1	0	0	0	0	0	0	0	1	0	20
0	0	0	1	0	0	0	0	0	0	0	1	25
0	0	0	0	14	0	0	0	10	0	39	34	8230

(CIMA Quantitative Techniques)

A4. The Hermes Manufacturing Company operates a three-shift system at one of its plants. In a certain section of the plant, the number of operators required on each of the three shifts is as follows:

	Shift	Number of Operators
Day	(6 a.m.–2 p.m.)	50
Afternoon	(2 p.m.–10 p.m.)	24
Night	(10 p.m.– 6 p.m.)	10

The company pays its operators at the basic rate of £2 per hour for those working on the day shift. For the afternoon and night shifts, the rates are one and a half times the basic rate and twice the basic rate respectively. In agreement with each operator at the commencement of his employment, he is allocated to one of three schemes-A, B or C. These are as follows:

A. Work (on average) one night shift, one afternoon shift, and two day shifts in every four shifts.

B. Work (on average) equal numbers of day and afternnon shifts.

C. Work day shifts only.

(In A and B, it is not necessary to work strictly alternating sequences of specified shifts, as long as the correct proportion of each shift is worked in the long run).

Required:

(a) Formulate a linear programming model to obtain the required number of operators at minimum cost..

(b) By solving the dual of the problem that you have formulated, determine how many operators must be employed under each of the three schemes. Does this result in over-provision of operators on any one of the three shifts?

(ACCA Quantitative Analysis)

EXERCISES WITHOUT ANSWERS

B1. Form the dual of the following problem.

$$\text{Maximise } 5A + 6B$$

subject to

$$\begin{aligned} A &\geq 10 \\ 4A + 16B &\leq 200 \\ 9A + 3B &\leq 500 \\ 2B &\leq 40 \\ B &\geq 0 \end{aligned}$$

B2. Form the dual of the following problem.

$$\begin{array}{llllllll} \text{Minimise} & 15x & + & 20y & + & 2z & & \\ \text{Subject to} & 3x & + & 6y & + & 4z & \geq & 150 \\ & 2x & & & + & 1z & \geq & 300 \\ & & & 2y & + & 2z & \geq & 100 \end{array}$$

EXAMINATION QUESTIONS WITHOUT ANSWERS

B3. Decibel p.l.c. manufactures classical and electric guitars. It operates a 48-week year, divided into 4-week periods.

The models, demand and selling prices are:

Model	*Expected demand per period (units)*	*Selling price (£)*
Folk	*200*	*110*
Junior	*–*	*–*
Electric	*150*	*90*
Mastersound	*130*	*130*
Mightysound	*50*	*240*

Each of two department stores has contracted to purchase 50 units per period of the Folk and Junior Electric guitars.

Decibels p.l.c. has three production departments, each with a largely skilled workforce, working 40 hours a week, with productive time in the company laboratoriés, where staff work a 35-hour week, also withe effective time being 75% of attendance time.

Details relating to the production of guitars are:

Department	*No. of operators*	*Folk (hrs)*	*Junior Electric (hrs)*	*Master-sound (hrs)*	*Mighty sound (hrs)*
Soundbox	*10*	*3.0*	*1.5*	*2.0*	*3.5*
Neck and Fingerboard	*10*	*2.0*	*2.0*	*3.5*	*4.0*
Assemble	*15*	*3.5*	*3.0*	*4.5*	*6.0*
Laboratory	*3*	*0.5*	*0.5*	*1.0*	*1.5*
Laboratory	*3*	*0.5*	*0.5*	*1.0*	*1.5*

Fixed costs are running at £14,000 per month and the contribution margins are £40, £30, £25, £80 per unit respectively for Folk, Junior Electric, Mastersound and Mightysound.

Decibels p.l.c. produce a linear programme to estimate monthly income from the above data. At **Appendix A** *top this question is the final tableau resulting from running the programme. The slack variables are arranged in the following order: 2 to 5 relate to production and laboratory test department operator constraints; 6 and 7 represent the stores' contracts and 8 to 11 represent the estimates demand per month. Row 1 is the objective row.*

You are required from the information given to:

(a) formulate the initial equations of the linear programme;

(b) interpret the results of the linear programme, including the dual (shodow) prices;

(c) state and explain whether it would be worthwhile to employ another member of staff in the test laboratory or permit overtime working of up to 8 hours per man per week. (Overtime is paid at $1\frac{1}{2}$ times normal rates, the latter being £3.5 per hour.)

(CIMA Quantitative Techniques)

APPENDIX A TO QUESTION B3

LINEAR PROGRAMMME FINAL TABLEAU

ROW	FOLK	JUNIOR ELECTRIC	MASTER SOUND	MIGHTY SOUND	SLACK VARIABLES										
					2	3	4	5	6	7	8	9	10	11	by
1	0.0	0.0	0.0	0.0	0.0	0.0	0.0	25.0	0.0	0.0	27.5	17.5	0.0	42.5	18,125
2	0.0	0.0	0.0	0.0	1.0	0.0	0.0	-2.0	0.0	0.0	-2.0	-0.5	0.0	-0.5	70.0
3	0.0	0.0	0.0	0.0	0.0	1.0	0.0	-3.5	0.0	0.0	-0.25	-0.25	0.0	1.25	72.5
4	0.0	0.0	0.0	0.0	0.0	0.0	1.0	-4.5	0.0	0.0	-1.25	-0.75	0.0	0.75	57.5
5	0.0	0.0	1.0	0.0	0.0	0.0	0.0	1.0	0.0	0.0	-0.5	-0.5	0.0	-1.5	65.0
6	0.0	0.0	0.0	0.0	0.0	0.0	0.0	0.0	1.0	0.0	1.0	0.0	0.0	0.0	150.00
7	0.0	0.0	0.0	0.0	0.0	0.0	0.0	0.0	0.0	1.0	0.0	1.0	0.0	0.0	100.00
8	1.0	0.0	0.0	0.0	0.0	0.0	0.0	0.0	0.0	0.0	1.0	0.0	0.0	0.0	200.00
9	0.0	1.0	0.0	0.0	0.0	0.0	0.0	0.0	0.0	0.0	0.0	1.0	0.0	0.0	150.00
10	0.0	0.0	0.0	0.0	0.0	0.0	0.0	-1.0	0.0	0.0	0.5	0.5	1.0	1.5	65.00
11	0.0	0.0	0.0	1.0	0.0	0.0	0.0	0.0	0.0	0.0	0.0	0.0	0.0	1.0	50.00

21 Transportation

INTRODUCTION.

1. The transportation problem is a particular form of the general linear programing model which is usually solved by a different technique to the Simplex method. This chapter describes transportation problems and shows a step by step method of solution. As with the simplex method all that is required is simple arithmetic and the ability to follow a set of rules.

TRANSPORTATION PROBLEMS DEFINED.

2. The typical transportation problem involves a number of sources of supply (eg warehouses) and a number of destinations (eg retail shops). The usual objective is to minimise the transportation cost of supplying quantities of a commodity from the warehouses to the shops. The major requirement is that there must be a constant transportation cost per unit ie if one unit costs £10 to transport from Warehouse A to Shop X, five units will cost £50. This will be recognised as the linearity requirement fundamental to all forms of LP.

THE TRANSPORTATION TECHNIQUE.

3. Although the method of solving transportation problems described below differs in appearance from the simplex method it has some basic similarities, as follows:

a. It is an iterative, step by step, process.

b. It starts with a feasible solution and each succeeding solution is also feasible.

c. At each stage a test is made to see whether transportation costs can be reduced.

d. Optimum is reached when no further cost reductions are possible.

TRANSPORTATION EXAMPLE.

4. The following simple example will be used as a basis for the step-by-step explanation of the transportation technique.

Example 1.

A firm of office equipment suppliers has three depots located in various towns. It receives orders for a total of 15 special filing cabinets from four customers. In total in the three depots there are 15 of the correct filing cabinets available and the management wish to minimise delivery costs by despatching the filing cabinets from the appropriate depot for each customer.

Details of the availabilities, requirements, and transport costs per filing cabinet are given in the following table.

Note.

The body of the table contains the transportation costs per cabinet from the depots to the customer. For example, it cost £14 to sent 1 cabinet from Depot Y to customer B (and £28 for 2, £42 for 3 etc.).

AVAILABLE \ REQUIRED	Customer A 3 cabinets	Customer B 3 cabinets	Customer C 4 cabinets	Customer D 5 cabinets	Total 15
DEPOT X 2 Cabinets	£13	11	15	20	Transportation
DEPOT Y 6 Cabinets	£17	14	12	13	cost per
DEPOT Z 7 Cabinets	£18	18	15	12	unit
TOTAL 15					

Table 1

STEP 1. Make an initial feasible allocation of deliveries. The method used for this initial solution does not affect the value of the optimum but a careful initial choice may reduce the number of iterations that have to be made. The method to be used in this manual is to select the cheapest route first, and allocate as many as possible then the next cheapest and so on. The result of such an allocation is as follows.

REQUIREMENTS

AVAILABLE		A 3	B 3	C 4	D 5
X	2 UNITS		2(1)		
Y	6 UNITS	1(4)	1(3)	4(2)	
Z	7 UNITS	2(5)			5(2)

Table 2

Note.

The numbers in the table represent deliveries of cabinets and the numbers in the brackets (1), (2), etc represent the sequence in which they are inserted, lowest cost first ie.

			£
1.	2 units X → B £11/unit	Total Cost	22
2.	4 units Y → C £12/unit	Total cost	48
	5 units Z → D £12/unit	Total cost	60
3.	The next lowest cost move which is feasible ie does not exceed row or column totals is 1 unit Y → B £14/unit		14
4.	Similarly the next lowest feasible allocation 1 unit Y → A £17/unit		17
5.	Finally to fulfil the row/column totals 2 units Z → A £18/unit		36
			197

STEP 2. Check solution obtained to see if it represents the minimum cost possible. This is done by calculating what are known as 'shadow costs' (ie an imputed cost of not using a particular route) and comparing these with the real transport costs to see whether a change of allocation is desirable.

This is done as follows:

Calculate a norminal 'despatch' and 'reception' cost for each occupied cell by making the assumption that the transport cost per unit is capable of being split between despatch and reception costs thus:

$$D(X) + R(B) = 11$$
$$D(Y) + R(A) = 17$$
$$D(Y) + R(B) = 14$$
$$D(Y) + R(C) = 12$$
$$D(Z) + R(A) = 18$$
$$D(Z) + R(D) = 12$$

where D (X), D(Y) and D(Z) represent Despatch cost from depots X, Y and Z, and R (A), R (B), R (C) and R(D) represent Reception costs at customers A, B, C & D.

By convention the first depot is assigned the value of zero ie D(X) = 0 and this value is substituted in the first equation and then all the other values can be obtained thus

R (A) =	14	D (X) =	0
R (B) =	11	D (Y) =	3
R (C) =	9	D (Z) =	4
R (D) =	8		

Using these values the shadow costs of the unoccupied cells can be calculated. The unoccupied cells are X:A, X:C, X:D, Y:D, Z:B, Z:C.

		SHADOW COSTS
∴ D(X) + R (A)	= 0 + 14 =	14
D(X) + R (C)	= 0 + 9 =	9
D(X) + R(D)	= 0 + 8 =	8
D(Y) + R(D)	= 3 + 8 =	11
D(Z) + R(B)	= 4 + 11 =	15
D(Z) + R(C)	= 4 + 9 =	13

These computed 'shadow costs' are compared with the actual transport costs (from Table 1), Where the ACTUAL costs are LESS THAN SHADOW COSTS, overall costs can be reduced by allocating units into that cell.

	ACTUAL COST	–	SHADOW COST		+ COST INCREASE – COST REDUCTION
Cell X:A	13	–	14	=	–1
X:C	15	–	9	=	+6
X:D	20	–	8	=	+12
Y:D	13	–	11	=	+2
Z:B	18	–	15	=	+3
Z:C	15	–	13	=	+2

The meaning of this is that total costs could be reduced by £1 for every unit that can be transferred into cell X : A. As there is a cost reduction that can be made the solution in Table 2 is not optimum.

STEP 3. Make the maximum possible allocation of deliveries into the cell where actual costs are less than shadow costs using occupied cells ie.

Cell X :A from Step 2, The number that can be allocated is governed by the need to keep within the row and column totals. This is done as follows:

REQUIREMENTS

		A	B	C	D
		3	3	4	5 UNITS
	X 2 UNITS	+	2 -		
AVAILABLE	Y 6 UNITS	1 -	1 +	4	
	Z 7 UNITS	2			5

Table 3

Table 3 is a reproduction of Table 2 with a number of + and - inserted. These were inserted for the following reasons.

Cell X: A, + indicates a transfer IN as indicated in Step 2.
Cell X: B, – indicates a transfer OUT to maintain Row X total.
Cell Y: B, + indicates a transfer IN to maintain Column B total
Cell Y: A, – indicates a transfer OUT to maintain Row Y and Column A totals.

The maximum number than can be transferred into Cell X : A is the lowest number in the minus cells ie cells Y : A, and X : B which is 1 unit.

∴ 1 unit is transferred in the + and – sequence described above resulting in the following table.

REQUIREMENTS

	A	B	C	D
	3	3	4	5 UNITS
X 2 UNITS	1	1		
Y 6 UNITS		2	4	
Z 7 UNITS	2			5

Table 4

The total cost of this solution is

			£
Cell X : A	1 unit @ £13	=	13
X : B	1 unit @ £11	=	11
Y : B	2 units @ £14	=	28
Y : C	4 units @ £12	=	48
Z : A	2 units @ £18	=	36
Z : D	5 units @ £12	=	60
			£196

The new total cost is £1 less than the total cost established in Step 1. This is the result expected because it was calculated in Step 2 that £1 would be saved for every unit we were able to transfer to Cell X : A and we were able to transfer 1 unit only.

Notes.

Always commence the + and – sequence with a + in the cell indicated by the (actual cost – shadow cost) calculation. Then put a – in the occupied cell in the same row which has an occupied cell in its column. Proceed until a – appears in the same column as the original +

STEP 4. Repeat Step 2 ie check that solution represents minimum cost. Each of the processes in Step 2 are repeated using the latest solution (Table 4) as a basis, thus:

Nominal despatch and reception costs for each occupied cell.

$$D(X) + R(A) = 13$$
$$D(X) + R(B) = 11$$
$$D(Y) + R(B) = 14$$
$$D(Y) + R(C) = 12$$
$$D(Z) + R(A) = 18$$
$$D(Z) + R(D) = 12$$

Setting D (X) at zero the following values are obtained

R (A) = 13		D (X) = 0	
R (B) = 11		D (Y) = 3	
R (C) = 9		D (Z) = 5	
R (D) = 7			

Using these values the shadow costs of the UNOCCUPIED cells are calculated. The unoccupied cells are X : C, X : D, Y : A, Y : D, Z : B, and Z : C.

$$\therefore D(X) + R(C) = 9$$
$$D(X) + R(D) = 7$$
$$D(Y) + R(A) = 16$$
$$D(Y) + R(D) = 10$$
$$D(Z) + R(B) = 16$$
$$D(Z) + R(C) = 14$$

The computed shadow costs are compared with actual costs to see if any reduction in cost is possible.

	ACTUAL COST		SHADOW COST		+ COST INCREASE –COST REDUCTION
Cell X : C	15	–	9	=	+6
X : D	20	–	7	=	+13
Y : A	17	–	16	=	+ 1
Y : D	13	–	10	=	+ 3
Z : B	18	–	16	=	+ 2
Z : C	15	–	14	=	+ 1

It will be seen that all the answers are positive, therefore no further cost reduction is possible and optimum has been reached.

OPTIMUM SOLUTION

1 UNIT X → A
1 UNIT X → B
2 UNITS Y → B
4 UNITS Y → C
2 UNITS Z → A
5 UNITS Z → D

with a total cost of £196

This solution is shown in the following tableau.

	A	B	C	D
X	1	1		
Y		2	4	
Z	2			5

Note.

In this example only one iteration was necessary to produce an optimum solution mainly because a good initial solution was chosen. The principles explained above would, of course, be equally suitable for many iterations.

UNEQUAL AVAILABILITY AND REQUIREMENT QUANTITIES.

5. Example 1 above had equal quantities of units available and required. Obviously this is not always the case and the most common situation is that there are more units available to be despatched than are required. The transportation technique can be used in such circumstances with only a slight adjustment to the initial table. A dummy destination, with zero transport costs, is inserted in the table to absorb the surplus available. Thereafter the transportation technique is followed. The following example explains the procedure.

TRANSPORTATION EXAMPLE WITH A DUMMY DESTINATION.

6. **Example 2.**

A firm of wholesale domestic equipment suppliers, with 3 warehouses, received orders for a total of 100 deep freezers from 4 retail shops. In total in the 3 warehouses there are 110 freezers available and the management wish to minimise transport costs by despatching the freezers required from the appropriate warehouses, Details of availabilities, requirements, and transport costs are given in the following table.

AVAILABLE		**REQUIRED** SHOP A	SHOP B	SHOP C	SHOP D		TOTAL REQUIRED
		25	25	42	8	=	100
Warehouse I	40 Freezers	£3	16	9	2		Transport
Warehouse II	20 Freezers	1	9	3	8		Costs per
Warehouse III	50 Freezers	4	5	2	5		freezer
TOTAL AVAILABLE 110							

Table 5

STEP 1. Add a DUMMY destination to Table 5 with a zero transport costs and a requirements equal to the surplus availability.

$\therefore$ Dummy requirement = 110 - 100 = 10 FREEZERS

AVAILABLE	SHOP A	SHOP B	SHOP C	SHOP D	DUMMY	TOTAL REQUIRED
	REQUIRED					
	25	25	42	8	10	110
Warehouse I 40 Freezers	£3	16	9	2	0	Transport
Warehouse II 20 Freezers	1	9	3	8	0	Costs per
Warehouse III 50 Freezers	4	5	2	5	0	freezer
TOTAL AVAILABLE 110						

Table 6

STEP 2. Now that the quantitiy available equals the quantity required (because of the insertion of the dummy) the solution can proceed in exactly the same manner described in Para. 4 Example 7 First set up an initial feasible solution.

			A	B	C	D	DUMMY
			REQUIRED				
			25	25	42	8	10
	I	40	5(4)	17(6)		8(3)	10(7)
AVAILABLE	II	20	20(1)				
	III	50		8(5)	42(2)		

Table 7

The numbers in the table represent the allocations made and the numbers in brackets represent the sequence they were inserted based on lowest cost and the necessity to maintain row/column totals. The residue of 10 was allocated to the dummy.

The cost of this allocation is

				£		£
I	→	A	5 units @	3	=	15
I	→	B	17 units @	16	=	272
I	→	D	8 units @	2	=	16
I	→	Dummy	10 units @	zero cost		
II	→	A	20 units @	1	=	20
III	→	B	8 units @	5	=	40
III	→	C	42 units @	2	=	84
						£447

STEP 3 Check solution to see if it represents the minimum cost possible in the same manner as previously described ie

Despatch & Reception Costs of used routes:

				£
D (I)	+	R(A)	=	3
D (I)	+	R(B)	=	16
D (I)	+	R(D)	=	2
D (I)	+	R(DUMMY)	=	0
D (II)	+	R(A)	=	1
D(III)	+	R(B)	=	5
D(III)	+	R(C)	=	2

Setting D (I) at zero the following values can be obtained:

R (A)	=	3	D(I)	=	0
R (B)	=	16	D(II)	=	-2
R (C)	=	13	D(III)	=	-11
R (D)	=	2			
R (DUMMY)	=	0			

Using these values the shadow costs of the unused routes can be calculated. The unused routes are I :C, 11:B, II:D, Dummy, III:A, III:D, and III:Dummy.

								SHADOW COSTS £
D(I)	+	R(C)	=	0	+	13	=	13
D (II)	+	R(B)	=	-2	+	16	=	14
D (II)	+	R(C)	=	-2	+	13	=	11
D (II)	+	R(D)	=	-2	+	2	=	0
D (II)	+	R(Dummy)	=	-2	+	0	=	-2
D (III)	+	R(A)	=	-11	+	3	=	-8
D (III)	+	R(D)	=	-11	+	2	=	-9
D (III)	+	R(Dummy)	=	-11	+	0	=	-11

The shadow costs are then deducted from actual costs.

		ACTUAL COST	–	SHADOW COST	=	+ COST INCREASE –COST REDUCTION
Cell I :	C	9	–	13	=	–4
II :	B	9	–	14	=	–5
II :	C	3	–	11	=	–8
II :	D	8	–	0	=	+8
II :	Dummy	0	–	(– 2)	=	+2
III :	A	4	–	(– 8)	=	+12
III :	D	5	–	(– 9)	=	+14
III :	Dummy	0	–	(– 11)	=	+11

It will be seen that total costs can be reduced by £8 per unit for every unit that can be transferred into Cell II : C.

STEP 4. Make the maximum possible allocation of deliveries into Cell II : C. This is done by inserting a sequence of + and -, maintaining row and column totals.

REQUIRED

			A	B	C	D	DUMMY
			25	25	42	8	10
	I	40	5 +	17 -		8	10
AVAILABLE	II	20	20 -		+		
	III	50		8 +	42 -		

Table 8

Note.

This is a reproduction of Table 7 with a sequence of + and - added starting with a + in Cell II : C and then - and + as necessary to maintain row and column balances. The maximum number that can be transferred is the lowest number in the minus cells ie 17 units in cell 1 : B.

This transfer is made and the following table results.

REQUIRED

			A	B	C	D	DUMMY
			25	25	42	8	10
	I	40	22			8	10
AVAILABLE	II	20	3		17		
	III	50		25	25		

Table 9

The cost of this allocation is

$$(22 \times 3) + (8 \times 2) + (10 \times 0) + (3 \times 1) + (17 \times 3) + (25 \times 5) + (25 \times 2) = £311$$

This can be verified by deducting from the cost of the original allocation (Table 7) the savings of £8 per unit for the 17 units transferred ie

$$£447 - (17 \times 8) = £311$$

STEP 5. Repeat Step 3 to check if cost is at a minimum. After setting D (I) = 0, the following values can be obtained.

R (A)	=	3	D (I)	=	0
R (B)	=	8	D (II)	=	- 2
R (C)	=	5	D (III)	=	- 3
R (D)	=	2			
R (DUMMY)	=	0			

These values are used to calculate the shadow costs of the unused routes.

SHADOW COSTS

			£
Cell I :	B	=	8
I :	C	=	5
II :	B	=	6
II :	D	=	0
II :	Dummy	=	- 2
III :	A	=	0
III :	D	=	- 1
III :	Dummy	=	- 3

When these shadow costs are deducted from the actual costs no negative values result : the allocation shown in Table 9 is optimum with a minimum transportation cost of £311.

Notes:

a. It will be seen that, apart from setting up the initial table with a Dummy destination, the solution method for Example 2 is identical to Example 1.

b. A frequently advocated method of making the initial feasible allocation is what is called the North-West corner method. This means filling the requirements starting from the top left hand cell regardless of the costings. The same optimum solution is reached but more iterations are usually required. Example 2, for instance, would take 5 iterations to reach optimum starting from a North-West corner initial allocation as opposed to 2 iterations when a more rational choice is made.

c. Frequently it is found that alternative solutions exist ie different series of allocations can be found with the same overall cost.

MAXIMISATION AND THE TRANSPORTATION TECHNIQUE.

7. Although transportation problems are usually minimising problems, on occasions problems are framed so that the objective is to make the allocations from sources to destinations in a manner which maximises contribution or profit. These problems are dealt with relatively easily as follows.

STEPS INVOLVED IN MAXIMISATION.

8. Using Example 1, paragraph 4, for comparison the following procedures should be followed.

See	MINIMISING TECHNIQUE	MAXIMISING TECHNIQUE
STEP 1	Make initial feasible allocation lowest cost first and so on.	Make initial feasible allocation on basis of maximum contribution first, then next highest and so on.
STEP 2	Test differences between actual and shadow costs on unused routes for optimality ie all positive If not, make allocation into cell with largest negative difference	For optimum, the differences between actual and shadow contributions for the unused routes should be ALL NEGATIVE. If not, make allocation into cell with the LARGEST POSITIVE difference.

Apart from the differences above the transportation technique can be followed as usual.

MAXIMISING AND DUMMIES.

9. It will be recalled from Para 5 that where availability and requirements are unequal a dummy destination with zero transport costs was introduced and thereafter the normal technique was followed. In a maximising problem where there are more items available than are required, a dummy destination with zero contribution should also be introduced and the maximising procedure in Para 8 followed.

DEGENERACY AND THE TRANSPORTATION TECHNIQUE.

10. If Tables 2, 3, 4, 5, 7, 8 and 9 are examined it will be seen in each case that the number of allocations made is 1 less than the number of rows added to the number of columns. For example, Table 9 (3 rows and 5 columns) has 7 allocations. To be able to calculate the shadow despatch and receiving costs this condition is essential but on occasions the number of allocations turns out to be less than ROWS + COLUMNS - 1. This condition is known as degeneracy.

DEALING WITH DEGENERACY.

10. If the number of allocations is less than, No. of ROWS + COLUMNS - 1, then it is necessary to make one or more zero allocations to routes to bring up the number of allocations to ROWS + COLUMNS - 1. This means that, for shadow cost calculation purposes, one or more cells with zero allocation are treated as occupied. For example in a 3 row, 5 column table if 6 allocations had been made which satisfied the requirements, any 1 cell would be given a zero allocations and treated as occupied. For moves following a zero allocation the cell with zero allocation is treated as a positive allocation and can therefore be moved to and from as with other allocations. The allocation must be into an *independent* cell.

SUMMARY.

11.

a. Flowchart 1 gives an outline of the transportation method for minimising problems and is cross referenced to appropriate parts of the chapter.

b. Maximising problems follow the same general pattern except that the initial feasible solution is made on the basis of maximum contribution first and optimum is recognised when all the values are negative after deducting shadow from actual contribution.

c. The number of allocations made must be one less than the number of rows plus the number of columns. If this does not happen after making the necessary actual allocations one or more cells, with zero allocation, must be treated as occupied.

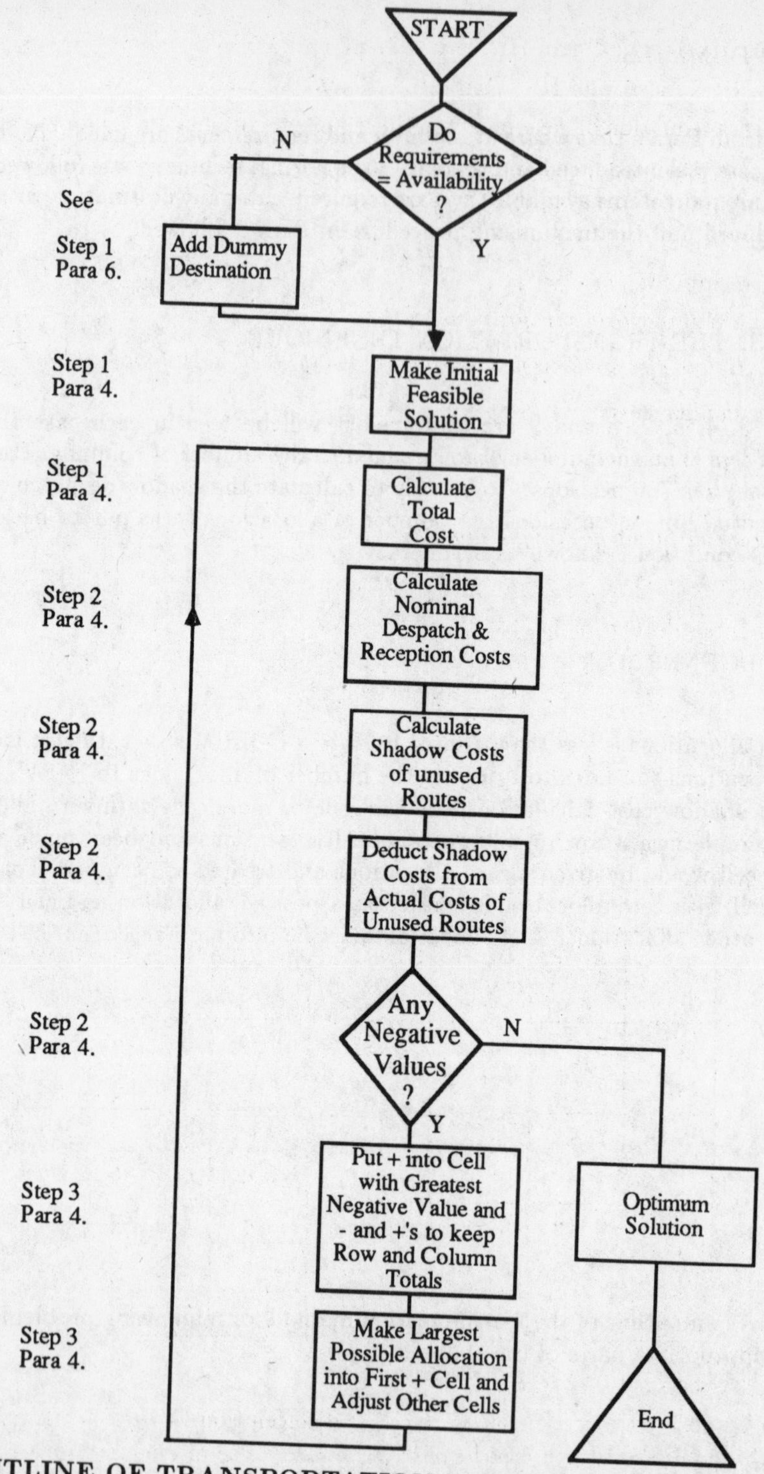

OUTLINE OF TRANSPORTATION METHOD FLOWCHART 1

POINTS TO NOTE.

12.

a. The transportation method is simple but tedious therefore reduce the number of iterations necessary by making the best possible choice of initial solution.

b. The figure obtained by deducting the shadow costs from actual costs is the netted result of the + and - sequence. For example in Table 8 the + and - sequence and costs were:

+ Costs in cells, I : A, II : C and III : B ie £3, £3 and £5 = £11

- Cost in cells, I : B, I : A and III : C ie £16, £1 and £2 = £19

making a net cost reduction of £8 which was the value indicated by the shadow cost calculations.

c. An Appendix to this chapter describes a shorter approach to solving Transportation problems using the principles developed in the Chapter.

SELF REVIEW QUESTIONS.

1. What is a typical transportation problem? (2)

2. What similarities to the simplex method has the usual transportation solution technique? (3)

3. What are the shadow costs? (4, Step 2)

4. How is the basic transportation technique modified to deal with the situation where there are more items available than are required? (5)

5. How is the transportation technique modified to solve maximising problems? (7 and 8)

6. What is degeneracy? (10)

7. How is degeneracy dealt with? (11)

APPENDIX.

The methodology developed and summarised in the Flow Chart 1 provides a detailed description of the principles involved in the Transportation Technique. However in the time constrained examination a shorter approach using the same principles can be employed.

Example 2 is reworked using such a technique.

The initial STEP 1 is repeated below.

→	A	B	C	D	Du	Total
	3	16	13	2	0	
W1	5 + x	17 - x	−4	8	10	
0	3	16	9 13	2	0	40
W2	20 -x	−5	x −8	8	2	
-2	1	9 14	3 11	8 0	0(-2)	20
W3	12	8 + x	42 -x	−4	11	
-11	4(-8)	5	2	5 9	0(-11)	50
Total	25	25	42	8	10	110

The initial feasible solution is inserted as in STEP 2.

STEP 3 proceeds with the insertion of Despatch and Receiption Costs for cells used. Put 0 in the box marked W1 to represent the despatch cost from Warehouse 1. The receipt cost in A is 3. This is put in the box labelled A. Repeat the process for B, D and Du. Row W1 can be linked to row W2 through column A. The despatch cost for W2 is -2. Row W1 can be linked to row W3 through Column B. The despatch cost for W3 is -11. The receipt cost for Column C is obtained from W3 through (W3 to C) and is 13.

Add together the receipt and despatch costs for unused cells and write them by the actual cost. These are the shadow costs to compare with the actual costs. The difference is noted in each cell. The only ones of interest are those which are circled. The minus values show savings and the maximum saving is through cell W2 to C. Let x units be put through this cell. This is exactly the same as STEP 4 in the main text. A closed loop of re-allocation is made. As before the maximum value of x is 17.

At this point the diagram is redrawn below:

	A	B	C	D	Du	Total
	3	8	5	2	0	Total
W1	22	[8]	[4]	8	10	
0	3	16 8	9 5	2	0	40
W2	3	[3]	17	[8]	[2]	
-2	1	9 6	3	8 0	0(-2)	20
W3	[4]	25	25	[1]	[3]	
-3	4 0	5	2	5(-1)	0(-3)	50
Total	25	25	42	8	10	110

The process described above is now repeated.

There are no more savings ie negative values in the circles and so the minimum cost allocation has been reached.

This technique is the same as that developed in the main text, except that all the calculations are performed on one diagram, thus saving valuable minutes in the examination.

EXERCISES WITH ANSWERS COMMENCING PAGE 488

A1. A firm has three shops with a total of 80 televisions. An order is received from the Local Authority for 70 sets to be delivered to 4 schools. The transport costs from shops to schools are shown below together with the availabilities and requirements.

		SCHOOLS				
		A	*B*	*C*	*D*	
AVAILABLE		*20*	*30*	*15*	*5*	*REQUIREMENTS*
SHOP I	*40 SETS*	*2*	*4*	*1*	*6*	
II	*20 SETS*	*4*	*3*	*3*	*3*	*COSTS*
III	*20 SETS*	*1*	*2*	*5*	*2*	

It is required to make the most economic deliveries.

Set up the initial tableau and make the initial feasible deliveries.

A2. Work out the shadow prices for the tableau in A1.

A3. Solve the problem in A1.

EXAMINATION QUESTIONS WITH ANSWERS COMMENCING PAGE 488

A4. In a certain region of the Republic of Pelion there are five coal mines which have the following outputs and production costs:

Mine	*Output (Tons/day)*	*Production Cost ($ /Ton)*
1	*120*	*25*
2	*150*	*29*
3	*80*	*34*
4	*160*	*26*
5	*140*	*28*

Before the coal can be sold, it must be 'cleaned' and graded at one of three coal preparation plants. The capactities and operating costs of these three plants are as follows:-

Plant	*Capacity (Tons/day)*	*Operating Cost ($ /Ton)*
A	300	2
B	200	3
C	200	3

All coal is transported by rail at a cost of $0.5 per ton kilometre, and the distances (in kilometres) from each mine to the three preparation plants are:

Preparation Plant	*Mine* 1	2	3	4	5
A	22	44	26	52	24
B	18	16	24	42	48
C	44	32	16	16	22

Required:

(a) Using a transportation model, determine how the output of each mine should be allocated to the three preparation plants.

(b) Following the installation of new equipment at coal mine number 3, the production cost is expected to fall to $30 per ton.

What effect, if any, will this have on the allocation of coal to the preparation plants?

(c) It is planned to increase the output of coal mine number 5 to 180 tons per day which can be achieved without any increase in production cost per ton. How will this affect the allocation of coal to the preparation plants?

(ACCA QUANTITATIVE ANALYSIS)

A5. A ladies fashion shop wishes to purchase the following quantities of summer dresses:

Dress size	I	II	III	IV
Quantity	100	200	450	150

Three manufacturers are willing to supply dresses. The quantities given below are the maximum they are able to supply of any given combination of orders for dresses:

Manufacturer	A	B	C
Total quantity	150	450	250

The shop expects the profit per dress to vary with the manufacturer as given below:

Manufacturer	*Sizes* I	II	II	IV
	£	£	£	£
A	2.50	4.00	5.00	2.00
B	3.00	3.50	5.50	1.50
C	2.00	4.50	4.50	2.50

You are required to:

a. use the transportation technique to solve the problem of how the orders should be placed on the manufacturers by the fashion shop in order to maximise profits;

b. explain how you know that there is no further improvement possible, showing your workings.

(CIMA QUANTITATIVE TECHNIQUES)

A6. As a result of an expansion in production capacity, the management of Minerva Manufacturing Ltd. has decided to take an additional employees at each of their 5 plants in the South West of England. The numbers required at each plant are:

Plant	1	2	3	4	5
Employees Required	45	74	50	82	63

All their employees currently come from three large towns in the area. Upon contracting the main employment agency in each town, Minerva finds that the numbers of suitable people available for employment are as follows:

Agency (town)	A	B	C
People Available	120	100	154

Because of the rural situations of the five plants, Minerva has agreed with the trades unions concerned that daily return travelling expenses from each town will be paid by the company to all employees. The rate is currently 12p per mile, and the distances (in miles) between each plant and each town are as follows:

	Plant				
Town	1	2	3	4	5
A	6	2	2	6	3
B	14	9	4	5	3
C	10	4	11	3	4

Required:

(a) How many men should Minerva aim to employ from each town in order to minimise the additional travelling expenses incurred? What is the minimum value of these expenses in connection with the additional 314 employees?

(b) In order to appear not to be unfair to potential employees from any one of the three towns, it has now been decided that the 60 people who are surplus to requirements should be spread equally between the three towns, i.e. 20 from each. How much more than in (a) would the company have to pay out each day in travelling expenses in order to achieve this at minimum cost?

ACCA, Quantitative Analysis.

EXERCISES WITHOUT ANSWERS

B1. A distributor has the following units to transport to various receiving points and wishes to do this at the lowest cost.

		Receiving Points				
Despatch		15	10	5	20	= 50 REQUIRED
Points		A	B	C	D	
I	15	8	2	6	4	
II	25	4	5	3	2	
III	10	3	3	5	6	
AVAILABLE	50					

The values in the table are the transportation costs per unit.

Solve using the single table method given in the Appendix.

B2. what is the solution to B1 if there are a total of 60 units available as follows: I 30 units, II 20 units, and III 10 units?

EXAMINATION QUESTIONS WITHOUT ANSWERS

B3. A wholesale company has nine storage depots which it proposes to rationalise. Four depots, Q, R, S and T are to be expanded and five depots, A, B, C, D and E are to be closed. Thirty six of the mechanical loaders in the depots to be closed will be required for use in the enlarged depots.

The mechanical loaders in the five depots to be closed are:

A : 5, B : 7, C : 11, D : 8 and E : 9.

The additional loaders required at the depots to be expanded are:

Q : 8, R : 9, S : 11 and T : 8

The cost of transporting one mechanical loader, in hundreds of pounds, between depots is given below:

Depots to be closed	Depots to be expanded			
	Q	R	S	T
A	3	3	7	9
B	6	5	3	3
C	6	4	8	7
D	5	4	5	4
E	4	3	6	5

You are required to:

a. show by calculation the minimum cost plan for meeting the rationalisation requirement by transfers between depots;

b. state at which depot there will be surplus loaders;

c. state with reasons whether or not your solution is unique.

(CIMA QUANTITATIVE TECHNIQUES)

B4. Multel Ltd. had decided to launch an addition to its product range. The new product may be distributed through any combination of the two company warehouses W1 and W2. The available annual production capacities for the new product are:
100 units at plant P1
200 units at plant P2
100 units at Plant P3

The three major concentrations of customer demand are at locations D1, D2 and D3 which are estimated to require each year:
90 units at D1
80 units at D2
90 units at D3

The unit production costs amount to £3, £4, £1 at P1, P2 and P3 respectively.

The unit handling costs at the warehouses amount to £2 and £3 at W1 and W2 respectively.

The unit trunking costs from plant to warehouse and unit delivery costs from warehouse to customer are as follows:

	W1	W2
P1	6	6
P2	5	5
P3	13	4

	D1	D2	D3
W1	3	5	8
W2	5	3	9

(All costs are in £'s)

Required:

a. Determine an optimum production and distribution schedule.

(Hint: first establish the least costly means of supplying each demand centre from each of the plants).

b. Assuming that each warehouse can handle a maximum 200 units a year, explain why it would be incorrect to solve the problem using the transportation technique to obtain a solution to the flows between plant and warehouse and then apply the technique again to the flows between the warehouses and the customers.

(ACCA Management Mathematics)

22 Assignment

INTRODUCTION.

1. A special form of the Transportation problem exists when there is only one item at each of the various sources and only one item is required at each of the various destinations. The assignment technique can be used for problems which are similar to normal transportation problems, eg assigning service engineers to service requests so as to minimise mileage, and also for problems such as assigning personnel to tasks. As with other LP techniques no advanced mathematics is required. The chapter covers in step-by-step fashion the techniques for both minimising and maximising assignment problems.

THE ASSIGNMENT TECHNIQUE FOR MINIMISING.

2. The following example will be used as a basis of the step-by-step explanation.

Example 1.

A company employs service engineers based at various locations throughout the country to sevice and repair their equipment installed in customers' premises. Four requests for service have been received and the company finds that four engineers are available. The distances each of the engineers is from the various customers is given in the following table and the company wishes to assign engineers to customers to minimise the total distance to be travelled.

CUSTOMERS

		W	X	Y	Z	
	Alf	25	18	23	14	
Service	Bill	38	15	53	23	Distances in miles from
Engineers	Charlie	15	17	41	30	engineers to customers
	Dave	26	28	36	29	

Table 1

STEP 1. Reduce each *column* by the smallest figure in that column. The smallest figures are 15, 15, 23 and 14 and deducting these values from each element in the columns produces the following table.

	W	X	Y	Z
A	10	3	0	0
B	23	0	30	9
C	0	2	18	16
D	11	13	13	15

Table 2

STEP 2. Reduce each row by the smallest figure in that row.

The smallest figures are 0, 0, 0 and 11 and deducting these values gives the following table.

	W	X	Y	Z
A	10	3	0	0
B	23	0	30	9
C	0	2	18	16
D	0	2	2	4

Table 3

Note.

Where the smallest value in a row is zero (ie as in rows A, B and C above) the row is, of course, unchanged.

STEP 3. Cover all the zeros in Table 3 by the MINIMUM POSSIBLE number of lines. The lines may be horizontal or vertical.

	W	X	Y	Z	
A	10	3	0	0	Line 2
B	23	0	30	9	Line 3
C	0	2	18	16	
D	0	2	2	4	
	Line 1				

Table 4

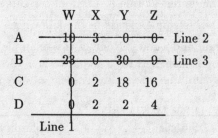

Note: Line 3, covering Row B, could equally well have been drawn covering column X.

STEP 4. Compare the number of lines with the number of assignments to be made (in this example there are 3 lines and 4 assignments). If the number of lines *EQUALS* the number of assignments to be made go to Step 6.

If the number of lines is LESS than the number of assignments to be made (ie as in this example which has three lines and four assignments) then

a. Find the smallest UNCOVERED element from Step 3, called X (in Table 4 this value is 2).
b. Subtract X from every element in the matrix.
c. Add back X to every element covered by a line. If an element is covered by two lines, for example, cell A: W in Table 4, X is added twice.

Note: The effect of these steps is that X is subtracted from all uncovered elements, elements covered by one line remain unchanged, and elements covered by two lines are increased by X.

Carrying out this procedure on Table 4 produces the following result:

In Table 4 the smallest element is 2. New table is

	W	X	Y	Z
A	12	3	0	0
B	25	0	30	9
C	0	0	16	14
D	0	0	0	2

Table 5

Note

It will be seen that cells A : W and B : W have been increased by 2; cells A : X, A : Y, A : Z, B : X, B : Y, B : Z, C : W and D : W are unchanged, and all other cells have been reduced by 2.

STEP 5. Repeat Steps 3 and 4 until the number of lines covering the zeros equals the number of assignments to be made.

In this example covering the zeros in Table 5 by the minimum number of lines equals the number of assignements without any further repetition, thus:

	W	X	Y	Z	
A	~~12~~	~~3~~	~~0~~	~~0~~	Line 1
B	~~25~~	~~0~~	~~30~~	~~9~~	Line 2
C	~~0~~	~~0~~	~~16~~	~~14~~	Line 3
D	~~0~~	~~0~~	~~0~~	~~2~~	Line 4

Table 6

STEP 6, When the number of lines EQUALS the number of assignments to be made, the actual assignments can be made using the following rules:

a. Assign to any zero which is unique to BOTH a column and a row.
b. Assign to any zero which is unique to a column OR a row.
c. Ignoring assignments already made repeat rule b. until all assignments are made.

Carrying out this procedure for our example results in the following:

a. (Zero unique to BOTH a column and a row). None in this example.
b. (Zero unique to column OR row). Assign B to X and A to Z.
The position is now as follows

	W	X	Y	Z
A	Row	Satisfied ↔		↕ Column Satisfied ↕
B	Row	Satisfied ↔		↕ Column Satisfied ↕
C	0	↕ Column Satisfied ↕	16	↕ Column Satisfied ↕
D	0	↕ Column Satisfied ↕	0	↕ Column Satisfied ↕

Table 7

c. Repeating rule b. results in assigning D to Y and C to W.

Notes.

a. Should the final assignment not be to a zero, then more lines than necessary were used in Step 3.
b. If a block of 4 or more zero's is left for the final assignment, then a choice of assignment exists with the same mileage.

STEP 7. Calculate the total mileage of the final assignment.

A to Z	Mileage	14
B to X		15
C to W		15
D to Y		36
		80 miles

THE ASSIGNMENT TECHNIQUE FOR MAXIMISING.

3. A maximising assignment problem typically involves making assignments so as to maximise contribution. To maximise only Step 1 from above differs - the columns are reduced by the LARGEST number in each column. From then on the same rules apply that are used for minimising.

MAXIMISING EXAMPLE.

4. **Example 2.**

The previous example No. 1 will be used with the changed assumption that the figures relate to *contribution* and not mileage and that it is required to maximise contribution. The solution would be reached as follows. (In each case the Step number corresponds to the solution given for Example No 1).

Original data.

	W	X	Y	Z	
A	25	18	23	14	
B	38	15	53	23	Contributions
C	15	17	41	30	to be gained
D	26	28	36	29	

Table 8

STEP 1. Reduce each column by LARGEST figure in that column and ignore the resulting minus signs.

	W	X	Y	Z
A	13	10	30	16
B	0	13	0	7
C	23	11	12	0
D	12	0	17	1

Table 9

STEP 2. Reduce each row by SMALLEST figure in that row.

	W	X	Y	Z
A	3	0	20	6
B	0	13	0	7
C	23	11	12	0
D	12	0	17	1

Table 10

STEP 3. Cover zeros by minimum possible number of lines.

	W	X	Y	Z
A	3	0	20	6
B	0	13	0	7
C	23	11	12	0
D	12	0	17	1

Table 11

STEP 4. If number of lines equals the number of assignments to be made go to Step 6. If less, (as in this example), carry out the 'uncovered element' procedure previously described. This results in the following table:

	W	X	Y	Z
A	0	0	17	6
B	0	16	0	10
C	20	11	9	0
D	9	0	14	1

Table 12

STEP 5. Repeat steps 3 and 4 until number of lines equals the number of assignments to be made. In this example this occurs without further repetition, thus:

	W	X	Y	Z
A	~~0~~	~~0~~	~~17~~	~~6~~
B	~~0~~	~~16~~	~~0~~	~~10~~
C	~~20~~	~~11~~	~~9~~	~~0~~
D	~~9~~	~~0~~	~~14~~	~~1~~

Table 13

STEP 6. Make assignments in accordance with the rules previously described which result in the following assignments:

C to Z
D to X
S to W
B to Y

STEP 7. Calculate contribution to be gained from the assignments.

	£
C to Z	30
D to X	28
A to W	25
B to Y	53
	£136

Notes.

a. It will be apparent that maximisng assignment problems can be solved in virutually the same manner as minimising problems.

b. The solution methods given are suitable for any size of matrix. If a problem is as small as the illustration used in this chapter, it can probably be solved merely by inspection.

UNEQUAL SOURCES AND DESTINATIONS.

5. To solve assignment problems in the manner described the matrix must be square, ie the supply must equal the requirements. Where the supply and requirements are not equal, an artificial source or destination must be created to square the matrix. The costs/mileage/contributions etc for the fictitious column or row will be zero throughout.

SOLUTION METHOD.

6. Having made the sources equal the destinations, the solution method will be as normal, treating the fictitious elements as though they were real. The solution method will automatically assign a source or destination to the fictitious row or column and the resulting assignment will incur zero cost or gain zero contribution.

SUMMARY.

7.

a. Flowchart 1 gives an outline of the assignment method and is cross referenced to appropriate parts of the chapter.

b. Because of the similarity in approach both MINIMISING and MAXIMISING problems can be dealt with the same flowchart.

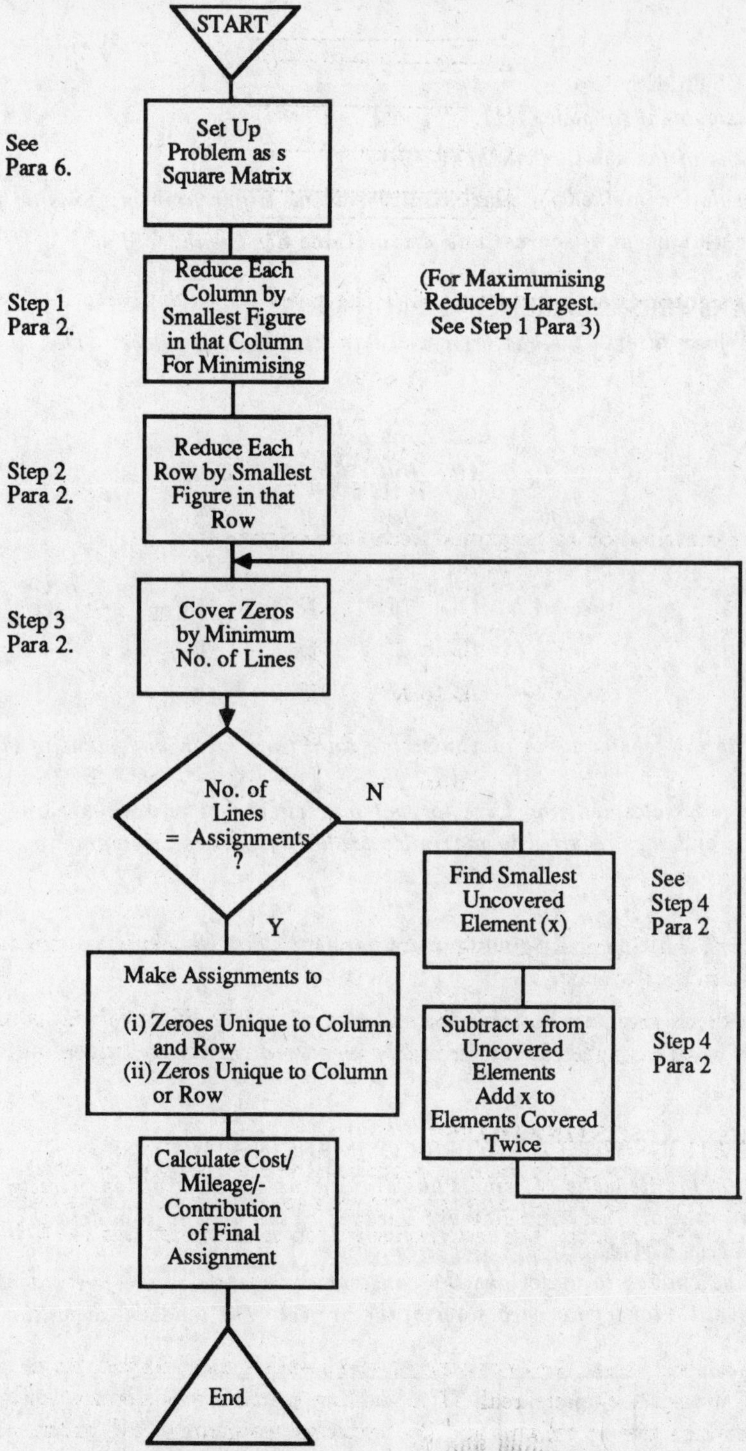

ASSIGNMENT TECHNIQUE FLOWCHART 1

POINTS TO NOTE.

8.

a. The assignment technique can be used for any pairing type of problem, eg taxis to customers, jobs to personnel.

b. Most practical problems of the size illustrated could be solved fairly readily using nothing more than commonsense. However, the technique illustrated can be used to solve much larger problems.

SELF REVIEW QUESTIONS.

1. *What is the assignment problem? (1)*
2. *What is the basis of the solution method? (2)*
3. *How does the solution method for maximising problems differ from minimising problems? (3)*
4. *How are unequal numbers of sources and destinations dealt with? (5)*

EXERCISES WITH ANSWERS COMMENCING PAGE 488

A1. A foremen has four fitters and has been asked to deal with five jobs. The times for each job are estimated as follows:

	Fitters			
	Alf	Bill	Charlie	Dave
Job 1	6	12	20	12
2	22	18	15	20
3	12	16	18	15
4	16	8	12	20
5	18	14	10	17

Allocate the men to the jobs so as to minimise the total time taken and identify the job which will not be dealt with.

A2. A company has four salesmen who have to visit four clients. The profit records from previous visits are shown in the table and it is required to maximise profits by the best assignments.

	A	B	C	D
Customer 1	£6	12	20	12
2	22	18	15	20
3	12	16	18	15
4	16	8	12	20

EXAMINATION QUESTIONS WITH ANSWERS COMMENCING PAGE 488

A3. The government of the Republic of Semele has decided, as a matter of top priority, to build a new road joining the two main cities of Areas and Boreas. Because of the need to complete the project as quickly as possible, the work has been divided into five stages which are to be built simultaneously. Within Semele there are six companies large enough to undertake the construction of any of the five stages and each company has been invited to submit a tender for each stage of the project. The tenders (in millions of Semele dollars) are as follows:

Company	Stage				
	1	2	3	4	5
A	49	84	63	82	68
B	53	92	62	no bid	67
C	54	86	67	78	68
D	46	86	62	76	no bid
E	57	94	66	83	70
F	50	82	65	80	72

Required:

(a) Assuming that none of the companies is large enough to undertake the work of more than one stage, advise the government how the five contracts should be allocated. What is the minimum total cost for the project?

(b) On speaking to representatives of the six companies, it is discovered that A, B, D and F have the capacity to undertake any 2 stages simultaneously and that C can undertake any 3 stages simultaneously. Show how the problem may now be formulated and solved using the 'transportation' algorithm. What is now the minimum cost allocation of contracts?

(ACCA, Quantitative Analysis)

A4. Amphion Airlines is a small air freight company based in Holland and operating throughout Western Europe. The company has 6 aircraft of different types, namely:

3 Type 'A'

2 Type 'B'

1 Type 'C'

whose operating costs and load carrying capacities are as follows:

Aircraft Type	Fixed Cost (£ per day)	Variable Cost (£) per mile	Variable Cost (£) per ton	Capacity (tons)
A	800	0.60	30	10
B	700	0.40	35	8
C	500	1.00	25	4

For any journey, variable costs are assigned on the basis of both the distance flown and the load being carried. All fixed and variable cost components are then added to obtain the relevant total cost.

On one particular day, there are 5 loads to be delivered to various destinations, the size of load and distances being:

Load	Size (tons)	Distance (miles)
1	10	200
2	2	550
3	8	320
4	5	280
5	3	450

The distances given above are direct from the company's base in Holland to the location involved and in each case there is no return load so that the aircraft will fly back empty. This means that mileage costs are incurred on both the outward and return journeys, but the tonnage cost is only incurred on the outward journey. All five return journeys can be completed within one day, and each aircraft can only fly one load in any one day. You may also assume that loads cannot be divided up and delivered in parts.

Required:

(a) For each of the five loads, determine the cost of delivery using each of the feasible aircraft types.

(b) Set up the cost matrix for assigning each load to each particular aircraft. Using an appropriate procedure, decide which aircraft should be used for delivering each load so that total cost is minimised. What is the total cost of all five deliveries.

(ACCA, Quantitative Analysis)

EXERCISES WITHOUT ANSWERS

B1. A company has 4 salesmen and 4 clients to visit. The profit per visit records are shown in the table and it is required to maximise profits by the best assignments.

Salesmen

	A	B	C	D
Client 1	*£9*	*12*	*7*	*15*
2	*13*	*14*	*15*	*10*
3	*8*	*10*	*20*	*6*
4	*11*	*15*	*13*	*10*

B2. Four engineers have to deal with four jobs. The costs for similar work are shown in the table and it is required to minimise the costs.

Engineer

	A	B	C	D
Job 1	*9*	*12*	*7*	*15*
2	*13*	*14*	*15*	*10*
3	*8*	*10*	*20*	*6*
4	*11*	*15*	*13*	*10*

EXAMINATION QUESTIONS WITHOUT ANSWERS

B3. A large oil company operating a number of drilling platforms in the North Sea is forming a high speed rescue unit to cope with emergency situations which may occur. The rescue unit comprises 6 personnel who, for reasons of flexibility, undergo the same comprehensive training program. The six personnel are assessed as to their suitability for various specialist tasks and the marks they received in the training program are given in the following table:

	TRAINEE NO.					
Specialist Task	*I*	*II*	*III*	*IV*	*V*	*VI*
Unit Leader	*21*	*5*	*21*	*15*	*15*	*28*
Helicopter Pilot	*30*	*11*	*16*	*8*	*16*	*4*
First Aid	*28*	*2*	*11*	*16*	*25*	*25*
Drilling Technology	*19*	*16*	*17*	*15*	*19*	*8*
Fire Fighting	*26*	*21*	*22*	*28*	*29*	*24*
Communications	*3*	*21*	*21*	*11*	*26*	*26*

Based on the marks awarded, what role should each of the trainees be given in the rescue unit?

B4. 'The assignment problem is a type of allocation problem.'
Required:
What do you understand by an assignment problem?
Explain one technique for solving such problems, illustrating your answer by means of a simple example.
(ACCA Management Mathematics)

23 Network Analysis – Introduction and Terminology

INTRODUCTION.

1. This chapter introduces the planning and control technique termed network analysis, defines the basic terminology used and the rules for drawing networks.

DEFINITION.

2. Network analysis is a generic term for a family of related techniques developed to aid management in the planning and control of projects. These techniques show the inter-relationship of the various jobs or tasks which make up the overall project and clearly identify the critical parts of the project. They can provide planning and control information on the time, cost and resource aspects of a project. Network analysis is likely to be of most value where projects are:

a. Complex, ie they contain many related and interdependent activities, and/or
b. Large, ie where many types of facilities, high capital investments, many personnel are involved; and/or
c. Where restrictions exists, ie where projects have to be completed within stipulated time or cost limits, or where some or all of the resources (material, labour) are limited.

BACKGROUND.

3. A basic form of network analysis was being used in the UK and USA in the mid-1950's in an attempt to reduce project times.

In 1958 the US Naval Special Projects Office set up a team to devise a technique to control the planning of complex projects. The outcome of the team's efforts was the development of the network technique known as PERT (Programme Evaluation and Review Technique). Pert was used to plan and control the development of the Polaris missile and was credited with saving two years in the missile's development.

Since 1958 the technique has been developed and nowadays many variants exist which handle, in addition to basic time factors, costs, resources, probabilities and combinations of all these factors. A variety of names exist and some of the more commonly used are:

Critical Path Planning	CPP
Critical Path Analysis	CPA
Critical Patch Scheduling	CPS
Critical Path Method	CPM
Programme Evaluation and Review Technique etc.	PERT, PERT/ COST

BASIC NETWORK TERMINOLOGY.

4. Only the basic elements of networks are covered to start with, other more complex features are introduced as required in later chapters.

Activity.

This is a task or job of work which takes *time* and resources eg Build a Wall, Verify the debtors in a sales ledger, Dig foundations etc. An activity is represented in a network by an arrow thus:

The head of the arrow indicates where the task ends and the tail where the tasks begins. The arrow points from left to right but is NOT drawn to scale. An essential preliminary to the use of network analaysis is establishing.

a. what activities are involved in the project.

b. their logical relationship eg the activity or Building a Wall must take place after the activity, Dig Foundations.

c. an estimate of the time the activity is expected to take. Note that the basic time estimate is always necessary but in addition other estimates of times, costs, resources, probabilities etc may also be required. These other factors are dealt with later.

Event.

This is a point in time and indicates the start or finish of an activity, or activities, eg Wall built, Debtors verified, Foundations Dug etc. An event is represented in a network by a *circle* or node thus:

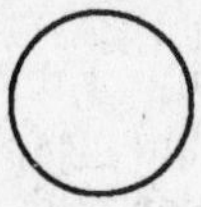

It will be noted that the establishment of activities automatically determines events because they are the start and finish of activities and represent the achievement of a specific stage of a project.

DUMMY ACTIVITY. This is an activity which does not consume time or resources. It is used merely to show clear, logical dependencies between activities so as not to violate the rules for drawing networks. It is represented on a network by a *dotted arrow* thus:

Note that dummy activities are not usually listed with the real activities but become necessary as the network is drawn. Dummy activity examples are given after the rules for drawing networks have been discussed.

NETWORK. This is the combination of activities, dummy activities and events in logical sequence acording to the rules for drawing networks. Thus a small network might appear as follows:

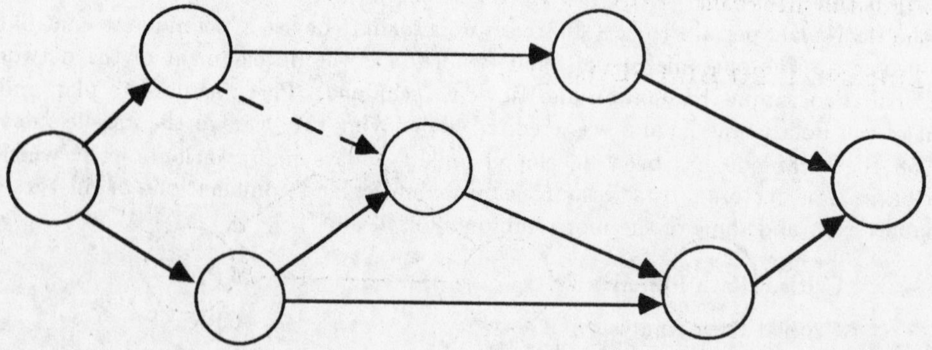

RULES FOR DRAWING NETWORKS.

5. The following rules are all logically based and should be thoroughly learned before attemtping to draw networks.

a. A complete network should have only one point of entry – a START event and only one point of exist – a FINISH event.

b. Every activity must have one preceding or 'tail' event and one succeeding or 'head' event. Note that many activities may use the same tail event and many may use the head event, eg.

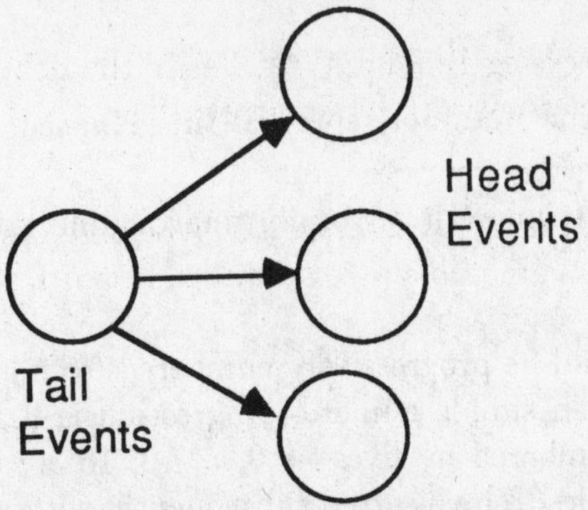

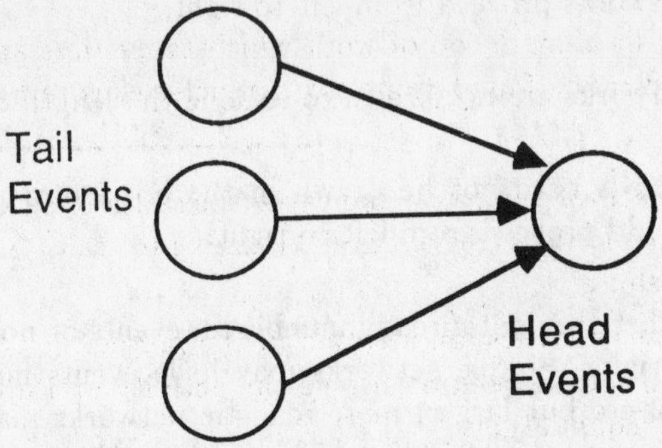

However an activity must not share the same tail event *AND* the same head event with any other activities (this is dealt with in detail in Para 8 on Dummies).

c. No activity can start until its tail event is reached.

d. An event is not complete until *all* activities leading in to it are complete.
This is an important rule and invariably has to be applied in examination questions.

e. 'Loops' ie a series of activities which lead back to the same event are not allowed because the essence of networks is a progression of activities always moving onwards in time.

'LOOPS' NOT TO BE USED

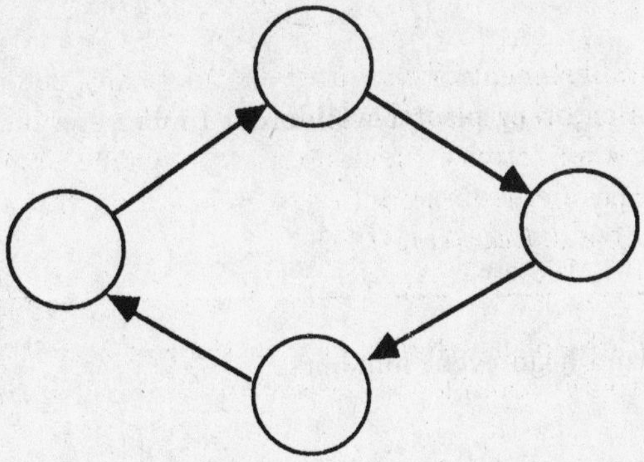

f. All activities must be tied into the network ie they must contribute to the progression or be discarded as irrelevant. Activities which do not link into the overall project are termed 'danglers'.

DANGLER. NOT TO BE USED.

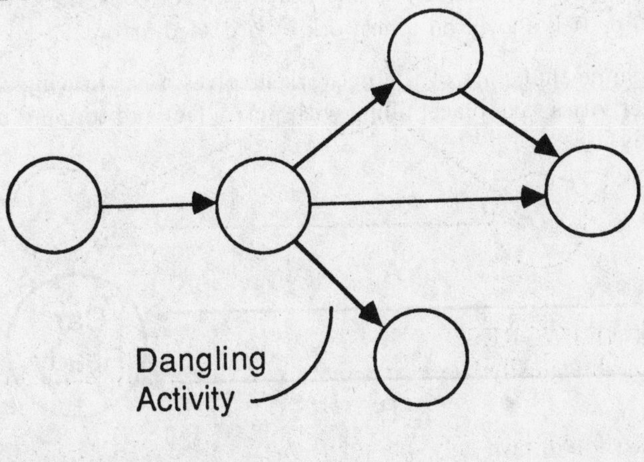

CONVENTIONS FOR DRAWING NETWORKS.

6. In addition to the Rules in Paragraph 5 above, which must not be violated, certain conventions are usually observed and for the sake of uniformity and easier communication students are recommended to follow the normal conventions.

a. Networks proceed from left to right.

b. Networks are not drawn to scale ie the length of the arrow does not represent time elapsed.

c. Arrows need not be drawn in the horizontal plane but unless it is totally unavoidable they should proceed from left to right.

d. If there are not already numbered, events or nodes should be progressively numbered from left to right. Simple networks may have events numbered in simple numeric progression ie 0, 1, 2, 3 etc but larger, more realistic networks may be numbered in 'fives' ie 0, 5, 10, 15 etc or 'tens' ie 0, 10, 20, 30 etc. This enables additional activities to be inserted subsequently without affecting the numbering sequence of the whole profject.

ACTIVITY IDENTIFICATION.

7. Activities may be identified in several ways and students should familiarise themselves with the various methods so that unfamiliar presentation does not cause confusion. Typical of the methods to be found include:

a. Shortened description of the job eg plaster wall, order timber etc.

b. Alphabetic or numeric code.

eg. A, B, C etc. or 100, 101, 108 etc.

c. Identification by the tail and head event numbers

eg 1-2, 2-3, 2-5 etc.

DUMMY ACTIVITIES.

8. It will be recalled that a dummy activity is one that does not consume time or resources but merely shows a logical relationship. It is shown on a network by a dotted arrow.

Dummy example. Assume that part of the network involves a car arrving at a service station during which two independent activities take place, filling with petrol (A) and topping up with oil (B). This could be shown thus (incorrectly)

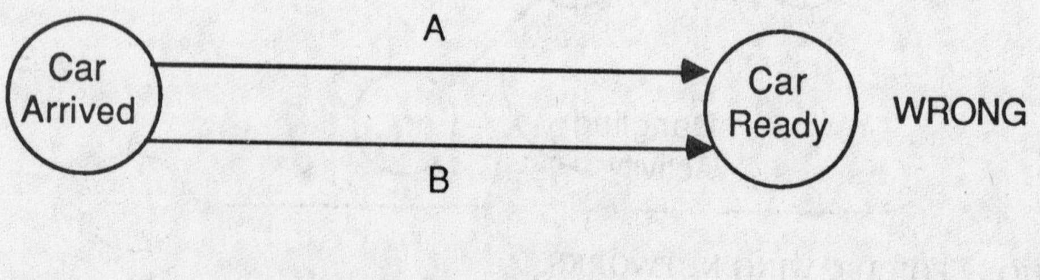

NB. This is wrong because it contravenes rule b. para 5.

By the use of a dummy activity it could be shown thus (correctly)

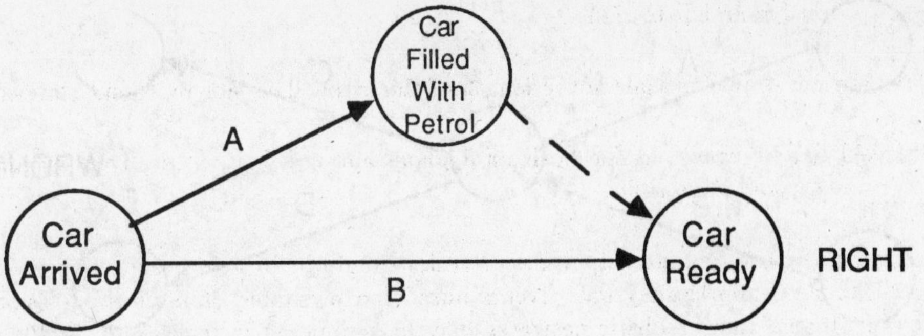

OR

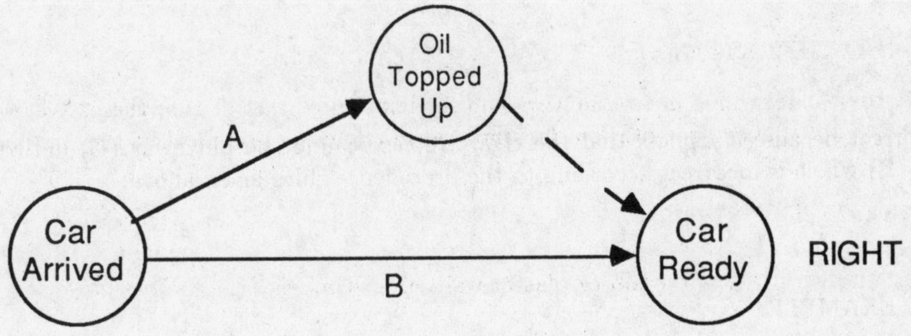

Further dummy example. Assume that part of a network involves a man lighting a cigarette. The activities involved, and their relationships are assumed to be as follows.

		Activity	Preceding Activity
A	–	Remove cigarette from case	(Relates to earlier part of network)
C	–	Put cigarette case away	A
B	–	Strike match	(Relates to earlier part of network)
D	–	Light cigarette	A, B

The network could be drawn thus

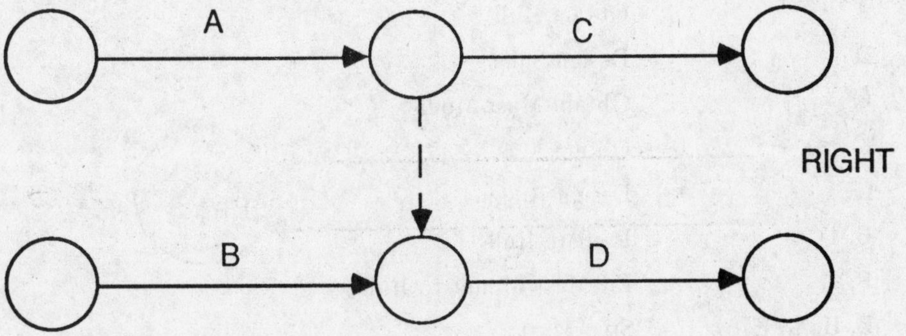

If the network had been drawn as follows it would have been incorrect.

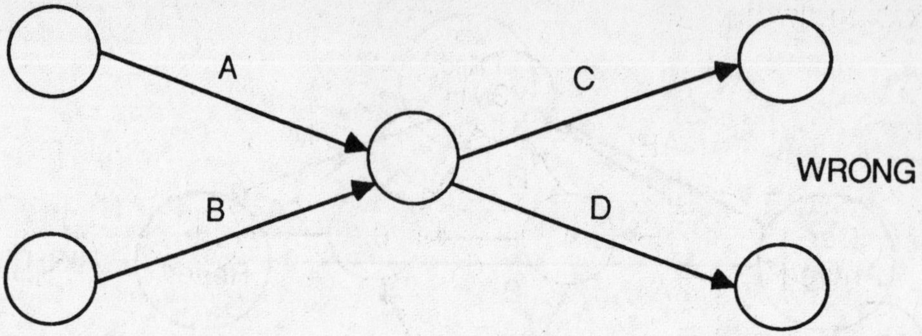

It is incorrect because it depicts that the cigarette case cannot be put away (C) until the match has been struck (B) which is incorrect according to the precedence rules given above.

NETWORK EXAMPLE.

9. To summarise the material so far, a simple network example is given. Try to draw the network yourself and compare the logic of your network with the solution given.

Project XXX Building a Boat.

Activity	Preceding Activity	Activity Description
A	-	Design Hull
B	-	Prepare Boat Shed
C	A	Design Mast and Mast mount
D	A	Obtain Hull
E	A	Design Sails
F	C	Obtain Mast Mount
G	C	Obtain Mast
H	C	Design Rigging
J	B, D	Prepare Hull
K	F, J	Fit Mast Mount to Hull
L	E, H, G, K	Step Mast
M	E, H	Obtain Sails and Rigging
N	L, M	Fit Sails and Rigging

PROJECT XXX NETWORK.

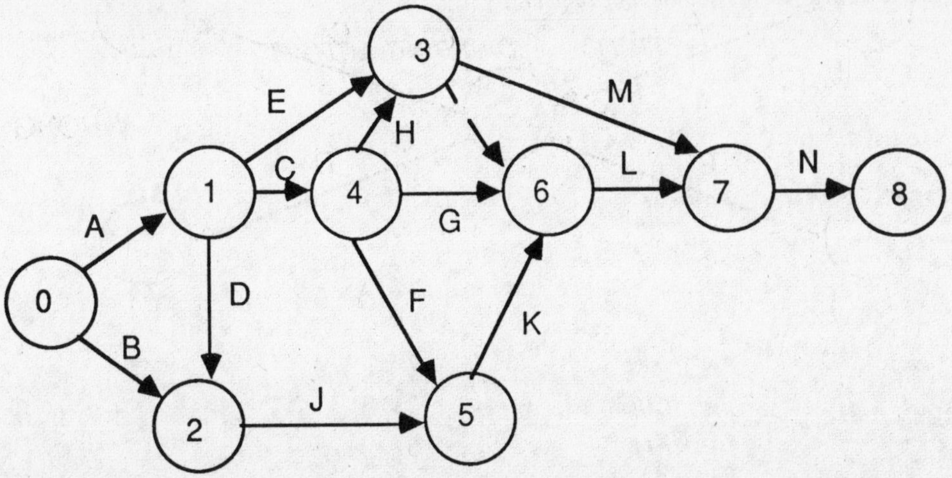

Notes on solution given.

a. The events have been numbered from 0, the start event, through to 7, the finish event.
b. A dummy (3-6) was necessary because of the preceding activity requirements of activity L. If activitites E, H had not been specified as preceding activity L, the dummy would not have been necessary.
c. The shape of the network is unimportant but the logic must be correct.

SUMMARY.

10.

a. Network analysis is used for the planning and control of large, complex projects.
b. Networks comprise activities (represented thus ⟶) and events (represented thus ○). Activities consume time and resources, events are points in time.
c. Networks have one start event and one end event. An event is not complete until *all* activities leading into it are complete.
d. The length of the arrows representing activities is not important because networks are not drawn to scale.
e. Dummy activities (represented thus — — — →) are necessary to show logical relationships. They do not consume time or resources. They become necessary as the network is drawn.

POINTS TO NOTE.

11.

a. Network analysis is a popular type of examination question.
b. Network analysis is an important management tool and in some industries notably civil engineering and construction, is used on a day by day basis.
c. Rarely does one draw a network in a neat, orderly fashion at the first attempt. Accordingly it is is a useful examination technique to do a draft and copy this out neatly for the official answer.

SELF REVIEW QUESTIONS.

1 What is Network Analysis? (2)

2 What are activities and events? (4)

3 What are the basic rules for drawing networks? (5)

4 Does the length of an activity arrow represent the time taken? (6)

5 What is a dummy activity? (8)

EXERCISES WITH ANSWERS COMMENCING PAGE 488

A1. Draw the network for the following problem.

ACTIVITY	PRECEDING ACTIVITY
1	–
2, 3, 4	1
5	2
6	3
7	5
8	6
9	7, 8
10	3
11	4
12	9,10,11

A2. draw the network in A1 except that Activity 8 is preceded by 6 and 2.

EXAMINATION QUESTIONS WITH ANSWERS COMMENCING PAGE 488

A3. An insurance company has decided to modernise and refit one of its branch offices. Some of the existing office equipment will be disposed of but the remainder will be returned to the branch on completion of the alterations. Estimates for the alterations are to be invited from a selection of builders and the builder chosen will be responsible for all aspects of the alterations with the exception of the prior removal of the old equipment and its subsequent replacement.

The major elements of the project have been identified as follows, along with their approximate durations and the immediately preceding elements:

	Element	Duration (weeks)	Preceding Element
A	Obtain estimates from selected builders	5	E
B	Decide on builder to be used	1	A
C	Arrange details with selected builder	2	B
D	Alterations take place	14	K
E	Design new premises	16	–
F	Decide which equipment is to be retained	1	E
G	Arrange storage of equipment to be retained	2	F
H	Arrange disposal of remaining equipment	3	F
I	Order new equipment	2	F
J	Take delivery of new equipment	3	I, L
K	Remove old equipment to storage or disposal	4	C,G,H
L	Clear up after builder has finished	2	D
M	Return old equipment from storage	2	I,L

Required:

(a) Draw a network to represent the inter-relationships between the various elements of the project.

(b) What is the minimum time that the alterations can take from commencement of the design stage?

(c) It has been suggested that if the number of builders invited to tender were reduced, the estimates could be obtained in three weeks. What effect would this have on the overall duration of the project?

(d) What is 'independent float'? Do any of the activities in your network possess it and, if so, which?

(ACCA Quantitative Analysis)

Do not attempt to answer parts (b), (c) and (d) yet.

EXERCISES WITHOUT ANSWERS

B1. Draw the network diagram for the following problem

Activity	*Preceding activity*
1	–
2	–
3	1
4	2
5	2
6	2
7	3,4
8	6

B2. Draw the network diagram for the following problem

Activity	*Preceding activity*
A	–
B	A
C	–
D	C
E	–
F	E
G	–
H	A
I	B,D,G
J	H,I
K	J,F
L	K
M	L

EXAMINATION QUESTIONS WITHOUT ANSWER

B3. The following tasks are to be completed on vehicles at a service station. Assume that all the jobs must be done, and that an unlimited number of men is available.

TASKS (Not necessarily in order)		Preceding Task
A	Driver arrives and stops	NONE
B	Driver selects brands of oil and petrol	A
C	Fill petrol tank	B
D	Prepare bill	C and L
E	Receive payment and give stamps	D
F	Wash windscreen	A
G	Polish windscreen	F
H	Check tyre pressure	A
J	Inflate tyres	H
K	Open bonnet	A
L	Check oil requirement	K
M	Add oil	B and L
N	Add distilled water to battery	K
P	Fill radiator	K
Q	Close bonnet	M,N and P
R	Driver departs from forecourt	E,G,J and Q

The radiator, sump and battery are all located under the bonnet for the benefit of this exercise. Draw a network diagram for the above.

24 Network Analysis – Time Analysis

INTRODUCTION.

1. This chapter deals with the main objective of network analysis which is to establish the overall completion time of projects by calculating what is known as the critical path. The basic time analysis of projects is then expanded to cover variable activities and probabilties.

ASSESSING THE TIME.

2. Once the logic has been agreed and the outline network drawn it can be completed by inserting the activity duration times.

a. Time estimates. The analysis of project times can be achieved by using;

i. Single time estimates for each activity. These estimates would be based on the judgement of the individual responsible or by technical calculations using data from similar projects, or.

ii. Multiple time estimates for each activity. The most usual multiple time estimates are three estimates for each activity ie Optimistic (0), Most Likely (ML), and Pessimistic (P). These three estimates are combined to give an expected time and the accepted formula is:

$$\text{Expected time} = \frac{0 + P + 4ML}{6}$$

For example assume that the three estimates for an activity are

Optimistic	11 days
Most likely	15 days
Pessimistic	18 days.

$$\text{Expected time} = \frac{11 + 18 + 4(15)}{6}$$

$$= 14.8 \text{ days}$$

b. Use of time estimates. As the three time estimates are converted to a single time estimate there is no fundamental difference between the two methods as regards the basic time analysis of a network. However, on completion of the basic time analysis, projects with multiple time estimates can be further analysed to give an estimate of the probability of completing the project by a scheduled date. (This is dealt with in detail in para 7).

c. Time units. Time estimates may be given in any unit ie minutes, hours, days, weeks, depending on the project. All times estimates within a project must be in the same units otherwise confusion is bound to occur.

BASIC TIME ANALYSIS – CRITICAL PATH.

3. However sophisticated the time analysis becomes, a basic feature is always the calculation of the project duration which is the duration of the*critical path*.

Critical path. The critical path of a network gives the shortest time in which the whole project can be completed. It is the chain of activities with the longest duration times. There may be more than one critical path in a network and it is possible for the critical path to run through a dummy. The following paragraphs give step by step, the procedure for establishing the critical path.

Earliest start times (EST), Once the activities have been timed it is possible to assess the total project time by calculating the EST's for each activity. The EST is the earliest possible time at which a succeeding activity can start and the method of calculation will be apparent from the following example.

Assume the following network has been drawn and the activity times estimated in days.

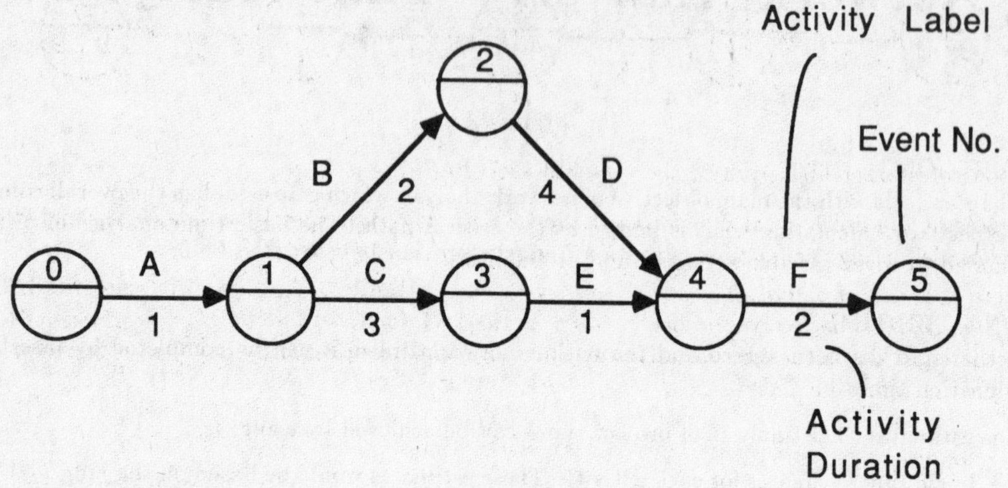

Figure 1

The EST's can be inserted as follows.
EST (Day No)

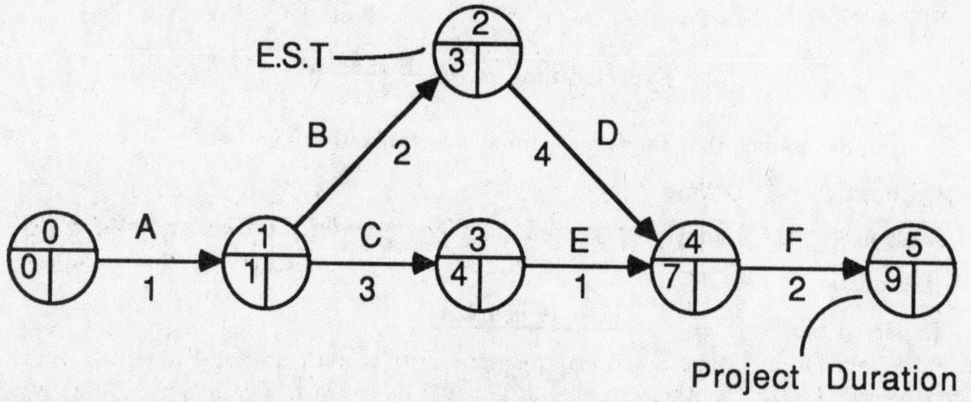

Figure 2

Notes on calculation of EST (termed the FORWARD PASS).

a. The EST of a head event is obtained by adding onto the EST of the tail event the linking activity duration starting from Event 0, time 0 and working forward through the network.

b. Where two or more routes arrive at an event the LONGEST route time must be taken, eg Activity F depends on completion of D and E. E is completed by day 5 and D is not complete until day 7 ∴ F cannot start before day 7.

c. The EST in the finish event No. 5 is the project duration and is the shortest time in which the whole project can be completed.

Latest start times (LST). To enable the critical path to be isolated, the LST for each activity must be established. The LST is the latest possible time at which a preceding activity can finish wihout increasing the project duration. Using the example above the LSTs are as follows.

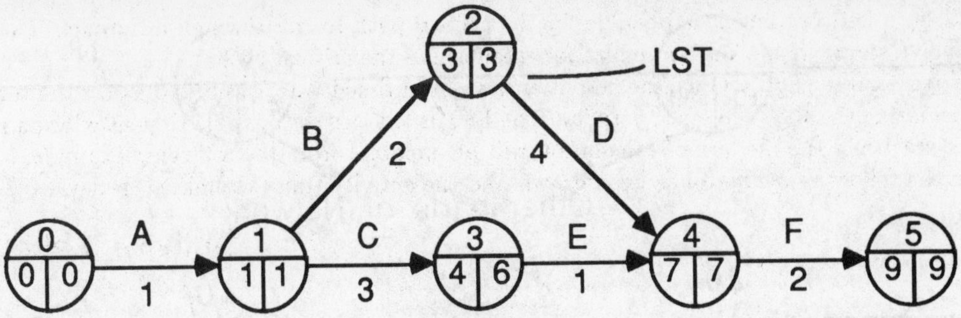

Figure 3

Notes on calculating LST (termed the BACKWARD PASS).

a. Starting at the finish event No. 5, insert the LST (ie day 9) and work backwards through the network deducting each activity duration from the previously calculated LST.

b. Where the tails of activities B and C join event No. 1, the LST for C is day 3 and the LST for B is day 1. The *lowest* number is taken as the LST for Event No. 1 because if event No. 1 occurred at day 3 then activities B and C could not be completed by day 7 as required and the project would be delayed.

CRITICAL PATH.

4. Examination of Figure 3 shows that one path through the network (A, B, D, F) has EST's and LST's which are identifical. This is the critical path which it should be noted is the chain of activities which has the longest duration. The critical patch can be indicated on the network either by a different colour or by two small transverse lines across the arrows along the path thus:

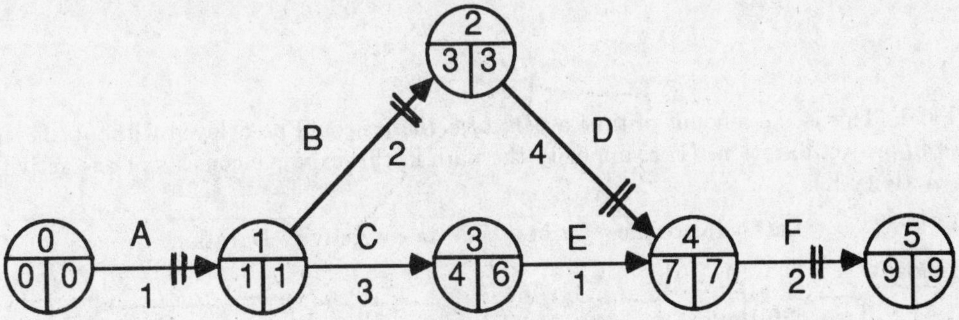

Figure 4

Critical path implications. The activities along the critical path are vital activities which must be completed by their EST's/LST's otherwise the project will be delayed. The non critical activities (in the example above, C and E) have spare time or *float* available ie C and/or E could take up to an additional 2 days in total without delaying the project duration. If it is required to reduce the overall project duration then the time of one or more of the activities on the critical path must be reduced perhaps by using more labour, or more or better equipment or some other method of reducing job times.

Note that for simple networks the critical path can be found by inspection ie looking for the longest route but the above procedure is necessary for larger projects and must be understood. The procedure is similar to that used by most computer programs dealing with network analysis.

FLOAT.

5. Float or spare time can only be associated with activities which are non-critical. By definition, activities on the critical path cannot have float. There are three types of float, Total Float, Free Float and Independent Float. To illustrate these types of float, part of a network will be used together with a bar diagram of the timings thus;

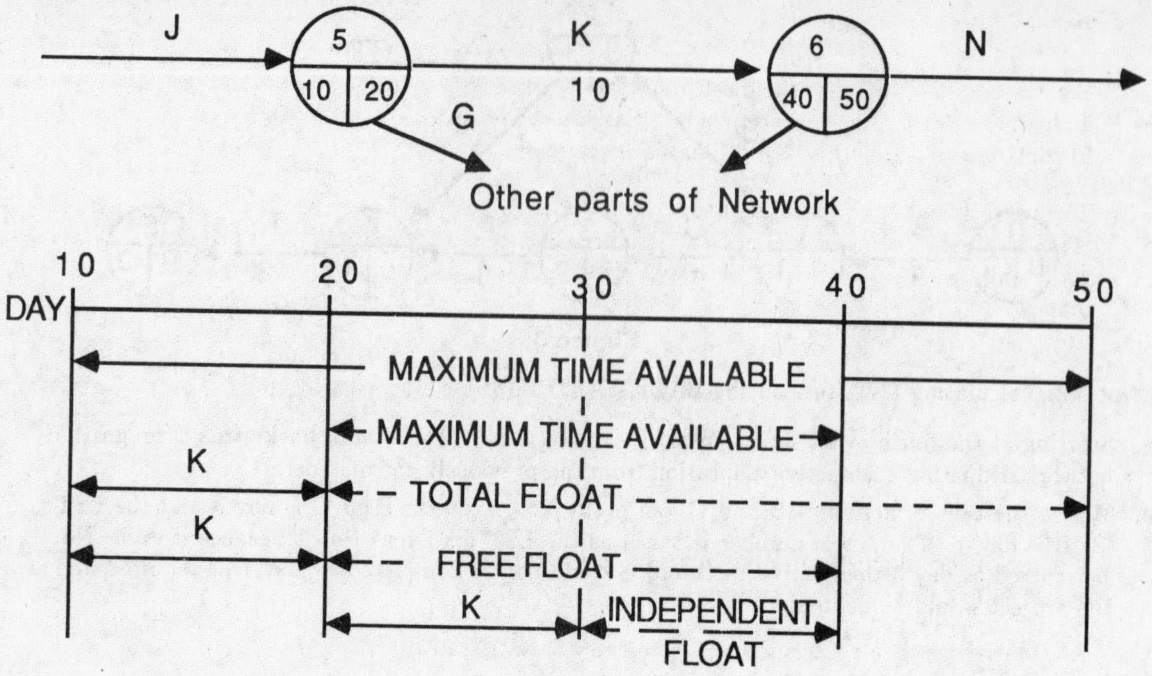

Figure 5

a. Total Float. This is the amount of time a *path of activities* could be delayed without affecting the *overall* project duration. (For simplicity the path in this example consists of one activitity only ie Activity K).

Total Float = Latest Headtime - Earliest Tail time - Activity Duration

Total Float = 50 - 10 - 10

= **30 days**

b. Free Float. This is the amount of time *an activity* can be delayed without affecting the commencement of a *subsequent activity* at its *earliest start time*, but may affect float of a *previous* activity.

Free Float = Earliest Head time - Earliest Tail time - Activity Duration

Free Float = 40 - 10 - 10

= **20 days**

c. Independent float. This is the amount of time an *activity* can be delayed when all preceding activities are completed as late as possible and all succeeding activities completed as early as possible. Independent float therefore does not affect float of either preceding or subsequent activities.

Independent float = Earliest Head time - Latest Tail time - Activity Duration

Independent float = 40 - 20 - 10

= **10 days**

Notes.

a. For examination purposes the most important type of float is Total Float because it is involved with the overall project duration. On occasions the term 'Float' is used without qualification. In such cases assume that Total Float is required.

b. The total float can be calculated separately for each activity but it is often useful to find the total float over chains of non-critical activities between critical events. For example in Figure 4 the only non-cricitical chain of activities is C, E for which the following calculation can be made:

Non-critical chain	Time Required	Time available	Total float over Chain
C,E	3 + 1 = 4 days	7 - 1 = 6 days	= 2 days

If some of the 'chain float' is used up on one of the activities in a chain it reduces the leeway available to other activities in the chain.

c. Alternative terms for Earliest Head Time and Latest Headtime are earliest.

Finishing Time (EFT) and Latest Finishing Time (LFT), respectively.

EXAMPLE OF FLOAT CALCULATIONS.

6. The example used in the preceding chapter is reproduced below with the addition of activity durations. It is required to find the critical path and all floats.

Project XXX Building a Boat

Activity	Preceding Activity	Activity Description	Activity Duration (Days)
A	—	Design Hull	9
B	—	Prepare Boat Shed	3
C	A	Design Mast and Mast Mount	8
D	A	Obtain Hull	2
E	A	Design Sails	3
F	C	Obtain Mast Mount	2
G	C	Obtain Mast	6
H	C	Design Rigging	1
J	B, D	Prepare Hull	4
K	F, J	Fit Mast Mount to Hull	1
L	E, H, G, K	Step Mast	2
M	E, H	Obtain Sails and Rigging	3
N	L, M	Fit Sails and Rigging	4

SOLUTION.

The network is shown in the normal manner in Figure 6 from which it will be seen that the critical path is:

Activities A, C, G, L, N with a duration of 29 days.

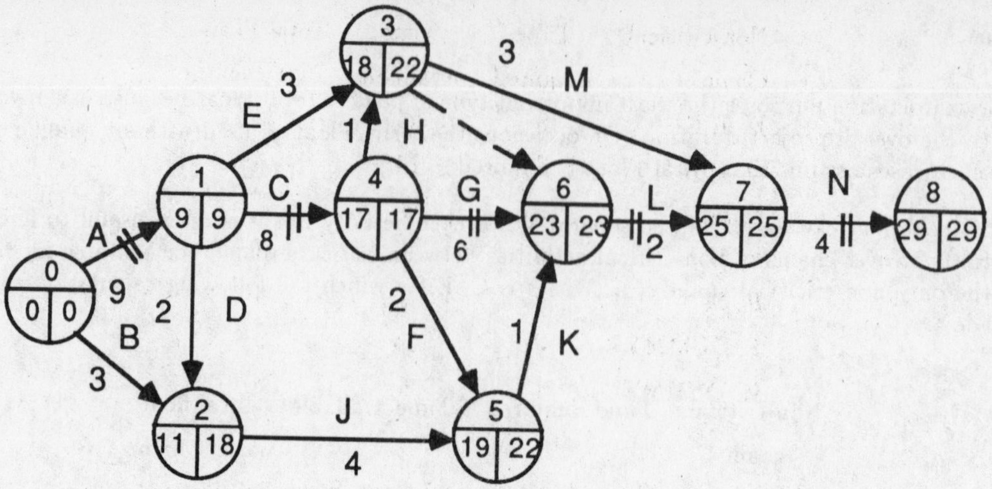

PROJECT XXX NETWORK Figure 6

The float calculations are shown in Table 1.

ACTIVITY		EST	LST	EFT	LFT	D	TOTAL FLOAT (LFT-EST-D)	FREE FLOAT (EFT-EST-D)	INDEPENDENT FLOAT (EFT-LST-D)
A	*	0	0	9	9	9	—	—	—
B		0	0	11	18	3	15	8	8
C	*	9	9	17	17	8	—	—	—
D		9	9	11	18	2	7	—	—
E		9	9	18	22	3	10	6	6
F		17	17	19	22	2	3	—	—
G	*	17	17	23	23	6	—	—	—
H		17	17	18	22	1	4	—	—
J		11	18	19	22	4	7	4	—
K		19	22	23	23	1	3	1	—
L	*	23	23	25	25	2	—	—	—
M		18	22	25	25	3	4	4	—
N	*	25	25	29	29	4	—	—	—

* CRITICAL ACTIVITIES

FLOAT CALCULATIONS
PROJECT XXX
TABLE 1

The total float on the non critical chains can also be calculated:

Non-Critical Chain	Time Required	Time Available	Total Float over chain
B, J, K	8	23	15
D, J, K	7	14	7
F, K	3	6	3
E, M	6	16	10
H, M	4	8	4
E, DUMMY	3	14	9
H, DUMMY	1	6	5

SLACK.

7. This is the difference between the ESt and LST for each *event.* Strictly it does not apply to activities but on occasions the terms are confused in examination questions and unless the context makes it abundantly clear that *event* slack is required, it is likely that some form of activitiy float is required. Events on the critical path have zero slack.

FURTHER PROJECT TIME ANALYSIS.

8. More sophisticated time analysis presupposes that some form of distribution is available for each activity time estimate, for example, the three time estimates described in Para 2. These can be used to make statements about the probability of achieving scheduled dates.

Probability example. Assume that a simple project has the following network. The activity times are in weeks and three estimates have been given for each activity thus:

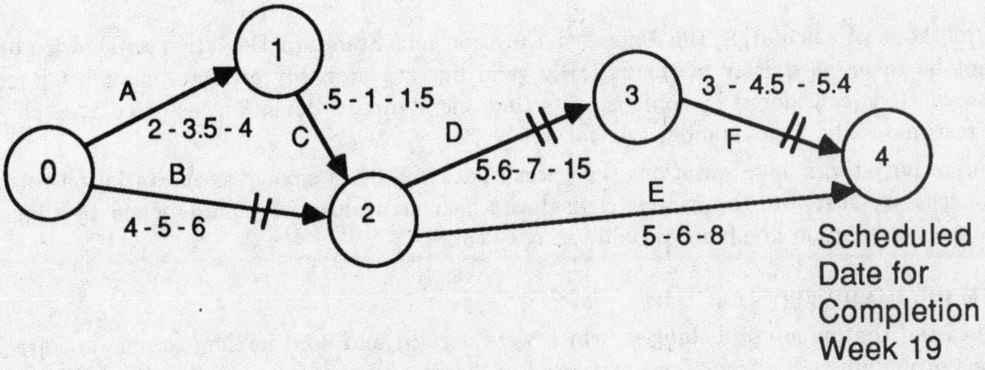

Figure 7

Critical Path (B, D, F) Expected Duration

$$B = \frac{4 + 6 + 4(5)}{6} = 5 \text{ weeks}$$

$$D = \frac{5.6 + 15 + 4(7)}{6} = 8.1 \text{ weeks}$$

$$F = \frac{3 + 5.4 + 4(4.5)}{6} = \underline{4.4}$$

$$\underline{17.5}$$

If the critical activities were to occur at their optimistic times, event 4 would be reached in 12.6 weeks and if the critical activities occurred at their pessimistic times, event 4 would be reached in 26.4 weeks. As these durations span the scheduled date of week 19 some estimate of the probability of achieving the schedule date must be calculated, as follows.

a. Make an estimate of the Standard Deviation for each of the critical activities. If no additional information is avilable the following formula can be used.

$$\frac{\text{PESSIMISTIC TIME} - \text{OPTIMISTIC TIME}}{6}$$

$$\text{ie Activity B} = \frac{6-4}{6} = .33$$

$$\text{Activity D} = \frac{15-5.6}{6} = 1.57$$

$$\text{Activity F} = \frac{5.4-3}{6} = .4$$

b. Find the standard deviation of event 4 by calculating the statistical sum (the square root of the sum of the squares) of the standard deviations of all activities on the critical path.

$$\text{ie Standard Deviation of Event 4} = \sqrt{(.33^2 + 1.57^2 + .4^2)}$$

$$= 1.65 \text{ weeks}$$

c. Find the number of event standard deviations that the scheduled date is away from the expected duration.

$$\text{ie } \frac{19-17.5}{1.65} = 91$$

d. Look up this value (.91) in a table of areas under the Normal Curve to find the probability (Table I). In this case the probability of achieving the scheduled date of week 19 is 82% .

Probability interpretation. If management consider that the probability of 82% is not high enough, efforts must be made to reduce the times or the spread of time of activities on the critical path. It is an inefficient use of resources to try to make the probability of reaching the scheduled date 100% or very close to 100% . In this case management may well accept the 18% chance of not achieving the schedule date as realistic.

Notes.

a. The methods of calculating the Expected Duration and Standard Deviation as shown above cannot be taken as strictly mathematically valid but are probably accurate enough for most purposes. It is considered by some experts that the standard deviation, as calculated above, underestimatest he 'true' standard deviation.

b. When activity times have variations the critical path will often change as the variations occur. It is necessary therefore to examine critical and near critical activity paths when tackling an examination question involving variable activity times.

DISCRETE PROBABILITIES.

9. Instead of the continuous probabilities, which were derived and used in the example in Para 7 above, on occasions probabilities are sometimes expressed in discrete terms. For example the time estimates for an activity could be given as follows:

	Estimates	
Activity	Time	Probability
A	8 weeks	.6
	11 weeks	.4 weeks

The expected time for activity A would be $(8 \times .6) + (11 \times .4) =$ 9.2 WEEKS.

Discrete probability example. Assume that time estimates have been made for the following network using discrete probabilities thus:

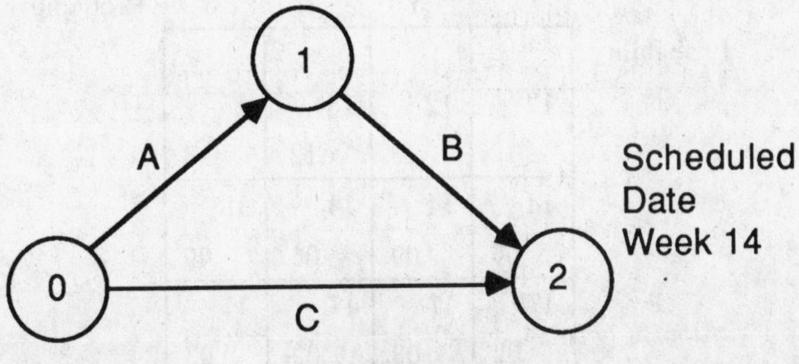

Figure 8

Activity	Estimates Time (Weeks)	Probability
A	6	.5
	10	.5
B	3	.4
	5	.6
C	12	.6
	14	.3
	17	.1

The expected times for the activities are:

$$A = (6 \times .5) + (10 \times .5) = 8$$
$$B = (3 \times .4) + (5 \times .6) = 4.2$$
$$C = (12 \times .6) + (14 \times .3) + (17 \times .1) = 13.1$$

On the basis of the expected times the critical path is C with a duration of 13.1 weeks. However, numerous other possibilities exist and the probabilities of the various completion times and thus of achieving the schedule date of week 14 can be evaluated as follows:

The A, B route can have four durations, each with an associated probability thus:

A, B route

Durations	9	11	13	15	weeks
Probability	.2	.3	.2	.3	

(These values are found by combining the durations and probabilities of Activities A and B. For example Activity A duration of 6 weeks, probability .5, can be combined with Activity B duration of 3 weeks, probability .4, to give 9 weeks duration and probability of .2(ie .5 × .4).

C route

Duration	12	14	17	weeks
Probability	.6	.3	.1	

The A, B route and the C route alternate as the critical path with varying probabilities as shown in the following table.

			A B ROUTE				
			9	11	13	15	Duration
			.2	.3	.2	.3	Probability
	Duration	Probability					
	12	.6	12 .12	12 .18	13 * .12	15 .18	
C ROUTE	14	.3	14 .06	14 .09	14 .06	15 .09	
	17	.1	17 .02	17 .03	17 .02	17 .03	

*This means that if the A, B route with 13 weeks duration, probability .2, occurs at the same time as the C route duration of 12 weeks, probability .6, the critical path would be 13 weeks ie the longer duration, with the probability of .12(.6 × .2)

SUMMARY OF POSSIBLE DURATIONS

12 WEEKS PROBABILITY (.12 + .18)	=	.30
13 WEEKS PROBABILITY (.12)	=	.12
14 WEEKS PROBABILITY (.06 + .09 + .06)	=	.21
15 WEEKS PROBABILITY (.18 + .09)	=	.27
17 WEEKS PROBABILITY (0.2 + 0.3 + .02 + 0.3)	=	.10
		1.00

Thus the probability of achieving 14 weeks or less is .62 (.30 + .12 + .21) and the probability of exceeding the scheduled date is .37

SUMMARY.

10.

a. Basic time analysis of a network involves calculating the critical path ie the shortest time in which the project can be completed.

b. The critical path is established by calculating the EST (Earliest Start Times) and LST (Latest Start Time) for each event and comparing them. The critical path is the chain of activities where the EST's and LST's are the same.

c. Float is the spare time available on non-critical activities. There are three types of float; total float, free float and independent float.

d. To calculate the probability of achieving scheduled dates it is necessary to establish what variability is likely to exist for each activity.

e. Given activity time estimates the expected value of the project duration is calculated and an estimate made of the activity standard deviations.

f. The activity standard deviations are combined to form the standard deviation of the overall project so that probability estimates can be made for various project duration possibilities.

POINTS TO NOTE.

11.

a. The problems of dealing with uncertainty occur again and again in quantitative techniques. Increasingly examination questions are likely to contain variable activity times and associated probabilities.

b. When variable time estimates are used, near critical paths may have more variability than the critical path so the near critical paths may influence probability estimates.

c. The basis of the Standard Deviation estimate given in para 7 is the Normal Distribution. It is known that virtually all of the distribution lies within the mean $\pm 3\sigma$ hence the formula given ie. $\frac{\text{max - min}}{6} = \sigma$.

However the tails of the distribution are unlikely to occur very often so the 95% concept may be used in which case the range becomes mean $\pm 2\sigma$. If this is thought to be realistic the revised formula below can be used.

$$\frac{\text{Pessimistic time - Optimistic time}}{4} = \sigma.$$

SELF REVIEW QUESTIONS.

1 What types of time estimates are made for activity durations? (2)

2 What is the critical path? (3)

3 What are the EST's and LST's (3)

4 How is the critical path determined? (4)

5 What is float? (5)

6 When multiple time estimates of activity durations are available how can an estimate be calculated of the probability of completing the network in a given time? (8)

EXERCISES WITH ANSWERS COMMENCING PAGE 488

A1. Find the critical path of the following network using the EST/LSTs.

Activity	*Preceding Activity*	*Duration (days)*
1	-	4
2	1	7
3	1	5
4	1	6
5	2	2
6	3	3
7	5	5
8	2, 6	11
9	7, 8	7
10	3	4
11	4	3
12	9, 10, 11	4

A2. Calculate the floats of the network in A1.

A3. The standard deviations of the activities on the critical path in A1 are: 1, 2, 1.5, 3, 2.5 and 3 respectively. Based on these values calculate the probability of achieving a scheduled time of 40 days for the project duration.

EXAMINATION QUESTIONS WITH ANSWERS COMMENCING PAGE 488

A4. On 1 September each year, Salemis Limited begins the task of preparing budgets for the coming year. The various stages in the budgeting process have been identified as follows:

	Stage	Preceding Stage(s)	Time (weeks)
A	*Estimate wage rates*	—	2
B.	*Develop a market forecast*	—	4
C.	*Fix selling prices*	—	3
D.	*Prepare sales quantities budget*	B	3
E.	*Prepare sales revenue budget*	C, D	1
F.	*Prepare selling expenses budget*	A, D	3
G.	*Prepare production quantities budget*	D	6
H.	*Prepare overheads budget*	A	4
I.	*Prepare manpower budget*	A, G	2
J.	*Prepare materials budget*	G	3
K.	*Prepare plant and equipment budget*	G	5
L.	*Produce overall profit forecast*	E, F, H, I, J, K	1

The whole process must be completed by the end of December which gives a period of 17 working weeks.
Required:

(a) Draw a network to represent the sequence of stages involved in the preparation of budgets. Can the whole process be completed within the required period of 17 weeks?

(b) If it is necessary to reduce the time taken to complete the budgeting process, which stages should be investigated and why?

(c) Explain the difference between total float, free float and independent float. Show that stage 1 has a free float of 3 weeks, of which 2 weeks is independent float.

(ACCA QUANTITATIVE ANALYSIS)

A5. Consider the following data for a small project

Activity	Estimated time (days)			Standard
	Optimistic	Mean	Pessimistic	deviation
1–2	2	4	6	1
1–3	11	13	15	1
1–4	2	5	8	1.5
2–4	3	6	9	1.5
2–3	1	3	5	1
2–5	2	4	6	1
3–6	3	7	11	2
4–6	4	8	12	2
5–6	4	9	14	2

The estimated times for each activity are independent of the estimates for any other activity.
You are required to:

(a) identify all the paths through the network;

(b) calculate and state the time for completion of the project, assuming that:

i. *the mean time for each activity is achieved*

ii. *the optimistic time for each activity is achieved;*

iii. *the pessimistic time for each activity is achieved;*

(c) calculate and state the variance of the critical path in (b) (i) and (b) (iii) above;

(d) calculate and state the probability of completing the critical path in (b) (i) and (b) (iii) above in 17 days or less, assuming that activity times are normally distributed.

(CIMA QUANTITATIVE TECHNIQUES)

A6. The Hydra Company manufactures a range of hair care cand shaving products, including disposable razors. A competitor has recently introduced a new style of disposable razor which, in the last six months, has taken a significant share of the market, with adverse effects on Hydra's sales. The management at Hydra has decided that a competitive product must be introduced as quickly as possible and has asked Jim Sharp, the management accountant, to draw up a plan for developing and marketing this new product.

As the first step in planning the project, Jim Sharp has identified the following major tasks which will be involved in the new product launch. He has also estimated how long each task will take and what other taks must precede each one.

	Task	Time (weeks)	Preceding Tasks
A.	Design new product	8	—
B.	Design packaging	4	—
C.	Organise production facilities	4	A
D.	Obtain production materials	2	A
E.	Manufacture trial batch	3	C, D
F.	Obtain packaging	2	B
G.	Decide on test market area	1	—
H.	Package trial batch	2	E, F
I.	Distribute product in test area.	3	H, G
J.	Conduct test market	4	I
K.	Assess test market results	3	J
L.	Plan national launch	4	K

Required:

(a) Draw a network to represent the logical sequence of tasks and determine how long it will be before the new product can be launched. (You may assume that the national launch can take place immediately after it has been planned.)

(b) Calculate the float which is available for each of the non-critical activities.

(c) The time taken to complete taks A, B, D, K and L is somewhat uncertain and so the following optimistic and pessimistic estimates have also been made to supplement the most likely figure given above. These additional estimates are:

Task	Optimistic Time (weeks)	Pessimistic Time (weeks)
A	5	13
B	2	6
D	1	4
K	2	6
L	2	8

What now is the expected time until the product can be launched and what is the probability of this time exceeding 35 weeks? (You should assume that the overall project duration follows a normal distribution.)

(ACCA Quantitative Analysis)

A7. The group chief accountant of the Nisus Car company has asked you to arrange a training course on 'Financial Planning Using Micro-Computers' for the accounts staff within the group's six subsidiary companies. Having decided upon a two-week course, you list the various jobs which will need doing along with their estimated times and any necessary preceding jobs, as follows:

	Job	Time (weeks)	Preceding Jobs
A	Arrange Programme	2	—
B	Prepare Publicity	3	A
C	Publicise Course	2	B
D	Receive Applications	4	C
E	Prepare Course Material	8	A
F	Decide on Location of Course	1	D
G	Arrange Accommodation	2	F
H	Arrange Computer Facilities	3	F
I	Run Course	2	E, G, H
J	Set Course Assignments	3	D, E
K	Mark Assignments	2	I, J
L	Post-Course Evaluation	1	I, K

Required:

(a) Assuming that the work of organising the course can start immediately, what is the minimum number of weeks that must elapse before the course can be run?

(b) After the post-course evaluation, you must report back to the group chief accountant on the success of the course. How long will it take (i.e. how many weeks) before you can begin to compile your report?

(c) Comment on how any uncertainty might be analysed within a situation such as this.

(ACCA Quantitative Analysis)

A8. Complete Question A3, Chapter 23.

EXERCISES WITHOUT ANSWERS.

B1.

Find the critical path of the following activities using EST/LST.

ACTIVITY	*PRECEDING ACTIVITY*	*DURATION (WEEKS)*
A	—	*3*
B	*A*	*4*
C	—	*6*
D	*C*	*5*
E	—	*4*
F	*E*	*3*
G	—	*5*
H	*A*	*6*
I	*B, D, G*	*8*
J	*H, I*	*6*
K	*J, F*	*8*
L	*K*	*1*
M	*L*	*2*

B2. Find the floats for the network in B1.

EXAMINATION QUESTIONS WITHOUT ANSWERS

B3. Delta Ltd., in planning a project to introduce a new product, has listed the following necessary activities.

Activity	*Preceding Activity*	*Expected Time (weeks)*
A	—	6
B	—	3
C	A	5
D	A	4
E	A	3
F	C	3
G	D	5
H	B, D, E	5
I	H	2
J	F, G, I	3

Required:

a. Draw the critical path network for the project and determine the critical path and its duration.

b. If the start of activity B is delayed by 3 weeks, activity E by 2 weeks and activity G by 2 weeks, how is the total time for the project affected?

c. Assume that the times given in the above table are the expected times of the activities, the durations of which are normally distributed with the following standard deviations:

Activity:	A	B	C	D	E	F	G	H	I	J
Standard Deviation	1	0.5	1	1	0.5	0.5	1	1	0.5	1

Ignoring the delays referred to in (b) and the possible effect of uncertainty in non-critical activities, determine a 95% confidence interval for the expected time on the critical path.

d. The costs of the projects are estimated to be £100,000. If it is completed within 24 weeks the expected returns should be about £1,000,000 but if the deadline of 24 weeks is not met, the product will fail to penetrate the market and a net revenue of only £20,000 is expected. Determine the expected profit on this project. (For simplicity, you should again ignore the delays referred to in (b) and the possible effect of uncertainty in non-critical activities.

(ACCA, Management Mathematics)

25 Network Analysis – Cost Scheduling

INTRODUCTION.

1. This chapter develops the analysis of networks and deals with the cost aspect of activities and the process of least cost scheduling sometimes known as 'crashing' the network.

COSTS AND NETWORKS.

2. A further important feature of network analysis is concerned with the costs of activities and of the project as a whole. This is sometimes known as PERT/COST.

Cost analysis objectives. The primary objective of network cost analysis is to be able to calculate the cost of various project durations. The *normal* duration of a project incurs a given cost and by more labour, working overtime, more equipment etc the duration could be reduced but at the expense of higher costs. Some ways of reducing the project duration will be cheaper than others and network cost analysis seeks to select the cheapest way of reducing the overall duration.

Penalties and Bonuses. A common feature of many projects is a penalty clause for delayed completion and/or a bonus for earlier completion. In examination questions, network costs analysis is often combined with a penalty and/or bonus situation with the general aim of calculating whether it is worthwhile paying extra to reduce the project time so as to save a penalty.

Cost and networks - basic definitions.

a. Normal cost. The costs associated with a normal time estimate for an activity. Often the 'normal' time estimate is set at the point where resources (men, machines etc) are used in the most efficient manner.

b. Crash cost. The costs associated with the minimum possible time for an activity. Crash costs, because of extra wages, overtime premiums, extra facility costs are always higher than normal costs.

c. Crash time. The minimum possible time that an activity is planned to take. The minimum time is invariably brought about by the application of extra resources, eg more labour or machinery.

d. Cost slope. This is the average cost of shortening an activity by one time unit (day, week, month as appropriate). The cost slope is generally assumed to be linear and is calculated as follows:

$$\text{COST SLOPE} = \frac{\text{CRASH COST - NORMAL COST}}{\text{NORMAL TIME - CRASH TIME}}$$

eg Activity A data:

Normal	Crash
Time | Cost	Time | cost
12 days at £480	8 days at £640

$$\text{Cost slope} = \frac{640 - 480}{12 - 8} = \underline{\mathbf{£40/day}}$$

e. Least cost scheduling or 'crashing'. The process which finds the least cost method of reducing the overall project duration, time period by time period. The following example shows the process step by step.

LEAST COST SCHEDULING RULES.

3. The basic rule of least cost scheduling is simply stated. Reduce the time of the activity on the critical path with the lowest cost slope and progressively repeat this process until the desired reduction in time is achieved. Complications occur when time reductions cause several paths to become critical simultaneously thus necessitating several activities to be reduced at the same time. These complications are explained below as they occur.

Least cost scheduling example.

A project has five activities and it is required to prepare the least cost schedules for all possible durations from 'normal time' – 'normal cost' to 'crash time' – 'crash cost'.

Project Data	Preceding	Time (Days)		Costs(£'s)		Cost (£)
Activity	Activity	Normal	Crash	Normal	Crash	Slope
A	-	4	3	360	420	60
B	-	8	5	300	510	70
C	A	5	3	170	270	50
D	A	9	7	220	300	40
E	B, C	5	3	200	360	80

PROJECT NETWORK.

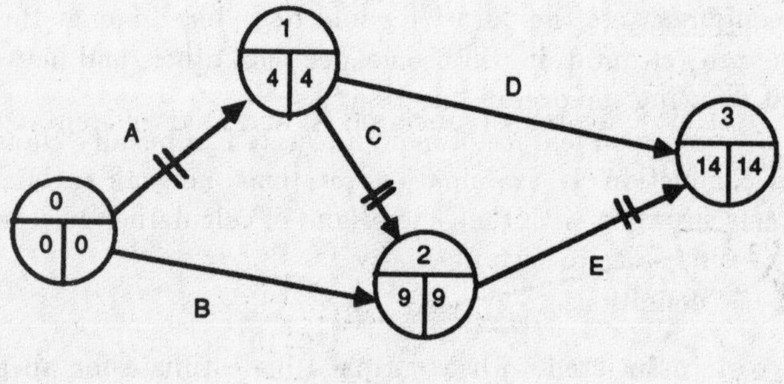

Figure 1

Project durations and costs.

a. Normal Duration **14 days.**
Critical path A, C, E
Project cost (ie cost of ALL activities at normal time) = £1250

b. Reduce by 1 day the activity on the critical path with the lowest cost slope.
Reduce activity C at extra cost of £50
Project Duration **13 days**
Project cost **£1300**
N.B. *All* activities are now critical.

c. Several alternative ways are possible to reduce the project time by a further 1 day but not 2 or 3 activities need to be shortened because there are several critical paths.
POSSIBILITIES AVAILABLE.

Reduce by 1 day	Extra Costs	Activities critical
A and B	£60 + 70 = £130	All
D and E	£40 + 80 = £120	All
B, C and D	£70 + 50 + 40 = £160	All
A and E	£60 + 80 = £140	A, D, B, E

An indication of the total extra costs apparently indicates that the second alternative (ie D and E reduced) is the cheapest. However, closer examination of the last alternative (ie A and E reduced) reveals that activity C is non-critical and with 1 day float. It will be recalled that Activity C was reduced by 1 day previously at an extra cost of £50. If in conjunction with the A and E reduction, Activity C is INCREASED by 1 day, the £50 is saved and all activities become critical. The net cost therefore for the 12 day duration is £1300 + (140 - 50) = £1390. The network is now as follows:

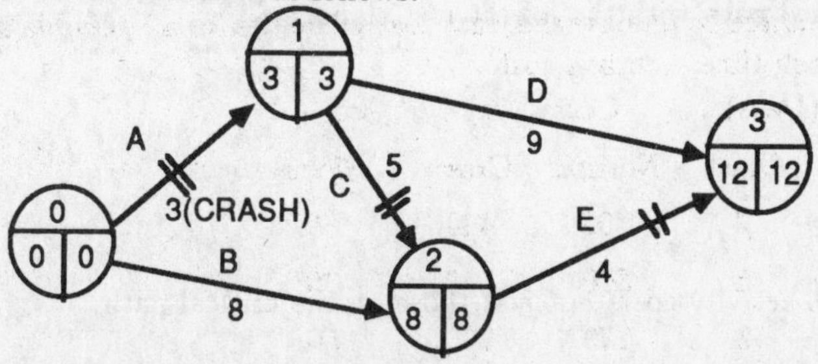

Duration **12 days**

Cost **£1390**

All activities critical

d. the next reduction would be achieved by reducing D and E at an increase of £120 with once again all activities being critical.

Project duration **11 days**

Project cost **£1510**

e. The final reduction possible is made by reducing B, C and D at an increased cost of £160. The final network becomes,

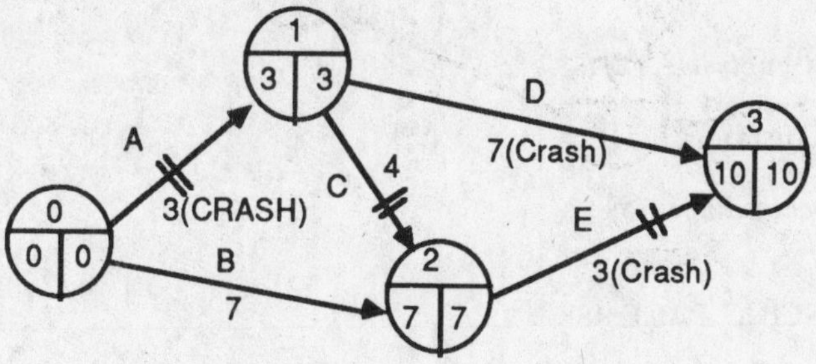

Duration **10 days**

Cost **£1670**

All activities critical

CRASHING NETWORKS IN EXAMINATIONS.

4. All the principles necessary to crash networks have already been covered and the following points may save time in an examination.

a. Only critical activities affect the project duration so take care not to crash non-critical activities.
b. The minimum possible project duration is not necessarily the most profitable option. It may be cost effective to pay some penalties to avoid higher crash costs.
c. If there are several independent critical paths then several activities will need to be crashed simultaneously. If there are several critical paths which are not separate ie they share an activity or activities, then it may be cost effective to crash the shared activities even though they may not have the lowest cost slopes.
d. Always look for the possibility of INCREASING the duration of a previously crashed activity when subsequent crashing renders it non-critical, ie it has float.

SUMMARY.

5.

a. Cost analysis of networks seeks the cheapest ways of reducing project times.

b. The crash cost is the cost associated with the minimum possible time for an actitivy, which is known as the crash time.

c. The average cost of shortening an activity by one time period (day, weeks etc) is known as the cost slope.

d. Least cost scheduling finds the cheapest method of reducing the overall project time by reducing the time of the activity on the critical path with the lowest cost slope.

POINTS TO NOTE.

6.

a. The total project cost includes *ALL* activity costs not just those on the critical path.

b. The usual assumption is that the cost slope is linear. This need not be so and care should be taken not to make the linearity assumption when circumstances point to some other conclusion.

c. The example used in this chapter includes increasing the time of a subcritical activity, which has already been crashed, so saving the extra costs incurred. Always look for such possibilities.

d. Dummy activities have zero slopes and cannot be crashed.

SELF REVIEW QUESTIONS.

1 What is the objective of network cost analysis? (2)

2 What are 'normal' costs and 'crash' costs? (2)

3 What is the basic rule of least cost scheduling? (3)

EXERCISES WITH ANSWERS COMMENCING PAGE 488

A1. Calculate the cost slopes and the critical path of the following network.

Activity	*Preceding Activity*	*TIME NORMAL*	*CRASH*	*COST NORMAL*	*CRASH*
1	—	*6*	*4*	*500*	*620*
2	—	*4*	*2*	*300*	*390*
3	*1*	*7*	*6*	*650*	*680*
4	*1*	*3*	*2*	*400*	*450*
5	*2, 3*	*5*	*3*	*850*	*1000*

A2. Construct a least cost schedule for the network in A1 showing all durations from normal time - normal cost to crash time – crash cost.

EXAMINATION QUESTIONS WITH ANSWERS COMMENCING PAGE

A3. Consider a project which requires the following activities:

Activity		*Activity time (in days)*		*Total Cost (£)*	
Initial node	*Terminal node*	*Normal*	*Crash*	*Normal*	*Crash*
0	1	12	9	800	950
0	2	8	6	750	850
0	4	14	8	1,060	1,500
2	3	4	2	550	750
3	4	1	1	200	200
1	5	9	6	770	950
1	6	12	10	950	1,400
4	5	8	8	760	760
5	7	7	1	620	750
6	7	4	4	540	540

Site costs are £200 per day.
Each activity must be completed either in normal time or crash time.
It is not possible to partly crash a particular activity.
Note: *critical paths should be described by the use of node numbers.*
You are required to:

(a) calculate and state the normal critical path, normal duration of the project and normal cost;

(b) calculate and state the minimum time in which the project could be completed, the related critical activities, and the associated minimum cost;

(c) calculate and state the minimum cost for which the project could be completed, the related critical activities and the associated minimum duration;

(d) comment briefly on **three** *of the problems which have to be overcome when using this technique to help complete a construction project within the edstimated cost and time.*

(CIMA Quantitative Techniques)

A4. Orbona Office Equipment Limited have recently developed a new colour copying machine and are planning to launch it at a forthcoming trade show. In the meantime, salesmen and service engineers will have to be trained to deal with the new copier, the necessary documentation and publicity material must be got ready, and the preparations for the show itself must be completed. In particular, the product manager has drawn up a list of the activities which will be involved and he has also estimated the order and approximate cost and duration of each activity as shown in the following table.

	Activity Description	*Preceding Activities*	*Cost (£'00)*	*Duration (weeks)*
A	*Train Salesman*	C,J	60	3
B	*Train Service Engineers*	C,I	80	4
C	*Prepare Instruction Manuals*	—	30	10
D	*Organise Trade Show Display*	G,J	20	4
E	*Train Staff for Trade Show*	D	5	1
F	*Arrange Pre-Release Publicity*	H,J	60	3
G	*Arrange Staff for Trade Show*	H	2	2
H	*Set up Sales Office*	—	45	5
I	*Have Service Contract Prepared*	—	30	5
J	*Produce Promotional Material*	I	120	8

Required:

(a) Represent the stages involved in the product launch in the form of an appropriate network of activities. Given that the trade show will take place in 6 months (i.e. 26 weeks time), can all the necessary activities be completed in time for the show?

(b) Draw a graph showing the week by week schedule of cumulative cash flows assuming that all activities commence at their earliest time. (You may also assume that, for each activity, the cost is incurred evenly over the duration of the activity.) Comment briefly on the form of your graph.

(ACCA Quantitative Analysis)

A5. The following activities, with associated costs and times, represent those necessary for the completion of a project to be started by your organisation next month.

Activity	Preceding activity(ies)	Normal Cost (£)	Normal Time (days)	Crash Cost (£)	Crash Time (days)
A	—	250	5	370	3
B	A	160	4	160	4
C	A	360	6	750	3
D	A,C	490	7	950	6
E	B,C	640	8	1,300	4
F	E,D	390	6	760	3
G	E,F	230	5	450	3

The cost and time in the 'crash' columns are the estimates for an alternative time, except for activity B, and represent the total (not extra) cost of the new, shorter time for each activity.

Site costs associated with the project are estimated at £300 per day.

You are required to:

(a) calculate, and state, the critical path(s) and the cost of completion in the normal time;

(b) calculate, and state, the critical path(s) and cost of completion in the crash time;

(c) calculate and state the minimum cost of completion and the associated critical path(s) and time;

(d) mention **two** *problems that have to be considered in the practical implemention of critical path analaysis.*

CIMA Quantitative Techniques.

EXERCISES WITHOUT ANSWERS

B1.

Activity	Preceding Activity	Duration Normal – Crash	Cost Slope £
A	—	8 – 4	900
B	—	4 – 3	300
C	B	2 – 1	1,200
D	A,C	3 – 1	600
E	D	3 – 2	1,800

Show all durations from normal to crash time and the extra costs incurred at each stage.

B2. . The activities in B1 represent the maintenance schedule for a peice of equipment and it has been estimated that £1000 per day is lost for each day the equipment is out of action.

What is the optimal duration?

EXAMINATION QUESTIONS WITHOUT ANSWERS

B3. Your managerial colleagues have recently heard of the techniques of Critical Path Analysis (CPA) and Program Evaluation and Review Technique (PERT).

They are considering a project which can be divided into activities A to H. Estimates have been made of the time and cost each will take under normal conditions and under 'crash conditions'.

Activity	Preceding activities	Normal days	program Cost	Crash days	program Cost
			£		£
A	—	3	160	1	240
B	—	4	230	2	270
C	A,B	4	280	2	300
D	B	5	240	2	290
E	C,D	8	440	4	600
F	E	6	320	4	450
G	A	18	700	10	1,500
H	G,F	6	320	5	400

Site costs are estimated at £300 per day.

Activity G, whose normal time was 18 days costing £700, can be reduced by one day at a time at an extra cost of £100 per day down to 10 days costing £1,500. The other activities can be completed either in normal time and cost or in crash time and cost.

You are required to:

(a) identify and state the different paths through the network.

(b) calculate and state the normal time for completion and the normal cost;

(c) calculate and state the minimum time for completion and the minimum cost of completion in this time;

(d) explain clearly the purpose, advantages and disadvantages of both CPA and PERT.

(CIMA Quantitative Techniques)

B4. The following information relates to a construction project for which your company is about to sign a contract.

Seven activities are necessary and the normal duration, cost, crash duration, crash cost have been derived from the best available sources.

Activity	Preceding activity	Duration in weeks Normal	Crash	Direct Cost Normal £	Crash £
a	—	15	12	4,500	5,250
b	—	19	14	4,000	4,500
c	—	9	5	2,500	4,500
d	a	6	5	1,700	1,940
e	a	14	9	4,300	5,350
f	b,d	9	6	2,600	3,440
g	c	8	3	1,800	3,400

Each activity may be reduced to the crash duration in weekly stages at a pro rata cost. There is a fixed cost of £500 per week.

You are required to:

a. draw, clearly labelled, a network and indicate the notation pattern used;

b. indicate the critical path and state the normal duration and cost;

c. calculate the minimum total cost, showing clearly your workings, and the revised duration and cost for each activity.

(CIMA QUANTITATIVE TECHNIQUES)

B5. Delco Ltd., a small engineering company, intends to produce a batch of machines to be used by a shoe manufacturer in the mass production of shoes.

The activities required in the design and manufacture of the machine are listed below, together with duration and costs.

	Activity	Preceding Activity	Duration (weeks)	Cost (£)
A	Draw up estimate of costs	—	2	400
B	Agree estimate	A	1	0
C	Purchase internal machinery	B	4	200
D	Prepare design drawings	B	6	450
E	Construct main frame	D	3	700
F	Assemble machinery	C,E	3	200
G	Test machinery	F	4	600
H	Determine model type	D	2	0
I	Design outer casing	D	3	250
J	Construct outer casing	H,I	8	600
K	Final assembly	G,J	2	450
L	Final check	K	2	200

In addition to the above cost figures, overheads of £250 per week will be incurred for the duration of the project.

Required:

a. What is the critical path and the duration of the project?

b. i. What would be the effect of a strike at the factory supplying the internal machinery thereby delaying its delivery for four weeks?

ii. What would be the effect if the test on the machinery had been done incorrectly and had to be redone, taking another four weeks?

c. The times of some of the activities could be reduced, the new times and costs being as follows:

Activity	*A*	*B*	*C*	*D*	*E*	*F*	*G*	*H*	*I*	*J*	*K*	*L*
Time (weeks)	*1*	*1*	*2*	*2*	*1*	*1*	*1*	*2*	*2*	*4*	*1*	*1*
Cost (£)	*800*	*0*	*450*	*1150*	*1200*	*600*	*1000*	*0*	*450*	*950*	*700*	*350*

In each activity can only be done in the original time or in the new time, what project time achieves minimum total cost?

(ACCA Management Mathmatics)

26 Network Analysis – Resource Scheduling

INTRODUCTION.

1. This chapter deals with the resource aspects of network analysis and shows how resources of men, machines etc could be scheduled over the project duration to be able to deal with resource and/or time constraints.

RESOURCES AND NETWORKS.

2. The usefulness of networks is not confined only to the time and cost factors which have been discussed so far. Considerable assistance in planning and controlling the use of resources can be given to management by appropriate development of the basic network techniques.

Project resources. The resources (men of varying skills, machines of all types, the required materials, finance, and space) used in a project are subject to varying demands and loadings as the project proceeds. Management need to know what activities and what resources are critical to the project duration and if resource limitations (eg shortage of materials, limited number of skilled craftsmen) might delay the project. They also wish to ensure, as far as possible constant work rates to eliminate paying overtime at one stage of a project and having short time working at another stage.

RESOURCE SCHEDULING REQUIREMENTS.

3. To be able to schedule the resource requirments for a project the following details are required.

a. The customary activity times, descriptions and sequences as previously described.

b. The resource requirements for each activity showing the classification of the resource and the quantity required.

c. The resources in each classification that are available to the project. If variations in availability are likely during the project life, these must also be specified.

d. Any management restrictions that need to be considered eg which activities may or may not be split or any limitations on labour mobility.

RESOURCES SCHEDULING EXAMPLE, USING A GANTT CHART.

4. A simple project has the following time and resource data (for simplicity, only the one resource of labour is considered but similar principles would apply to other types of inter-changeable resources).

PROJECT DATA.

ACTIVITY	PRECEDING ACTIVITY	DURATION (DAYS)	LABOUR REQUIREMENTS
A	–	1	2 men
B	–	2	1 man
C	A	1	1 man
D	–	5	1 man
E	B	1	1 man
F	C	1	1 man

Resource constraint 2 men only available

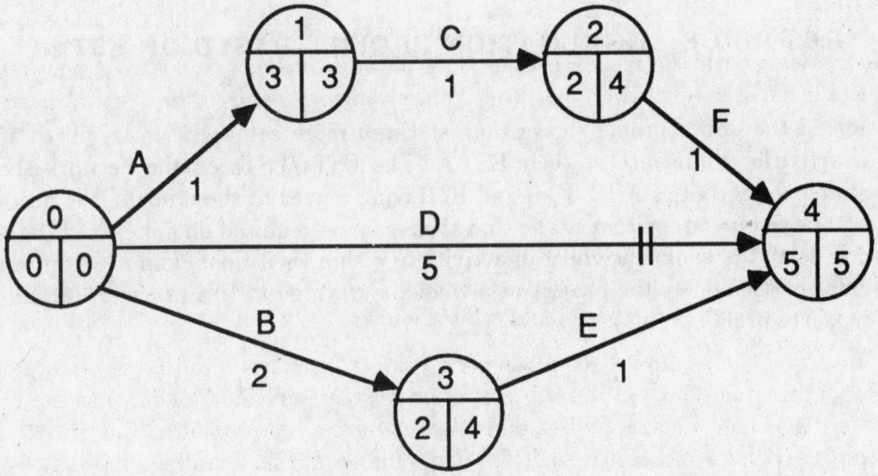

CRITICAL PATH – ACTIVITY D – DURATION 5 DAYS
(Without taking account of the resource constraint).

Resource Scheduling Steps

a. Draw the activity times on a Gantt or Bar Chart based on their ESTs

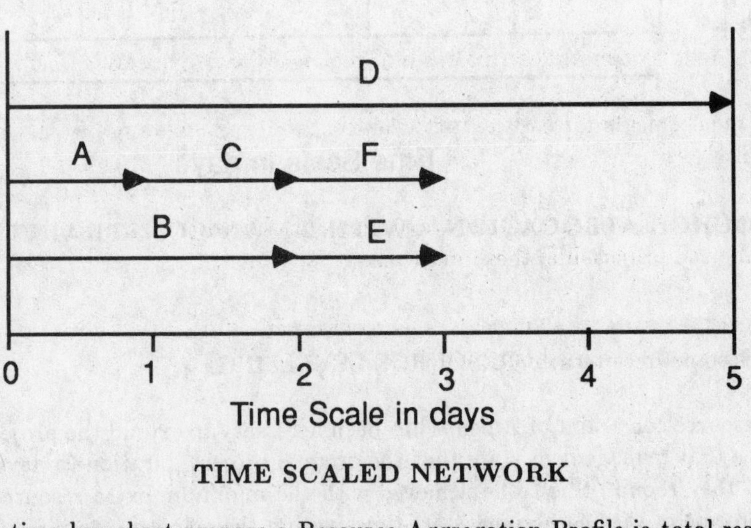

TIME SCALED NETWORK

b. Based on the time bar chart prepare a Resource Aggregation Profile ie total resource requirements in each time period.

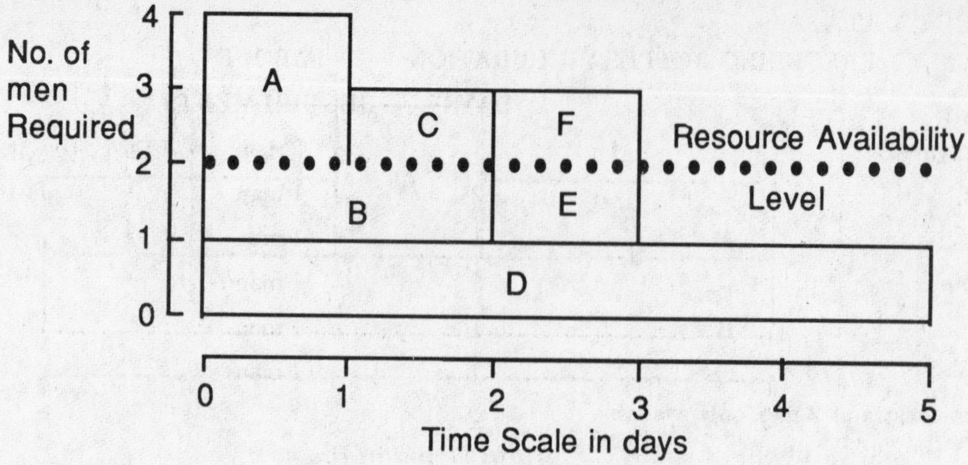

RESOURCE AGGREGATION PROFILE BASED ON EST's

c. Examination of the above profile shows that at times more resources are required than are available if activities commence at their EST's. The ESTs/LSTs on the network show that float is available for activities A, C, F, B and E. Having regard to these floats it is necessary to 'smooth out' the resource requirements so that the resources required do not exceed the resource constraint, ie delay the commencement of activities (within their float) and if this procedure is still not sufficient then delay the project as a whole. Carrying out this procedure results in the following resource profile.

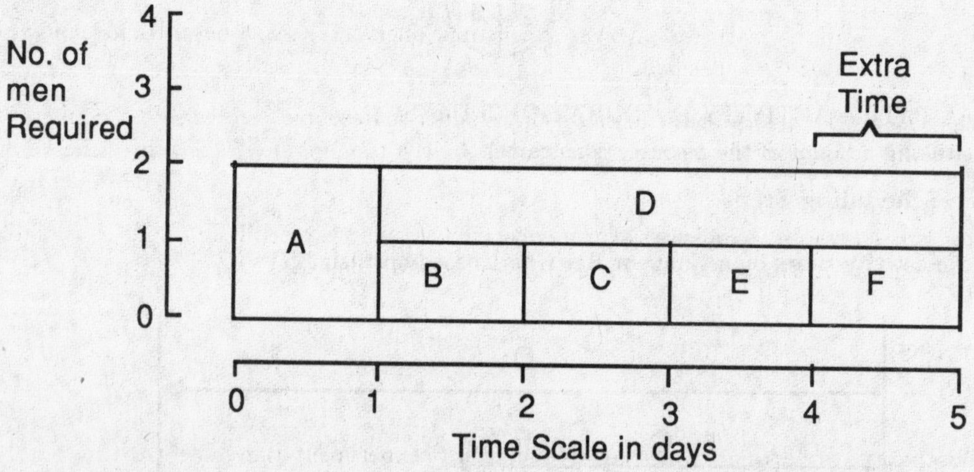

RESOURCE ALLOCATION – WITH 2 MAN CONSTRAINTS

Note.

This procedure is sometimes termed RESOURCE LEVELLING.

d. Because of the resource constraint of 2 men it has been necessary to extend the project duration by 1 day. Assume that management state that the original project duration (5 days) must not be extended and they require this to be achieved with the minimum extra resources. In such cases a similar process of varying activity start times within their float is carried out, resulting in the following resource profile.

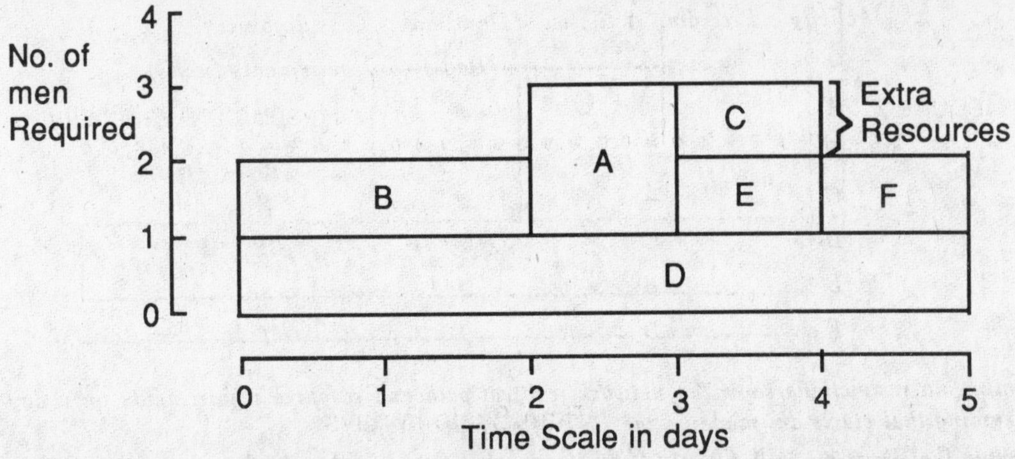

RESOURCE ALLOCATION PROFILE - WITH 5 DAY CONSTRAINT

e. The above profile shows that to achieve the 5 day duration it is necessary to have 3 men available from day 2 to day 4.

SUMMARY.

5.

a. To enable resource scheduling to be carried out the resource requirements for each activity must be specified.

b. In addition the various resources involved (men, machinery etc) must be classified and the availability and constraints specified.

c. After calculating the critical path in the usual manner a Resource Aggregation Profile(s) is prepared ie the amount of the resource(s) required in each time period of the project based on the EST's of each activity.

d. If the resource aggregation indicates that a constraint is being exceeded, and float is available the resource usage is 'smoothed' i.e. the start of activities is delayed.

POINTS TO NOTE.

6.

a. The smoothing of resource profiles is largely a matter of experimentation but if the time for the project is fixed concentrate attention on those activities with free float (described in Chapter 24).

SELF REVIEW QUESTIONS.

1 What data are required to be able to carry out resource scheduling on a network? (3)

2 What is a resource aggregation profile? (4b)

3 What is resource levelling? (4c)

EXERCISES WITH ANSWERS COMMENCING PAGE 488

A1. A project has the following activity durations and resource requirements.

Activity	Preceding Activities	Duration (Days)	Resource Requirements (units)
A	—	6	3
B	—	3	2
C	—	2	2
D	C	2	1
E	B	1	2
F	D	1	1

Assuming no restrictions show the network, critical path and resource requirements on a day by day basis, assuming that starts are made on the EST of each activity.

A2. Assume that there are only 6 units of resources what would be the plan?

EXAMINATION QUESTIONS WITH ANSWERS COMMENCING PAGE 488

A3. Each autumn the Quantitative Accountants Association prepares and distributes an annual programme. The programme gives dates of meetings and a list of speakers with summaries of their talks. Also included is an up-to-date list of paid-up members. The activities to be carried out to complete the prepation of the programme are as follows:

	Activity	Immediate predecessor	Estimated time (days)
A	Select dates for programme	—	4
B	Secure agreement from speakers and prepare summaries of their talks	A	12
C	Obtain advertising material for programme	A	11
D	Mail membership renewal notices	—	20
E	Prepare list of paid-up members	D	6
F	Send membership list to printer and read proofs	B,C,E	7
G	Print and assemble programme	F	10
H	Obtain computer printed address labels of members	E	5
I	Send out programmes	G,H	4

Required:

a. Draw a network for the scheme of activities set out above. Include full information on earliest and latest event times and indicate the critical path.

b. Draw a bar chart for the scheme and state the total float for each activity.

c. If each activity requires one member of the office staff of the association, so that the activities may be completed in the estimated times, what is the minimum number of staff that should be allocated to the scheme?

d. What would be effect on the total time if one of the allocated staff was taken ill for the duration of the scheme and not replaced?

(ACCA, Management Mathematics)

A4. Consider the project which requires the following activities

Activity		*Activity time in days*		*Total cost (normal)*	*Resources normal number of men per day*
Initial node	*Terminal node*	*Normal*	*Crash*		
				£	
0	9	6	3	480	4
0	10	10	5	900	5
10	7	7	4	490	5
7	8	9	2	540	4
9	2	8	4	560	6
3	4	5	2	300	4
7	3	6	3	500	4
6	11	6	3	520	6
1	6	7	4	510	5
8	4	10	5	920	6
4	5	8	4	580	6
2	8	10	5	940	5
0	1	9	6	560	4
11	4	8	4	480	4

The activities that can be 'crashed' must either take the normal time or the crash time. There is no opportunity to reduce the time of an activity by one or two days. The cost of crashing any activity is £100 per day.

You are required:

a. calculate the normal duration of the project, its normal cost and the critical path;

b. state the number of different paths from start to finish.

c. calculate the minimum time in which the project can be completed and state the critical activities.

d. state the maximum number of men required to complete the project if all activities commence at the earliest start date.

(CIMA, Quantitative Techniques)

EXERCISES WITHOUT ANSWERS.

B1. The following information is available about a project.

Activity	*Preceding Activity*	*Duration*	*Resource(Units)*
1	—	6	18
2	—	10	9
3	2	4	12
4	1	2	12
5	1	12	15
6	4	6	18
7	3,5	6	9

Assuming each activity starts on its EST what is the critical path and units of resource required?

B2. Replan the project in B1 to complete in the minimum time using the minimum units of resource.

EXAMINATION QUESTIONS WITHOUT ANSWERS

B3. The activities comprising a certain project have been identified as follows:

Activity	*Preceding activity*	*Duration (weeks)*	*Number of men required for activity*
A	—	4	1
B	—	7	1
C	—	8	2
D	A	5	3
E	C	4	1
F	B,E	4	2
G	C	11	2
H	G,F	4	1

Required:

i. For the above project, determine the critical path and its duration.

ii. If there were only three men available at any one time, how long would the project take and how would you allocate the men to the activities?

iii. If there were no restrictions on the amount of labour available, explain how you might schedule the activities, commenting on different criteria that might be used.

(ACCA, Management Mathematics)

27 Network Analysis – Activity on Nodes

INTRODUCTION.

1. This chapter explains as alternative method of drawing networks known as Activity on Node diagrams and compares this approach to the more conventional approach previously explained. In addition a brief resume of the use of computers in network analysis is given.

ACTIVITY ON NODE NETWORKS.

2. This type of network, sometimes known as PRECEDENCE DIAGRAM, is an alternative form of presentation based on similar estimates to those previously described.

Activity on Node Network Characteristics.

a. The activities are shown on boxes, not as arrows.
b. No events appear.
c. Boxes are linked by lines to indicate their sequence or precedence.
d. A box appears for the START and another for the FINISH of a project.
e. No dummies are necessasry.

COMPARISON WITH CONVENTIONAL NETWORKS.

3. The Activity on Node approach is best illustrated by comparison with the procedures for drawing conventional networks.

EXAMPLE | CONVENTIONAL NETWORK | ACTIVITY ON NODE NETWORK

A. Activity X depends upon Activity Y

B. Activity Z depends upon Activities X and Y

C. Activity C depends upon Activity A. Activity D depends upon Activities A and B.

D. Activity B can start immediately Activity A is Complete. Durations are 8 days and 6 days respectively.

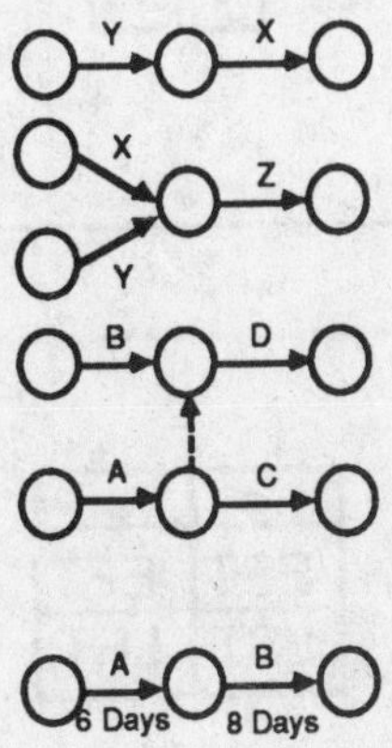

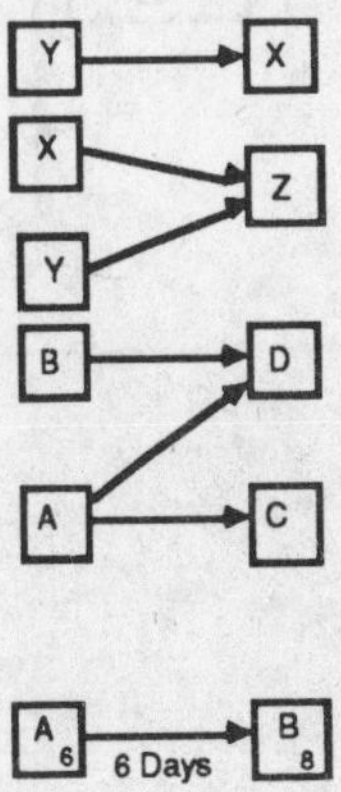

Notes.

a. Events as such do not appear in Activity on Node (A/N) networks.
b. The lines shown in A/N networks indicate precedences and are not activities. The activities are represented by the square boxes.

c. From example C it will be seen that dummies are not necessary in A/N networks.
d. The time (6 days) shown on the A/N network in Example D is known as the Dependency time.

ACTIVITY ON NODE EXAMPLE.

4. Based on the conventions described above a full A/N network is shown below. This uses the same activities, sequences and durations already used in in Par 4, Chapter 26.

CONVENTIONAL NETWORK (From Chapter 26)

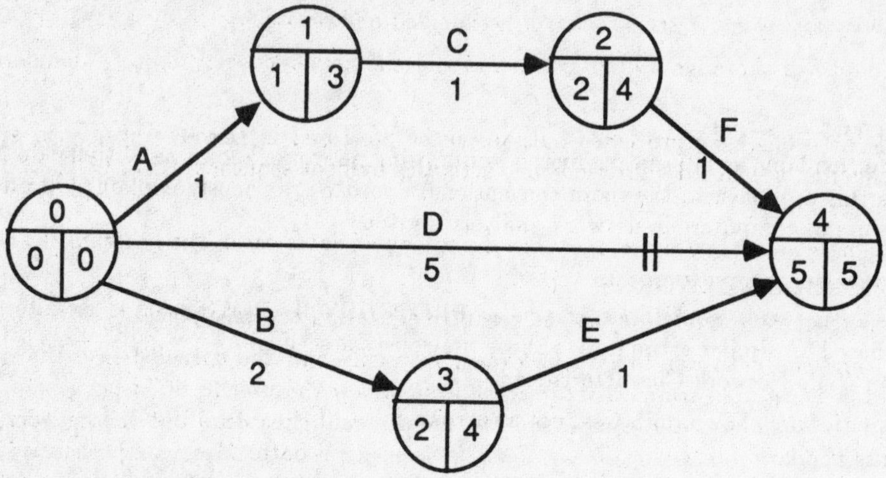

ACTIVITY ON NODE NETWORK

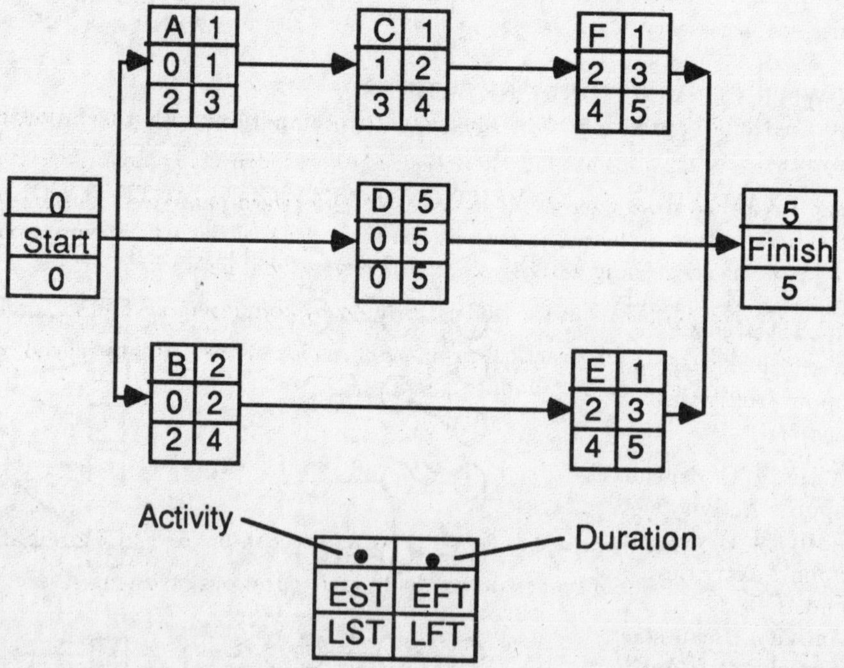

Notes on Activity on node network.

a. The lines joining the boxes are NOT activities, they are precedences as originally specified.
b. The ESTs/LSTs in the boxes are calculated by the same process as previously described but note that they are not the same values as shown in the events of the conventional network.
c. The EFT (Earliest Finish Time) and LFT (Latest Finish Time) are calculated by adding the activity time on to the EST and LST respectively.
d. The critical path is found by the usual method of comparing the EST and the LST (or EFT and LFT).

NETWORKS AND COMPUTERS.

5. So far only the manual handling of networks has been considered but in practice most network analysis is handled by computers. Most installations have standard packages to deal with this technique and there are a number of advantages in utilising these facilities.

a. By virtue of their speed computers can handle large networks with ease. Beyond a certain number of activities (say 50-100) networks become very difficult to handle manually and errors are almost certain to occur.

b. Full activity and event descriptions can be handled and printed out.

c. 'Input' data has thorough validation checks and the network logic ('loops', 'danglers' etc) is tested.

d. Once the data has been processed output can be presented in various ways, eg in activity or event sequence, scheduled data sequence, activities by float sequence, EST, LST, EFT or LFT sequence etc.

e. When changes in activity times, resources, or scheduled dates occur, the program can be quickly rerun to produce the new results.

f. More comprehensive time analysis and resource allocation can take place.

g. At one time the networks had to be drawn manually and the data fed into the computer. Packages are now appearing on the market which allow the user to build up a network using the graphics facilities of the computer. The package will then draw out the network diagram and calculate the project duration and isolate the critical path. More comprehensive packages will undertake cost scheduling and resource scheduling.

SUMMARY.

6.

a. Activity on node networks are an alternative method of presentation to conventional networks.

b. A/N networks do not show events but show the links (precedences) between activities.

c. Forward and backward passes are made as usual. The forward pass gives the same EST as in conventional networks, but the backward pass gives the LST of the activity in the node rather than the LST of the succeeding activity as in the conventional networks.

d. The critical lpath is established in the normal manner by comparing EST/LST, or EFT/LFT.

e. Computers are widely used for practical problems because of their greater speed, calculating ability and the existence of many standard packages.

POINTS TO NOTE.

7.

a. It is claimed that A/N networks are easier to draw and so can be used by more people.

b. At least one of the professional bodies occasionally have questions involving A/N networks.

SELF REVIEW QUESTIONS.

1 What are the features of activities on Node networks? (2)

2 What do the arrows represent in Activity on Node networks? (3)

3 How is the critical path established in A/N networks? (4)

4 Why are comptuers invariably used for solving practical network analysis problems? (5)

EXERCISES WITH ANSWERS COMMENCING PAGE 488

A1. Draw an activity on node diagram for the following project.

ACTIVITY	PRECEDING ACTIVITY	DURATION (DAYS)
1	—	4
2	1	7
3	1	5
4	1	6
5	2	2
6	3	3
7	5	5
8	2,6	11
9	7,8	7
10	3	4
11	4	3
12	9,10,11	4

A2. Calculate the EST/LST/ and LFT values for each box

EXAMINATION QUESTIONS WITH ANSWERS COMMENCING PAGE 488

A3. The following activity-on-node network shows the relationship between the 11 activities which make up a particular stage of a large construction project. Within each activity box, the letter denotes the 'name' of the activity, and the number is its duration in weeks.

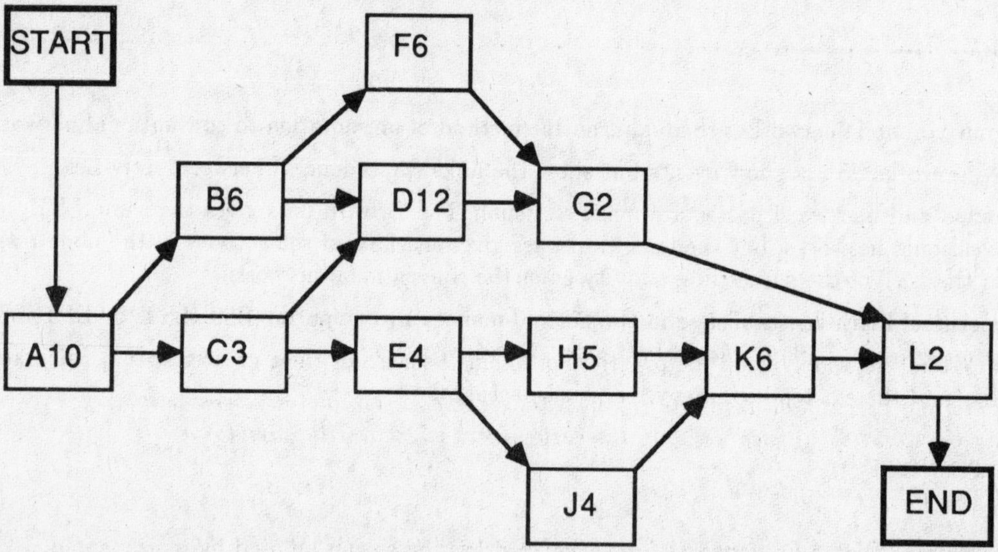

Required:

(a)

i. *How long will it take to complete this stage of the project?*

ii. *What is the critical path?*

iii. *By how much would the duration of activity J have to increase before it becomes critical?*

iv. *What would be the effect, if any, on both the duration of the project and the critical path if activity D does not have to be preceded by activity B?*

(b) The cash required to complete each activity is as follows:

Activity	A	B	C	D	E	F	G	H	J	K	L
Cash (£000)	30	18	12	12	8	12	6	15	16	12	6

What is the maximum amount of cash required in any one week and when will this occur?

You should assume that all activities start at their earliest time and that the necessary cash is used at a uniform rate throughout the duration of each activity.

(ACCA Quantitative Analysis)

A4. There are at least two different diagrammatic representations of networks, one in which the activity is represented by the line joining two nodes (arrow diagram) and the other in which the activity is represented by the node itself (AON).

The following information on the project upon which you have been asked to advise has been collected.

Activity	Immediate predecessors	Estimated duration, in days	Normal cost per day £	Days that could be 'saved'	Cost per day of saving 1 day £
a	b	2	50	1	20
b	—	3	60	1	60
c	b	4	70	2	30
r	c,a	2	40	—	—
p	r	3	30	1	40
n	p	1	75	—	—
q	b	15	20	6	70
m	q,n	3	50	1	90

You are required to:

a. draw the arrow diagram clearly, indicating the meaning of any notation you have used and including the duration of each activity, the earliest and lates starting times.

b. draw the activity-on-node (AON) diagram clearly, explaining any symbols that you have used and including the duration of each activity, the earliest and latest starting times;

c. state the critical activities

d. calculate and state the duration at normal cost and the total cost of the project on the normal cost basis.

e. calculate the minimum cost of completing the project in 16 days.

(CIMA QUANTITATIVE TECHNIQUES)

EXERCISE WITHOUT ANSWERS

B1. Draw the activity on node diagram of question B1 in Chapter 24.

EXAMINATION QUESTIONS WITHOUT ANSWERS

B2. Consider the activities required to complete the processing of a customer's order.

Activities	Preceeding activities	Average time in days	Normal variable cost per day £
1. Receipt of order, checking credit rating, etc.	—	2	5
2. Preparation of material specification, availability of material, etc.	1	4	10
3. Inspection, packing, etc.	2	1	7
4. Arrangement of transport facilities etc.	1	5	5
5. Delivery	3,4	3	2

The time for activities 1, 3 and 5 are fixed; for activity 2 there is a 0.5 probability that it will require 2 days and a 0.5 probability that it will require 6 days; for activity 4 a 0.7 probability of taking 4 days, 0.2 of taking 6 days and 0.1 of taking 10 days.

You are required to:

a. draw the network (it is very simple) twice, first using an arrow diagram and secondly an activity-on-node presentation, clearly indicating the meaning of any symbols that you use.

b. indicate the critical path, calculate average duration and variable cost under normal conditions;

c. calculate the minimum and maximum times and the probabilities associated with them.

(CIMA, Quantitative Techniques)

28 Financial Mathematics

INTRODUCTION.

1. Many aspects of business and accounting eg depreciation, loans, interest calculations, investments appraisals, have as their basis some relatively simple formulae. This chapter reviews the more important areas of financial mathematics and provides the most common formulae in a concise form. The full derivation of each formula is not given but an example is shown of a practical application of every formula.

SERIES.

2. Basic to many financial calculations is the concept of allocating or paying out or receiving money at regular intervals. Typical examples include: depreciation calculations, investing funds, loan repayment, cash flow analysis. These situations can be represented by series of which the two most common types are arithmetic and geometric progressions.

ARITHMETIC PROGRESSION.

3. A series of quantities where each new value is obtained by adding a constant amount to the previous value. The constant amount is sometimes called the common difference.

An arithmetic progression has the form

$$a, a+d, a+2d..........., a+(x-1)d$$

where a is the first value

d is the common difference

x is the number of terms in the series.

Example 1.

A firm rents its premises and the rental agreement provides for a regular annual increase of £2650. If the rent in the first year is £8500, what is the rent in the tenth year?

$$\begin{aligned} \text{Rent in 10th year} &= a+(x-1)d \\ &= 8500 + (10 - 1)\ 2650 \\ &= \underline{\underline{\pounds 32{,}350}} \end{aligned}$$

Example 2.

A firm buys a power press for £32500 which is expected to last for 20 years and to have a scrap value of £7500. If depreciation is on the straight line method, how much should be provided for in each year?

In such a problem the numberof terms in the series is 1 more than the number of years because the cost is the value at the *beginning* of the first year and the scrap value is at the *end* of the final year.

$$a = 32,500 \quad x = 21$$

$$\begin{aligned} 7500 &= a+(x-1)d \\ 7500 &= 32500+20d \\ d &= -1250 \end{aligned}$$

Straight line depreciation is £1250 pa

SUM OF ARITHMETIC PROGRESSIONS.

4. One way to find the sum of an arithmetic progression is to evalue each of the successive terms and add them up. This could be lengthy if numerous terms are involved, so the following formula can be used.

$$S = n[a + \tfrac{1}{2}(x-1)d]$$

where S = sum of the progression.

Example 3.

How much rent in total did the firm in Example 1 pay for its premises over the ten years?

$$a = 8500 \quad x = 10 \quad d = 2650$$

$$\begin{aligned} S &= 10[8500 + \tfrac{1}{2}(10-1)2650] \\ &= \underline{\underline{\pounds 204{,}250}} \end{aligned}$$

Example 4.

An employee, who received fixed annual increments had a final salary of £9000 pa after 10 years. If his total salary was £65000 over the 10 years, what was his initial salary?

$$\begin{aligned} 65000 &= 10[a + \tfrac{1}{2}(10-1)d] \\ \underline{6500} &= \underline{a + 4.5d} \ldots\ldots\ldots\ldots(i) \end{aligned}$$

and from Para 3 we know that

$$\begin{aligned} 9000 &= a + (10-1)d \\ \underline{9000} &= \underline{a + 9d} \ldots\ldots\ldots\ldots(ii) \end{aligned}$$

(i) and (ii) are simultaneous equations and (ii) - (i) gives

$$\begin{aligned} 2500 &= 4.5d \\ \therefore\ d &= \pounds 555.55 \end{aligned}$$

substituting we obtain a = £4000

Initial salary is $\underline{\underline{\pounds 4000}}$ and

annual increment is $\underline{\underline{\pounds 555.55}}$

GEOMETRIC PROGRESSIONS.

5. A series of quantities where each value is obtained by multiplying the previous value by a constant which is called the common ratio.

A geometric progress has the form.

$a, ar, ar^2, ar^3, \ldots\ldots, ar^{x-1}$

where a is the first value

r is the common ratio

x is the number of terms in the series.

Example 5.

Given the same details as in example 2 what would be the depreciation rate as a percentage if the depreciation was to be calculated on the reducing balance method?

$$a = 32{,}500 \quad x = 21 \quad \text{scrap value} = 7500$$

$$7500 = ar^{x-1}$$

$$7500 = 32500r^{20}$$

$$r^{20} = \frac{7500}{32500}$$ which may be solved using logs, or the scientific function on a calculator.

$$\text{ie} \log r = \frac{\log 7500 - \log 32500}{20}$$

$$\log r = 1.968159$$

$$\therefore r = .92927$$

$\therefore$ reducing balance depreciation rate

$$= 1 - .92927$$

$$\text{or} = 7\%$$

Example 6.
A building cost £500,000 and it is decided to depreciate it at 10% pa on the reducing balance method. What will its written down value be after 25 years?

a = 500,000 $x = 26$ $r = (1 - d)$where
d =depreciation rate

$$\text{Value after 25 years} = ar^{x-1}$$

$$= 500,000(1 - .1)^{26-1}$$

$$\therefore \text{ log 25th year value} = \log 500,000 + 25 \log (1 - d)$$

$$\text{log 25th year value} = 5.69897 + 25(9.95424 - 10)$$

$$\text{log 25th year value} = 4.55497$$

$$\therefore \text{ 25th year value} = \underline{\underline{\pounds 35,890}}$$

Notes.

a. The common ratio, r, in depreciation problems is always obtained by deducting the depreciation rate from 1, ie if the depreciation rate is 20% then $r = (1 - .2)$ ie .8.
b. Make sure you can deal with the multiplication and division of negative logarithms.

SUM OF GEOMETRIC PROGRESSIONS.

6. In a similar fashion to an arithmetic progression the individual terms could be evaluated and added together but a simple formula exists:

$$S = \frac{a(r^x - 1)}{r - 1}$$

where S is the sum of the progression

Example 7.
A company sets up a sinking fund and invests £10,000 each year for 5 years at 9% compound interest. What will the fund be worth after 5 years?
(Note: From such a question it can be inferred that the £10,000 invested at the end of each year so that the last allocation earns no interest).
To clarify the problem the whole series is set out below.

$$\pounds(10,000 \times 1.09^4) + \pounds(10,000 \times 1.09^3) + \pounds(10,000 \times 1.09^2) + \pounds(10,000 \times 1.09) + \pounds10,000$$

From this it will be seen that the series is the reverse of the usual order and that the number of terms in the series (x) is 5, ie the same as the number of years.

$$a = 10,000 \qquad r = 1.09 \quad x = 5$$
$$S = \frac{a(r^x - 1)}{r - 1} \qquad = \qquad \frac{10,000(1.09^5 - 1)}{1.09 - 1}$$
$$S = \underline{\pounds 59847}$$

SIMPLE AND COMPOUND INTEREST.

7. Of particular interest to accountants and businessmen are the concepts of simple and compound interest. The solution to such problems involve the concepts of progressions as discussed above. Common practice uses the following terminology which will be followed in this manual.

P = a sum at the present time

S = a sum arising in the future

n = number of interest bearing periods usually, but not exclusively, expressed in years

r = rate of interest invariably expressed in an interest rate per annum

I = total amount of interest

SIMPLE INTEREST.

8. Where interest only accrues on the principal this is known as simple interest, ie the interest is not re-invested to earn more interest.

$$\begin{aligned} I &= S - P \\ \text{and } r &= \frac{I}{Pn} \\ \text{and } I &= Prn \\ \text{and } S &= P + I = P + Prn = P(1 + rn) \end{aligned}$$

Example 8.

How much will £ 10,000 amount to at 8% simple interest over 15 years?

$$\begin{aligned} S &= \pounds 10,000(1 + .08(15) + \pounds 10,000 \\ &= \underline{\underline{\pounds 22,000}} \end{aligned}$$

Example 9.

How long will it take for a sum of money to double itself at 10% pa simple interest?

$$\text{Let } P = 1 \qquad \text{and } S = 2 \quad I = 1$$
$$\begin{aligned} I &= Prn \\ 1 &= (1)(0.10)(n) \\ n &= \frac{1}{0.10} \end{aligned} \qquad = \underline{\underline{\textbf{10years}}}$$

COMPOUND INTEREST.

9. Of considerably more practical use is the principle of compound interest whereby interest is paid on the principal plus the re-invested interest so that the successive terms of the series form a geometric progression. The principles of compound interest form the basis of annuity calculations and discounting so that a clear understanding is vital.

The basic compounding formula is

$$S = P(1+r)^n$$

Because of its importance and frequency of occurrence, compound interest tables have been calculated which show the compound interest factor for various rates of interest (r) over various numbers of year(n). See Table VII

Example 10.

How much will £ 10,000 amount to at 8% pa compound interest over 15 years?

$$S = 10,000(1+.08)^{15}$$

(Note: The compound interest factor (1 + .08)15 could be evaluated by logarithms or calculator but tables are more commonly used - look up in Table VII under 8% for 15 years and the factor is 3.172)

$$\begin{aligned} S &= \text{£}10,000(3.172) \\ &= \underline{\underline{\textbf{£31,720}}} \end{aligned}$$

Note: Contrast this amount with Example 8.

Example 11.

What compound rate of interest will be required to produce £ 5000 after five years with an initial investment of £ 4000?

$$\begin{aligned} 5000 &= 4000(1+r)^5 \\ \frac{5000}{4000} &= (1+r)^5 \\ (1+r)^5 &= 1.25 \end{aligned}$$

Look in Table VII along the 5 year line for a compound interest factor of 1.25. It will be seen that the factor for 4% is 1.217 and for 5% 1.276. ∴ the solution to this problem is between 4% and 5% and is just over 4 $\frac{1}{2}$%.

Example 12.

How long will it take for a given sum of money to double itself at 10% pa compound interest? (see Example 9)

$$\begin{aligned} 2 &= 1(1+.1)^n \\ \therefore (1+.1)^n &= 2 \end{aligned}$$

Once again the tables can be used as a short cut method. Look in Table VII down the 10% column to see the factor closest to 2 which is found to be 7 years having a factor of 1.949. The factor for 8 years is 2.144 so that the period required is approximately 7.3 years.

DISCOUNTING.

10. The basic compounding principle, given in Para. 9, essentially looks forward from a known present amount (P) together with re-invested interest, equalling some terminal value (S) . It will be apparent that there are occasions when the future value (S) is known and it is required to calculate the present value (P). The basic compounding formula can be restated in terms of discounting to a present value as follows:

$$P = \frac{S}{(1+r)^n}$$

Note.

This formula is the basis of all discounting methods and is particularly useful as the basis of Discounted Cash Flow techniques which are dealt with in the chapters which follow.

Example 13.

How much will have to be invested now to produce £ 20,000 after 5 years with a 10% compound interest rate?

(Alternatively the question could be framed; what is the present value of £ 20,000 received in 5 years time at a discount rate of 10% ?)

$$P = \frac{S}{(1+r)^n}$$
$$P = \frac{20,000}{(1+.1)^5}$$
$$= \underline{\underline{£12,420}}$$

Note.

The expression could be evaluated by logarithms or a calculator but because discounting is a common process, discount factor tables have been calculated, see Table VIII. The discount factor for 10% for 5 years is 0.621.

$$20,000 \times 0.621 = \underline{\underline{£12,420}}$$

DISCOUNTING A SERIES.

11. Many problems are not concerned merely with discounting one value but involve a whole series of cash flows which are required to be discounted to a present value.

In such circumstances the formula given in Para 10 becomes

$$P = \sum_{i=1}^{i=n} \frac{A_i}{(1+r)^i}$$

where A_i; represents the cash flows arising at the end of year 1, 2, 3,........,n.

Example 14.

What is the present value of receiving £ 1000 in 1 year's time, £ 2000 in 2 years time, and £ 3000 in 3 years time when the discount rate is 10% .

$$\therefore P = \frac{1000}{(1+.1)^1} + \frac{2000}{(1.1)^2} + \frac{3000}{(1+.1)^3}$$

The discount factors are .909, .826, and .751 (Table VIII)

$$P = 1000(.909) + 2000(.826) + 3000(.751)$$
$$= \underline{\underline{£4814}}$$

Where the cash flows vary from year to year there is no single all embracing formula which can be used. A separate calculation has to be made for each year and added together. However, when the cash flows are regular, certain short cuts are possible.

ANNUITIES.

12. Where the cash flows received are constant for all years the series is known as an annuity. The present value could be calculated using the formula given in Para 11, ie discounting each term and adding them togehter, but the series of expressions can be brought into one formula, thus

$$P = \frac{A[1-(1+r)^{-n}]}{r}$$

where A is the regular cash receipt.

Example 15.

What is the present value of an annuity of £ 500 pa received for 10 years when the discount rate is 10% .

$$P = \frac{500[1 - \frac{1}{(1+.1)^{10}}]}{.1}$$
$$\simeq \underline{\underline{£3072}}$$

Note.

Once again, because annuities are commonly encountered, tables have been calculated for the annuity factor

$$\text{ie} \quad \frac{1-(1+r)^{-n}}{r} \quad \text{(see Table IX)}$$

If Table IX is examined for the 10% rate for 10 years the factor 6.145 is obtained

$\therefore$ present value is £ 5000 × 6.145 = <u>£ 3072</u>

Because of the frequency with which annuities are encountered a shorthand way of writing such problems is used, ie $a_{n\rceil r}$, which means the annuity factor for n years at r rate of interest. Example 15 could have been written as follows:

$$£500a_{10\rceil 10\%} \simeq £3072.$$

PERPETUITIES.

13. Where a steam of cash flows goes on for ever the expression in square brackets in the annuity formula reduces to 1 and the formula dramatically simplifies to

$$P = \frac{A}{r}$$

Example 16.

What is the present value of a perpetual annuity of £ 500 pa at 10% (alternatively £ $500a_{\infty\rceil 10\%}$)?

$$\begin{aligned} P &= \frac{500}{.1} \\ &= \underline{£5000} \end{aligned}$$

Example 17.

What is the rate of interest when a £ 5000 investment now provides a perpetual annuity of £ 3000 pa?

$$\begin{aligned} r = \frac{A}{P} &= \frac{300}{5000} \\ &= \underline{6\%} \end{aligned}$$

Note.

This simple concept is important and is used subsequently when investment appraisal and DCF is considered.

CASH FLOWS GROWING (OR DECLINING) AT A COMPOUND RATE.

14. On occasion it is required to find the present value of a series of cash flows which are expected to grow (or decline) at a compound rate eg a series of dividends which are expected to grow at a rate of 8% pa.

$$\begin{aligned} \text{Let g} &= \text{\% growth pa} \\ \text{then P} &= \frac{A}{(1+g)} a_{n\rceil r_0}\% \quad \text{where } r_0 = \frac{r-g}{1+g} \end{aligned}$$

($a_{n\rceil r_0}\%$ is, of course the annuity factor described in Para 12)

Example 18.

what is the present value of a dividend stream which is expected to commence in a year's time with a dividend of £ 440 and thereafter increase at 10% pa. The dividends are expected to last 10 years and the discount rate is 32%.

$$P = \frac{A}{1+g} a_{\overline{n}|r_0}\% \qquad \text{where } r_0 = \frac{r-g}{1+g}$$

$$r_0 = \frac{.32-.10}{1.10} = \frac{.22}{1.10} = \underline{\underline{.20}}$$

and $A/1+g = 440/1.10 = £400$

$$\therefore P = £400a_{\overline{10}|20\%}$$

$$= 400 \times 4.192$$

$$= \underline{\underline{£1677}}$$

Note.

The factor 4.192 is obtained from Table IX

Example 19.

What would be the present value of Example 18 if the dividend stream was considered to last indefinitely?

As in example 18

$$r_0 = .20a\frac{A}{1+g} = £400$$

$$\therefore P = £400a_{\overline{\infty}|20\%}$$

$$= \frac{400}{.2}$$

$$= \underline{\underline{£2000}}$$

Example 20.

Assume the same situation as example 18 except that the dividend was expected to *reduce* by 10% pa.

$$g = -0.10$$

$$r_0 = \frac{.32+0.01}{1-0.10} = 0.466$$

$$\text{and } \frac{A}{1+g} = \frac{440}{.9} = £489$$

$$\therefore P = £489a_{\overline{10}|46.2/3\%}$$

$$P = £489.2 \times 2.09650$$

$$P = \underline{\underline{£1025}}$$

Note.

When some large value of r_0 is obtained tables may not be obtainable so that the annuity factor can be found by using a calculator or logarithms.

COMPOUNDING/DISCOUNTING AT INTERVALS OTHER THAN ANNUAL

15. The assumption so far has been that cash flows have been received or paid out at year ends and that interest is always applied annually. These are the normal assumptions in examination questions but on occasions discounting or compounding may be required at some other interval, eg monthly, quarterly, half yearly or even continuously. Continuous compounding or discounting requires special tables which are used in exactly the same way as normal tables based on discrete periods. The normal tables (Table VIII and IX) can be simply used for periods other than a year as shown by the following example.

Example 21.

How much will have to be invested now to produce £ 20,000 after 5 years where a rate of 10% pa is compounded half yearly? (Alternatively, what is the present value of £ 20,000 received in 5 years time discounted half yearly at 10% pa?)

Calculate the number of interest/discount periods, ie $5 \times 2 = 10$
Calculate interest/discount rate per period ie

$$\frac{\text{Interest/discount rate pa}}{\text{No. of periods pa}} = \frac{10}{2} = \underline{\underline{5\%}}$$

Look up the tables for 10 periods at 5% (ie treat the years column as 'periods').
From Table VIII the factor obtained is 0.614

$$\text{Present value} = £20,000 \times 0.614$$
$$= \underline{\underline{£\ 12{,}280}}$$

Contrast this answer with Example 13.

Note.

Whether compounding or discounting a single value or a series, similar principles apply. Calculate the number of interest/discount periods and the rate of interest per period. the more frequently a value is compounded/discounted, the larger/smaller will be the answer.

NOMINAL AND ACTUAL INTEREST RATES.

16. Most interest rates are expressed a per annum figures even when the interest is compounded or discounted over periods of less than one year. In such cases the given interest rate is called a *nominal rate.*

Depending on whether the compounding or discounting is done daily, weekly, monthly, quarterly or six monthly the ***actual rate*** or ***actual percentage rate*** (APR) will vary by differing amounts from the nominal rate. The discrepancy between the nominal rate and the APR gets larger as the frequency of compounding or discounting and the number of years increases. The APR is an important figure and, by law, must be quoted in finance loan and hire purchase agreements.

Given a nominal annual rate of interest the APR can be calculated using the following formula:

$$\text{APR} = (1 + \tfrac{i}{n})^n - 1$$

where i = nominal rate per compounding period

n = number of compounding periods in one year.

Example 22.

A finance company loans money at 20% nominal interest but compounds monthly. What is the APR?

SOLUTION.

Monthly nominal rate $= \frac{0.20}{12} = 0.0166 \therefore$ APR $= (1 + 0.0166)^{12} - 1 = 0.2194$ or $\underline{21.94\%}$

SUMMARY.

17.

a. Many financial calculations are based on series. The two most common types are arithmetic and geometric progressions.
b. In an arithmetic progression each new value is obtained by adding a constant amount to the previous value.
c. In a geometric progression each new value is obtained by multiplying the previous value by a constant.
d. Where interest accrues only upon the principal it is known as *simple interest*
e. Where interest accrues on the principal plus the re-invested interest it is known as ***compound interest*** Many annuity and discounting problems have the principle of compound interest as their basis.
f. The basic compounding principle looks forward in time to some future date, whereas discounting starts with a known future sum and arrives at its value in present day terms.
g. The basic discounting formula

$$P = \sum_{i=1}^{1=n} \frac{A_i}{(1+r)^i}$$

is important and is the basis of the Discounted Cash Flow (DCF) techniques described in subsequent chapters.

h. Annuities are constant amounts received annually for a given number of years.

i. Perpetuities are constant amounts received annually for ever. Clearly this is not a strictly realistic assumption but it is one occasionally made.

j. Although interest and discount rates are normally applied at yearly intervals this is not always the case. The tables (Table VIII, VIII, IX) can still be used by calculating the number of interest bearing periods and adjusting the annual interest/discount rate according to the time period required.

POINTS TO NOTE.

18.

a. Financial mathematics are the basis of many accounting and business techniques (including depreciation, discounting) and so the contents of this chapter should be thoroughly learned.

SELF REVIEW QUESTIONS.

1 What are the two common series widely used in financial matters? (3 and 5)

2 What is simple interest and what is the formula to calculate a future sum given a present sum and a rate of interest? (8)

3 What is compound interest and what is the equivalent formula to 2. above? (9)

4 What is the relationship between discounting and compounding? (10)

5 What is the formula for calculating the present value of a series? (11)

6 What is an annuity? (12)

7 What is a perpetuity and how is the present value calculated? (13)

8 If interest is compounded or discounted at intervals other than annually how is this dealt with? (15)

EXERCISES WITH ANSWERS COMMENCING PAGE 488

A1. Find the value of the 12th term and the sum of the first 20 terms of the progression
4, 8, 16, 32, 64...

A2. How long will it take for a given sum to treble itself;
(a) at 15% simple interest?
(b) at 15% compound interest?

A3. What is the present value of
(a) £200 p.a. received for 10 years at 10% ?
(b) £200 p.a. received for 10 years commencing in 5 years time, at 10% ?
(c) A dividend of £500 p.a. growing at 5% p.a., with a discount rate of 26% , which is expected to last for 10 years?

EXAMINATION QUESTIONS WITH ANSWERS COMMENCING PAGE 488

A4. A client of yours has received confusing advice from three different investment advisers and has come to you for help. He wishes to invest £5,000 for two years (with interest compounded) but with the right to withdraw at a moment's notice.

Silas O'Fenton, one of the investment advisers, has recommended the Not-nef Building Society currently offering an interest rate of 8% pa. AFTER TAX, with interest paid half yearly. Tiny Tim Brokers have recommended investing with the T.T. Bank at an interest rate of 10% pa BEFORE TAX, interest paid half yearly.

Ebenezer S Finance Investigators have suggested investing with the E. Scrooge bank which is offering an interest rate of 9% pa BEFORE TAX, interest paid every three months. (All interest rates are nominal).

Required.

a. After carrying out a suitable analysis, make recommendations to your client regarding which of the three pieces of investment advice he should take.

(Assume a standard rate of tax of 35%)

b. What is the effective annual interest rate, after tax of your recommended proposal?

c. What situations might occur that would make you wish to reconsider your advice?

Table for evaluating $(x)^n$

(Use if required)

1 + i	n			
	2	4	6	8
1.0225	1.046	1.093	1.143	1.195
1.04	1.082	1.170	1.265	1.369
1.045	1.092	1.193	1.302	1.422
1.05	1.103	1.216	1.340	1.477
1.08	1.166	1.360	1.587	1.851
1.09	1.188	1.412	1.677	1.993
1.10	1.210	1.464	1.772	2.144

where i = rate of interest per time period.

(ACCA , Management Mathematics)

a. In order to purchase a property for £20,000 a loan of £15,000 is negotiated with a finance company. The balance of £5,000 is to be paid out of personal resources.

The terms of the loan are as follows:

Duration of the loan is for 15 years.

Rate of interest is fixed at 10% per annum throughout the 15 years. The annual interest charge is to be calculated on the balance outstanding at the beginning of each year.

Repayment is to be in 15 equal annual instalments. Each instalment will include both interest and capital.

b. If property values were to appreciate at the rate of 7% per annum, what would be the value, in 15 years time, of the property purchased now for £20,000?

(CIMA BUSINESS MATHEMATICS)

EXERCISES WITHOUT ANSWERS

B1. Find the value of the 8th term and the sum of the first 12 terms of the progression.

2, 6, 18, 54,...

B2. An employee who receives fixed annual increments had a final salary of £20,000 after 6 years. If his total salary over the 6 years was £80,000 what was his initial salary?

B3. (a) What is the present value of receiving £2,000 after 1 year, £1,500 after 2 years and £2,500 after 5 years at 20% ?

(b) What is the equivalent five year annuity at 20% to the series in (a) above.

EXAMINATION QUESTIONS WITHOUT ANSWERS

B4. Mr. Able, aged 40 on his next birthday, wishes to take out an insurance policy which will pay him £10,000 on his 50th birthday, £15,000 on his 55th birthday and £20,000 on his 60th birthday, assuming he lives long enough. The insurance company calculates the total premium payable by determining the expected payout (discounted at 12% per annum) using standard mortality tables. It then adds on a service charge of 2% of the amount calculated, plus a fixed charge of £50.

Required:

a. Using the mortality table calculate the probabilities that Mr. Able will live to ages 50, 55 and 60 years respectively.

b. Determine the once and for all premium charged by the insurance company which would be paid by Mr. Able on his 40th birthday.

c. Calculate the annual payment if the premium is paid in ten equal annual instalments, the first payment being paid on Mr. Able's 40th birthday (assume a discount rate 12% p.a. throughout the question.

Mortality Table

Age Number	*living**
40	883,342
45	852,554
50	810,900
55	754,191
60	677,771

**Assumes 1,000,000 alive at age 1*

The present value of an annuity of £1 paid at the end of each period for n periods discounted at 100i% is given by B(n, i) where

$$B(n,i) = \frac{1-(1+i)^{-n}}{i}$$

$i = 0.12$	
n	$(1+i)^{-n}$
8	0.4039
9	0.3606
10	0.3220
11	0.2875
12	0.2567
15	0.1827
20	0.1037

(ACCA, Management Mathematics)

29 Investment Appraisal – Background and Techniques

INTRODUCTION.

1. Many quantitative techniques aid management decision making and on important area of application is concerned with investment decisions. This chapter considers the reasons for investment and explains in detail the various appraisal criteria. The 'traditional' techniques of accounting rate of return and payback are described together with their limitations. Discounted Cash Flow (DCF) is explained and the two principal techniques of Net Present Value (NPV) and Internal Rate of Return (IRR) are discussed in detail. Their use in typical situations is shown and a detailed comparison is made of their relative advantages and disadvantages. The latter part of the chapter discusses the treatment of inflation in investment appraisal.

LONG RUN DECISION MAKING.

2. Investment decisions are long run decisions where consumption and investment alternatives are balanced over time in the hope that investment now will generate extra returns in the future. There are many similarities between shortrun and long-run decision making, for example, the choice between alternatives, the need to consider future costs and revenues and the importance of incremental changes in costs and revenues but there is the additional requirement for investment decisions that, because of the time scale involved, the time value of the money invested must be considered. The time scale also makes the consideration of uncertainty and inflation of even greater importance than when considering short term decisions.

Assuming that finance is available the decision to invest will be based on three major factors:

a. The investor's beliefs in the future. In business the beliefs would be based on forecasts of internal and external factors including: costs, revenues, inflation and interest rates, taxation and numerous other factors.

b. The alternatives available in which to invest. This is the stage at which the various techniques used to appraise the competing investments would be used. The various techniques are covered in detail in this chapter.

c. The investor's attitude to risk. Because investment decsions are often on a large scale, analysis of the investor's attitude to risk and the project uncertainty are critical factors in an investment decision and are dealt with in the following chapter.

Investment decision making is invariably a top management exercise. This is because of the scale and long term nature of the consequences of such decicion. Although the final decision would be made by management the analyst would assess the alternatives available, analyse the data using the most appropriate techniques and present the results of this exercise to management so that hopefully, better decisions are made.

TRADITIONAL INVESTMENT APPRAISAL TECHNIQUES.

3. Two particular methods of comparing the attractiveness of competing projects have become known as the 'traditional techniques'. These are the Accounting Rate of Return and Payback which are described below.

ACCOUNTING RATE OF RETURN.

4. This is the ratio of average annual profits, after depreciation, to the capital invested. This is a basic definition only and variations exist, for example

– profits may be before or after tax – capital may or may not include working capital – capital invested may mean the initial capital investment or the average of the capital invested over the life of the project.

Note: An alternative term is Return on Capital Employed (ROCE).

Example 1. Accounting Rate of Return

A firm is considering three projects each with an initial investment of £1000 and a life of 5 years. The profits generated by the projects are estimated to be as follows:

AFTER TAX AND DEPRECIATION PROFITS

YEAR	PROJECT 1	PROJECT II	PROJECT III
	£	£	£
1	200	350	150
2	200	200	150
3	200	150	150
4	200	150	200
5	200	150	350
TOTAL	1000	1000	1000

Calculate the account rate of return (ARR) on
(a) Initial Capital
(b) Average Capital.

Accounting rate of return on Initial Capital:

	Project 1	Project II	Project III
Average Profits	$= \frac{1000}{5}$	$\frac{1000}{5}$	$\frac{1000}{5}$
	= £200 p.a.	= £200 p.a.	= £200 p.a.
∴ ARR is	$\frac{200}{100} = 20\%$	$\frac{200}{1000} = 20\%$	$\frac{200}{100} = 20\%$

Accounting rate of return on Average Capital:

	Project I	Project II	Project III
Average Capital	$= \frac{1000}{2}$	$\frac{1000}{2}$	$\frac{1000}{2}$
	= £500	= £500	= £500
∴ ARR is	$\frac{200}{500} = 40\%$	$\frac{200}{500} = 40\%$	$\frac{200}{500} = 40\%$

Note: Average capital is calculated according to the usual accounting convention that the initial investment is eroded steadily to zero over the life of the project so that the average capital invested is

$$\frac{\text{Initial Investment}}{2}$$

ADVANTAGES AND DISADVANTAGES OF ARR.

5. The only advantage that can be claimed for the ARR is simplicity of calculation, but the disadvantages are more numerous.

Disadvantages:

a. Does not allow for the timing of outflows and inflows. The three projects in Example 1 are ranked equally even though there are clear differences in timings.

b. Uses as a measure of return the concept of accounting profit. Profit has subjective elements, is subject ot accounting conventions and is not as appropriate for investment appraisal purposes as the cash flows generated by the project.

c. There is no universally accepted method of calculating ARR.

PAYBACK.

6. Numerous surveys have shown that payback is a popular technique for appraising projects either on its own or in conjunction with other methods. Payback can be defined as the period, usually expressed in years which it takes for the project's net cash inflows to recoup the original investment. The usual decision rules is to accept the project with the shortest payback period. The following example demonstrates the technique.

Example 2

Calculate the payback periods for the following three projects:

NET CASH FLOWS

Year	PROJECT I		PROJECT II		PROJECT III	
	Cash Flow	Cumulative Cash Flow	Cash Flow	Cumulative Cash Flow	Cash Flow	Cumulative Cash Flow
0	-1500	-1500	-1500	-1500	-1500	-1500
1	+ 600	- 900	+ 400	-1100	+ 300	-1200
2	+ 500	- 400	- 500	- 600	+ 500	- 700
3	+ 400	NIL	+ 600	NIL	+ 400	- 300
4	—		—		+ 300	NIL
5	—		—		+ 300	+ 300
6	—		—		+ 300	+ 600

(Note: The usual investment appraisal assumptions are adopted for the above table and all subsequent examples, that Year 0 means now, Year 1 means at the end of 1 year, Year 2 the end of 2 years and so on, and that a negative cash flow represents a cash outflow and a positive sign represents a cash inflow).

Payback Periods	Project I	=	3 years
	Project II	=	3 years
	Project III	=	4 years

ADVANTAGES AND DISADVANTAGES OF PAYBACK.

7. Advantages:

a. Simple to calculate and understand.

b. Uses project cash flows rather than accounting profits and hence is more objectively based.

c. Favours quick return projects which may produce faster growth for the company and enhance liquidity.

d. Choosing projects which payback quickest will tend to minimise those risks facing the company which are related to time. However, not all risks are related merely to time.

Disadvantages:

a. Payback does not measure overall project worth because it does not consider cash flows after the payback period. In Example 2, Project III is ranked after Project I and II, even though it produces cash flows over a 6 year period.

b. Payback provides only a crude measure of the timing of project cash flows. In Example 2, Projects I and II are ranked equally, even though there are clear differences in the timings of the cash flows.

In spite of any theoretical disadvantages, payback is undoubtedly the most popular appraisal criterion in practice.

DISCOUNTED CASH FLOW (DCF).

8. There is growing use of DCF techniques for appraising projects and for assisting investment decision making. The use of DCF overcomes some of the disadvantages of the traditional techniques but it must be stressed that DCF itself has problems and contains many assumptions so that it should be used with care and with an awareness of its limitations. The main DCF techniques of Net Present Value (NPV) and Internal Rate of Return (IRR) are described in this chapter but it is necessary first to consider two features common to all DCF methods: the use of cash flows and the time value of money.

USE OF CASH FLOWS.

9. All DCF methods use cash flows and not accounting profits. Accounting profits are invariably calculated for stewardship purposes and are period orientated (usually monthly, quarterly or annually) thus necessitating accrual accounting with its attendant conventions and assumptions. For investment appraisal purposes a project orientated approach using cash flows is to be preferred for the following reasons.

a. Cash flows are more objective and in the end are what actually count.
Profits cannot be spent.

b. Accounting conventions regarding revenue/capital expenditure classifications, depreciation calculations, stock valuations become largely redundant.

c. The whole life of the project is to be considered, therefore it becomes unnecessary and misleading to consider accounting profits which are related to periods.

d. The timing or expected timing of cash flows is more easily ascertained.

WHAT CASH FLOWS SHOULD BE INCLUDED?

10. the all embracing answer to this question is the net after tax incremental cash flow effect on the firm by accepting the project, i.e. the comparison of cash flows with and without the project. Many of the cash flow items are readily identifiable, e.g. the initial outlay on a new machine, but others are less easily identified yet are nevertheless just as relevant, e.g. the increase or reduction in sales income of an existing product when a new product is introduced. Typical cash flow items include:

a. Cash Inflows

i. The project revenues

ii. Government grants

iii. Resale or scrap value of assets

iv. Tax receipts

v. Any other cash inflows caused by accepting the project

b. Cash Outflow

i. Initial investment in acquiring the assets

ii. Project costs (labour, materials etc)

iii. Working capital investment

iv. Tax payments

v. Any other cash outflow caused by accepting the project.

Notes:

a. The relevant costs in investment decisions, as with all other decisions, are opportunity costs and not historical accounting costs. For example, if a project occupies storage space rented by the firm at £5/square metre which could be sublet by the firm at £7/square metre, then the relevant cash flow is the benefit foregone of £7/square metre.

b. It will be noted that depreciation is not included. Depreciation is NOT a cash flow but an accounting convention. The capital outlay is already represented by the cash outflow of the initial investment, so to include depreciation would involve double counting. The only role of depreciation in investment appraisal is in determining the tax payments of the project, which are, of course, real cash flows.

c. Similarly, interest payments are not included because the discounting process itself takes account of the time value of money and to include interest payments and to discount would be to double count.

TIME VALUE OF MONEY.

11. Investment appraisal is concerned with long run decisions where costs and income arise at intervals over a period. Monies spent or received at different times cannot be compared directly, they must be reduced to equivalent values at some common date. This could be at any time during the project life but appraisal methiods which take account of the time factor use either now, the present time, or the end of the project as the common date.

Both discounting and compounding methods allow for the time value of money and could thus be used for investment appraisal but on the whole discounting methods are more frequently used. In general it is preferable to receive a given sum earlier rather than later because the sum received earlier can be put to use by earning interest or some productive investment within the business i.e. money has a time productivity.

It should be noted that the time value of money concept applies even if there is zero inflation. Inflation obviously increases the discreptancy in value between monies received at different times but it is not the basis of the concept.

ASSUMPTIONS IN BASIC DCF APPRAISAL.

12. In describing the two main DCF methods certain assumptions are made initially so that the underlying principles can be more easily understood. These are as follows:

a. Uncertainty does not exist
b. Inflation does not exist
c. The appropriate discount rate to use is known
d. A perfect capital market exists i.e. unlimited funds can be raised at the market rate of interest.

Subsequently these assumptions will be removed and the problems of dealing with uncertainty, inflation, and capital rationing are dealt with. The choice of an appropriate discount rate involves Financial Management and is outside the scope of this manual.

NET PRESENT VALUE (NPV).

13. The NPV method utilises discounting principles which should be familiar from the previous chapter.

The NPV method involves calculating the present values of expected cash inflows and outflows (i.e. the process of discounting) and establishing whether in total the present value of cash inflows is greater than the present value of cash outflows.

The formula is

$$NPV = \sum_{i=0}^{i=n} \frac{C_i}{(1+r)^i}$$

where C is the net cash flow in the period, i is the period number, and r is the discount rate.

Where the discount rate is the cost of capital of the firm the usual decision rule, given the assumptions in para 12., is that a project is acceptable if it has a positive NPV.

Example 3.

An investment is being considered for which the net cash flows have been estimated as follows:

Year 0	Year 1	Year 2	Year 3	Year 4
-9,500	+3,000	+4,700	+4,800	+3,200

What is the NPV if the discount rate is 20% ? Is the project acceptable?

Note: Conventional year end cash flows have been assumed i.e . Year 0 means now, Year 1 means after 1 year and so on.

Solution

From Table VIII the discount factors are 0.833, 0.694, 0.579 and 0.482

$\therefore$ NPV $= -9,500 + (0.833 \times 3,000) + (0.694 \times 4,700) + (0.597 \times 4,800) + (0.482 \times 3,200)$

NPV = + £582 and, given the assumptions contained in the basic DCF model the investment would be acceptable.

MEANING OF NPV.

14. If the NPV of a project is positive this can be interpreted as the potential increase in consumption made, possible by the project valued in present day terms. This is illustrated by Table 1 based on Example 3 which shows the position if £9,500 is borrowed at 20% p.a. to finance the project on overdraft terms where interest is paid on the balance outstanding at the end of each year.

	Amount Owing b/fwd	+	Year's Interest	–	Year's Cash Flow	=	Balance o/s c/fwd
End Year 1	9500	+	1900	–	3000	=	8400
End Year 2	8400	+	1680	–	4700	=	5380
End Year 3	5380	+	1076	–	4800	=	1656
End Year 4	1656	+	331	–	3200		

giving a final surplus of £1213

Table 1

This shows that if £9500 is borrowed at 20% the principal and interest could be repaid from the project cash flows leaving a cash balance at the end of Year 4 of £1212. This balance is known a Net Terminal Value and has a present value of £584 (£1213 × 0.482) which, allowing for the approximations contained in three figure tables, is the NPV of Example 3.

INTERNAL RATE OF RETURN (IRR).

15. Alternative names for the IRR include: DCF yield, marginal efficiency of capital, trial and error method, discounted yield and the actuarial rate of return.

The IRR can be defined as the discount rate which gives zero NPV. Except by chance the IRR cannot be found directly; it can be found either by drawing a graph known as a present value profile or, more normally, by calculations involving linear interpolation. Both methods are illustrated below using the data from Example 3.

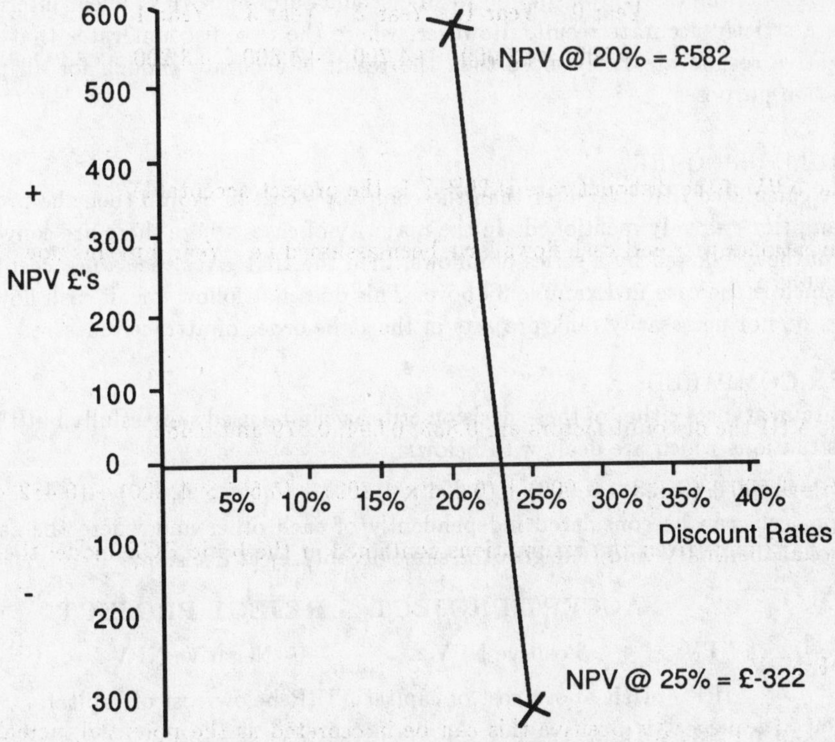

Figure 1 Present Value Profile

Notes on Figure 1.

a. At least one discount rate must be chosen which gives a negative NPV so that the present value line crosses the horizontal axis.

b. The present value line crosses the axis at approximately 23% which is a close enough estimate for most practical purposes.

FINDING THE IRR BY LINEAR INTERPOLATION.

16. Based on the data from Example 3 the IRR can be calculated as follows:

$$\text{IRR} = \underset{(a)}{20\%} + \underset{(b)}{5\%} \left(\frac{\overset{(c)}{582}}{\underset{(d)}{904}} \right)$$

$$= \underline{23.2\%}$$

Where

(a) is a discount rate which gives a positive NPV. In this example 20% gives £582.

(b) is the difference between (a) and the rate which gives a negative NPV.
In this example 25% - 20% = 5%

(c) is the positive NPV at the discount rate chosen in (a). In this example it is £582.

(d) is the total range of NPV at the rates chosen. In this example + 582 to – 322 is a range of £904.

Notes:

a. A simple way of obtaining a rough estimate of the IRR is to take the reciprocal of the payback period. This works best with relatively long payback periods. With short payback periods as in Example 3 the method is a poor estimator.

b. As there is a non-linear relationship between discount rates and NPV, linear interpolation does not give a strictly accurate result. However, where the two discount rates that give positive and negative results are fairly close then the result is accurate enough for all practical and examination purposes.

DECISION RULE USING IRR.

17. Where the calculated IRR is greater than the company's cost of capital then the project is acceptable, given the assumptions already mentioned. In the majority of cases where there are conventional cash flows i.e. an initial outflow followed by a series of inflows, then the IRR gives the same accept or reject decision as the NPV which is the case in Example 3 above. This does not follow for all cash flow patterns and the two techniques do not necessarily rank projects in the same order of attractiveness.

NPV AND IRR COMPARED.

18. In many circumstances either of these decision criteria can be used successfully but there are differences in particular situations which are dealt with below.

a. Accept/Reject decisions.
Where projects can be considered independently of each other and where the cash flows are conventional then NPV and IRR give the same accept/reject decision.

	ACCEPT PROJECT	**REJECT PROJECT**
NPV	Positive NPV	Negative NPV
IRR	IRR above cost of capital	IRR below cost of capital

b. Absolute and Relative measures.
NPV is an absolute measure of the return on a project whereas IRR is a relative measure relating the size and timing of the cash flows to the initial investment. Thus the NPV reflects the scale of a project whereas the IRR does not.

Example 4

Assume a project has the following cash flows:

		Year 0	Year 5
Project x		–£20,000	+£40,241
NPV @ 10%	=	£4,990	
IRR	=	15%	

∴ Project acceptable by both methods - assuming 10% is the cost of capital
Now assume that the project is scaled up by a factor of 10

		Year 0	Year 5
Project 10x		–£200,000	+£402,410
NPV @ 10%	=	£49,900	
IRR	=	15%	

The NPV method clearly discriminates between Project x and Project 10x whereas the IRR remains unchanged at 15% .

c. Mutually Exclusive Projects.
An important class of projects is that concerned with mutually exclusive decisions e.g. where only one of several alternative projects can be chosen. For example, where several alternative uses of the same piece of land are being considered, when one is chosen the others are automatically excluded.

Mutually exclusive decisions are commonly encountered and make it necessary to rank projects in order of attractiveness and to choose the most profitable. In such circumstances NPV and IRR may give conflicting rankings.

Example 5 (Mutually exclusive projects of differing scale)

A property company wishes to develop a site it owns. Three sizes of property are being considered and the costs and revenues are as follows:

	Year 0	Year 1 to perpetuity
	Expenditure	Rentals p.a.
	£m	£m
Small development	2	0.6
Medium development	4	1
Large development	6	1.35

The cost of capital is 10% and it is required to rank the projects by NPV and IRR and to select the most profitable.

The projects are mutually exclusive because the building of one size of development excludes the others.

Solution

	Expenditure	P.V. of rentals	NPV	IRR
	£m	£m	£m	%
Small	2	6	4	30
Medium	4	10	6	25
Large	6	13.5	7.5	22.5

The ranking obtained by NPV and IRR differ and in such circumstances the NPV ranking is preferred (i.e. large develoment in this example) because it leads to the greatest increase in wealth for the company.

Although safer and simpler to rank by NPV , IRR can be used by adopting an incremental approach and comparing the incremental IRR at each increment with the cost of capital. Example 5 is reworked using this approach.

	Incremental Expenditure	Incremental Rental	Incremental IRR
	£m	£m	%
Stage 1 (small)	2	0.6	30
Stage 2 (medium – small)	2	0.4	20
Stage 3 (large – medium)	2	0.35	17.5

It will be seen that the IRR of each successive stage, although declining, is greater than the 10% cost of capital so that each successive increment is worthwhile. Although this method leads to the correct conclusion it is cumbersome and the simpler, more direct NPV method is preferable.

Example 6 (Mutually exclusive projects, same scale)

Two mutually exclusive investments have cash flows as follows:

	Year 0	Year 1	Year 2	Year 3
Project A	-24000	+ 8000	+ 12000	+ 16000
Project B	-24000	+ 16000	+ 10000	+ 8000

The cost of capital is 10%

The NPV and IRR of these projects is as follows:

	NPV @ 10%	IRR
		%
Project A	+2600	20.65
Project B	+2406	22.8

Thus it will be seen that the ranking differ and, assuming that 10% is the appropriate discount rate, the ranking given by the NPV, i.e. Project A being preferred, gives the maximum wealth to the company.

Note: The conflict in ranking shown abnove is but a reflection of the differing time profile of the project cash flows. Such time profiles produce different NPV rankings using different discount rates; for example, the NPV's of the above projects at 20% discount rate are £1256 and £900 respectively, giving a B - A ranking instead of the A - B ranking at 10%.

NON-CONVENTIONAL CASH FLOWS. (THE MULTIPLE RATE PROBLEM).

19. The projects considered so far have had conventional cash flows i.e. an intial outflow followed by a series of inflows. Where the cash flows vary from this they are termed non-conventional. The following are examples.

Example 7. Non-Conventional Cash-flow Patterns

	Year 0	Year 1	Year 2
Project X	-2000	+4700	-2750
Project Y	+2000	-4000	+4000

Project X has 2 outflows and is thus non-conventional

Project Y has an outflow in a year's time instead of initially and is thus non-conventional.

When a project has non-conventional cash flows it may have

i. one IRR

ii. multiple IRR's

iii. no IRR

Multiple Rates:- If the present value profile for Project x in Example 7 is drawn it can be seen that it is a multiple IRR project having two IRR's, at 10% and 25% .

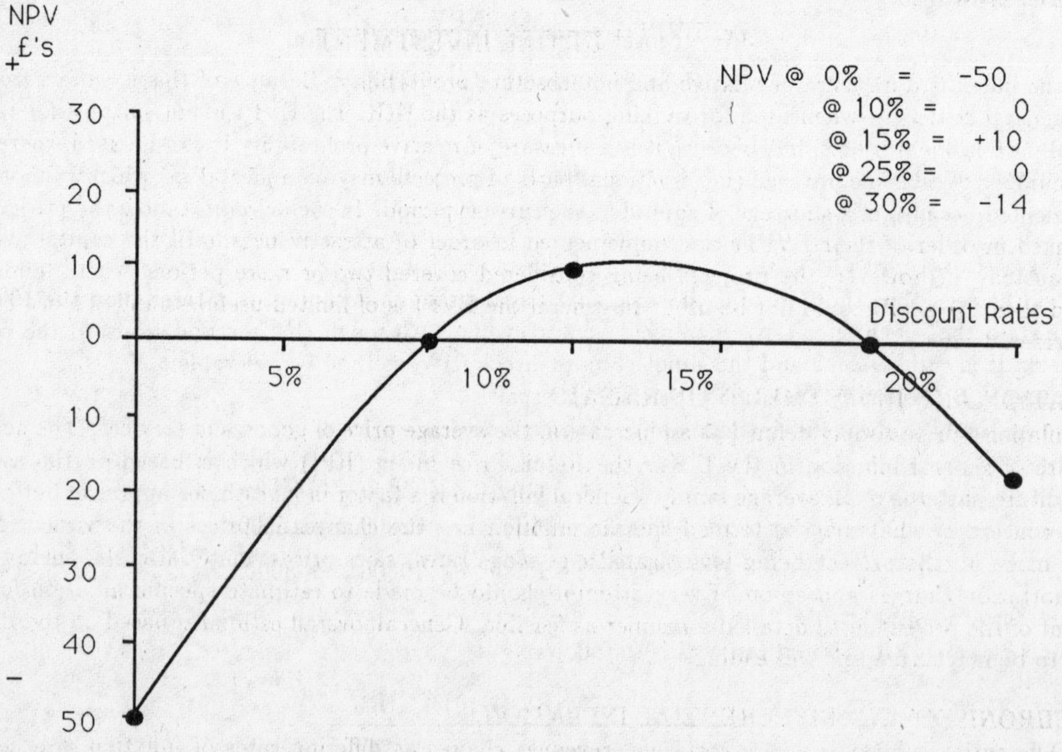

Figure 2 Present Value Profile of Project X

No IRR: Project Y in Example 7 above is an example of a project where it is not possible to calculate a real rate of return.

To be able to calculate a real IRR it is necessary to solve for i in the following expression:

$$+2000 - \frac{4000}{(1+i)^1} + \frac{4000}{(1+i)^2} = 0$$

Solving for i produces $i = \sqrt{-1}$ which is not a real number.

In circumstances with non-conventional cash flow patterns which produce multiple IRR's or no real IRR the use of IRR is not recommended.

The NPV method gives clear, unambiguous results whatever the cash flow pattern.

Project X above has positive NPV's at discount rates between 10% and 25% and negative NPV's at lower and higher rates. Project Y has a positive NPV at any discount rate.

SUMMARY OF NPV and IRR COMPARISON.

20.

a. NPV is technically superior to IRR and is simpler to calculate.

b. Where cash-flow patterns are non-conventional there may be nil or several internal rates of return making the IRR impossible to apply.

c. NPV is superior for ranking investments in order of attractiveness.

d. With conventional cash flow patterns both methods give the same accept or reject decision.

e. Where discount rates are expected to differ over the life of the project such variations can be readily incorporated into NPV calculations, but not in those for the IRR.

f. Notwithstanding the technical advantages of NPV over IRR, IRR is widely used in practice so that it is essential that students are aware of its inherent limitations.

EXCESS PRESENT VALUE INDEX (EVPI) OR PROFITABILITY INDEX.

21. The EVPI is merely a variant of the basic NPV method and is the ratio of the NPV of a project to the initial investment.

$$\text{i.e. EVPI} = \frac{\text{NPV}}{\text{INITIAL INVESTMENT}}$$

Thus the index is a measure of relative and not absolute profitability. Because of this it suffers from the same general criticisms when used for ranking purposes as the IRR. The EVPI is not suitable for ranking mutually exclusive projects, but because it is a measure of relative profitability it can be used where there are a number of divisible projects (i.e. fractional parts of projects may be undertaken) which cannot all be implemented because of a shortage of capital in the current period. In such circumstances the projects can be ranked in order of their EVPI's and implemented in order of attractiveness until the capital available is exhausted. If, however, the projects being considered covered two or more periods where funds were limited then the EVPI could not be used. In general the EVPI is of limited usefuless and the use of NPV is considered safer.

INFLATION AND INVESTMENT APPRAISAL.

22. Inflation can be simply defined as an increase in the average price of goods and services. The accepted measure of general inflation in the U.K.is the Retail Price Index (RPI) which is based on the assumed expenditure patterns of an average family. General inflation is a factor in investment appraisal but of more direct concern is what may be termed specific inflation i.e. the changes in prices of the various factors which make up the project being investigated e.g. wage rates, sales prices, material costs, energy costs, transportation charges and so on. Every attempt should be made to estimate specific inflation for each element of the project in as detailed a manner as feasible. General, overall estimates based on the RPI are likely to be inaccurate and misleading.

SYNCHRONISED AND DIFFERENTIAL INFLATION.

23. Differential inflationis where costs and revenues change at differing rates of inflation or where the various items of cost and revenue move at different rates. This is the normal situation but the concept of synchronised inflation - where costs and revenues rise at the same rate - although unlikely to be encountered in practice, is useful for illustrating various facets of projects appraisals involving inflation.

MONEY CASH FLOWS AND REAL CASH FLOWS.

24. Money cash flows are the actual amounts of money changing hands whereas 'real' cash flows are the purchasing power equivalents of the actual cash flows. In a world of zero inflation there would be no need to distinguish between money and real cash flows as they would be identical. Where inflation does exist then a difference arises between money cash flows and their real value and this difference is the basis of the treatment of inflation in project appraisal.

DEALING WITH INFLATION.

25. The following example will be used to illustrate the way that inflation is dealt with in investment appraisal.

Example 8.

A labour saving machine costs £60,000 and will save £24,000 p.a. at current wage rates. The machine is expected to have a 3 year life and nil scrap value. The firm's cost of capital is 10% .

Calculate the project's NPV

a. With no inflation

b. With general inflation of 15% which wage rates are expected to follow (i.e. synchronised inflation).

c. With general inflation of 15% and wages rising at 20% p.a. (i.e. differential inflation)

Solution

a. NPV - No inflation

$$-60,000 + 24000A_{3]10\%}$$
$$= -60,000 + 24000 \times 2.487 = -£312$$

∴ Project unacceptable as it has a negative NPV at company's cost of capital

b. General inflation 15%, wages increasing at 15%

Wage savings p.a. with no inflation	Wage savings p.a. with 15% inflation
24000	27600
24000	31740
24000	36501

With no inflation the appropriate discounting rate was 10% . With inflation at 15% , the 10% discounting rate is insufficient to bring cash sums arising at different periods into equivalent purchasing power terms. Without inflation £1 now was deemed equivalent to £1.10 a year hence. With a 15% inflation rate the sum required would be £1.10 (1.15) = £1.265, thus the discount rate to be used is $26\frac{1}{2}\%$.

Project NPV with 15% synchronised inflation

Year	Cash Flow	$26\frac{1}{2}\%$ Discount Factors	Present Value
0	-60,000	1,000	-60,000
1	+27,600	0.792	21,859
2	+31,740	0.624	19,806
3	+36,501	0.494	18,031
		NPV =	-£304

∴ Project unacceptable

It will be seen that the answers with no inflation and with 15% synchronised inflation are virtually the same, (the difference being due to roundings in three figure tables). This equivalence is to be expected, as with synchronised inflation the firm, in real terms, is no better or no worse off.

c. Project with 15% general inflation and wages rising at 20% p.a. (differential inflation)

Wages per annum

Year 1	24000 (1.20)	=	£28,800
2	24000 $(1.20)^2$	=	£34,560
3	24000 $(1.20)^3$	=	£41,472

Project NPV with differential inflation

Year	Cash Flows	$26\frac{1}{2}$% Discount Factors	Present Value
0	-60,000	1,000	-60,000
1	+28,800	0.792	22,810
2	+34,560	0.624	21,565
3	+41,472	0.494	20,487
		NPV =	£4,862

∴ Project unacceptable

Thus it will be seen that with differential inflation the project is acceptable. In this case this is to be expected because it was a labour saving project so that, in real terms, the firm is better off if the rate of wage inflation is greater than the general rate of inflation.

Frequently differential inflation works to the disadvantage of the firm, for example, when costs are rising faster than prices. Each case is different and detailed, individual analysis is required - not generalised assumptions.

MONEY AND REAL DISCOUNT RATES.

26. The $26\frac{1}{2}$% discount rate used in Example 1 was a money discount factor and was used to discount the money cash flows of the project. The relationship between real and money discount factors is as follows:

$$\text{Real discount factor} = \frac{1 + \text{Money discount factor}}{1 + \text{Inflation Rate}} - 1$$

Using the data from Example 1 the real discount factor can be calculated.

$$\text{Real discount factor} = \frac{1 + .265}{1 + .15} - 1 = 0.1 \text{ i.e. } \underline{\underline{10\%}}$$

In this case, of course, the real discount factor was already known and the above calculation was for illustrative purposes only.

The real discount factor can be used providing that the money cash flows are first converted into real cash flows by discounting at the general inflation rate as follows.

Example 9.

Rework part (c) of Example 8 using real cash flows and the real discount factor.

Real Cash Flow Evaluation

Year	Money Cash Flow	General Inflation 15% Discount Factors	Real Cash Flows	Real Discount Factors 10%	Present Values
0	-60,000	1,000	-60,000	1.000	-60,000
1	+28,800	0.870	25,056	.909	22,776
2	+34,560	0.756	26,127	.826	21,581
3	+41,472	0.658	27,289	.751	20,494
				NPV =	£4,851

From which it will be seen that (table rounding differences apart) the two methods give identical results.

Thus it will be seen that there are two approaches to investment appraisal where inflation is present.

SINGLE DISCOUNTING – MONEY CASH FLOWS DISCOUNTED BY MONEY DISCOUNT FACTOR

TWO STAGES DISCOUNTING – MONEY CASH FLOWS DISCOUNTED BY GENERAL INFLATION RATE AND THEN THE REAL CASH FLOWS PRODUCED DISCOUNTED BY REAL DISCOUNT FACTOR

The two approaches produce the same answer because the money discount factor includes the inflation allowance. Because of this and because money cash flows are the most natural medium in which estimates will be made, it is recommended that money cash flows should be discounted at an appropriate money discount factor. Take GREAT CARE never to discount money cash flows by a real discount factor or real cash flows by a money discount factor. If real cash flows are directly provided in a question take care to discount once only using a real discount factor.

TAXATION AND INVESTMENT APPRAISAL.

27. Because taxation causes a change in cash flows it is a factor to be considered in project appraisal. Indeed in some practical situations the taxation implications are dominant influences on the final investment decision. Any consideration of tax intricacies is clearly outside the scope of this manual and the analyst is strongly recommended to seek advice from a tax specialist when dealing with project appraisal.

The payment of tax reduces the cash flows of a project so that in outline, the analyst will need to know the amount of the tax liability and the time when the tax liability and the time when the tax must be paid.

SUMMARY.

28.

a. Investment decisions are long run decisions where consumption and investment opportunities are balanced over time.
b. The decision to invest is based on many factors including; the investor's beliefs in the future, the alternatives available and his attitude to risk.
c. The 'traditional' investment appraisal techniques are the accounting rate of return and payback. Payback is shown by recent surveys to be the most widely used technique.
d. Payback is the number of period's cash flows to recoup the original investment. The project chosen is the one with the shortest payback period.
e. Discounted Cash Flow (DCF) techniques use cash flows rather than profits and take account of the time value of money.
f. The formula for Net Present Value is

$$NPV = \sum \frac{Ci}{(1+r)^i}$$

and given the assumption of the basic model, a project is acceptable if it has a positive NPV

g. NPV can be interpreted as the potential increase in consumption made possible by the project valued in present day terms.

h. Internal Rate of Return (IRR) is the discount rate which gives zero NPV and can be found graphically or by linear interpolation.

i. With conventional projects IRR and NPV give the same accept or reject decision NPV is an absolute measure whereas IRR is a relative one.

j. NPV is a more appropriate measure for choosing between mutually exclusive projects and in general is technically superior to IRR.

k. The discount rate used in DCF calculations is known as the cost of capital.

l. Specific inflation is of more direct concern in investment appraisal and differential inflation is commonly encountered.

m. The general treatment of inflation in investment appraisal and differential inflation is commonly encountered.

n. The amount and timing of tax payments and other tax effects must be considered.

POINTS TO NOTE.

29.

a. It is arguable that the existence of a stream of potentially worthwhile investment opportunities is of far greater importance to the firm than the particular appraisal method used.

b. A recent survey of the capital budgeting practices of large companies by Dr R. Pike showed that over 75% of companies used payback as an appraisal method, often in conjunction with other techniques. The same survey showed that only 17% on companies used NPV as their primary evaluation technique in spite of the generally acknowledged technical superiority of NPV over payback. This would seem to suggest that much of the academic preoccupation with refining measurement techniques may be misplaced.

c. Successful investment appraisal is entirely dependent on the accuracy of cost and revenue estimates. No appraisal technique can overcome significant inaccuracies in this area.

SELF REVIEW QUESTIONS.

1 Why are investment decisions important? (2)

2 Define the accounting rate of return and give its advantages and disadvantages? (4)

3 What is payback and what is the normal decision rule using payback? (6)

4 Why are cash flows used in DCF calculations and not accounting profits? (6)

5 What cash flows should be included in the appraisal? (10)

6 Why has money a time value? (11)

7 Define NPV and state the basic formula (13)

8 What is Net Terminal Value? (14)

9 What is the Internal Rate of Return and how is it calculated? (15 and 16)

10 What are the major differences between NPV and IRR? (18)

11 What is the multiple rate problem? (19)

12 What is the EVPI or Profitability Index and when can it be used effectively? (21)

13 What type of inflation is most relevant to investment appraisal? (22)

14 What is the general method of dealing with inflation in investment appraisal? (25)

15 Distinguish between money and real discount rates? (26)

16 What is the importance of taxation in investment appraisal? (27)

EXERCISES WITH ANSWERS COMMENCING PAGE 488

A1. What is the present value of the following series at 10% and its IRR?

0	1	2	3	4
-2000	+800	+600	+700	+500

A2. Draw a present value profile of the following project and determine the IRR. Is the project acceptable at 10% cost of capital?

	Year 0	Year 1	Year 2
Cash Flows	-4000	+10,200	-6,300

A3. A firm is considering a project with a cash outlay of £1,000 now and 5 yearly cash inflows of £500.

(a) What is the NPV at 10% ?

(b) What is the NPV assuming a general inflation rate of 8% and an increase in cash flows to £510 per annum?

EXAMINATION QUESTIONS WITH ANSWERS COMMENCING PAGE 488

A4. You have been appointed a chief management accountant of a well-established company with a brief to improve the quality of information supplied for management decision-making. As a first task you have decided to examine the system used for providing information for capital investment decisions. You find that discounted cash flow techniques are used but in a mechanical fashion with no apparent understanding of the figures produced. The most recent example of an investment appraisal produced by the accounting department showed a positive Net Present Value of £35,000 for a five-year life project when discounted at 14% which you are informed 'was the rate charged on the bank loan raised to finance the investment'. You note that the appraisal did not include any consideration of the effects of inflation nor was there any form of risk analysis.

You are required to:

(a) explain the meaning of a positive Net Present Value of £35,000;

(b) comment on the appropriateness or otherwise of the discounting rate used;

(c) state whether you agree with the treatment of inflation and, if not, explain how you would deal with inflation in investment appraisals;

(d) explain what is meant by 'risk analysis' and describe ways this could be carried out in investment appraisals and what benefits (if any) this would bring.

CIMA Management Accounting Techniques

A5. An accountant is using the concept of net present value (NPV) to assess three alternative methods of paying for a new computer system which is expected to have a commercial life of eight years before replacement.

(a) Rent the system for eight years at £120,000 per annum, payable annually in advance, inclusive of all servicing and maintenance.

(b) Outright purchase for £0.5 million, with a service contract of £40,000 payable annually in advance. After eight years the system would have a re-sale value of 10% of its original purchase price.

(c) Hire purchase of a deposit of £150,000 and seven further annual payments of £100,000, inclusive of all servicing, after which time (i.e. after eight years) the company would own the system, then worth £50,000.

You are required to find which method is the most economical, assuming the cost of capital to be 15%, and comment on your answer.

(CIMA Quantitative Methods)

A6. Romulus Products plc operates 30 day terms for all its customers. Experience has shown that 80% of all accounts are settled within 1 month, and 70% of the remainder are settled during the second month after the customer has been sent a standard 'overdue account' letter. Of those accounts still unpaid after 2 months, 50% are settled during the third month after a 'final demand' has been sent.

Any accounts still not paid after 3 months are dealt with in one of two ways. If the amount owing exceeds £1,000, the company institutes legal proceedings to recover the money. Taking into account the legal costs involved, the proportion of the original sum owing which is ultimately recovered varies as follows:

Proportion Recovered	*Probability*
0% - 40%	*0.1*
40% - 60%	*0.3*
60% - 80%	*0.4*
80% -100%	*0.2*

This process takes a further 3 months before payment is finally received.

If the amount owing is less than £1,000, the debt is sold to a debt collecting company in return for 50% of the sum involved, which is obtained after a further month i.e. at the end of month 4.

In recent months, the size of the accounts issued by Romulus is shown by the following distributions:

Size of Account	*Probability*
£0 - £200	*0.1*
£200 - £500	*0.2*
£500 - £1,000	*0.3*
£1,000 - £2,000	*0.3*
£2,000 - £5,000	*0.1*

You may assume that there is no relationship between the size of the account, when it is settled and the proportion recovered; and that all accounts are settled on the last day of the month. The company's cost of capital is the equivalent of 1.5% per month.

Required:

(a) What is the probability that, for any particular account, payment is received at the end of

i. the second month

ii. the third month

iii. the fourth month

iv. the sixth month?

(b) What is the expected present value of a new account which has £2,000 outstanding?

Monthly discount factors are:

Month	*1*	*2*	*3*	*4*	*5*	*6*
Factor	*0.9852*	*0.9707*	*0.9563*	*0.9422*	*0.9283*	*0.9145*

(c) Show how the system as a whole may be simulated by using the folliwng random digits to determine the present value of two simulated accounts.

Account 1:	*8*	*8*	*7*	*5*	*7*
Account 2:	*9*	*9*	*8*	*2*	*9*

ACCA Quantitative Analaysis

EXERCISES WITHOUT ANSWERS

B1. What is the value of the following series at 20% and its IRR?

0	*1*	*2*	*3*
-5,000	*+2,500*	*+2,000*	*+2,000*

B2. A firm is considering the following mutually exclusive projects.

	OUTLAY NOW	*Year 1*	*2*	*3*
PROJECT A	*-7,000*	*3,430*	*3,430*	*3,430*
PROJECT B	*-12,000*	*5,520*	*5,520*	*5,520*

Based on the cash flows above and a 10% cost of capital calculate:
(a) the NPV and IRR's of the projects
(b) select the better project

B3. Draw present value profiles of the projects in B2 and comment on the graph

B4. Prove the results in B2 by using the incremental IRR method.

EXAMINATION QUESTIONS WITHOUT ANSWERS

B5. Phil the farmer at Pond Farm in the village of Upper Lake has previously raised ducks for the Christmas market. Having been so successful he now wants to supply a local deep freeze company throughout the year. He buys the young ducklings at a local market for £0.50 each. The price at which he sells the ducks depends upon their weight. He estimates that he should receive £1.00 per 1lb of duck.

A local mathematician has calculated that the weight of a duck depends upon its age and may be represented by the following equation:

$$W = 0.25 + 0.5x - 0.001x^3 \text{ for } 0 \leq x \leq 14$$

where
W = weight in lbs
x = number of weeks the farmer has had the duck
Phil estimates that the weekly cost of feeding each duck on a high nutrient diet is £0.40 a week.

When the duck has been at the farm for 3 weeks she starts to lay eggs at an average of 5 eggs a week. These eggs can be sold at £0.60 for 12 eggs, the cash being received at the end of each week.

Required:

a. Determine the time after purchase at which the farmer should sell the ducks if he is to maximise his profit. (Round to nearest week). What is the profit per duck?

b. How is the solution to part (a) changed if the opportunity cost of money is taken into account? (Assume all cash flows take place at the end of the week apart from the initial £0.50 cost of duckling which is incurred at the beginning of the week.) Use a discount rate of 1/2% per week for which appropriate present value factors are given in the following table.

Present Value Factors

Week	$\frac{1}{2}\%$
1	
2	0.990
3	0.985
4	0.980
5	0.975
6	0.971
7	0.966
8	0.961
9	0.956
10	0.951
11	0.947
12	0.942
13	0.937
14	0.933

(ACCA Management Mathematics)

30 Investment Appraisal – Uncertainty and Capital Rationing

INTRODUCTION.

1. This chapter continues the study of investment appraisal and considers the various methods of analysing uncertainty in investment decisions. These include time based methods, probabilistic analysis, portfolio analysis and consideration of the decision maker's attitude to risk. The chapter concludes with an explanation of the ways of dealing with capital rationing.

UNCERTAINTY IN INVESTMENT APPRAISAL.

2. Uncertainity is a major factor to be considered in all types of decision making. It is of particular importance in investment appraisal because of the long time scale and amounts of resources involved in a typical investment decision.

In general, risky or uncertain projects are those whose future cash flows, and hence the returns on the project, are likely to be variable - the greater the variability, the greater the risk. Unfortunately, elements of uncertainty can exist even if future cash flows are known with certainty. For example, if a lease is being appraised the future cash flows are known and fixed but their value may vary because of changes in the rate of inflation.

There are three stages of the overall appraisal and decision process in which risk and uncertainty merit special attention:

a. The risk and uncertainty associated with the individual project.

b. The effect on the overall risk and uncertainty of the firm when the project being considered is combined with the rest of the firm's operations – the portfolio effect.

c. The decision maker's attitude to risk and its effect on the final decision.

These three elements are dealt with below:

UNCERTAINTY AND THE INDIVIDUAL PROJECT.

3. Various methods of considering the uncertainty associated with projects are described below. They have the general objective of attempting to assess or quantify the uncertainty surrounding a project by some form of analysis which goes beyond merely calculating the overall return expected from the project. In this way further information is provided for the ultimate decision maker so that, hopefully, a better decision will be made. It must be emphasised, however that the methods do not of themselves reduce the uncertainties surrounding a proposed investment. If this is feasible, it can only be done by management action.

The methods to be described can be separated into three groups.

a. Time based.

b. Probability based

c. Sensitivity analysis and simulation.

TIME BASED.

4. The three methods of incorporating uncertainty which are based on time are Payback, Risk Premium and Finite Horizon. These methods rest on the assumption that project risks and uncertainty are related to time ie the longer the project the more uncertain it is. Whilst it is reasonable to assume that uncertainty does often increase with time it is by no means universally true and there are many projects which are shortlived and risky whilst others are long term and relatively safe. The three methods are described below:

PAYBACK.

5. This is the number of periods cash flows required to recoup the original investment. Apart from its use as an accept/reject criterion, payback can be used as a measure of risk, often in conjunction with a DCF measure such as NPV or IRR. If two projects A and B had approximately the same NPV and A had the shorter payback period then A would be preferred.

Advantages:

a. Simplicity of calculation.

b. General acceptability and ease of understanding

Disadvantages:

a. Assumes that uncertainty relates only to the time elapsed.

b. Assumes that cash flows within the calculated payback period are certain.

c. Makes a single blanket assumption - that uncertainty is a function of time - and does not attempt to consider the variabilities of the cash flows estimated for the particular project being appraised.

RISK PREMIUM.

6. On occasions the discount rate is raised above the cost of capital in an attempt to allow for the riskiness of projects. The extra percentage being known as the risk premium. Such an inflated discount rate raises the acceptance hurdle for projects and can be shown to treat risk as a function of time by more heavily discounting later cash flows as demonstrated in the following example.

Example 1.

The cash flows for a project are shown below. The cost of capital is 10% and as the project is considered to be risky, a risk premium of 5% is to be added to the basic rate. The effects of the two discount rates are shown.

Year	0	1	2	3	4	5	NPV
Estimated Cash Flows	-10,000	+2,000	+3,000	+2,500	+3,000	+3,500	
10% Discount Factors	1.000	0.909	0.826	0.751	0.683	0.621	
P.V. @ 10%	-10,000	1818	2478	1877	2049	2173	+395
15% Discount Factors	1.000	0.870	0.756	0.658	0.572	0.495	
P.V. @ 15%	-10,000	1740	2268	1645	1716	1732	-899
Percentage reduction of P.V's caused by risk premium		4%	8%	12%	16%	20%	

Table 1.

The bottom line shows the progressively increased discounting which takes place on later cash flows demonstrating that the risk premium concept treats uncertainty as being related to time elapsed.

Advantages of a risk premium.

a. Simple to use

Disadvantages of a risk premium.

a. Makes the implicit assumption that uncertainty is a function of time.

b. By making the same overall, blanket assumption for all projects it does not consider the individual project characteristics nor does it explicitly consider the variability of the project cash flows.

c. It creates the problem of deciding upon a suitable risk premium. Should it be the same for all projects or should it be adjusted for different projects?

Note: One of the theories relating to business profits is that it is the reward for taking uninsurable risks. If this is correct, and it has some intuitive appeal, then a more subtle and long term effect of using a risk premium is that the firm will tend to move towards a portfolio of projects which, although potentially high yielding, have high risks - which is the opposite effect to that intended.

FINITE HORIZON.

7. In this method, which is the simplest of all to apply, project results beyond a certain period (eg 10 years) are ignored. All projects are thus appraised over the same time period.

Advantage:

a. Simplicity.

Disadvantages:

a. The establishment of any fixed time horizon is arbitrary. Projects do vary in length and this should be reflected in the appraisal.

b. Project cash flows within the time horizon are considered certain.

c. Does not explicitly consider the variabilities of cash flows.

SUMMARY OF TIME-BASED METHODS OF CONSIDERING UNCERTAINTY.

8. These methods are simple to apply and require little, if any, extra calculation. They are for the most part arbitrary and unreliable. Although obviously uncertainty tends to increase with time there is not a straightforward relationship and the time based methods fail to examine the characteristics of individual projects and merely make one blanket assumption covering all projects. The whole purpose of investment appraisal is to distinguish between projects and accepting one overall assumption is likely to mask rather than highlight the differences between the investment opportunities being considered.

PROBABILITY BASED METHODS OF ASSESSING UNCERTAINTY.

9. The methods to be described rest on the assumption that meaningful estimates of the subjective probabilities associated with the various cash flows can be established. For example, the project analyst might ask a manager to make three estimates of the cash flow of a period (optimistic, most likely, pessimistic) instead of just a single estimate, and in addition ask the manager to assess the likelihood of each of three estimates. Following such a request the manager might make the following estimate:

	Cash Flow in Period x	
Optimistic	£ 8,000	with a probability of 10% (.1)
Most likely	£ 4,500	with a probability of 65% (.65)
Pessimistic	£ 3,000	with a probability of 25% (.25)

The estimates thus obtained form a probability distribution of the cash flows. It follows that if the individual cash flows are expected to vary then the overall return for the project will also vary. The main objectives of probability based methods is to demonstrate the likely variations in the result, whether NPV or IRR, due to the estimated variations in the cash flows. In this way the effects of uncertainty are more clearly shown and hopefully a more informed decision may be taken. The three methods to be described which use subjective probabilities are Expected Value, Discrete Probabilistic Analysis and Continuous Probabilistic Analysis.

EXPECTED VALUE (EV).

10. This has been covered in detail earlier. It will be recalled that EV is Probability x Value and EV can be used for individual cash flows or project NPV's. The following simple example illustrates the technique.

Example 2.

The cash flow and probability estimates for a project are shown below.
Calculate

a. Expected value of the cash flows in each period and
b. Expected value of the NPV when the initial project outlay is £ 11,000 and the cost of capital is 15% .

CASH FLOW AND PROBABILITY ESTIMATES

		CASH FLOWS			
	Probability	Period 1	2	3	4
		£	£	£	£
Optimistic	0.3	5000	6000	4500	5000
Most likely	0.5	3500	4000	3800	4500
Pessimistic	0.2	3200	3600	3100	4000
Expected value of cash flows		3890	4520	3870	4550

The NPV is found by discounting the expected value of cash flows in the normal manner.

$NPV = -11,000 + (3890 \times 0.870) + (4520 \times 0.756) + (3870 \times 0.658) + (4550 \times 0.572) = \underline{\pounds 950}$

The advantages and disadvantages of expected value as a decision criterion have already been covered and these apply equally to the use of Expected Value in investment appraisal.

It is worth repeating that expected value, in spite of its limitations, is the decision rule which should normally be employed unless the problem clearly indicates something to the contrary.

DISCRETE PROBABILISTIC ANALYSIS (DPA).

11. DPA can be considered as an extension of the expected value procedure described above. As its basis it requires similar estimates of cash flows and associated probabilities, but instead of merely averaging these estimates it uses the component parts of the estimates to show the various outcomes and probabilities possible. The following example illustrates the techniques.

Example 3.

The NPV of Example 5 was £ 950 and management consider this somewhat marginal and wish to explore the range of outcomes possible. Further investigation reveals that two capital costs are possible; the £ 11,000 as stated with a probability of 0.8 and £ 15,000 with a probability of 0.2. This results in a new expected NPV of + £ 150 using the new expected capital cost of £ 11,800. The full range of outcomes and probabilities is shown in Table 2.

	Most Likely Capital Cost P = 0.8 £ 11,000		Pessimistic Capital Cost P = 0.2 £ 15,000	
Optimistic Cash Flows P = 0.3	3707	(0.24)	- 293	(0.06)
Most Likely Cash Flows P = 0.5	143 *	(0.4)	-3857	(0.1)
Pessimistic Cash Flows P = 0.2	-1167	(0.16)	-5167	(0.04)

Table 2

The table shows the NPV resulting from each possible combination of the original estimates of cash flows and the capital costs and gives the probability of the combination occurring. For example, the cell marked * is calculated thus:

Present value of most likely cash flows	=	£ 11,143
less most likely capital cost		11,000
NPV	=	143

The combination has a probability of $0.5 \times 0.8 = \underline{0.4}$

From Table 2 it will be seen that the outcomes range from +3707 to -£ 5167 and that the probability of making a loss is $0.16 + 0.1 + 0.04 = \underline{0.36}$ or alternatively, the probability of at least breaking even is 0.64.

Management now has more information on which to base a decision.

Advantages of DPA.

a. Simple to apply and understand
b. Gives some indication of the range of possible outcomes and their probabilities
c. Consideres the detailed variations in the cash flows and investment required for a project rather than merely making one overall assumption such as that uncertainty is directly related to time elapsed.

Disadvantages of DPA.

a. Uses discrete estimates whereas a continuous distribution may be a better representation of a particular project.
b. Increases the amount of subjective estimation necessary.

CONTINUOUS PROBABILISTIC ANALYSIS (CPA).

12. CPA has the same overall objective as DPA which has been described above. That is, to show the variability of the project outcome which results from the variability of the individual cash flows thus enabling the analyst to make probability assessments of the likelihood of various outcomes. It differs from DPA in that continuous distributions and aspects of statistical theory are used instead of the discrete estimates which are a feature of D.P.A.

CPA can be shown diagrammatically as follows:

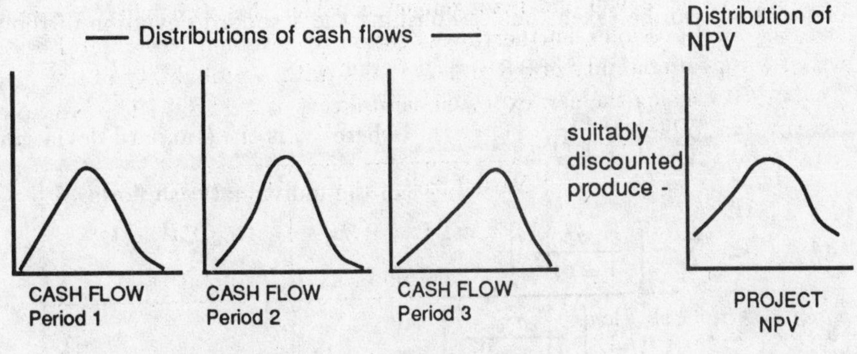

Figure 1

To be able to combine the distributions as shown and to be able to make probability statements about the project outcome, it is first necessary to establish the mean (or most likely value) and a measure of the dispersion of each of the individual period's cash flows.

ESTABLISHING THE MEANS AND DISPERSION OF CASH FLOWS.

13. In general, there is little problem in estimating the mean of the period's cash flows, this being equivalent to the most likely value. A more significant problem is to establish a suitable measdure of the variability

or dispersion of the period's cash flows. The most useful measure for statistical purposes is the standard deviation but invariably there is insufficient data to calculate the standard deviation in the conventional statistical manner so that some form of subjective estimation becomes necessary.

This could be done as follows:

Assume that the most likely value of the cash flow in a given period was estimated to be £ 30,000 and it was considered that there was likely to be some variability.

The managers responsible for the estimate could be asked a question similar to the following.

'Given that the most likely value of the cash flow is £ 30,000, within what limits would you expect the cash flow to be 50% of the time?'

Assume that the answer to the above question was £ 25,000 to £ 35,000.

It is known from Normal Area Tables (Table I) that 50% of a distribution lies between the mean $\pm\frac{2}{3}\sigma$ (approximately)

$\therefore$ £10,000(*ie*.35,000 – 25,000) $= \frac{4}{3}\sigma$

$\therefore$ $\hat{\sigma} \simeq$ <u>£ 7500</u>

An alternative to the question asked above would be to ask the manager,

'what is the total range of cash flow that might be expected?'

If the manager was consistent he would answer, '£ 7,500 to £ 52,500'.

It is known that the whole of a normal distribution is within the range of the mean $\pm 3\sigma$ (approximately). Accordingly, the estimate of the standard deviation would be,

$$\hat{\sigma} = \frac{£52,500 - 7,500}{6} = \underline{\underline{£7,500}}$$

It is clear that the estimation process outlined above is crude and lacks statistical rigour. However, subjective estimation is an unavoidable aspect of all investment appraisals and the procedure does enable some sort of assessment to be made of the probability of achieving various outcomes.

Having obtained the estimates of the means and standard deviations these must be combined to give the mean and standard deviation of the overall project NPV.

COMBINING THE MEANS AND STANDARD DEVIATIONS OF THE CASH FLOWS.

14. There is little problem in obtaining the mean of the project NPV. This is simply the means, or most likely values, of the cash flows discounted in the usual manner. The project standard deviations is obtained by combining the discounted standard deviations of the individual cash flows using what is known as the statistical sum.

Standard deviaitons cannot be combined directly but it is possible to add variances, when this is done the square root of the result can be taken thus establishing the standard deviation of the project's NPV, ie. σ_{NPV}

$$\therefore \sigma^2_{NPV} = \sum \left[\frac{\sigma_i}{1+r)^i} \right]^2$$

where σ_i is the standard deviation of the individual cash flows.

$$\sigma^2_{NPV} = \sum \left[\frac{\sigma_i^2}{1+r)^{i2}} \right]$$

$$\sigma_{NPV} = \sqrt{\sum \left[\frac{\sigma_i^2}{(1+r)^{i2}} \right]}$$

This formula is used in the following example

Example 4.

The means and standard deviations of the cash flows of a project are shown below and it is required to calculate.

a. The project NPV (ie. the mean)
b. The variability of the project NPV (ie. σ_{NPV})

c. The probability of obtaining
   – a negative NPV
   – a NPV of at least £ 20,000

It can be assumed that the cash flows in each period are independent ie. variations in one period are independent of variations i n other periods and that the cost of capital is 10% .

Period	0	1	2	3	4	5
Net cash flow (most likely value)	-200,000	+55,000	+48,000	+65,000	+70,000	+40,000
Variability expected (ie Standard deviation of cash flow)	0	4,000	4,500	3,500	4,500	3,000
Discount Factors @ Cost of Capital of 10%	1.00	.909	.826	.751	.683	.621

Solution.

a. The project NPV is found in the usual way ie

$$-200,000+(55,000\times0.909)+(48,000\times0.826)+(65,000\times0.751)+(70,000\times0.683)+(40,000\times0.621)$$

∴ Project NPV (ie. the mean) = **£ 11,108**

b. The standard deviation of the NPV is found by inserting the various estimated cash flow standard deviations into the formula.

$$\sigma_{NPV} = \sqrt{\sum\left[\frac{4000^2}{(1+.1)^2} + \frac{4500^2}{(1+.1)^4} + \frac{3500^2}{1+.1)^6} + \frac{4500^2}{(1+.1)^8} + \frac{3000^2}{(1+.1)^{10}}\right]}$$

$\therefore\ \sigma_{NPV} = £6,847$

It will be seen that the squaring of the denominator has the effect of requiring discount factors at 2, 4, 6, 8 and 10 years instead of the usual 1, 2, 3, 4 and 5 years.

c. The probability of obtaining a negative NPV (or the probability of any value of NPV) is found by using standard statistical test of normal area ie. find the 'z' score or standardised variate and obtain the resulting probability from Normal Area Table I follows.

$$z = \left|\frac{£11,108 - 0}{6847}\right|$$

$$= \underline{1.622}$$

and from the Tables we find that the probability of the NPV being above zero is 0.947 (ie 0.5 + 0.4474) thus there is approximately a 5.3% chance (1 - 0.9474) of there being a negative NPV.

The probability of there being at least £ 20,000 NPV is found by a similar process.

$$Z = \left|\frac{20,000 - 11,108}{6847}\right|$$

$$= \underline{1.299}$$

and using the Tables we find that the probability of obtaining at least £ 20,000 NPV is approximately 9.7% .

The distribution of the project NPV can also be shown diagrammatically as in Figure 2.

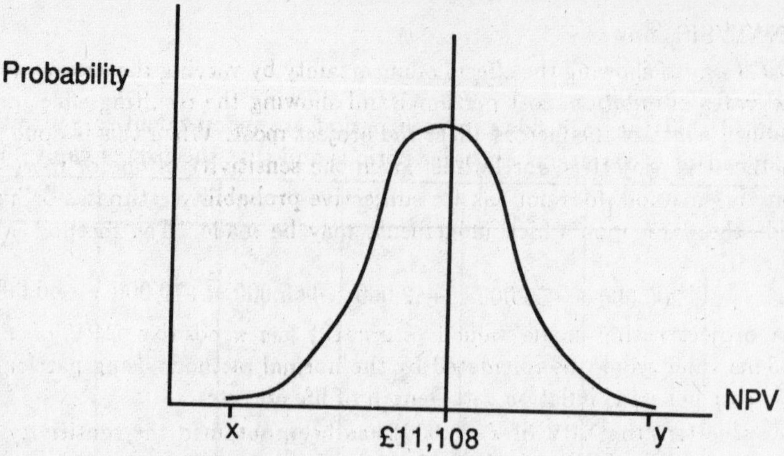

Probability Distribution of Project. Figure 2

Point x on the diagram is approximately £11,108 – (3 × 6847) = £ – 9433 and point y is approximately £11,108 + (3 × 6847) = £31,649

COMPARISON OF PROJECTS USING CPA.

15. Having calculated the means and standard deviations of various project the project distributions can be compared quite simply. The distributions could be drawn on the same graph and visually examined or the relative variability of the distributions could be calculated using their coeffcients of variations.

The coefficient of variation is found as follows:

$$\text{Coefficient of variation} = \frac{\sigma}{\bar{x}}\ 100\%$$

For example, two projects have estimated results as under

Project –A mean = £ 80,000 s.d. = £ 12,500

–B mean = £ 130,000 s.d. = £ 17,500

What are the coefficients of variation and which is the relatively less risky project?

$$\text{Coefficient of variation A} = \frac{12,500}{80,000} \times 100\% = \underline{15.6\%}$$

$$\text{Coefficient of variation B} = \frac{17,500}{13,000} \times 100\% = \underline{13.5\%}$$

∴ Project B is relatively less risky assuming that the standard deviation is a reasonable measure of the riskiness of the projects.

SUMMARY OF CPA.

16. The analysis outlined above can be extended to cover situations where the projects are not independent and/or where the individual distributions are not normal or near normal. All the methods have the same overall objective, which is to find the mean and variability (riskiness) of the project NPV.

Advantages of CPA.

a. Produces a distribution of the NPV rather than a single figure.
b. Enables probability statements to be made about the project's outcome which relfect the variabilities expected in each period's cash flows.
c. Enables the NPV distributions of competing projects to be compared.
d. Uses the more realistic assumption of continuous rather than discrete values.

Disadvantages.

a. Introduces a further element of subjective estimation.
b. More complex than DPA, so therefore may not be properly understood or used by decision makers.

SENSITIVITY ANALYSIS.

17. This is a practical way of showing the effects of uncertainty by varying the values of the key factors (eg. sales volume, price, rates of inflation, cost per unit) and showing the resulting effect on the project. The objective is to establish which of the factors affect the project most. When this is done it is management's task to decide whether the project is worthwhile, given the sensitivity of one or more of the key factors. It will be seen that this method does not ask for subjective probability estimates or likely outcomes, but attempts to provide the data upon which judgements may be made. The method is illustrated by the following example.

Example 5.

Assume that a project (using single valued estimates) has a positive NPV of £ 25,000 at a 10% discounting rate. This value would be calculated by the normal methods using particular values for sales volume, sales price, cost per unit, inflation rate, length of life etc, etc.

Once the basic value (ie. the NPV of £ 25,000) has been obtained the sensitivity analysis is carried out by flexing, both upwards and downwards, each of the factors in turn.

An abstract of the results of a sensitivity analysis for the project above might be as follows:

SENSITIVITY ANALYSIS ABSTRACT

Original NPV = £ 25,000

A	B	C	D	E	F
Element to be varied	Alteration from Basic	Revised NPV £	Increase + Decrease – £	Percentage Change	Sensitivity Factor ie $\frac{E}{B}$
Sales	+15%	46,000	+21,000	84	5.6
Volume	+10%	33,000	+ 8,000	32	3.2
(Basic Value	–10%	17,000	– 8,000	32	3.2
8000 units in					
Period 1,	–15%	14,000	–11,000	44	2.9
8500 in					
Period 2 etc)	–20%	9,000	–16,000	64	3.2
Sales	+20%	42,000	+17,000	68	3.4
Price	+10%	31,000	+ 6,000	24	2.4
(Basic Value	–10%	17,000	– 8,000	32	3.2
£ 6 unit in					
Period 1,	–15%	11,000	–14,000	56	3.73
£ 6.25 in					
Period 2 etc)	–20%	2,000	–23,000	92	4.6
Cost/Unit	+25%	–12,000	–37,000	148	5.9
(Basic Value	+10%	6,000	–19,000	76	7.6
£ 2.50 in					
Period 1	–5%	34,000	+9,000	36	7.2
£ 2.60 in					
Period 2 etc)	–10%	47,000	+22,000	88	8.8

Table 3

From such an analysis the more sensitive elements can be identified. Once identified further analysis and study can take place on these factors to try to establish the likelihood of variability and the range of values that might be expected so as to be able to make a more reasoned decision whether or not to proceed with the project.

Advantages of Sensitivity Analysis.

a. Shows the effect on project outcome of varying the value of the elements which make up the project (eg. Sales, Costs, etc).

b. Simple in principle.

c. Enables the identification of the most sensitive variables.

Disadvantages of Sensitivity Analysis.

a. Gives no indication of the likelihood of a variation occuring.

b. Considerable amount of computation involved.

c. Only considers the effect of a single change at a time which may be unrealistic.

RISK AND THE PORTFOLIO EFFECT.

18. So far in this chapter we have studied the risks associated with each project considered in isolation. This is an important matter but it will be apparent that of greater significance to the firm is the aggregate risk from all projects accepted which could be termed its portfolio of projects.

The effect on the firm of the risks of individual projects may be neutralised or enhanced when all the individual projects are considered together. A simple example would be where a firm is operating in a cyclical industry with variable (ie. risky) returns on its existing projects. A new project is being considered which, although variable or risky, is expected to follow a different cyclical pattern to existing operations. When existing operations are experiencing low activity the new project is expected to have substantial activity so that the overall risk to the firm from its portfolio, including the new project, will be minimised. This is, of course, a major reason why firms diversify their operations.

The analysis of this aspect of risk and uncertainty was developed for stock market investment portfolio analysis of Markowitz and others. There are many restrictive assumptions behind the analysis and there are some difficulties in applying it to project investment within the firm but the general reasoning is valid and is of considerable importance.

ASSESSING THE PORTFOLIO RISK.

19. The general procedure for assessing the extent to which the proposed project(s) add to or subtract from the risk of existing operations is to calculate the covariance between the returns of the project(s) and returns of existing operations and to use the covariance(s) to obtain the coefficient of correlation between the project(s) returns and the returns of existing operations.

The interpretation of the correlation coefficients is as follows:-

Coefficient of correlation	=	-1	risk fully neutralised
	=	0	risk unaltered
	=	$+1$	risk fully enhanced

The following example illustrates the general procedure.

Example 6.

A firm with £ 100,000 to invest is considering two projects, X and Y each requiring an investment of £100,000. The returns from the proposed projects and from existing operations under three possible views of expected market conditions are shown in Table 4 together with the calculated standard deviations of returns ie. the measure of riskiness used by the company.,

MARKET STATE	I	II	III
PROBABILITY OF MARKET STATE	0.3	0.4	0.3
Rate of return PROJECT X	20%	20%	$-1\frac{2}{3}$%
Standard deviation of returns, Project X = 22%			
Rate of Return PROJECT Y	-2%	15%	27%
Standard deviation of returns, Project Y = 15%			
Rate of Return of existing operations	-9%	$18\frac{1}{4}$%	28%
Standard deviation of returns on existing operations = 18%			

Table 4

The firm considers that the risk and return of their existing operations are similar to the market as a whole and that a reasonable estimate of a risk free interest rate is 8% .

Which, if either, of the two proposed investments should be initiated and why?

Solution.

The first stage is to calculate the expected returns for X and Y and existing operations.

Expected Returns ($\bar{R}$)

Project X

$$\overline{R_x} = (0.20 \times 0.3) + (0.20 \times 0.4) + (-0.01667 \times 0.3) = 0.135$$
$$= \underline{13.5\%}$$

Project Y

$$\overline{R_x} = (-0.02 \times 0.3) + (0.15 \times 0.4) + (0.27 \times 0.3) = 0.135$$
$$= \underline{13.5\%}$$

Existing Operations

$$\overline{R_O} = (-0.09 \times 0.3) + (0.1825 \times 0.4) + (0.28 \times 0.3) = 0.13$$
$$= \underline{13\%}$$

It will be seen that the expected returns of Project X and Y are the same and as the standard deviation of Project Y is lower than Project X then Project Y is the preferred project if the projects are considered in isolation from existing operations.

However, this is too superficial a view and further analysis is required on the effects of adding either project to the existing portfolio.

A project's risk can be separated into two elements – systematic and unsystematic risk. The unsystematic risk is the diversifiable risk which can be reduced or eliminated when the project is part of an appropriate portfolio. The systematic risk is the proportion which cannot be eliminated (it applies to the economy or market as a whole) and thus the project's returns must be considered against this residual element.

Portfolio analysis can be used to find the minimum required return for Project X and Y given their risk levels by calculated the covariances between project returns and existing operations and using these values to calculate the correlation coefficients thus;

Covariance between Project X return(R_x) and Company Return (R_0)

	$(R_x - \overline{R}_x)*$	×	$(R_0 - \overline{R}_0)*$	×	Market state probability	=	Covariance
State I	0.065	×	−0.22	×	0.3	=	−0.00429
State II	0.065	×	0.0525	×	0.4	=	0.001365
State III	−0.15167	×	0.15	×	0.3		−0.00682
					Covariance	=	−0.009745

*These values are found by deducting the calculated expected return ($\overline{R}$) from the actual return given in Table 4. For example the value -0.15167 is found as follows: (-0.01667 - 0.135) = -0.15167.

The value of the co-variance is then used to find the correlation coefficient between Project X returns and returns from existing operations (0)

Correlation coefficient

$$\text{between } X \text{ and } 0 = \frac{\text{covariance}(x,o)}{\sigma_x.\sigma_0} = \frac{-0.009745}{0.22 \times 0.18}$$

$$\therefore \text{Correlation}(x,o) = \underline{\underline{-0.246}}$$

Covariance between Project Y return (R_y)and Company Return (R_0)

	$(R_y - \overline{R}_y)$	×	$(R_0 - \overline{R}_0)$	×	Market state probability	=	Covariance
State I	−0.155	×	−0.22	×	0.3	=	0.01023
II	0.015	×	0.0525	×	0.4	=	0.000315
III	0.135	×	0.15	×	0.3	=	−0.006075
							+0.01662

Correlation coefficient

$$\text{between } Y \text{ and } O = \frac{\text{Covariance}(y,o)}{\sigma_y.\sigma_0} = \frac{+0.01662}{0.15 \times 0.18}$$

$$\text{Correlation}(y,o) = \underline{\underline{+0.615}}$$

These values can be used to calculate the required return from project X and Y given that the risk free interest rate is 8% . (R_F)

Required return of Project X

$$= R_F + \frac{R_0 - R_F}{\sigma_0}.\sigma_x \text{ Correlation}_{(x,o)}$$

$$= 0.08 + \frac{0.13 - 0.08}{0.18}.0.22 - 0.246$$

$$= 0.08 - 0.015 = 0.065 = \underline{\underline{6.5\%}}$$

Required return of Project Y

$$= R_F + \frac{R_0 - R_F}{\sigma_0}.\sigma_y.\text{ Correlation}(y,o)$$

$$= 0.08 + \frac{0.13 - 0.08}{0.18}.0.15.0.615$$

$$= 0.08 + 0.0256 = \underline{\underline{10.56\%}}$$

Based on the Portfolio analysis, Project X is the preferred project for the following reasons.

a. Project X provides the greatest excess of actual return over minimum return ie. 13.5% c.f.6.5% whereas Project Y is 13.5% c.f.10.56. Thus Project X maximises the company's wealth.

b. The negative correlation coefficient of Project X, -0.246 means that its pattern of returns to some extent neutralises the overall portfolio risk when Project X is combined with current operations. Although Project Y has a lower individual risk its correlation coefficient of + 0.615 means that it enhances risk when combined with current operations.

Note: It will be seen that the decision following analysis of the Portfolio effects is the opposite to that when the project's riskiness is considered in isolation.

It is feasible to work manually through a problem with as few projects as Example 8 but the number of relationships rises dramatically as the number of projects increases so it is likely that the application of the above principles to any practical sized problem would require computer assistance.

DECISION MAKER's ATTITUDE TO RISK.

20. Having dealt with the riskiness of individual projects and of combinations of projects, the third aspect of risk in investment appraisal can now be considered; that of the decision maker's attitude to risk and its influence on the final investment decision.

Surveys and studies have shown that individuals differ in their attitudes to risk and that for serious decisions such as investment appraisals in business, decision makers are risk averters. This means that in general, decision makers would prefer a less risky (less variable) investment even though it may have a lower expected value than a higher return yet riskier investment.

This may be demonstrated by the following.

Two investments are being considered.

Investment A – Return of £ 100,000 with a probability of 1 ie. certainty

Investment B { Return of £300,000 with a probability of 0.5; Return of zero with a probability of 0.5 }

The expected returns are:

Investment A **£100,000**

Investment B (£300,000 × 0.5) + (0 × 0.5)= **£150,000**

It will be apparent that virutally every investor would prefer the certainty of Investment A to the uncertainty or risk involved in Investment B even though it has the higher expected value. Such behaviour is risk aversion.

Implicit in such behaviour is an assumption about the utility or satisfaction derived from money. The utility function of a risk averter declines as the level of income or wealth rises ie. a declining marginal utility. A 'risk neutral' investor regards each increment of income or wealth as having the same value whereas a 'risk seeker' is a person whose utility function increases as his level of income or wealth increases. These three possibilities are shown in Figure 3.

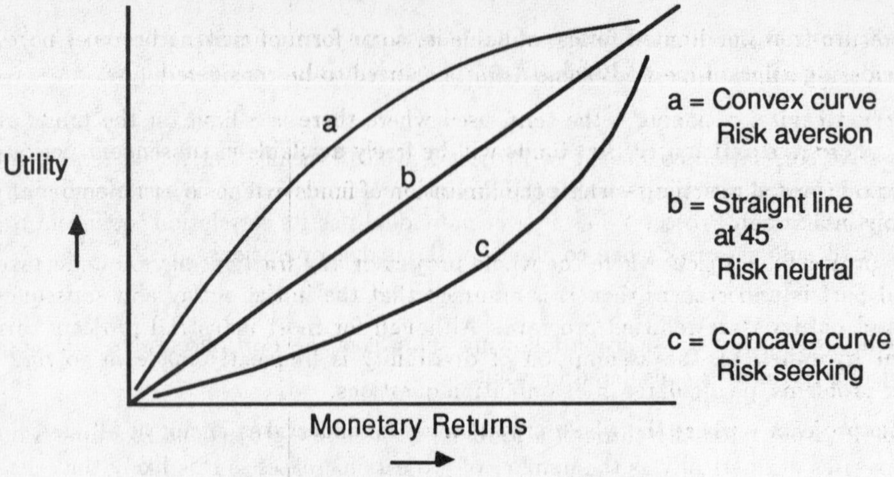

Utility Function of Money. Figure 3

UTILITY AND CERTAINTY EQUIVALENT.

21. Utility theory applied to decision making in risky conditions postulates that individuals attempt to optimise something termed utility and assumes that for any individual a formal, quantifiable relationship can be established between utility and money.

The theoretical way that an individual's utility function is established is by the use of certainty equivalents. These are derived in the following fashion.

Assume that an individual owns an sweepstake ticket which offers a 50% chance of winning £ 200,000 and a 50% chance of winning nothing. He would be asked what amount of cash he would accept for the lottery ticket. If he would sell the ticket for £ 75,000 this is the **certainty equivalent** ie. the value at which he is indifferent between the certain £ 75,000 and the chance of winning £ 200,000. This certainty equivalent would be assigned a utile value of 0.5 (a utile is the unit of utility). From such questions the person's utility function can be derived and then asked to make choices in investment decisions.

However, whilst these processes have theoretical appeal they are virtually impossible to apply in practice because of the extreme difficulty in establishing any form of meaningful utility function. However, risk aversion and varying individual attitudes to risk are very real phenomena although difficult to quantify. Accordingly, it is essential that the project analyst produces some form of risk analysis, both for projects in isolation and in combination, so that the decision maker has more information upon which to make a decision. There are variable or risky elements of every project and to ignore this aspect in the project appraisal can be positively misleading to the decision maker.

CAPITAL RATIONING-DEFINITION.

22. This is where the firm is unable to initiate all projects which are apparently profitable because insufficient funds are available. Under the assumptions given for the basic DCF model, a perfect capital market was presumed, ie as much finance as required could be raised at the market rate of interest. In imperfect capital market conditions capital may be raised, but at increasing rates of interest; but there will be some point where there is an absolute limit to the amount that could be raised. This is known as external capital rationing. Alternatively, the effects of capital rationing may develop for internal purposes, for example, it may be decided that investment should be limited to the amount that can be financed solely from retained earnings or kept within a given capital expenditure budget. The external and internal factors which impose quantitative limits have led to two opposing view-points developing, known as the 'hard' and 'soft' views of capital rationing. The 'hard' view is that there is an absolute limit on the amount of money a firm may borrow or raise externally whereas the 'soft' view is that rationing by a quantitative limit such as an arbitrary capital expenditure budget should only be seen as a temporary, administrative expedient because such a limit is not determined by the market (the assumption being that any amount of funds is available, at a price) and such a limit would not be imposed by a profit maximising firm.

Whatever the causes of the limited capital supply available for investment purposes it means that, not only must each project cover the cost of capital but that the project or batch of projects selected must maximise the return from the limited funds available ie. some form of ranking becomes necessary.

Before considering solution methods some definitions need to be considered.

a. Single period capital rationing – the term used where there is a limit on the funds available now but where it is anticipated that funds will be freely available in subsequent periods.

b. Multi-Period Capital rationing – where the limitation of funds extends over a number of periods or possibly indefinitely.

c. Divisible projects – projects where the whole project or any fraction may be undertaken. If a fractional part is undertaken, then it is assumed that the initial outlay and subsequent cash inflows and outflows are reduced pro rata. Although for most industrial projects this seems somewhat hypothetical, the assumption of divisibility is frequently made in solving capital rationing problems, particularly in examination questions.

d. Indivisible projects – where the whole project must be undertaken or not at all.

PROJECT SELECTION UNDER CAPITAL RATIONING.

23. Where capital rationing exists the normal DCF decision rule ie. accept all projects which have a positive NPV at the cost of capital is insufficient to make the appropriate project selection.

The objective where capital rationing exists is to maximise the return from the batch of projects selected having regard to the capital limitation. This means that the investment decision changes from simply being 'accept or reject' to what is in effect a ranking problem. Ways of achieving this objective are shown below for the following rationing situations.

- single period capital rationing with divisible projects.
- single period capital rationing with divisible projects where some are mutually exclusive
- single period capital rationing with indivisible projects
- multi period capital rationing with divisible projects.

SINGLE PERIOD CAPITAL RATIONING – DIVISIBLE PROJECTS.

24. This is the simplest situation and the solution method is to rank the projects in order of their EVPI (i.e. NPV per £ of outlay as described earlier) and to choose projects, or fraction of a project, until the supply of capital for investment is exhausted.

Example 7.

CR Ltd has a cost of capital of 15% and has a limit of £ 100,000 available for investment in the curent period. It is expected that capital will be freely available in the future. The investment require, the NPV at 15% and the the EVPI for each of the 6 projects currently being considered are shown below.

What projects should be initiated?

PROJECT	OUTLAY	NPV @ 15%	EPVI $\left(\frac{NPV}{OUTLAY}\right)$
	£	£	
A	20,000	8,000	0.4
B	40,000	28,000	0.7
C	35,000	37,500	1.07
D	50,000	31,000	0.63
E	15,000	3,500	0.23
F	45,000	−5,000	−0.11

Solution.

Ranking by EVPI is C, B, D, A and E. Project F cannot be considered because it fails the initial hurdle of achieving a positive NPV.

∴ Optimal Investment Plan

PROJECT	FRACTION UNDERTAKEN	INVESTMENT	NPV
		£	£
C	1.00	35,000	37,500
B	1.00	40,000	28,000
D	0.50	25,000	15,750
		£ 100,000	£ 81,250

It will be seen that this solution method uses the well known management accounting principle of maximising return per unit of the limiting factor - in this case NPV per £ of capital available for investment. It will be recalled that this principle is appropriate where there is a **single constraint only** – in this investment finance for one period.

SINGLE PERIOD CAPITAL RATIONING WITH MUTUALLY EXCLUSIVE DIVISIBLE PROJECTS.

25. Where two or more of the projects are mutually exclusive the solution method of ranking of EVPI can still be used but the projects have to be divided into groups each containing one of the mutually exclusive projects. This is shown below.

Example 8.

Assume the same data as Example 9 except that projects B and D are mutually exclusive.

What projects should be initiated?

Solution.

It is necessary to divide the projects into two groups, rank by EVPI, select projects up to the capital limit and to compare the total NPV obtainable from each group.

Group I			**Group II**		
Project	Investment	EVPI	Project	Investment	EVPI
	£			£	
A	20,000	0.4	A	20,000	0.4
B	40,000	0.7	C	35,000	1.07
C	35,000	1.07	D	50,000	0.63
E	15,000	0.23	E	15,000	0.23

Ranking the groups and choosing the projects up to the investment limit produces the following:

Group I				**Group II**			
Project	Fraction	Investment	NPV	Project	Fraction	Investment	NPV
		£	£			£	£
C	1.00	35,000	37,000	C	1.00	35,000	37,500
B	1.00	40,000	28,000	D	1.00	50,000	31,500
A	1.00	20,000	8,000	A	$\frac{3}{4}$	15,000	6,000
E	$\frac{1}{3}$	5,000	1,167				
		£ 100,000	£ 74,667			£ 100,000	£ 75,000

It will be seen that, by a narrow margin, Group II with the proportions indicated, has the greatest NPV and would be chosen.

SINGLE PERIOD CAPITAL RATIONING – INDIVISIBLE PROJECTS.

26. Where projects have to be accepted in their entirety or not at all, then EVPI ranking procedure does not necessarily produce the optimal solution. Providing that relatively few projects are involved a trial and

error approach can be used to find a solution. Where projects are indivisible then it is likely that some of the capital available for investment may be unused and in such circumstances a full analysis should include the returns from external investment of under-utilised funds.

Example 9.

Lloyds Ltd. has a cost of capital of 10% and has a limit of £ 100,000 available for investment in the current period. Capital is expected to be freely available in future periods. The following indivisible projects are being considered.

Project	Initial Investment	NPV @ 10%
	£	£
A	35,000	17,500
B	40,000	22,500
C	65,000	38,000
D	48,000	31,500
E	23,000	9,000

It is required to calculate the optimal investment plan

a. where there are no alternative investments available for any surplus funds.

b. where surplus funds can be invested to produce 12% in perpetuity

SOLUTION.

a. Various combinations are tried to see which combination produces the maximum NPV. Table 5 shows a few examples.

Project Combinations	Total Outlay for combinations	Surplus Funds	Total NPV of combination
	£	£	£
AC	100,000	—	55,500
ABE	98,000	2,000	49,000
AD	83,000	17,000	49,000
BD	88,000	12,000	54,000
BE	63,000	37,000	31,500
CE	88,000	12,000	47,000
DE	71,000	29,000	40,500

Table 5

It will be seen from Table 5 that the best investment plan is A and C which utilises all the funds available and produces a combined NPV of £ 55,500.

b. When surplus funds can be invested externally each of the combinations in Table 5 which have surplus funds must be examined to see if the project NPV plus the return on external investment is greater than £ 55,000.

Each £ 1,000 invested at 12% in perpetuity yields £ 200 NPV

i.e. $\left(\frac{1,000 \times .12}{.1}\right) - 1,000 = £200$

The project combinations and total NPV (Projects + External Investment) are shown in Table 6.

Combination	Total Project Outlay	Funds Externally Invested	External Investment NPV	+	Project NPV	=	Total NPV
	£	£	£		£		£
ABE	98,000	2,000	400	+	49,000		49,400
AD	83,000	17,000	3,400	+	49,000		52,400
BD	88,000	12,000	2,400	+	54,000		56,400*
BE	63,000	37,000	7,400	+	31,500		38,900
CE	88,000	12,000	2,400	+	47,000		49,400
DE	71,000	29,000	5,800	+	40,500		46,300

Table 6

*When external investment is considered then projects B D should be intiated and £ 12,000 invested externally to produce a total NPV of £ 54,500. It will be seen that this slightly better than the A C combination shown in Table 5.

Note: Although ranking by EVPI in conditions of single-period capital rationing with indivisible projects does not necessarily produce the correct ranking it usually provides an excellent guide to the best group of projects.

MULTI-PERIOD CAPITAL RATIONING.

27. This has been previously defined to be where investment funds are expected to be limited over several periods. In such circumstances it becomes difficult to choose the batch of projects (some starting immediately, some one period hence, two periods hence, etc.) which yield the maximum return and yet which remain within the capital limits. The problem becomes one of optimising a factor (e.g. NPV) where resources are limited, i.e. the funds available over the periods being considered. This will be recognised as a situation where Linear Programming (LP) can be used (covered previously) and LP has been used successfully in solving Multi-Period Capital Rationing problems.

MULTI-PERIOD RATIONING – LP SOLUTION.

28. To use LP as a solution method means making the assumption that projects are divisible i.e. fractional parts of a project can be undertaken. This is not necessarily a realistic assumption, but it is one frequently made for examinations purposes. The following example will be used to illustrate the LP formulation solution and interpretation of multi-period capital rationing problems,.

Example 10.

Trent Ltd has a cost of capital of 10% and is considering which project or projects it should initiate. The following projects are being considered:

Estimate Cash Flows

Project	Year O	Year 1	Year 2	Year 3	Year 4
A	-15,000	-25,000	30,000	30,000	20,000
B	-25,000	-15,000	30,000	29,000	30,000
C	-35,000	-15,000	40,000	44,000	30,000

Capital is limited to £ 40,000 now and £ 35,000 in Year 1. The projects are divisible.

Solution.

Step 1. Calculate the project NPV's in the usual manner.

These are as follows:

A = £ 23,245

B = £ 28,414

C = £ 37,939

Step 2. Formulate the problem in LP terms which means defining the objective function and the constraints. The objective for Trent Ltd. is to maximise NPV and this may be expressed as:

$$\text{Maximise } 23,245X_A + 28,414X_B + 37,939X_c$$

where X_A is the proportion of Project A to be initiated

X_B is the proportion of Project B to be initiated

X_C is the proportion of Project C to be initiated

The constraints in this problem are the budgetary limiations in Periods 0 and 1.
Capital at time 0

$$15,000X_A + 25,000X_B + 25,000X_C \leq 40,000$$

Capital at time 1

$$25,000X_A + 15,000X_B + 15,000X_C \leq 35,000$$

In addition it is necessary to specify the formal constraints regarding the proportions of projects accepted to ensure that a project cannot be accepted more than once or that 'negative' projects are accepted.

$$i.e. X_A, X_B, X_C \leq 1$$
$$X_A, X_B, X_C \geq 0$$

The whole formula appears thus:

$$\begin{array}{lrcrcrl}
\text{Maximise} & 23,245X_A & + & 28,414X_B & + & 37,939X_C & \\
\text{Subject to} & 15,000X_A & + & 25,000X_B & + & 35,000X_C & \leq 40,000 \\
 & 25,000X_A & + & 15,000X_B & + & 15,000X_C & \leq 35,500 \\
 & X_A & & & & & \leq 1 \\
 & & & X_B & & & \leq 1 \\
 & & & & & X_C & \leq 1 \\
 & X_A & & & & & \geq 0 \\
 & & & X_B & & & \geq 0 \\
 & & & & & X_C & \geq 0
\end{array}$$

Step 3. Solve the LP Problem.
The above formulation can then be solved by the Simplex method. It will be apparent that even with a highly simplified problem such as this manual solution methods are exceedingly tedious and accordingly it is unlikely that a student would have to work through the method in examinations.
However, formulation of the problem and interpretation of results are possible topics.
The solution of the above problem is as follows:

Project	Fraction Accepted
A	0.988
B	0
C	0.719

Value of objective function £ 50,244

Shadow prices	1st constraint (i.e. £ 40,000 Year 0 budget)	=	0.922
	2nd constraint (i.e. £ 35,000 Year 1 budget)	=	0.3755

Step 4. Interpretation of Solution.

The solution indicates that 0.988 of Project A and 0.719 of Project C should be initiated. This investment plan uses all the funds available in Year 0 and 1.

The shadow prices indicate the amount by which the NPV of the optimal plan (i.e. £ 50,244) could be increased if the budgetary constraints could be increased. For every £ 1 relaxation of the constraint in Period 0, £ 0.922 extra NPV would be obtained. The shadow prices indicate that extra funds in Period 0 are worth approximately three times those in Period 1. This fact may give a management some guidance in their considerations of various alternative sources of capital.

Note: It will be remembered the assumption made in this example is that these projects are divisible. It is appreciated that this is not necessarily a very practical assumption, but it appears to be one frequently made in examinations. Being divisible the NPV is scaled down by the proportion of the project accepted. This is a way of checking the result obtained. In this example the value of NPV obtained is £ 50,244 i.e. $(0.988 \times £23,245) + (0.719 \times 37,939)$.

Where projects are not divisible the only feasible solution method is Integer Programming which is outside the scope of the syllabuses at which this book is aimed.

RESERVATIONS OVER THE LP METHOD OF SOLVING CAPITAL RATIONING PROBLEMS.

29. There is no doubt that in the right circumstances LP can be useful method of dealing with multi-period capital rationing problems. There are, however, numerous assumptions and limitations which must be kept in mind if the use of the technique is being considered. The major ones are as follows:

a. Is the asumption of linearity for all functions realistic?
b. Are projects truly divisible and capable of being scaled in a linear fashion?
c. Are all investment opportunities included for each of the periods contained in the model?
d. Are all projects and constraints independent of one another as assumed in the LP model?
e. Are all cash flows, resources, constraints known with the certainty assumed in the model? (The way that uncertainty is ignored is possibly the most significant reservation)
f. Is the choice of discount rate a realistic one? Under 'hard' capital rationing. (i.e. externally imposed) the opportunity cost of funds cannot be known until the investment plan is formulated which, of course, requires the cost of funds to be known - a classic circular argument!

SUMMARY

30.

a. Uncertainty and risk are important factors to be considered in investment appraisal. Three aspects are of special concern: individual project uncertainty, the 'portfolio' effect and the decision makers' attitude to risk.
b. Individual project uncertainty can be analysed by three groups of techniques: time based, probability based, and senstivity analysis and simulation.
c. The main problem with the time based methods is that they do not explicitly consider the variability of cash flows.
d. The probability based methods use subjective probabilities and range from expected value through to methods employing statistical analysis based on the properties of distributions.
e. Arguably of more importance than individual project risk is the aggregate risk of the firm's portfolio of projects. New projects may, to some extent, neutralise or enhance existing risks.
f. Using the covariance of project returns and returns on existing operations the correlation coefficients of new and existing projects can be calculated.
g. The decision maker's attitude to risk is of critical importance but is extremely difficult to quantify. In general, decision makers are risk averters.

h. Capital rationing is where all apparently profitable projects cannot be initiated because of shortage of capital.

i. The decision rule where capital rationing exists is to maximise the return from the project(s) selected rather than simply accept/reject decisions of projects in isolation.

j. Single period rationing with divisible projects is dealt with by ranking in order of EVPI, having due regard to mutually exclusive projects. Where the projects are indivisible then a trial and error combination approach can be used.

k. Multi-period capital rationing with divisible projects is usually solved by LP which produces the optimal solution quantities (i.e. the projects to be initiated) the value of the objective function (i.e. the total NPV) and the shadow costs (i.e. opportunity costs of the binding constraints).

l. Although useful there are a number of reservations of using LP for solving capital rationing problems.

POINTS TO NOTE.

31.

a. The treatment of such matters as inflation and uncertainty have been dealt with in the context of investment appraisal. However the concepts and techniques described have a much wider application than just investment decisions. For example, the uses of expected values, sensitivity analysis and the concept of the real as opposed to the nominal value of money are applicable in virtually every area of planning and decision making.

b. Because of the amount of data involved and the complexity of the techniques used, computers are widely employed for investment appraisals, particularly in the are of risk evaluation and sensitivity analysis.

SELF REVIEW QUESTIONS.

1 In which stages of the appraisal and decision process should uncertainty and risk be considered? (2)

2 What are the time based methods of considering uncertainty? What is their underlying assumption and their major limitation? (4-8)

3 Describe the method of using Expected Value in project appraisals? (10)

4 How does discrete probabilistic analysis extend the expected value technique? (11)

5 What is continuous probabilistic analysis and, if used, how are the means and dispersions of the cash flows established? (12-13)

6 How is the standard deviation of the NPV established and how is this used? (14)

7 What is the objective of sensitivity analysis and how is it carried out? (17)

8 Why is it important to consider not only the risks of individual projects but the aggregate risk of combinations of projects?

9 What is the general procedure for assessing the portfolio risk? (19)

10 What are risk averters? (20)

11 What is a certainty equivalent? (21)

12 What is the difference between 'hard' and 'soft' capital rationing? (22)

13 How would the investment decision be made if single period rationing existed with divisible projects? (24)

14 How would the answer to 13 change if some of the projects were mutually exclusive? (25)

15 What is multi-period capital rationing and what is a possible solution method? (27)

16 What reservations exist regarding the use of LP to solve capital rationing problems? (29)

EXERCISES WITH ANSWERS COMMENCING PAGE 488

A1. Calculate the Expected NPV of the following project which has an outlay of £10,000 and a 10% cost of capital.

	CASH FLOWS			
	P	Year 1	2	3
Optimistic	0.2	£5500	£7000	£5500
Most Likely	0.5	4000	5500	5000
Pessimistic	0.3	3000	4500	3000

A2. The standard deviations of the cash flows in A1 have been estimated as follows

	Year 1	Year 2	Year 3
Estimated s.d.	£400	£500	£350

What is the probability of obtaining an expected NPV of zero or less?

A3. A firm has the following 5 divisible projects. There is a limit of capital for this period only of £150,000. Which projects should be selected?

Project	Outlay	NPV
A	£80,000	£15,000
B	£50,000	£15,000
C	£60,000	£25,000
D	£50,000	£23,000
E	£30,000	£ 8,000

EXAMINATION QUESTIONS WITH ANSWERS COMMENCING PAGE 488

A4. The distribution of cash flows for two investment projects is given below:

Project A		Project B	
Net Cash flow (£)	Probability	Net cash flow (£)	Probability
1,000	1/3	0	1/3
3,000	1/3	3,000	1/3
5,000	1/3	6,000	1/3

Either project A or B but not both may be undertaken.

You are required to:

(a) calculate the expected values of projects A and B and their respective variances.

(b) discuss general criteria for making a choice between projects such as A and B, and to determine which project should be selected, giving reasons for your conclusions;

(c) discuss briefly the use which may be made of the coefficient of variations in helping to decide between projects such as A and B, illustrating your answer with regard to these two potential investments.

(CIMA Quantitative Techniques)

A5. The managers of a dairy are planning to launch a new range of real cream ices and the marketing department has produced the following information.

Project horizon: six years

Annual total contribution of new range (Undiscounted) and estimated probabilities:

	Years 1 – 3	Years 4 – 6	Probabilities
If demand is high	£40,000	£30,000	0.75
If demand is low	£15,000	£10,000	0.25

If the present range of ice creams is continued and the new range is not introduced it is expected that sales will decline and the present contribution of £30,000 p.a. will reduce by 5% p.a. meaning that contribution in Year 1 is expected to £28,500.

It is possible to commission a market research survey, at a cost of £12,000, to assess likely demand. The market research company has been used before and its reliability can be summarised as follows:

Outcome of survey	*Subsequent sales performance*	
	High	*Low*
'High' forecast	*70% **	*20%*
'Low' forecast	*30%*	*80%*

**this means that when sales were high the survey had forecast this 70% of the time.*

It has been decided that if the survey predicts high demand for the new range then £15,000 will be invested in new equipment and there will be increased marketing effort which it is estimated will increase contribution by £20,000 p.a. if demand is high and by £10,000 p.a. if demand is low. However, if the survey predicts low demand then it has been decided that the company will continue with the old range of ice creams.

The diary has a cost of capital of 20% per annum.

Using decision tree analysis, you are required to:

(a) calculate the expected present value of the new project without a market research survey;

(b) calculate the expected present value of continuing with the old range;

(c) calculate the expected present value of the new project if the market research survey is carried out;

(d) recommend a course of action to the firm.

(CIMA Management Accounting Techniques)

A6. Mentor Products plc are considering the purchase of a new computer controlled packing machine to replace the two machines which are currently used to pack product X. The new machine would result in reduced labour costs because of the more automated nature of the process and, in addition, would permit production levels to be increased by creating greater capacity at the packing stage. With an anticipated rise in the demand for product X, it has been estimated that the new machine will lead to increased profits in each of the next three years. Due to uncertainty in demand however, the annual cash flows (including savings) resulting from purchase of the new machine cannot be fixed with certainty and have therefore been estimated probabilistically as follows:

Annual Cash Flows (£'000)

Year 1	*Prob*	*Year 2*	*Prob*	*Year 3*	*Prob*
10	*0.3*	*10*	*0.1*	*10*	*0.3*
15	*0.4*	*20*	*0.2*	*20*	*0.5*
20	*0.3*	*30*	*0.4*	*30*	*0.2*
		40	*0.3*		

Because of the overall uncertainty in the sales of product X, it has been decided that only 3 year's cash flows will be considered in deciding whether to purchase the new machine. After allowing for the scrap value of the existing machines, the net cost of the new machine will be £42,000.

The effects of taxation should be ignored.

Required:

(a) Ignoring the time value of money, identify which combinations of annual cash flows will lead to an overall negative net cash flow, and determine the total probability of this occurring.

(b) On the basis of the average cash flow for each year, calculate the net present value of the new machine given that the company's cost of capital is 15%. Relevant discount factors are as follows:

Year	Discount Factor
1	0.8696
2	0.7561
3	0.6575

(c) Analyse the risk inherent in this situation by simulating the net present value calculation. You should use the random numbers given at the end of the question to simulate 5 sets of cash flows. On the basis of your simulation results, what is the expected net present value and what is the probability of the new machine yielding a negative net present value?

	Set 1	Set 2	Set 3	Set 4	Set 5
Year 1	4	7	6	5	0
Year 2	2	4	8	0	1
Year 3	7	9	4	0	3

(ACCA Quantitative Analysis)

A7. A company has the following six investment opportunities open to it:

Project	Years 0	1	2	3	4	5	NPV
	Annual cash flow						
	£000	£000	£000	£000	£000	£000	£000
A	-200	-100	-50	+200	+200	+200	20.53
B	-60	-80	+100	+100			25.94
C	—	-120	-50	+170	+210		89.69
D	—	—	-250	+240	+120	+110	92.07
E	-80	-100	+100	+150	+150	-100	43.33
F	-150	-150	+200	+180	+50		17.33

The company cannot permit more than £300,000 to be spent on capital projects in any one year. The Net Present Value (NPV) have been arrived at by discounting each project at 15% . Projects are divisible and can be repeated more than once. Project timings cannot be advanced or delayed.

The outcome of a linear programme used to make an initial analysis of the above data for the company's capital budget is given below:

Row	A	B	C	D	E	F	Slack variables 2	3	4	5	
1	57.28	21.58	0.0	0.0	16.07	71.37	0.0	0.59	0.37	0.0	288.67
2	200.00	60.00	0.0	0.0	80.00	150.00	1.0	0.00	0.00	0.0	300.00
3	0.83	0.67	1.0	0.0	0.83	1.25	0.0	0.01	0.00	0.0	2.50
4	0.03	-0.13	0.0	1.0	-0.18	-0.25	0.0	-0.00	0.00	0.0	0.70
5	0.00	0.00	0.0	0.0	100.00	0.00	0.0	0.00	0.00	1.0	300.00

Note: Row 1 is the objective row. Numbers have been rounded to two decimal places.

You are required to:

(a) formulate the linear programme for the company;

(b) provide a full interpretation of the outcome of the linear programme.

(c) discuss three limitations of the use of a linear programme in these circumstances.

(CIMA Quantitative Techniques)

EXERCISES WITHOUT ANSWERS

B1. The NPVs of a project with variable cash flows and capital costs are shown in the table below:

	Capital Cost	
	Most likely	*Pessimistic*
	£20,000	*£25,000*
	P = 0.7	*P = 0.3*
Cash Flows		
OPTIMISTIC		
P = 0.2	*£8,000*	*£1,000*
MOST LIKELY		
P = 0.6	*£3,000*	*-2,500*
PESSIMISTIC		
P = 0.2	*£200*	*-6,000*

Calculate the probability of each NPV and the probability of making a loss.

B2. Two projects have estimated results as follows:

Project X: NPV £50,000 s.d. = £5,000

Project Y: NPV £80,000 s.d. = £9,000

Calculate

(a) which project is relatively less risky.

(b) the probability of achieving £55,000 NPV in project X

B3. A firm has a cost of capital of 10% and a limit of £200,000 for investment in the current period after which capital is expected to be freely available. The following indivisible projects are being considered:

Project	*Outlay*	*NPV @ 10%*
R	50,000	20,000
S	75,000	37,000
T	90,000	35,000
U	45,000	15,000
V	115,000	42,000

Calculate the optimal investment plan when

(a) there are no alternative investment opportunities and

(b) surplus funds can be invested at 15% in perpetuity.

EXAMINATION QUESTIONS WITHOUT ANSWERS

B4. Improved economic conditions mean that Equipment Supplies p.l.c. has a number of potentially profitable investments to choose from. However, finance will be insufficient to undertake all investments.

The following data are given:

Project No	Present value of cash outlays		Net present value of net cash income
	Period 1	Period 2	
	£000	£000	£
1	500	50	50,000
2	200	800	80,000
3	400	600	60,000
4	600	200	20,000
5	100	200	30,000

Finance available in Period 0 (the present) is £1.2 million and in Period 1 (one year ahead) is £1.4 million. Projects may be invested in only once and are divisible. (Fractional values of less than 1 are permitted.)

You are required to:

(a) use the above data and information to formulate a linear programme to maximise the net present value of the investment opportunities.

(b) describe how you would deal with the situation if you were now told that each project could be invested in once and that fractional values were not permitted.

(c) state what information you would expect to obtain from the dual values derived as a result of running the linear programme in (a) above (You are not *required to solve the L.P.);*

(d) indicate the changes in the constraints which would be necessary if it were possible to transfer any unused capital funds from one period to the next at a given rate of interest.

(CIMA Quantitative Techniques)

31 Matrix Algebra

INTRODUCTION.
1. This chapter defines a matrix and explains the more important rules of matrix algebra and gives examples of how matrices can be used in business.

PRESENTATION OF INFORMATION.
2. Accountants and businessmen are well used to presenting information in tabular form or writing information in rows and columns. Often one set of information in tabular form eg depreciation by category of fixed asset, is worked upon to produce a subsequent set of information based upon the first table, eg depreciation by category of fixed asset spread over cost centres. Although not generally referred to as such the foregoing are examples of matrices. An understanding of matrices and matrix algebra may provide short cut methods of calculation and will provide further insights into improved methods of presenting and manipulating data.

MATRIX DEFINITION.
3. A matrix is a rectangular array of numbers whose value and position in the matrix is significant. A matrix is usually, but not always, shown in brackets thus,

$$\begin{bmatrix} 1 & 8 \\ 3 & 7 \end{bmatrix}$$

Example 1.

The size of a matrix is given by the number of rows and the number of columns, ie rows x columns. The symbols most commonly used being m (columns) x n (rows). The matrix in example 1 is a 2 x 2 matrix, and as the number of columns equals the number or rows, it is known as SQUARE MATRIX. The following are further examples of matrices:

$$\begin{bmatrix} x_1 & x_2 \\ x_3 & x_4 \\ x_5 & x_6 \end{bmatrix} \qquad \begin{bmatrix} 5 & 9 & 16 \\ 2 & 8 & 4 \end{bmatrix} \qquad \begin{bmatrix} 8 & 12 & 6 \\ 9 & 5 & 1 \\ 7 & 0 & 2 \end{bmatrix}$$

Example 2 (a 3 × 2 matrix) Example 3 (a 2 × 3 matrix) Example 4 (a 3 × 3matrix ie square)

The standard notation for an element in a matrix is as follows

$x_{i,j}$ = the element in Row i Column j

thus

$x_{2,3}$ = the element in the second row, column three.

VECTORS.
4. A single row matrix is called a row vector and a single column matrix is called a column vector.

$$\begin{bmatrix} 9 & 5 & 8 & 2 \end{bmatrix}$$

Example 5

(Row Vector)

$$\begin{bmatrix} 16 \\ 5 \\ 2 \\ 9 \end{bmatrix}$$

Example 6

(column vector)

MATRIX ALGEBRA.

5. The particular rules applying the manipulation of data in matrix form are given in the following sections on MATRIX ADDITION, MATRIX SUBTRACTION, MATRIX MULTIPLICATION and MATRIX INVERSION. As a form of shorthand matrices are often referred to by capital letters, for example.

$$A = \begin{bmatrix} 1 & 6 \\ 5 & 2 \\ 8 & 3 \end{bmatrix} \qquad C = \begin{bmatrix} 3 & 2 \\ 1 & 6 \end{bmatrix}$$

Example 7

MATRIX ADDITION.

6. The only rule is that matrices to be added (or subtracted) must be the same size as one another, ie. they must have the same number of columns and the same number of rows, for example

$$A = \begin{bmatrix} 1 & 11 & 2 \\ 6 & 2 & 9 \end{bmatrix} \qquad B = \begin{bmatrix} 2 & 0 & 7 \\ 5 & 9 & 6 \end{bmatrix}$$

$$A + B = \begin{bmatrix} 1 & 11 & 2 \\ 6 & 2 & 9 \end{bmatrix} + \begin{bmatrix} 2 & 0 & 7 \\ 5 & 9 & 6 \end{bmatrix}$$

$$= \begin{bmatrix} 1+2 & 11+0 & 2+7 \\ 6+5 & 2+9 & 9+6 \end{bmatrix}$$

$$A + B = \begin{bmatrix} 3 & 11 & 9 \\ 11 & 11 & 15 \end{bmatrix}$$

Example 8

It will be noted that numbers in the same locations have been added giving a matrix with the same dimensions as those added, ie a 2×3 matrix. Note that A + B = B + A, ie it does not matter in which sequence the matrices are added. It follows that any number of matrices can be added together providing that they are the same size. If the matrices are not the same size they cannot be added, for example.

$$\text{if } X = \begin{bmatrix} 1 & 4 \\ 8 & 2 \end{bmatrix} \text{ and } Y = \begin{bmatrix} 6 \\ 5 \end{bmatrix}$$

Example 9

X + Y has no meaning because the matrices involved are not the same size.

MATRIX SUBTRACTION.

7. Subtraction involves matrices uses the same general rules as for matrix addition.
For example, using the same matrices as in Example 8 calculate

$$A - B$$

$$\text{ie} \begin{bmatrix} 1 & 11 & 2 \\ 6 & 2 & 9 \end{bmatrix} - \begin{bmatrix} 2 & 0 & 7 \\ 5 & 9 & 6 \end{bmatrix}$$

$$A - B = \begin{bmatrix} 1-2 & 11-0 & 2-7 \\ 6-5 & 2-9 & 9-6 \end{bmatrix}$$

$$= \begin{bmatrix} -1 & 11 & -5 \\ 1 & -7 & 3 \end{bmatrix}$$

Example 10

It will be seen that minus numbers appear in the final matrix. If minus numbers appear in the original matrix then the usual rules of arithmetic apply, for example minus a minus equal a plus. It is important to note that whereas $A + B = B + A$, $A - B \neq B - A$, for example reversing example 10 above to calculate

$$B - A \text{ gives}$$

$$\begin{bmatrix} 2 & 0 & 7 \\ 5 & 9 & 6 \end{bmatrix} - \begin{bmatrix} 1 & 11 & 2 \\ 6 & 2 & 9 \end{bmatrix}$$

$$B - A = \begin{bmatrix} 2-1 & 0-11 & 7-2 \\ 5-6 & 9-2 & 6-9 \end{bmatrix} = \begin{bmatrix} 1 & -11 & 5 \\ -1 & 7 & -3 \end{bmatrix}$$

Example 11

It will be seen that this is a different result to that in Example 10.

MATRIX MULTIPLICATION.

8. There are two aspects of matrix multiplication, the multiplication of a matrix by a single number, called a scalar, and the multiplication of a matrix by another matrix.

SCALAR MULTIPLICATION.

9. A scalar is an ordinary number such as 3, 6, 8.2 etc. The rule for this is simple - multiply each element in the matrix by the scalar, for example.

$$\text{Let } A = \begin{bmatrix} 5 & 2 \\ 8 & 3 \end{bmatrix}$$

and it is required to find 4× A

$$4 \times A = 4 \times \begin{bmatrix} 5 & 2 \\ 8 & 3 \end{bmatrix} = \begin{bmatrix} 20 & 8 \\ 32 & 12 \end{bmatrix}$$

Example 12

MATRIX MULTIPLICATION.

10. The main rule to be remembered when it is required to multiply a matrix by another matrix is that the number of columns in the 1st matrix MUST EQUAL the number of rows in the 2nd matrix, ie a 2×3 matrix can be multiplied with a 3×2 matrix (ie the number of columns, 3 = number of rows,) but a 2×3 matrix cannot be multiplied with another 2×3 matrix.

The method of matrix multiplication will be shown using the following matrices as a basis

$$A = \begin{bmatrix} 3 & 1 \\ 2 & 4 \\ 7 & 4 \end{bmatrix} \qquad \text{ie a } 3 \times 2 \text{ matrix}$$

$$B = \begin{bmatrix} 8 & 0 & 5 & 4 \\ 3 & 2 & 11 & 1 \end{bmatrix} \qquad \text{ie a } 2 \times 4 \text{ matrix}$$

Calculate AB, ie $A \times B$

		Rows		Columns
First check if feasible	$A =$	3	$\times$	2
	$B =$	2	$\times$	4

$\therefore$ No. of Columns of A = No. of rows of B $\therefore$ Multiplication is feasible.

The new matrix AB is produced by the following steps

$$AB = \begin{bmatrix} 3 \times 8 + 1 \times 3 & 3 \times 0 + 1 \times 2 & 3 \times 5 + 1 \times 11 & 3 \times 4 + 1 \times 1 \\ 2 \times 8 + 4 \times 3 & 2 \times 0 + 4 \times 2 & 2 \times 5 + 4 \times 11 & 2 \times 4 + 4 \times 1 \\ 7 \times 8 + 4 \times 3 & 7 \times 0 + 4 \times 2 & 7 \times 5 + 4 \times 11 & 7 \times 4 + 4 \times 1 \end{bmatrix}$$

$$AB = \begin{bmatrix} 27 & 2 & 26 & 13 \\ 28 & 8 & 54 & 12 \\ 68 & 8 & 79 & 32 \end{bmatrix}$$

which, of course would normally be shown in the usual more compact form

$$AB = \begin{bmatrix} 27 & 2 & 26 & 13 \\ 28 & 8 & 54 & 12 \\ 68 & 8 & 79 & 32 \end{bmatrix}$$

The steps in obtaining AB were,

Multiply 1st element in 1st row in A by 1st element in 1st column in B (ie 3×8).

Multiply 2nd element in 1st row in A by 2nd element in 1st column in B (ie 1×3)

(This multiplication process would be continued until the n'th element in 1st row of the first matrix had been multiplied by the n' element in the first column the second matrix).

All these products are added to give the 1st element in 1st row and 1st column of the new matrix AB, ie $(3 \times 8) + (1 \times 3) = 27$

Then every number in the 2nd row of matrix A is multiplied with every number in the 1st column of matrix B ie (2×8) and (4×3) and these are added to give the second element in the first column of matrix AB, ie 28.

This process is continued until every row of matrix A has been multiplied by the 1st column of matrix B. When this is done, the new matrix, AB, has its first column.

The process of multiplying each row of matrix A with each column of matrix B continues until all the elements of the new matrix, AB, are calculated.

Note:

The size of AB is 3×4 ie it has the number of rows of A and the number of columns of B.

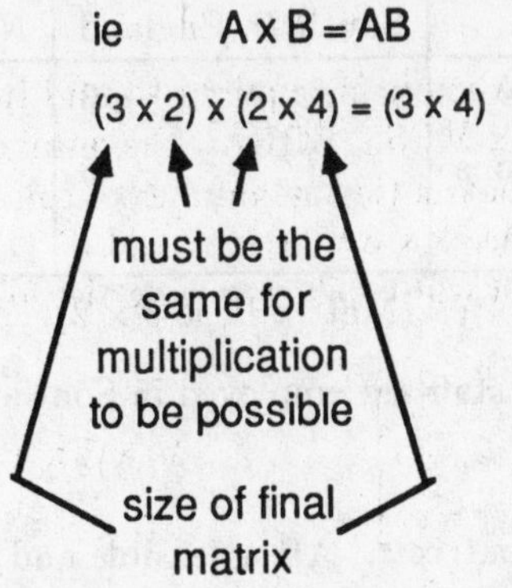

Notes.

a. $A \times B$ does NOT equal $B \times A$. This is unlike ordinary multiplication of numbers where $3 \times 6 = 18$ and so does $6 \times 3 = 18$.

b. If $A \times B$ is possible it does not follow that $B \times A$ is possible.

VECTOR MULTIPLICATION.

11. The process to be followed when multiplying a matrix by a vector is the same as detailed in Para 10. This will be shown by the following example:

$$A = \begin{bmatrix} 5 & 6 & 7 \end{bmatrix} \quad B = \begin{bmatrix} 4 & 3 \\ 1 & 2 \\ 8 & 9 \end{bmatrix}$$

ie a 1×3 matrix (or a row vector) ie a 3×2 matrix

$$\therefore AB = \begin{bmatrix} 5 & 6 & 7 \end{bmatrix} \times \begin{bmatrix} 4 & 3 \\ 1 & 2 \\ 8 & 9 \end{bmatrix}$$

$$= \begin{bmatrix} 5 \times 4 + 6 \times 1 + 7 \times 8 & 5 \times 3 + 6 \times 2 + 7 \times 9 \end{bmatrix}$$

$$AB = \begin{bmatrix} 82 & 90 \end{bmatrix}$$ ie a 1×2 matrix or row vector.

AN EXAMPLE OF MATRIX MULTIPLICATION.

12. A group operates a chain of filling stations in each of which are employed cashiers, attendants and mechanics as shown

	Types of Filling Stations		
	Large	Medium	Small
Cashier	4	2	1
Attendants	12	6	3
Mechanics	6	4	2

(Matrix A ie 3 × 3

The number of filling stations are

	Southern England	Northern England
Large Stations	3	7
Medium Stations	5	8
Small Stations	12	4

(Matrix B, ie 3 × 2)

How many of the various types of staff are employed in Southern England and in Northern England?
Example 13

Solution.

A is a 3 × 3 matrix, B is a 3 × 2 matrix ∴ AB is feasible and will be a 3 × 2 matrix

$$\begin{array}{ccccc} A & \times & B & = & AB \\ \begin{bmatrix} 4 & 2 & 1 \\ 12 & 6 & 3 \\ 6 & 4 & 2 \end{bmatrix} & \times & \begin{bmatrix} 3 & 7 \\ 5 & 8 \\ 12 & 4 \end{bmatrix} & = & \begin{bmatrix} x_{11} & x_{12} \\ x_{21} & x_{22} \\ x_{31} & x_{32} \end{bmatrix} \end{array}$$

$$\begin{aligned} x_{11} &= (4 \times 3) + (2 \times 5) + (1 \times 12) &= 34 \\ x_{12} &= (4 \times 7) + (2 \times 8) + (1 \times 4) &= 48 \\ x_{21} &= (12 \times 3) + (6 \times 5) + (3 \times 12) &= 102 \\ x_{22} &= (12 \times 7) + (6 \times 8) + (3 \times 4) &= 144 \\ x_{31} &= (6 \times 3) + (4 \times 5) + (2 \times 12) &= 62 \\ x_{32} &= (6 \times 7) + (4 \times 8) + (2 \times 4) &= 82 \end{aligned}$$

∴ AB is

	South	North
Cashiers	34	48
Attendants	102	144
Mechanics	62	82

ZERO MATRIX.

13. In matrix algebra a zero is represented by the zero matrix which is any square matrix in which every element is zero. As with normal numbers if a matrix is multiplied by a zero matrix we obtain a zero matrix, ie

$$\begin{bmatrix} 3 & 4 \\ 5 & 6 \end{bmatrix} \times \begin{bmatrix} 0 & 0 \\ 0 & 0 \end{bmatrix} = \begin{bmatrix} (3 \times 0) + (4 \times 0) & (3 \times 0) + (4 \times 0) \\ (5 \times 0) + (6 \times 0) & (5 \times 0) + (6 \times 0) \end{bmatrix}$$

$$= \begin{bmatrix} 0 & 0 \\ 0 & 0 \end{bmatrix}$$

UNITY MATRIX.

14. In matrix algebra unity is any square matrix whose top left to bottom right diagonal consists of 1's where all the rest of the matrix consists of zero's. This matrix is important and is always given the symbol **I** thus

$$\mathbf{I} = \begin{bmatrix} 1 & 0 \\ 0 & 1 \end{bmatrix} \quad \text{or } \mathbf{I} = \begin{bmatrix} 1 & 0 & 0 \\ 0 & 1 & 0 \\ 0 & 0 & 1 \end{bmatrix} \quad \text{or } \mathbf{I} = \begin{bmatrix} 1 & 0 & 0 & 0 \\ 0 & 1 & 0 & 0 \\ 0 & 0 & 1 & 0 \\ 0 & 0 & 0 & 1 \end{bmatrix}$$

Matrices are only equal where they are the same size and have the same elements in the same place, ie

$$\begin{bmatrix} 1 & 0 \\ 0 & 1 \end{bmatrix} \neq \begin{bmatrix} 1 & 0 & 0 \\ 0 & 1 & 0 \\ 0 & 0 & 1 \end{bmatrix}$$

As with normal numbers where a number multiplied by one equals itself ($3 \times 1 = 3$) so with matrices. A matrix multiplied by the unity matrix equals itself, ie

$\mathbf{AI} = \mathrm{A}$ and $\mathbf{IA} = \mathrm{A}$

$$\mathrm{A} = \begin{bmatrix} 1 & 6 \\ 2 & 3 \end{bmatrix} \quad \text{for example}$$

$$\mathbf{AI} = \begin{bmatrix} 1 & 6 \\ 2 & 3 \end{bmatrix} \times \begin{bmatrix} 1 & 0 \\ 0 & 1 \end{bmatrix} = \begin{bmatrix} 1 \times 1 + 6 \times 0 & 1 \times 0 + 6 \times 1 \\ 2 \times 1 + 3 \times 0 & 2 \times 0 + 3 \times 1 \end{bmatrix}$$

$$= \begin{bmatrix} 1 & 6 \\ 2 & 3 \end{bmatrix} \quad \text{similarly}$$

$$\mathbf{IA} = \begin{bmatrix} 1 & 0 \\ 0 & 1 \end{bmatrix} \times \begin{bmatrix} 1 & 6 \\ 2 & 3 \end{bmatrix} = \begin{bmatrix} 1 \times 1 + 0 \times 2 & 1 \times 6 + 0 \times 3 \\ 0 \times 1 + 1 \times 2 & 0 \times 6 + 1 \times 3 \end{bmatrix}$$

$$= \begin{bmatrix} 1 & 6 \\ 2 & 3 \end{bmatrix} \quad \text{thus proving that } \mathbf{AI} = \mathbf{IA} = \mathrm{A}.$$

Note:
The unit matrix, **I**, must always be square.

MATRIX INVERSION.

15. In matrix algebra the function of division is changed to that of invesion. The inverse (or reciprocal) of a matrix has the same property as that of the inverse of an ordinary number. The inverse of 8 is 1/8 so that

$$8 \times \frac{1}{8} = 1 = \frac{1}{8} \times 8$$

In matrix algebra the inverse of a matrix is denoted A^{-1} and

$$\mathrm{A} \times \mathrm{A}^{-1} = \mathbf{I} = \mathrm{A}^{-1} \times \mathrm{A}$$

Only SQUARE matrices can have inverses which follows from

$$\mathrm{A} \times \mathrm{A}^{-1} = \mathrm{A}^{-1} \times \mathrm{A}$$

which expression implies that rows and columns are equal.

FINDING THE INVERSE.

16. Several methods exist for finding A^{-1} given A, but the following step by step method is simplest and is quite manageable for the size of matrices likely tobe encountered in examinations.

Assume that it is required to find the inverse of matrix A

$$A = \begin{bmatrix} a_{11} & a_{12} \\ a_{21} & a_{22} \end{bmatrix} = \begin{bmatrix} 1 & 2 \\ 3 & 4 \end{bmatrix}$$

This is done by carrying out row by row operations on A with the objective of transforming it into a unity matrix, I. At the same time the same row by row operations are carried out on a unity matrix which at the end of the operations becomes A^{-1}.

STEP 1. Place a unity matrix alongside A

$$\begin{bmatrix} 1 & 2 \\ 3 & 4 \end{bmatrix} \begin{bmatrix} 1 & 0 \\ 0 & 1 \end{bmatrix}$$

STEP 2. As a_{11} is already 1 we wish to make a_{21} into zero, ie Row 2 – (3× Row 1)

$$\text{Row } 2 - (3 \times \text{ Row } 1) \text{ gives } \begin{bmatrix} 1 & 2 \\ 0 & -2 \end{bmatrix} \begin{bmatrix} 1 & 0 \\ -3 & 1 \end{bmatrix}$$

STEP 3. We now require a_{22} to be 1, therefore we multiply Row 2 by $-\frac{1}{2}$

$$\text{Row } 2 \times -\frac{1}{2} \text{ gives } \begin{bmatrix} 1 & 2 \\ 0 & 1 \end{bmatrix} \begin{bmatrix} 1 & 0 \\ 1\frac{1}{2} & -\frac{1}{2} \end{bmatrix}$$

STEP 4. Finally we wish to make a_{12} into zero, ie Row 1 - (2× Row 2)

$$\text{Row } 1 - (2 \times \text{ Row } 2) \text{ gives } \begin{bmatrix} 1 & 0 \\ 0 & 1 \end{bmatrix} \begin{bmatrix} -2 & 1 \\ 1\frac{1}{2} & -\frac{1}{2} \end{bmatrix}$$

A becomes **I** and the original **I** becomes A^1

Notes.

The row by row operations shown are similar to those used in the simplex method of solving LP problems given earlier.

To prove that the matrix obtained in Step 4 is A^{-1} we can multiply it by A and we should obtain a unity matrix, ie.

A

$$A \times A^{-1} = \mathbf{I}$$

$$ie \begin{bmatrix} 1 & 2 \\ 3 & 4 \end{bmatrix} \times \begin{bmatrix} -2 & 1 \\ 1\frac{1}{2} & -\frac{1}{2} \end{bmatrix} = \begin{bmatrix} 1 \times -2 + 2 \times 1\frac{1}{2} & 1 \times 1 + 2 \times -\frac{1}{2} \\ 3 \times -2 + 4 \times 1\frac{1}{2} & 3 \times 1 + 4 \times -\frac{1}{2} \end{bmatrix}$$

$$= \begin{bmatrix} 1 & 0 \\ 0 & 1 \end{bmatrix} = \mathbf{I}$$

Note.

a. Not every square matrix has an inverse, for example

$$\begin{bmatrix} 1 & 1 \\ 1 & 1 \end{bmatrix} \text{ has no inverse}$$

b. The product of two matrices, neither of which is a zero matrix, may give a zero matrix as an answer, for example

$$A = \begin{bmatrix} 1 & 1 \\ 1 & 1 \end{bmatrix} \qquad \text{and B} = \begin{bmatrix} 1 & -1 \\ -1 & 1 \end{bmatrix}$$

$$AB = \begin{bmatrix} 1 & 1 \\ 1 & 1 \end{bmatrix} \times \begin{bmatrix} 1 & -1 \\ -1 & 1 \end{bmatrix}$$

$$= \begin{bmatrix} 0 & 0 \\ 0 & 0 \end{bmatrix}$$

FINDING THE INVERSE USING DETERMINANTS.

17. An alternative method of finding an inverse uses determinants. A determinant of matrix A is denoted by |A| or Det A and is defined as follows: (for a 2 × 2 matrix).

$$\text{If A} = \begin{bmatrix} a & b \\ c & d \end{bmatrix} \text{ then } |A| = ad - bc$$

For example, matrix A from para 16 is

$$\begin{bmatrix} 1 & 2 \\ 3 & 4 \end{bmatrix} \therefore |A| = (1 \times 4) - (3 \times 2) = \underline{\underline{-2}}$$

A determinant is used as follows:

$$\text{If A} = \begin{bmatrix} a & b \\ c & d \end{bmatrix} \text{ then } A^{-1} = \frac{1}{|A|}\begin{bmatrix} d & -b \\ -c & a \end{bmatrix}$$

This procedure will be used to invert matrix A from Para 16 for which the determinant is -2, as calculated above.

$$A = \begin{bmatrix} 1 & 2 \\ 3 & 4 \end{bmatrix} \text{ and } |A| = -2$$

$$\therefore A^{-1} = \frac{1}{-2}\begin{bmatrix} 4 & -2 \\ -3 & 1 \end{bmatrix}$$

which, multiplied in the usual manner gives

$$A^{-1} = \begin{bmatrix} -2 & 1 \\ 1\frac{1}{2} & -\frac{1}{2} \end{bmatrix}$$

which is the same result obtained by using the row by row operations in the preceding paragraph.

SOLVING SIMULTANEOUS EQUATIONS BY MATRIX ALGEBRA.

18. Matrix algebra can be useful for solving simultaneous equations. To be able to find a unique solution there must be an equal number of equations and unknowns (or more equations than unknowns) so that a square matrix can be established. The solution method is similar to the method of finding the inverse of a matrix, ie row by row operations. This will be demonstrated using the following example:

Solve, using matrix algebra, the following simultaneous equations.

$$3x + 4y = 10$$

$$2x + 7y = 11$$

Setting out the problem in matrix form gives

$$\begin{bmatrix} 3 & 4 \\ 2 & 7 \end{bmatrix} \begin{bmatrix} 10 \\ 11 \end{bmatrix}$$

from which it is required to produce

$$\begin{bmatrix} 1 & 0 \\ 0 & 1 \end{bmatrix} \begin{bmatrix} x \\ y \end{bmatrix}$$

giving a numeric answer for x and y
STEP 1. Set out the equations in matrix form (ie as above)

$$\begin{bmatrix} 3 & 4 \\ 2 & 7 \end{bmatrix} \begin{bmatrix} 10 \\ 11 \end{bmatrix}$$

STEP 2. make a_{11} into 1 by substracting Row 2.

$$\text{Row 1} - \text{ Row 2 gives } \begin{bmatrix} 1 & -3 \\ 2 & 7 \end{bmatrix} \begin{bmatrix} -1 \\ 11 \end{bmatrix}$$

STEP 3. Make a_{21} into a zero by subtracting 2× Row 1

$$\text{Row 2} - (2 \times \text{ Row 1) gives } \begin{bmatrix} 1 & -3 \\ 0 & 13 \end{bmatrix} \begin{bmatrix} -1 \\ 13 \end{bmatrix}$$

STEP 4. Make a_{22} into 1 by dividing Row 2 by 13

$$\text{Row 2} \div 13 \text{ gives } \begin{bmatrix} 1 & -3 \\ 0 & 1 \end{bmatrix} \begin{bmatrix} -1 \\ 1 \end{bmatrix}$$

STEP 5. Make a_{12} into a zero by adding to Row 1 three times Row 2.

$$\text{Row 1} + (3 \times \text{ Row 2) gives } \begin{bmatrix} 1 & 0 \\ 0 & 1 \end{bmatrix} \begin{bmatrix} 2 \\ 1 \end{bmatrix}$$

$\therefore\ x = 2 \quad y = 1$

which can be checked by substituting in the original equations,

$$3x + 4y = 10$$

$$2x + 7y = 11$$

$$\text{ie} \quad 3 \times 2 + 4 \times 1 = 10$$

$$2 \times 2 + 7 \times 1 = 11$$

PROBABILITY TRANSITION MATRICES.

19. These are matrices in which the individual elements are in the form of probabilities eg. 0.5, 0.70, 0.1 etc.

The probabilities represent the probability of one event following another event ie. the probability of the transition from one event to the next. The probabilities of the various changes, applied to the initial state by matrix multiplication, give a forecast of the succeeding state. This process can be repeated indefinitely but usually it will be found that after several cycles the values will stablise within a restricted range.

Applications of this process, known as the MARKOV process, occur in the marketing area when brand switching is being investigated and in forecasting rates of breakdown in machinery so as to determine appropriate replacement programmes. It can also be applied to other problems where one event succeeds another and the transition probabilities are known.

An application of probability transition matrices.

Assume that two products, Gleem and Sparkle, currently share the market with shares of 60% and 40% each respectively.

Each week some brand switching takes place. Of those who bought Gleem the previous week, 70% buy it again whilst 30% switch to Sparkle. Of those who bought Sparkle the previous week 80% buy it again whilst 20% switch to Gleem.

How can this information be used to find the proportion of the market the brands will eventually hold? The first step is to construct the probability transition matrix of the switching probabilities.

	Gleem	Sparkle
Gleem	0.7	0.2
Sparkle	0.3	0.8

The columns show the switching probabilities and total 1.

Next a vector is constructed representing the initial market shares in % .

Gleem	60
Sparkle	40

The matrix and vector are multiplied to give the new market share for the following week.

$$\begin{bmatrix} 0.7 & 0.2 \\ 0.3 & 0.8 \end{bmatrix} \begin{bmatrix} 60 \\ 40 \end{bmatrix} = \begin{bmatrix} 50 \\ 50 \end{bmatrix}$$

ie. the market shares are now 50:50 for Gleem and Sparkle.

To obtain the forecast for the following week the original branch switching probabilities must be multiplied by the new market share.

$$\begin{bmatrix} 0.7 & 0.2 \\ 0.3 & 0.8 \end{bmatrix} \begin{bmatrix} 50 \\ 50 \end{bmatrix} = \begin{bmatrix} 45 \\ 55 \end{bmatrix} \text{ which is}$$

the latest market share position.

This process can be continued indefinitely if required but it will be found that the market shares settle down around particular values. In this example, after five cycles, Gleem's share is 40.625 and Sparkle's share is 59.375 which are close to the eventual share of the market. If it is required to find these equilibrium values this can be done as follows.

At equilibrium

$$\begin{bmatrix} 0.7 & 0.2 \\ 0.3 & 0.8 \end{bmatrix} \begin{bmatrix} G \\ S \end{bmatrix} = \begin{bmatrix} G \\ S \end{bmatrix}$$

where G and S represent the equilibrium shares.

$$\text{As } G+S=1 \quad S=1-G$$

$\therefore\ 0.7G+0.2(1-G)=G$

and substituting

$$0.7G+0.2(1-G)=G$$

$$\therefore 0.5G=0.2$$

$$\therefore G=0.4$$

$\therefore$ Equilibrium shares are Gleem 40% and Sparkle 60%

SUMMARY

20.

a. A matrix is a rectangular array of numbers. Where the number of columns is the same as the number of rows it is a square matrix.

b. Matrix addition and subtraction. Each matrix must be the same size and corresponding elements are added or subtracted.

c. Matrix multiplication by scalar. Any size matrix can be multiplied by a number, a scalar, each element being multiplied by the scalar.

d. Matrix multiplication. A matrix of size $m \times n$ can be multiplied by a matrix of size $n \times p$ producing a matrix of size $m \times p$. Each row of matrix A is multiplied by each column in matrix B . $AB \neq BA$.

e. Two special matrices are the zero matrix, ie any square matrix where all the elements are zero, and the unity matrix (I), ie any square matrix with 1's in a diagonal from top left to bottom right with the rest of the elements being zero.

f. Matrix inversion. The inverse of a matrix, denoted A^{-1} or C^{-1} etc, is found by carrying out row by row operations on the original matrix and a unity matrix with the objective of changing the original matrix into I. The inverse is the matrix which has replaced the original unity matrix.

POINTS TO NOTE.

21.

a. There is a strong relationship between the usual algebraic method of solving LP problems, the Simplex method, and matrix inversion.

SELF REVIEW QUESTIONS.

1 How is the size of a matrix described? (3)

2 What is a vector (4)

3 What is the rule regarding the size of matrices that are to be added? (6)

4 Does $A-B=B-A$? (7)

5 What is scalar multiplication? (8)

6 What is the size rule for matrix multiplication? (10)

7 How is matrix multiplication carried out? (10)

8 What is the unity matrix? (14)

9 Does $A \times A^{-1}=A^{-1} \times A$? (15)

10 What are the steps in matrix inversion? (16)

11 What are the essential conditions for simultaneous equations to be solved by matrix algebra. (18)

12 What are probability transition matrices and what are they used for? (19)

EXERCISES WITH ANSWERS COMMENCING PAGE 488

A1.

$$X = \begin{bmatrix} 3 & 11 & 6 \\ 9 & -3 & 8 \\ 5 & 0 & 9 \end{bmatrix}$$

$$Y = \begin{bmatrix} 1 & 2 & 0 \\ 0 & -4 & 5 \\ 5 & -8 & 7 \end{bmatrix}$$

Calculate

(a) $X + Y$

(b) $X - Y$

A2. Multiply the matrices X and Y given in A1

A3. Let

$$M = \begin{bmatrix} 6 & 4 \\ 3 & 1 \end{bmatrix}$$

Find M^{-1} using determinants and check your answer using row by row operations.

EXAMINATION QUESTIONS WITH ANSWERS COMMENCING PAGE 488

A4. a. The allocation of service department costs to production departments and other service departments is one area where matrix algebra may be used.

	Service departments		*Production departments*	
	Maintenance	*Electricity*	*Machining*	*Assembly*
Manhours of maintenance time	—	*3,000*	*16,000*	*1,000*
Units of electricity consumed	*20,000*	—	*130,000*	*50,000*
Department costs before any allocation of service departments	*£50,000*	*£4,000*	*£140,000*	*£206,000*

You are required to:

i. calculate the total costs to be allocated to the production departments using matrix algebra (formulate the problem and show all workings);

ii. explain clearly the advantages of this method over the traditional allocation procedures.

b. An employee profit sharing scheme entitled the employees to share 10% of the profit after tax. The payment made to the employees under this scheme is tax deductible. Tax is to be taken at 50% . In the year to 31st March, 1977 the pre-tax profit was £100,000 before charging the employees' share of the profit.

You are required to calculate the amount to which the employees are entitled using matrix algebra. Formulate the problem and show all workings.

(CIMA Quantitative Techniques)

A5.

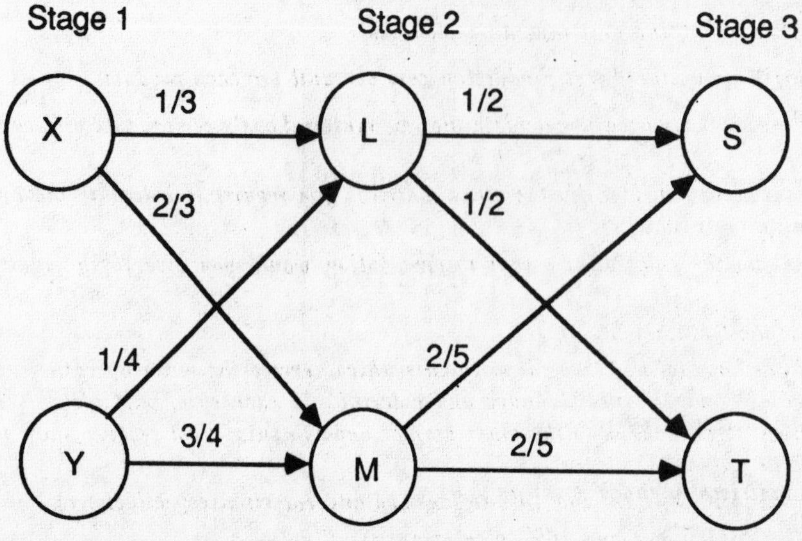

In the above network the fraction along each link represent the probability that a flow from the previous node will occur along that route.

Required:

i. Write down the 2 × 2 probability transition matrices A and B such that A represents the flow between Stage 1 and Stage 2 and B represents the flow between Stage 2 and Stage 3.

ii . Determine the matrix product AB and show that it represents the flow between stage 1 and Stage 3.

b. The probability transition matrix for the movement of a particular share price on two successive days is:

		Movement Tomorrow	
		Up	Down
Movement	Up	1/2	1/2
Today	Down	2/3	1/3

Required:

i. If the price goes up today, calculate the probability that the price will go up

a. Tomorrow

b. In two days time

c. In three days time

ii. Noticing that the above probabilities are stabilizing, what is the probability that the price will go up on a particular day a long way into the future?

(ACCA, Management Mathematics)

A6. The Trix Manufacturing Co. Ltd. produces four products, A, B, C and D.

Each product is made from three raw materials, P, Q and R

One unit of product A requires 2 units of P, 1 unit of Q and 4 units of R.

One unit of product B requires 5 of P and 3 of R.

One unit of product C requires 4 of P, 3 of Q and 2 of R.

One unit of product D requires 4 of P, 1 of Q and 2 of R.

The costs of each unit of raw material are P £2, Q £3, R £6. The direct production costs per unit are A £4, B £2, C £3, D £5.

The product selling prices are A £40, B £40, C £36, D £32.

The weekly demands for each product are A 400 units, B 500 units, C 600 units, D 200 units.

Required:

a. Prepare the following matrices:

i. W : 4 × 3 matrix giving the component requirements.

ii. $X : 1 \times 4$ *matrix giving the weekly demands for each product*

iii. $Y : 3 \times 1$ *matrix giving the unit raw material costs.*

iv. $Z : 4 \times 1$ *matrix giving the direct production cost per unit for each product*

b. Identify the matrices required to calculate the raw material costs per product and calculate them using matrix methods.

c. Using your result in (b), identify the other matrices you require to calculate the total weekly contribution and determine the result.

d. Without making the calculation, what interpretation would you give to the matrix T *where* $T = XWY$*?*

(ACCA Management Mathematics)

A7. (a) St. Swithin's hospital has three departments which service the main operating departments of the hospital. The three are maintenance, laundry and catering. In each case, part of the services provided is within the department itself and/or to the other service departments. Past records show the proportions of such services to be as follows:

Maintenance: 5% to itself, 25% and 10% to laundry and catering respectively.

Laundry: 5% to maintenance and 10% to catering

Catering: 5% to itself, 10% and 15% to maintenance and laundry respectively.

In a given period, direct costs allocated to the operating of each of these departments are shown as:

Maintenance:	*£56,000*
Laundry:	*£250,000*
Catering:	*£35,000*

You are required to:

(i) draw up the cost equations to derive the gross operating cost of each of the service departments;

(ii) demonstrate, both algebraically and numerically, the matrix algebra steps which would lead to obtaining the inverse matrix to solve the unknown values in the equations of (i) above. (Do not attempt to invert the matrix.)

(b) You are given the following as the inverse matrix for the problem of (a) above:

1.083	*0.067*	*0.125*	*(Figures rounded to*
0.293	*1.034*	*0.194*	*three decimal places)*
0.145	*0.116*	*1.086*	

You are required, using the inverse matrix, to obtain the gross cost of operation of each service department. Workings must be shown.

(CIMA Quantitative Techniques)

A8. The following data relate to the retail trade in category Z:

Table 1 Number of different grades of employees

Grade	*Type of outlet*		
	Branch of multiple store	*Supermarket*	*Independent*
Supervisors	*1*	*5*	*nil*
Cashiers	*4*	*10*	*2*
Storekeepers	*3*	*15*	*1*

Table 2 Number of outlets in different areas

Outlet	Midlands	Other areas
Branch of multiple store	36	104
Supermarket	18	75
Independent	25	30

You are required to:

(a) state the purpose of using matrix algebra and give two business situations in which it may be used;

(b) present the data in table 1 in a matrix format (subsequently referred to as A);

(c) present the data in table 2 in a matrix format (subsequently referred to as B);

(d) calculate by means of matrix multiplication, showing clearly all the steps, AB, and explain what the product mean.

(CIMA QUANTITATIVE TECHNIQUES)

EXERCISES WITHOUT ANSWERS

B1.

$$A = \begin{bmatrix} 0 & 6 & 16 \\ -3 & 7 & 9 \\ 21 & 0 & -5 \end{bmatrix}$$

$$B = \begin{bmatrix} -4 & 6 & 12 \\ 0 & 5 & -3 \\ 9 & 0 & 6 \end{bmatrix}$$

Calculate

(a) $A + B$

(b) $B - A$

B2. Multiply the matrices A and B in B1

B3.

$$N = \begin{bmatrix} -2 & 6 \\ -3 & 4 \end{bmatrix}$$

Find N^{-1}

EXAMINATION QUESTIONS WITHOUT ANSWERS

B4. A company consists of three service departments (S_1, S_2 S_3) and two production departments (P_1, P_2)

Analysis of the service department activities shows:

Services supplied by	Services supplied to (%)				
	S_1	S_2	S_3	P_1	P_2
S_1		50		30	20
S_2	20		20	20	40
S_3	20			30	50

Costs directly allocated to the service departments are (per annum):

Dept.	Variable (£)	Fixed (£)	Total (£)
S_1	40,000	30,000	70,000
S_2	120,000	80,000	200,000
S_3	60,000	40,000	100,000

You are required:

(a) to derive the cost equations to show the gross total operating costs of each of the service departments;

(b) to calculate the gross total operating costs of each service department after reapportionment of the intra-service department costs;

(c) if P_1 and P_2 respectively produce 400,000 and 200,000 units of finished product per annum, to determine the service department charge in each of the product costs;

(d) given that S_3, produces 90,000 units of service per annum, to comment on whether it would be advisable to accept an offer from an outside supplier to supply this quantity at £0.90 per unit.

(CIMA QUANTITATIVE TECHNIQUES)

32 Replacement Analysis

INTRODUCTION.

1. This chapter deals with the cost effects of replacement. The two most commonly encountered replacement situations - sudden failure and deteriorating items - are explained and analysed and the minimum cost decision rules are exemplified.

REPLACEMENT DECISIONS.

2. Most items of equipment (ie components, parts, vehicles, machinery) need replacement at some time or other. Replacement analysis is the process by which the various cost consequences involved are studied so that the optimum replacement decision can be taken. The two most common replacement problems relate to.

a. Parts or components that work adequately up to a point and then fail eg. fan belts, light bulbs, some types of tools.

b. Items that deteriorate. These are usually relatively expensive items which could be kept functioning with increasing amounts of maintenance eg. vehicles, machine tools, boilers.

These two categories are dealt with below.

SUDDEN FAILURE ITEMS.

3. Often these items are inexpensive in themselves but the cost consequence of their failure and/or the installation costs involved in replacing them can be considerable. It is therefore necessary to estimate the various costs involved and choose the least cost position. The three categories of cost are:

a. The replacement cost of the item; usually the purchase price at the time of replacement.

b. The consequential costs of failure which might be trivial say, if an electric bulb failed, but could be substantial if a small component failure caused an assembly line stoppage.

c. The costs involved in the actual replacement of the item. Because of location and/or accessibility problems consideration is often given to group replacement at intervals or on the failure of one item. For example, if a single electric bulb failed in an overhead lamp cluster in a factory then all the bulbs might be replaced at the same time even though many are still functioning.

As a result of the need to minimise the various costs involved several decision alternatives are usually explored and the least cost alternative chosen. For example, assume that a mchine contains 50 components whose maximum life is 4 weeks. The various alternatives are,

a. Replace on failure only.

b. Replace on failure and all components at end of Week 1

c. Replace on failure and all components at end of Week 2.

d. Replace on failure and all components at end of Week 3.

e. Replace on failure and all components at end of Week 4.

Using the probabilities of a component failing at the end of each week the expected cost of each alternative can be found and compared.

ILLUSTRATION OF REPLACEMENT FOR SUDDEN FAILURE ITEMS.

4. The following example will be used to illustrate the approach to this type of problem.

Example 1.

A special component is used throughout a large machine tool. The component has a limited life and the following data have been collected on failures.

	Week after Replacement			
	1	2	3	4
Percentage of components which have failed by the end of that week (cumulative)	20	50	80	100

500 components are in use at any one time and they can be replaced on a mass replacement basis for £ 2 per component. If they are replaced individually as they fail the cost is £ 10 representing £ 1 for the component and £ 9 labour charges.

It is required to establish the least cost replacement policy comparing individual replacement on failure with mass replacement at the end of the various weeks together with individual replacement of components which have failed in the preceding interval.

Solution to Example 1.

Proportions failing each week

Week 1	20%
" 2	30%
" 3	30%
" 4	20%
	100%

∴ Average life of a component

$= (1 \times 0.2) + (2 \times 0.3) + (3 \times 0.3) + (4 \times 0.2)$

$= \underline{2.5 \text{ weeks}}$

∴ Average number of replacement per week $= \frac{500}{2.5} = \underline{\underline{200}}$

∴ Cost of individual replacement on failure $= 200 \times £10 = \underline{\underline{£\ 2000 \text{ per week}}}$

Mass Replacement.

To calculate the costs involved it is necessary to find the number of failures each week which include the proportion of original components which fail *plus* the replaced components which fail.

The number of individual failures is shown in Table 1 which applies the proportions failing each week to the original batch of 500 and then to the individual failures which are replaced.

FAILURE TABLE

	WEEK 1	WEEK 2	WEEK 3	WEEK 4
500 batch (original Batch)	100	150	150	100
100 batch (week 1 replacement)		20	30	30
150 batch (week 2 replacement)			30	45
150 batch (week 3 replacements)				30
20 batch (week 2 replacements)			4	6
60 batch (30 + 30) (week 3 replacements)				12
TOTAL FAILURES	100	170	214	223

Table 1.

The total cost is then the cost of mass replacement plus the cost of individual failures.

		TOTAL COST £	AVERAGE WEEKLY COST £
WEEK 1	100 × £10 + £1000	2000	2000
2	270 × £10 + £1000	3700	1350*
3	484 × £10 + £1000	5840	1947
4	707 × £10 + £1000	8070	2018

Thus the best strategy is to replace en masse in Week 2.

REPLACEMENT OF ITEMS THAT DETERIORATE.

5. A lorry could be kept operating with satisfactory performance for say, 15 years, but to do so would incur increasing amounts of maintenance so that careful cost analysis is needed to choose the most economical replacement time.

There are two major cost consequences involved: the annual capital loss each year (the difference between the market value at the beginning and end of the year) and the maintenance charges. The two costs are accumulated and averaged over the number of years to find the minimum average annual cost.

This is illustrated by the following example.

Example 2.

A lorry cost £ 15,000 and it is required to find the least cost point to replace it with a new vehicle. The following data have been estimated.

Year	1	2	3	4	5	6	7	8
Resale value at year end	£ 12000	9500	7500	5700	4200	3900	2900	2000
Annual Maintenance Cost	£ 600	800	1050	1400	2100	3500	5000	6800

Ignore the time value of money and inflation.

Year	Annual Capital Loss	Cumulative Capital Loss	Annual Maintenance Cost	Cumulative Maintenance Cost	Cumulative Annual Cost	Average Annual Cost
	£	£	£	£	£	£
1	3000	3000	600	600	3600	3600
2	2500	5500	800	1400	6900	3450
3	2000	7500	1050	2450	9950	3317
4	1800	9300	1400	3850	13150	3287
5	1500	10800	2100	4950	15750	3150*
6	1300	12100	3500	8450	20550	3425
7	1000	13100	5000	13450	26550	3793
8	900	14000	6800	20250	36250	4531

*Best replacement point at end of the fifth year.

SUMMARY.

6.

a. Replacement analysis seeks the least cost point at which to replace items.

b. The main costs involved with sudden failure items are: cost of the replacement item, consequential costs, installation costs.

c. For sudden failure items, typically individual replacement on failure is compared with group replacement and the least cost policy chosen.

d. The main costs involved with deteriorating items are the capital loss each year and the (increasing) annual maintenance costs.

e. The average annual cost is calculated and the least cost position chosen.

POINTS TO NOTE.

7.

a. Simple replacement analysis assumes that there are no changes in performance or technology. In practice there are frequently advantages to be gained in the potential improvement in performance from a new item. In such cases the extra output or contribution becomes a relevant factor in the analysis.

b. Particularly for expensive items, liquidity and taxation implictions frequently are dominant factors in replacement decisions.

SELF REVIEW QUESTIONS.

1 What is the objective of replacement cost analysis? (2)

2 What are the three categories of cost associated with sudden failure items? (3)

3 What is the procedure for finding the minimum cost point for items that deteriorate? (5)

EXERCISES WITH ANSWERS COMMENCING PAGE 488

A1. A part is used in an equipment handling system. The component has a limited life and data have been collected on failures.

	Week after replacement		
	1	*2*	*3*
Cumulative percentage of failures	*30*	*75*	*100*

1000 components are in use and they can be replaced en masse for £5 per component. If replaced individually they cost £30 per component.

Calculate:

(a) average component life

(b) average number of replacement per week.

(c) cost of individual replacement per week.

A2. Calculate the cost of mass replacement at the end of each week for the components in A1 and determine the best replacement strategy.

EXAMINATION QUESTIONS WITH ANSWERS COMMENCING PAGE 488

A3. A. An engineering company is studying a replacement strategy for its metal cutting tools. It has collected the following data on tool life relating to normal load and operating conditions.

	Month after replacement				
	1	2	3	4	5
Percentage of original tools which have failed by the end of the month (cumulative)	10	25	50	80	100

1,000 cutting tools are in use at any given time. They could be replaced by new tool on a mass replacement basis for £1.00 per tool. Alternatively, they may be replaced individually as they fail at cost of £4 per tool. In each case, the actual cost of the tool itself is 50 pence, the remainder representing labour and overhead charges.

At present, the company replaces tools as they fail.

You are required to:

a. compare the costs of the current tool replacement system with the alternative of replacing all tools at a certain fixed monthly interval together with individual replacements of those tools which have failed in the preceding interval;

b State the best strategy for the company to follow.

B. A transport company is considering the possibility of adding a new 12 ton lorry to its vehicle fleet. It bases its pricing and cost calculations on the expectation of running the vehicle on average three-quarters loaded at 500 miles per week over 40 weeks of the year, ie. 180,000 ton-miles per annum. Past experience shows that for a variety of reasons there is a standard deviation of 60,000 ton-miles per annum for this class of vehicle.

The company intends to charge £0.50 per ton-mile; variable operating costs are calculated as £0.45 per ton-mile and fixed costs as £6,500 per annum.

You are required to:

a. calculate the break-even positon for operating the lorry;

b. calculate the expected annual profit;

c. calculate the probability that the lorry will:

i. at least break-even;

ii. make a profit of at least £2,000 per annum;

iii. make a profit of at least £5,000 per annum;

d. state the value to management of information of this nature.

(CIMA Quantitative Techniques)

A4. In an industrial process, certain pressure valves become subject to random failure after 600 hours operational life. Present company policy is to replace each valve as it fails, but, having kept records of the valve failures, the company is now reviewing that policy.

The following are data on failures (occurring after the 600-hour period has passed):

Length of valve life (to nearest 100 hours)	*Number of valves*
100	*15*
200	*45*
300	*30*
400	*10*

Replacement is a complex task and the cost of replacing an individual valve is £40. Treated as a group replacement, this reduces to £23 per valve, though any failures during the period prior to group replacement would continue to be replaced individually.

The company decides to investigate a policy of group replacement at intervals of 100, 200, 300 and 400 hours.

You are required:

(a) to calculate (to the nearest whole number) the costs of:

(i) continuing to replace failed valves on an individual basis;

(ii) group replacement

(b) to prepare a brief report on the results;

(c) given that the replacement costs are estimated figures, to state how you would attempt to assess the sensitivity of your calculations to changes in cost.

(CIMA Quantitative Techniques)

EXERCISES WITHOUT ANSWERS

B1. A component is used in large quantities in a machine. Data on failure rates have been collected as follows:

	Month after replacement			
	1	*2*	*3*	*4*
Cumulative percentage of failures	*25*	*50*	*85*	*100*

Calculate

(a) average component life

(b) average number of replacement per month where the quantity in the machine is 750.

(c) cost of individual replacement per month at £3 per component.

B2. Calculate the cost of mass replacement at the end of each month for the component in B1 and determine the best replacement strategy if the replacement cost falls to 50p per component.

EXAMINATION QUESTIONS WITHOUT ANSWERS.

B3. In the context of operational research, what do you understand by a replacement problem? Your answer should distinguish between situations involving sudden failure and situations involving gradual deterioration. For each of these two situations, explain the nature of the model used and its information requirements. What are the underlying assumptions of each model and what factors are generally ignored in the simpler model formulation?

ACCA, Management Mathematics

Statistical and Financial Tables

TABLE I

AREAS UNDER THE STANDARD NORMAL CURVE
from 0 to Z

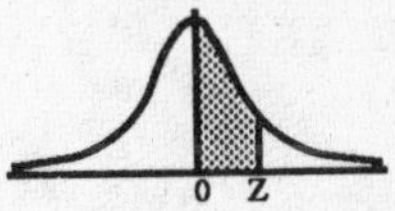

z	0	1	2	3	4	5	6	7	8	9
0.0	0.0000	0.0040	0.0080	0.0120	0.0160	0.0199	0.0239	0.0279	0.0319	0.0359
0.1	0.0398	0.0438	0.0478	0.0517	0.0557	0.0596	0.0636	0.0675	0.0714	0.0754
0.2	0.0793	0.0832	0.0871	0.0910	0.0948	0.0987	0.1026	0.1064	0.1103	0.1141
0.3	0.1179	0.1217	0.1255	0.1293	0.1331	0.1368	0.1406	0.1443	0.1480	0.1517
0.4	0.1554	0.1591	0.1628	0.1664	0.1700	0.1736	0.1722	0.1808	0.1844	0.1879
0.5	0.1915	0.1950	0.1985	0.2019	0.2054	0.2088	0.2123	0.2157	0.2190	0.2224
0.6	0.2258	0.2291	0.2324	0.2357	0.2389	0.2422	0.2454	0.2486	0.2518	0.2549
0.7	0.2580	0.2612	0.2642	0.2673	0.2704	0.2734	0.2764	0.2794	0.2823	0.2852
0.8	0.2881	0.2910	0.2939	0.2967	0.2996	0.3023	0.3051	0.3078	0.3106	0.3133
0.9	0.3159	0.3186	0.3212	0.3238	0.3264	0.3289	0.3315	0.3340	0.3365	0.3389
1.0	0.3413	0.3438	0.3461	0.3485	0.3508	0.3531	0.3554	0.3577	0.3599	0.3621
1.1	0.3643	0.3665	0.3686	0.3708	0.3729	0.3749	0.3770	0.3790	0.3810	0.3830
1.2	0.3849	0.3869	0.3888	0.3907	0.3925	0.3944	0.3962	0.3980	0.3997	0.4015
1.3	0.4032	0.4049	0.4066	0.4082	0.4099	0.4115	0.4131	0.4147	0.4162	0.4177
1.4	0.4192	0.4207	0.4222	0.4236	0.4251	0.4265	0.4279	0.4292	0.4306	0.4319
1.5	0.4332	0.4345	0.4357	0.4370	0.4382	0.4394	0.4406	0.4418	0.4429	0.4441
1.6	0.4452	0.4463	0.4474	0.4484	0.4495	0.4505	0.4515	0.4525	0.4535	0.4545
1.7	0.4554	0.4564	0.4573	0.4582	0.4591	0.4599	0.4608	0.4616	0.4625	0.4633
1.8	0.4641	0.4649	0.4656	0.4664	0.4671	0.4678	0.4686	0.4693	0.4699	0.4706
1.9	0.4713	0.4719	0.4726	0.4732	0.4738	0.4744	0.4750	0.4756	0.4762	0.4767
2.0	0.4772	0.4778	0.4783	0.4788	0.4793	0.4798	0.4803	0.4808	0.4812	0.4817
2.1	0.4821	0.4826	0.4830	0.4834	0.4838	0.4842	0.4846	0.4850	0.4854	0.4857
2.2	0.4861	0.4864	0.4868	0.4871	0.4875	0.4878	0.4881	0.4884	0.4887	0.4890
2.3	0.4893	0.4896	0.4898	0.4901	0.4904	0.4906	0.4909	0.4911	0.4913	0.4916
2.4	0.4918	0.4920	0.4922	0.4925	0.4927	0.4929	0.4931	0.4932	0.4934	0.4936
2.5	0.4938	0.4940	0.4941	0.4943	0.4945	0.4946	0.4948	0.4949	0.4951	0.4952
2.6	0.4953	0.4955	0.4956	0.4957	0.4959	0.4960	0.4961	0.4962	0.4963	0.4964
2.7	0.4965	0.4966	0.4967	0.4968	0.4969	0.4970	0.4971	0.4972	0.4973	0.4974
2.8	0.4974	0.4975	0.4976	0.4977	0.4977	0.4978	0.4979	0.4979	0.4980	0.4981
2.9	0.4981	0.4982	0.4982	0.4983	0.4984	0.4984	0.4985	0.4985	0.4986	0.4986
3.0	0.4987	0.4987	0.4987	0.4988	0.4988	0.4989	0.4989	0.4989	0.4990	0.4990
3.1	0.4990	0.4991	0.4991	0.4991	0.4992	0.4992	0.4992	0.4992	0.4993	0.4993
3.2	0.4993	0.4993	0.4994	0.4994	0.4994	0.4994	0.4994	0.4995	0.4995	0.4995
3.3	0.4995	0.4995	0.4995	0.4996	0.4996	0.4996	0.4996	0.4996	0.4996	0.4997
3.4	0.4997	0.4997	0.4997	0.4997	0.4997	0.4997	0.4997	0.4997	0.4997	0.4998
3.5	0.4998	0.4998	0.4998	0.4998	0.4998	0.4998	0.4998	0.4998	0.4998	0.4998
3.6	0.4998	0.4998	0.4999	0.4999	0.4999	0.4999	0.4999	0.4999	0.4999	0.4999
3.7	0.4999	0.4999	0.4999	0.4999	0.4999	0.4999	0.4999	0.4999	0.4999	0.4999
3.8	0.4999	0.4999	0.4999	0.4999	0.4999	0.4999	0.4999	0.4999	0.4999	0.4999
3.9	0.5000	0.5000	0.5000	0.5000	0.5000	0.5000	0.5000	0.5000	0.5000	0.5000

TABLE II

(i) Normal distribution 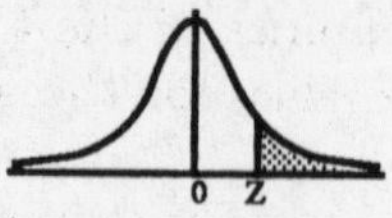 (shaded area = p)

Z	0.0	0.1	0.2	0.3	0.4	0.5	0.6	0.7	0.8	0.9
p	0.500	0.460	0.421	0.382	0.345	0.308	0.274	0.242	0.212	0.184
Z	1.0	1.1	1.2	1.3	1.4	1.5	1.6	1.7	1.8	1.9
p	0.159	0.136	0.115	0.097	0.081	0.067	0.055	0.045	0.036	0.029
Z	2.0	2.1	2.2	2.3	2.4	2.5	2.6	2.7	2.8	2.9
p	0.023	0.018	0.014	0.011	0.008	0.006	0.005	0.003	0.003	0.002
Z	3.0	3.1	3.2	3.3	3.4					
p	0.0013	0.0010	0.0007	0.0005	0.0003					

TABLE III

Percentage points of the t distribution

The table gives the values for the area in both tails.

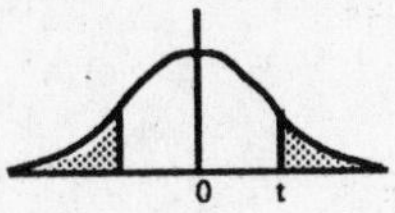

The table shows the total of the shaded areas

Degrees of Freedom	Area in Both Tails Combined .10	.05	.02	.01
$\nu = 1$	6,314	12,706	31,821	63,657
2	2,920	4,303	6,965	9,925
3	2,353	3,182	4,541	5,841
4	2,132	2,776	3,747	4,604
5	2,015	2,571	3,365	4,032
6	1,493	2,447	3,143	3,707
7	1,895	2,365	2,998	3,499
8	1,860	2,306	2,896	3,355
9	1,833	2,262	2,821	3,250
10	1,812	2,228	2,764	3,169
11	1,796	2,201	2,718	3,106
12	1,782	2,179	2,681	3,055
13	1,771	2,160	2,650	3,012
14	1,761	2,145	2,624	2,977
15	1,753	2,131	2,602	2,947
16	1,746	2,120	2,583	2,921
17	1,740	2,110	2,567	2,898
18	1,734	2,101	2,552	2,878
19	1,729	2,093	2,539	2,861
20	1,725	2,086	2,528	2,845
21	1,721	2,080	2,518	2,831
22	1,717	2,074	2,508	2,819
23	1,714	2,069	2,500	2,807
24	1,711	2,064	2,492	2,797
25	1,708	2,060	2,485	2,787
26	1,706	2,056	2,479	2,779
27	1,703	2,052	2,473	2,771
28	1,701	2,048	2,467	2,763
29	1,699	2,045	2,462	2,756
30	1,697	2,042	2,457	2,750
40	1,684	2,021	2,423	2,704
60	1,671	2,000	2,390	2,660
120	1,658	1,980	2,358	2,617
∞	1,645	1,960	2,326	2,576

TABLE IV

THE χ^2 DISTRIBUTION

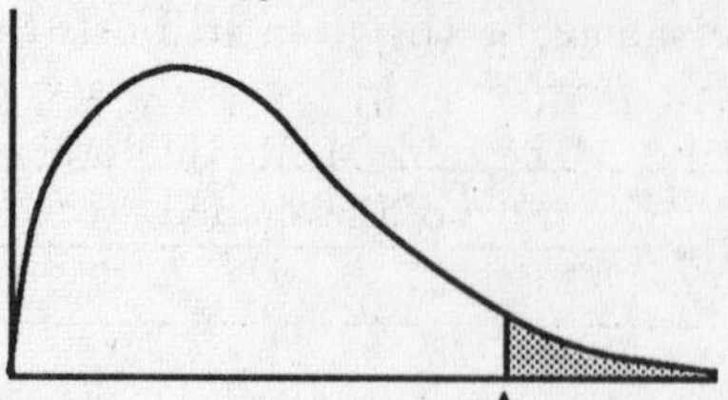

Degrees of Freedom	LEVEL OF SIGNIFICANCE	
	5%	1%
$\nu = 1$	3,841	6,635
2	5,991	9,210
3	7,815	11,345
4	9,488	13,277
5	11,070	15,086
6	12,592	16,812
7	14,067	18,475
8	15,507	20,090
9	16,919	21,666
10	18,307	23,209
11	19,675	24,725
12	21,026	26,217
13	22,362	27,688
14	23,685	29,141
15	24,996	30,578
16	26,296	31,999
17	27,587	33,409
18	28,869	34,805
19	30,144	36,191
20	31,410	37,566
21	32,671	38,932
22	33,924	40,289
23	35,172	41,638
24	36,415	42,979
25	37,652	44,314

TABLE V
PERCENTAGE POINTS OF THE F DISTRIBUTION
VALUES OF F

RIGHT TAIL OF THE DISTRIBUTION FOR P = .05
RIGHT TAIL OF THE DISTRIBUTION FOR P = .01 (IN BRACKETS)

ν_2 = Degrees of Freedom for Denominator	ν_1 = Degrees of Freedom for Numerator											
	1	2	3	4	5	6	7	8	9	10	11	12
1	161	200	216	225	230	234	237	239	241	242	243	244
	(4,052)	(4,999)	(5,403)	(5,625)	(5,764)	(5,859)	(5,928)	(5,981)	(6,022)	(6,056)	(6,082)	(6,106)
2	18.51	19.00	19.16	19.25	19.30	19.33	19.36	19.37	19.38	19.39	19.40	19.41
	(98.49)	(99.01)	(99.17)	(99.25)	(99.30)	(99.33)	(99.34)	(99.36)	(99.38)	(99.40)	(99.41)	(99.42)
3	10.13	9.55	9.28	9.12	9.01	8.94	8.88	8.84	8.81	8.78	8.76	8.74
	(34.12)	(30.81)	(29.46)	(28.71)	(28.24)	(27.91)	(27.67)	(27.49)	(27.34)	(27.23)	(27.13)	(27.05)
4	7.71	6.94	6.59	6.39	6.26	6.16	6.09	6.04	6.00	5.96	5.93	5.91
	(21.20)	(18.00)	(16.69)	(15.98)	(15.52)	(15.21)	(14.98)	(14.80)	(15.68)	(14.64)	(14.45)	(14.37)
5	6.61	5.79	5.41	5.19	5.05	4.95	4.88	4.82	4.78	4.74	4.70	4.68
	(16.26)	(13.27)	(12.06)	(11.39)	(10.97)	(10.67)	(10.45)	(10.27)	(10.15)	(10.05)	(9.98)	(9.89)
6	5.99	5.14	4.76	4.53	4.39	4.28	4.21	4.15	4.10	4.06	4.03	4.00
	(13.75)	(10.92)	(9.78)	(9.15)	(8.75)	(8.47)	(8.26)	(8.10)	(7.98)	(7.87)	(7.79)	(7.72)
7	5.59	4.74	4.35	4.12	3.97	3.87	3.79	3.73	3.68	3.63	3.60	3.57
	(12.25)	(9.55)	(8.45)	(7.85)	(7.46)	(7.19)	(7.00)	(6.84)	(6.71)	(6.62)	(6.54)	(6.47)
8	5.32	4.46	4.07	3.84	3.69	3.58	3.50	3.44	3.39	3.34	3.31	3.28
	(11,26)	(8.65)	(7.59)	(7.01)	(6.93)	(6.37)	(6.19)	(6.08)	(5.91)	(5.82)	(5,74)	(5.67)
9	5.12	4.26	3.83	3.63	3.48	3.37	3.29	3.23	3.18	3.13	3.10	3.07
	(10.56)	(8.02)	(6.99)	(6.42)	(6.06)	(5.80)	(5.62)	(5.47)	(5.35)	(5.38)	(5.18)	(5.11)
10	4.96	4.10	3.71	3.48	3.33	3.22	3.14	3.07	3.02	2.97	2.94	2.91
	(10.04)	(7.58)	(6.55)	(5.99)	(5.64)	(5.39)	(5,21)	(5.06)	(4.93)	(4.85)	(4.76)	(4.71)
11	4.84	3.98	3.59	3.36	3.20	3.09	3.01	2.95	2.90	2.86	2.82	2.79
	(9.65)	(7.20)	(6.22)	(5.67)	(5.32)	(5.07)	(4.88)	(4.74)	(4.63)	(4.54)	(4.46)	(4.40)
12	4.75	3.88	3.49	3.26	3.11	3.00	2.92	2.85	2.80	2.70	2.73	2.69
	(9.33)	(6.93)	(5.95)	(5.41)	(5.06)	(4.82)	(4.65)	(4.50)	(4.39)	(4.30)	(4.23)	(4.18)

TABLE VI

(a) TABLE OF INDIVIDUAL POISSON PROBABILITIES

Mean (m)	NUMBER OF OCCURRENCES (x) 0	1	2	3	4	5	6
0.1	0.9048	0.9048	0.0905	.0045	0.000	0.000	0.000
0.2	0.8187	0.1637	0.0164	0.0011	0.0011	0.000	0.000
0.3	0.7408	0.2222	0.0333	0.0033	0.0003	0.000	0.000
0.4	0.6703	0.2681	0.0536	0.0072	0.0007	0.0001	0.000
0.5	0.6065	0.3033	0.0758	0.0126	0.0016	0.0002	0.000
0.6	0.5488	0.3293	0.0988	0.0198	0.0030	0.0004	0.000
0.7	0.4966	0.3476	0.1217	0.0284	0.0050	0.0007	0.0001
0.8	0.4493	0.3595	0.1438	0.0383	0.0077	0.0012	0.0002
0.9	0.4066	0.3659	0.1647	0.0494	0.0111	0.0020	0.0003
1.0	0.3679	0.3679	0.1839	0.0613	0.0153	0.0031	0.0005

Table shows probability of a given number of occurrences for a given mean (m)

(b) TABLE OF CUMULATIVE POISSON PROBABILITIES

Mean (m)	NUMBER OF OCCURRENCES (x) 0	1	2	3	4	5	6
0.1	0.9048	0.9953	0.9998	1.00	1.00	1.00	1.00
0.2	0.8187	0.9824	0.9988	0.9999	1.00	1.00	1.00
0.3	0.7408	0.9630	0.9963	0.9996	0.9999	1.00	1.00
0.4	0.6703	0.9384	0.9920	0.9992	0.9999	1.00	1.00
0.5	0.6065	0.9098	0.9856	0.9982	0.9998	1.00	1.00
0.6	0.5488	0.8781	0.9769	0.9967	0.9997	1.00	1.00
0.7	0.4966	0.8442	0.9659	0.9943	0.993	1.00	1.00
0.8	0.4493	0.8088	0.9526	0.9909	0.9986	0.9998	1.00
0.9	0.4066	0.7725	0.9372	0.9866	0.9977	0.9997	1.00
1.0	0.3679	0.7358	0.9197	0.9810	0.9963	0.9994	0.9999

Table shows probability of finding x or fewer occurrences for a given mean (m)

TABLE VII

COMPOUND INTEREST, TABLE SHOWS AMOUNT OF £1 AT COMPOUND INTEREST $(1 + r)^n$

YEARS (n)	INTEREST RATES (r)% 1	2	3	4	5	6	7	8	9	10	11	12	13	14	15	16	17	18	19	20	25	30
1	1.010	1.020	1.030	1.040	1.050	1.060	1.070	1.080	1.090	1.100	1.110	1.120	1.130	1.140	1.150	1.160	1.170	1.180	1.190	1.200	1.250	1.300
2	1.020	1.040	1.061	1.082	1.102	1.124	1.145	1.166	1.188	1.210	1.232	1.254	1.277	1.297	1.322	1.346	1.367	1.392	1.416	1.440	1.562	1.690
3	1.030	1.061	1.093	1.125	1.158	1.191	1.225	1.260	1.295	1.331	1.368	1.405	1.443	1.481	1.521	1.561	1.602	1.643	1.685	1.728	1.953	2.197
4	1.041	1.082	1.126	1.167	1.216	1.262	1.311	1.360	1.412	1.464	1.518	1.573	1.630	1.689	1.749	1.811	1.874	1.939	2.005	2.074	2.441	2.856
5	1.051	1.104	1.159	1.217	1.276	1.338	1.403	1.469	1.539	1.610	1.685	1.762	1.842	1.925	2.011	2.100	2.192	2.288	2.386	2.488	3.052	3.713
6	1.061	1.126	1.194	1.265	1.340	1.419	1.501	1.587	1.677	1.772	1.870	1.974	2.082	2.195	2.313	2.436	2.565	2.700	2.840	2.986	3.815	4.827
7	1.072	1.149	1.230	1.316	1.407	1.504	1.606	1.714	1.828	1.949	2.076	2.211	2.353	2.502	2.660	2.826	3.001	3.186	3.379	3.583	4.768	6.275
8	1.083	1.172	1.267	1.369	1.477	1.594	1.718	1.851	1.993	2.144	2.304	2.476	2.658	2.853	3.059	3.278	3.511	3.759	4.021	4.300	5.960	8.157
9	1.094	1.195	1.305	‘.423	1.551	1.689	1.838	1.999	2.172	2.358	2.558	2.773	3.004	3.252	3.518	3.803	4.108	4.435	4.785	5.159	7.451	10.604
10	1.105	1.219	1.344	1.480	1.629	1.791	1.967	2.159	2.367	2.594	2.839	3.106	3.395	3.707	4.046	4.411	4.807	5.234	5.695	6.192	9.313	13.786
11	1.116	1.243	1.384	1.539	1.710	1.898	2.105	2.332	2.580	2.853	3.152	3.478	3.836	4.226	4.662	5.117	5.624	6.176	6.777	7.430	11.641	17.922
12	1.127	1.268	1.426	1.601	1.796	2.012	2.252	2.519	2.813	3.138	3.498	3.896	4.334	4.818	5.350	5.936	6.580	7.288	8.064	8.916	14.552	23.298
13	1.138	1.294	1.468	1.665	1.886	2.133	2.410	2.720	3.066	3.452	3.883	4.363	4.898	5.492	6.153	6.886	7.699	8.599	9.596	10.699	18.190	30.287
14	1.149	1.319	1.513	1.732	1.980	2.261	2.578	2.937	3.342	3.797	4.310	4.887	5.535	6.261	7.076	7.988	9.007	10.147	11.420	12.839	22.737	39.374
15	1.161	1.346	1.558	1.801	2.079	2.397	2.759	3.172	3.642	4.177	4.785	5.474	6.254	7.138	8.137	9.265	10.539	11.974	13.589	15.407	28.422	51.186
20	1.220	1.486	1.806	2.191	2.653	3.207	3.870	4661	5.604	6.727	8.062	9.646	11.523	13.743	15.366	19.461	23.106	27.393	32.429	38.338	86.736	190.050
25	1.282	1.641	2.094	2.666	3.386	4.292	5.427	6.848	8.623	10.835	13.585	17.000	21.230	26.462	32.920	40.874	50.658	62.669	77.388	95.396	264.698	705.641

TABLE VIII

PRESENT VALUE FACTORS: PRESENT VALUE OF £1 $(1+r)^{-n}$

DISCOUNT RATES (r)%

Periods (n)	1%	2%	4%	6%	8%	10%	12%	14%	15%	16%	18%	20%	22%	24%	25%	26%	28%	30%
1	0.990	0.980	0.962	0.943	0.926	0.909	0.893	0.877	0.870	0.862	0.847	0.833	0.820	0.806	0.800	0.794	0.781	0.769
2	0.980	0.961	0.925	0.890	0.857	0.826	0.797	0.769	0.756	0.743	0.718	0.694	0.672	0.650	0.640	0.630	0.610	0.592
3	0.971	0.942	0.889	0.840	0.794	0.751	0.712	0.675	0.658	0.641	0.609	0.579	0.551	0.524	0.512	0.500	0.477	0.455
4	0.961	0.924	0.855	0.792	0.735	0.683	0.636	0.592	0.572	0.552	0.516	0.482	0.451	0.423	0.410	0.397	0.373	0.350
5	0.951	0.906	0.822	0.747	0.681	0.621	0.567	0.519	0.497	0.476	0.437	0.402	0.370	0.341	0.328	0.315	0.291	0.269
6	0.942	0.888	0.790	0.705	0.630	0.564	0.507	0.456	0.432	0.410	0.370	0.335	0.303	0.275	0.262	0.250	0.227	0.207
7	0.933	0.871	0.760	0.665	0.583	0.513	0.452	0.400	0.376	0.354	0.314	0.279	0.249	0.222	0.210	0.198	0.178	0.159
8	0.923	0.853	0.731	0.627	0.540	0.467	0.404	0.351	0.327	0.305	0.266	0.233	0.204	0.179	0.168	0.157	0.139	0.123
9	0.914	0.837	0.703	0.592	0.500	0.424	0.361	0.308	0.284	0.263	0.225	0.194	0.167	0.144	0.134	0.125	0.108	0.094
10	0.905	0.820	0.676	0.558	0.463	0.386	0.322	0.270	0.247	0.227	0.191	0.162	0.137	0.116	0.107	0.099	0.085	0.075
11	0.0896	0.804	0.650	0.527	0.429	0.350	0.287	0.237	0.215	0.195	0.162	0.135	0.112	0.094	0.086	0.079	0.066	0.056
12	0.887	0.788	0.625	0.497	0.397	0.319	0.257	0.208	0.187	0.168	0.137	0.112	0.192	0.076	0.069	0.062	0.052	0.043
13	0.879	0.773	0.601	0.469	0.368	0.290	0.229	0.182	0.163	0.145	0.116	0.093	0.075	0.061	0.055	0.050	0.040	0.033
14	0.870	0.758	0.577	0.442	0.340	0.263	0.205	0.160	0.141	0.125	0.099	0.178	0.062	0.049	0.044	0.039	0.032	0.025
15	0.861	0.743	0.555	0.417	0.315	0.239	0.183	0.140	0.123	0.108	0.084	0.065	0.051	0.040	0.035	0.031	0.025	0.020
16	0.853	0.728	0.534	0.394	0.292	0.218	0.163	0.123	0.107	0.093	0.071	0.054	0.042	0.032	0.028	0.025	0.019	0.015
17	0.855	0.714	0.513	0.371	0.270	0.198	0.146	0.108	0.093	0.080	0.060	0.045	0.034	0.026	0.023	0.020	0.015	0.012
18	0.836	0.700	0.494	0.350	0.250	0.180	0.130	0.095	0.081	0.069	0.051	0.038	0.028	0.021	0.018	0.016	0.012	0.009
19	0.828	0.686	0.475	0.331	0.232	0.164	0.116	0.083	0.070	0.060	0.043	0.031	0.023	0.017	0.014	0.012	0.009	0.007
20	0.820	0.675	0.456	0.312	0.215	0.149	0.104	0.073	0.061	0.051	0.037	0.026	0.019	0.014	0.012	0.010	0.007	0.005
21	0.811	0.660	0.439	0.294	0.199	0.135	0.093	0.064	0.053	0.044	0.031	0.022	0.015	0.011	0.009	0.008	0.006	0.004
22	0.803	0.647	0.422	0.278	0.184	0.123	0.083	0.056	0.046	0.038	0.026	0.018	0.013	0.009	0.007	0.006	0.004	0.003
23	0.795	0.634	0.406	0.262	0.170	0.112	0.074	0.049	0.040	0.033	0.022	0.015	0.010	0.007	0.006	0.005	0.003	0.002
24	0.788	0.622	0.390	0.247	0.158	0.102	0.066	0.043	0.035	0.028	0.019	0.011	0.008	0.006	0.005	0.004	0.003	0.002
25	0.780	0.610	0.375	0.233	0.146	0.092	0.059	0.038	0.030	0.024	0.016	0.010	0.007	0.005	0.004	0.003	0.002	0.001

TABLE IX

PRESENT VALUE ANNUITY FACTORS: PRESENT VALUE OF £1 RECEIVED ANNUALLY FOR n YEARS $\left(\frac{1-(1+r)^{-n}}{r}\right)$

DISCOUNT RATES (r)%

Years (n)	1%	2%	4%	6%	8%	10%	12%	14%	15%	16%	18%	20%	22%	24%	25%	26%	28%	30%
1	0.990	0.980	0.962	0.943	0.926	0.909	0.893	0.877	0.870	0.862	0.847	0.833	0.820	0.806	0.800	0.794	0.781	0.769
2	1.970	1.942	1.886	1.833	1.783	1.736	1.690	1.647	1.626	1.605	1.566	1.528	1.492	1.457	1.440	1.424	1.392	1.361
3	2.941	2.884	2.775	2.675	2.577	2.487	2.402	2.322	2.283	2.246	2.174	2.106	2.042	1.981	1.952	1.923	1.868	1.816
4	3.902	3.808	3.610	3.465	3.312	3.170	3.037	2.914	2.855	2.798	2.690	2.589	2.494	2.404	2.362	2.320	2.241	2.166
5	4.853	4.713	4.452	4.212	3.996	3.791	3.605	3.433	3.352	3.274	3.127	2.991	2.864	2.745	2.689	2.635	2.532	2.436
6	5.795	5.601	5.242	4.917	4.623	4.355	4.111	3.889	3.784	3.685	3.498	3.326	3.167	3.020	2.951	2.885	2.759	2.643
7	6.728	6.472	6.002	5.582	5.206	4.868	4.564	4.288	4.160	4.039	3.812	3.605	3.416	3.242	3.161	3.083	2.937	2.802
8	7.652	7.325	6.733	6.210	5.747	5.335	4.968	4.639	4.487	4.344	4.078	3.837	3.619	3.421	3.329	3.421	3.076	2.925
9	8.566	8.162	7.435	6.802	6.247	5.759	5.328	4.946	4.772	4.607	4.303	4.031	3.786	3.566	3.463	3.366	3.184	3.019
10	9.471	8.983	8.111	7.360	6.710	6.145	5.650	5.216	5.019	4.833	4.949	4.192	3.923	3.682	3.571	3.465	3.269	3.092
11	10.368	9.787	8.760	7.887	7.139	6.495	5.988	5.453	5.234	5.029	4.636	4.327	4.035	3.766	3.656	3.544	3.335	3.147
12	11.255	10.575	9.385	8.384	7.536	6.814	6.194	5.660	5.421	5.197	4.793	4.439	4.127	3.851	3.725	3.606	3.387	3.190
13	12.114	11.343	9.986	8.853	7.904	7.103	6.424	5.842	5.583	5.342	4.910	4.533	4.203	3.912	3.780	3.656	3.427	3.223
14	13.004	12.106	10.563	9.295	8.244	7.367	6.628	6.002	5.724	5.468	5.008	4.611	4.265	3.961	3.824	3.965	3.459	3.249
15	13 865	12.849	11.118	9.712	8.559	7.606	6.811	6.142	5.847	5.575	5.092	4.675	4.315	4.001	3.859	3.726	3.483	3.268
16	14.718	13.578	11.652	10.106	8.851	7.824	6.974	6.265	5.954	5.669	5.162	4.730	4.357	4.033	3.887	3.751	3.503	3.283
17	15.562	14.292	12.166	10.477	9.122	8.022	7.120	6.373	6.047	5.749	5.222	4.775	4.391	4.059	3.910	3.771	3.518	3.295
18	16.328	14.992	12.659	10.828	9.372	8.201	7.250	6.467	6.128	5.818	5.273	4.812	4.419	4.080	3.928	3.786	3.529	3.304
19	17.226	15.678	13.134	11.158	9.604	8.365	7.366	6.550	6.198	5.877	5.316	4.844	4.442	4.097	3.942	3.799	3.539	3.311
20	18.046	16.351	13.590	11.470	9.818	8.514	7.469	6.623	6.259	5.929	5.353	4.870	4.460	4.110	3.954	3.808	3.546	3.316
21	18.857	17.011	14.029	11.764	10.017	8.649	7.562	6.687	6.312	5.973	5.384	4.891	4.476	4.121	3.963	3.816	3.551	3.320
22	19.660	17.658	14.451	12.042	10.201	8.772	7.645	6.743	6.369	6.011	5.410	4.909	4.488	4.130	3.970	3.822	3.556	3.323
23	20.456	18.292	14.857	12.303	10.371	8.883	7.718	6.792	6.399	6.044	5.432	4.925	4.499	4.137	3.976	3.827	3.559	3.325
24	21.243	18.914	15.247	12.550	10.529	8.985	7.784	6.815	6.434	6.073	5.451	4.937	4.507	4.143	3.981	3.831	3.562	3.327
25	22.023	19.523	15.622	12.783	10.675	9.077	7.843	6.873	6.464	6.097	5.467	4.948	4.514	4.147	3.985	3.834	3.564	3.329

Examination Technique

INTRODUCTION

If you are a genius and/or can calculate and reproduce facts and figures with the speed of a computer and/or know the examiner then there is no need for you to read this section. On the other hand if you do not fall into any of the above categories then you will stand more chance of passing your examinations first time if you study this section carefully and follow the simple rules.

WELL BEFORE THE EXAMINATION

No amount of examination room technique will enable you to pass unless you have prepared yourself thoroughly beforehand. The period of preparation may be years or months long. It is no use expecting to pass with a feverish last minute bout of swotting.

Plan your study and preparation systematically. Allocate specific times for study and stick to them. At a minimum your pre-examination preparation should include the following:

a. Obtain the official syllabus of the examination.
b. Systematically follow a course of study directed towards the examination.
c. Obtain past examination papers for say the last five years.
d. Make sure you can answer *every* question previously set.
e. Analyse the questions. Are some topics more popular than others?
f. Make sure you enter the examination in good time and receive official confirmation.

IMMEDIATELY BEFORE THE EXAMINATION

a. Make sure you know exact time, date and location of examination.
b. Carefully check your travel arrangements. Leave yourself adequate time.
c. Check your examination equipment:-
   Calculator? Spare Battery? Pens? Pencils? Slide Rule? Tables? Watch?
   Sweets? Cigarettes? etc, etc.
d. Check your examination number.

IN THE EXAMINATION ROOM

If you have followed the rules so far you are well prepared; you have all the equipment you need; you did not have to rush - YOU ARE CALM AND CONFIDENT.

Before you start writing:

a. Carefully read the whole examination paper including the rubric.
b. Decide what questions you are going to answer.
c. Decide the sequence you will tackle the questions. Generally, answer the easiest question first.
d. Decide the time allocation for each question. In general the time allocation should be in direct proportion to the marks for each question.
e. Read the questions you have decided to answer again. Do you know *exactly* what the examiner is asking? Underline the key words in the question and keep these in your mind when answering.

DEALING WITH THE QUESTIONS

a. Make sure you plan each question first. Make a note of the main points or principles involved. If you are unable to finish the question you will gain some marks from these points.

b. Attempt all questions required and each part of each question.

c. Do not let your answer ramble on. Be as brief as possible consistent with covering all the points you know.

d. Follow a logical sequence in your answers.

e. Write neatly, underline headings and if the question asks for a particular sequence of answer then follow that sequence.

f. If diagrams graphs or tables are required give them plenty of space, label them neatly and comprehensively, and give a key to symbols, lines etc used. A simple clear diagram showing the main points can often gain a good proportion of the marks for a question.

When you have finished writing:

a. Check that you have followed the examination regulations regarding examination title, examination number, candidates number and sequence of answer sheets.

b. If you have time carefully read each and every part of each answer and check each calculation.

General points

a. Concentrate on answering the questions set not some relaed topic which you happen to know something about.

b. Do *not* leave the examination room early. Use every minute for checking and rechecking or adding points to questions answered.

c. Always attempt every question set and every part of each question.

Solutions to Exercises and Examination Questions

CHAPTER 1

SOLUTION A1

'Systems approach to OR' – This can be answered directly from the text.

The second part of the question relates to the very real problems of coming to grips with large, complex, interconnected systems. Because of problems of time and resources, operational researchers often have to consider particular sub-systems more or less independently from the rest of the system. Although this is not ideal and could lead to sub-optimality, providing that there are only minor connections with other sub-systems, this is a practical solution.

It must be recognised that dealing with parts of the system separately does conflict with the pure systems approach but it is something that occasionally has to be done for practical reasons.

SOLUTION A2

a. If Operational Research is to provide a valid contribution it must take into account the conditions of the world in which problems exist. Being deterministic implies certainty, of say, cost, of the relationship between variables, the level of sales or the length of time a task takes. Probabilistic or stochastic implies uncertainly and risk.
When learning, certainty is easier to cope with so deterministic models of often taught first. Indeed in basic OR courses some techniques are never taken beyond the deterministic stage. Examples include:

   Linear programming
   stock control
   project planning (critical path)
   investment appraisal

   In contrast queueing theory is almost wholly stochastic in nature. Similarly forecasting techniques using confidence intervals imply a probabilistic approach.
   However further developments in the deterministic models quoted above strip away certainty linear programming under uncertainty is a major area. The classic EOQ model gives way to a probabilistic model. Investment appraisal develops expected N P V'S and their variances, P E R T has been developed to cope with risk and uncertainty in project planning.
   Ultimately every deterministic technique is developed into a probabilistic method. However in many cases a decision has got to be made, and so, say a probabilistic Linear programming model which gives a range of outputs for a given product and their associated probabilities is not really much use to the production manager who has to run the factory! Probability must not be used as an excuse for sloppy thinking. Think about the three time estimates for P.E.R.T! The proposition in the question is true but in the end decisions have to be made. The Manager has to determine a level of output. The finance Manager has to ask for a level of funding and the manpower manager has to engage labour. They will be right or wrong but they must decide.

b. Basic cost-volume profit analysis is concerned with the way in which profit changes in relation to changes in the level of activity of the organisation.

If P = profit

R = revenue per unit

C = variable cost per unit

X = number of units produced

F = fixed costs of the organisation

then

$$P = XR - XC - F$$
$$= X(R - C) - F$$

Breakeven point is defined as P = O and so occurs when

$$X(R - C) - F = O$$

OR

$$X(R - C) = F$$

or when $X = \frac{F}{R - C}$

The above assumes that R, C & F are known with certainty. R is possibly the only variable over which the organisation has control but in a competitive situation the managers may have to have a range of values in mind to respond to competitive pressures. There are two ways to handle uncertainty. The first is called sensitivity analysis. This involves varying the values of R. C and F individually to ascertain what the effect will be on profit. The second approach is the use of a probability distribution which overcomes the major weakness of sensitivity analysis – lack of probability. This second approach may be considered from two viewpoints – discrete and continuous probability distributions. The discrete approach brings in set figures for each variable with some attempt to set a probability. For example the managers may try to determine a price range i.e. revenue per unit.

Revenue per unit	Probability
50p	0.1
60p	0.6
70p	0.3

From the table above, an expected revenue per unit may be produced. Similarly a calculation may be made for expected cost and fixed costs. These may be combined to produce an expected breakeven point.

The most sophisticated approach may be to use a continuous distribution such as the normal distribution and make use of its attributes. Care must be taken however to ensure that the data involved does fit a normal distribution. If all valves, R, C and F were examined a continuous distribution of breakeven points could be produced.

SOLUTION A3.

a. This section can largely be answered from the chapter. Note, especially the power of mathematical modelling to ensure efficient utilisation of finance, time, labour and materials.

b. Benefits may not be always achieved because

   i. inaccurate, incomplete or biassed data.

   ii. wrong choice of model

   iii. inaccurate or incomplete specification of variables

   iv. poor interpretation &/or implementation of results.

c. Procedures to ensure better results

i. prompt and accurate data capture

ii. better training

iii. senstivity analyses

iv. better model development

v. detailed planning of whole process

vi. regular feed back and review

SOLUTION A4

It is normal practice to start with a simple model and gradually refine the model in order to reflect more accurately the inherent complexities of practical problems. This process is known as model development or enrichment. All model building and use must be an iterative process whereby the model is developed, manipulated and the results and/or projections tested against reality. It is this process which points the way towards the most worthwhile development of the model.

All models are simplifications of reality and the best model is the simplest that fulfills the objectives.

The 'start simple, then elaborate' process is practical, enables some sort of results to be obtained reasonably quickly and enables experience to be gained in model development both by OR specialists and management. The disadvantages of this approach is that perhaps a superficial and positively misleading view is taken of the underlying real problem and that the model is not developed in the right manner to solve the real problem.

The 'elaborate model' approach does have the advantages that there is more likelihood of the real problem being defined during the system investigation but suffers from the problem of cost and the practical problem of managers understanding the interactions and facilities of the model sufficiently to be able to suggest improvements.

CHAPTER 2

SOLUTION A1

$$\begin{aligned} \text{P(King)} &= \tfrac{4}{52} \\ \text{P (heart)} &= \tfrac{13}{52} \\ \text{P (King and heart)} &= \tfrac{1}{52} \\ \therefore\ \text{P(King or heart)} &= \tfrac{4}{52} + \tfrac{13}{52} - \tfrac{1}{52} = \tfrac{16}{52} = \tfrac{4}{13} \end{aligned}$$

SOLUTION A2

$$\begin{array}{lll} \text{10 REQUESTS:} & \text{P(5 AND 5)} = 0.3 \times 0.3 & = 0.09 \\ \text{11 REQUESTS:} & \left\{ \begin{array}{l} \text{P(5 AND 6)} = 0.3 \times 0.7 = 0.21 \\ \text{P(6 AND 5)} = 0.7 \times 0.3 = 0.21 \end{array} \right\} & = 0.42 \\ \text{12 REQUESTS:} & \text{P(6 AND 6)} = 0.7 \times 0.7 & = \underline{0.49} \\ & & \quad \underline{1.00} \end{array}$$

SOLUTION A3

This exercise uses Bayes Theorem which has the general form

$$P(A|B) = \frac{P(A).\ P(B—A)}{P(B)}$$

Let H = hot weather

G = Good holiday

then P(G) = 0.75, P(H) = 0.6

and P(G|H) = 0.9

$$\therefore \; P(H|G) = \frac{P(H).P(G|H)}{P(G)} = \frac{0.6.0.9}{0.75} = \underline{\underline{0.72}}$$

SOLUTION A4

a. The first stage is to calculate the Conditional Profit i.e. the profit at each sales/stock position. this is shown in the following table.

STOCK (dozens)

Sales (dozens)	30	31	32	33	34	35	36
30	£ 18.00	£ 17.76	£ 17.52	£ 17.28	£ 17.04	£ 16.80	£ 16.56
31	18.00	18.60	18.36	18.12	17.88	17.64	17.40
32	18.00	18.60	19.20	18.96	18.72	18.48	18.24
33	18.00	18.60	19.20	19.80	19.56	19.32	19.08
34	18.00	18.60	19.20	19.80	20.40	20.16	19.92
35	18.00	18.60	19.20	19.80	20.40	21.00	20.76
36	18.00	18.60	19.20	19.80	20.40	21.00	21.60

TABLE OF CONDITIONAL PROFITS

Note.

The method of calculation for each entry in the table follows the pattern of the following two examples:

Sales 30/stock 33 entry of £ 17.28

Profit on sales = (30 × 12)× (15p - 10p) = £ 18.00

less Loss on unsold stock =

(3 × 12)× (8p - 10p) = <u>72</u>

<u>£ 17.28</u>

Sales 35/stock 34 entry of £ 20.40

If stock is only 34 but a sales potential of 35 exists, obviously only 34 can be sold.

Profit = (34 × 12)× (15p - 10p) = <u>£ 20.40</u>

Each entry in the conditional profit table is then multiplied by the relative frequency (probability) of the sales to produce the Expected Profits (to two decimal places) as shown in the following table:

STOCK QUANTITY

Probability Sales	30	31	32	33	34	35	36
0.01	0.18	0.18	0.18	0.17	0.17	0.17	0.17
0.09	1.62	1.67	1.64	1.63	1.61	1.59	1.57
0.16	2.88	2.98	3.07	3.03	3.00	2.96	2.92
0.25	4.50	4.65	4.80	4.95	4.89	4.83	4.77
0.30	5.40	5.58	5.76	5.94	6.12	6.05	5.98
0.11	1.98	2.04	2.11	2.18	2.24	2.31	2.28
0.08	1.44	1.49	1.54	1.58	1.63	1.68	1.73
Total Expected Profit	18.00	18.59	19.10	19.48	19.66 *	19.59	19.42

TABLE OF EXPECTED PROFITS

*Best quantity to purchase is 34 dozens given an expected profit of £ 19.66 per day.

b. If the bakery had perfect information about sales, then they would purchase the exact quantity required, ie if sales were 30 they would stock 30 and so on. In such circumstances the expected profit would be the total of the diagonal terms in the Table of Expected Profits.

ie Maximum Expected Profit = £ 0.18 + £ 1.67 + £ 3.07 + £ 4.95 + £ 6.12 + £ 2.31 + £ 1.73

= **£ 20.03 per day**

∴ value of perfect information

= £20.03 – £19.66 = **£0.37perday**.

Solution A5

a. i. The five firms may be visited in any order and so the number of possible ways is given by

$$5! = 5 \times 4 \times 3 \times 2 \times 1 = 120 \text{ ways}$$

The probability of following one given route is thus

$$\frac{1}{120} = 0.0083$$

ii. Week 1: 120 routes out of 120
Week 2: 119 routes out of 120
Week 3: 118 routes out of 120
Week 4: 117 routes out of 120

Given that week one has passed the probability of choosing a different route on the next three occasions is given by

$$\frac{120}{120} \times \frac{119}{120} \times \frac{118}{120} \times \frac{117}{120} = 0.9507604 = 0.951$$

iii. There are two approaches to this; one is far easier than the other
If A and B are to be visited consecutively let them be linked and called X giving

X, C, D E four firms

The four firms can be visited

$$4! \text{ ways} = 4 \times 3 \times 2 \times 1 = 24 \text{ ways}$$

However A could come first or B could come first and so there are $24 \times 2 = 48$ ways.
There are 120 ways to visit all five firms and so the probability of A and B being visited consecutively is

$$\frac{48}{120} = \underline{\underline{0.4}}$$

Case 3
probability of C or D or E first is $\frac{3}{5}$. Fix C as first and there are four firms remaining. The probability of D or E being second is given by

$$\frac{1}{4} + \frac{1}{4} = \frac{1}{2}$$

Probability of A being third is now $\frac{1}{3}$ and if A is third the probability of B fourth is $\frac{1}{2}$.
∴ The joint outcome is $\frac{3}{5} \times \frac{1}{2} \times \frac{1}{3} \times \frac{1}{2} = \frac{1}{20}$
Case 4 is similar to Case 3
probability of C or D or E first is $\frac{3}{5}$. Fix C and the probability of D or E second is $\frac{2}{4}$ or $\frac{1}{2}$. Fix D as second and probability of E being third is $\frac{1}{3}$. This leaves A and B. Probability of A fourth is now $\frac{1}{2}$ and since only B remains, its probability of being fifth is unity.

iv. A, B, and C may be visited in
$3!$ ways $= 3 \times 2 \times 1 = 6$ ways
D and E may be visited in
$2!$ ways $= 2 \times 1 = 2$ ways
This means there are now $6 \times 2 = 12$ routes
a (i) becomes $\frac{1}{12}$ or 0.083
a (ii) becomes

week 2 $\frac{11}{12}$
week 3 $\frac{10}{12}$
week 4 $\frac{9}{12}$

The joint outcome is

$$\frac{11}{12} \times \frac{10}{12} \times \frac{9}{12} = 0.5729166 = 0.573$$

a (iii) becomes X C and D E
X, C has $2! \times 2 = 4$ ways
D, E has $2! = 2$ ways
There are now $4 \times 2 = 8$ routes
8 routes out of 12 gives a probability of

$$\frac{8}{2} = 0.67$$

a (iii) can also be expressed as

1 A B C

2 C A B

Case 1 is analysed as follows:

probability A first = $\frac{1}{3}$

probability B second = $\frac{1}{2}$ if A first

Joint outcome $\frac{1}{3} \times \frac{1}{2} = \frac{1}{6}$

Case 2 is treated as follows:

probability C first = $\frac{1}{3}$. Let C be first. The probability of A being second is now $\frac{1}{2}$. If A is second, B can only be third and this has a probability of unity or 1.

The joint outcome is

$$\frac{1}{3} \times \frac{1}{2} \times 1 = \frac{1}{6}$$

Cases 1 and 2 are mutually exclusive and so their joint outcome is

$$\frac{1}{6} + \frac{1}{6} = \frac{1}{3}$$

However as, B could come first the required probability is

$$2 \times \frac{1}{3} = \frac{2}{3} = 0.67.$$

v. This differs from (b) in (a) (ii) in that on each occasion after the first there are only 11 routes available.

Week 1 12 routes out of 12

Week 2 11 routes out of 11

Week 3 10 routes out of 11*

Week 4 9 routes out of 11**

* must be different from week 2

** must be different from week 3 but could be the same as week 2.

The required probability is given by

$$\frac{12}{12} \times \frac{11}{11} \times \frac{10}{11} \times \frac{9}{11} = \underline{\underline{0.7438}}$$

Solution A6

a. The opportunity losses are calculated in the usual manner by establishing the short-fall from the best possible result. This gives the following table with the stated probabilities.

	Poor	Fair	Good	∴ Expected
	p = 0.3	0.5	0.2	opportunity loss
CONV	0	0.5	0.2	0.65
NC	0.5	0	1	0.35
CNC	2.0	1.0	0	1.10

Table 1

∴ Ranking is NC, CONV, and CNC

b. The choice based on expected opportunity loss is NC ie. £ 350,000.
With perfect information the opportunity loss would be zero.
∴ Value of perfect information

$$= £350,000 - 0 = \underline{\underline{£350,000}}$$

c. Note: This part of the question involves conditional probabilities ie. the probability of one event *given* that another event has occurred.

Let PM = poor market size
FM = fair market size
GM = good market size
R = research group findings

Market probabilities	CONDITIONAL PROBABILITIES	JOINT PROBABILITY
	P (R|PM)	P(PM) × P(R|PM)
	I = 0.7	0.21
P(PM) = 0.3	II = 0.2	0.06
	III = 0.1	0.03
	P(R|FM)	P(FM) × P(R|FM)
	I = 0.2	0.1
P(FM) = 0.5	II = 0.7	0.35
	III = 0.1	0.05
	P(R|GM)	P(GM) × P(R|GM)
	I = 0	0
P(GM) = 0.2	II = 0.2	0.04
	III = 0.8	0.16

Table 2

The probabilities for the three market size indications I, II and III can be totalled from the table.

$$P(I) = 0.21 + 0.10 + 0 = 0.31$$
$$P(II) = 0.06 + 0.35 + 0.04 = 0.45$$
$$P(III) = 0.03 + 0.05 + 0.16 = 0.24$$
$$\underline{\underline{1.00}}$$

The relative probabilities of the actual market given a particular market research indicator.

Given State 1

$$P(PM|I) = \frac{0.21}{0.31} = 0.677$$
$$P(FM|I) = \frac{0.10}{0.31} = 0.323$$
$$P(GM|I) = \frac{0}{0.031} = \underline{0}$$
$$\underline{\underline{1.00}}$$

Given State II

$$P(RM|II) = \frac{0.06}{0.45} = 0.133$$
$$P(FM|II) = \frac{0.35}{0.45} = 0.778$$
$$P(GM|II) = \frac{0.04}{0.45} = \underline{0.089}$$
$$\underline{1.000}$$

Given State III

$$P(PM|III) = \frac{0.03}{0.24} = 0.125$$
$$P(FM|III) = \frac{0.05}{0.24} = 0.208$$
$$P(GM|III) = \frac{0.16}{0.24} = \underline{0.667}$$
$$\underline{1.000}$$

These relative probabilities are then used to calculate the expected opportunity losses using the calculated opportunity losses in Table 1.

Given State I

	Poor	Fair	Good	∴ Expected
	p = 0.677	0.323	0	Opportunity Loss
CONV	0	0.5	2.0	0.161 *
NC	0.5	0	1.0	0.338
CNC	2.0	1.0	0	1.667

Given State II

	Poor	Fair	Good	
	p = 0.133	0.778	0.089	
CONV	0	0.5	2.00	0.567
NC	0.5	0	1.00	0.156*
CNC	2.0	1.0	0	1.044

Given State III

	Poor	Fair	Good	
	p = 0.125	0.208	0.667	
CONV	0	0.5	2.0	1.408
NC	0.5	0	1.0	0.729
CNC	2.0	1.0	0	0.458 *

*indicates the minimum EOL and thus the appropriate machine in the various circumstances.

d. Maximum amount to pay for market research.

The machine chosen should be that which minimises the expected opportunity loss but this depends on the market research indications.

Market Research Indicator	Machine	Minimum EOL of Each State
State I	Conv	0.161
State II	NC	0.156
State III	CNC	0.458

∴ overall EOL is the EOL for each state times the probabilities of the market research indicators.

$$(0.31 \times 0.161) + (0.45 \times 0.156) + (0.25 \times 0.458) = 0.23$$

Therefore, by using the market research information the overall EOL is reduced from 0.35 (from Table 1) to 0.23 ie. a saving of 0.12 ie. £ 120,000 which represents the value of the market research information.

SOLUTION A7
Profit per unit sale = £ 6 - 4 = £ 2
Loss per unit unsold = £ 4 - 1 = £ 3

Conditional and Expected Profit Table

DEMAND	10 P = 0.24		20 P = 0.28		30 P = 0.32		40 P = 0.16		
PURCHASE	CP	EP	CP	EP	CP	EP	CP	EP	TOTAL
10	20	4.8	20	5.6	20	6.4	20	3.2	20
20	-10	-2.4	40	11.2	40	12.8	40	6.4	28
30	-40	-9.6	10	2.8	60	19.2	60	9.6	22
40	-70	-16.8	-20	5.6	30	9.6	80	12.8	0

∴ Purchase 20 units per day.

e. Expected sales

$$= (10 \times 0.24) + (20 \times 0.28) + (30 \times 0.32) + (40 \times 0.16) = 24$$

There are two alternatives
Purchase 20 giving a profit of 20 × £2 = £ 40 day
or Purchase 30 and sell an average of 24 per day and with 6 per day sold to staff.

$$24 \times £2 - 6 \times £3 = £30 \text{ per day}$$

∴ Best policy is to order 20 per day and store when demand drops to 10 per day. It would be worth (£ 40 - 28) £ 12 per day for the storage facility.

CHAPTER 3

SOLUTION A1

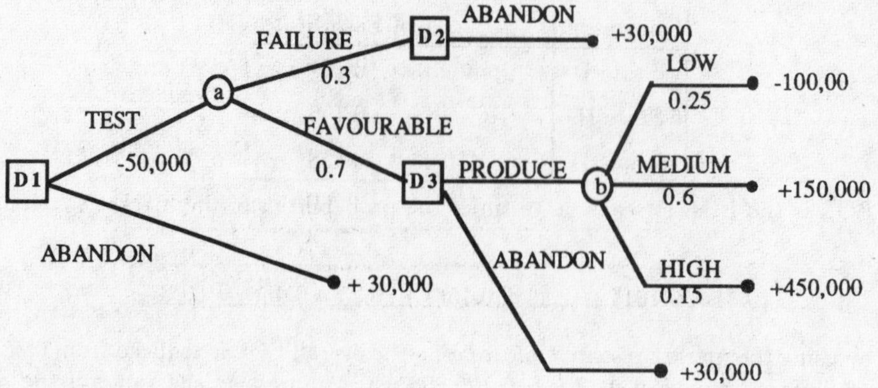

SOLUTION A2

Expected value at Node b

$$(0.25 \times -100,000) + (0.6 \times 150,000) + (0.15 \times 450,000) = \underline{£132,500}$$

∴ comparison at D3 is + 30,000 and + 132,500

∴ PRODUCE WITH EV OF £ 132,500

EV at Node A

$$(0.3 \times 30,000) + (0.7 \times 132,500) = \underline{£101,750}$$

∴ comparison at D1 is

$$101,750 - 50,000 = \underline{51,750} \text{ and } 30,000$$

∴ Test market at cost of £ 50,000 and produce if there are favourable indications.

SOLUTION A3

Decision Tree

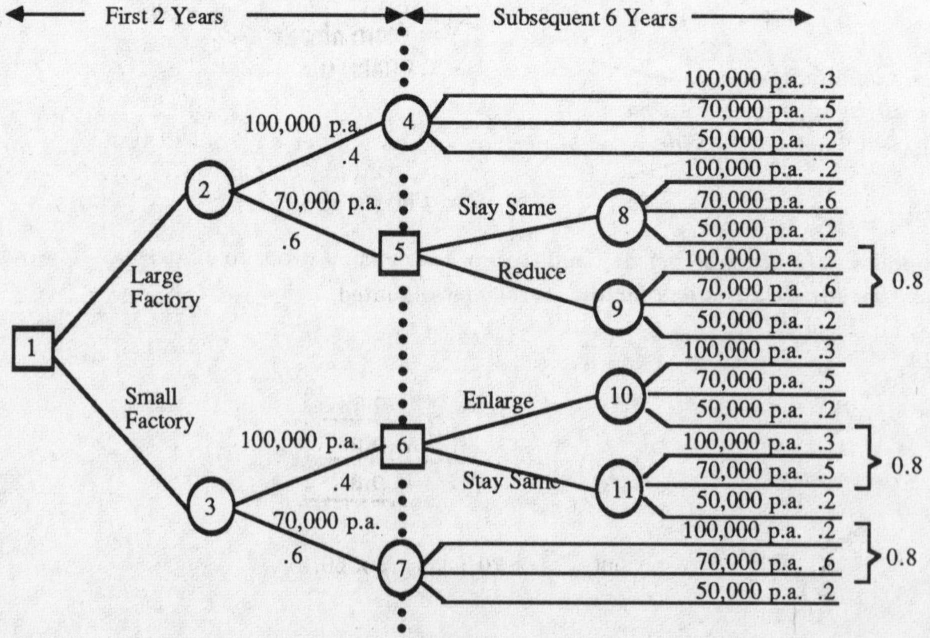

(Note.

The three bracketed probabilities on Nodes 9, 11 or 7 are because, in each case, capacity is a maximum of 70,000 units, so that the 100,000 demand potential cannot be realised and its probability can be added to the 70,000 p.a. demand).

The decision tree can then be evaluated from RIGHT to LEFT.

The expected value of the various demand possibilities (ie circular nodes) are given below together with extracts from the main diagram showing the nodes concerned.

LARGE FACTORY.

NODE 4

$$\therefore EV = 6 \times (.3 \times 100,000 + .5 \times 70,000 + .2 \times 50,000) \times £1 = \underline{\underline{\mathbf{£450,000}}}$$

NODE 8

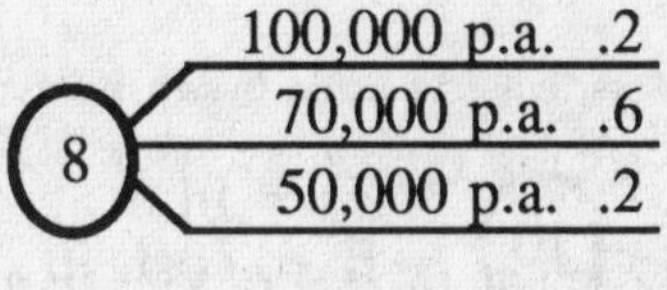

$$\therefore EV = 6 \times (.2 \times 100,000 + .6 \times 70,000 + .2 \times 50,000) \times £1 = \underline{\underline{\mathbf{£432,000}}}$$

NODE 9

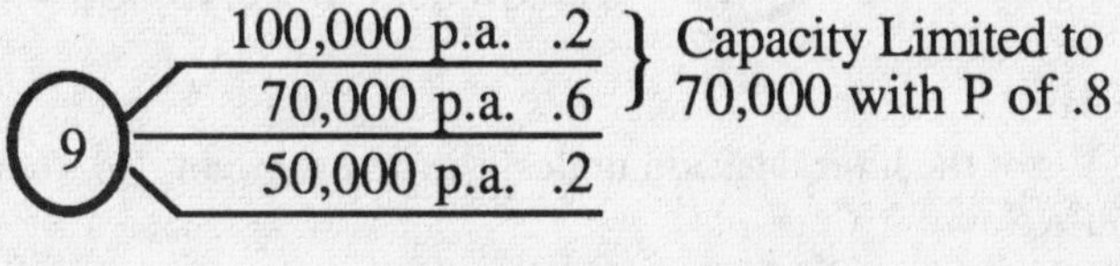

$$\therefore EV = 6 \times (.8 \times 70,000 + .2 \times 50,000) \times £1 = \underline{\underline{\mathbf{£396,000}}}$$

Having obtained these EV's the later decision node 5 can be evaluated

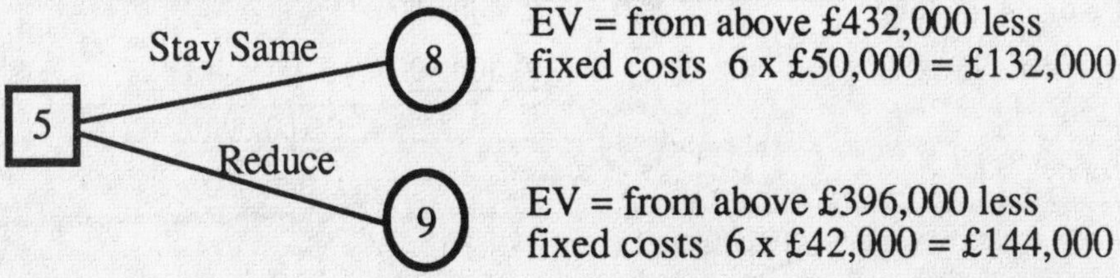

$\therefore$ choose to reduce.

In a similar fashion in the small factory nodes are evaluated.

SMALL FACTORY

NODE 10

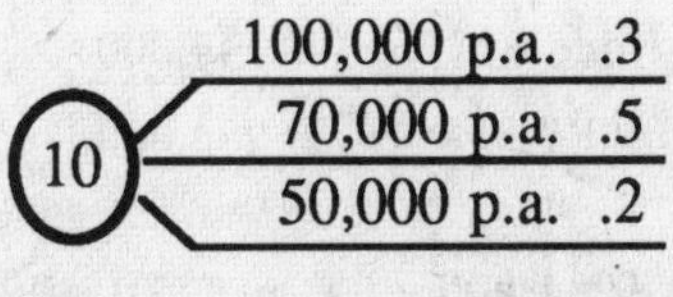

$$\therefore EV = 6 \times (.3 \times 100,000 + .5 \times 70,000 + .2 \times 50,000) \times £0.9 = \underline{\underline{\mathbf{£405,000}}}$$

NODE 11

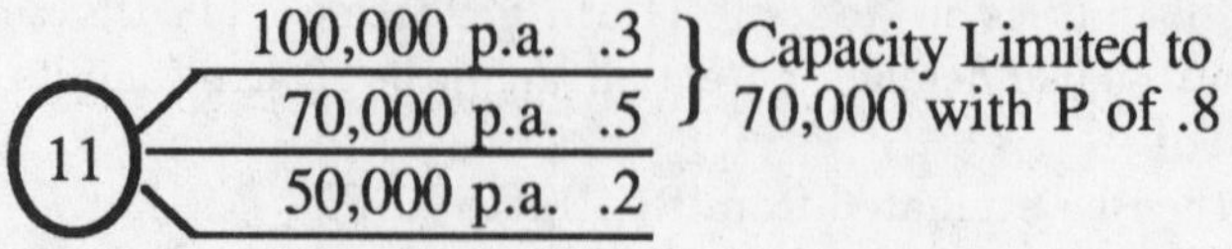

$$\therefore EV = 6 \times (.8 \times 70,000 + .2 \times 50,000) \times £0.9 = \underline{\underline{\mathbf{£356,400}}}$$

Having obtained these EV's the later decision node 6 can be evaluated.

NODE 7

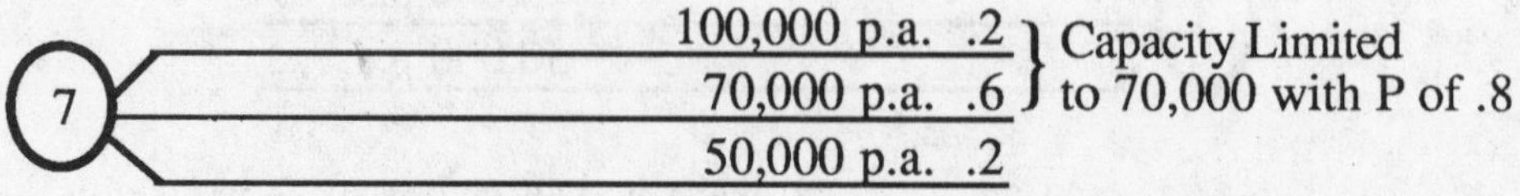

$$\therefore EV = 6 \times (.8 \times 70,000 + .2 \times 50,000) \times £0.9 = \underline{\underline{\mathbf{£356,400}}}$$

Having obtained these EV's the later decision node 6 can be evaluated.

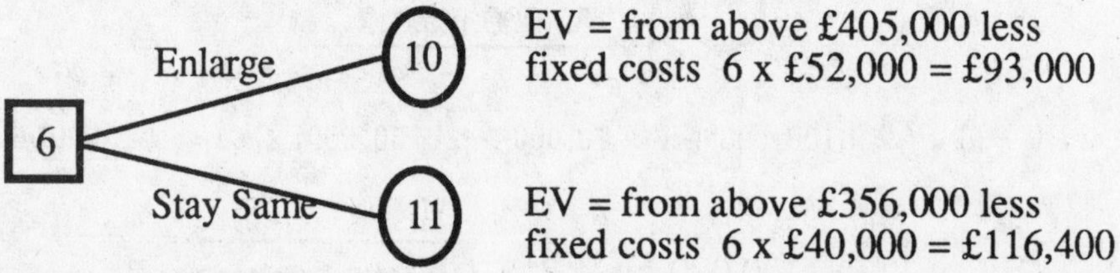

∴ Choose to stay the same

Having evaluated the EV's of the later decision nodes, the first decsion, No. 1 can be made by calculating the expected values at Nodes 2 and 3 thus:-

Node 2. Expected Value

If 100,000 demand p = 0.4

Contribution Limit = £ 1 ∴ over 2 years	=		£ 200,000
plus EV of Node 4 demand	=	£ 450,000	
less 6 years Fixed Costs	=	£ 300,000	
			£ 150,000
			£ 350,000

$$£350,000 \times 0.4 = \underline{\underline{\mathbf{£140,000}}}$$

If demand is 70,000 p = 0.6

Contribution/Unit =£ 1 ∴ over 2 years	=	£ 140,000
Plus Expected Value of Decision Node 5	=	£ 144,000
		£ 284,000

$$£284,000 \times 0.6 = \underline{\underline{\mathbf{£170,400}}}$$

∴ Total EV of Node 2 = £ 140,000 + £ 170,400 = **£ 310,400**

Node 3 Expected Value If demand is 100,000 p.a. p = 0.4 but node 3 will only be reached if the small factory unit is built,

∴ Sales will be limited to 70,000 whatever the demand. ∴ Contribution/unit = £ 0.90 and over 2 years the contribution is

$$140,000 times \text{ times } £0.90 \quad = \quad £126,000$$
$$\text{plus expected value of Node 6} \quad \underline{116,400}$$
$$242,400$$
$$£242,400 \text{ times } 0.4 \quad = \quad \underline{£96,960}$$

The situation when demand is 70,000 units is obviously the same as above so that the Expected Value is

$$£\ 242,400 \times 0.6 \quad = \quad \underline{£\ 145,440}$$
$$\therefore \text{ Total EV of Node 3} \quad = \quad £\ 96,960 + £\ 145,440$$
$$= \quad \underline{\underline{\mathbf{£\ 242,400}}}$$

∴ The company should build the large factory (EV given above of £ 310,400) and reduce its capacity if demand is initially 70,000 units p.a. for the first 2 years (ie the 'reduce' decision from Node 5, EV of £ 144,000)

SOLUTION A4

a.

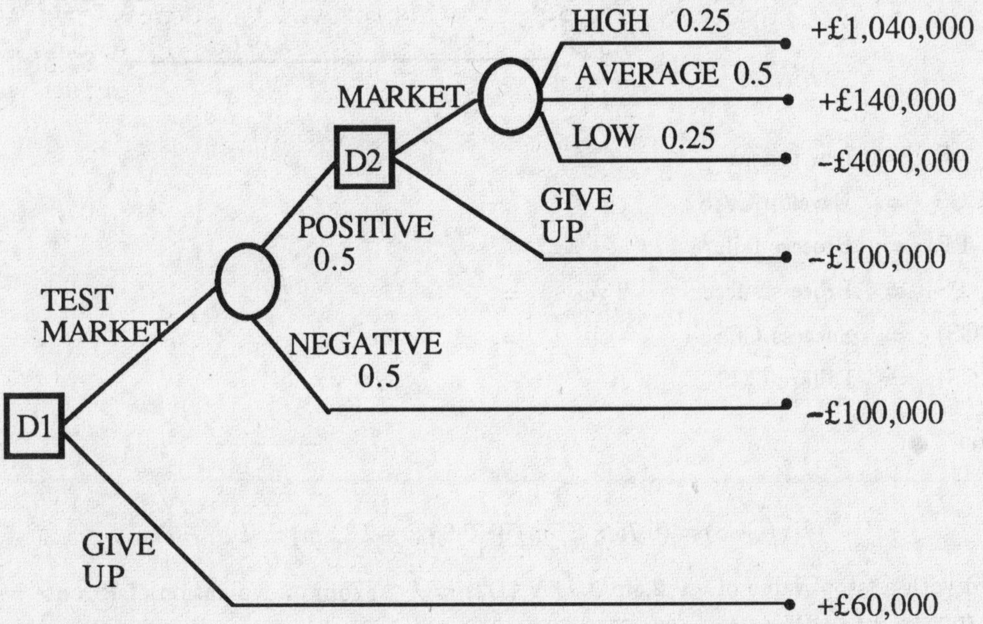

b. Decision 2

EV (Market) = $(0.25 \times £1,040,000) + (0.5 \times £140,000) + (0.25 \times -£400,000)$

= $\underline{£\ 230,000}$

EV (Give up) = - $\underline{£\ 100,000}$

∴ Market at D2

Decision 1

EV (Test Market) = $(0.5 \times £230,000) + (0.5 \times -£100,000) = \underline{£\ 65,000}$

EV (Give up) = £ 60,000

∴ on basis of E.V. the, decision should be 'test market and if positive' market nationally.

c. There are numerous estimates involved and gross simplifications eg the assessment of probabilities and the number and value of outcomes. In the circumstances given because of the closeness of the values it is likely that the firm would choose the less risky option of £ 60,000 and give up the project.

SOLUTION A5.

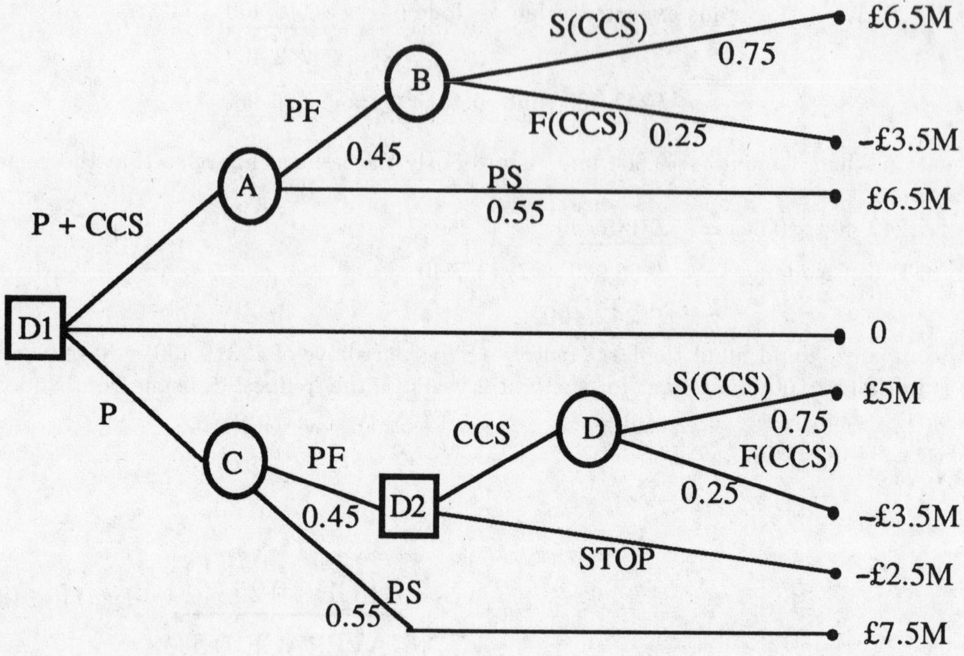

Key

P	=	new process
CCS	=	Develop C.CS
PF	=	Process failure
PS	=	Process success
S(CCS)	=	Success CCS
F(CCS)	=	Failure CCS

Evaluation

D2

$$EV(CCS) = (0.75 \times £5m) + (0.25 \times -£3.5m) = £2.875m$$

Compared with a 'stop' value of - £ 2.5m ∴ EV (D2) = £ 2.875m ∴ Valuation of P route back to D1

= $(0.55 \times £1.5m) + (0.45 \times £2.875)$

= £ 5.41875M

Evaluation Node B

$$= (0.75 \times £6.5m) + (0.25 \times -£3.5m) = \underline{£4M}$$

Node A

$$= (0.45 \times £4m) + (0.55 \times £6.5m) = \underline{£5.375m}$$

b. The three decision routes at D1

are D + CCS = £ 5.375m

P = £ 5.4m

Stop = 0

∴ Choose new Process initially and develop CCS if process is a failure

c. The two alternatives are

$$E(P + CCS) = (p \times £6.5m) + (1 - p) \times £4m)$$
$$= \underline{2.5p + 4}$$
$$E(P) = (p \times £7.5m) + (1 - p) \times £2.875m)$$
$$= 4.625p + 2.875$$

where p = probability of success

To be indifferent

$$E(P + CCS) = E(p)$$
$$\therefore\ 2.5P + 4 = 4.625P + 2.875$$
$$\therefore\ = \underline{0.53}$$

Thus if the probability of a successful new process is less than 0.53 it is better to begin the new process and the CCS development simultaneously.

SOLUTION A6

a. Various decsion criteria are discussed in Chapter 3, e.g. Expected Value, Minimax, Maximax.

b. Decision tree with probabilities.

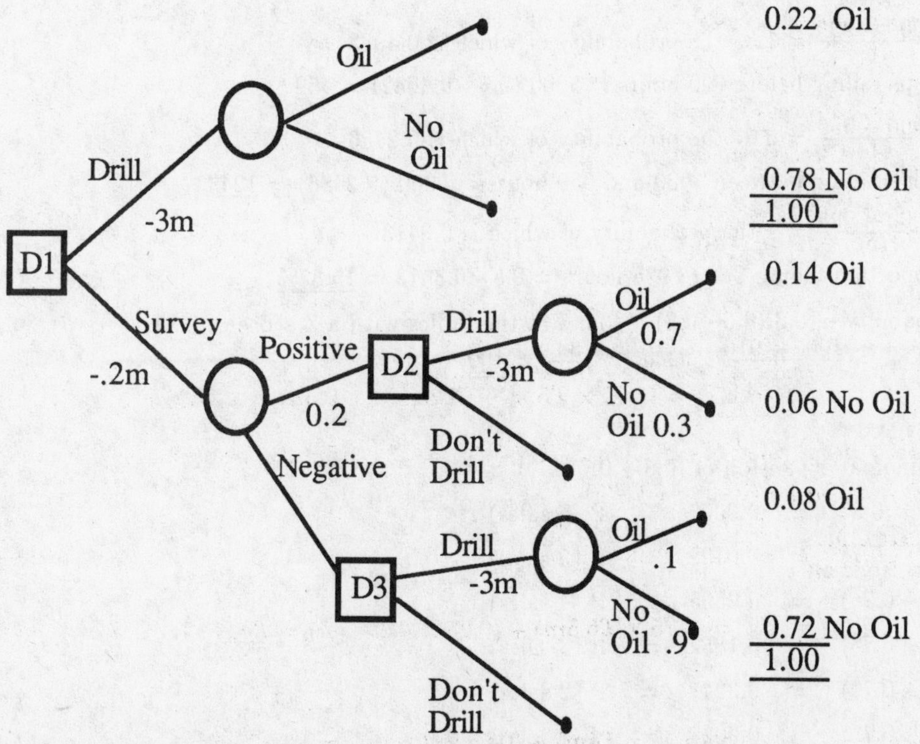

The return from the various options using expected values are:

EXPECTED VALUES

D3

0.1 × 30m	=	3m
Less drilling		
cost		3m
		0

∴ Do not drill if survey negative

D2

0.7 × 30m	=	21m
Less drilling		
cost		3m
		18m

∴ Drill if survey positive

∴ Expected value of survey arm of D1

= (.2 × 18m) + (0.8 × 0) − 0.2m = 3.4m

Expected value of drilling arm of D1

= (0.22 × 30m) + (0.78 × 0) − 3m = 3.6m

∴ Drill without survey, based on returns and probabilties given.

CHAPTER 4

SOLUTION A1

$$\bar{x} = 52.44 \quad \sigma = 33.68$$

SOLUTION A2

a. $Z = \frac{1000 - 900}{75} = 1.33$ the probability of which is 0.4082

∴ lamps failing before 900 hours = 5000 (0.5 - 0.4082) = 459

b. $Z = \frac{1000 - 950}{75} = 0.67$ the probability of which is 0.2486

∴ lamps failing between 1000 and 950 hours = 5000 (0.2486) = 1243

c. $Z = \frac{1000 - 925}{75} = 1$ the probability of which is 0.3413

∴ Proportion failing before 925 hours = 0.5 - 0.3413 = 15.87%

d. A probability of 0.3 (0.5 - 0.2) is found in the tables with a Z score of 0.84,

Thus $0.84 = \frac{1000 - 916}{\text{s.d.}}$ ∴ $\text{s.d.} = \frac{84}{0.84} = 100$

SOLUTION A3

Binomal expansion of $(0.3 + 0.7)^6$

$$
\begin{aligned}
0.3^6 &= 0.0007 = \text{P (6 sales)}\\
6(0.3^5 + 0.7) &= 0.0102 = \text{P (5 sales)}\\
15(0.3^4 + 0.7^2) &= 0.0595 = \text{P (4 sales)}\\
20(0.3^3 + 0.7^3) &= 0.1852 = \text{P (3 sales)}\\
15(0.3^2 + 0.7^4) &= 0.3241 = \text{P (2 sales)}\\
6(0.3 + 0.7^5) &= 0.3025 = \text{P(1 sale)}\\
0.7^6 &= 0.1176 = \text{P(0 Sales)}
\end{aligned}
$$

SOLUTION A4

a. a. and b. can be answered directly from the chapter.

b. $Sk = \frac{3(\text{mean - median}}{\sigma} = \frac{3(15-16)}{6}$ Skewness =-0.5

This shows that the distribution is slightly negatively skewed.

ii. An alternative measure of skewness uses the upper and lower quartiles ie. the values $\frac{3}{4}$ and $\frac{1}{4}$ along the distribution.

The formula is

$$\frac{(Q_1 + Q_3) - 2(\text{Median})}{Q_3 - Q_1}$$

So assuming $Q_1 = 10$ and $Q_3 = 20$ the skewness $= \frac{(10+20) - 2 \times 16}{20-10} = \frac{-2}{10} = -0.2$

c. Many distributions exhibit varying degrees of skewness and calculation of a measure of skewness gives insight into the properties of the distributions. Examples include distributions of wealth and earnings.

SOLUTION A5

a. i. z measures the number of standard deviations a given value is away from the mean.

ii. The standardised value z has a mean of 0 and a standard deviation of 1.

iii. Using the Tables

i. z = 1.96

ii. z = 3.29

b. i.

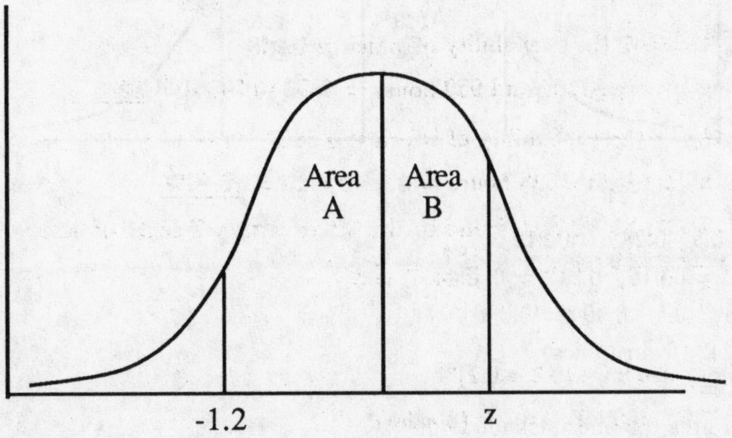

Area A + B = 0.523

Area A (from tables) = 0.3849

∴ Area B = 0.523 - 0.3849

= 0.1381

and from the tables the z score is found to be

$z \simeq 0.353$

ii.

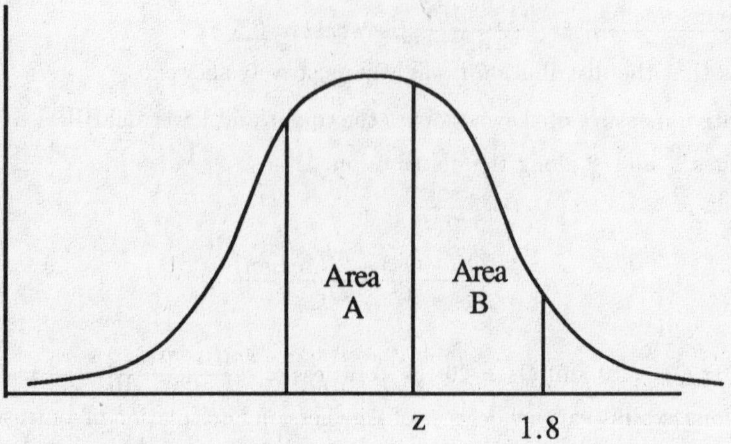

Area A + B = 0.4641 (from tables)

∴ Area A = 0.4641 - 0.355 = 0.1091

∴ z = 0.277 (from tables)

iii.

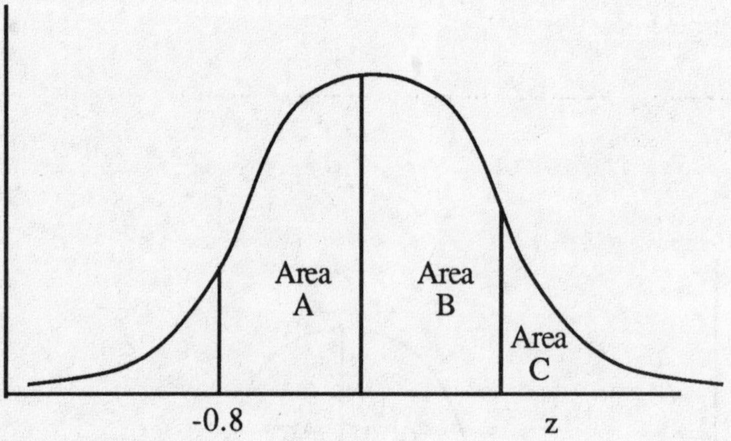

Area A = 0.5 - 0.288 = 0.212

∴ Area C = 0.616 - 0.212 = 0.404

∴ Area B = 0.5 - 0.404 = 0.096

∴ z = 0.242 (from tables)

Total area = 1

∴ Shaded area 0.2 and unshaded 0.8

∴ Area between mean and z is 0.5 - 0.2 = 0.3

∴ z = 0.841

SOLUTION A6

a. i. The probability is found by calculating the area between 5500 and 6500 hours thus <u>at 5500 hours</u>

$$z = \frac{5500 - 5000}{1000} = 0.5 \text{ and area from the tables is } \underline{0.1915}$$

at 6500 hours

$$z = \frac{6500 - 5000}{1000} = 1.5 \text{ and area from tables is } \underline{0.4332}$$

∴ P(Tube life 550 to 6500 hrs) = 0.4332 - 0.1915 <u>0.2417</u>

ii. The *expected* life of a tube is the mean life ∴ 50% of tubes have a life less than 1000 hours.

b. Five years use at 1500 hours per year = 7500 hrs.
   ∴ $z = \frac{7500 - 5000}{1000} = 2.5$ and area from tables = 0.4938
   ∴ $P(z < 2.5) = 0.5 + 0.4938 = \underline{0.9938}$

c. Life is failure in 3 years or less = 4500 hours
   ∴ $z = \frac{4500 - 5000}{1000} = 0.5$ and value from tables = 0.1915
   ∴ $P(z \leq 0.5) = 0.5 - 0.1915 = \underline{0.3085}$
   Probability of failure between 3 and 5 years
   = 0.9938 (from (b) above) - 0.3085 = 0.6853
   ∴ Expected payout (£80 × 0.3085) + (£40 × 0.6853) = £ 52.09 and as the charge for the guarantee is £ 25 there is an expected loss to the company of <u>£ 27.09</u>

SOLUTION A7

A Decision Tree

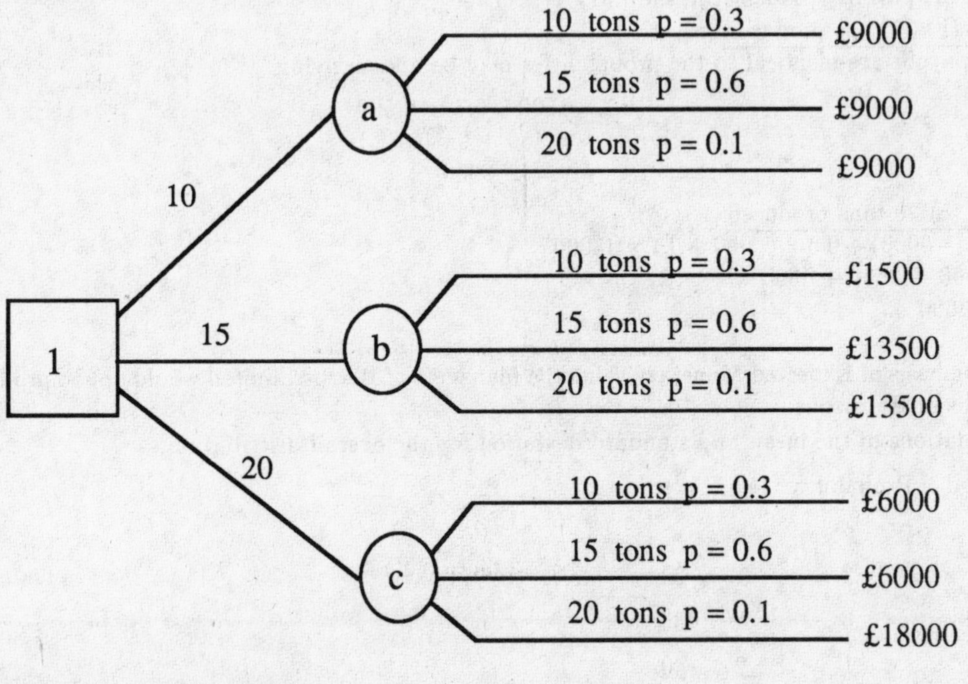

a. Calculations for Decision Tree

<u>Let 10 tons be produced</u>

If 10, 15, or 20 tons are demanded then contribution will be

$$10(2400 - 1500) = £9,000$$

<u>Let 15 tons be produced</u>

If 10 tons are demanded

$$\begin{aligned} \text{Contribution} &= 10 \times 2400 - 15 \times 1500 \\ &= 24{,}000 - 22{,}500 \\ &= £\ 1500 \end{aligned}$$

If 15 tons or 20 tons are demanded

Contribution = 15 (2400 - 1500)

= £ 13500

Let 20 tons be produced

If 10 tons are demanded

Contribution = $10 \times 2400 - 20 \times 1500$

= 24000 - 30000

= - £ 6000

If 15 tons are demanded

Contribution = $15 \times 2400 - 20 \times 1500$

= 36000 - 30000

= £ 6,000

If 20 tons are demanded

Contribution = 20(2400 - 1500)

= £ 18000

These are the payoffs on the decision tree

b. Calculations of Expected Monetary Values

Node (a) 10 tons produced

Since the payoffs are identical, the EMV is £ 9,000

Node (b) 15 tons produced

Two payoffs are identical so the probabilities may be added giving

$$0.3 \times 1500 + 0.7 \times 13500$$
$$= 450 + 9450$$
$$= £\ 9900$$

Node (c) 20 tons produced

$0.3 \times (-6000) + 0.6 \times 6,000 + 0.1 \times 18000$

= -1800 + 3600 + 1800

= £ 3600

On the basis of Expected Monetary value the managers of Hetros Limited would opt to produce 15 tons of Hetrozone.

c. Calculations of the mean and standard deviation for the overall distribution.

Demand x	Probability p	xp	x^2p
10	.3	3	30
15	.6	9	135
20	.1	2	40
		14	205

$$\mu = \sum xp = 14 \text{ tons}$$
$$\sigma^2 = \sum x^2p - (\sum xp)^2$$
$$= 205 - 14^2$$
$$= 205 - 196$$
$$= 9$$
$$\sigma = \sqrt{9}$$
$$= 3 \text{ tons}$$

If the demand pattern is assumed to be normal then the distribution may be sketched as follows:

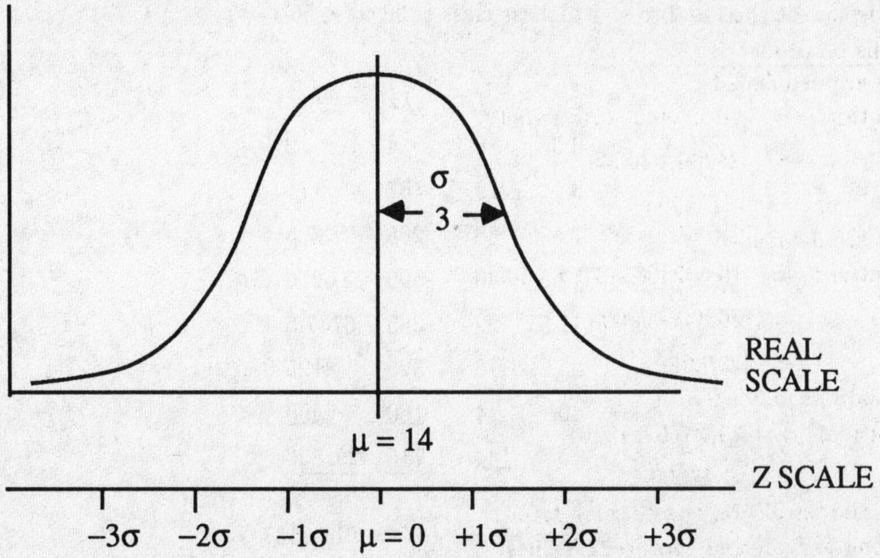

probability is represented by the area under the normal curve

$$v/p = 1500/2400 = 0.625$$

The area required is that which contains 62.5% of the are in the upper part of the curve. Since 50% of the area lies above $\mu = 14$ tons the optimum value of Q must lie below $\mu = 14$ tons.

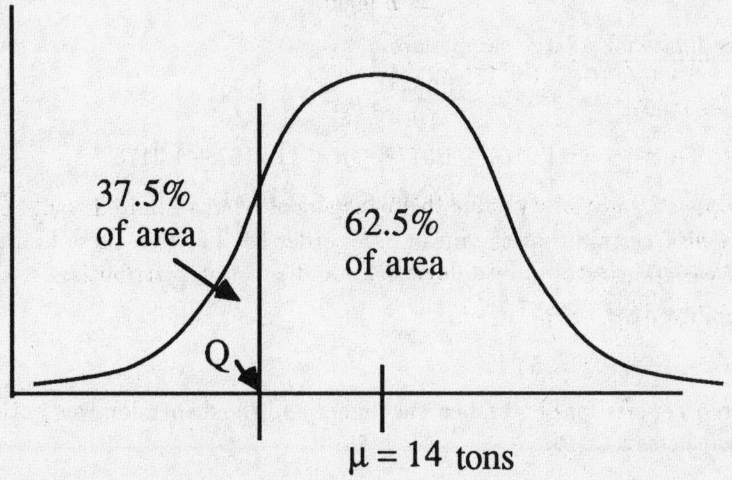

It is easier to work with the complement of the required area i.e. 100 - 62.5 giving 37.5% or 0.375.
0.375 lies between 0.382 (z = 0.3) and 0.345 (z = 0.4)
A crude linear interpolation below gives an estimate of z = 0.32

Since $Q < \mu$ work with - 0.32

$$\text{Using } Z = \frac{x-\mu}{\sigma}$$

$$-0.32 = \frac{Q-14}{3}$$

$$-0.96 = Q - 14$$

$$-0.96 + 14 = Q$$

$$Q = 13.04 \text{ tons}$$

Say 13 tons for an integer solution.

SOLUTION A8

a. Assuming lowest class is 0 to < 1 highest class is 30 to < 50
midpoints

x	f	fx	fx^2
0.5	8	4	2
3	19	57	171
7.5	38	285	2137.5
12.5	40	500	6250
17.5	22	385	6737.5
25	13	325	8125
40	4	160	6400
	144	1,716	29,823

$$\therefore \overline{x} = \frac{fx}{f} = \frac{1716}{144} = £11.9167$$

$$S = \sqrt{\frac{\sum fx^2}{\sum f} - \left(\frac{\sum fx}{\sum f}\right)^2}$$
$$= \sqrt{\frac{29,823}{144} - \left(\frac{1716}{144}\right)^2}$$
$$= \underline{£8.068}$$

b. 95% confidence limits for a large sample are

$$\overline{x} - \frac{1.96s}{\sqrt{n}} \leq \mu \leq \overline{x} + \frac{1.96s}{\sqrt{n}}$$
$$= 11.9167 - 1.3178 \leq \mu \leq 11.9167 + 1.3178$$
$$= £10.60 \leq \mu \leq £13.24$$

thus we can be 95% certain that the mean of all order lies between these limits.

c. Coefficients of variation

April $= \dfrac{8.068}{11.9167} = 67.7\%$

September $= \dfrac{7.05}{13.28} = 53.1\%$

Thus the mean order size for September was higher and the dispersion was both absolutely and relatively less dispersed.

SOLUTION A9

a. If p = proportion of rooms occupied then 120p = number occupied and 120pq are let as single rooms and 120p (1 - q) are let as double rooms.

$\therefore$ Revenue from rooms = 120 pq × 45 + 120 p(1 - q) × 2 = 120p (70 - 25q)

Number of residents = 120pq × 1 + 120p (1 - q) = 120p(2 - q)

$\therefore$ Revenue from meals = 0.6 × 9 × 120p(2 - q)

= 648p(2 - q)

$\therefore$ Total revenue = Room + Meal revenue

= 120p (70 - 25q) + 648p(2 - q)

= <u>96p (101 - 38q)</u>

b.

When q = 0.1   R = 96p (101 - 3.8)   = 9,331.2p

q = 0.2   R = 96p (101 - 7.6)   = 8,996.4p

q = 0.3   R = 96p (101 - 11.4)   = 8,601.6p

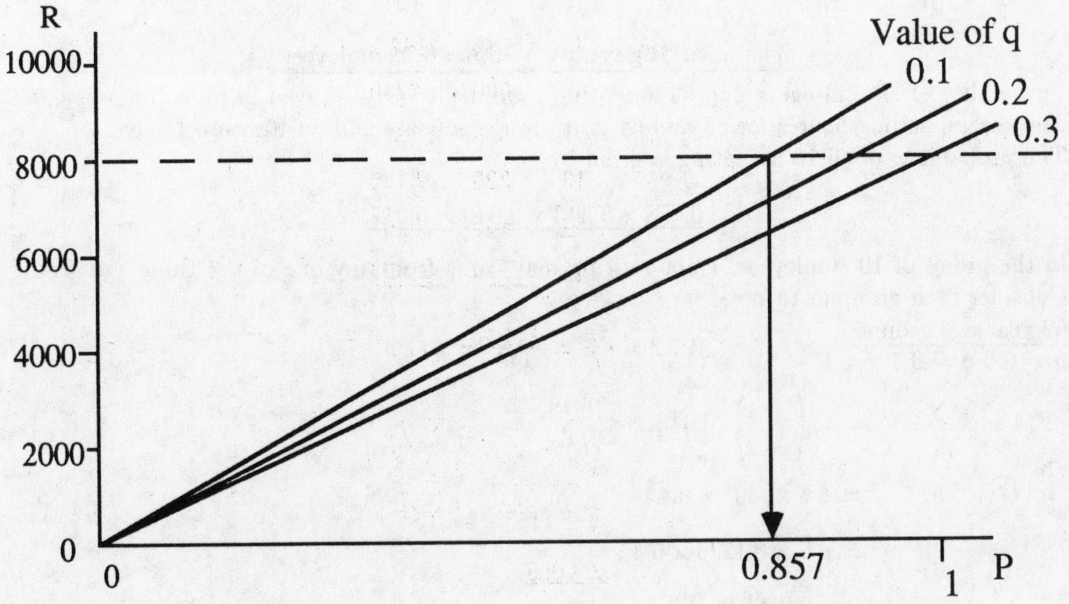

From the graph, the lowest value of p to yield an expected daily revenue of £ 8,000 occurs when q = 0.1

∴ 9,331.2p = 8,000

i.e. p = 8,000/9,331.2 = 0.857 = 85.7%

c. If the three values of q have probabilities of 0.3, 0.5 and 0.2 respectively then the expected daily revenue is

$$E(R) = 0.3 \times 9,331.2p + 0.5 \times 8,966.4p + 0.2 \times 8,601p$$

$$= 9,002.88p = £\ 9,000p$$

d. Alternatively, if q has a normal distribution with a mean of 19% and a standard deviation of 7%, the 95% limits of q are

$0.19 - 1.96 \times 0.07$ and $0.19 + 1.96 \times 0.07$

i.e. 0.05 and 0.33

Substituting these limits in the expression for R gives

Lower limit = 96p $(101 - 38 \times 0.05) = £9,513.6p$

Upper limit = 96p $(101 - 38 \times 0.33) = £8,492.2p$

Therefore, with 95% probability, the daily revenue will fall between approximately £ 8,500p and £ 9,500p

SOLUTION A10

Employees in each age group may retire or not retire early and so each age group may be considered as a Binomial Distribution where p is defined as the probability of success and pn is the probability of n successes in a trial.

a. The expected number accepting early retirement.

Age Group	n	p	np	p^n
62	5	0.6	3.0	0.078
63	3	0.7	2.1	0.343
64	2	0.8	1.6	0.640
	10		6.7	

The mean is given by $\sum$ np = 6.7 employees

Probability of all 5 in age group 62 accepting retirement early is given in pn column as 0.078.
The corresponding figures for 63 and 64 year groups is 0.343 and 0.640 respectively.
The probability of all 10 accepting is given by

$$0.078 \times 0.343 \times 0.640 = 0.017$$

b. In the group of 10 employees, 1 not retiring may come from any one of the three age groups. Consider each group in turn

62 year age group

p = 0.6 q = 0.4 n = 5

$$\begin{aligned} P(4 \text{ successes}) &= \binom{5}{4} 0.6^4 \times 0.4^1 \\ &= 5 \times 0.6^4 \times 0.4 \\ &= 5 \times 0.1296 \times 0.4 \\ &= 0.2592 \end{aligned}$$

$$NB \binom{5}{4} = \frac{5!}{4!(5-4)!} = \frac{5 \times 4 \times 3 \times 2 \times 1}{4 \times 3 \times 2 \times 1 \times 1} = 5$$

The 5 remaining members to retire will come from the 63 and 64 year age groups
63 year group $0.7^3 = 0.343$
64 year group $0.8^2 = 0.640$
The overall probability is thus

$$0.2592 \times 0.343 \times 0.640 = 0.057$$

63 year age group

p = 0.7 q = 0.3 n = 3

$$\begin{aligned} p(2 \text{ - successes}) &= \binom{3}{2} \times 0.7^2 \times 0.3^1 \\ &= 3 \times 0.49 \times 0.3 \\ &= 0.441 \end{aligned}$$

The 7 remaining members to retire will come from the 62 and 64 year groups
62 year group 0.65 = 0.078
64 year group 0.82 = 0.64
The overall probability is thus

$$0.078 \times 0.441 \times 0.64 = 0.022$$

64 year age group

p = 0.8 q = 0.2 n = 2

$$\begin{aligned} p(1 \text{ success}) &= \binom{2}{1} \times 0.8^1 \times 0.2^1 \\ &= 2 \times 0.8 \times 0.2 \\ &= 0.32 \end{aligned}$$

The 8 remaining members to retire will come from the 62 and 63 year age groups

62 year group $0.6^5 = 0.0768$

63 year group $0.7^3 = 0.343$

The overall probability is thus

$\underline{0.078 \times 0.343 \times 0.32 = 0.009}$

These are three mutually exclusive outcomes and so the probability of any nine employees accepting early retirment is given by

$\underline{0.057 + 0.022 + 0.009 = 0.088}$

c. The overall variance is the sum of the individual age group variances and may be calculated as follows:

Age Group	n	p	q or 1 - p	np(1 - p) or npq
62	5	0.6	0.4	1.20
63	3	0.7	0.3	0.63
64	2	0.8	0.2	0.32
				2.15

The variance is thus 2.15

The use of the Normal distribution which is a continuous distribution to estimate Binomial probabilities require the use of the continuity correction factor. Treated as a continuous variable 8 extends from 7,.5 to 8.5 and so at least 8 starts at 7.5 on the x scale of the normal distribution below where;

$\mu = 6.7$ employees

$\sigma = \sqrt{2.15} = 1.47$ employees

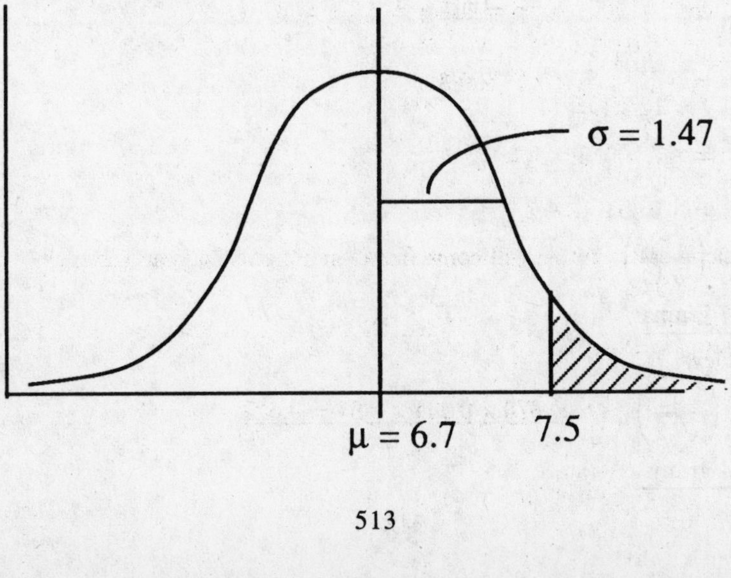

$$
\begin{aligned}
Z &= \frac{7.5-6.7}{1.47} \\
&= \frac{0.8}{1.47} \\
&= 0.5442
\end{aligned}
$$

For Z = 0.5442 the area in the tail from the table is

$$0.5 - 0.2054 = \underline{\underline{0.2946}}$$

CHAPTER 5

SOLUTION A1

$$\text{Standard Error} = \frac{s}{\sqrt{n}} = \frac{3.45}{\sqrt{529}} = \underline{0.15}$$

At 99% level the average faults are in the range 8 ± 2.58 (0.15)

$$= 7.613 \text{ to } 8.387$$

At the 95% level the average faults are in the range 8 ± 1.96 (0.15)

$$= 7.706 \text{ to } 8.294$$

SOLUTION A2

$$
\begin{aligned}
p &= 0.03 \quad q = 1 - p = 0.97 \\
d &= \text{degree of accuracy required and} \\
s &= \sqrt{\frac{pq}{n}}
\end{aligned}
$$

∴ at 99% level

$$
\begin{aligned}
d &= 2.58\sqrt{\frac{pq}{n}} \\
\therefore d^2 &= \frac{2.58^2 pq}{n} \\
\therefore n &= \frac{2.58^2 pq}{d^2}
\end{aligned}
$$

and substituting when d = 0.01

$$
\begin{aligned}
\therefore n &= \frac{2.58^2(0.03)(0.97)}{0.01^2} \\
&= \underline{\underline{1937}}
\end{aligned}
$$

SOLUTION A3

$$
\begin{aligned}
\overline{x} &= 50 \quad s = 9 \quad v = 12 - 1 = 11 \\
\mu &= \overline{x} \pm t\frac{s}{\sqrt{n}}
\end{aligned}
$$

at 95% confidence level

$$
\begin{aligned}
\mu &= 50 \pm 2.262\left(\frac{9}{\sqrt{12}}\right) \\
&= \underline{50 \pm 5.877 \text{ grams}}
\end{aligned}
$$

at 99% confidence level

$$
\begin{aligned}
\mu &= 50 \pm 3.25\left(\frac{9}{\sqrt{12}}\right) \\
&= \underline{50 \pm 8.444 \text{ grams}}
\end{aligned}
$$

SOLUTION A4

Note: Part (a) does not involve statistics

a. Let p = proportion of customers who purchase, then total contribution £ $4000 \times 100p - 60,000$

∴ Contribution for each of the proportions given is:

p	0.04	0.08	0.12	0.16	0.20
CONTRIBUTION	-£ 44,000	-£ 28,000	£ -12,000	+£ 4,000	+£ 20,000

The opportunity losses for the two decisions possibilities (develop or not) are as follows:

	Customer proportions				
	0.04	0.08	0.12	0.16	0.20
DEVELOP	£ 44,000	£ 28,000	£ 12,000	-	-
NOT DEVELOP	-	-	-	£ 4,000	£ 20,000

∴ Expected opportunity losses

if decision is DEVELOP: EOL $= (44000 \times 0.1) + (28000 \times 0.1) + (12000 \times 0.2)$

$= \underline{£\ 9{,}600}$

If decision is to

NOT DEVELOP: EOL $= (4000 \times 0.4) + (20000 \times 0.2) = \underline{£\ 5{,}600}$

∴ on basis of EOLs do not develop

b. The first step is to calculate the breakeven proportion of customers who purchase thus: £ $4000 \times 100p = £60,000$

∴ p at breakeven = 0.15

This means that the product should be developed if more than 15% of customer purchase.

For each value of p given in the question the table can be used to determine the probability of at least 3 favourable responses in a sample of 20.

p	Probability of at least 3 (from Table)
0.04	0.0439
0.08	0.2121
0.12	0.4369
0.16	0.6420
0.20	0.7939

However the probability is given in the question of each value of p so it is possible to calculate the joint probability of a given value of p and at least three favourable responses in a sample of 20.

p	(a) P(p)	(b) P (at least 3)	Joint probability (a × b)	
0.04	0.1	0.0439	0.00439	}
0.08	0.1	0.2121	0.02121	} 0.11298
0.12	0.2	0.4369	0.08738	}
0.16	0.4	0.6420	0.25680	
0.20	0.2	0.7939	0.15878	
	1.00		0.52856	

∴ The probability of at least 3 favourable responses is 0.52856. However, there is a combined probability that 3 favourable responses will be as a result of p being less than 15% when we should not develop.

∴ probability that it would be wrong to develop with 3 or more favourable responses.

$$= \frac{0.11298}{0.52856} = \underline{0.2137}$$

Note: Strictly speaking because sampling in this case would be without replacement the population is finite and the Binomial Distribution should not be used. The correct distribution is the Hypergeometric but in this case it makes very little difference to the result.

SOLUTION A5

As n = 60, large sampling theory based on the Normal Distribution can be used but note that as the sample is greater than 5% of the population (395) the Finite Population Correction Factor must be used.

The first stage is to calculate the sample statistics $\overline{x}$ and s.

The most relevant formulae to use for grouped data with unequal class intervals are:

$$\overline{x} = \frac{\sum fx}{n} \text{ and } s = \sqrt{\frac{\sum fx^2 - (\sum fx)^2/n}{n-1}}$$

where f = frequency x = midpoint of class interval n = number in sample

x	f	fx	fx^2
40	4	160	6400
90	9	810	72900
210	16	3360	705600
270	11	2970	801900
330	6	1980	653400
390	2	780	304200
	60	11860	2,814,400

$$\overline{x} = \frac{11860}{60} = \underline{197.67}$$

$$s = \sqrt{\frac{2,814,400 - (11860)^2/60}{60-1}}$$

$$= \underline{89.26}$$

∴ 95% confidence interval for the mean invoice value of the population.

$$= 197.67 \pm 1.96 \left(\frac{89.26}{60}\sqrt{1-\frac{60}{395}}\right)$$

$$= 197.67 \pm 20.80$$

and as the confidence interval for T (the Total Value) is required it is necessary to multiply the average value by N, thus:

$$T = 395\ (197.67 \pm 20.80)$$

$$\text{ie } \underline{£\ 69,863.65 \text{ to } £\ 86,295.65}$$

a. There are three possible causes of T being outside the confidence interval.

i. Bias in the sampling procedures

ii. The 5% (1 in 20) chance expected at the 95% confidence level. To check this a further sample could be taken.

iii. Calculation errors or incorrect formulae.

SOLUTION A6

Apart from part (f) this is answerable direct from the chapter.

a. Sampling with probability proportional to size.
This is a system used in multi-stage sampling to ensure that the probability of the selection of a sub-unit is proportional to the number of elements of the population in the sub-unit. Thus the selection of geographic areas for a national survey would be arranged so that an area with 2 million population would have twice the probability of being chosen to one with 1 million.

CHAPTER 6

SOLUTION A1

S.e. Man A $= \frac{6}{\sqrt{50}} = 0.849$

S.e. Man B $= \frac{5}{\sqrt{60}} = 0.645$

S.E. of difference of means $= \sqrt{0.849^2 + 0.645^2} = 1.066$

$$Z = \frac{30-32}{1.066} = 1.876$$

Z score for two tailed test at the 5% level is 1.96 $\therefore$ difference not significant.

SOLUTION A2

a. S.e. $= \sqrt{\frac{pq}{n}} = \sqrt{\frac{0.1 \times 0.9}{.80}} = 0.033$
where p = proportion late
actual p $= \frac{6}{80} = 0.075$
$\therefore \quad \frac{0.1 - 0.075}{0.033} = 0.75$ standard errors.
This is less than the standard errors at the 5% level ±1.96 so we conclude there is no significant improvement in deliveries.

b. ± 0.75 standard errors from the mean would cover ± 0.2734 i.e. 54.68% , say 55% of the population so the MD's claim could be accepted at any level of confidence below 55% , which is a very low level of confidence.

SOLUTION A3

Calculated mean of sample = 4.68 gms

Calculated sample s.d. = 1.968

$\therefore$ best estimate of population s.d. $= 1.986\sqrt{\frac{n}{n-1}} = 1.986\sqrt{\frac{10}{9}} = 2.093$

$\therefore$ std. error of mean $= \frac{2.093}{\sqrt{10}} = 0.66$

There are 10 - 1 = 9 d.f and it is a one tailed test. From table III the 5% value for a one tail test is 1.833.

$\therefore$ The sample mean should be within 1.833 x 0.66 gms = 1.21 gms.

The actual difference is 4.68 - 3.8 gms = 0.88 gms so the figures do not support the Purchasing Managers assertion.

SOLUTION A4

Note: This should be recognised as a two-way classification or contingency table and an appropriate question in which to apply χ^2.

The null hypothesis is

H_0 - No relationship between class of company and its status as a payer.

This assumption is used to calculate the *expected frequencies* in the normal manner, as shown below.

EXPECTED FREQUENCIES

Payer Status	Class of Customer Company $< £1m$	$> £1m$	Public	Total
Very Slow	17.60	11.73	10.67	40
Slow	18.48	12.32	11.20	42
Average	19.36	12.91	11.73	44
Prompt	10.56	7.04	6.40	24
Total	66	44	40	150

To find χ^2 it is necessary to evaluate $\sum \frac{(O-E)^2}{E}$ as follows:

O	E	$(O-E)$	$(O-E)^2$	$\frac{(O-E)^2}{E}$
20	17.60	2.40	5.76	0.33
16	18.48	-2.48	6.15	0.33
22	19.36	2.64	6.97	0.36
8	10.56	-2.56	6.55	0.62
10	11.73	-1.73	2.99	0.25
14	12.32	1.68	2.82	0.23
12	12.91	-0.91	0.83	0.06
8	7.04	0.96	0.92	0.13
10	10.67	-0.67	0.45	0.04
12	11.20	0.80	0.64	0.06
10	11.73	-1.73	2.99	0.25
8	6.40	1.60	2.56	0.40
				$\chi^2 = \underline{3.06}$

There are (4 - 1) (3 - 1) = 6 degrees of freedom
$\therefore$ $\chi^2_{0.05}$ (where v = 6) = 12.592 (from Table IV)
$\therefore$ As the calculated score is less than this there is no evidence to reject the null hypothesis.

SOLUTION A5

a. i. Given a normal distribution with a standard deviation of 0.2 litres the z score (from Table I) to give an area in the tail of 1% is 2.33σ

$\therefore$ mean must be

$$\mu = 10 \text{ litres } + (2.33 \times 0.2) = \underline{10.466\text{litres}}$$

ii. Because of the modification the mean fill can be slightly lower ie.

$$\mu = 10 + (2.33 \times 0.15) \text{ litres} = \underline{10.349 \text{ litres}}$$

$\therefore$ Saving per container = 10.466 - 10.349 = 0.117 litre
$\therefore$ Total saving = $£(100,000 \times 0.117 \times 0.1) = £1.1760$

b. i. The statement is not correct
The variance of the distribution of the difference between sample means is calculated by adding the variances of the distribution of sample means i.e. the standard errors squared providing that the sample are independent.

ii.

$$\sigma^2_{(\bar{x}-\bar{y})} = \left(\frac{\sigma_x}{\sqrt{n_x}}\right)^2 + \left(\frac{\sigma_y}{\sqrt{n_y}}\right)^2 = \frac{\sigma_x^2}{n_x} + \frac{\sigma_y^2}{n_y}$$

SOLUTION A6

a. The total number of respondents is 1295.
The overall proportions are:

	Number	percentage
Yes	676	52.20
No	441	34.05
Don't know	178	13.75
	1295	100.00

The ratio of Yes to No is 676 to 441 or 1.53 to 1.00.
Analysis by age group reveals

	30 or under		over 30	
	number	percentage	number	percentage
Yes	262	46.95	414	56.17
No	167	29.93	274	37.18
Don't know	129	23.12	49	6.65
	558	100.00	737	100.00

The ratio of Yes to No is

30 or under	262 to 167	or	1.57 to 1
Over 30	414 to 274	or	1.51 to 1

The acceptability of the scheme seems similar in both age groups. There appears to be a higher percentage of Don't knows in the 30 or under age group, and this may distort the degree of acceptability of the scheme in this age group.
Analysis by Marital Status indicates

	Married		Single	
	Number	Percentage	Number	Percentage
Yes	471	59.32	205	40.92
No	250	31.49	191	38.12
Don't know	73	9.19	105	20.96
	794	100.00	501	100.00

The ratios of yes to No is

Married	471 to 250	or	1.88 to 1
Single	205 to 191	or	1.07 to 1

There is a very distinct difference here, the ratio being much lower for single people. There is also a much higher percentage of don't knows in the single category.

b. The don't knows do not know by definition and so are best disregarded.
The most appropriate form of test is the χ^2 test for the difference between two proportions which can be handled the same way as a contingency table.

	30 or Under	Over 30	Total
Yes	[11] 262 (259.6)	[12] 414 (416.4)	676
No	[21] 167 (169.4)	[22] 274 (271.6)	441
TOTAL	429	688	1117

The null hypothesis is that there is no difference in the proportion who said 'Yes' in the two age groups.

The expected scores under Ho are calculated below:

Cell 11 $\frac{429}{1117} \times \frac{675}{1117} \times 1117 = 259.6$ (1 dp is enough)

Cell 12 $676 - 259.6 = 416.4$

Cell 21 $429 - 259.6 = 169.4$

Cell 22 $441 - 169.4 = 271.6$

The χ^2 statistic is calculated below:

O	E	0 - E	$(O - E)^2/E$
262	259.6	2.4	0.022
414	416.4	-2.4	0.013
167	169.4	-2.4	0.034
274	271.6	+2.4	0.021
1117	1117.0	0	0.090

$$\chi^2 = 0.09$$

For $(2-1) \times (2-1) = 1$df at 5% χ^2 from tables is 3.8

Since $0.09 < 3.8$ there is not enough evidence to reject Ho and so the conclusion is that the proportions in the two age groups is the same.

Analysis by Marital Status

	Married	Single	Total
YES	[11] 471 (436.3)	[12] 205 239.7	676
NO	[21] 250 284.7	[22] 191 156.3	441
TOTAL	721	396	1117

The null hypothesis is that there is no difference in the proportion who said yes in the two marital groups.

The expected scores are calculated below.

Cell 11 $\frac{721}{1117} \times \frac{676}{1117} \times 1117 = 436.3$

Cell 12 $676 - 436.6 = 239.7$

Cell 21 $721 - 436.3 = 284.7$

Cell 22 $441 - 284.7 = 156.3$

The X^2 statistic is calculated as follows:

O	E	O - E	(O - E)²/E
471	436.3	+34.7	2.76
205	239.7	-34.7	5.02
250	284.7	-34.7	4.23
191	156.3	+34.7	7.70
			19.71

$\chi^2 = 19.71$

For 1 df and 5% significance level χ^2 from tables is 3.8

$19.71 > 3.8 \therefore$ reject the null hypothesis and conclude that there is a difference in proportion saying "yes" between the two marital groups.

NB These two tests should have been undertaken using the parametric technique of difference between two proportions.

c. Possible Treatment of Don't Knows

1) Ignore the group of Don't knows

The intention of don't knows is unknown by definition! Ultimately they must choose and so are a passing phenomenon.

2) Combine the group into the Yes or No groups

There is no rational basis for doing this unless there is some indication of how "don't knows" will choose! in which case they are not 'don't knows'

3) Split the Don't knows in the proportions of the Yes and No groups

This assumes that the Don't knows are representative of the group. Don't knows are often Don't knows because they are not representative. Incorporating them may not therefore be a valid course of action.

4) Maintain the group as a separate one for analysis

This is a most valid option the higher the proportion the Don't knows are of the whole. If the don't knows are a high proportion, it means that there may be some reason beyond apathy for the don't know response, say a failure to communicate on the part of management. It is interesting to note the low level of Don't knows in the married group over 30's group.

SOLUTION A7

a. The number of invoices with at least one error is given by

1 Error:	2 + 8 + 8	=	18
2 Errors:	2 + 8 + 6	=	16
	TOTAL	=	34

Total Errors = 200

Sample proportion = 34/200 = 0.17

The 95% confidence interval is equal to $0.17 \pm 1.96\sqrt{\frac{0.17(1.017)}{200}} = 0.17 \pm 1.96 \times 0.02656 = 0.17 \pm 0.052$

b. The appropriate test is the χ^2 with a contingency table which is shown below:

ERRORS

	0	1	2	Total
1 – 5	11 60 (53.12)	12 2 (5.76)	13 2 (5.12)	64
6 – 10	21 74 (74.7)	22 8 (8.10)	23 8 (7.20)	90
10+	31 32 (38.18)	32 8 (4.14)	33 6 (3.68)	46
TOTAL	166	18	16	200

The null hypothesis stated verbally is that there is no association between the number of errors observed per invoice and the size of the invoice.
Under the null hypothesis the expected value in cell 11 is

$$\frac{64}{200} \times \frac{166}{200} \times 200 = 53.12$$

This is shown in brackets
The remaining cells are calculated in a similar manner.
The statistic is calculated below.

O	E	0 - E	$(O - E)^2/E$
60	53.12	+6.88	0.891
2	5.76	-3.76	2.454
2	5.12	-3.12	1.901
74	74.70	-0.70	0.007
8	8.10	-0.10	0.001
8	7.20	+0.80	0.089
32	38.18	-6.18	1.000
8	4.14	+3.86	3.599
6	3.68	+2.32	1.463
200	200.00	0	11.405

$\chi^2 = 11.405$
for $(3 - 1) \times (3 - 1) = 4$ df χ^2 from tables is 9.5
$11.405 > 9.5$ $\therefore$ Reject Ho and conclude that there is a relationship between the number of errors observed and the invoice size.

c. The total number of errors is:

Invoice	Number of Errors			
Items	1	2		
1 - 5	2 + 2 × 2		=	6
6 - 10	8 + 2 × 8		=	24
10 +	8 + 2 × 6		=	20
50				50

If the errors were equally likely to occur on invoices of any size then the following pattern will emerge.

Invoice Items	Proportion of total		Expected Number	
1 – 5	$\frac{64}{200}$ =	0.32	.32 × 50 =	16.00
6 – 10	$\frac{90}{200}$ =	0.45	.45 × 50 =	22.5
10+	$\frac{46}{200}$ =	0.23	.23 × 50 =	11.50

A χ^2 test is required to ascertain whether the expected values are significantly different from the observed values:

O	E	O - E	$(O - E)^2/E$
6	16	-10	6.250
24	22.5	1.5	0.100
20	11.5	8.5	6.283
50	50.00	0	12.633

1 piece of information is obtained from the data i.e. the total 50.

∴ 1 degree of freedom is lost

for 3 - 1 = 2 df χ^2 from tables for 5% significance is 6.0

12.633 > 6 Reject the Null Hypothesis that there is no difference between the expected and observed values.

SOLUTION A8

Ho = Variances are equal

t test with $12 + 12 - 2 = 22$ d.f.

Value from Table III for a two tailed test at 5% = 2.074

$$\text{FORMULA} = \frac{\overline{x}_1 - \overline{x}_2}{\sqrt{\frac{\sigma^2 + \sigma_2^2}{n}}}$$

$$= \frac{5.2083 - 5.1250}{\sqrt{\frac{0.8390 + 1.0057}{12}}}$$

$$= \underline{0.2125}$$

This value is much less than the table value of 2.074 so we conclude there is no significant difference between the two towns.

SOLUTION A9

a. This test involves the test for the difference of two means based on independent samples. Let schools be x and offices y

SCHOOLS: Sample 1

COST

x	$x-\overline{x}$	$(x-\overline{x})^2$
28	-2	4
31	+1	1
26	-4	16
27	-3	9
23	-7	49
38	+8	64
37	+7	49
210		192

$$x = \frac{\sum x}{n_1} = \frac{210}{7} = 30$$

$$S^2 = \frac{\sum(x-\overline{x})^2}{n_1 - 1} = \frac{192}{6}$$

OFFICES Sample 2

COST

y	$y-\overline{y}$	$(y-\overline{y})^2$
37	0	0
42	5	25
34	-3	9
37	0	0
35	-2	4
185		38

$\overline{y} = \frac{\sum y}{n_2} = \frac{185}{5} = 37$

$S^2 = \frac{\sum(y-\overline{y})^2}{n_2 - 1} = \frac{37}{4}$

Assuming that the population variances for offices and schools are equal, the pooled variance may be calculated thus:

$$S_p^2 = \frac{S_1^2(n_1-1) + S_2^2(n_2-1)}{n_1+n_2-2}$$

$$\frac{\frac{192}{6} \times 6 + \frac{37}{4} \times 4}{7+5-2}$$

$$= \frac{192+37}{10}$$

$$= \frac{229}{10}$$

$$= 22.9$$

$\therefore\ S_p = \sqrt{22.9} = 4.79$

The standard error of the difference between two means is given by

$S_p\sqrt{\frac{1}{n_1} + \frac{1}{n_2}}$

$= 4.79\ \sqrt{\frac{1}{7} + \frac{1}{5}}$

$= 4.79 \times 0.59$

$= 2.81$

The test is formulated as follows:
H_o: μ Office blocks $= \mu$ schools or $\mu_2 = \mu_1$
H_1: $\mu_2 > \mu_1$
The conventional level of significance is 5% and the measurement is in one direction ∴ one tail test

$n_1 + n_2 - 2 < 30$ ∴ t distribution

Test Statistic

$$t = \frac{\mu_2 - \mu_1}{Sp\sqrt{\frac{1}{n_1} + \frac{1}{n_2}}}$$
$$= \frac{37 - 30}{2.81}$$
$$t = 2.49$$

For $n_1 + n_2 - 1 = 10$ degrees of freedom the tabulated value of t = 1.81
Since 2.49 > 1.81 the evidence is strong enough to reject Ho and conclude that the mean cost per square metre for offices is greater than that for schools.

b. The additional data indicates that the populations are now finite and so the finite population correction factor must be used to estimate the standard error and this is given by:

$$Sp \sqrt{\frac{1}{n_1}\left(\frac{N_1 - n_1}{N_1 - 1}\right) + \frac{1}{n_2}\left(\frac{N_2 - n_2}{N_2 - 1}\right)}$$
$$= 4.79 \times \sqrt{\left(\frac{1}{7} \times \frac{17}{23}\right) + \left(\frac{1}{5} \times \frac{22}{26}\right)}$$
$$= 4.79 \times \sqrt{0.10559 + 0.16923}$$
$$= 4.79 \times 0.5242$$
$$= 2.511$$

The test statistic now becomes

$$t = \frac{37 - 30}{2.511}$$

$$= 2.79$$

At 5% 2.79 > 1.81 but at 1% 2.79 > 2.76 (just).
This reduces the probability of committing a type I error from 5% to 1% .

c. Strictly an F ratio test should have been performed to ascertain whether $\sigma_1^2 = \sigma_2 2$. In addition the normality of the two parent populations should have been examined. However this test is known to be robust in practice. It is questionable whether schools should be compared with offices as the contractual conditions and materials used are often quite different.

SOLUTION A10

Ho = no difference in practice between UK and US
The table is a 4 x 2 table
∴ degrees of freedom = (4 – 1)(2 – 1) = 3 and chi-square values are; at 0.05 = 7.81 at 0.01 = 11.34
Based on the table the Expected Values are:

	UK	US
DCF	142.3	127.7
Payback	115.95	104.05
ROCE	68.51	61.49
Non-financial	63.24	56.76

O - E	$\frac{(O - E)^2}{E}$
-42.30	12.57
14.05	1.7
11.49	1.93
16.76	4.44
42.30	14.01
-14.05	1.90
-11.49	2.15
-16.76	4.95
$\chi^2 =$	43.65

The calculated value is much greater than both the table values so we conclude there is a significant difference in the approaches in the two countries.

a. The test would be valid when

   i. all methods and terminology are consistent between companies

   ii. the sample must be random

CHAPTER 7

SOLUTION A1

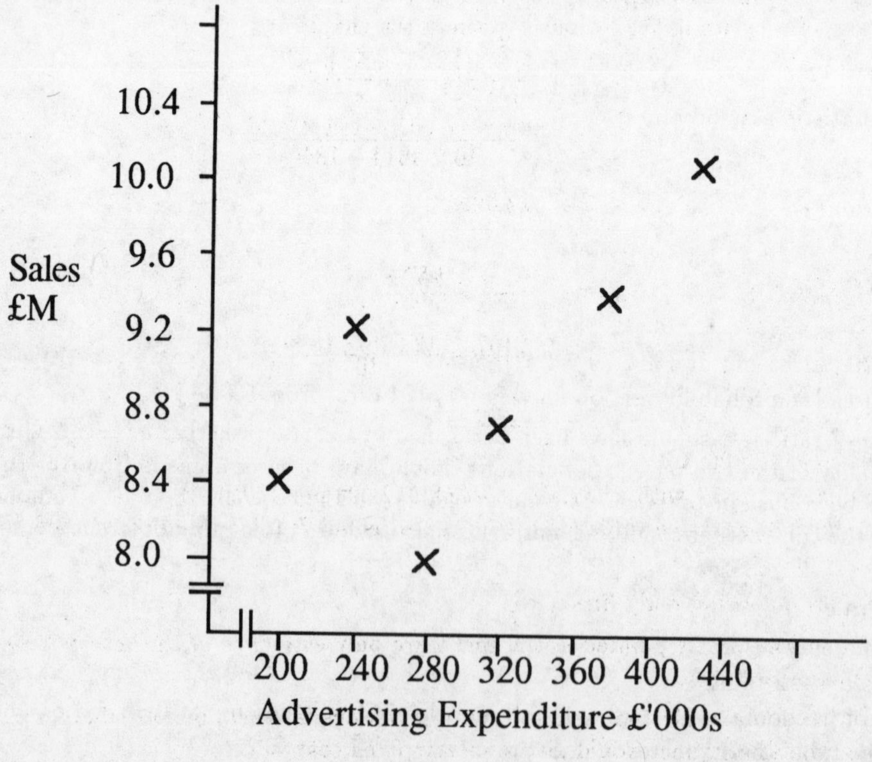

There is a positive correlation between advertising expenditure and sales but it is far from perfect.

SOLUTION A2

$$r = \frac{n\sum xy - \sum x \sum y}{\sqrt{n\sum x^2 - (\sum x)^2}.\sqrt{n\sum y^2 - (\sum y)^2}}$$

x	y	x^2	y^2	xy
8.5	210	72.25	44,100	1785
9.2	250	84.64	62,500	2300
7.9	290	62.41	84,100	2291
8.6	330	73.96	108,900	2838
9.4	370	88.36	136,900	3478
10.1	410	102.01	168,100	4141
53.7	1860	483.63	604,600	16833

$$r = \frac{6 \times 16833 - 53.7 \times 1860}{\sqrt{6 \times 483.63 - 53.7^2}.\sqrt{6 \times 604,600 - 1860^2}}$$

$= \underline{0.64}$

There is a reasonably strong positive correlation betwen sales advertising expenditure.

SOLUTION A3

$$r^2 = 0.64^2 = \underline{0.41}$$

$\therefore$ factors other than advertising cause 1 - 0.41 = 59% of variations in sales.

SOLUTION A4

a. Note: As the examiner has kindly done most of the calculations, the coefficients, a and b can be found directly by using the formulae given in the chapter.

$$\begin{aligned} b &= \frac{n\sum xy - \sum x \sum y}{n\sum x^2 - (\sum x)^2} \\ &= \frac{10 \times 47,667 - 184 \times 2157}{10 \times 4014 - 184^2} \\ &= \underline{12.696} \end{aligned}$$

$$\begin{aligned} a &= \frac{\sum y}{n} - \frac{b\sum x}{n} \\ &= \frac{2157}{10} - \frac{12.696 \times 184}{10} \\ &= \underline{-17.9} \end{aligned}$$

$\therefore$ Y = -17.9 + 12.696 X

b. The fixed cost is - £179 with a variable cost of £126.96 per 100 switches.
It is clear that the negative value for the fixed cost is not feasible when considered alone.
This may be due to:

i. The data not being truly linear.

ii. Sampling errors. As pointed out a and b are only estimates of the true population parameters a and B.

iii. Extrapolation outside the range of the observations ie. there is not value for a zero production level which would give a specific fixed cost value.

iv. An error in the figures provided in the question (which is the case in this instance).

c. Note: The formulae given is an alternative to the Standard Error formula given in the chapter. Fortunately the standard Error has already been calculated by the examiner.

As the sample size is small, the 't' distribution with 10 - 2 = 8 degrees of freedom is used.

The 95% value from Table V when $\nu = 8$ is 2.306.

Mean Value of costs with batch size of 4000 (ie. 40 in units of 100).

= £- 179 + 126.96(40)

= £4899

$\therefore$ 95% confidence limits = £4899 ± 2.306(2200) <u>£4899 ± £5073</u>

Note: The above calculation is based on the standard error given in the question but as will be seen it gives confidence limits so broad as to be almost meaningless as a result of an error in the figures supplied in the question. $\sum xy = 46248$ not 47667 and this results in changes in all values.

The question has been reworked using the correct figure.

Rework of Q2

$$b = \frac{10 \times 46248 - 184 \times 2157}{10 \times 4014 - (184)^2} = \underline{10.438}$$

$$a = \frac{2157}{10} - \frac{10.438 \times 184}{10} = \underline{23.64}$$

$\therefore\ y = 23.64 + 10.438x$

The Standard error is

$$\sqrt{\frac{\sum y^2 - a\sum y - b\sum xy}{n-2}}$$

$$= \sqrt{\frac{535187 - 23.64 \times 2157 - 10.438 \times 46248}{8}}$$

$$= 13.50 (\text{in } £10 \text{ units})$$

Mean value of costs with 400 batch (ie. 40 in units of 100)

$$= 23.64 + 10.438(40)$$

$$= \underline{£4{,}412}$$

$\therefore$ 95% confidence limits

$$= £4412 \pm 2.306(135)$$

$$= \underline{\underline{£4412 \pm 311}}$$

SOLUTION A5

a.

$$
\begin{aligned}
b &= \frac{n\sum xy - \sum x \sum y}{n\sum x^2 - (\sum x)^2} \\
&= \frac{10 \times 82780 - 241 \times 3230}{10 \times 6225 - (241)^2} \\
&= 11.84
\end{aligned}
$$

$$
\begin{aligned}
a &= \frac{\sum y}{n} - \frac{b\sum x}{n} \\
&= \frac{3230}{10} - \frac{11.84 \times 241}{10} \\
&= \underline{37.66}
\end{aligned}
$$

$$\therefore y = £37.66 + 11.84x$$

or Labour Cost = £ 37.66 + 11.84 (batch size)

b. The standard error is

$$
\begin{aligned}
S_e &= \sqrt{\frac{\sum y^2 - a\sum y - b\sum xy}{n-2}} \\
&= \sqrt{\frac{1,103,900 - 37.66 \times 3230 - 11.84 \times 82780}{8}} \\
&= \underline{16.37}
\end{aligned}
$$

The t value for 95% confidence limits = 2.306.

$\therefore$ 95% confidence limits are $y \pm 2.306 \times 16.37 = y \pm 37.75$

c. The statistic that summarises how well the regression line explains the variability is the coefficient of determination, r^2.

The most appropriate formula to use (given the various calculated figures in the question) is

$$
\begin{aligned}
r^2 &= \frac{(n\sum xy - \sum x \sum y)^2}{(n\sum x^2 - (\sum x)^2)n\sum y^2 - (\sum y)^2} \\
r^2 &= \frac{(10 \times 82780 - 241 \times 3230)^2}{(10 \times 6225 - 2412)10 \times 1,103,900 - 3230^2} \\
&= \underline{0.965}
\end{aligned}
$$

This value means that 96 1/2% of the variability is explained by the variability in batch size.

d. Direct labour cost for a batch of 25

= £37.66 + 11.84(25)

= <u>£333.60</u>

e. See Figure 1.

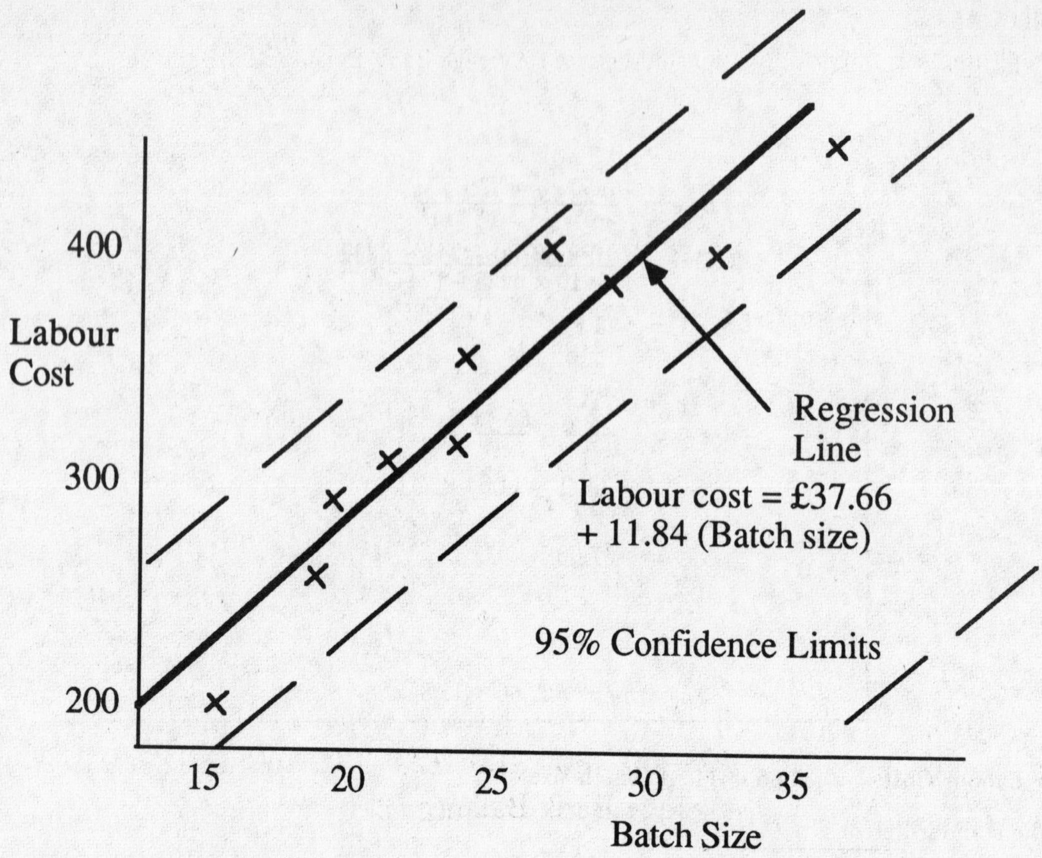
400
300
200
Labour
Cost
15
20
25
30
35
Batch Size
Regression
Line
Labour cost = £37.66
+ 11.84 (Batch size)
95% Confidence Limits

Figure 1

SOLUTION A6

a. Graph Representing the Relationship between Average Bank Balance and Bank charges.

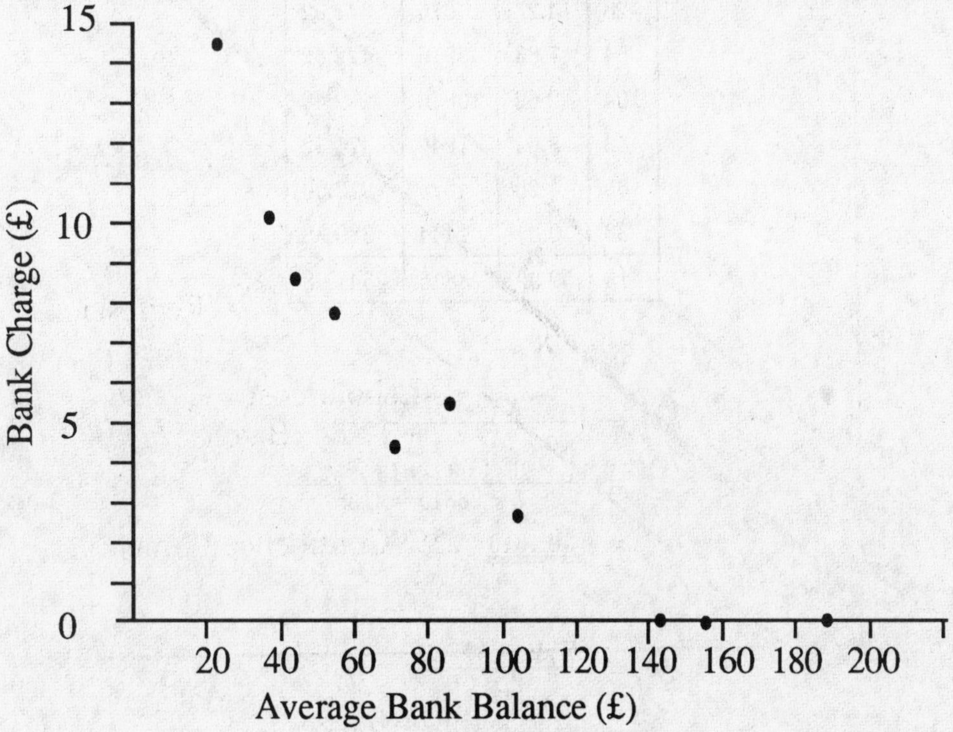

The model by which the bank charges are calculated may be summarised as follows:
If the bank balance is less than £50 the charge equals fixed account charge times number of transactions minus interest rate times daily balance plus overdraft charge if the daily balance is less than zero. The effect of this is that as the balance increases the charges decrease.
The graph above reveals that the relationship is not linear and this is caused by the condition that if the balance is more than £50 there are no charges. In many cases the nominal interest may be well above £50 but the customer is not allowed to have the extra. If customers were allowed this money as interest the graph could well look like the sketch below:

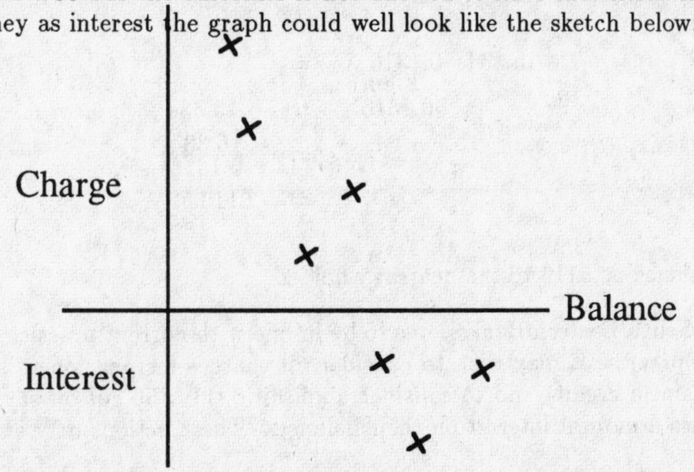

The graph also shows that the higher bank charges are associated with bank balances that generally have a mean balance of less than £50.

b. When undertaking calculations, then accounts 6, 7 and 10 should be ignored as they distort the pattern.
The calculation of the least squares relationship is given below:

X	Y	X^2	XY
83	5.42	6889	449.86
26	14.27	676	371.02
54	7.83	2916	422.82
104	2.62	10816	272.48
43	8.64	1849	371.52
65	4.20	4225	273.00
38	10.01	1444	380.38
413	52.99	28815	2541.08

$$\begin{aligned} b &= \frac{n\sum XY - \sum X \sum Y}{n\sum X^2 - (\sum X)^2} \\ &= \frac{7 \times 2541.08 - 413 \times 52.99}{7 \times 28815 - 413^2} \\ &= \underline{\underline{-0.1316}} \end{aligned}$$

$$\begin{aligned} a &= \frac{\sum Y}{n} - \frac{b\sum X}{n} \\ &= \frac{52.99}{7} - \frac{(-0.1316)}{7} \times 413 \\ &= \underline{\underline{15.334}} \end{aligned}$$

Bank charge = 15.334 - 0.1316 × mean balance

The minimum mean bank balance to attract nil charges is found when

$$\begin{aligned} 15.334 - 0.1316\,X &= 0 \\ 0.1316X &= 15.334 \\ X &= \frac{15.334}{0.1316} \\ &= £116.52 \end{aligned}$$

The minimum balance is £116 to the nearest whole £

c. The London and South Eastern Bank seems to be in line with current practice in a comprehensive survey of its practice it may wish to consider nil charges for pensioners and students (so long as they remain in credit) and to consider abolishing the £50 cut-off say, for charities so that they may earn a modest interest on their balances. These actions may attract customers.

SOLUTION A7

a. The calculation of the least squares should be based on quarters rather than months as given in the question.

Age in Quarters x	Service Cost s	x^2	xs
1	51	1	51
4	69	16	276
6	81	36	486
10	112	100	1120
5	70	25	350
6	89	36	534
8	104	64	832
4	82	16	328
3	55	9	165
7	102	49	714
54	815	352	4856

$$
\begin{aligned}
b &= \frac{n\sum xs - \sum x \sum s}{n\sum x^2 n(\sum x)^2} \\
&= \frac{10 \times 4856 - 54 \times 815}{10 \times 352 - 542} \\
&= \underline{7.5331} \\
a &= \frac{\sum s}{n} - \frac{b\sum x}{n} \\
&= \frac{815}{10} - \frac{7.5331 \times 54}{0} \\
&= \underline{40.8212}
\end{aligned}
$$

Thus $s = 40.82 + 7.53x$

This means that the service cost has a fixed element of £40.82 and that the total charge s increases by £7.53 for each quarter that is added to the age of the car.

b. The working assumption must be that a car is serviced immediately prior to trade in at the end of a quarter.

The servicing costs may be built up as an arithmetic progression.

Service	Cost
1 st	a + b
2nd	a + 2b
3rd	a + 3b
4 th	a + 4b
5th	a + 5b
nth	a + nb

The mean service cost may be ascertained by noting a simple but useful relationship when a set of numbers is evenly spaced the arithmetic mean is delivered from

$$\frac{\text{first} + \text{last}}{2}$$

Split the cost into a and b terms. The mean of 'a' is 'a' since it is constant. The 'b' element becomes

$$b(1+2+3+4+5....+n)$$

The mean is $\frac{b(1+n)}{2}$

The mean service cost is thus

$a + b(1+n)/2$

$= 40.8218 + 8.5331(1+n)/2$

$= 40.8218 + 3.7666(1+n)$

$= \underline{44.5884 + 3.7666n}$

Capital cost is measured by original cost - Trade-in value.

Trade-in Value = 4000 - 225n

where n = number of quarters of ownership and £225 is the quarterly decline in trade in value.

After n quarters the capital cost of trade in will be

$$\begin{aligned}&4200-(4000-225n)\\&=4200-4000+225n\\&=200+225n\end{aligned}$$

The mean value of this term is

$$\frac{200+225n}{n}$$

$$=\frac{200}{n}+225$$

The table below shows whether or not the proposition in part (b) is correct

1yr = 4 qtrs

2yrs = 8 qtrs

3yrs = 12 qtrs

n	mean Capital Cost	mean Service Cost	Total mean Cost
4	275*	59.66**	334.66
8	250	74.72	324.72
12	241.67	89.79	331.46

Specimen calculations

$$*\frac{200}{4}+225=275$$

$$**\,44.5884+4\times 3.7666=59.66$$

SOLUTION A8

Thus the minimum total mean holding cost occurs if the car is kept for 2 years.

$$a = \frac{\sum y}{n} - \frac{b\sum x}{n}$$

$$b = \frac{n\sum xy - \sum x \sum y}{n\sum x^2 - (\sum x)^2}$$

$$b = \frac{7 \times 242,804 - 1845 \times 917}{7 \times 486,791 - 1845^2}$$

$$= \underline{2.21}$$

$$a = \frac{917}{7} - \frac{2.21 \times 1845}{7}$$

$$= \underline{-451.49}$$

$$\therefore \ Y = 2.21x - 451.49$$

(b) when x = 276
Y = 2.21 × 276 – 451.49 = $\underline{158.47}$
when x = 280
Y = 2.21 × 280 – 451.49
= 167.31

(c) standard error of regression $= \sqrt{\frac{\sum y^2 - a\sum y - b\sum xy}{n-2}}$

$= \sqrt{\frac{122,679 - (451.49) \times 917 - 2.21 \times 242,804}{5}}$

$= \underline{4.44}$

standard error of slope $= \frac{S_e}{\sum x^2 - \frac{(\sum x)^2}{n}}$

$S_b = \frac{4.44}{486,791 - \frac{1845^2}{7}}$

$= 0.198$

$\therefore \ t = \frac{2.21 - 0}{0.198} = \underline{11.16}$

From Table III the critical value at 5% with 5 d.f. is 2.571 and as the calculated value exceeds this we conclude that there is a significant difference between b and 0.

(d) Note: It is assumed that what is required here are the 95% confidence intervals for α and β i.e. the regression coefficients and not for the regression line as a whole. This is because the calculation of the curved confidence intervals for the regression line is a lengthy detailed series of calculations which would not be feasible as one part of a five part question.

$S_b = 0.198$ previously calculated

Standard error of intercept $= S_a = S_e\sqrt{\frac{\sum x^2}{n\sum x^2 - (\sum x)^2}}$

$= 4.44\sqrt{\frac{486,791}{7 \times 486,791 - 1845^2}}$

$= \underline{52.32}$

$\therefore$ Confidence intervals

$$\alpha = a \pm t\ S_a$$

$$= \underline{\underline{-451.49 \pm 134.51}}$$

$$\beta = b \pm t\ S_b$$

$$= 2.21 \pm 2.571(0.198)$$

$$= \underline{\underline{2.21 \pm 0.51}}$$

(e) There is strong correlation with a highly significant regression coefficient so that the calculation values would appear to be suitable for prediction.

Other measures that could be investigated include

the coefficient of determination
multiple regression
non-linear regression

CHAPTER 8

SOLUTION A1

$$r^2_{x_1} = 0.78$$

This is the coefficient of determination of miles travelled to cost and means that 78% of total cost is attributable to mileage.

$r^2_{x_2} = 0.16$ i.e. 16% of cost is accounted for by the type of journey

$R^2 = 0.88$ is the overall coefficient of determinationa nd indicates that the multiple regression equation accounts for 88% of the total valuation in costs.

The coefficients in the equation are:

a = £ 86 = fixed costs

b_1 = 0.37 = amount per mile

b_2 = 0.08 = influence of the type of journey

SOLUTION A2

10% learning curve

Learning curve = ax^b

where:

$$b = \log(1 - 0.1)/\log 2 = -0.152$$

$$\therefore \text{ Time for 20th unit } = 30.20^{-0.152}$$

$$= 19.03 \text{ minutes}$$

SOLUTION A3

30% learning curve

$$b = \log(1 - 0.3)/\log 2 = -0.5146$$

$$\therefore \text{ Time for 20th unit } = 30.20^{-0.5146}$$

$$= 6.42 \text{ minutes}$$

SOLUTION A4

a. Straight line regression

Treating the years as 1, 2, 3, 4 and 5 gives the following table

Years = x	Sales = y		
x	y	x^2	xy
1	1.5	1	1.5
2	1.6	4	3.2
3	1.8	9	5.4
4	2.2	16	8.8
5	2.7	25	13.5
$x = 15$	$y = 9.8$	$x^2 = 55$	$xy = 32.4$

and substituting in the formulae for a and b

$$\text{ie a} = \frac{\sum y}{n} - \text{b}\frac{\sum x}{n}$$

$$\text{b} = \frac{n\sum xy - \sum x \sum y}{n\sum x^2 - (\sum x)^2}$$

we obtain

$$\text{b} = \frac{5 \times 32.4 - 15 \times 9.8}{5 \times 55 - 15^2} = \frac{15}{50} = 0.3$$

$$\text{a} = \frac{9.8}{5} - \frac{0.3 \times 15}{5} = 1.96 - 0.9 = 1.06$$

∴ straight line equation is $\underline{\underline{y = 1.06 + 0.3x}}$

b. logarithmic Curve

$$y = ax^b$$

To solve, this is made into the logarithmic linear form

x	y	$\log x$	$\log y$	$(\log x)^2$	$\log x \log y$
1	1.5	0	0.1761	0	0
2	1.6	0.3010	0.2041	0.0906	0.0614
3	1.8	0.4771	0.2553	0.2276	0.1218
4	2.2	0.6021	0.3424	0.3625	0.2062
5	2.7	0.6990	0.4314	0.4886	0.3015
	$\log x =$	2.0792	$\log y =$ 1.4093	$(\log x)^2 =$ 1.1693	$\log x \log y =$ 0.6909

and substituting in the formulae we obtain

$$b = \frac{5 \times 0.6909 - 2.0792 \times 1.4093}{5 \times 1.1693 - (2.0792)^2} = \underline{\underline{0.344}}$$

$$\log a = \frac{1.4093}{5} - 0.344 \times \frac{2.0792}{5} = 0.1387$$

and the antilog is $\underline{\underline{0.376}}$

∴ logarithmic equation is $\underline{\underline{y = 1.376x^{0.344}}}$

a.

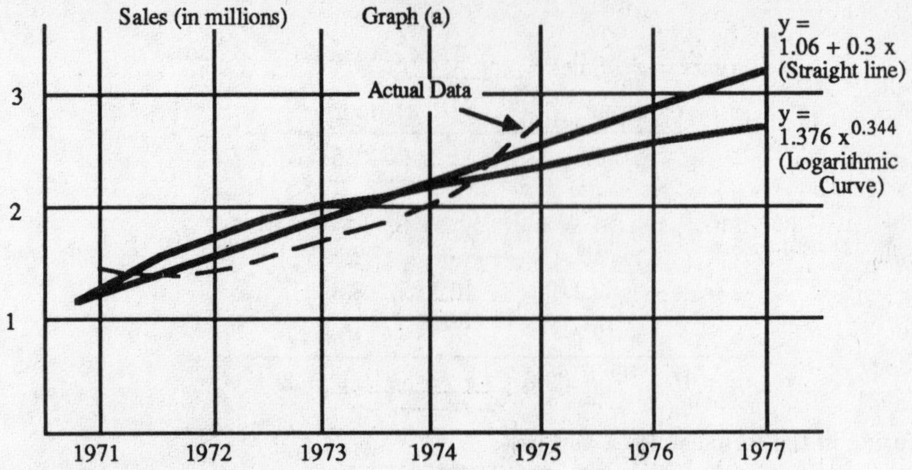

b. Forecast Sales Figures for 1977 (ie Year 7)
Straight line forecast when x = 7

$$y = 1.06 + 0.3x$$
$$= 1.06 + 0.3(7)$$
$$= \underline{\underline{3.16}}$$

logarithmic curve when x = 7

$$y = 1.376x^{0.344}$$
$$= 1.376.7^{0.344}$$
$$= \underline{\underline{2.69}}$$

Note:
Both these extrapolations have been shown on the graph.

c. On the evidence of the graph the straight line seems to be the better curve to use although it should be pointed out that neither of the two forms appear to be a very good fit. From the shape of the curve of the actual data some form of exponential curve would seem to be more appropriate, ie the form $y = ab^x$.

d. The results obtained from both the curve suggest do not appear to differ markedly over the period of the data, ie 1971 - 1975, but if the growth factor which appears to be apparent in the data continues, both forecast types will get progressively out of line. The lesson to be drawn is that great care is necessary in choosing the right type of trend line. In this case, as pointed out above, some form of exponential curve would appear to be appropriate.

e. The main advantage of these types of functions is that an objective forecast is obtained based on past data and if past trends continue, such forecasts, based on the appropriate curve, may be reasonable approximations. However, many limitations exist, for example.

   i. It is assumed that the variable to be forecast depends only upon time, whereas many complex and interrelated factors influence sales and demand.

   ii. Time series analysis assumes that patterns and trends will continue in the future as they have in the past, whereas patterns, tastes, and other factors do change over time.

   iii. Generally all previous data, particularly using the curves mentioned in this question, are given equal weight, despite their different ages and appropriateness to current and future situations.

SOLUTION A5

a.

x : Output y : Total Power Costs

x	y	x^2	y^2	xy
12	6.2	144	38.44	74.4
18	8.0	324	64.00	144.0
19	8.6	361	73.96	163.4
20	10.4	400	108.16	208.0
24	10.2	576	104.04	244.8
30	12.4	900	153.76	372.0
123	55.8	2705	542.36	1206.6

$$\begin{aligned} b &= \frac{n\sum xy - \sum x \sum y}{n\sum x^2 - (\sum x)^2} \\ &= \frac{6(1206.6) - 123(55.8)}{6(2705) - (123)^2} \\ &= \frac{7239.6 - 6863.4}{16230 - 15129} \\ &= \frac{376.2}{1101.0} \\ &= 0.3416893 \\ &= +0.342(\text{gradient}) \end{aligned}$$

$$\begin{aligned} a &= \frac{\sum y}{n} - b\frac{\sum x}{n} \\ &= \frac{55.8}{6} - \frac{0.342(123)}{6} \\ &= 9.3 - 7.011 \\ &= 2.289(\text{intercept}) \end{aligned}$$

The linear relationship between total power costs and output.
Power Costs = 2.289 + 0.342× Output

Part (b)

$$r = \frac{n\sum xy - \sum x \sum y}{\sqrt{(n\sum x^2 - (\sum x)^2(n\sum y^2 - (\sum y)^2)}}$$

$$\begin{aligned} \text{NB. } n\sum y^2 - (\sum y)^2 &= 6(542.36) - 55.8^2 \\ &= 3254.16 - 3223.64 \\ &= 140.52 \end{aligned}$$

$$\begin{aligned} r &= \frac{376.2}{\sqrt{(1101.0)(140.52)}} \\ &= \frac{376.2}{\sqrt{154712.52}} \\ &= 376.2/393.33512 \\ &= +0.9564363 \\ &= \underline{+0.956} \end{aligned}$$

Part (b)

The introduction of the extra variable of time has not brought about much increase in the value of r ie 0.956 to 0.976 and so the improvement in the level by which it is possible to predict power costs is very marginal. The respective coefficients of determination would be

$$0.956^2 = 0.913936 = 0.914$$

$$0.976^2 = 0.952576 = 0.953$$

The t value of time is low in comparison with the t value for output.

Observation would indicate that the Time variable is likely to be fairly highly correlated with the output level. This being so then the inclusion of time is not going to improve the fit very much.

There are three possible ways to predict the power costs in period 7 the first is to treat the information as a simple regression analysis and use the equation in Part (a) to predict power cost.

The second approach is to treat the data as a time series and work out an equation to elate time and power cost.

The third method is to do what was done in the question and that is to develop a multiple regression model.

The second method would not take into account because cost would include inflation as well as real change in cost generated by a change in output.

It might be worth taking past data and applying the three models to this to see which has the least forecast error, from comparing predicted and actual past data.

SOLUTION. A6

Note: The question is based on the use of the transformation required for the use of the Hyperbolic Function.

a. The curve $y = a + \frac{b}{x}$ belongs to a set of equations which have the quality that they can be transposed into the form

$$y = a + bx$$

and as such are amenable to handling by linear least squares regression.

The graph of $y = a + \frac{b}{x}$ for the data is shown below based on the following calculations:

x	$\frac{1}{x}$
5	0.200
2	0.500
10	0.100
8	0.125
1	1.000
3	0.333

The y values are not transposed.

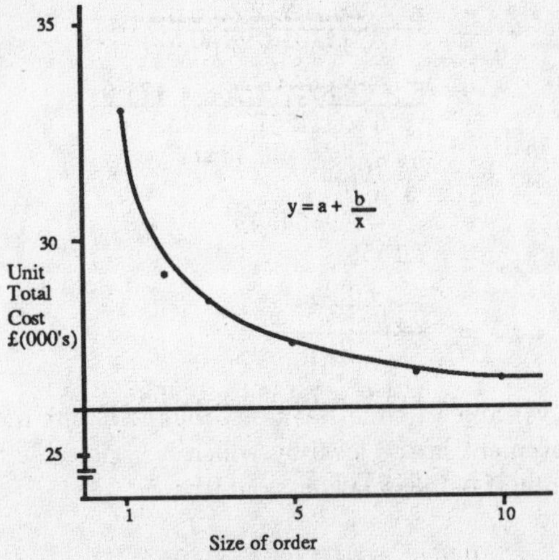

GRAPH 1

The above graph is NOT required in the question but shows the pattern of the untransformed data.
The graph required for the question is shown below.

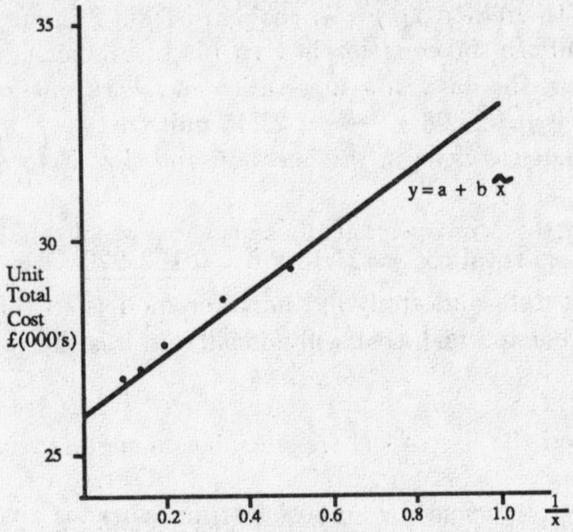

GRAPH 2

The line of best fit $y = a + b\tilde{x}$ where $\overline{x} = \frac{1}{x}$ is based on the calculations in part (b)

b. The calculations for Least Squares Linear Regression are given below:

$\frac{1}{x}$	y	$(\frac{1}{x})^2$	$(\frac{1}{x})y$
0.200	27.5	0.0400	5.50
0.500	29.2	0.2500	14.60
0.100	26.7	0.0100	2.67
0.125	26.8	0.0156	3.35
1.000	33.2	1.0000	33.20
0.333	28.5	0.1111	9.50
2.258	171.9	1.4267	68.82

If $\frac{1}{x} = \tilde{x}$

$$b = \frac{n\sum \tilde{x}y - \sum \tilde{x}\sum y}{n\sum \tilde{x}^2 - (\sum \tilde{x})^2}$$

$$= \frac{6 \times 68.82 - 2.258 \times 171.9}{6 \times 1.4267 - 2.258^2}$$

$$= \frac{24.7698}{3.4616}$$

$$= 7.1556$$

$$a = \frac{\sum y - b\sum \tilde{x}}{n}$$

$$= \frac{171.9 - 7.1556 \times 2.258}{6}$$

$$a = 25.9571$$

Thus $y = 25.96 + \frac{7.16}{x}$ to 2 dp
For the completion of figure 2,
If $\frac{1}{x} = 0$ then $y = 25.96$
If $\frac{1}{x} = 1.0$ then $y = 25.96 + 7.16 = 33.12$
The line of best fit is plotted from these two values of y
Total cost for 6 coaches ie x = 6

$$y = 25.96 + \frac{7.16}{6} = 27.15 \text{ unit cost}$$

$$\therefore \text{ total cost} = 27.15 \times 6 = \underline{£162,920}$$

c. The value a is a fixed value below which cost will not fall and b is the rate by which total costs fall as order size increases.

SOLUTION A7

The calculation of the learning coefficient for an 80% learning curve is given in the chapter

$$y = ax^{-b} = ax^{-0.322}$$

Strategy 1 - production to October

Overall time per batch $= 52 \times \left(\frac{175000}{10}\right)^{-0.322}$
Total Production time = 17500 × 2.237 = 39148 hours
$\therefore$ Labour cost = 39148 × £6 = £234,888

Strategy 1 - production November - January

using a similar process gives a labour cost of £ 103,678

Strategy 11 - production to October

Labour cost £ 138,181

Strategy 11 - production November to January

Labour cost £ 177,044

PROFIT STATEMENTS

Strategy 1	9 months to October	November - January	TOTAL
	£	£	£
Sales Revenue	568,750	312,500	881,250
Materials	52,500	37,500	90,000
Variable ohds	19,250	13,750	33,000
	71,750	51,250	123,000
Labour Costs	234,888	103,678	338,566
	306,638	154,928	461,566
Advertising	180,000	105,000	285,000
Fixed Costs	40,500	13,500	54,000
	527,138	273,428	800,566
Tooling	40,000	–	40,000
Total Costs	567,138	273,428	840,566
Profit	1,612	39,072	40,684
Net Cash Flow (90%)	1,451		£ 36,616

A similar process brings for
Strategy II

Profit (loss)	(76,481)	171,556	95,075
Cash Flow	(68,833)		85,568

∴ On basis of profits cash flows Strategy II is preferable.

b.

WITH COMPETITION

Strategy I	9 months to October	November - January	TOTAL
	£	£	£
Sales Revenue	487,500	200,000	687,500
Materials & Ohds	61,500	32,800	94,300
Labour	211,817	71,219	283,036
Advertising	110,000	80,000	190,000
Fixed	40,500	13,500	54,000
Tooling	40,000	=	40,000
Total Costs	463,817	197,519	661,336
Profit	23,683	2,481	26,164
Cash Flow	21,315		23,548
Strategy 11 on same basis			
Profit (Loss)	(79,952)	84,408	4,456
Cash Flow	(71,958)		4,010

∴ Strategy I is better

Pay Off Matrix

	Competitor	
	Enters	Not Enters
Strategy I	26,164	40,684
Strategy II	4,456	95,075

Regret Matrix

			Row Maxima
Strategy I	0	54,391	54,391
Strategy II	27,708	0	21,708

∴ Choose Strategy II

SOLUTION A8

a. i. b_i is a measure of the variation in the ith regression coefficient

ii. the t statistic is used for testing the hypothesis that $b_i = 0$

iii. the multiple correlation coefficient is a measure of the strength of the correlation.

iv. Col 1 shows the total of the sum of the squares and of the regression and, by deduction the residuals.

Col 2 shows the d.f. for the total variation (ie $n - 1$). The regression d.f. matches the number of variables and once again, by deduction the balance is the residuals.

$$\text{The mean squares} = \frac{3.341}{3} = 1.114$$

$$= \frac{0.354}{7} = 0.051$$

The F statistic is the ratio of the two figures above i.e. 1.114: 0.051 but note some rounding has taken place at earlier stages.

b. F value of 3 and 7 d.f. at 5% from Table V is 4.35. The computed value is 22.05 which is significantly higher.

∴ the null hypothesis can be rejected.

The one tailed t value for 7 d.f. from Table III is 1.895 and only x_2 is greater than this.

In summary the regression equation is significant overall but only one of the variable x_2 is significant.

c. Although overall the regression equation could be used for prediction it is of some concern that only x_2 is significant so perhaps some other predictor (possibly non-linear) should be found.

d. the coefficient of multiple determination.

CHAPTER 9

SOLUTION A1

	SALES	3 MONTH M.A.	6 MONTH M.A.
JANUARY	1,200		
FEBRUARY	1,280		
MARCH	1,310		
APRIL	1,270	1,263	
MAY	1,190	1,287	
JUNE	1,290	1,257	
JULY	1,410	1,250	1,257
AUGUST	1,360	1,297	1,292
SEPTEMBER	1,430	1,353	1,305
OCTOBER	1,280	1,400	1,325
NOVEMBER	1,410	1,357	1,327
DECEMBER	1,390	1,373	1,363

SOLUTION A2

Exponential smoothing forecasts for February onwards $\alpha = 0.3$

FEBRUARY	1,200
MARCH	1,224
APRIL	1,250
MAY	1,256
JUNE	1,233
JULY	1,250
AUGUST	1,283
SEPTEMBER	1,327
OCTOBER	1,358
NOVEMBER	1,335
DECEMBER	1,357

SOLUTION A3

	SALES	3 MONTH MA	FORECAST ERROR	SQUARED	6 MONTHS MA	FORECAST ERROR	SQUARED
APRIL	1270	1263	7	49			
MAY	1190	1287	97	9409			
JUNE	1290	1257	33	1089			
JULY	1410	1250	160	25600	1257	153	23409
AUGUST	1360	1297	63	3969	1292	68	4624
SEPTEMBER	1430	1353	77	5929	1305	125	15625
OCTOBER	1280	1400	120	14400	1325	45	2025
NOVEMBER	1410	1357	53	2809	1327	83	6889
DECEMBER	1390	1373	17	289	1363	27	729
Sum JULY-DECEMBER				52996			53301

Thus over the same comparative period the 3 month M.A., is slightly the better forecast but only just.

SOLUTION A4

a. i. Subjective

Delphi Method
Historical Analogy
Surveys

ii. Statistical

Moving Averages
Exponential smoothing

iii. Casual Models

Regression Analysis
Correlation

b. Eight factors which limit accuracy

i. Incomplete data

ii. Badly specified model

iii. Assumption of linearity when non-linear

iv. Inflation

v. Changes in economy/industry

vi. Omission of key variables

vii. Government legislation

viii. Unforeseen competitive changes

c. Great care must be taken to specify fully all the + and - factors which make up cash flow. This is more important than using any particular statistical technique.

CHAPTER 10

SOLUTION A1

(a) 6 (b) $\frac{-2}{x^3}$

(c) $\frac{1}{\sqrt{1+2x}}$ (d) $-\frac{1}{2x\sqrt{x}}$

SOLUTION A2

$$\frac{dc}{dQ} = 2Q - 30$$

$$\therefore Q = 15 \text{ at minimum}$$

NOTE: $\frac{d^2C}{dQ^2} = 2$ which is positive indicating a minimum value

SOLUTION A3

$$\frac{\partial P}{\partial D} = 9 - 0.001D + 0.06A$$

$$\frac{\partial P}{\partial A} = 0.06D - 160A$$

$$\therefore D = \frac{160A}{0.06} = 2667A$$

$$\therefore 9 - 0.001\,(2667A) + 0.06A$$

$$9 = 2.727A \therefore A + \underline{3.3 \text{ pages}}$$

and substituting

$$9 - 0.001D + 0.06\,(3.3)$$

$$9.198 = 0.001D$$

$$\therefore D = \underline{9{,}198 \text{ copies}}$$

SOLUTION A4

a. Profit p = Revenue - Cost, where revenue = Px.

$$\begin{aligned} \therefore p &= Px - c \\ &= (157 - 3x)x - (1064 + 5x + 0.04x^2) \\ &= 157x - 3x^2 - 1064 + 5x + 0.04x^2 \\ &= -3.04x^2 + 152x - 1,064 \end{aligned}$$

$$\frac{dp}{dx} = 6.08x + 152 \text{ and } \frac{d^2p}{dx^2} = -6.08$$

$\therefore$ set $\frac{dp}{dx}$ to zero ie. $0 = -6.08x + 152$

$\therefore$ $x = 25$ which gives a maximum of p as the second derivative is negative.

When $x = 25$ $P = 157 - (3x25) = 82$ ie. $\underline{\underline{£\ 82{,}000}}$

b. Revenue with the tax, t is

$$\begin{aligned} (P-t)x &= (157 - 3x - t)x \\ \therefore profitp &= (157 - 3x - t)x - (1064 + 5x + 0.04x^2) \\ &= -3.04x^2 + (152 - t)x - 1064 \end{aligned}$$

$\therefore\ \frac{dp}{dx} = 6.08x + 152 - t$

and $\frac{d^2p}{dx^2}$ is -6.08

$\therefore$ When $\frac{dp}{dx} = 0$ profit is a maximum

$\therefore\ 6.08x = 152 - t$

$\therefore\ x = \underline{25 - 0.164t}$

Thus price $= 157 - 3(25 - 0.164t) = 82 + 0.492t$

ie $\underline{£82,000 + 492t}$ is price to maximise profit

c. The introduction of the tax causes the price to move from £ 82,000 to £ 82,000 + 492 t. This means that 49.2% of the tax is passed on to the customer.

d. With no tax profit is

$$p = 25 \times 82 - (1064 + (5 \times 25) + 0.04(25^2))$$
$$= 836 \text{ ie } \underline{£\ 836{,}000}$$

With a tax of 4 (in '000s)

$$\text{Quantity sold} = 25 - 0.164 \times 4 = 24.344$$
$$\text{and price} = 82 + 0.492 \times 4 = 83.968$$
$$\therefore \text{Profit with tax} = 24{,}344\ (83.968 - 4) - (1064 + (5 \times 24.344) + 0.04\ (24.344^2))$$
$$= 737{,}316 \text{ ie } £\ 737{,}316$$

$\therefore$ Reduction in profit is £ 836,000 - 737,316 = $\underline{\underline{£\ 98{,}684}}$

SOLUTION A5

i. Revenue function is

$$R = pq = (600 - 2q^2)q$$
$$= 600q - 2q^3$$

$\therefore\ \frac{dR}{dq} = 600 - 6q^2 = 0$ for maximum because $\frac{d^2R}{dq} = -12q$ ie. is negative.

$\therefore\ q = 10$ and $p = 600 - 2(10^2) = £400$

$\therefore$ Maximum revenue $= 10 \times £400 = £4000$

(Alternatively $R = 600q - 2q^3 = 600(10) - 2(10^3) = £4000$).

ii. Point of maximum profit is when Marginal Cost = Marginal Revenue.

$$MC = \frac{dc}{dq} = 216$$

$\therefore\ 216 = 600 - 6q^2$

$\therefore\ q = 8$ and $p = 600 - 2(8^2) = \underline{£472}$

The maximum profit (P) $R - C$ when $q = 8$

$\therefore\ p = £(8 \times 472) - (100 + 216 \times 8) = \underline{\underline{£1948}}$

$$E = \frac{p}{q}\frac{dq}{dp}$$
$$p = 600 - 2q^2 \text{ as given}$$

iii. $\therefore\ \frac{dp}{dq} = -4q$

$\therefore\ \frac{dq}{dp} = -\frac{1}{4q}$ (ie. the reciprocal of $\frac{dp}{dq}$)

$\therefore\ E = \frac{p}{q}\frac{dq}{dp} = \frac{p}{q}(-1/4q) = -\frac{p}{4q^2}$

At maximum revenue $q = 10$ and $p = £400$

$\therefore\ E = \frac{400}{4(10^2)} = -1$

At maximum profit q = 8 and p = £ 472

$\therefore\ E = \frac{472}{4(8^2)} = -1.84$

When $E = -1$ this means that this is a point of constant revenue ie. a 10% increase in price will cause the quantity demanded to fall by 10% resulting in constant revenue.

When E is less than 1 (ie. $E > -1$) eg. - 0.6 demand is said to be inelastic whereas if E is greater than 1 ie. ($E < 1$) eg. as in this example when $E = -1.84$, demand is *elastic.*

Normally the negative sign is omitted in elasticity of demand values because it is taken for granted that q decreases as p increases.

iv. Note: This section of the questions works back from derivatives using simple integration procedures.

If $E = \frac{p}{10q^2}$ this means that

$$\frac{p}{q}\frac{dq}{dp} = -\frac{p}{10q^2}$$

$$\therefore\ \frac{dq}{dp} = -\frac{1}{10q} \quad \text{the reciprocal of which is}$$

$$\frac{dp}{dq} = -10q \quad \text{which is the marginal demand}$$

function which, if integrated gives the new demand function ie.

$$\int -10q dp = -5q^2 + C \text{ where } C \text{ is a constant}$$

The initial condition of price being £ 256, giving a demand of 10, means that

$256 = -5(10^2) + C$

$\therefore\ C = 756$

$\therefore$ the new demand function is

$p = 756 - 5q^2$

$\therefore$ Revenue $(R) = (756 - 5q^2)q$

$= 756q - 5q^3$

$\therefore$ Marginal Revenue MR $= 756 - 15q^2$

Maximum profit is when MC = MR

$\therefore$ 216 = 756 - $15q^2$

$\therefore\ Q = 6$ and $p = £576$

$\therefore$ Total Revenue − Total Cost = Profit

$(£576 \times 6) - (100 + (216 \times 6) = \underline{£2060}$

SOLUTION A6

a.

$$\begin{aligned} p &= R - C \\ &= (100x - x^2) - (100 + 23x + \tfrac{1}{2}x^2) \\ &= -100 + 77x - 1.5x^2 \\ \frac{dp}{dx} &= 77 - 3x \left(\frac{d^2p}{dx^2} = -3 \right) \end{aligned}$$

set $77 - 3x = 0 \therefore\ x = \underline{25.7 \text{ tonnes}}$

b. $P = 0$ means that

$-100 + 77x - 1.5x^2 = 0$

or

$3x^2 - 154x + 200 = 0$ ie a quadratic which can be solved using the quadratic formula

$$x = \frac{-b \pm \sqrt{b^2 - 4ac}}{2a}$$

$$= \frac{154 \pm \sqrt{154^2 - 4 \times 3 \times 200}}{2 \times 3}$$

$$\therefore x = \underline{1.3 \text{ tonnes} \, or \, 50 \text{ tonnes}}$$

c.

$$R = 100x - x^2$$

$$\therefore \frac{dR}{dx} = 100 - 2x \left(\frac{d^2R}{dx^2} = -2 \right)$$

$$\therefore 100 - 2x = 0$$

$$\therefore x = \underline{50 \text{ tonnes}}$$

d. Graph of cost and revenue

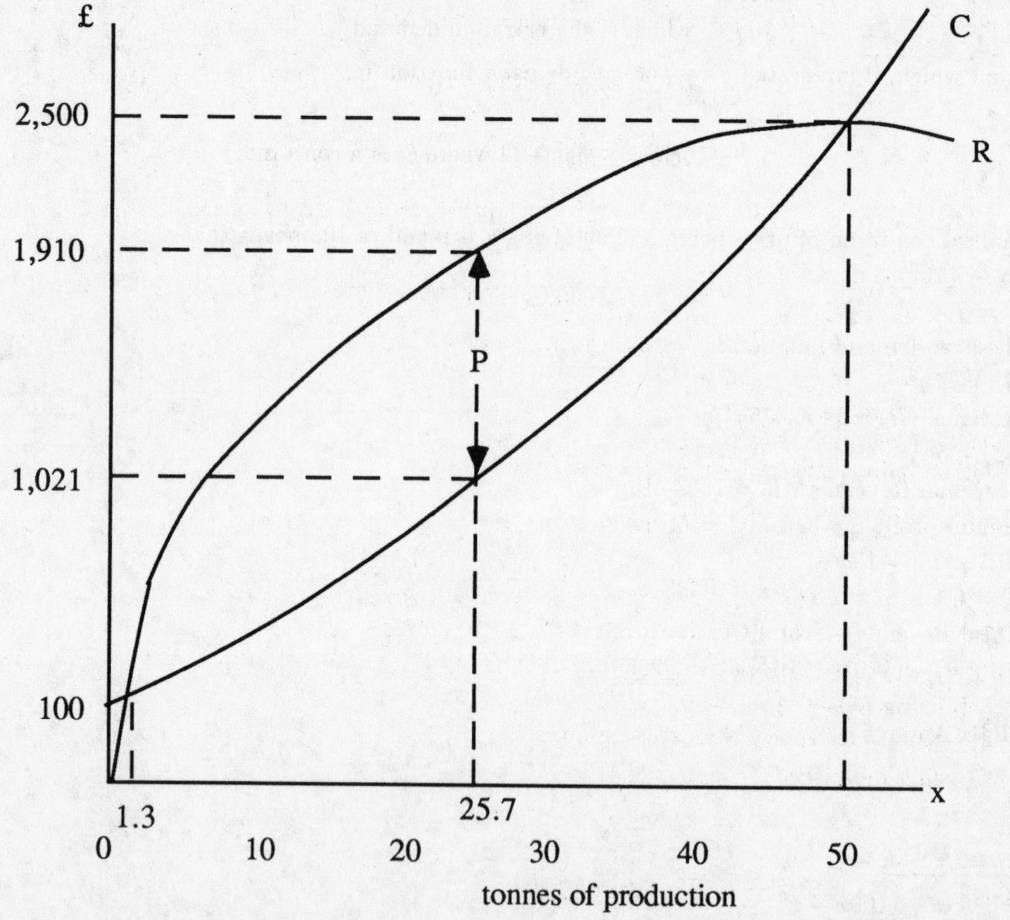

e. If possible 25.7 tonnes would be produced but failing this an output of 1.3 to 50 tonnes should be produced.

SOLUTION A7

a. Expected time for Gracious Gardens

$$
\begin{aligned}
E(t) &= {}_0\int^{30} t\left(\frac{1}{4500}\ t\ (30-t)\right) dt \\
&= {}_0\int^{30} \frac{1}{4500}t^2(30-t)dt \\
&= {}_0\int^{30} \frac{1}{4500}(30t^2 - t^4)dt \\
&= \frac{1}{4500}\left[\frac{30t^3}{3} - \frac{t^4}{4}\right]_0^{30} \\
&= \frac{1}{4500}\left(\left(\frac{30^4}{4} - \frac{30^4}{4}\right) - 0\right) \\
&= 15 \text{ days}
\end{aligned}
$$

Expected time for Speedy Landscaping

$$
\begin{aligned}
E(t) &= {}_0\int^{30} t\left(\frac{3}{40000}\ t^2\ (20-t)\right) dt \\
&= {}_0\int^{20} \frac{3}{40000}t^3(20-t)dt \\
&= {}_0\int^{20} \frac{3}{40000}(20t^3 - t^4)dt \\
&= \frac{3}{40000}\left[\frac{20t^4}{4} - \frac{t^5}{5}\right]_0^{30} \\
&= \frac{3}{40000}\left(\left(\frac{20^5}{4} - \frac{20^5}{5}\right) - 0\right) \\
&= \underline{12\text{days}}
\end{aligned}
$$

b. Gracious Gardens
P(Job being unfinished) = 1 - P (Job being finished)

$$
\begin{aligned}
\text{P(Job being finished)} &= {}_0\int^{15} \frac{1}{4500} \quad t(30 - t)\ dt \\
&= \frac{1}{4500} \quad \left[\frac{30t^2}{2} - \frac{t^3}{3}\right]_0^{15} \\
&= 0.5
\end{aligned}
$$

∴ P(Job being finished) = 1 – 0.5 =<u>0.5</u>
A similar process for speedy landscaping gives

$$
\begin{aligned}
\text{P (Job being unfinished)} &= 1 - 0.3125 \\
&= \underline{0.6875}
\end{aligned}
$$

c. <u>Expected costs</u>
Gracious Gardens = £ 250 + 15 × 20 = <u>£ 550</u>
Speedy Landscaping = £ 220 + 12 × 30 = <u>£ 580</u>

d. Gracious Gardens have a lower expected cost and a higher probability of completing on time so would be the recommended choice.

CHAPTER 11

SOLUTION A1

a. This can be answered directly from the text Paragraphs 3 and 4.
b. This is largely answerable from the text Paragraphs 5-9 inclusive. Emphasis must be given to the three key questions.

- How many to order?
- When to order?
- How many items should be held in stock to cater for demand and lead time variabilities?

CHAPTER 12

SOLUTION A1

$$\text{Reorder Level} = 2000 \times 20 = \underline{40,000}$$

$$\text{Minimum Level} = 40,000 - (1300 \times 17\tfrac{1}{2})$$
$$= \underline{17,250}$$

$$\text{Maximum Level} = 40,000 + 30,000 - (900 \times 15)$$
$$= \underline{56,500}$$

SOLUTION A2

a. The main advantage of a periodic review system are:-

i. All stock holdings are reviewed periodically. Therefore obsolete stocks can be eliminated.

ii. Specialist labour can be gainfully employed.

iii. Where there is a cost advantage in placing a batch of orders, normally a number of items from one supplier, it can be exploited.

iv. Cost advantages may be gained from certain production sequences. For example, where changing from one production run to another is easier than re-setting.
The main disadvantages are:-

v. It requires additional labour to review items of stock at times other than when receipts and issues are being posted.

vi. Larger stocks are often required, as re-order levels must take account of the period between reviews, as well as lead time.

vii. Slow to respond to changes in consumption. Should the rate of usage change shortly after a review a stockout may well occur before the next review.

viii. Difficult to set periods for review. Fluctuating, spasmodic usage may render it impossible.

b. Re-order point = Safety stock + normal usage in lead time.

$$\therefore = 20,000 + (\frac{50,000}{25} \times \frac{15}{1})*$$
$$= 20,000 + 30,000 = 50,000$$

Therefore re-order point is when stocks fall to $\underline{\underline{50,000}}$

* assuming lead time refers to working days.

Should the 15 days refer to calender days then the re-order level would be:-

Safety stock + normal usage in lead time.

$$= 20,000 + (50,000 \times \frac{15}{30})*$$
$$= 20,000 + 25,000 = 45,000$$

Therefore re-order point is when stock falls to $\underline{\underline{45{,}000}}$

* assuming 30 calendar days per month.

c. Current Costs (p.a.)

				£
i	Cost of supplies	=	annual usage × cost price	
			$(50,00 \times 12) \times 0.25$	150,000
ii	Cost of holding	=	Average stock × holding cost	
iii	Average stock	=	Safety Stock + $\frac{\text{Order quantity}}{2}$	
iv	Holding cost	=	cost price × 20%	
v	from ii	=	$(20,000 + \frac{50,000}{2}) \times (0.25 \times \frac{20}{100})$	
		=	$45,000 \times 0.05 =$	£ 2,250
			TOTAL ANNUAL COST	**£ 152,250**

Cost of Proposed Scheme (p.a.)

				£
i	Cost of supplies	=	$(50,000 \times 12) \times 0.23$	138,000
ii	Cost of holding	=	$(20,000 + \frac{200,000}{2}) \times (0.23 \times \frac{20}{100})$	
		=	$120,000 \times 0.046$	5,520
iii	Additional fixed costs			6,000
			TOTAL ANNUAL COST	**£ 149,520**

Adopting of the proposed policy will show an annual saving of £ 2,730 without considering the savings on ordering costs. it is therefore recommended providing usage remains at its current level.

SOLUTION A3.

This can be answered directly from the chapter.

CHAPTER 13

SOLUTION A1

Reorder level $= 710 \times 20 = 14200$

Minimum level $14200 - (560 \times 17.5) = 4,400$

Maximum level $14200 + 10,000 - (240 \times 15) = 20,600$

SOLUTION A2

a.

$$\text{EOQ} = \sqrt{\frac{2 \times 250 \times 100,000}{3 \times 0.12}}$$

$$= \underline{11,785}$$

b. EOQ with gradual replenishment

$$= \sqrt{\frac{2 \times 250 \times 100,000}{3 \times 0.12(1 - \frac{100,000}{600,000})}}$$

$$= \underline{12909}$$

SOLUTION A3

$$\text{EOQ} = \sqrt{\frac{2 \times 5000 \times 100}{5 \times 0.2}} = 1,000$$

ORDER QTY	1000	1200	1400	1500
AVERAGE ORDERS P.A	5	4.16	3.57	3.33
ORDER COST SAVINGS	-	84	143	167
PRICE SAVINGS P.A.	-	2500	3750	5000
EXTRA STOCK HOLDING COST	-	40	95	100
TOTAL GAIN		2544	3798	5067

∴ Order in 1500 lots.

SOLUTION A4

a.

COST SUMMARY

ORDERS P.A.	20	40	60	80	100
SIZE OF ORDER	2400	1200	7800	600	480
AVERAGE STOCK	1200	600	400	300	240
	£	£	£	£	£
STOCK HOLDING	2880	1440	960	720	576
ORDERING	1000	2000	3000	4000	5000
TOTAL COST	3880	3440	3960	4720	5576

b.

$$\text{EBQ} = \sqrt{\frac{2cd}{h}}$$

$$= \sqrt{\frac{2 \times 50 \times 48000}{2.4}} = \underline{1414 \text{ units}}$$

Using EBQ costs are:

	£
Average stock holding cost $= \frac{1414}{2} \times £2.40$	1697
No of orders $\frac{48000}{1414} \times £50$	1700
	3397
+ Purchase cost	48,000
	£ 51,397

c. 5% discount and 2000 order quantity

Stock holding $\frac{2000}{2} \times £2.40$	2400
Order $\frac{48,000}{2,000} \times £50$	1200
Purchase cost $48,000 \times £0.95$	45600
	£ 49,200

There is a £ 2,197 saving overall because of the discount.

SOLUTION A5

a. Using the E.O.Q. Model

$$Q^* = \sqrt{\frac{2DCo}{P.i}}$$

$$TC^* = \frac{D}{Q^*}.Co + \frac{Q^*}{2}.P.i.$$

$$N^* = \frac{D}{Q^*} = \text{number of times to buy.}$$

D = demand

Co = order cost

P = price to buy

i = cost of capital

Q* = optimum order quantity

TC* = optimum stock management cost

Substituting into the formulae above and using one year as the period.

D = 25 x 50 = 1250

Co = 10

P = £ 0.5 ie £ 5 for 10

i = 0.20

$$Q^* = \sqrt{\frac{2(1250)(10)}{0.5(0.2)}}$$

$$= \sqrt{\frac{25000}{0.1}}$$

$$= \sqrt{250000}$$

$$Q^* = 500$$

$$TC^* = \frac{1250}{500}(10) + \frac{500}{2}(.5)(0.2)$$

$$= 25 + 25$$

$$= £\ 50$$

$$N^* = \frac{1250}{50} = 25 \text{ times per year}$$

Total annual cost (TAC) including both purchase cost and stock management cost is given by

TAC = 1250 (0.5) + 50

= 625 + 50

= £ 675

Average cost = $\frac{675}{1250}$ = £ 0.54

Markup = 0.54 (0.20) = £ 0.108

Price = 0.54 + 0.108

= 0.648

= <u>65p each</u>

The advice to the manager is

(a) to buy 50 units at a time, 25 times per year

(b) to sell at 65p per unit.

b. 95% of 50p = 47.5p or £ 0.475

Let the manager order 1000 units at a time

$$N = \frac{D}{Q} = \frac{1250}{1000} = 1\tfrac{1}{4} \text{ times or once every 40 weeks.}$$

This may be looked upon as 5 orders every 4 years

$$\begin{aligned}
\text{Order cost} &= 1.25\ (10) = 12.50 \\
\text{Holding cost} &= \frac{1000}{2}\ (0.475)\ (0.2) \\
&= 47.50 \\
\text{TC} &= 12.50 + 47.50 \\
&= 60 \\
\text{TAC} &= £\ 60 + 1250 \times £0.475 \\
&= £\ 60 + 593.75 \\
&= \underline{£\ 653.75} \\
\text{Average cost} &= \frac{£653.75}{1250} \\
&= £\ 0.523 \\
\text{Mark up} &= 0.2\ (0.523) = £\ 0.1046 \\
\text{Price} &= 0.523 + 0.10446 \\
&= £\ 0.6276 \\
&= £\ 062.76\text{p} \\
&= \underline{63\text{p each}}
\end{aligned}$$

The advice to the manager is

(a) buy 1000 units at a time only qualifying this by asking if the manager is confident that demand will not fall off.

(b) price the component at 63p each

c. To find a value for i such that total annual cost from buying 500 at a time is equal to that from buying 1000. This will happen when

$$\frac{1250}{500}(10) + \frac{500}{2}(0.5)i + 625 = \frac{1250}{1000}(10) + 1000/2(0.475)i + 593.75$$

$$25 + 125i + 625 = 12.5 + 237.5i + 593.75$$

$$112.5i = 43.,75$$

$$i = \frac{43.75}{112.50} = 0.39$$

The value of i, the cost of capital, which will make the manager indifferent between the two policies is 0.39 or 39%.

A cost of capital figure of 39% does seem rather high and so it is likely that the manager would opt for the discount price.

SOLUTION A6

a. The small van will be more economical if its total collection and stock holding costs are less than those for the large van.

Let Ts = small van total cost

Tl = large van total cost

Annual Demand D = 240 units

Unit Cost C = £ 100

Order Quantities

Qs = 20 units

Ql = 30 units

Order or Delivery Costs

Ds = 50

Dl = 70

Small van : Total Costs

$$Ts = \frac{240}{20} \times 50 + \frac{20}{2} \times 100 \times i$$

$$= 600 + 1000i$$

Large van: Total Costs

$$Tl = \frac{240}{30} \times 70 + \frac{30}{2} \times 100 \times i$$

$$= 560 + 1500i$$

if $Ts < Tl$

$$\text{then } 600 + 1000i < 560 + 1500i$$

$$40 < 500i$$

$$\text{or } 500i > 40$$

$$i > \frac{40}{500}$$

$$i > 0.08 \text{ or } 8\%$$

This if the cost of capital is more than 8% the use of a smaller van will be cheaper.
This gives a lower limit on i.
The above analysis was based on the assumption of full vans being used but they need not be full.
It may be worth investigating beyond what value of i partial loads are worth considering. This may be done as follows:
Small van incomplete load $Q < 20$

$$\sqrt{\frac{2 \times 240 \times 50}{100i}} < 20$$

$$\frac{24000}{100i} < 400$$

$$24000 < 40000i$$

$$\text{or } 40000i > 24000$$

$$i > \frac{24000}{60000}$$

$$i > 0.6 \text{ or } 60\%$$

Thus from 8% to 60% values of i it would be more economical to use a small van fully laden.
Beyond 60% partial loads should be considered.

b. For 40 unit small van deliveries

Ds becomes £ 75

Ts may be re-named Ts_2

Os becomes 40 units

$$Ts_2 = \frac{240 \times 75}{40} + \frac{40}{2} \times 100 \times i$$

$$Ts_2 = 450 + 2000i$$

The double delivery will be more economical if

$$450 + 2000\,i < 600 + 1000\,i$$
$$1000i < 150$$
$$i < 15\%$$

If $i < 15\%$ then it is worth the customer taking double deliveries.
The threshold of 8% should be considered.

$$Ts_2 = \frac{240 \times 75}{40} + \frac{40}{2} \times 100 \times 0.08$$
$$= 450 + 160$$
$$= £\,610$$
$$Tl = \frac{240 \times 70}{30} + \frac{30}{2} \times 100 \times 0.8$$
$$= 560 + 120$$
$$= £\,680$$

Since £ 610 < £ 680 double small van deliveries are more economical than Large van deliveries assuming full loads.

c. The results about may be summarised as follows:

i	Decision
O to 15%	Small van double trip
15 to 60%	Small van single trip
60% +	Small van partial load

SOLUTION A7

a.

$$\text{EOQ} = \sqrt{\frac{2 \times 15 \times 10,000}{0.25 \times 30}} = 200 \text{ Kgs}$$

b. i. Increasing stockholding costs by 35% will cause the EOQ to be multiplied by a factor of

$$\sqrt{\frac{0.25}{0.35}} = 0.845$$

$\therefore$ New EOQ = 200 × 0.845 = 169 Kgs

ii. Reducing price to £ 20 Kg

$$\sqrt{\frac{30}{20}} = 1.225$$

$\therefore$ New EOQ = 200 × 1.225 = 245 kgs

iii. Increase to 250 Kgs

$$\sqrt{\frac{250}{200}} = 1.118$$

$\therefore$ New EOQ = 200 × 1.118 = 224 Kgs

c. The change in EOQ is proportional to the square root of the change in the variable.

SOLUTION A8

a.

$$\text{Part F EOQ} = \sqrt{\frac{2 \times 5000 \times 150}{2}} = \underline{866}$$

$$\text{Part b EOQ} = \sqrt{\frac{2 \times 10,000 \times 50}{2}} = \underline{1225}$$

b.

	Costs		
	F		G
Purchase	125,000		320,000
Order Cost			
$\frac{5000}{866} \times 150$	866	$\frac{10,000}{1,225} \times 150$	1,225
Holding Cost	866		1,225
Total Cost	£ 126,732		£ 322,540

c. Let maximum price = p

$$\text{Total cost} = 12 \times £250 + \tfrac{1}{2}\frac{15,000}{12} \times £2 \times £15,000 \times \text{p}$$
$$= £\ 4,250 + £\ 15,000\text{p}$$

This must equal the minimum cost from existing supplier

$$\text{ie } 4250 + 15000\text{ p} = £\ 126,732 + £\ 322,540$$
$$\therefore \text{p} = £\ 29.66$$

which is the price at which a change would be worthwhile

SOLUTION A9

a. (a) and (b) Can be answered directly from Chapter 13.

b. (i) $\text{EOQ} = \sqrt{\frac{2 \times 30 \times 12000}{25}} = 170$

(ii) $\text{EOQ} = \sqrt{\frac{2 \times 30 \times 12000}{25\left(1 - \frac{12000}{50000}\right)}} = \underline{195}$

c. With instantaneous replenishment the average stock level is higher thus the EOQ formula with gradual replenishment enables the order quantity to be increased.

SOLUTION A10

a. Using outside supplier

$$\text{EOQ} = \sqrt{\frac{2 \times 10000 \times 30}{2}} = 548$$

$\therefore$ Total cost = Carrying cost + Ordering cost + cost of parts

$$= \tfrac{1}{2}(548 \times 2) + \frac{10,000 \times 30}{548} + 10,000 \times 12 = \underline{£\ 121,095}$$

b. Using subsidiary company.

$$EOQ = \sqrt{\frac{2 \times 10,000 \times 25}{2}} = \underline{500}$$

Total cost

$$= \tfrac{1}{2}(500 \times 2) + \frac{10,000 \times 25}{500} + 10,000 \times 13 = \underline{£131,000}$$

c. If holding costs were £ 5 per item.

Outside supplier

$$EOQ = \sqrt{\frac{2 \times 10,000 \times 30}{5}} = \underline{346}$$

Costs =

$$\tfrac{1}{2}(346 \times 5) = \frac{10,000 \times 30}{346} + 10,000 \times 12 = \underline{£121,732}$$

Subsidiary Company

$$EOQ = \sqrt{\frac{2 \times 10,000 \times 25}{5}} = \underline{316}$$

Costs

$$\tfrac{1}{2}(316 \times 5) + \frac{10,000 \times 25}{316} + 10,000 \times 13 = \underline{131,581}$$

The EOQs fall and the total costs increase because of the increased carrying costs.

CHAPTER 14

SOLUTION A1

Expected usage $= (80 \times 0.2) + (90 \times 0.5) + (100 \times 0.3) = 91$

Cost Tabulation

ORDER LEVEL	SAFETY STOCK	HOLDING COST £	SHORTAGES	P	ORDERS p.a.	COST OF SHORTAGES + HOLDING COST	£
90	1	2	1	0.5	4	$1 \times 0.5 \times 3 \times 4 + 2 =$	8
			9	0.3	4	$9 \times 0.3 \times 3 \times 4 + 2 =$	34.4
							42.4
95	4	8	5 ×	0.3	4	$5 \times 0.3 \times 3 \times 4 + 8 =$	26
100	9	18	-			=	18

∴ 100 is most economical order quantity

SOLUTION A2

Average demand in lead time $= 50 \times 20 = 1000$

∴ Safety stock given 10% of area is above the mean $+1.286\sigma$

$= 1.28 \times 5 \times \sqrt{20}$

$= \underline{28.62}$

Suggested reorder level is 1028.62

Note: An alternative way of dealing with the variability of demand is to combine the variances of demand.

s.d. of demand = 5 ∴ variance $= 5^2 = \underline{25}$

∴ variance of demand over lead time $= 20 \times 25 = \underline{500}$

∴ s.d. of demand over lead time $= \sqrt{500} = 22.36$

∴ Safety stock giving 90% confidence $= 1.28 \times 22.36 = \underline{28.62}$ as previously

SOLUTION A3

a. The standard EOQ formula can be used

ie $\text{EOQ} = \sqrt{\frac{2.\text{Co}.\text{D}}{\text{Cc}}}$

$\text{Co} = \text{Orders cost} = £\ 32$

$\text{D} = \text{Demand} = 200{,}000$

$\text{Cc} = \text{Carrying Cost} = £8 \times 0.1 = £0.8$

$\therefore \quad \text{EOQ} = \sqrt{\frac{2.32.200{,}000}{0.8}} = \underline{\underline{4000 units}}$

$\therefore$ No. of order p.a. $= \frac{200{,}000}{4000} = \underline{\underline{50}}$

b. Order Costs = £ (50 × 32) = **£ 1600**

$\therefore$ Total inventory cost = £ 1600 + 1600 = £ 3200

c. If the previous EOQ of 4000 is used then $\frac{242{,}000}{4000}$ orders p.a. will be required,

= 60.5orders p.a.

Total Order Cost = 60.5 × £32 = £ 1936
The holding costs for a 4000 batch size are £ 1600 as calculated in c.
$\therefore$ Total order + holding costs = £ 1936 + 1600 = £ 3536
Recalculating EOQ for new demand.

$$= \sqrt{\frac{2 \times 32 \times 242{,}000}{0.8}} = \underline{\underline{4400 \text{ units}}}$$

$\therefore$ No. of orders p.a. $= \frac{242{,}000}{4400} = 55$

Total order cost = £ (55 × 32) = £ 1760

Total holding cost = $(\frac{1}{2} \times 4400) \times 0.8$ = £ 1760

Total = £ 1760 + 1760 = **£ 3520**

$\therefore$ loss due to non-optimal ordering

= 3536 - 3520 = £ 16 p.a.

d. The question states that demand was underestimated at 200,000 and true demand was 242,000. This represents a 17.36% underestimate. This demand underestimate resulted in a £ 16 difference to costs which is approximately $\frac{1}{2}$% of costs.
The conclusion is that an approximate error of 17% in demand causes approximately $\frac{1}{2}$% increase in costs so that the basic EOQ is insensitive to changes in demand.
Note:
As pointed out in the text, the bottom of the total cost curve for the EOQ's is relatively flat, producing a range of EOQ sizes with optimal or near optimal costs.

SOLUTION A4

a. The total cost model for this company comprises the following elements:

i. Allocated fixed costs £ 2500

ii. Warehouse fixed costs £ 4000

iii. £ 0.01 per item ordered

iv. Total variable costs

iii and iv must be determined from the data supplied.
Total variable costs per component are:
Cost of holding mean stock plus
£ 25 per order placed.
The mean stock calculation may be aided by using a diagram.

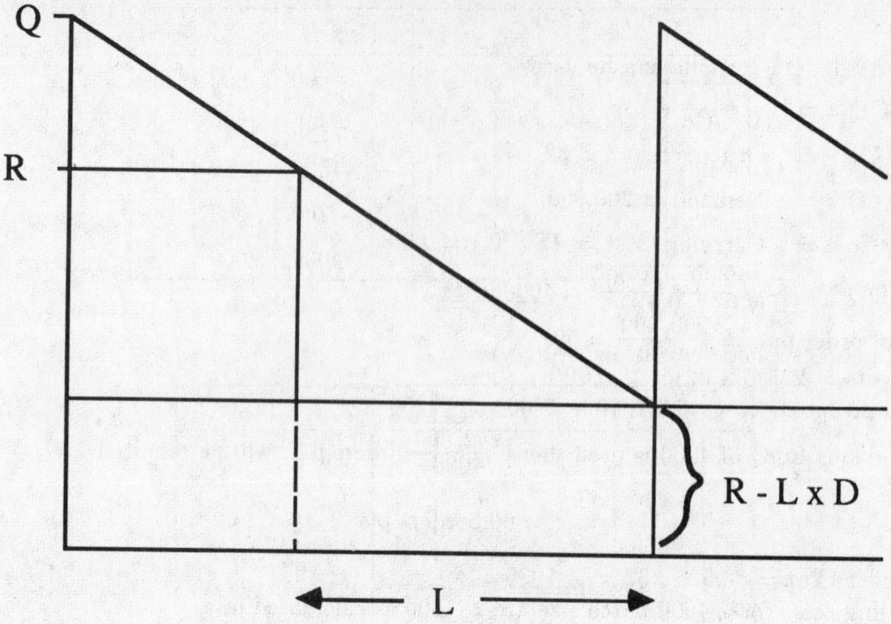

R	=	Re-order level
L	=	Lead-time in weeks
D	=	Demand in lead time
Q	=	Re-order quantity
P	=	Purchase price per unit
N	=	Number of orders per annum
M	=	Mean stock

Lead-time usage = $L \times D$

Minimum stock = $R - (L \times D)$

Maximum stock = $R - (L \times D) + Q$

Mean stock $= M = \dfrac{Q + R - (L \times D) + R - (L \times D)}{2}$

$= \dfrac{Q + 2R - D(L \times D)}{2}$

M $= \dfrac{Q}{2} + R - (L \times D)$

The number of orders placed per annum is developed from the

$$\frac{\text{Number of working weeks} \times D}{Q}$$

The number of working weeks $= \dfrac{5000}{100} = 50$

$N = \dfrac{50 \times D}{Q}$ as in basic EOQ model

The expression for £ 25 per order can now be given as £ 25n

The variable cost can be stated as 0.2 x M x P per annum

The two above cost expression may be added to give

Total annual variable cost $= 0.2 \times M \times P + 25 \times N$

The mean stocks for each item are calculated in the table below along with the value of N

	$\frac{Q}{2}$	R	L	D	$-(L \times D)$	M	N
A	500	500	2	200	- 400	600	10
B	1000	1000	4	200	- 800	1200	5
C	2500	2000	3	500	-1500	3000	5
D	250	300	2	100	- 200	350	10
E	5000	5000	8	500	-4000	6000	2.5
TOTAL WEEK UNITS				1500			

The total annual variable cost is shown below:

	0.2M	P	02M xP	N	25N	TOTAL
A	120	7	840	10	250	1090
B	240	4	960	5	125	1085
C	600	2	1200	5	125	1325
D	70	10	700	10	250	950
E	1200	1	1200	2.5	62.5	1262.5
						5712.5

The cost of £ 0.01 per item ordered can now be dealt with.
Total weekly items ordered = 1500
Annual Total = 50 × 1500 = 75000
75000 @ 0.01 = £ 750

Summary of Total Costs

Allocated Cost	2500
Warehouse Cost	4000
Variable Cost	5712.5
Item Ordered Cost	750
TOTAL ANNUAL COST	£ 12962.5

b. A minimum variable cost model may be developed using the basic EOQ model

$$Q = \sqrt{\frac{2 \times 50D \times 25}{0.2 \times P}}$$

$$Q = \sqrt{\frac{2500D}{0.2P}}$$

The table below gives the five Q values

	D	2500D	P	0.2P	Q*
A	200	500000	7	1.4	598
B	200	500000	4	0.8	791
C	500	1250000	2	0.4	1768
D	100	250000	10	2.0	354
E	500	1250000	1	0.2	2500

Since at equilibrium

$$TC = \frac{d}{Q^*} \times 25 + \frac{Q^*}{2} \times 0.2 \times P$$

$$\text{and } \frac{D}{Q^*} \times 25 = \frac{Q^*}{2} \times 0.2\,P$$

then total cost may be written as

$$2 \times \frac{Q^*}{2} \times 0.2P$$

$$= Q^* \times 0.2P$$

The total costs for each commodity can be calculated from the above table

A	598 × 1.4	=	837.2
B	791 × 0.8	=	632.8
C	1768 × 0.4	=	707.2
D	354 × 2.0	=	708.0
E	2500 × 0.2	=	500.0
Total variable cost			£3,385.2

The saving by using an EOQ Policy is

5712.5	
- 3385.2	
£ 2327.3	per annum

SOLUTION A5

a. Reorder point with certainty
EOQ = 140 and orders every 10 days
∴ demand per day = $\frac{140}{10} = 14$
∴ demand in lead time = 7 × 14 = 98 = reorder level

b.

Cost Table

Reorder Point	Usage 49	98	147	Expected Cost
49	0	147	294	147
98	49	0	147	58.8
147	98	49	0	49
Probability	0.3	0.4	0.3	

∴ Best re-order point = 147 at a cost of £ 49

c. Probabilities of all possible re-order points

LEAD TIME	P	DEMAND	P	RE-ORDER POINT	P
6	0.4	7	0.5	42	0.2
7	0.2	7	0.5	49	0.1
8	0.4	7	0.5	56	0.2
6	0.4	21	0.5	126	0.2
7	0.2	21	0.5	147	0.1
8	0.4	21	0.5	168	0.2

Using the reorder points the costs can be shown using the £ 1 and £ 3 values

Reorder	Consumption in lead time						Expected
Point	42	49	56	126	147	168	Value
42	0	21	42	252	315	378	168
49	7	0	21	231	294	357	152.6
56	14	7	0	210	273	336	140
126	84	77	70	0	63	127	70.2
147	105	98	91	21	0	63	65.8
168	126	117	112	42	21	0	70
Probability	0.2	0.1	0.2	0.2	0.1	0.2	

∴ Best point is 147 with an expected value of £ 65.8

SOLUTION A6

a. $EOQ = \sqrt{\dfrac{2 \times 4000 \times 11}{0.20 \times 1.1.}} = \underline{632 \text{ units}}$

b. Consumption in average lead time = 2 × 80 = 160

Orders p.a. = $\frac{4000}{632}$ = 6.329 . The excess of 30 would occur on 15% of occasions i.e. 0.15 × 6.329 = 0.95 times p.a.

∴ Lost sales = 30 × 0.95 × 40p = <u>£ 11.4</u>

holding the extra 30 is 30 × 0.02 × 1.1. = £ 6.6

∴ Best reorder point is 160 + 30 = <u>190</u>

(c) and (d) can be answered from the chapter.

CHAPTER 15

SOLUTION A1

<u>10mm team</u>

$$\lambda = 5 \quad \mu = \frac{60}{10} = 6$$

Average time in system $= \frac{1}{\mu - \lambda} = \frac{1}{6-5} = \underline{1\text{ hour}}$

Cost of 10 man team	=	10 × £3 × 8	=	<u>£ 240</u>
Cost of lorries waiting	=	40 × 1× £ 10	=	<u>£ 400</u>

∴ Total cost = £ 640 per day

<u>14 man team</u>

$$\lambda = 5 \quad \mu = \frac{60}{7} = 8.57$$

$$\text{Time in system} \frac{1}{\mu - \lambda} = \frac{1}{857.5} = \frac{1}{357} = \underline{17 mins}$$

Cost of team = 14 × £3 × 8 = £336
Lorries = 40 × $\frac{17}{60}$ × £10 = £113
∴ Total cost = £ 449
∴ 14 man team best

SOLUTION A2

2 Channel system	3 channel system
$\lambda = 30$	$\lambda = 30$
C = 2	C = 3
$\mu = 18$	$\mu = 14$
$\therefore\ \rho = \frac{30}{2 \times 18} = \underline{0.83}$	$\therefore\ \rho = \frac{30}{3 \times 14} = \underline{0.71}$

For 2 channel system

$$\text{Po} = \frac{2 \times (1 - 0.83)}{(2 \times 0.83)^2 + 2(1 - 0.83)(1 + 2 \times 0.83)} = \underline{\underline{0.213}}$$

For a 3 channel system

$$\text{Po} = \frac{6 \times (1 - 0.71)}{(3 \times 0.71)^3 + 6(1 - 0.7)(1 + 3 \times 0.71 + \frac{1}{2}(3 \times 0.71)^2)} = \underline{\underline{0.076}}$$

SOLUTION A3

Average time in system

<u>2 channels</u>

$$\frac{(0.83 \times 2)^2}{2 \times (1 - 0.083)2 \times^2 2 \times 18} \times 0.213 + \frac{1}{18} = \frac{2.76}{2.081} \times 0.213 + \frac{1}{18} = \underline{0.338\text{ hrs}}$$

∴ Total Cost = 30 × 0.338 × £6 + £80 = <u>£140.84</u>

<u>3 Channels</u>

$$\frac{(0.71 \times 2)^2}{6 \times (1 - 0.71)^2 \times 3 \times 14} \times 0.076 + 0.071 = \frac{2.016}{21.19} \times 0.076 + 0.071 = \underline{0.078}$$

∴ Total Cost = 30 × 0.078 × £6 + £100 = <u>£114.04</u>
∴ 3 channel system is cheaper.

a. This can be answered from the chapter

   i. Traffic intensity $= \frac{20}{30} = \underline{0.667}$

   Average time in system $= \frac{1}{30} - 20 = \underline{6 minutes}$

   ii. Cost of system

	£
Service point	100
Variable 20 × £20	400
Total Cost	£ 500

b. i. Service rate is now 40

   $\therefore$ Traffic intensity $= \frac{20}{40} = \underline{0.5}$

   Average time in system

$$\frac{1}{40-20} = \underline{3\text{minutes}}$$

   ii. Cost of system

	£
Service point	120
Variable 20 × £25	500
Total Cost	620

SOLUTION A5.

This question can be largely answered from the chapter. Particular mention should be made of the assumptions inherent in the 'simple queue model' which constitute the major limitations to the use of queueing theory. In general, these limitations make the use of analytical queueing methods inappropriate for most practical situations and in such circumstances the normal method is to use simulation.

During your studies look out for examples of queueing behaviour in such places as banks, building societies, bus queues, petrol stations. Note how queues are dealt with say in shops public houses in contrast to banks.

SOLUTION A6

a. The pre-delivery inspection stage may be regarded as a multiple server (M/M/2) queueing system if:-

   i. the cars waiting to be serviced are treated as a single queue and cars are moved into service on a first come first served basis.

   ii. the mean time that it takes to service a car in channel one is the same as that for channel two and that the service time in each channel is described by the negative exponential probability distribution.

b.

$$\begin{aligned} \rho &= \frac{\lambda}{c\mu} \\ \lambda &= 38 \text{ per week. c} = 2 \\ \mu &= \frac{40}{2} = 20 \text{ per week} \\ \text{Thus } \rho &= \frac{38}{2 \times 20} = \frac{38}{40} = 0.95 \end{aligned}$$

$$Po = \left\{ \sum_{i=o}^{c-1} \frac{(\rho^c)^i}{i!} + \frac{(\rho C)^c}{c!(1-\rho)} \right\}^{-1}$$

Take the first Element first ie

$$\sum_{1=o}^{c-1} \frac{(\rho c)^i}{i!}$$

$$\text{If } i = 0 \frac{(0.95 \times 2)^o}{0!} = 1$$

$$\text{If } i = 1 \frac{(0.95 \times 2)^2}{1!} = 1.90$$

Take the second element

$$\frac{(\rho C)^c}{C!(1-\rho)} = \frac{(0.95 \times 2)^2}{2(1-0.95)} = \frac{3.61}{0.10} = 36.1$$

$$\text{Thus Po} = (1 + 1.90 + 36.10)^{-1} 0.025641$$

This accords with the value given in the question.
The time elapsing between an order being placed and the car being delivered to the show room may be looked upon as mean time in that system. This is given as

$$\frac{(\rho C)^c Po}{C!(1-\rho)^2 C\mu} + \frac{1}{\mu}$$

in the question. There is an extra day to add on to account for the transportation to the showroom from the compound/service section.
Substitution into the formula gives

$$\frac{(0.95 \times 2)^2 \times 0.0256}{2(1-0.95)^2 \times 2 \times 20} + \frac{1}{20} = 0.51208\text{weeks}$$

This is (0.51208 × 5) days which is 2.56 days. Add the one day delivery. This gives 3.56 days.

a. The number of men per inspection bay is to be doubted. This reduces the service duration to 1.5 hours.

   The queueing formulae must now be used to calculate new values.

   $\lambda = 38 \qquad C = 2$

   $\mu = \frac{40}{1.5} = 26.67$

   $\rho = \frac{38}{2 \times 26.67} = 0.7125$

   Po is calculated as above in part (b)

   $\text{If i} = 0 \quad \frac{(0.7125 \times 2)^0}{0!} = 1$

   $\text{If i} = 1 \quad \frac{(0.7125 \times 2)^1}{1!} = 1.425$

$$\text{and } \frac{(0.7125 \times 2)^2}{2!(1-0.7125)}$$

$$= \frac{2.030625}{0.575}$$

$$= 3.5315217$$

   $\text{Po} = (1 + 1.425 + 3.5315217)^{-1} = (5.957)^{-1} = 0.1679$

   The mean time in the system is

$$\frac{(0.7125 \times 2)^2 \times 0.1679}{2!(1-0.7125)^2 \times 2 \times 26.67} + \frac{1}{26.67}$$

$$= \frac{0.33485}{8.8177688} + \frac{1}{26.67}$$

$$= 0.0379744 + 0.0374953 = 0.0754697 \text{ weeks } or 0.377 \text{ days}$$

The saving on days is thus

$$2.56 - 0.377 = 2.183 \text{ days}$$

The saving in monetary terms is

$$£2 \times 2.183 = \underline{£4.366}$$

On a mean through put of 38 cars per week the saving is

$$38 \times 4.366 = \underline{£165.908}$$

The cost of generating this saving is £ 110 per engineer making £ 220 in total.

On this basis it is not worth employing the two extra mechanics, but there are two factors which may count more than the above costs.

1. The customer has a much speedier delivery. 1.38 days instead of 3.56.

2. The idle time which has increased from 0.05 of the time to 0.2875 of the time (i.e. by an amount of 0.2375) may be used say for tuning customers cars. This would amount to 40 × 0.2375 = 9.5 hours per week.

CHAPTER 16

SOLUTION A1

Note.

The question does not ask for the simulations to be done but asks for descriptions of how they might be done.

a. **Simulation of present policy**

The basis of any simulation is to construct a model of the situation. The main factors in constructing a model are:

i. Clearly identify the objectives of the simulation.

ii. Clearly identify the critical variables and their relationships to the logic of the model. In this example the logic will be shown as a flowchart.

i. The following are the *assumed* objectives of the present policy simulation,.

General: The priority scheme related to the council's housing policy.
Specific: Average time to be housed for each group and for all groups.
Average number of applicants of each group and for all groups on the housing list. Average length of time on housing list for each group.

Note.

In practice one would not assume objectives, but ascertain by investigation and questioning what are the real objectives.

ii. The critical variables in this simulation are:

Arrival of applicants

Classification of applicants

Applicant's progress on housing list

The process of seeking accommodation

Being housed.

The relationship of these factors (ie the logic of the simulation - the model) is given in Flowchart 1.

OUTLINE FLOWCHART OF HOUSING POLICY SIMULATION

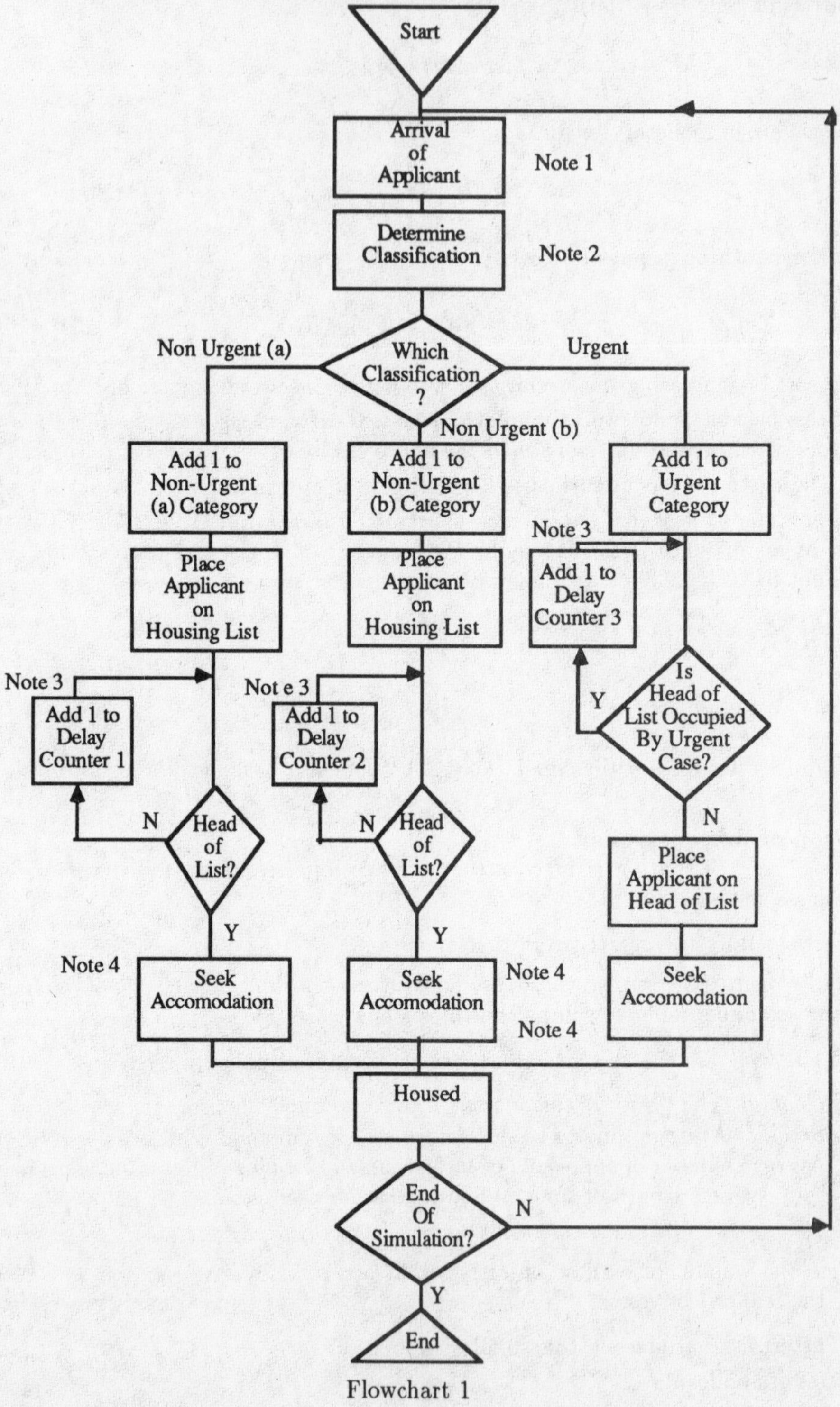

Flowchart 1

General note on flowchart.

The flowchart shows the main logic only and some detailed elements have been omitted for clarity. The flowchart would be worked through for the number of iterations thought necessary for a realistic simulation and each iteration would represent a working day.

Note 1. The arrival rate is given as 'two per week'. Although not stated, this presumably must be an average and arrivals/week must surely vary. Accordingly some distribution must be assumed for variable arrival rates with an average of 2 per week. More correctly the matter would be investigated to establish the probability pattern, eg as shown for the case types.

Note 2. A probability pattern is supplied for the case types so that it is necessary to classify arrivals, at random, in a way which reflects this pattern. This could be done using random numbers as follows:

URGENT CASES	ASSIGNED DIGIT	0
Non-Urgent (a) cases	Assigned digits	1-8
Non-Urgent (b) cases	Assigned digit	9

Then single digit random numbers are selected and applicants classified accordingly.

Note 3. The delay counters merely clock up on every iteration so that the length of time on the waiting list for each category can be determined.

Note 4. In a similar fashion to the arrival rate there must be some variation in the time to seek accommodation. The most appropriate distribution should be found by investigation and a selection made after the fashion of Note 2.

b. **Simulation of New Policy.**

Any further simulation involves speculation about future policies. A possible new policy might be to include groups other than the destitute (eg the disabled) into the urgent category or to allow groups such as the disabled to move to the head of the queue behind urgent cases. To carry out such simulations the same basic flowchart could be used, but separate housing lists for the categories would need to be maintained.

If, however, the priority logic was to be altered, the appropriate part of the flowchart would need to be amended.

c. The major way in which chance variations would be smoothed out is to allow the simulation to work through sufficient iterations so that the underlying probability distributions are accurately refflected. It is difficult to be specific about the number of iterations necessary, but at least 100 days simulations is likely to be necessary.

SOLUTION A2

Part (a)

The situation facing the clerk may be looked upon as a simple single queue single server situation.

Working on an hourly basis it is possible to look upon the mean hourly arrival rate of 5 orders per hour as λ, and the mean time of 10 minutes to produce an invoice as $60/10 = 6$ per hour as μ. These really are the components of a simple queueing system.

The assumptions are as follows:

1) Arrivals are random and follow a Poisson Distribution.

In this context this assumption is questionable because in most organisations there is one delivery of the post each day. It is more realistic however if orders are received by telephone.

2) The service rate follows a negative exponential distribution.

Without empirical evidence it is impossible to say whether or not the creation of an invoice follows the distribution noted above.

3) Queue Discipline is first in first served.

This is highly improbable unless there is a spike from the bottom of which the clerk draws the invoice. If orders are received by telephone the first in first served idea is probably more valid.

4) In this context the assumption of not baulking and no reneging are not relevant.

a. The simulation could be carried out using the logic shown in Figure 1.

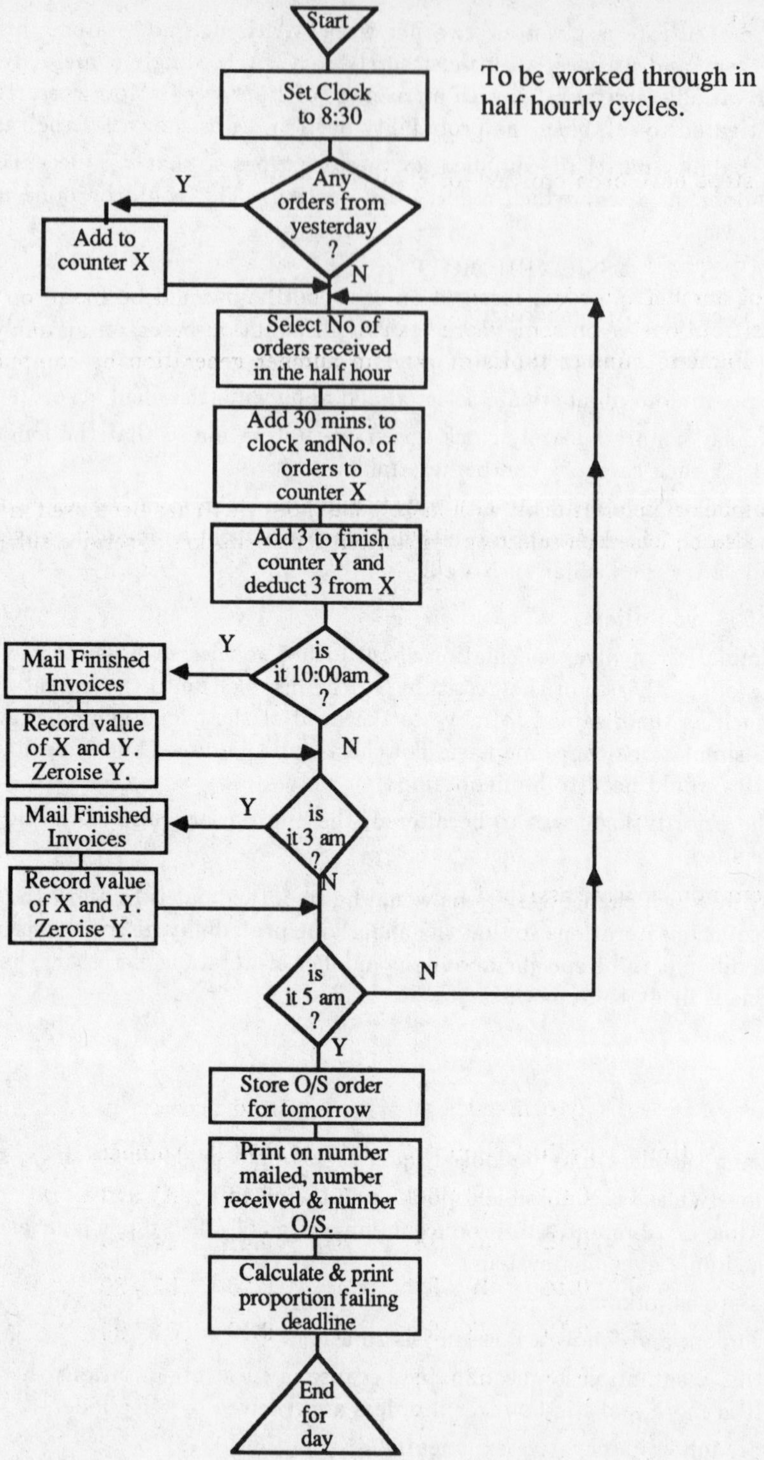

Figure 1 Simulation Flowchart

Notes on Flowchart

a. Many detailed steps have been omitted for clarity

b. The selection of number of orders received on each half hour could be based on the negative exponential distributions or on some more realistic distribution based on an analysis of actual arrival times. Random number tables or random number generation by computer would be necessary.

c. The average number of invoices dealt with in each half hour (ie 3) has been used in the flowchart but this could also be based on selecting times from a distribution of service times.

SOLUTION A3

a. First the random numbers are assigned.

Daily demand			Lead time		
Units	Prob.	Numbers	Units	Prob.	Numbers
4	0.07	00 - 06	3	0.14	00 - 13
5	0.12	07 - 18	4	0.41	14 - 54
6	0.14	19 - 32	5	0.26	55 - 80
7	0.19	33 - 51	6	0.19	81 - 99
8	0.18	52 - 69			
9	0.13	70 - 82			
10	0.09	83 - 91			
11	0.05	92 - 96			
12	0.03	97 - 99			

The simulation can be set out in tabular form as below

Opening balance is 60

Day	b/f	del	tot	RN	dem	c/f	ord	RN	lead	carry cost	order cost	s/out cost	total cost
1	60			03	4	56				28.00			28.00
2	56			97	12	44				22.00			50.00
3	44			16	5	39				19.50			69.50
4	39			12	5	34				17.00			86.50
5	34			55	8	26	42	47	4	13.00	10		109.50
6	26			16	5	21				10.50			120.00
7	21			84	10	11				5.50			125.50
8	11			63	8	3				1.50			127.00
9	11			33	7	(-4)				0.00		8	135.00
10	0	42	42	57	8	34				17.00			152.00
11	34			18	5	29	39	74	5	14.50	10		176.50
12	29			26	6	23				11.50			188.00
13	23			23	6	17				8.50			196.50
14	17			52	8	9				4.50			201.00
15	9			37	7	2				1.00			202.00
16	2			70	9	(-7)				0.00		14	216.00
17	0	39	39	56	8	31				15.50			231.50
18	31			99	12	19	49	76	5	9.50	10		251.00
19	19			16	5	14				7.00			258.00
20	14			31	6	8				4.00			262.00
21	8			68	8	0				0.00			262.00
22	0			74	9	(-9)				0.00		18	280.00
23	0			27	6	(-6)				0.00		12	293.00
24	0	49	49	00	4	45				22.50			314.50

The average demand from the acutal data is 7.27 and the average demand from the simulation is calculated below

Units	Frequency	Units x f
4	2	8
5	5	25
6	4	24
7	2	14
8	6	48
9	2	18
10	1	10
11	0	0
12	2	24
	24	171

$\therefore$ average demand $= \frac{171}{24} = \underline{7.125}$

which is close to the original mean suggesting that the simulation is reasonably realistic

b. Average daily stock cost $= \frac{314.50}{24} = \underline{£13.10}$

c. The simulation shows a gradual reduction ins tocks and an increasing number of stock-outs. This suggests that the re-order point or reorder quantity should be increased.

d. can be taken from the chapter.

SOLUTION A4

a. To perform the simulation, random number ranges must be allocated to the three distributions based on the probabilities given in each. The mid-points are used as a representative figure for each class interval. The random numbers supplied in the question are single digits.

Wages and Salaries

Mid-point	Probability	Random Number
11	0.3	0 - 2
13	0.5	3 - 7
15	0.2	8 - 9

Raw Materials

Mid-point	Probability	Random Number
7	0.2	0 - 1
9	0.3	2 - 4
11	0.3	5 - 7
13	0.2	8 - 9

Sales Revenue

Mid-point	Probability	Random Number
32	0.1	0
36	0.3	1 - 3
40	0.4	4 - 7
44	0.2	8 - 9

Wages and Salaries (£ 000)

Month	Random Number	Cash Flow
1	2	-11
2	7	-13
3	9	-15
4	2	-11
5	9	-15
6	8	-15

Raw Materials (£ 000)

Month	Random Number	Cash Flow
1	4	-9
2	4	-9
3	1	-7
4	0	-7
5	3	-9
6	4	-9

Sales Revenue (£ 000)

Month	Random Number	Cash Flow
1	0	+32
2	6	+40
3	6	+40
4	8	+44
5	0	+32
6	2	+36

Summary of Cash Flow Months 1 - 6

Month	Sales	Wages and Salaries	Raw Materials	Fixed Costs	Balance
0					50
1	32	-11	-9	-14	(D)48
2	40	-13	-9	-14	(U)52
3	40	-15	-7	-14	(U)52
4	44	-11	-7	-14	(U)68
5	32	-15	-9	-14	(D)62
6	36	-15	-9	-14	(D)60

(D) = Down on previous month

(U) = Up on previous month

In three out of the six months the cash balance fell over the previous month and so the probability of a net cash out flow is

$$\frac{3}{6} = 0.5$$

Based on the results of the simulation the closing cash balance is £ 60,000.

b. The expected cash balance may be determined by calculating the mean values of the three distributions

Wages and Salaries

X	P	XP
11	0.3	3.3
13	0.5	6.5
15	0.2	3.0
		12.8

Raw Materials

X	P	XP
7	0.2	1.4
9	0.3	2.7
11	0.3	3.3
13	0.2	2.6
		10.0

Sales Revenue

X	P	XP
32	0.1	3.2
36	0.3	10.8
40	0.4	16.0
44	0.2	8.8
		38.8

The individual means may be combined into an overall mean for each month

Sales	+38.8
Wages and Salaries	-12.8
Raw Materials	-10.0
Fixed Costs	-14.0
	36.8

Cash Flow = 38.8 − 36.8 = +2

Cash flow for 6 months = +2 × 6 = +12

The expected cash balance at the end of 6 months is thus 50,000 + 12 = 62 = £ 62,000

There is a difference or "error" of £ 2000

The expected value is based on probabilities which have presumably been derived from a reasonable period of past experience and so would have settled down at the given value.

The simulation (and allocated random number ranges) whilst being based on the derived probability distributions has only been run once and so may not be representative of a pattern which would develop it a large number of runs or simulations were undertaken. As the number of simulations increases some will be under the expected value and some over this figure, but the size of the error will diminish with the number of runs.

a. The two major assumptions upon which the simulation was run were that

1) All cash flows took place at the end of the month

2) All cash flows were independent.

Whilst salaries may be a monthly outflow, wages in general, are not, being normally paid weekly. Thus a positive cash flow for the month as a whole might hide a substantial negative cash flow within the month itself. Sales revenue and raw materials payments may not fit a neat month end pattern. This means that the managers of the company may wish to consider a weekly simulation period and the weeks during the month would have to be identified, ie week 1, week 2 and so on because the probabilitty patterns may not be the same.

The second assumption concerning the independence of cash flows may not be valid. For example, if there is a seasonal pattern, production in anticipation of a peak will affect raw materials and wages. Sales revenue will be affected on a lagged basis accorfding to the credit period. Thus there is a linkage between the cash inflows and outflows on a seasonal pattern which makes them dependent.

For a simulation to be valid, these dependencies must be built into the model.

SOLUTION A5

a. Simulation

Day	R.N.	Demand	Lost Sales	Wastage
1	93	60	20	
2	53	40	-	
3	81	50	10	
4	93	60	20	
5	88	60	20	
6	23	30		10
7	22	30		10
8	96	60	20	
9	79	50	10	
10	06	20		20
TOTAL		460	100	40

b.

	£
Sales 360 × £30	£ 10,800
Cost of Sales 10 × 40 × £20	(8,000)
Lost sales 100 × £6	(600)
Profit	£ 2,200

c. If daily order increased to 50

Lost sales would be reduced by 10 on 6 days

∴ Total lost sales = 100 - 60 = 40

Wast would be increased on 4 days

∴ Total waste = 40 + 40 = 80

Profit calculations

	£
Revenue 420 × £30	12,600
Cost of sales 10 × 50 × £20	(10,000)
Lost Sales 40 × £5	(240)
Profit	£ 2,360

d. Simulation of daily order of 50 with free storage.

Day	Random Number	Demand	Lost Sales	Stock
1	93	60	10	
2	53	40		10
3	81	50		10
4	93	60		
5	88	60	10	
6	23	30		20
7	22	30		40
8	96	60		30
9	79	50		30
10	6	20		60
TOTAL		460	20	

The profit calculations now become:

Sales revenue	(460 - 20) @ £ 30	=	13,200
Cost of sales	(10 × 50) @ £ 20	=	(10,000)
Lost sales	20 @ £ 6	=	(120)
Profit		=	3,080
Value of closing stock	60 @ £ 20	=	1,200
Total profit			£ 4,280

Thus there is an increased profit of £ 4,280 - £ 2,360 = £ **1,920**

e. Can be taken from chapter.

SOLUTION A6

a. Random allocation of questions between the four sections of the syllabus may be achieved by using random numbers. The weights are given as percentages, thus the random numbers chosen must be two digits and correspond to the weightings. This is shown below:

Section	Weight	Random Number
A	35	00 - 34
B	15	35 - 49
C	20	50 - 69
D	30	10 - 99

Let seven random numbers be generated and linked to sections.

16 - A

82 - D

91 - D

42 - B

39 - B

60 - C

21 - A

Such an allocation would give a distribution of questions as follows:

Section A	2
Section B	2
Section C	1
Section D	2

The weakness of this approach is that, quite by chance, one section could be over represented at the expense of other sections.

b. One possibility is to ensure that each paper is fully representative of the four sections. This would involve the following breakdown of questions.

A	0.35×7	=	2.45
B	0.15×7	=	1.05
C	0.20×7	=	1.40
D	0.30×7	=	2.10

This could be achieved if a question were drawn from more than one section, (as indeed this question is). A less restrictive solution might be to expect that over a range of say, 6 settings, the overall percentages should, fit the section percentages as published. This will be achieved if the examiners consciously set questions such that the percentages are maintained. This means that no one paper may fit exactly the proportions laid down, but that say over a period the topics examined to match the published sections.

c. The expected number of questions to be set for each section over six settings giving 42 questions is

Section	Weight	Expected	
A	0.35×42	=	14.7
B	0.15×42	=	6.3
C	0.20×42	=	8.4
D	0.30×42	=	12.6
			42.0

Adding across the rows for the data given shows the following frequencies:

A	17
B	5
C	7
D	13
	42

The most appropriate way to test whether the observed values fit the expected values is to use the chi-square test.

O	E	O-E	$(O-E)^2/E$
17	14.7	2.3	0.3599
5	6.3	-1.3	0.2683
7	8.4	-1.4	0.2333
13	12.6	0.4	0.0127
			0.8742

There are four "cells" in the data A, B, C, D. The only outcome provided by the data is the section when a question is devised, and so there are 3 degrees of freedom.

Thus for a 5% significance level the tabulated value of $\chi^2 = 7.8$. This is much greater than 0.87. Thus the evidence suggests that there is no significant difference between the published percentages and the actual pattern of questions set.

CHAPTER 17

SOLUTION A1.

Maximise $20A + 25B + 12C + 30D$

Subject to:

$$6A + 4B + 2C + 5D \leq 20{,}000$$
$$2A + 8.3B + 5C + 9D \leq 100{,}000$$
$$10A + 4B + 8C + 2D \leq 65{,}000$$
$$1.5A + 2C + 8D \leq 220{,}000$$
$$A, B, C \text{ and } D \geq 0$$

SOLUTION A2

Minimise $8R + 2S + 3T + U$

Subject to

$$R + S + T + U \geq 1{,}000$$
$$0.5R + 0.1S + 0.3T \geq 400$$
$$0.3R + 0.15S + 0.05T + 0.05U \geq 250$$
$$0.15R + 0.5S + 0.3T + 0.05U \geq 300$$
$$0.05R + 0.15S + 0.3T + 0.3U \geq 50$$
$$R, S, T, U \geq 0$$

SOLUTION A3

This can be taken from various earlier chapters of the manual. Note: Statistical Decision Theory is a term for the incorporation of uncertainty and variability into the analysis. An example is Expected Value.

SOLUTION A4.

a. The answer to this question requires the problem to be stated in the standard manner.
Step 1. Establish the objective function.
Clearly the objective is to produce the maximum return from the optimum production mix. To do this contribution/unit of each product must be calculated because fixed costs presumably remain the same in total and will not vary directly with the units produced.

CONTRIBUTION/UNIT

Product	A	B	C	D	E
	£	£	£	£	£
Selling Price	48	42	35	31	27
less Variable Costs					
(Materials + Labour)	33	30	22	19	20
CONTRIBUTION	£15	£12	£16	£12	£7

Let A, B, C, D and E represent the number of units of the product per week
Objective Function
Maximise $15A + 12B + 16C + 12D + 7E$
Step 2. Establish the constraints. Constraints exist regarding demand, labour and materials.

Demand. Any optimum solution must be within the demand expectations so that the demand constraints are:

$$\begin{array}{lllll} A & & & & \leq 1500 \\ & B & & & \leq 1200 \\ & & C & & \leq 900 \\ & & & D & \leq 600 \\ & & & & E \leq 600 \end{array}$$

Labour Constraints.

To establish the number of hours per unit of each product the labour costs given in the question have to be divided by £ 1.50 to establish the number of hours per unit. This results in a constraint as follows.

$12A + 10\,2/3B + 4C + 2\,2/3D + 2\,2/3E \leq 20{,}000$

but this is somewhat clumsy because of the fractions so that it is easier to consider the constraint in terms of labour costs ie $20,000 \times £1.50 = £30,000$. The constraints becomes $18A + 16B + 6C + 4D + 4E \leq 30000$

Material Constraints.

There are two constraints regarding materials; the special component availability and expenditure.

The special component constraint is

$A + B + 3C + 4D + 5E \leq 5800$

The expenditure constraint is

$15A + 14B + 16C + 15D + 16E \leq 30{,}000$

Finally the non negativity constraints should be formally stated, ie

A, B, C, D and E ≥ 0

The full LP formulation is given below.

Maximise $15A + 12B + 16C + 12D + 7E$

Subject to (Demand Constraints)

$$\left[\begin{array}{lllll} A & & & & \leq 1500 \\ & B & & & \leq 1200 \\ & & C & & \leq 900 \\ & & & D & \leq 900 \\ & & & & E \leq 600 \end{array}\right.$$

(Labour Constraint)

$18A + 16B + 6C + 4D + 4E \leq 30000$

(Material Constraints)

$$\left[\begin{array}{l} A + B + 3C + 4D + 5E \leq 5{,}800 \\ 15A + 14B + 16C + 15D + 16E \leq 30{,}000 \end{array}\right.$$

(Non negativity constraints) A, B, C, D, E ≤ 0

b. the usual problems associated with LP problems which no doubt apply to Fenton Enterprises Ltd. are

   i. Linearity - Is the assumption of linear relationships realistic?

   ii. Non-integer solutions - LP may produce fractional solutions which presumably are inappropriate in this problem. This may be avoided by the use of integer programming (ie a programming method which produces whole number solutions but is complex and time consuming). In practice the rounding of fractional solutions may not make a material difference to the optimum solution.

iii. Accuracy of estimates. The LP solution is obviously only as good as the accuracy of the input data.

SOLUTION A5

a. **Objective Function**

Let the manager buy

			£
£ a	worth of A at 13.5%	Redemption yield	0.135a
£ b	worth of B at 12.2%	Redemption yield	0.122b
£ c	worth of C at 14.3%	Redemption yield	0.143c
£ d	worth of D at 14.9%	Redemption yield	0.149d
£ e	worth of E at 15.1%	Redemption yield	0.151e

Maximise Z = 0.135a + 0.122b + 0.143c + 0.149d + 0.151e

Constraints

1. Overall Capital available to invest

a + b + c + d + e ≤ 100000

2. Short Term investment (A Treasury 1984) a ≥ 30000
3. Long term (D Treasury 1998 E Treasury 1999) d + e ≤ 40,000
4. Interest-only Running Yield

$$\frac{0.9(100)}{94\frac{1}{2}}a + \frac{.12(100)}{91\frac{1}{8}}b + \frac{.115(100)}{82\frac{3}{4}}c + \frac{.14(100)}{92}d$$

$$+\frac{.10(100)}{78\frac{1}{4}} \geq 0.13(a + b + c + d + e)$$

0.095238a + 0.1316872b + 0.1389728c + 0.1521739d + 0.1277955e

≥ 0.13a + 0.13b + 0.13c + 0.13d + 0.13e

Gathering terms gives

-0.034762a + 0.0016872b + 0.0089728c + 0.021739d - 0.0022045e ≥ 0

these could be made more convenient by multiplication by 100

- 3.476a + 0.169b + 0.897c + 2.17d - 0.220e ≥ 0

The solution is continued in the solutions for CHAPTER 18.

CHAPTER 18

SOLUTION A1

Maximise 8X + 10Y

Subject to

(Labour)	3X + 5Y ≤ 500	(L)
Material A	4X + 2Y ≤ 350	(A)
Material B	6X + 8Y ≤ 800	(B)

SOLUTION A2

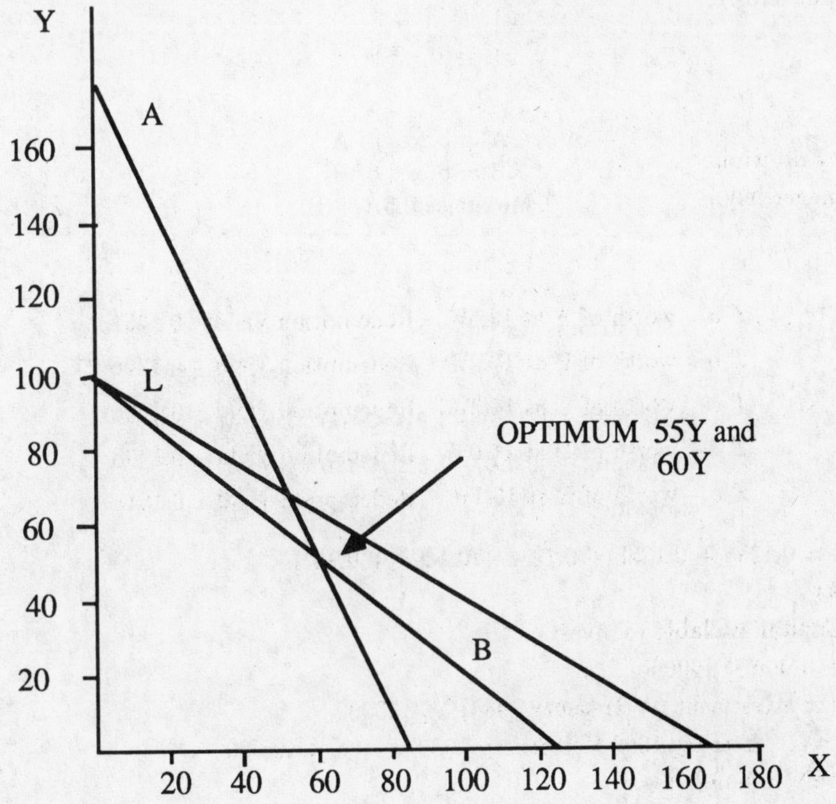

Optimum Solution 55Y and 60X
giving 60(8) + 55(10) = £ 1030

SOLUTION A3

Shadow price calculations

Optimum solution	
Objective	8X + 10Y
Subject to	$4X + 2Y \leq 350$
	$6X + 8Y \leq 800$

Dual formulation

Minimise	350S + 800T
Subject to	$4S + 6Y \geq 8$
	$2S + 8T \geq 10$
Solving	
	$4S + 6T = 8$
	$2S + 8T = 10$
=	$5T = 6$
	$\therefore\ T = 1.2$
	$S = 0.2$

Proof 350(0.2) + 800(1.2) = £ 1,030

Shadow prices Material A £ 0.2 Material B £ 1.2

SOLUTION A4

a.

A = boxes of A
B = boxes of B
Maximise 0.5A + B

b.

Constraints

		Constraint
Mixing	$1.25A + 1.2B \leq 480$	M
Cooking	$0.5A + 1.5B \leq 480$	C
Boxing	$1.5A + 0.5B \leq 480$	B

$A ; B \geq 0$

c.

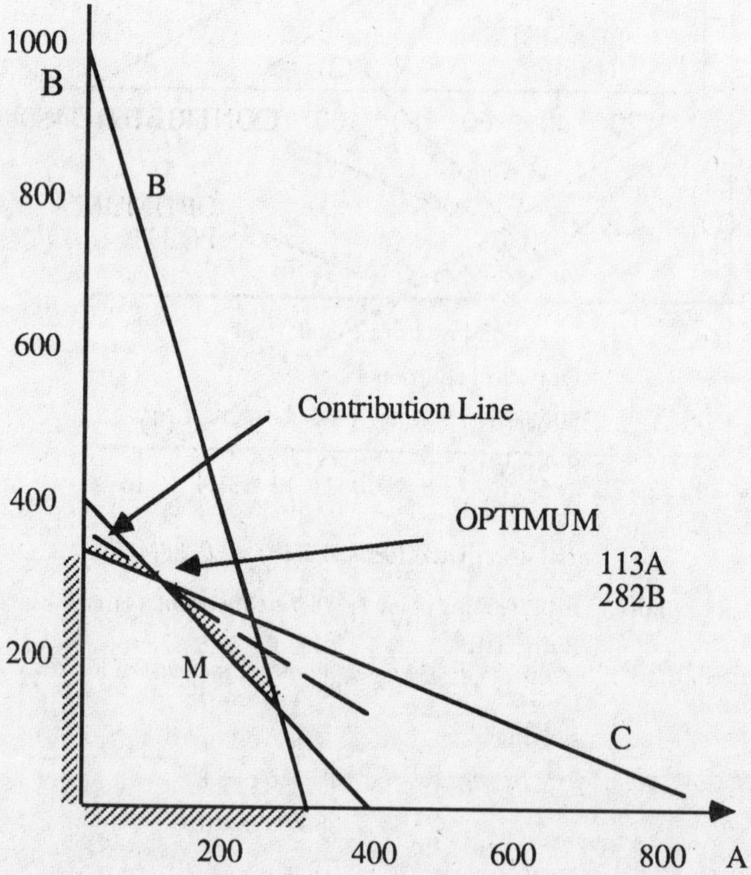

The optimum values can be found by solving the simultaneous equations.

Constraint M $1.25A + 1.2B = 480$

C $0.5A + 1.5B = 480$

Solving gives A = 113 B = 282

d. Contribution = 113(0.5) + 282 = <u>£338.5</u>

e. Can be taken from the manual.

SOLUTION A5

a. X = Value of new house building Y = Value of repair work
The LP model is

Maximise	0.2X + 0.25Y	(Contribution)
Subject to:		
(1)	$Y \geq 4$	(Repairs at least £ 4m)
(2)	$X - Y \geq 0$	(Repairs no more than half)
(3)	$X + Y \geq 10$	(Overheads covered by 5% charge)
(4)	$2X + 3Y \leq 30$	(Sufficient skilled labour)
	$X\ Y \geq 0$	

b.

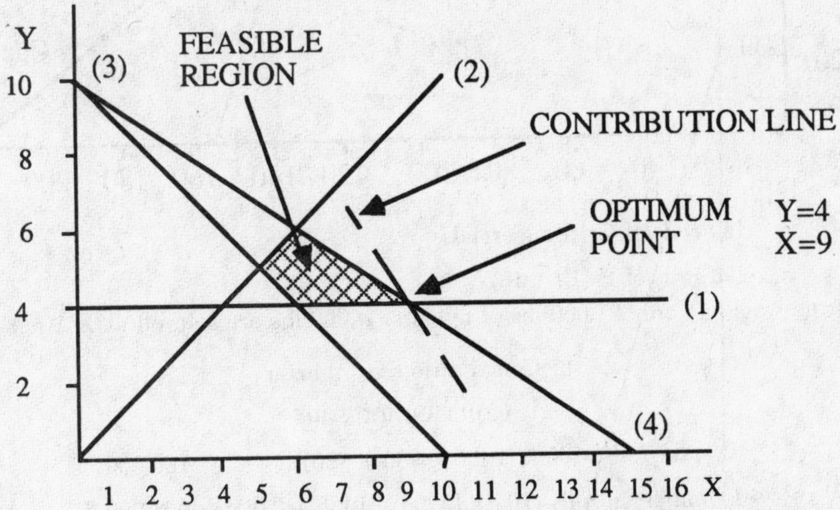

Contribution = 0.2(9) + 0.25(4) = <u>£ 2.8M</u>

c. If constraint (1) is removed the optimum point is where constraint (4) cuts the X axis ie X = 15
This gives a contribution of 0.2×15 = <u>£ 3M</u> resulting in an increase of 3 - 28 = <u>£ 200,000 p.a.</u>

SOLUTION A6

Maximise 1860P + 2530C

Subject to:

(wool)	$40P + 200C \leq$	24,000
(Nylon)	$160P + 50C \leq$	25,000
(Cap)	$30P + 36C \leq$	6,600

This is graphed as below

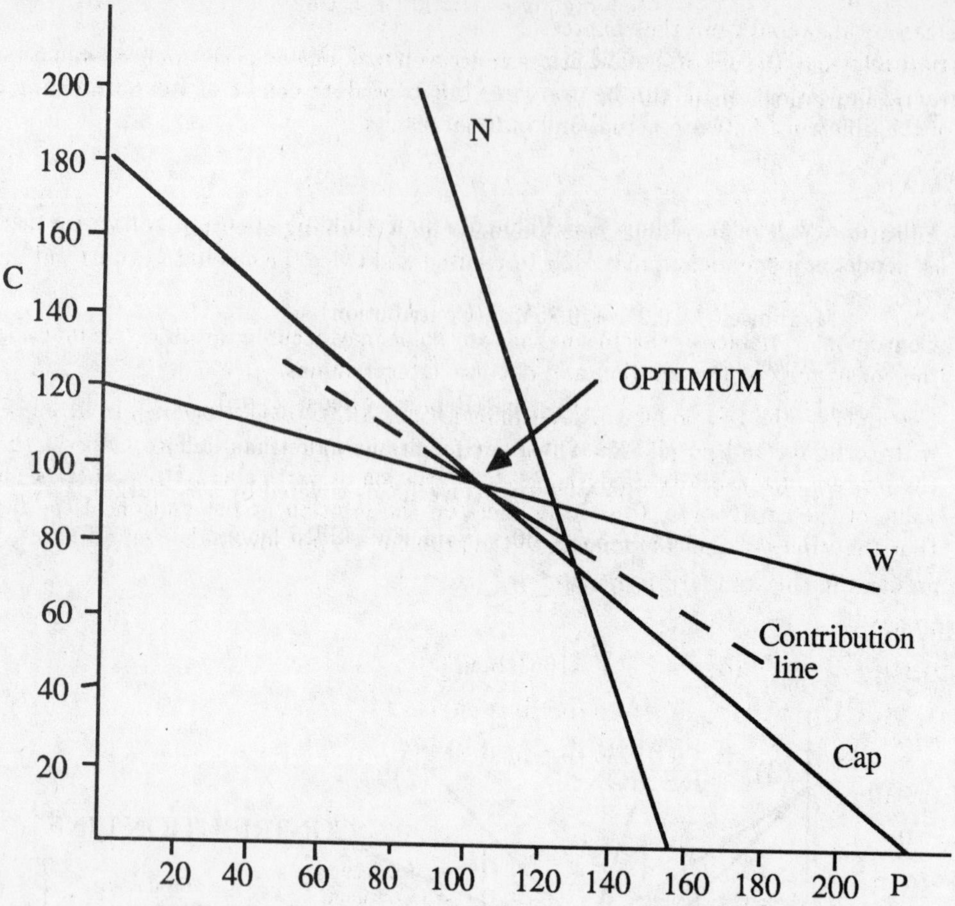

OPTIMUM = 100 rolls of C (commercial)

= 100 rolls of P (Private)

This uses all the wool but only 21,000 lbs of nylon so 4,000 lbs are sold off at £ 1 per lb.

∴ Contribution for quarter

	£
Private rolls (100 × (2400 − 980 + 180))	160,000
Commercial rolls (100 × (3200 − 1436 + 216))	198,000
Less Nylon loss	(4,000)
= Total	354,000

Note:

Calculation of contributions for objective functions is based on the fact that the materials costs are sunk costs ie do not increase with sales volume. Normally historic costs would be used resulting in an objective function of 1600P + 1980C.

Even if these values were used the same solution would be found in this case.

b.

Changes in objective function

P = £ 1860 - 110 = 1750

C = 2530 - 40 = 2490

∴ new function 1750P + 2490C

Although the slope changes the optimum solution does not.

c. This can be answered from the chapter.

d. this part relates to the use of shadow prices in decision making and performance evaluation. Providing that the general limitations of LP can be overcome this procedure can be of value providing an objective valuation of the difference between actual and optimal results.

SOLUTION A7

a. i. Linearity — all relationships must be linear ie. a doubling of output will cause twice as many components and materials to be used and twice the amount of contributions to be earned.

ii. Continuous variables — this means that any value may occur in the objective function, the constraints or the solution and not just integer values.

iii. Certainty — the LP model is a deterministic one. All factors are deemed to be known with certainty and no allowance is made for random elements. (Note however that the process of sensitivity analysis, ie. the variation of particular factors, such as the value of the constraints, to see the effect on the solution, is recognition of the fact that the values of the components of the problem are not always known exactly.)

b. The problem in the standard format is

maximise 4A + 3B

subject to A + 2B ≤ 110 (labour)

A ≤ 70 (production)

B ≤ 150 (production)

and the graph is

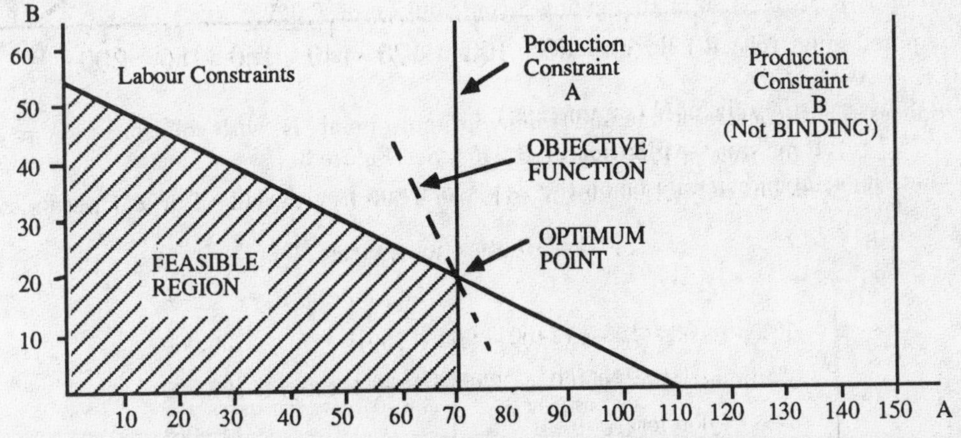

Figure 1

∴ Optimum is 20B and 70A resulting in a contribution of 4(70) + 3(20) = £ 340

c. The new objective function is 4A + 2B

Examination of figure 1 will show that the objective function will give the same optimal point until its slope is equal to that of the labour constraint which is when the ratio of contributions is 1 : 2 ie. $\frac{1}{2}$.

∴ Any ratio above $\frac{1}{2}$ gives the same optimum.

The ratio of the new objective function is $\frac{4}{2} = 2$ so the optimum is still 20B and 70A resulting in the following contribution.

4(70) + 2(20) = £ 320

ii. 10 hour increase in labour hours. This changes the labour constraint to A + 2B ≤ 120

The graph is redrawn with the labour constraint moved outwards parallel to the original constraint resulting in a new optimum at point Q where A = 70 and B = 25 resulting in a total contribution of £ 355. See Figure 2.

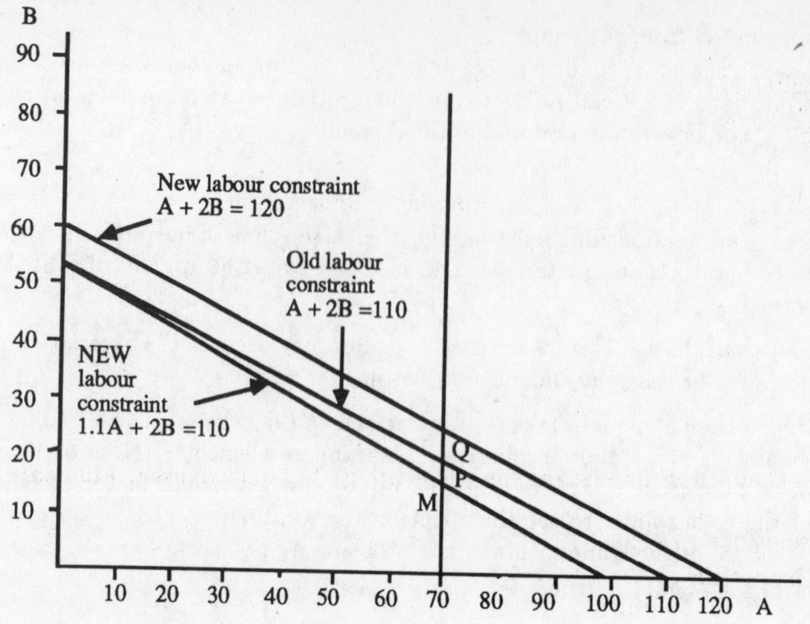

Figure 2

iii. 10% increase in labour hours per unit of A.
This change results in an alteration in the slope of the line. The new constraint is
$1.1A + 2B \leq 110$
This new constraint gives a new optimum at point M. See Figure 2.
The solution is $A = 70$ $\quad B = 16.5$ giving a contribution of <u>£ 329.5</u>

d. If B is required input to A it follows that the output of A cannot exceed that of B.
ie. $A \leq B$ or $A - B \leq 0$
This produces a new constraint line and a new optimum point, N, with solutions of $A = 36.7$ and $B = 36.7$ resulting in a contribution of <u>£ 256.9</u> See Figure 3.
Note: that the solution can only be on the new constraint line, $A - B = 0$

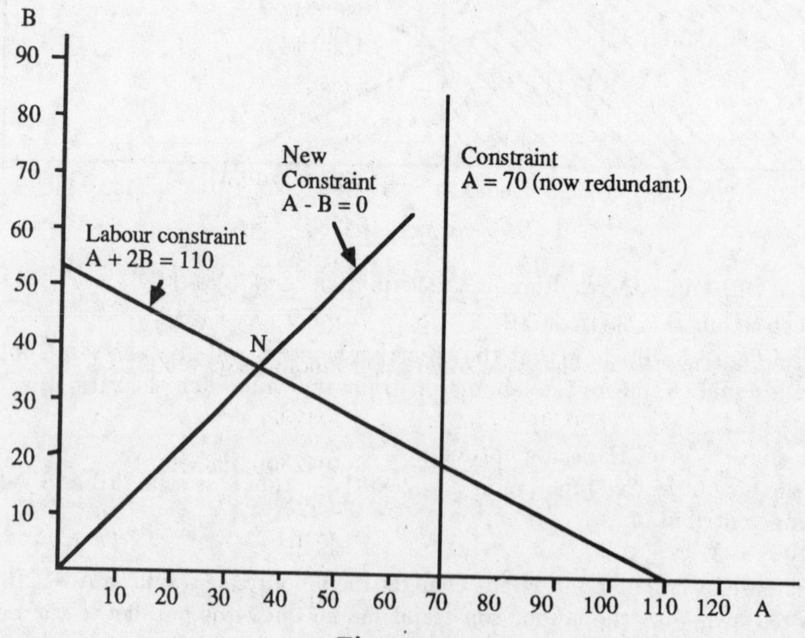

Figure 3

SOLUTION A8

a. (See A5 Chapter 17)

b. 'a' must be £ 30,000
Rank the Stock

Stock	Running Yield	Redemption Yield
B	3	4
C	2	3
D	1	2
E	4	1

D dominates C and B, E has 1st rank in the attribute to be maximised. Eliminate B and C (b and c)
Set A at £ 30,000 ie (a = 30000)

Objective Function

Maximise Z = 0.149d + 0.151e

Constraints

1. Capital Outlay
Deduct 30000
Thus
$d + e \leq 70000$

2. Interest-only running Yield

$$- 30000\,(3.476) + 0.217d - 0.22e \geq 0$$
$$2.17d - 0.22e \geq 104280$$

Graphical Solution
Capital Outlay

$$\begin{aligned}
d + e &= 70{,}000 \\
\text{If } d = 0 \; e &= 70{,}000 \text{ Plot} \\
e = 0 \; d &= 70{,}000 \text{ Plot} \\
2.17d - 0.22\,e &= 104280 \\
e = 0 \; 2.17\,d &= 104280 \\
d &= 48055.299 \text{ Plot} \\
d = 0 - 0.22\,e &= 104280 \\
e &= \frac{-104280}{0.22} \\
&= -\,474000
\end{aligned}$$

This is most awkward to plot ∴ let d be some other amount say + 50000

$$\begin{aligned}
2.17\,(50000) \; - 0.22e &= 104280 \\
- 0.22e &= 104280 - 108500 \\
- 0.22e &= -4220 \\
e &= \frac{4220}{0.22} \\
e &= 19181.81
\end{aligned}$$

This can be plotted allowing the graph to be in a single quadrant.
The solution lies at a corner of the triangle XYZ in Figure 1

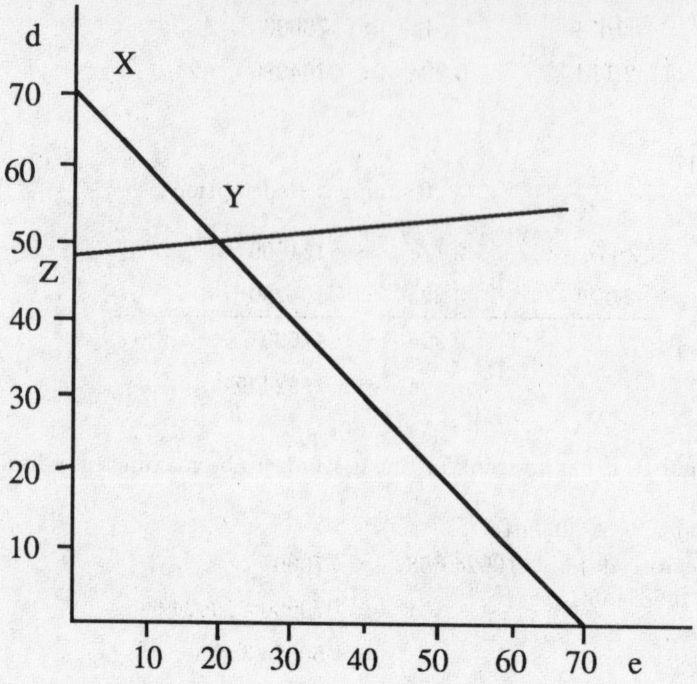

Figure 1

Test for the solution point.

Slope $= \frac{d}{e}$

Capital Outlay $\frac{1}{1} = 1$*

Interest Only Running Yield

$\frac{2.17}{0.22} = +\ 9.86$

Objective function

$\frac{0.149}{0.151} = 0.98$*

*These constraints are actually negative in slope. Usually this does not mater but on this occasion there is a constraint with a positive slope and so 1 should be written as -1 and 0.98 as -0.98 and so the optimum point is found by taking.

$$-1 < -0.98 < 9.86$$

This means that the optimum point is at Y in Figure 1.

$$
\begin{aligned}
1d + \quad 1e &= 70000 \cdots 1 \\
2.17d - \quad 0.22e &= 104280 \cdots 2
\end{aligned}
$$

multiply 1 by 2.17

$$
\begin{aligned}
2.17d + \quad 2.17e &= 151900 \\
2.17d - \quad 0.22e &= 104280 \\
\hline
2.39e &= 47620 \\
e &= 19924.686
\end{aligned}
$$

Substitute into 1

$$
\begin{aligned}
d + \quad 19924.686 &= 70000 \\
d &= 70000 - 19924.686 \\
&= 50075.314
\end{aligned}
$$

Check constraints for violation

$$d + e = 70000$$

$$50075.314 + 19924.686 = 70000$$

The constraint is satisfied

$$2.17d - 0.22e \geq 104280$$

$$108663.43 - 4383.4309 = 104280$$

The constraint is satisfied

Both constraints are actually binding.
Thus given the relaxation of the long term constraint the investment portfolio will be:

Invest £ 30,000 in A
£ 50,075 in D
£ 19,925 in E

The Redemption Yield on this will be

			£
A	30000 (0.135)	=	4050.000
D	50075 (0.149)	=	7461.175
E	19925 (0.151)	=	3008.675
			14519.850

Expressed as a percentage of £ 100,000 this is

$$\frac{14519.85}{100000.00}(100) = 14.52\%$$

CHAPTER 19

SOLUTION A1

INITIAL SIMPLEX TABLEAU

SOLUTION VARIABLE	X	Y	Z	S_1	S_2	S_3	
S_1	5	3	6	1	0	0	3000
S_2	2	5	3	0	1	0	2500
S_3	8	10	3	0	0	1	10000
	20	18	16	0	0	0	0

SOLUTION A2

FIRST ITERATION

	X	Y	Z	S_1	S_2	S_3	
X	1	$\frac{3}{5}$	$\frac{6}{5}$	$\frac{1}{5}$	0	0	600
S_2	0	$3\frac{4}{5}$	$\frac{3}{5}$	$-\frac{1}{5}$	1	0	1300
S_3	0	$5\frac{1}{5}$	$-6\frac{3}{5}$	$-1\frac{3}{5}$	0	1	5200
	0	6	-8	-4	0	0	12000

SOLUTION A3

Produce 276 A, 68B and 127C giving a contribution of £ 48,600

520 units of material unused Shadow prices of:
Machine hours = £ 12.5
Sales restriction = £ 25

SOLUTION A4

a. Model Formulation

Let A units of Aldex)
B units of Betdex)
C unitsof Gamdex)
} be produced each month

(1) Constraints

These are made up from the percentage constituents and the market units

	A	B	C	MAX $\leq$
X	0.20	0.10	0.10	1500
Y	0.10	0.10	0.20	1200
Z	0.05	0.10	0.15	1000

This produces the constraints

$$0.20A + 0.10B + 0.10C \leq 1500$$
$$0.10A + 0.10B + 0.20C \leq 1200$$
$$0.05A + 0.10B + 0.15C \leq 1000$$

The market constraint on C is $C \leq 1200$

The constraints may be used to develop the objective function.

2. Objective Function

		A	B	C
Revenue/unit		5.60	4.80	8.70
Variable Cost				
X	£ 3.50	0.20	0.10	0.10
	Cost £	0.70	0.35	0.35
Y	£ 4.20	0.10	0.10	0.20
	Cost £	0.42	0.42	0.84
Z	£ 6.80	0.05	0.10	0.15
	Cost £	0.34	0.68	1.02
		A	B	C
Cost Summary		1.46	1.45	2.21
Contribution		4.1	3.35	6.49

The complete model is formulated thus

maximise

Z = 4.14A + 3.35B + 6.49C

Subject to:

Y*	0.20A + 0.10B + 0.10C	≤	1500
X	0.10A + 0.10B + 0.20C	≤	1200
W	0.05A + 0.10B + 0.15C	≤	1000
V	1C	≤	1200

b. The dual problem is written as follows
* Let the dual variables be V W X Y
Minimise
1200V + 1000W + 1200X + 1500Y
Subject to:

	0.05W + 0.10X	0.20Y	≥	4.14
	0.10W + 0.10X	0.10Y	≥	3.35
1.00V +	0.15W + 0.20X	0.10Y	≥	6.49

The aim of the dual is to find the value of the scarce resources used in the primal solution.

c. i. This involves the interpretation of the final simplex table. Since there is a unique 1 in each of the A, B and C columns, all three are in the final solution.
Reading along the rows for the columns A, B, C the optimum values are:

A = 4200

B = 5400

C = 1200

ii. The missing value in the final column/final row is the value of Z which is:
4.14 × 4200 + 3.35 × 5400 + 6.49 × 1200 = 17388 + 18090 + 7788 = £ 43266 per month.
The missing value in the final column/third row must be unused Z because there is a unique 1 in the Z column, and a zero in the final row for Z column, meaning it has a zero dual value.
Substitute into

$0.05A + 0.10B + 0.15C \leq 1000$

$0.05 \times 4200 + 0.10 \times 5400 + 0.15 \times 1200 \leq 1000$

$210 + 540 + 180 \leq 1000$

$930 \leq 1000$

The difference is 70

$\therefore$ Z = 70 litres per month.

iii. Solution to dual problem.

V corresponds to the market constraint for C

W corresponds to the Z chemical constraint

X corresponds to the Y chemical constraint

Y corresponds to the X chemical constraint

Thus, reading from the simplex table

$$\left.\begin{array}{lcr} V & = & 0.58 \\ W & = & 0 \\ X & = & 25.6 \\ Y & = & 7.9 \end{array}\right\} \text{These represent}$$

the values of one extra unit fo the scare resource in question.

The value of the dual objective function is

$1200 \times 0.58 + 1200 \times 25.6 + 1500 \times 7.9 = 696 + 30720 + 11850 = \underline{£\ 43266}$

This is the minimum sum per month that Calyce Chemicals would be prepared to lease out the resources available to them.

2. To a certain extent this final part has been touched upon.

7.9 is the value to the company of one extra litre of X chemical.

25.6 is the value of one extra litre of chemical.

1 is the value of one extra litre of Z and this is so because the company has 70 litres unused.

If the marketing constraint on C were relaxed then profit or contribution would rise be £ 0.58 per each extra litre of C sold.

SOLUTION A5

a. Mr Wong has already agreed the purchase price of pineapples and so his problem is really now to use the stock that he will have to take delivery of to best advantage. Thus the cost of the pineapples should be treated as a fixed cost to be deducted from the objective function value once the model has been developed and run. The above comments conform to the general principle of linear programming that the model itself only takes account of variable quantities.

b. Model formulation

(1) Constraints

Large Pineapples – availability

$$Xj + Xc + Xs \leq 80,000$$

Small Pineapples – availability

$$Yj + Yc \leq 120,000$$

Demand for Juice $\leq$ 17000 litres

Juice comes from all pineapples as a by-product in varying degrees.

Xj and Yj pineapples are used for juice and 350 litres of juice come from 1000 kg of pineapples. This gives.

$$\frac{350}{1000}(Xj + Yj)$$

Xc and Yc pineapples are used for chunks but give a by product of 10 litres juice per 1000 kg of fruit. This gives

$$\frac{10}{1000}(Xc + Yc)$$

Xs pineapples are used for slices but give a by-product of 5 litres of juice.
This gives

$$\frac{5}{1000}Xs$$

The constraint is thus

$$\frac{350}{1000}(Xj + Yj) + \frac{10}{1000}(Xc + Yc) + \frac{5}{1000}Xs \leq 17000$$

Demand for chunks $\leq$ 60000 cans
Chunks come from the fruit at the rate of 750$\times$ 1kg cans from 1000 kg of fruit. This gives.

$$\frac{750}{1000}(Xc + Yc) \leq 60,000$$

Demand for slices $\leq$ 50000 cans
Slices come from the fruit at the rate of 500$\times$ 1kg cans from 1000 kg of fruit. This gives

$$\frac{500}{1000}Xs \leq 50000$$

2. The Objective Function.
The total variable costs per product may be taken from the question with the cost of pineapples missed out.

	Juice	Chunks	Slices
Revenue \$	2.21	2.40	2.81
Variable Cost \$	1.21	1.36	1.56
Contribution \$	1.00	1.04	1.25
Unit	litre	can	can

These may be multiplied by the inputs from the constraints above.
JUICE

$1.00 \left\{\frac{350}{100}(Xj + Yj) + \frac{10}{1000}(Xc + Yc) + \frac{5}{1000}Xs\right\}$

CHUNKS

$1.04 \left\{\frac{750}{1000}(Xc + Yc)\right\}$

SLICES

$1.25 \left\{\frac{500}{1000}Xs\right\}$

The model may be summarised (with the brackets cleared) as follows:
Maximise
$Z = 0.35Xj + 0.35Yj + 0.79Xc + 0.79Yc + 0.63Xs$
Subject to:
$1Xj + 1Xc + 1Xs + 1S1 = 80000$
$1Yj + 1Yc + 1S2 = 120000$
$0.35Xj + 0.35Yj + 0.01Xc + 0.01Yc + 005Xs + 1S3 = 17000$
$0.5Xs + 1S5 = 50000$
$S1$, $S2$, $S3$, $S4$ and $S5$ are the slacks associated with the constraints.

c. The solution is:

Yj	=	40,000	small pineapples for juice
Yc	=	80,000	small pineapples for chunks
Xs	=	80,000	large pineapples for slices
$S3$	=	1,800	unsatisfied juice demand
$S5$	=	10,000	unsatisfied slice demand
Xj	=	0	large pineapples for juice
Xc	=	0	large pineapples for chunks
$S1$	=	0	large pineapple slack
$S2$	=	0	small pineapple slack
$S4$	=	0	Unsatisfied chunk demand

The product mix is thus

JUICE:	Yj	0.35 × 40000	=	14,000
	Yc	0.01 × 80000	=	800
	Xs	0.005 × 80000	=	400
		Total Litres	=	15,200
	$S3$	Unsatisfied demand	=	1,800
CHUNKS:	Yc	0.75 × 80000	=	60,000
		There is no unsatisfied demand		
SLICES:	Xs	0.5 × 80000	=	40000
	$S5$	Unsatisfied demand	=	10000

Summary of Product mix
Juice 15200 litres
Chunks 60000 cans
Slices 40000 cans
The contribution is the sum of

15200 × 1.00	=	$15,200
60000 × 1.04	=	$62,400
40000 × 1.25	=	$50,000
		$127,600

The fixed costs are

80, 000 × 0.21	=	$16,800
120000 × 0.16	=	$19,200
		$36,000

The Net Profit is thus

Contribution	$127,600
Fixed Costs	$ 36,000
	$ 91,600

SOLUTION A6

a. Contributions

	Selling Price	-	Material Cost	-	Manufacturing Cost	=	Contribution
X_1	83	-	51	-	11	=	21
X_2	81	-	45	-	11	=	25
X_3	81	-	54	-	11	=	16

LP Formulation:-

Maximise $21X_1 + 25X_2 + 16X_3$

Subject to

$$0.1X_1 + 0.1X_2 + 0.2X_3 \leq 1200$$
$$0.1X_1 + 0.2X_2 + 0.1X_3 \leq 2000$$
$$0.2X_1 + 0.1X_2 + 0.1X_3 \leq 2200$$
$$X_1, X_2, X_3 \geq 0$$

b. Initial Simplex tableau

	X_1	X_2	X_3	X_4	X_5	X_6	SOLUTION
X_4	0.1	0.1	0.2	1	0	0	1200
X_5	0.1	0.2	0.1	0	1	0	2000
X_6	0.2	0.1	0.1	0	0	1	2200
	21	25	16	0	0	0	0

c. This follows the pattern of the chapter ie enter X_2 column (best contribution) constrained by X_5 (smallest value from division $\frac{2000}{0.2}$)

d. Produce 4000 tonnes X_1
8000 tonnes X_2
Contribution £ 284,000
All Nitrate and Phospate used but 600 tonnes of Potash unused
Shadow prices

$$X_3 = £\ 22$$
$$X_4 = £\ 170$$
$$X_5 = £\ 40$$

e. i. 100 tonnes extra Nitrate (X_4)

∴ New Values

$$X_1 = 4000 + (20 \times 1000) = 6{,}000$$
$$X_2 = 8000 + (-10 \times 1000) = 7{,}000$$
$$X_6 = 600 + (-3 \times 100) = 300$$
$$Z = £\ 284{,}000 + (170 \times 1000) = £\ 301{,}000$$

∴ New solution: Produce 6000 tonnes X_1 and 7,000 tonnes X_2 giving £ 301,000 contribution.

ii. Minimum contract of 200 tonnes X_3

This will result in a <u>reduction</u> in contribution because X_3 is not in the optimal solution. As above the simplex multipliers provide the answer:

$$X_1 = 4000 - (3 \times 2000) = 3400$$
$$X_2 = 8000 - (-1 \times 200) = 8200$$
$$X_6 = 600 - (-0.4 \times 200) = 680$$
$$Z = 284{,}000 - (22 \times 200) = 279{,}600$$

∴ New Solution:
Produce 3400 tonnes X_1, 8200 tonnes X_2, 200 tonnes X_3 for a contribution of £ 279,600.

SOLUTION A7

a. Return =- plant yield per acre × £0.80

Cost of Super X = 38p + 2p = 40p

Cost of Base Y = 23p + 2p = 25p

The net contribution per fertiliser combination can be set out in a table:

Fertiliser Combination	Quantity "Super X"	Quantity "Base Y"	Estimated S.P.	Cost per acre	Return per acre
A	0	0	320	0.00	320.00
B	50	50	480	32.50	447.50
C	100	50	544	52.50	491.50
D	150	50	560	72.50	487.50
E	50	100	504	45.00	459.00
F	100	100	600	65.00	535.00
G	150	100	640	85.00	555.00
H	50	200	544	70.00	474.00
I	100	200	624	90.00	534.00
J	150	200	640	110.00	530.00

The objective function is thus:
Maximise 320A + 447.5B + 491.5C + 487.5D + 459D + 535F + 555G + 474H + 534I + 530J

The various costs per acre must not exceed £ 50 so the subsidy constraint is:
32.5B + 52.5C + 72.5D + 45E + 65F + 85G + 70H + 90I + 110J ≤ 50

The various fertiliser proportions must not exceed, so the acreage constraint is:
A + B + C + D + E + F + G + H + I + J ≤ 1

These are the only two constraints so we expect only 2 values in the optimum solution.

b. Interpretation
Optimum Mixture

0.461538 units of B
0.538462 units of F giving a return of £ 494.615387 per acre

(Note: It is assumed that the comma in the question should be a decimal point)

Reduced Cost:
These are the negative Shadow costs ie if variable A is included in the solution contribution would fall by £ 40 per acre.

Dual Prices
Row (2) the Subsidy row. If the Subsidy is raised from £ 50 the marginal increase is £ 2.69 per £ 1 of increase.
Row (3) this dual price relates to the acreage constraint which had a maximum value of 1 ie 100%. Thus £ 360 = 100% and every 1% reduction in coverage would cause a drop of £ 3.6
Ranges in which basis is unchanged.
Objective coefficients.
These show the values by which the variables could increase decrease by before the variable become of the optimum plan.
if A increased by 40 it would become part of the plan.
Row 2 (subsidy constraint).

The values show that the existing £ 50 per acre subsidy could range from £ 50 + 15 = 65 to £ 50 - 17.5 = £ 32.50 before the plan would change.

Row 3 (acreage constraint)

As this can only have a maximum value of 1 the increase shown is meaningless but it shows that this constraint could decrease by .230769 or 23%.

CHAPTER 20

SOLUTION A1.

Maximise	2000L	+	300M	+	650N		
Subject to	5L	+	2M	+	8N	$\leq$	30
	10L	+	3M	+	6N	$\leq$	60
	15L	+	1M	+	4N	$\leq$	20
	L,		M,		N	$\leq$	0

SOLUTION A2

Maximise	55R	+	40S		
Subject to	6R	+	9S	$\leq$	200
	10R	+	7S	$\leq$	250
	3R			$\geq$	100
	(or -3R			$\leq$	-100)
			3S	$\leq$	50
			S	$\leq$	0

SOLUTION A3.

a. The standard formulation is maximise $80x_1 + 70 \times_2 +95 \times_3 +90\times_4$ subject to

(Production time constraint)	$5x_1 +$	$5x_2 +$	$4x_3 +$	$4x_4$	$\leq$	450
(Finishing time constraint)	$x_1 +$	$x_2 +$	$x_3 +$	x_4	$\leq$	120
(Packaging time constraint)	$2x_1 +$	$2.5x_2 +$	$3.5x_3 +$	$3.5x_4$	$\leq$	280
	$0.5x_1 +$	$0.5x_2 +$	$0.5x_3 +$	$0.5x_4$	$\leq$	80
Demand Constraints	x_1				$\leq$	30
		x_2			$\leq$	40
			x_3		$\leq$	20
				x_4	$\leq$	25

where x_1, x_2, x_3, x_4 represent number of cases of the products in '000's.

b. The dual of the above maximising problem is a *MINIMISING* problem with:

4 constraints ie. the number of variables in the original objective function.

8 variables in the new objective function ie. the number of constraints in the original problem.

The dual variables are defined as y_5 to y_{12} and the dual problem is:

Subject to:

Minimise

$450y_5 + 120y_6 + 280y_7 + 80y_8 + 30y_9 + 40y_{10} + 20y_{11} + 25y_{12}$

Subject to:

$$5y_5 + y_6 + 2y_7 + 0.5y_8 + y_9 \geq 80$$
$$5y_5 + y_6 + 2.5y_7 + 0.5y_8 + y_{10} \geq 70$$
$$4y_5 + y_6 + 3.5y_7 + 0.5y_8 + y_{11} \geq 95$$
$$4y_5 + y_6 + 3.5y_7 + 0.5y_8 + y_{12} \geq 90$$

The above minimising problem represents the LP formulation for minimising the cost of manufacture subject to achieving a given level of contribution per product.

c. Interpretation of final tableau of the primal problem (i.e. maximising). To achieve maximum contribution produce

30,000 cases of talcum power (x_1)

24,000 cases of shaving foam (x_2)

20,000 cases of hair spray (x_3)

25,000 cases of deodorant (x_4)

This produces a total contribution of £8230

Only four of the constraints are binding.

		Shadow prices
ie. Production time	(x_5)	14
Demand for talcum cases	(x_9)	10
Demand for Hairspray cases	(x_{11})	39
Demand for Deodorant cases	(x_{12})	34

This means that if the amounts of these constraints could be increased by 1 unit the contribution would be increased by the amount of the shadow price.

SOLUTION A4.

a. Model Formulation

The aim is to minimise total operator cost.

Let a operators work on scheme A
Let b operators work on scheme B
Let c operators work on scheme C

Constraints

A convenient way to handle the constraints is to think in proportions of the time spent on the various schemes. This is shown in the table below:

	A	B	C	Requirement
DAY	$\frac{1}{2}$	$\frac{1}{2}$	1	50
AFTERNOON	$\frac{1}{4}$	$\frac{1}{2}$	-	24
NIGHT	$\frac{1}{4}$	-	-	10

This table may be developed into a set of constraints thus:

D: $\frac{1}{2}a + \frac{1}{2}b + 1C \geq 50$

A: $\frac{1}{4}a + \frac{1}{2}b \geq 24$

N: $\frac{1}{4}a \geq 10$

The objective function

Rates of Pay

			£
Day	2×1	=	2
Afternoon	$2 \times 1\frac{1}{2}$	+	3
Night	2×2	=	4

The number of men appear on the left hand side of the constraints

D: $2(\frac{1}{2}a + \frac{1}{2}b + 1C)$

A: $3(\frac{1}{4}a + \frac{1}{2}b)$

N: $4(\frac{1}{4}a)$

Clear the brackets to give

D	a	+	b	+	2c
A	$\frac{3}{4}$a	+	$\frac{3}{2}$b		
N	1a				
TOTAL	$\frac{11}{4}$a	+	$\frac{5}{2}$b	+	2c

The model is thus

Minimise $Z = \frac{11}{4}a + \frac{5}{2}b + 2C$

Subject to:

$$\left.\begin{array}{lll} \frac{1}{2}a + \frac{1}{2}b + 1c & \geq & 50 \quad z \\ \frac{1}{4}a + \frac{1}{2}b & \geq & 24 \quad y \\ \frac{1}{4}a & \geq & 10 \quad x \end{array}\right\} \text{dual variables}$$

b. The dual of this problem is maximise 10x + 24y + 50z subject to:

$$\begin{array}{rcll} \frac{1}{4}x + \frac{1}{4}y + \frac{1}{2}z & \leq & \frac{11}{4} & (1) \\ \frac{1}{2}y + \frac{1}{2}z & \leq & \frac{5}{2} & (2) \\ 1\,z & \leq & 2 & (3) \end{array}$$

This requires the simplex method and the initial Tableau is as follows:

1		x	y	z	S_1	S_2	S_3	RHS	Ratio
R_1	S_1	$\frac{1}{4}$	$\frac{1}{4}$	$\frac{1}{2}$	1	0	0	$\frac{11}{4}$	$5\frac{1}{2}$
R_2	S_2	0	$\frac{1}{2}$	$\frac{1}{2}$	0	1	0	$\frac{5}{2}$	5
R_3	S_3	0	0	1	0	0	1	2	$\frac{2}{1} = 2$*
R_4	z	10	24	50	0	0	0	0	

↑ PIVOT COLUMN

*Lowest ratio gives pivot row, Z to enter, S3 to leave

Following the usual simplex interations the optimum tableau is reached:

4		x	y	z	S_1	S_2	S_3	RHS	RATIO
R_1	x	1	0	0	4	-2	-1	4	
R_2	y	0	1	0	0	2	-1	3	
R_3	z	0	0	1	0	0	1	2	
R_4	z	0	0	0	-40	-28	-16	-212	

*

*Cells are zero therefore the process of operations is complete

$$x = 4 \quad S_1 = 0$$
$$y = 3 \quad S_2 = 0$$
$$z = 2 \quad S_3 = 0$$

All dual constraints are binding meaning that a, b, c have values

a is associated with dual constraint 1, the shadow price of which is 40.

b is associated with dual constraint 2, the shadow price of which is 28

c is associated with dual constraint 3, the shadow price of which is 16.

Thus

a = 40 operators for A

b = 28 operators for B

c = 16 operators for C

Z = £212 per hour

CHAPTER 21

SOLUTION A1

		A	B	C	D	Dummy
		20	30	15	5	10
I	40		15(5)	15(1)		10 (6)
II	20		15(4)		5(3)	
III	20	20(2)				

NB solution is degenerate

∴ Treat DIII B as occupied

SOLUTION A2

D1	→	B	=	4	
D1	→	C	=	1	
D1	→	Dummy	=	0	
D11	→	B	=	3	
D11	→	D	=	3	
D111	→	A	=	1	
D111	→	B	=	2	(zero allocation)

∴ if D1 = 0

B	=	4
D11	=	-1
D	=	4
D111	=	-2
A	=	3
C	=	1
Dummy	=	0

Shadow costs of unused routes

1 + A	=	4
1 + D	=	3
11 + A	=	2
11 + C	=	0
11 + Dummy	=	- 1
111 + C	=	-1
111 + D	=	3
111 + Dummy	=	- 2

Actual - shadow

1 + A	=	2 - 4	=	-4
1 + D	=	6 - 3	=	3
11 + A	=	4 - 2	=	2
11 + C	=	3 - 0	=	3
11 + Dummy	=	0 - (-1)	=	1
111 + C	=	5 - (-1)	=	6
111 + D	=	2 - 3	=	-1
111 + Dummy	=	0 - (-2)	=	2

SOLUTION A3

New allocation

	A	B	C	D	Dummy
I	15		15		10
11		15		5	
111	5	15			

D1	→	A	=	2
D1	→	C	=	1
D1	→	Dummy	=	0
D11	→	B	=	3
D11	→	D	=	3
D111	→	A	=	1
D111	→	B	=	2

∴ If	D1	=	0
	A	=	2
	B	=	3
	C	=	1
	D11	=	0
	D111	=	- 1
	Dummy	=	0
	D	=	3

Unused routes

	ACTUAL	-	SHADOW		
I + B	4	-	3	=	1
1 + D	6	-	3	=	3
II + A	4	-	2	=	2
II + C	3	-	1	=	2
II + DUMMY	0	-	0	=	0
III + C	5	-	0	=	0
III + D	2	-	2	=	0
III + DUMMY	0	-	0	=	0

∴ OPTIMUM

SOLUTION A4

a. Supply and demand do not match so a dummy Mine is necessary. The costs within the table comprise.
Production cost + transportation cost + operating cost
The Initial tableau

	PREPARATION PLANT			OUTPUT
MINE	A	B	C	
1	38	37	50	120
2	53	40	48	150
3	49	49	45	80
4	54	50	37	160
5	42	55	42	140
D	0	0	0	50
Capacity	300	200	200	700

Using the single table approach and making the initial allocations on a least cost basis produces the following table.

PLANT

MINE	A		B		C		TOTAL	SHADOW COST
1	38		37	120	50		120	0
2	53	70	40	80	48		150	3
3	49	40	49		45	40	80	-1
4	54		50		37	160	160	-9
5	42	140	55		42		140	-8
D	0	50	0		0		50	-50
TOTAL		300		200		200	700	
SHADOW COST	50		37		46			

There is a saving of 12 for allocations into 1A so the maximum allocation of 70 is made resulting in the following table.

PLANT

MINE	A		B		C		TOTAL	SHADOW COST
1	38	70	37	50	50		120	0
2	53		40	150	48		150	3
3	49	40	49		45	40	80	11
4	54		50		37	160	160	3
5	42	140	55		42		140	4
D	0	50	0		0		50	-38
TOTAL		300		200		200		
SHADOW COST	38		37		34			

There are no further savings to be made so this represents the optimum allocation. Note that there is spare capacity of 50 tons at A.

b. Reducing Mine 3 costs by $4 will reduce the shadow cost in the final table from 11 to 7 which does not affect the solution.

c. For mine 5, Plant A has minimum cost AND spare capacity so the output should go to A.

SOLUTION A5.

a. The total requirements of the shop are

$$100 + 200 + 450 + 150 = 900 \text{ dresses}$$

but the total availability is only

$$150 + 450 + 250 = 850 \text{ dresses.}$$

Accordingly a DUMMY manufacturer capable of providing 50 dresses must be included so that the table balances. The DUMMY will be given zero profit per dress.
In this example the initial allocation is made to give maximum profit and this results in the following table.

Manufacturer \ Sizez	I	II	III	IV	Quantity Available
A	100 (3) 2.5	4	5	50 (4) 2	150
B	3	3.5	450 (1) 5.5	1.5	450
C	2	200 (2) 4.5	4.5	50 (3) 2.5	250
Dummy	0	0	0	50 (5) 0	50
Quantity required by shop	100	200	450	150	900 / 900

Table 1

Notes:

a. The bottom right hand figure in each square represents the actual profits as given in the question.

b. The number in the middle of each square represents the allocation of dress sizes to manufacturers and the small ringed number represents the sequence of allocation eg. Cell B/III shows 450 (1) ie an allocation of 450 dresses made first because it has the highest profit per dress, £5.50.

c. It will be seen that six allocations have been made. It will be recalled that a degenerate solution exists if the number of allocations is less than (no of columns + no of rows - 1). A DEGENERATE situations exists in this example because there should be 7 allocations ie (4 + 4 - 1) but only 6 have been made. Accordingly a zero allocation must be made and so that the shadow profits can be calculated, Cell A/III will be deemed to be occupied with a zero allocation.

d. As stated, the zero allocation must be made so that the shadow profits can be calculated. Shadow profits can be calculated when there is a linkage in the shadow profit calculations. It will be seen from Table 1 that there is no overlapping allocation with Cell B/III from the A row. Accordingly the zero allocation is made in Cell A/III so Cell B/III can be evaluated. If, for example, the zero allocation had been made in Cell A/II, Cell B/III could not have been evaluated because neither B nor III was linked.

The next step is to test the initial allocation for optimality by calculating the shadow profits and comparing these with actual profits to see whether any improvement to the initial allocation can be made.

Shadow Profit Calculation.

OCCUPIED CELLS

Cell A/1	=	£2.5 profit	
Cell A/111	=	£5 profit	(ie the zero allocation cell)
Cell A/1V	=	£2 profit	
Cell B/111	=	£5.5 profit	
Cell C/11	=	£4.5 profit	
Cell C/1V	=	£2.5 profit	
Cell DUMMY/1V	=	0	

Setting a = 0 the following values can be calculated:

A = 0   B = 0.5   C = 0.5   Dummy = -2

1 = 2.5   11 = 4   111 = 5   IV = 2

These values are used to calculate the shadow profits of the unused routes, ie

Cell	A/11	=	£4
	B/1	=	£3
	B/11	=	£4.5
	C/1	=	£3
	C/111	=	£3.3
	Dummy/1	=	£0.5
	Dummy/11	=	£2
	Dummy/111	=	£3

These shadow profits are compared with the actual profits resulting in the following table.

Notes on Table 2.

a. The bottom right hand figure in each square represents actual profit.

b. The top left hand figure in each square represents the shadow profit as calculated.

c. The top right hand figures in each square are the differences between actual and shadow profits.

Manufacturer \ Sizes	I	II	III	IV	Quantity Available
A	100 [2.5]	[4.0] [0] [4]	[5]	50 [2]	150
B	[3.0] [0] [3]	[4.5] [-1.0] [3.5]	450 [5.5]	[2.5] [-1.0] [1.5]	450
C	[3.0] [-1.0] [2]	200 [4.5]	[5.5] [-1] [4.5]	50 [2.5]	250
Dummy	[0.5] [-0.5] [0]	[2] [-2.0] [0]	[3.0] [-3.0] [0]	50 [0]	50
Quantity required by shop	100	200	450	150	900 / 900

Table 2

d. A study of the profit differences shows that the initial allocation is optimum.

The allocations which yield maximum profit are

			£
Manufacture A	100 Size 1 Dresses Profit	=	250
	50 Size IV Dresses Profit	=	100
Manufacture B	450 Size III Dresses Profit	=	2475
Manufacture C	200 Size II Dresses Profit	=	900
	50 Size IV Dresses Profit	=	125
	Total Profit		£3850

a. No improvement to this profit is possible because of the Actual/Shadow profit comparisons given in Table 2.
However, where there is a zero difference between actual and shadow profit, this indicates that an alternative solution exists giving the same profits.
For example, some dresses could be ordered from Manufacturer A in Sizes 11 and 111 and from Manufacturer B in Size 1.

SOLUTION A6.

a. Addition of demand and supply figures reveal that there is a surplus of 60 people, thus a dummy column of zero cost is created.
The first allocation is shown below.

	1_8	2_2	3_2	4_1	5_1	Du_{-2}	Total
A_o	x - (2) 6 8	70 -x 2	50 2	(5) 6 1	(2) 3 1	(2) 0 (-2)	120
B_2	(4) 14 10	(5) 9 4	(0) 4 4	(2) 5 3	63 3	37 0	100
C_2	45 - x 10	4 + x 4	(7) 11	82 3	(1) 4 3	23 0	154
Total	45	74	50	82	63	60	374

This is based on least cost allocation. The maximum savings or cost reduction occur in cell (A → 1). The minimum value for x is 45 and the new allocation is shown below.

	1_6	2_2	3_2	4_1	5_1	Du_{-2}	Total
A_o	45 6	25 + x 2	50 - x 2	(5) 6 1	(2) 3 1	(2) 0 (-2)	120
B_2	(6) 14 8	(5) 9 4	x (0) 4 4	(2) 5 3	63 3	37 - x 0	100
C_2	(2) 10 8	49 - x 4	(7) 11 4	82 3	(1) 4 3	23 + x 0	154
Total	45	74	50	82	63	60	374

There are no more cost savings, but since there is a zero saving in cell B 3 an alternative minimum cost solution is available.

Using the second table the actual number of men allocated and the transport costs can be calculated.

Town	Plant	Men	Miles	Men/Miles
A	1	45	6	270
A	2	25	2	50
A	3	50	2	100
B	5	63	3	189
B	Du	37	0	0
C	2	49	4	196
C	3	82	3	246
C	Du	23	0	0
				1051

Return journey 105 1 × 2 = 2102

Cost = 2102 × 0.12 = £252.24 per day.

a. This requires a transportation model with the 60 surplus deducted from each town.

	1_1	2_2	3_2	4_{-6}	5_1	Total
A_o	(5) 6 1	74 - x 2	26 + x 2	(12) 6 (-6)	(2) 3 1	100
B_2	(11) 14 3	(5) 9 4	17 4	9 5 (-4)	63 3	80
C_9	45 10	x (-7) 4 11	7 - x 11	82 3	(-6) 4 10	134
Total	45	74	50	82	63	314

The initial allocation is based on least cost cells. The maximum savings is in the cell (c - 2) and the value of x is 7,. The new allocation is shown below.

	1_8	2_2	3_2	4_1	5_1	Total
A_o	x (−2) 6 8	67 - x 2	33 2	(5) 6 1	(2) 3 1	100
B_2	(4) 14 10	(5) 9 4	17 4	(2) 5 3	63 3	80
C_2	45 - x 10	7 + x 4	(7) 11 4	82 3	(1) 4 3	134
Total	45	74	50	82	63	314

The maximum savings is in cell (A - 1). The value of x is 45. The new allocation is below.

	1_6	2_2	3_2	4_1	5_1	Total
A_o	45 6	22 2	33 2	(5) 6 1	(2) 3 1	100
B_2	(6) 14 8	(5) 9 4	17 4	(2) 5 3	63 3	80
C_2	(2) 10 8	52 4	(7) 11 4	82 3	(1) 4 3	134
Total	45	74	50	82	63	314

There are no more savings to be made and so the optimum solution has been located. The number of men allocated and cost are now calculated.

Town	Plant	Men	Miles	Men/Miles
A	1	45	6	270
A	2	22	2	44
A	3	33	2	66
B	3	17	4	68
B	5	63	3	189
C	2	52	4	208
C	4	82	3	246
				1091

Return journey 1091 × 2 = 2182
Cost = 2182 × 0.12 = £261.84 per day.
The difference in cost is
£261.84 - £252.24
= £9.60 per day

CHAPTER 22

SOLUTION A1

Dummy fitter inserted to Square matrix

	A	B	C	D	DUMMY
1	6	12	20	12	0
2	22	18	15	20	0
3	12	16	18	15	0
4	16	8	12	20	0
5	18	14	10	17	0

Reduce columns by smallest element and cover by lines

~~0~~	~~4~~	~~10~~	~~0~~	~~0~~
16	10	5	8	0
6	8	8	3	0
~~10~~	~~0~~	~~2~~	~~8~~	~~0~~
~~12~~	~~6~~	~~0~~	~~5~~	~~0~~

4 lines so not optimum, smalles element 3

∴ reduce uncovered elements by 3 and increase elements crossed by 2 lines by 3

~~0~~	~~4~~	~~10~~	~~0~~	~~3~~
~~13~~	~~7~~	~~2~~	~~5~~	~~0~~
~~3~~	~~5~~	~~5~~	~~0~~	~~0~~
~~10~~	~~0~~	~~2~~	~~8~~	~~3~~
~~12~~	~~6~~	~~0~~	~~5~~	~~3~~

5 lines so optimum.

Assignments

B to 4

C to 5

A to 1

Dummy to 2

D to 3

Job 2 not done

SOLUTION A2

Deducting each value from 22, the largest value gives.

16	10	2	10
0	4	7	2
10	6	4	7
6	14	10	2

Step 1

14	8	0	8
0	4	7	2
6	2	0	3
4	12	8	0

Step 2

14	6	0	8
0	2	7	2
6	0	0	3
4	10	8	0

At least 4 lines are required, so this is optimum.

Assignment

	Profit
C to Customer 1	20
A to Customer 2	22
B to Customer 3	16
D to Customer 4	20
	£78

SOLUTION A3

a. 1. Make the matrix square ie 6 × 6, and deduct the smallest value from each column from each element in the column.

3	2	1	6	1	0
7	10	0	M	0	0
8	4	5	2	1	0
0	4	0	0	M	0
11	12	4	7	3	0
4	0	3	4	5	0

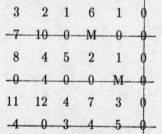

The M's refer to no bid situation.

2. There are no unique zero's and so an optimum solution has not been located. Find the minimum number of lines which will cover all the zero values. This must equal the number of rows/columns. The number is four.

3. Deduct the smalles element in the table from ALL uncovered values. Add this element to ALL intersections of lines. Leave elements under a single line unchanged. This gives.

2	1	0	5	0	0
7	10	0	M	0	1
7	3	4	1	0	0
0	4	0	0	M	1
10	11	3	6	2	0
4	0	3	4	5	1

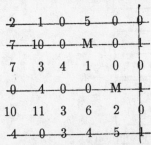

Draw minimum number of lines to cover the zero elements. Five are drawn, six are required. The solution is not unique.

4. Repeat 3.

2	1	0	5	0	1
7	10	0	M	0	2
6	2	3	0	0	0
0	1	0	0	M	2
9	10	2	5	1	0
4	0	3	4	5	2

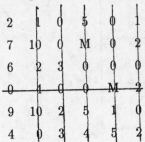

number of lines is now six so the optimum solution has been located.

5. Interpret solution by relating the last table to the original data.

	1	2	3	4	5
A	49	84	63	82	68
B	53	92	62	-	67
C	54	86	67	78	68
D	46	86	62	76	-
E	57	94	66	83	70
F	50	82	65	80	72

Stages 1 and 2 must be allocated to D and F respectively.

D is out for stage 3 and so it is either A or B

D is out for stage 4, so it must be C

C is out for stage 5 and so it must be B or A, according to what is chosen for stage 3.

The choice of alternatives does not affect total cost.

The allocation is summarised as follows:

	1	2	3	4	5	
A			63		68	
B		62			67	
C				78		
D	46					
E						
F		82				TOTAL
1	46	82	63	78	67	336
2	46	82	62	78	68	336

whichever allocation is made, the total cost is the same at <u>$336 million.</u>
A transportation model may be developed as below. The allocation is made using least cost cells.

	1_{46}	2_{82}	3_{62}	4_{76}	5_{67}	Du_0	
A_0	49	84	63	82	68	2 o	2
B_0	53	92	1 62	M	1 67	E 0	2
C_0	54	86	67	78	68	3 0	3
D_0	1 46	86	62	1 76	M	E o	2
E_0	57	92	66	83	70	1 0	1
F_0	50	1 82	65	80	72	1 0	2
	1	1	1	1	1	7	12

The cost of this allocation is

Company	Stage	$
B	3	62
B	5	67
D	1	46
D	4	76
F	2	<u>82</u>
		<u>333</u>

The solution is however degenerate, there being only 9 channels in use rather than the 11 required to test for optimality, two fictitious channels need to be introduced. The table above has been drawn up with the despatch and receipt costs entered. Inspection will reveal that there are no more savings to be made. The solution is thus optimal.

SOLUTION A4

a. To avoid calculations for infeasible loads a plane/load matrix may be drawn up:

Load	1	2	3	4	5
SIZE	10	2	8	5	3
PLANE					
A	Y	Y	Y	Y	Y
B	N	Y	Y	Y	Y
C	N	Y	N	N	Y

Y = feasible N = infeasible

The delivery cost for each type of aircraft for each type of load is built up below in £

Aircraft/ load Cost	Fixed Cost per mile*	Variable Cost per mile	Capacity cost per ton	Total
A1	800	400 × 0.6	30 × 10	1340
A2	800	1100 × 0.6	30 × 2	1520
A3	800	640 × 0.6	30 × 8	1424
A4	800	560 × 0.6	30 × 5	1286
A5	800	900 × 0.6	30 × 3	1430
B1	—	—	—	—
B2	700	1100 × 0.4	35 × 2	1210
B3	700	640 × 0.4	35 × 8	1236
B4	700	560 × 0.4	35 × 5	1099
B5	700	900 × 0.4	35 × 3	1165
C1	—	—	—	—
C2	500	1100 × 1.0	25 × 2	1650
C3	—	—	—	—
C4	—	—	—	—
C5	500	900 × 1.0	25 × 3	1475

*The mileage has been doubled to account for the return journey.

b. The cost matrix is formed from the calculations in part (a) and appears as follows:

Air-	Load				
Craft	1	2	3	4	5
A1	1340	1520	1424	1286	1430
A2	1340	1520	1424	1286	1430
A3	1340	1520	1424	1286	1430
B1	—	1210	1236	1099	1165
B2	—	1210	1236	1099	1165
C	—	1650	—	—	1475

The most appropriate procedure here is the assignment technique. The matrix is not square, and so a dummy column of zero values must be added. For convenience, the side values are missed off.

The assignment model matrix appears as follows: (M is used to denote an infeasible channel).

1340	1520	1424	1286	1430	0
1340	1520	1424	1286	1430	0
1340	1520	1424	1286	1430	0
M	1210	1236	1099	1165	0
M	1210	1236	1099	1165	0
M	1650	M	M	1475	0

Following the normal assignment routine results in the table below.

0	122	0	0	77	0
0	122	0	0	77	0
0	122	0	0	77	0
M	0	0	1	0	1
M	0	0	1	0	1
M	252	M	M	122	0

The number of lines is now six and so an optimum value has been reached. It may not be unique, but the various alternatives will produce an equal cost minimum cost solution.

Removing the dummy column, the matrix becomes.

	1	2	3	4	5
A1	0	122	0	0	77
A2	0	122	0	0	77
A3	0	122	0	0	77
B1	M	0	0	1	0
B2	M	0	0	1	0
C	M	252	M	M	122

ONE OPTIMUM SOLUTION IS

A1	-	LOAD 1	£1340
A2	-	LOAD 3	£1424
A3	-	LOAD 4	£1286
B1	-	LOAD 2	£1210
B2	-	LOAD 5	£ 1165
		TOTAL COST =	£6425

CHAPTER 23

SOLUTION A1

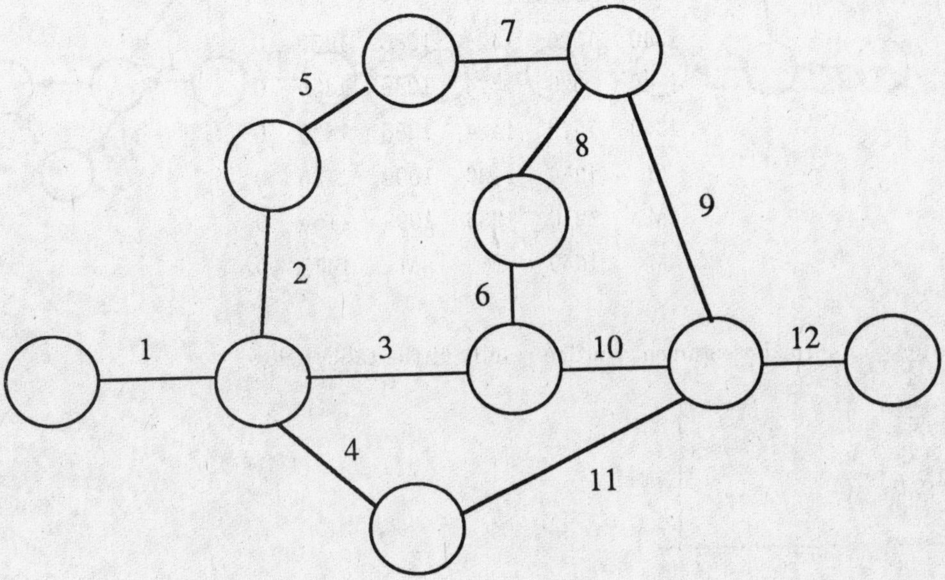

SOLUTION A2

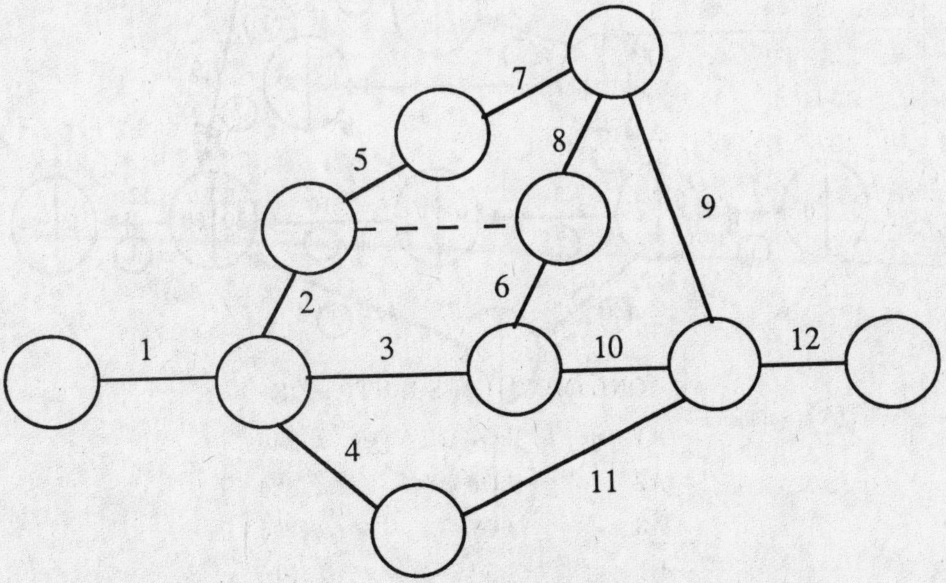

SOLUTION A3 (a)

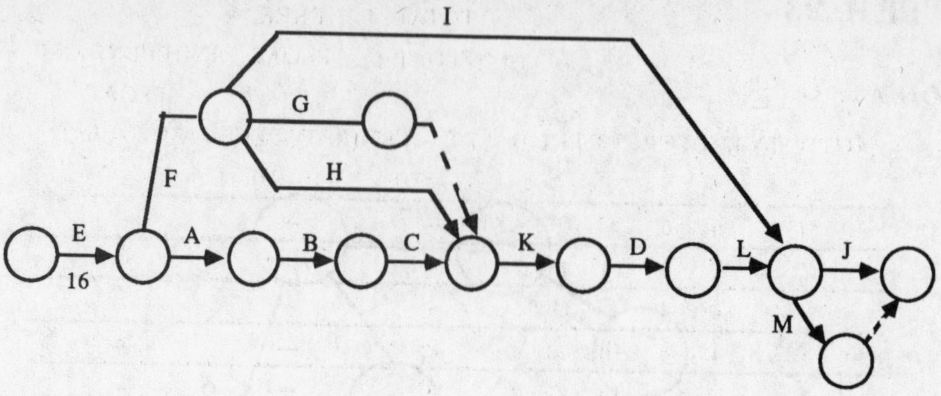

CHAPTER 24

SOLUTION A1

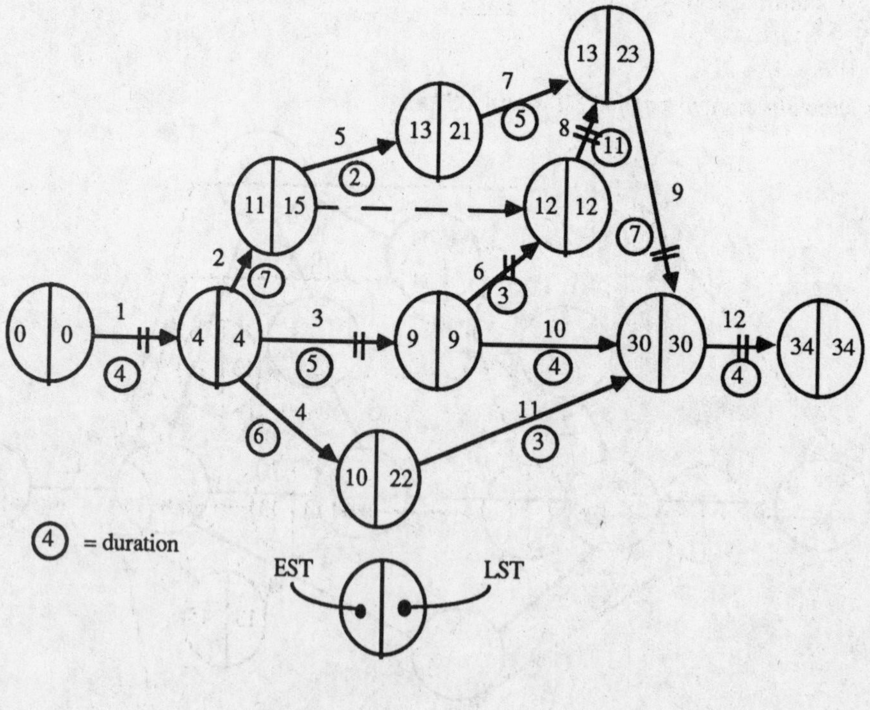

SOLUTION A2

ACTIVITY	EST	LST	EFT	LFT	D	TOTAL FLOAT (LFT − EST − D)	FREE FLOAT (EFT − EST − D)	INDEPENDENT FLOAT (EFT − LST − D)
*1	0	0	4	4	4	—	—	—
2	4	4	11	15	7	4	—	—
*3	4	4	9	9	5	—	—	—
4	4	4	10	22	6	12	—	—
5	11	15	13	21	2	8	—	—
*6	9	9	15	15	3	—	—	—
7	13	21	23	23	5	5	5	—
*8	12	12	23	23	11	—	—	—
* 9	23	23	30	30	7	—	—	—
10	9	9	30	30	4	17	17	17
11	10	22	30	30	3	17	17	5
*12	30	30	34	34	4	—	—	—

SOLUTION A3

S.d of critical path $= \sqrt{1^2 + 2^2 + 1.5^2 + 3^2 + 2.5^2 + 3^2} = \underline{5.61}$

$\therefore\ Z = \frac{40 - 37}{5.61} = 0.534$

From Table 1 the probability is just over $\underline{20\%}$.

SOLUTION A4.

a. Network showing critical path, EST's and LSTs

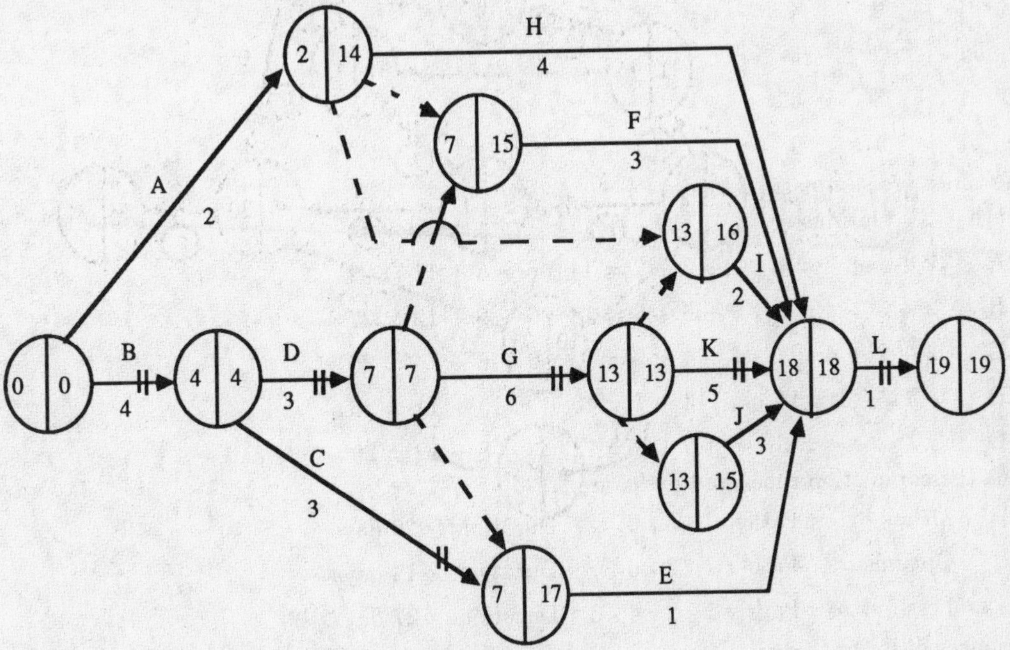

Duration 19 weeks

∴ cannot be completed in 17 weeks.

b. To reduce overall time only activities on the critical path will be effective ie B D G K and L. A reduction of 2 weeks is required which would also make activity J critical.

c. The type of floats are explained in the chapter.
Activity I
Free float = 18 - 13 - 2 = 3 days
Independent floats = 18 - 14 (i.e. Act A via DUMMY) - 2 = 2 days

SOLUTION A5

a. The network is

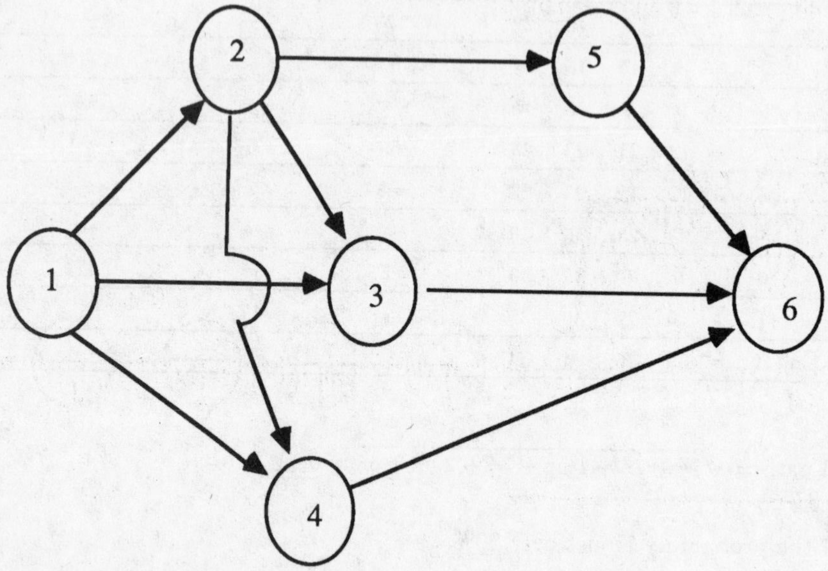

∴ Paths through network are

A 1 - 2 - 3 - 6

B 1 - 2 - 4 - 6

C 1 - 2 - 5 - 6

D 1 - 3 - 6

E 1 - 4 - 6

b. The times are summarised below:

Path	Optimistic	Mean	Pessimistic
A	2 + 1 + 3 = 6	4 + 3 + 7 = 14	6 + 5 + 11 = 22
B	2 + 3 + 4 = 9	4 + 6 + 8 = 18	6 + 9 + 12 = 27
C	2 + 2 + 4 = 8	4 + 4 + 9 = 17	6 + 6 + 14 = 26
D	11 + 3 = 14	13 + 7 = 20	15 + 11 = 26
E	2 + 4 = 6	5 + 8 = 13	8 + 12 = 20

Thus the completion times and paths are:

(i)	Mean	Path	1 - 3 - 6	Duration: 20 days
(ii)	Optimistic	Path	1 - 3 - 6	Duration: 14 days
(iii)	Pessimistic	Path	1 - 2 - 4 - 6	Duration: 27 days

c. Variances of paths

i. path 1 - 3 - 6 = $1^2 + 2^2 = \underline{5}$ and sd = $\sqrt{5} = \underline{2.236}$

ii. path 1 - 2 - 4 - 6 = $1^2 + 1.5^2 + 2^2 = \underline{7.25}$ and sd = $\sqrt{7.25} = \underline{2.693}$

d. path 1 - 3 - 6 has mean 20 days and sd 2.236

$\therefore$ $Z = \left| \frac{17-20}{2.236} \right| = 1.342$

and probability = 0.5 - 0.41 = $\underline{\underline{9\%}}$

path 1 - 2 - 4 - 6

$Z = \left| \frac{17-27}{2.693} \right| = 3.713$

and probability = 0.5 - 0.4998 = $\underline{\underline{0.02\%}}$

SOLUTION A6

a.

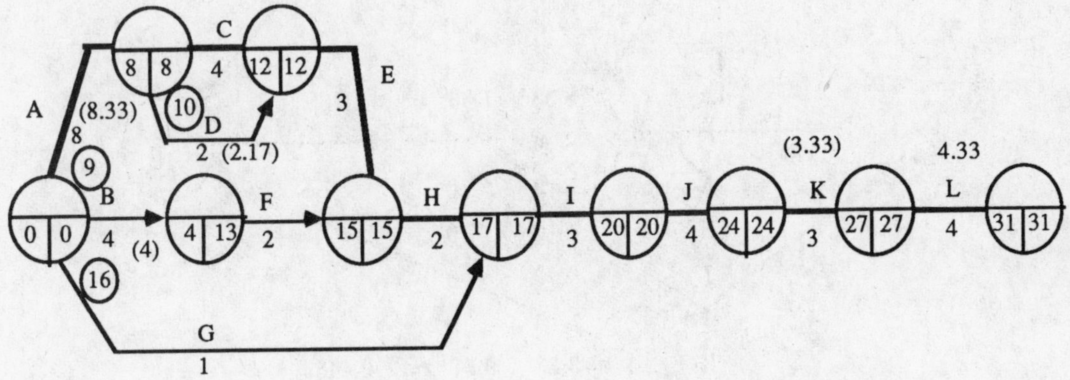

b. Calculation of floats.

The floats may be calculated from latest State Time - Earliest Start Time

Activity	L.S.T.	E.S.T.	FLOAT
B	9	0	9
D	10	8	2
F	13	4	9
G	16	0	16

c. Using the principles of P.E.R.T.

mean durations $= \frac{0 + 4M + P}{6}$

Standard deviation $= \frac{P - 0}{6}$

The necessary calculations are shown below:

Mean durations:

Task $\frac{1}{6}(4 \times M + 0 + P)$

A	$\frac{1}{6}(4 \times 8 + 5 + 13)$	=	8.33
B	$\frac{1}{6}(4 \times 4 + 2 + 6)$	=	4.00
D	$\frac{1}{6}(4 \times 2 + 1 + 4)$	=	2.17
K	$\frac{1}{6}(4 \times 3 + 2 + 6)$	=	3.33
L	$\frac{1}{6}(4 \times 4 + 2 + 8)$	=	4.33

Standard deviations

Task	$\frac{1}{6}$(P - 0)	
A	$\frac{1}{6}(13-5)$	= 1.33
B	$\frac{1}{6}(6-2)$	= 0.67
D	$\frac{1}{6}(4-1)$	= 0.50
K	$\frac{1}{6}(6-2)$	= 0.67
L	$\frac{1}{6}(8-2)$	= 1.00

The mean or expected times are shown in brackets on the project planning diagram above. The critical path is not affected but the duration becomes

Critical TASK	Duration	Variance	
A	8.33	1.33^2 =	1.768
C	4	0	
E	3	0	
H	2	0	
I	3	0	
J	4	0	
K	3.33	0.67^2 =	0.4489
L	4.33	1.00^2 =	1.0000
	32.00		3.2178

The project standard deviation is 1.79

The probability that the project will take more than 35 weeks is calculated below:L

$$Z = \left| \frac{35-32}{1.79} \right| = 1.67 \text{ which is 0.4525 in Table 1.}$$

∴ Probability that duration will exceed 35 weeks is 0.0475 ie 0.5 - 0.4525).

SOLUTION A7

a. The project planning diagram below shows that the task "Run Course" I may begin only after 15 working weeks have elapsed.

b. The duration of the project is 20 weeks. Only after this can the report to the Group Chief Accountant be made.

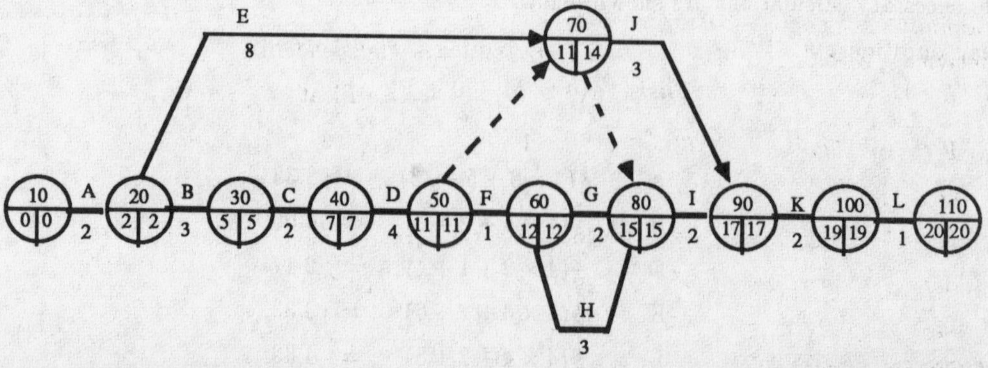

c. This can be answered from the manual.

SOLUTION A8 (Completion of A3, CHAPTER 23).

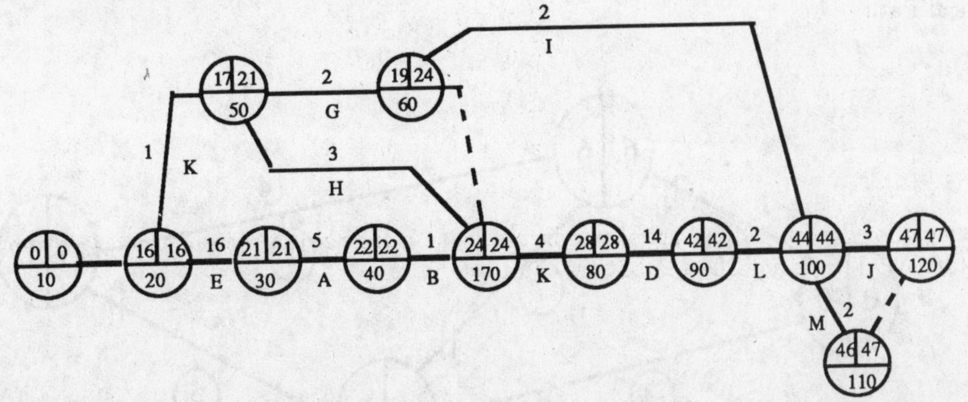

a.

b. By undertaking the forward pass on the arrow diagram in Part (a) it can be seen that the project duration is 47 working weeks.

c. The critical path has been located using the backward pass and is

$$E \rightarrow A \rightarrow B \rightarrow C \rightarrow K \rightarrow D \rightarrow L \rightarrow J$$

A is on the critical path, and if its duration becomes three weeks instead of five then there is a possibility of project time being reduced. There is a float of four weeks on the parallel path, and so the project duration may be reduced by the full two weeks to 45 weeks.

d. "Independent float" is the amount of time an activity can be delayed when all preceding activities are completed as late as possible and all succeeding activities are completed as early as possible.

Independent float = Earliest Head Time - Latest Head Time - Activity Duration

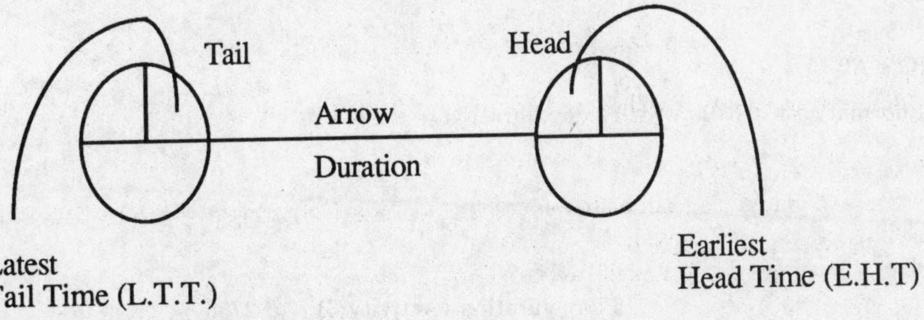

Examination of non-critical activities

Activity	E.H.T.	-	L.T.T.	-	Duration	=	Independent Float
F	17	-	16	-	1	=	0
G	24	-	21	-	2	=	1
H	24	-	21	-	3	=	0
I	44	-	21	-	2	=	21
M	47	-	44	-	2	=	1

*Ignore the dummy here

CHAPTER 25

SOLUTION A1

Critical Path

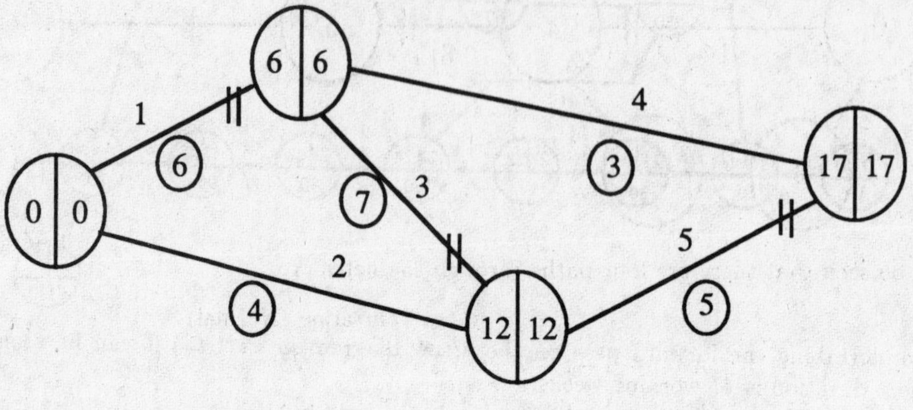

COST SLOPES

ACTIVITY	COST SLOPE
1	£ 60
2	45
3	30
4	50
5	75

SOLUTION A2

Total normal cost £ 3700 with 17 day duration

	COST
16 day duration (Activity 3)	£ 2730
15 day duration (Activity 1)	£ 2790
14 day duration (Activity 1)	£ 2850
13 day duration (Activity 5)	£ 2925
12 day duration (Activity 5)	£ 3000

SOLUTION A3

a. The network is

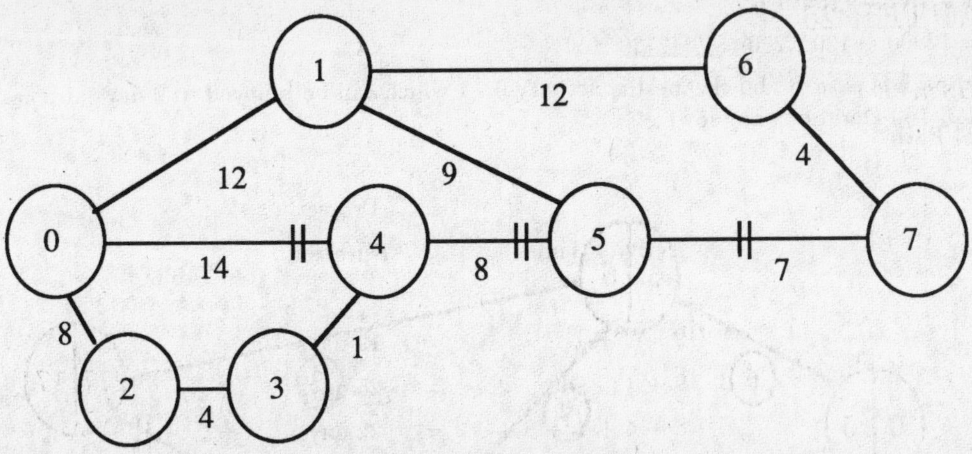

It will be seen that there are four paths through the network

		Duration (Normal)
A	0 – 1 – 5 – 7	28
B	0 – 1 – 6 – 7	28
C	0 – 2 – 3 – 4 – 5 – 7	28
D	0 – 4 – 5 – 7	29

∴ Path D is critical with a 29 day duration.
Cost of project is the sum of <u>all</u> normal costs + 29 × £200.
ie £ 7000 + 29 × 200 = £ 12,800

b. Minimum time for project can be found by crashing all activities on the four paths.

		Crash time	
A	0 – 1 – 5 – 7	9 + 6 + 1	= 16 days
B	0 – 1 – 6 – 7	9 + 10 + 4	= 23 days
C	0 – 2 – 3 – 4 – 5 – 7	6 + 2 + 1 + 8 + 1	= 18 days
D	0 – 4 – 5 – 7	8 + 8 + 1	= 17 days

Thus the minimum time is 23 days on Path B
The minimum cost is found by crashing, activity by activity, based on the cost slopes thus:

Activity	Saving	Cost	Cost slope
0 – 1	3	150	50
0 – 2	2	100	50
0 – 4	6	440	73
2 – 3	2	200	100
1 – 5	3	180	60
1 – 6	2	450	225
5 – 7	6	130	22

The other activities cannot be crashed.
Working from the original 29 day duration at normal times the least cost schedules are as follows:
Reduce 5 – 7 by 6 days (cheapest)

Duration 28 days (path B)

Cost = 12800 + 130 - 200 = <u>£ 12730</u>

Critical path is path B and cheapest is activity 0 - 1 which can be reduced to 9 days at a crash cost of £ 150 Durations are now:

	Activity Times		Project Duration
A	9 + 9 + 1	=	19 days
B	9 + 12 + 4	=	25 days
C	8 + 4 + 1 + 8 + 1	=	22 days
D	14 + 8 + 1	=	23 days

∴ Critical path now B @ 25 days

$$\text{Cost } = £12800 + 150 - 600 = £12,280$$

The only activity on B which can be crashed is 1 – 6 which can be reduced to 10 days and this is crashed next at a cost of £ 450, resulting in the following durations.

	Activity Times		Project Duration
A	9 + 9 + 1	=	19 days
B	9 + 10 + 4	=	23 days
C	8 + 4 + 1 + 8 + 1	=	22 days
D	14 + 8 + 1	=	23 days

Critical path is B and the project cost is

$$£12,280 + 450 - 400 = \underline{£12,330}$$

Thus the cost a minimum duration of 23 days is <u>£ 12,330</u>

c. The minimum cost is at a duration of 25 days ie Path B (0 – 1 – 6 – 7) at a cost of £ 12,280

d. Three possible problems:

i. accuracy of time estimates

ii. accuracy of cost estimates

iii. availability &/or scheduling problems with labour and equipment required.

SOLUTION A4

a. Project Diagram

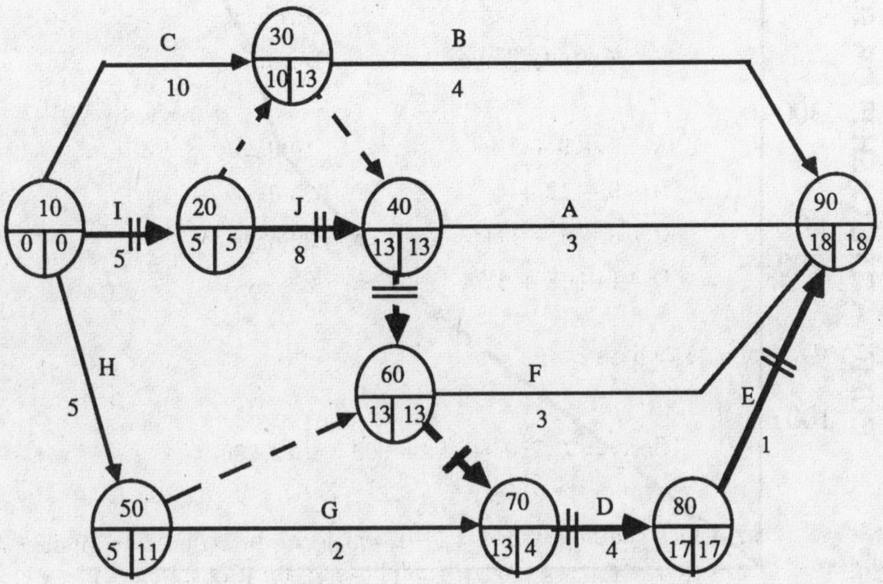

Project Duration 18 weeks

Given that there are no crises involving a delay of more than 8 weeks in project completion, there should be no problem in completing in time for the show.

b. The calculation of weekly and cumulative cash flow is given below:

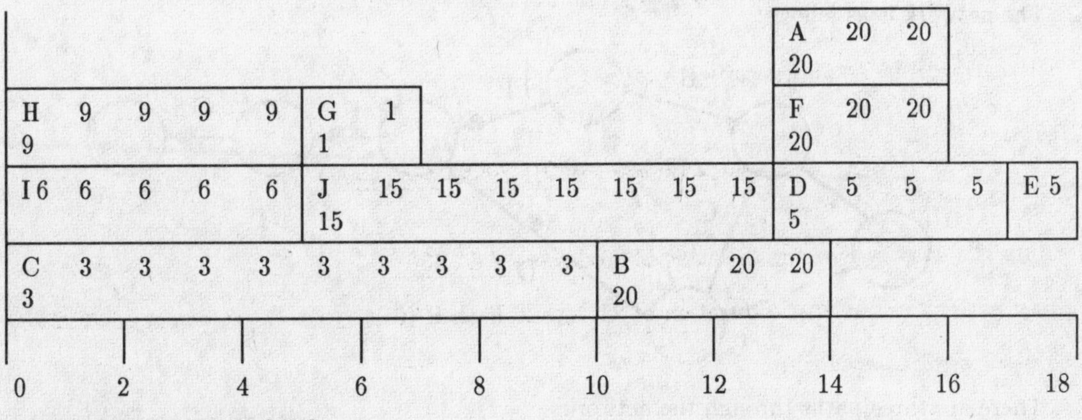

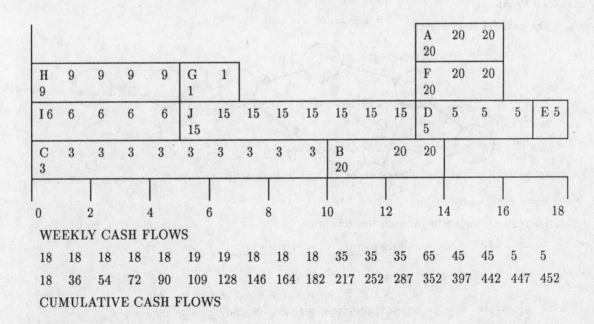

WEEKLY CASH FLOWS

18	18	18	18	18	19	19	18	18	18	35	35	35	65	45	45	5	5
18	36	54	72	90	109	128	146	164	182	217	252	287	352	397	442	447	452

CUMULATIVE CASH FLOWS

The graph of cumulative cash flow (y) against elapsed project time (x) is drawn below.

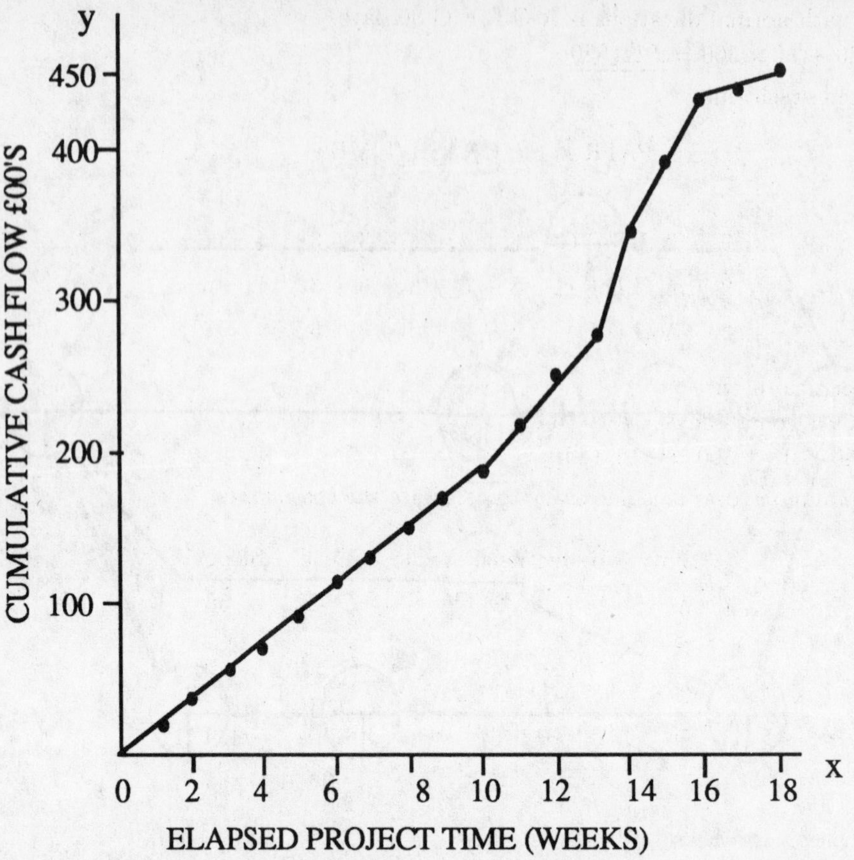

The outflow of cash is very even for the first 10 weeks at around £ 1800/£ 1900 pounds per week. The weekly outflow increase to £ 3500 per week in weeks 11, 12, and 13, then peaks at £ 6500 in week 14. It then tails off to £ 500 per week in weeks 17 and 18.

SOLUTION A5

a. The network is as follows:

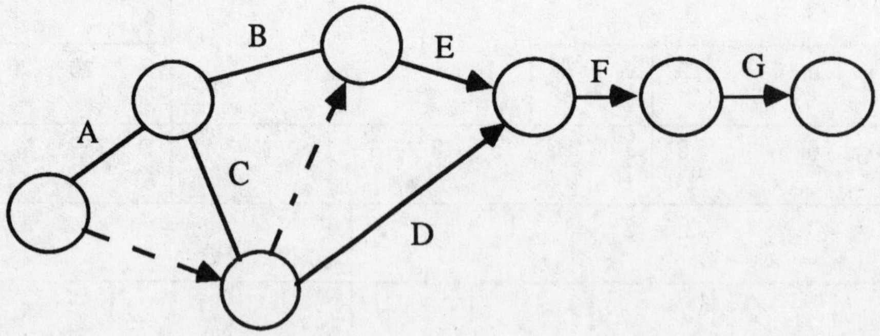

There are three paths through the network:

	PATH	DURATION		
1	A B E F G	5 + 4 + 8 + 6 + 5	=	28
2	A C E F G	5 + 6 + 8 + 6 + 5	=	30
3.	A C D F G	5 + 6 + 7 + 6 + 5	=	29

Critical path with normal durations is A C E F G 30 days.
Cost is £ 2520 + 30 × 300 = £11,520

b. Crash costs and crash time

	PATH	CRASH TIME		
1	A BE F G	3 + 4 + 4 + 3 + 3	=	17
2.	A C E F G	3 + 3 + 4 + 3 + 3	=	16
3.	A C D F G	3 + 3 + 6 + 3 + 3	=	18

Thus 'crash' critical path
A C D F G, duration 18 days
Cost = £ 4740 + 18 × 300 = £10, 140

c. To find the minimum costs it is necessary to calculate the cost slopes

Activity	Reduction Possible	Cost	Slope
A	2	£ 120	£ 60
B	–	–	–
C	3	390	130
D	1	460	460
E	4	660	165
F	3	370	123.3
G	2	220	110

The cost slopes are used to guide the progressive crashing of the network.

ACTIVITY CRASHED	PATH 1	PATH 2	PATH 3	CRITICAL PATH	COST CHANGE	OVERALL COST
ALL NORMAL	28	30	29	2	–	11520
(Crash A cheapest on critical path)						
A	26	28	27	2	120-600	11040
(Crash G)						
G	24	26	25	2	220 – 600	10660
(Crash F)						
F	21	23	22	2	370 – 600	10130
(Crash C)						
C	21	20	19	1	390 – 600	9920
(Crash E)						
E	17	16	19	3	660 – 600	99980
(Crash D)						
D	17	16	18	3	460 – 300	10140

∴ Minimum cost is £ 9920, critical path is Path 1 (A B E F G), duration 21 days.

d. This can be answered from the chapter, and from the answers to other questions.

CHAPTER 26

SOLUTION A1

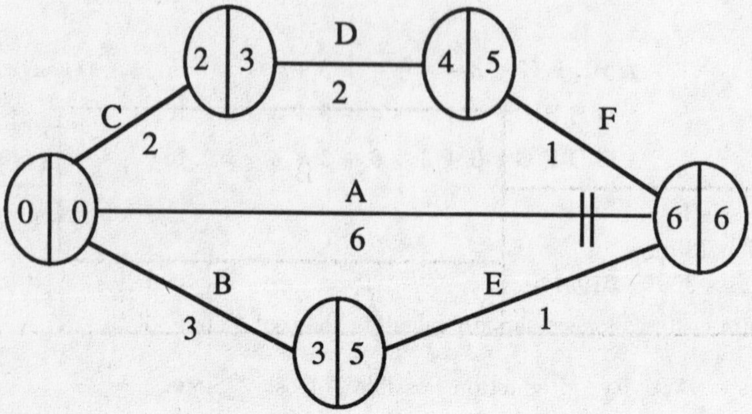

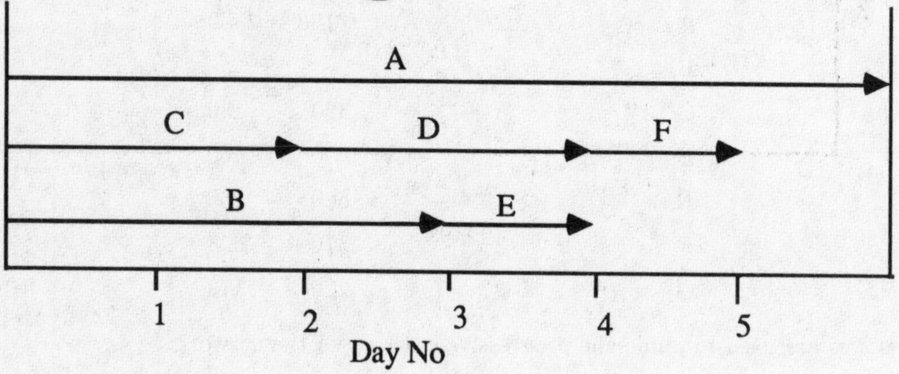

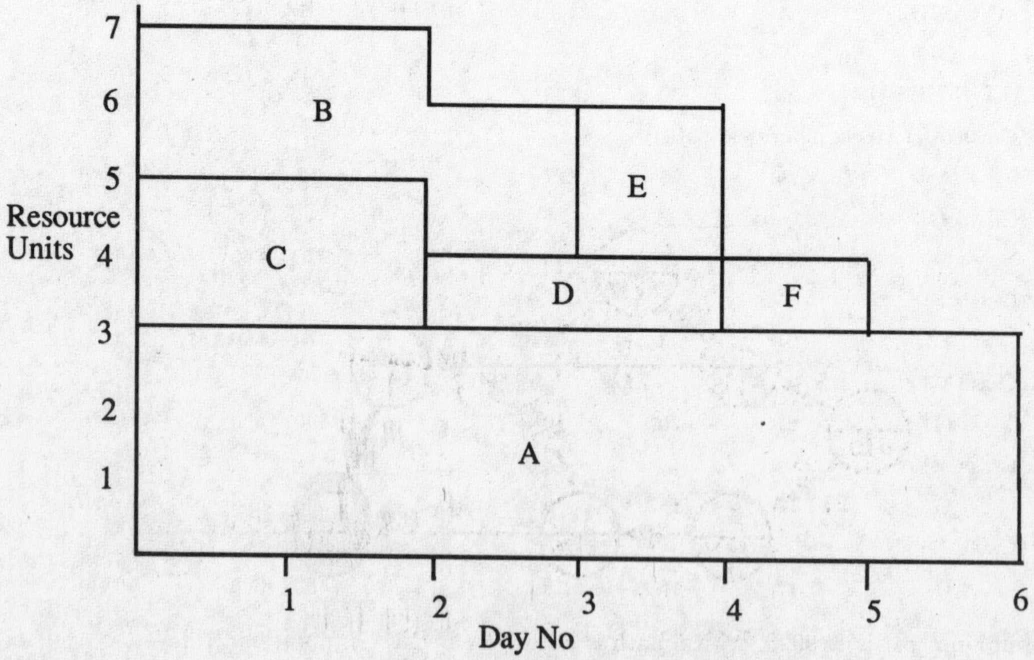

SOLUTION A2

Delay start of B/E until day 2 resulting in

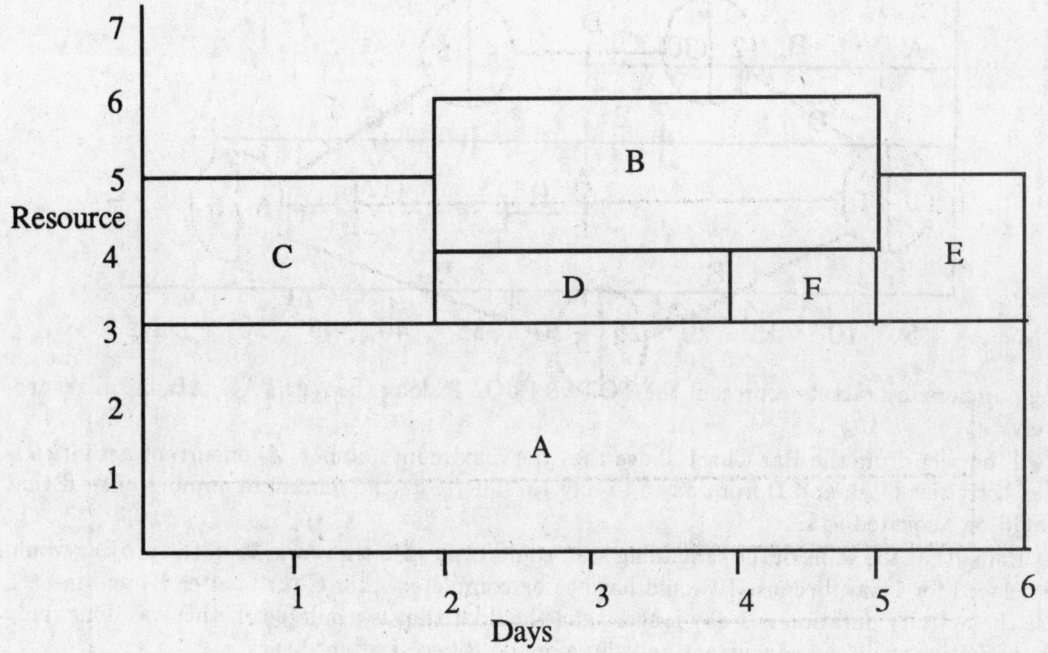

SOLUTION A3

a.

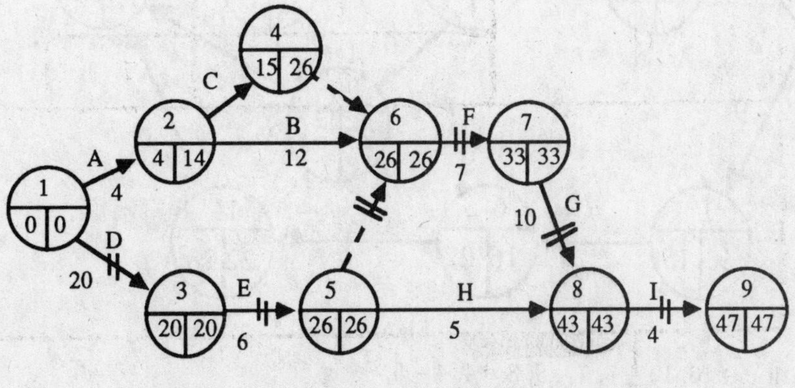

Critical path D, E, F, G, I duration 47 days

b.

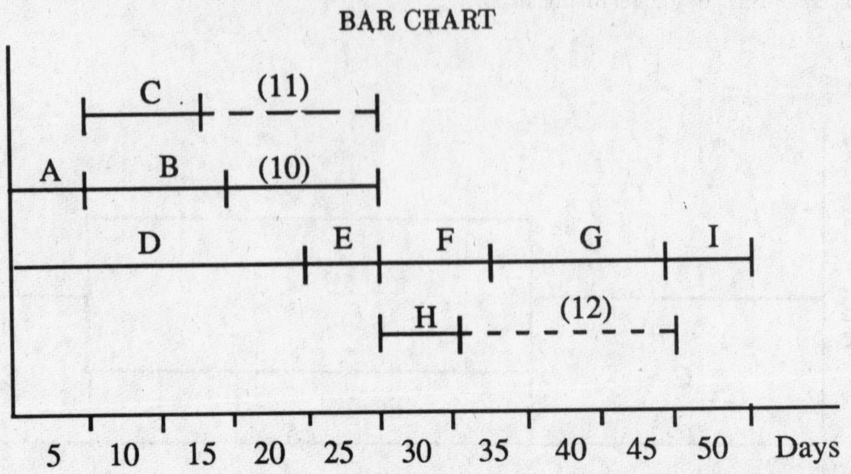

The numbers in brackets represent the TOTAL FLOAT along the paths AC, AB and H respectively.

c. It will be seen from the Bar Chart above that the maximum number of concurrent activities is 3, ie Activities C, B, and D from day 5 to day 15. Therefore the minimum number of staff that should be allocated is 3.

d. Assuming that the skills of the remaining staff could cope with the work, then the project would be delayed for 1 day, because B would have to be completed after C (or C after B) and in each case the activity duration is 1 day longer than the float that is available. If this was done, only two activities would be concurrent and therefore only two staff necessary.

SOLUTION A4

a.

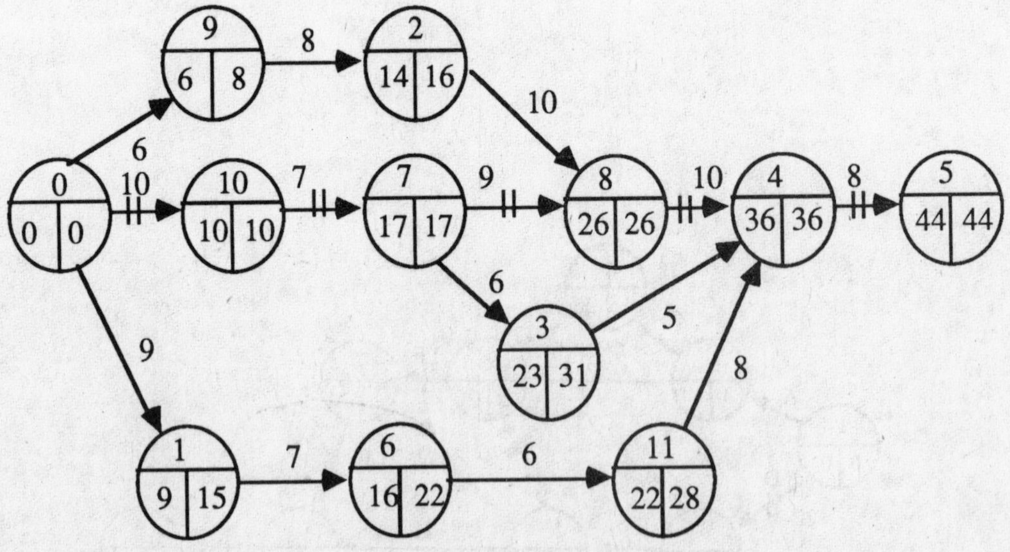

Figure 1

Critical Path 0 – 10, 10 – 7, 7 – 8, 8 – 4, 4 – 5.
Duration 44 days
Normal Cost (ie. total of the table in the question) = £ 8280

b. Number of different paths = 4

c. Minimum time for project ie. all activities crashed.

Activity	Crash time Days	Earliest Start time	Latest Finish time
0 — 9*	3	0	3
0 — 10	5	0	6
10 — 7	4	5	10
7 — 8	2	9	12
9 — 2*	4	3	7
3 — 4	2	12	17
7 — 3	3	9	15
6 — 11*	3	10	13
1 — 6*	4	6	10
8 — 4*	5	12	17
4 — 5*	4	17	21
2 — 8*	5	7	12
0 — 1*	6	0	6
11 — 4*	4	13	17

*Critical activities. Note that the critical path has changed and is now the lower loop in the network shown in part (a)

The minimum duration is the latest finish time for activity 4 – 5 ie. 21 days.

d. Although not stated, this part refers to normal times ie. as shown in the network, because the resources are specified as normal.

The following bar chart plots the various activities at their earliest start dates with their labour requirements.

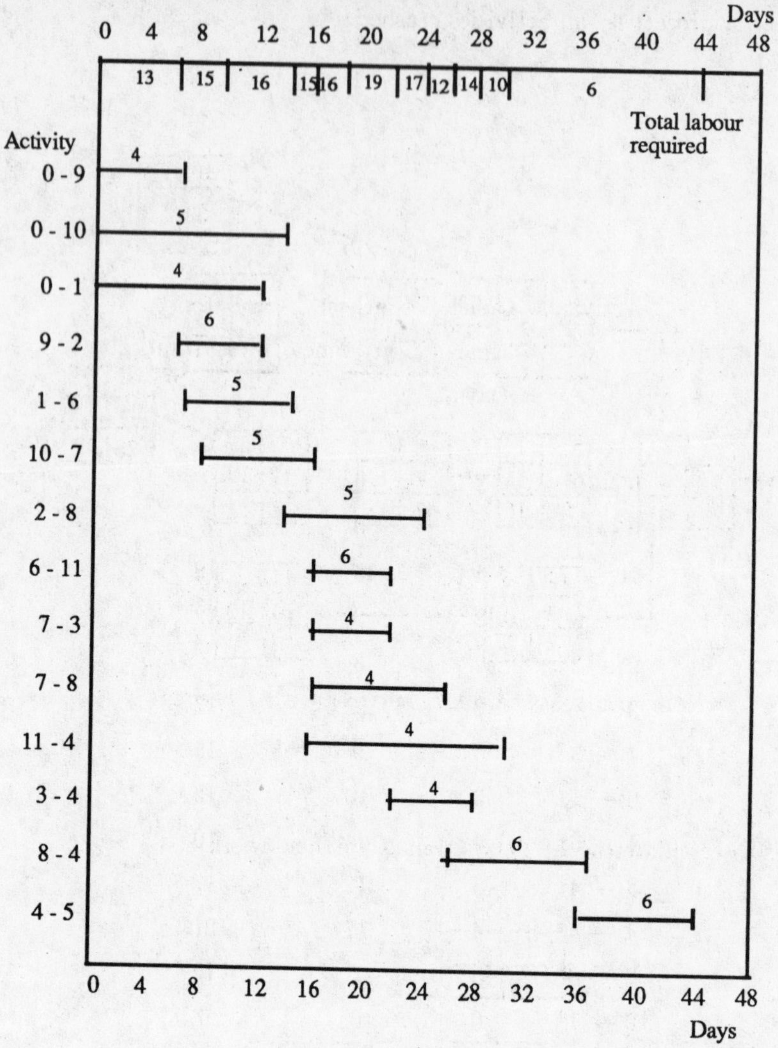

RESOURCE BARCHART. Figure 2

Figure 2 shows that the maximum requirement is 19 men between day nos 17 and 22.

*Labour requirements.

CHAPTER 27

SOLUTIONS A1 & A2

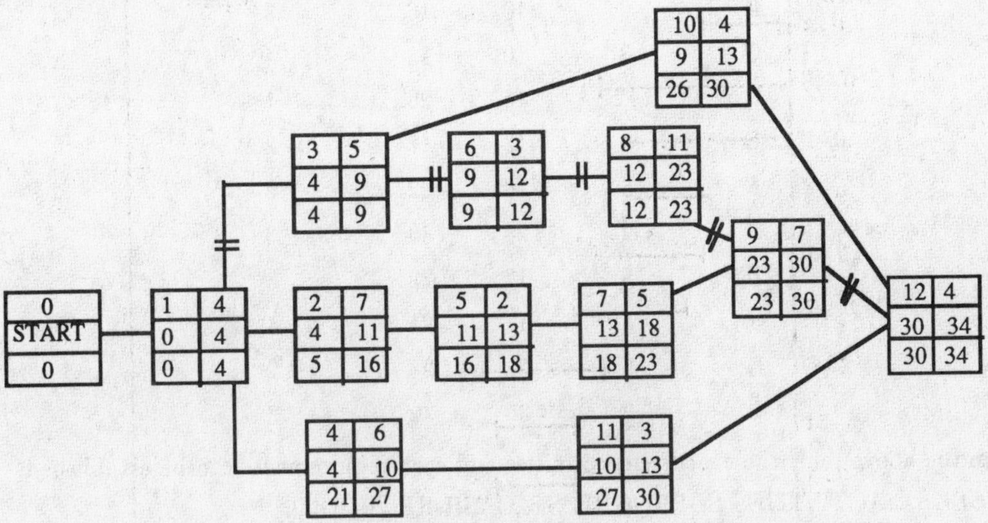

Note: contrast the above network with A1, chapter 24.

SOLUTION A3

The first stage is to calculate the EST/LST values for the nework:

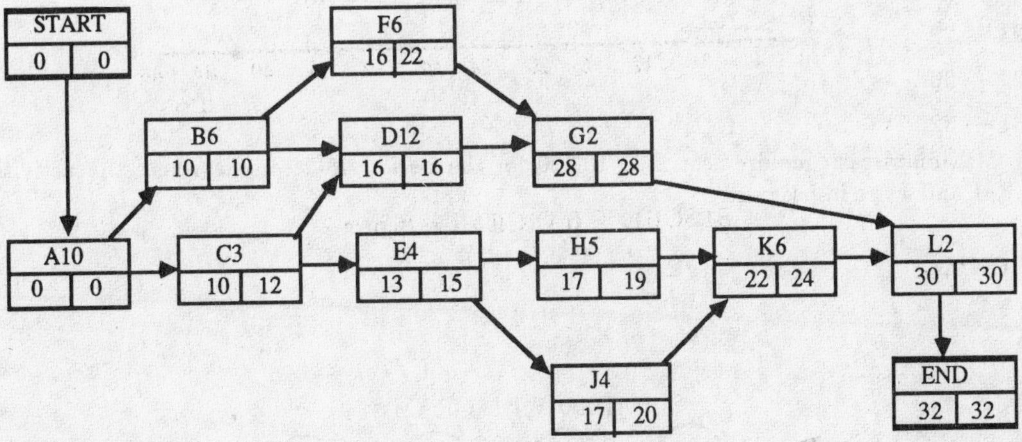

a. i. Completion time = 32 weeks

ii. Critical path A B D G L

iii. 3 weeks

iv. The removal of the link from B to D would alter the critical path to A – C – E – H – K – L, duration 30 weeks.

b. Table of EST's and cash required per week.

Activity	Duration	Start	Finish	Cash per week £ 000
A	10	0	10	3
B	6	10	16	3
C	3	10	13	4
D	12	16	28	1
E	4	13	17	2
F	6	16	22	2
G	2	28	30	3
H	5	17	22	3
J	4	17	21	4
K	6	22	28	2
L	2	30	32	3

From the above table the concurrent activities and cash requirements can be established.

WEEKS	ACTIVITIES IN PROGRESS	CASH REQUIRED		
1 — 10	A			3
11 — 13	B,C	3+4	=	7
14 — 16	B,E	3+2	=	5
17	D,E,F	1+2+2	=	5
18 — 21	D,F,H,J	1+2+3+4	=	10
22	D,F,H	1+2+3	=	6
23 — 28	D,K	1+2	=	3
29 — 30	G			3
31 — 32	L			3

∴ Maximum cash requirement is £ 10,000 for the period 18-21 weeks where the activities D,F,H and J are in progress.

SOLUTION A4

a.

ARROW DIAGRAM

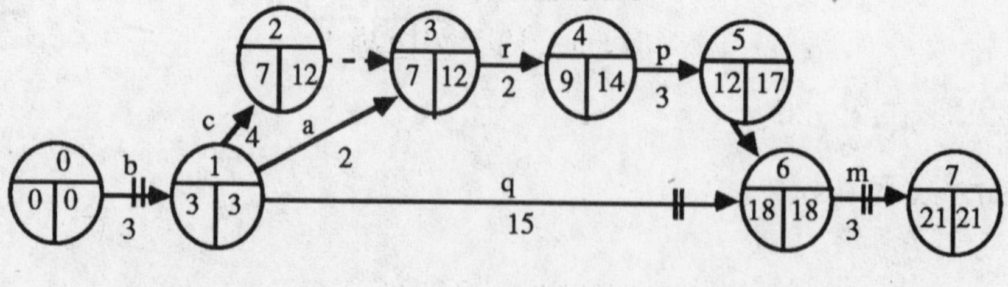

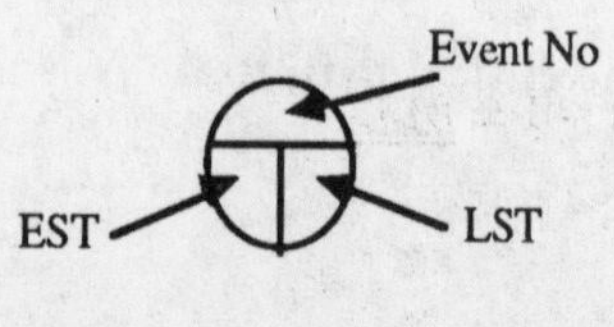

Critical Path b,q m

b.

ACTIVITY-ON-NODE DIAGRAM

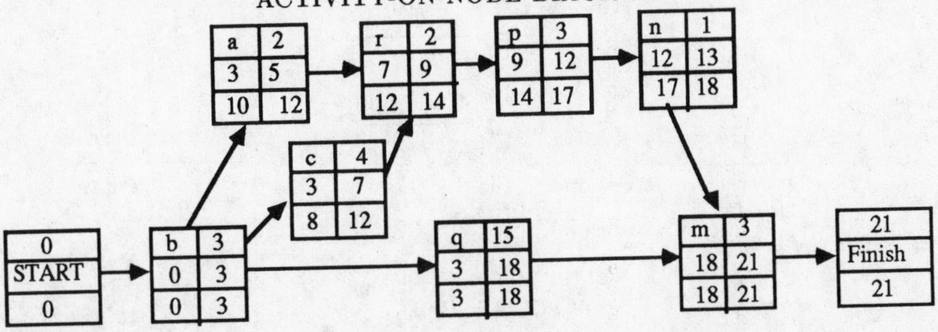

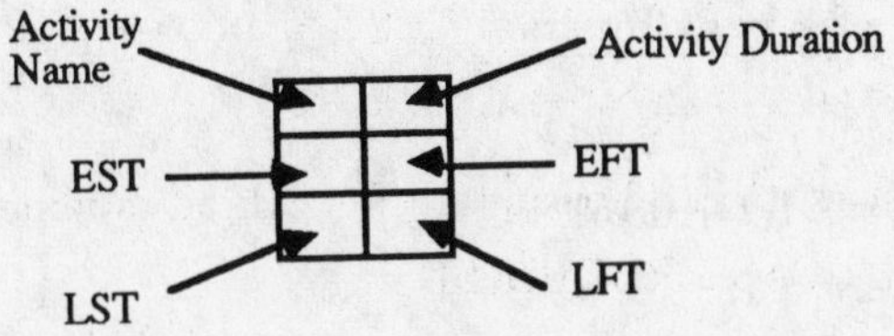

Critical Activities b, q, m

(Note.
The EFT'S and LFT's were not asked for in the question but have been included for completeness).

c. Critical activities are where the EST's and LST's are the same ie b, q and m.

d.

Normal duration = 21 days

Normal Cost = £ (2 × 50) + (3 × 60) + (4 × 70) + (2 × 40) + (3 × 30) + (1 × 75) + (15 × 20) + (3 × 50)

= **£ 1255**

e. To reduce the time of the project, activities on the critical path must be crashed cheapest first and so on ie in the sequence b, q, m.

i. Reduce b by 1 day - extra cost = £ 60

ii. Reduce q by 4 days - extra cost = 4 × £70 = £280

Total additional cost to reduce project time to 16 days is £ 340.
Minimum cost of whole project is

£1255 + 340 = **£1595**

CHAPTER 28

SOLUTION A1

This is a geometric progression with a common ratio of 2

$$\therefore \text{ Value of 12th term} = 4.2^{12-1} = \underline{8192}$$

Sum of first 20 terms

$$\begin{aligned} \text{Sum} &= \frac{a(r^n - 1)}{r - 1} \\ &= \frac{4(2^{20} - 1}{2 - 1} \\ &= \underline{\underline{4,194,300}} \end{aligned}$$

SOLUTION A2

a. Let $P = 1$, $S = 3$ $I = 2$

$$\therefore 2 = Prn$$

$$2 = 1 \times 0.15 \times n$$

$$\therefore n = \frac{2}{0.15} = \underline{13.3 \text{ years}}$$

b.

$$\begin{aligned} 3 &= 1(1 + 0.15)^n \\ 3 &= 1.15^n \\ \therefore n &= \underline{\underline{7.86 \text{ years}}} \end{aligned}$$

SOLUTION A3

a. £ 200 $a_{10\rceil 10\%}$ = 200 × 6.145 = £1229

b. £ 1229 discounted for 5 years @ 10% = £ 1229 × 0.621 = £763.2

c.

$$\begin{aligned} r_0 &= \frac{r - g}{1 + g} = \frac{0.26 - 0.05}{1.05} = \underline{20\%} \\ P &= \frac{A}{1 + g} = \frac{500}{1.05} = 476 \end{aligned}$$

$\therefore$ P = 476× $a_{10\rceil 20\%}$ = 476 × 4.192 = £1995

SOLUTION A4.

a. **Building Soceity Interest**

Amount (after tax) at end of two years.

$$\begin{aligned} &= £5000(1.04)^4 \\ &= 5000 \times 1.170 = \underline{\underline{£5850}} \end{aligned}$$

(Note

Interest rate of 8% p.a., compounded half yearly for 2 years is equivalent to 4% compounded for 4 periods ie 1.170 from table).

TT Bank Investment

Amount (before tax) at end of year 1

$$= £5000(1.05)2 = £5000 \times 1.103 = £5515$$

Amount (after tax) at end of year 1

$$\begin{aligned} &= £5515 - \text{Tax on interest of} £515 \\ &= £5515 - (£515 \times 0.35) = £5335 \end{aligned}$$

Amount (before tax) at end of year 2

$$= £5335(1.05)2 = £5335 \times 1.103 = £5885$$

$$\text{Interest in Year 2} = 5885 - 5335 = £550$$

Amount (after tax) at end of year 2

$$= £5885 - (£550 \times 0.35) = \underline{\underline{£5692}}$$

or £5690 to three figure accuracy.

E. Scrooge Bank Investment
Amount (before tax) at end of Year 1

$$= £5000(1.0225)^4 = £5000 \times 1.093 = £5465$$

Amount (after tax) at end of Year 1

$$= £5465 - (465 \times 0.35) = £5302$$

Amount (before tax) at end of Year 2

$$= £5302.25(1.0225)^4 = 5302.25 \times 1.093 = £5795$$

$$\text{Interest in Year 2} = £5795 - 5302 = £493$$

Amount (after tax) at end of year 2.

$$= £5795 - (493 \times 0.35) = £5622$$

∴ On basis of above analysis the Building Society is the best investment.

Note
The full calculation is given above but a short cut to the same conclusion would have been to compare the annual factor of 1.093 for E Scrooge with the annual factor of 1.103 for TT Bank showing the Scroog is inferior to TT Bank which is itself inferior to the Building Society.

b. Effective Annual interest rate of building society investment can be calculated as follows:

Let r = annual interest rate

$$\begin{aligned} \text{then} \quad £5000(1-r)^2 &= £5850 \\ (1+r)^2 &+ \frac{5850}{5000} \\ &= 1.17 \\ \therefore 1+r &= \sqrt{1.17} \\ &= 1.0817 \\ r &= 8.17\% \end{aligned}$$

Note
Alternatively this can be read directly from Table VII ie 4% for 2 years gives a factor of 1.082 which is 8.2% , close enough for all practical purposes.

c. Numerous factors would cause a reconsideration of the recommendation, for example

i. Client being a non-standard rate tax payer
ii. Changes in tax levels or rules governing Building Society investment
iii. Changes in interest rates in relation to each other
iv. Level of inflation may make all the investments unattractive
v. Changes in withdrawal rights etc.

SOLUTION A5

a. Rate of interest = r = 10%

Number of years = n = 15

Annual payment = A

Value of annual payment = Ri ie the annual payment, A, suitably discounted.

$$
\begin{aligned}
\text{Total loan} &= T = £15,000 \\
& \quad i = 15 \\
\therefore\ T &= \textstyle\sum_{i=1} R_i \\
\text{where } R_1 &= \frac{A}{(1+r)^{15}} \\
\text{where } R_2 &= \frac{A}{(1+r)^{14}} \\
& | \\
& | \\
& | \\
& | \\
R_{15} &= \frac{A}{(1+r)}
\end{aligned}
$$

(Note
An alternative way of looking at this problem which may help to explain the formula and method used is to ask, what annual amount, discounted at 10% over 15 years, has a present value of £ 15,000? This will be seen to be a normal annuity problem except that, in this case, the present value is given and the the annual amount unknown.)

$$\therefore \sum_{i=1}^{i=15} R_i = \sum_{i=1}^{i=15} \frac{A}{(1+r)^1} = £15,000$$

$$\therefore$$

$$15000 = \sum_{i=1}^{1=15} \frac{A}{1.1^1}$$

$$15000 = A\frac{1}{1.1^{15}} \cdot \frac{1-1.1^{15}}{1-1.1}$$

$$15000 = \frac{A}{1.1^{15}} \cdot \frac{1.1^{15}}{0.1}$$

$$\frac{1}{A} = \frac{1.1^{15}-1}{15000 \times 1.1^{15} \times 0.1}$$

$$A = \frac{15000 \times 1.1^{15} \times 0.1}{1.1^{15}-1}$$

$$A = \frac{15000 \times 0.4178}{3.177}$$

$$A = \underline{\underline{\mathbf{£1972}}}$$

(Note
The full calculation has been given above but, if the appropriate tables are available, a much simpler approach is possible. As shown above

$$15000 = \sum_{i=1}^{i=15} \frac{A}{(1+r)^1}$$

ie £ 15000 is present value of an annuity of Amount A at 10%

Look up in Table IX under 10% for 15 years and a factor of 7.606 will be obtained.

$$A = \frac{15000}{7.606}$$

$$= £1872)$$

b. Value in 15 years of £ 20,000 appreciating at 7% compound =

$$\begin{aligned} V_{15} &= V_0(1+0.07)^{15} \\ &= 20,000(1.07)^{15} \\ &= 20,000 \times 2.759 \text{ (Factor from Table VII)} \\ &= \underline{\underline{\mathbf{£55,180}}} \end{aligned}$$

CHAPTER 29

SOLUTION A1

$$NPV@10\% - 2000 + (800 \times 0.909) + (600 + 0.826) + (700 \times 0.751) + (500 \times 0.683)$$

$$= \underline{£90NPV}NPV@16\% = -£140$$

$\therefore$ IRR = 10 + 6 $(\frac{90}{230})$ = $\underline{\underline{12.34\%}}$

SOLUTION A2

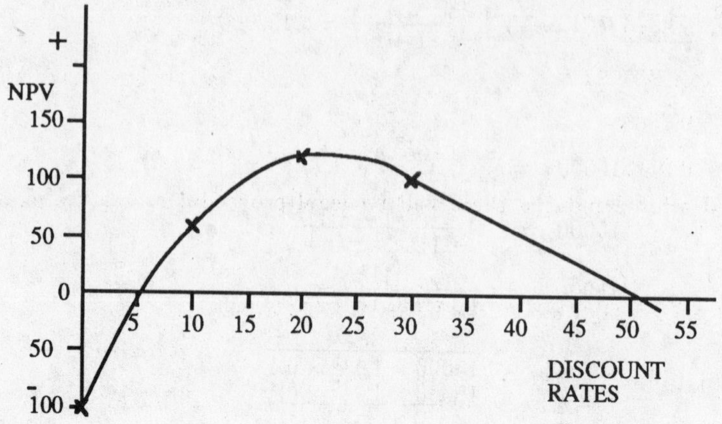

IRR 5% and 50%

Project acceptable at 10% cost of capital

SOLUTION A3

a. NPV @ 10% = £ 895.5

b. Discount rate with 8% inflation
 = 1.10 (1.08) = 1.188 say 19%
 ∴ NPV of 5 year series of £ 510 per annum and outlay of £ 1000 is - 1000 + 1559

 = +£559.4

This should be contrasted with the value in part (a)

SOLUTION A4

a. This is dealt with in the chapter

b. In general the discount rate should be representative of the long term pool of all capital sources and not just one of the sources as in this question.

c. and (d) Can be answered from the manual.

SOLUTION A5

a. NPV = $120,000 \times 4.160 + 120,000$ = £ 619,200

b. = $40,000 \times 4.160 + 540,000 - 50,000 \times .327$ = £ 690,050

c. = $100,000 \times 4.160 + 150,000 - 50,000 \times .327$ = £ 549,650

∴ Hire purchase, option C is preferable.

SOLUTION A6

a. i. P(payment at end of month 2) = $0.2 \times 0.7 = 0.14$

ii. P(payment at end of month 3) = $0.06 \times 0.5 = 0.03$

iii. If the account is not settled by the end of month 3 (P = 0.03) then payment is received at end of month 4 if sum is less than £ 1000 (P = 0.6)

∴ P(payment at end of month 4) = $0.03 \times 0.6 = 0.018$

iv. P(payment at end of month 6) $= 0.03 \times 0.4 = \underline{\underline{0.012}}$

b. For a sum of £ 2000 payment will be received after 1, 2, 3 or 6 months. This has a probability distribution of

Payment after (months)	Prob	PV Factor
1	0.8	0.9852
2	0.14	0.9707
3	0.03	0.7563
6	0.03	0.9145

If payment is not received after 3 months there will be legal proceedings and the expected proportion recovered is:

$$20 \times 0.1 + 50 \times 0.3 + 70 \times 0.4 + 90 \times 0.2 = 63\%$$

$\therefore$ Expected NPV overall is

$$2000 \times (0.8 \times 0.9852 + 0.14 \times 0.9707 + 0.03 \times 0.9563 + 0.03 \times 0.9145 + 0.9145 \times 0.63)$$

$$= \underline{\underline{£1940}}$$

c. There are three distributions that need to be sampled to simulate this system ie when payment received, the size of account and if necessary, the proportion recovered from legal proceedings. These distributions are allocated random numbers as follows:

When payment received:

TABLE A

Month	Probability	Random Numbers
1	0.80	00-79
2	$0.2 \times 0.7 = 0.14$	80 -93
3	$0.2 \times 0.3 \times 0.5 = 0.03$	94-96
3	0.003	97-99

Size of account

TABLE B

Account Size	Probability	Random Numbers
0 - 200	0.1	0
200 - 500	0.2	1-2
500 - 1000	0.3	3-5
1000 - 2000	0.3	6-8
2000 - 5000	0.1	9

Proportion recovered

TABLE C

Proportion	Probability	Random Numbers
0 - 40%	0.1	00 - 09
40 - 60%	0.3	10 - 29
60 - 80%	0.4	30 - 79
80 - 100	0.2	80 - 99

Simulation Account 1

Digits 88/7/57

Table A: 88 = Payment End of Month 2

Table B: 7 = Size of account = £ 1500

(Table C not required because of values already obtained)

Simulation Account 2

Digits 99/8/29

Table A: 99 = Not received by end of Month 3

Table B: 8 = Size of account = £ 1500

Table C: 29 = Proportion recovered 50%

ie mid-point

$\therefore PV = 1500 \times 0.9145 \times 0.5 = \underline{\pounds 685.88}$

CHAPTER 30

SOLUTION A1

Expected Cash Flows

Year 1	2	3
4,000	5500	4500

$$\therefore NPV = -10,000 + 11,558 = 558$$

SOLUTION A2

$$\sigma_{NPV} = \sqrt{\sum \left[\frac{400^2}{(1+.1)^2} + \frac{500^2}{(1+.1)^4} + \frac{350^2}{(1+.1)^6} \right]} = £881$$

$$\therefore Z = \frac{558 - 0}{881} = 0.633$$

$$\text{Probability} = 0.5 = 0.2357$$

$$\text{P(zero or less)} = \underline{26.43\%}$$

SOLUTION A3

Project	EVP1
A	0.1875
B	0.300
C	0.417
D	0.46
E	0.26

		CUMULATIVE OUTLAY	NPV
∴ Projects:	All D	£ 50,000	£ 23,000
	All C	110,000	48,000
	4/5 B	150,000	60,000

a. EV project A = 1/3 (1,000 + 3,000 + 5,000) = £ 3,000
   EV Project B = 1/3 (0 + 3,000 + 6,000) = £ 3,000
   Variance A = $1/3(2,000^2 + 0 + 2,000^2)$ = £ 2.67 M
   (ie the deviations from the three estimates from the mean)

b. Project A is preferable; both project have the same mean but A is less variable.

c. The coefficient of variation is a relative measure of dispersion and is:

$$\frac{\text{standard deviation}}{\text{mean}}$$

$$\therefore \text{coefficient of variation A} = \frac{\sqrt{2.67M}}{3,000} = \underline{0.544}$$

$$\text{coefficient of variation B} = \frac{\sqrt{6M}}{3,000} = \underline{0.816}$$

demonstrating the relative greater variability of B.

SOLUTION A5

The decision tree is shown complete with outcomes and probabilities, the calculations for which follow:

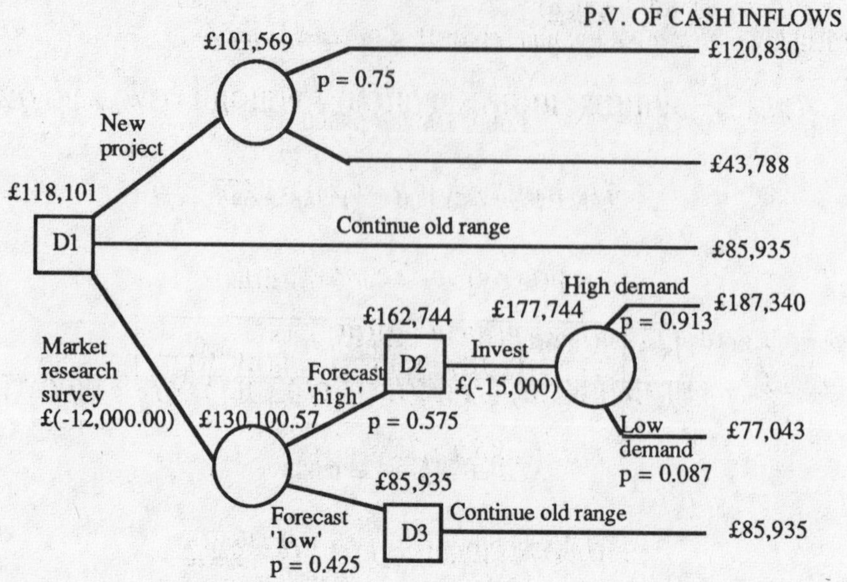

a. Expected NPV without survey.

High demand	Year 1	2	3	4	5	6
Cash Flows(000's)	40	40	40	30	30	30
Low demand	15	15	15	10	10	10

PV @ 20% = High Demand £ 120,830

Low Demand £ 43,788

$$\therefore \text{ENPV} = (0.75 \times 120,830) + (.25 \times 43,788) = \underline{\underline{£101,569}}$$

b. Expected NPV old range

	Year 1	2	3	4	5	6
Cash Flow	28,500	27,075	25,721	24,435	23,213	22,053

$$\therefore \text{PV@20\%} = \underline{£85,935}$$

c. Expected NPV with survey.

	Year 1	2	3	4	5	6
Forecast High and Result High Cash Flows (000's)	60	60	60	50	50	50
Forecast High and Result Low Cash Flows ('000)	25	25	25	20	20	20

∴ PVs

High/High = £ 187,340

High/Low = £ 77,043

To calculate the ENPV we must allow for the expenditures and calculate the required probabilities re P($\underline{\text{HIGH}}$) and P(HIGH | $\underline{\text{HIGH}}$) where:
P($\underline{\text{HIGH}}$) = P(Forecast will be $\underline{\text{high}}$)
P(HIGH | $\underline{\text{HIGH}}$) = P(Demand is high given that forecast is $\underline{\text{high}}$)

$$\therefore\ P(\underline{\text{HIGH}}) = P(\underline{\text{HIGH}} \mid \text{HIGH}) \times P(\text{HIGH}) + P(\underline{\text{HIGH}} \mid \text{LOW}) \times P(\text{LOW})$$

$$= (0.7 \times 0.75) + (0.2 \times 0.25) = \underline{0.575}$$

$$\therefore P(\text{LOW}) = 1 - 0.575 = \underline{0.425}$$

Bayes theorem is needed to calculate P(HIGH | $\underline{\text{HIGH}}$) thus

$$P(\text{HIGH} \mid \underline{\text{HIGH}}) = \frac{P(\underline{\text{HIGH}} \mid \text{HIGH}) \times P(\text{HIGH})}{P(\underline{\text{HIGH}} \mid \text{HIGH}) \times P(\text{HIGH}) + P(\underline{\text{HIGH}} \mid \text{LOW}) \times P(\text{LOW})}$$

$$= \frac{0.7 \times 0.75}{0.575} = \underline{0.913}$$

$$\therefore\ P(\text{LOW} \mid \underline{\text{HIGH}}) = 1 - 0.913 = \underline{0.087}$$

$\therefore$ ENPV is forecast is HIGH is:-

$$£(0.913 \times £187,340) + (0.087 \times 77,043) - 15,000 = \underline{\underline{£162,744}}$$

and ENPV with survey is:-

$$£(0.575 \times 162,744) + (0.425 \times 85,935) - 12,000 = \underline{\underline{£118,101}}$$

d. Decision
Carry out survey and make extra investment if forecast is high.

SOLUTION A6

a. There are 3 × 4 × 3 possible cash flow combinations but only those which yield a total of less than £ 42,000 are of interest.
A quicker way to identify the required combinations than listing all 36 is to write them as follows:

1	2	3
10	10	10
15	$\underline{20}$	$\underline{20}$
$\underline{20}$	30	30
	40	

values below the lines cannot be accepted because the will violate the requirement of less than 42,000. The remaining cashflows may be chosen by inspection.

	1	2	3	TOTAL
①	10	10	10	30
②	10	10	20	40
③	10	20	20	40
④	15	10	10	35
⑤	20	10	10	40

All totals are less than 42 and so the cash flow is negative.
Assuming that outcomes are independent the probabilities of the joint outcomes are given below:

	1		2		3		
①	0.3	×	0.1	×	0.3	=	0.009
②	0.3	×	0.1	×	0.5	=	0.015
③	0.3	×	0.2	×	0.3	=	0.018
④	0.4	×	0.1	×	0.3	=	0.012
⑤	0.3	×	0.1	×	0.3	=	0.009
							0.063

The overall probability of negative cash flow is 0.063 or 6.3%

b. Using the probability distributions the expected cash flows are calculated below:

	X	P	XP	
	10	0.3	3	Mean Cash Flow
Year 1	15	0.4	6	
	20	0.3	6	£ 15,000
			15	

	X	P	XP	
	10	0.1	1	Mean Cash Flow
Year 2	20	0.2	4	
	30	0.4	12	£ 29,000
	40	0.3	12	
			29	

	X	P	XP	
	10	0.3	3	Mean Cash Flow
Year 3	20	0.5	4	
	30	0.2	6	£ 19,000
			19	

Net present values:

Year	Mean Cash Flow	Discount Factor	Discounted Cash Flow
0	-42	1.000	−42,000
1	+15	0.8696	13,044
2	+29	0.7561	21,927
3	+19	0.6575	12,493
			5,464

The expected net present value for the project is thus £ 5,464.

c. Random numbers must be allocated to the probabilities associated with each cash flow.

YEAR 1

X	P	RANDOM NUMBER
10	0.3	0-2
15	0.4	3-6
20	0.3	7-9

YEAR 2

X	P	RANDOM NUMBER
10	0.1	0
20	0.2	1-2
30	0.4	3-6
40	0.3	7-9

YEAR 3

X	P	RANDOM NUMBER
10	0.3	0-2
20	0.5	3-7
30	0.2	8-9

Simulation year 1 (DCF Factor 0.8696)

SET	RANDOM NUMBER	CASH FLOW	DISCOUNTED CASH
1	4	15	13.044
2	7	20	17.392
3	6	15	13.044
4	5	15	13.044
5	0	10	8.696

Simulation Year 2 (DCF Factor 0.7561)

SET	RANDOM NUMBER	CASH FLOW	DISCOUNTED CASH
1	2	20	15.122
2	4	30	22.683
3	8	40	30.244
4	0	10	7.561
5	1	20	15.122

Simulation Year 3 (DCF Factor 0.6575)

SET	RANDOM NUMBER	CASH FLOW	DISCOUNTED CASH
1	7	20	13.150
2	9	30	19.725
3	4	20	13.150
4	0	10	6.575
5	3	20	13.150

The overall position is thus:
Simulation Results in D.C.F Terms

SET	YEAR 0	YEAR 1	YEAR 2	YEAR 3	NPV
1	−42	13.04	15.12	13.15	−0.69
2	−42	17.39	22.68	19.73	+17.80
3	−42	13.04	30.24	13.15	14.43
4	−42	13.04	7.56	6.58	−14.82
5	−42	8.70	15.12	13.15	− 5.02
					11.69

This value, £ 11,690, is produced over 5 simulations, and so to compare it with the expected value, the total must be divided by 5 giving:

$$\frac{11690}{5} = £2338$$

This is much below the £ 5,464 but given many more simulations the value would approach much closer to the expected figure.
Out of .5 simulations 3 give negative N.P.V. figures and so the probability of a negative net present value is:

$$\frac{3}{5} = \underline{\underline{0.6}}$$

SOLUTION A7

a. The objective is to maximise NPV so the LP formulation is
Maximise,

$$20.53A + 25.94B + 89.69C + 92.07D + 43.33E + 17.33F$$

Subject to:

Year					
0	200A + 60B		+ 80E + 150F	≤	300
1	100A + 80B	+ 120C	+ 100E + 150F	≤	300
2	50A	+ 50C + 250D		≤	300
5			+ 100E	≤	300

$$A, B, C, D, E, F \geq 0$$

Years 3 and 4 do not have outflows so are not constraints.

b. Interpretation

NPV over the period = £ 288,670

Initiate 2.5 Project C and 0.70 project D.
There is a surplus of £ 300,00 available in Periods 0 and 5.
The dual values 0.59 and 0.37 mean that an extra £ 1,000 available in periods 1 and 2 would produce £ 590 and £ 370 respectively.
From row 1, columns A, B, E, F it can be seen that if these projects are included in the optimum solution the return would fall by

£ 57,280 for A
£ 21,580 for B
£ 16,070 for E
£ 71,370 for F

Alternatively these values represent what the NPV of the various projects would have to increase to enter the optimum solution.

c. Can be answered from the manual.

CHAPTER 31

SOLUTION A1

$$X + Y = \begin{bmatrix} 3+1 & 11+2 & 6+0 \\ 9+0 & -3+(-4) & 8+5 \\ 5+5 & 0+(-8) & 9+7 \end{bmatrix}$$

$$= \begin{bmatrix} 4 & 13 & 6 \\ 9 & -7 & 13 \\ 10 & -8 & 16 \end{bmatrix}$$

$$X - Y = \begin{bmatrix} 2 & 9 & 6 \\ 9 & 1 & 3 \\ 0 & 8 & 2 \end{bmatrix}$$

SOLUTION A2

$$X \times Y = \begin{bmatrix} 33 & -86 & 97 \\ 49 & -34 & 41 \\ 50 & -62 & 63 \end{bmatrix}$$

SOLUTION A3

$$M = \begin{bmatrix} 6 & 4 \\ 3 & 1 \end{bmatrix} \quad |M| = -6$$

$$\therefore M^{-1} = \frac{1}{-6}\begin{bmatrix} 1 & -4 \\ -3 & 6 \end{bmatrix}$$

$$= \begin{bmatrix} -\frac{1}{6} & \frac{2}{3} \\ \frac{1}{2} & -1 \end{bmatrix}$$

Using row by row operations

$$\text{Row } 1 - 6 = \begin{bmatrix} 1 & \frac{2}{3} \\ 0 & -1 \end{bmatrix} \begin{bmatrix} \frac{1}{6} & 0 \\ -\frac{1}{2} & 1 \end{bmatrix}$$

$$\text{New Row } 2 \times -1 = \begin{bmatrix} 1 & \frac{2}{3} \\ 0 & 1 \end{bmatrix} \begin{bmatrix} \frac{1}{6} & 0 \\ \frac{1}{2} & -1 \end{bmatrix}$$

$$\text{New Row } 1 - \tfrac{2}{3}\text{ (New Row 2)} \begin{bmatrix} 1 & 0 \\ 0 & 1 \end{bmatrix} \begin{bmatrix} -\frac{1}{6} & \frac{2}{3} \\ \frac{1}{2} & -1 \end{bmatrix}$$

Thus providing inversion.

SOLUTION A4

a. The first stage is to set out the information given in the form of simulataneous equations which can then be solved using matrix algebra.

   i. Let M = total cost maintence dept. including an allocation of electricity costs.
   Let E = total cost of electricity including an apportionment of maintenance costs.
   Proportion of maintenance time consumed by electricity dept. is

$$\frac{3000 \text{ hrs}}{300 + 16,000 + 1000 \text{ hrs}} = .15 \text{ ie } 15\% \text{ or } \frac{3}{20}$$

   of maintenance dept. costs should be apportioned to electricity dept.

$$\text{E} = £4000 + 0.15\text{M} \quad \text{(Equation 1)}$$

   Similarly the proportion of electricity consumed by maintenance is

$$\frac{20,000 \text{ units}}{20,000 + 130,000 + 50,000 \text{ units}} = .10 \text{ ie } 10\% \text{ or } \frac{1}{10}$$

   of electricity costs should be apportioned to the maintenance dept.

$$\text{M} = £50,000 + 0.1\text{E (Equation 2)}$$

   Setting out equations 1 and 2 in the normal simultaneous manner gives

$$-0.15\text{M} + \text{E} = 4000$$

$$\text{M} - 0.1\text{E} = 50,000$$

   Check for feasibility of solution - Does number of equations = number of unknowns? - Yes.

∴ matrices to be solved are

$$\begin{bmatrix} -0.15 & 1 \\ 1 & -0.1 \end{bmatrix} \begin{bmatrix} 4000 \\ 50000 \end{bmatrix}$$

Exactly similar steps as shown in Para. 16 will now be followed, ie
Row 1 multiplied by $\frac{1}{0.15}$ gives

$$\begin{bmatrix} 1 & -6.66 \\ 1 & -0.1 \end{bmatrix} \begin{bmatrix} -26,666.66 \\ 50,000 \end{bmatrix}$$

Row 2 − Row 1 gives

$$\begin{bmatrix} 1 & -6.66 \\ 0 & 6.56 \end{bmatrix} \begin{bmatrix} -26,666.66 \\ 76,666.66 \end{bmatrix}$$

Row 2 divided by 6.56 gives

$$\begin{bmatrix} 1 & -6.66 \\ 0 & 1 \end{bmatrix} \begin{bmatrix} -26,666.66 \\ 11,675 \end{bmatrix}$$

Finally Row 1 + (6.66 × Row 2) gives

$$\begin{bmatrix} 1 & 0 \\ 0 & 1 \end{bmatrix} \begin{bmatrix} 51,168 \\ 11,675 \end{bmatrix}$$

Thus the value for M = £ 51,167 and E = £ 11,675
Having thus obtained the Service Dept. costs, including apportionments between themselves, the apportionments to the production departments can be made thus:
Proportions of maintenance and electricity consumed by production departments:

	Maintenance	Electricity
Machining	$\frac{16,000}{20,000} = 0.8$	$\frac{130,000}{200,000} = 0.65$
Assembly	$\frac{1,000}{20,000} = 0.05$	$\frac{50,000}{200,000} = 0.25$

Accordingly the apportionments of maintenance department costs to the production departments is:

$$\begin{bmatrix} 0.8 & 0.65 \\ 0.05 & 0.25 \end{bmatrix} \begin{bmatrix} M \\ E \end{bmatrix}$$

$$= \begin{bmatrix} 0.8 & 0.65 \\ 0.05 & 0.25 \end{bmatrix} \begin{bmatrix} 51,168 \\ 11,675 \end{bmatrix}$$

$$= \begin{bmatrix} 0.8 \times 51,168 + 0.65 \times 11,675 \\ 0.05 \times 51,168 + 0.25 \times 11,675 \end{bmatrix} = \begin{bmatrix} £48,523 \\ £5,477 \end{bmatrix}$$

ie £ 48,523 to machining and £ 5,477 to Assembly, a total of £ 54,000.

ii. The use of matrix algebra for this type of procedure formalises the procedures and permits the extension of the exercise to any number of departments. The calculations can be performed automatically usually by standard computer packages thus speeding up the whole process.

b. This in principle an identical problem and is solved in a similar manner.

Let E = employees share of profit

T = Tax payable

As employees are entitled to 10% or profits after tax

$$E = 0.1(\pounds 100,000 - T) \text{ and}$$

$$T = 0.5(100,000 - E)$$

From these equations we obtain

$$\begin{aligned} E + 0.1T &= 10,000 \\ 0.5E + T &= 50,000 \text{ and the matrices are} \end{aligned}$$

$$\begin{bmatrix} 1 & 0.1 \\ 0.5 & 1 \end{bmatrix} \begin{bmatrix} 10,000 \\ 50,000 \end{bmatrix}$$

To set a_{21} to zero, Row 2 - ($\frac{1}{2}\times$ Row)

$$\begin{bmatrix} 1 & 0.1 \\ 0 & 0.95 \end{bmatrix} \begin{bmatrix} 10,000 \\ 45,000 \end{bmatrix}$$

To set a_{22} to 1, multiply Row 2 $\times \frac{1}{0.95}$

$$\begin{bmatrix} 1 & 0.1 \\ 0 & 1 \end{bmatrix} \begin{bmatrix} 10,000 \\ 47,368 \end{bmatrix}$$

Finally, to set A_{12} to zero, Row 1 - ($\frac{1}{10}\times$ Row2)

$$\begin{bmatrix} 1 & 0 \\ 0 & 1 \end{bmatrix} \begin{bmatrix} 5,263 \\ 47,368 \end{bmatrix}$$

Employees are entitled to £ 5,263 and tax payable is £ 47,368

SOLUTION A5

The two probability transition matrices are:

$$A = \begin{matrix} & L & M \\ X & \frac{1}{3} & \frac{2}{3} \\ Y & \frac{1}{4} & \frac{3}{4} \end{matrix} \qquad B = \begin{matrix} & S & T \\ L & \frac{1}{2} & \frac{1}{2} \\ M & \frac{2}{5} & \frac{3}{5} \end{matrix}$$

$$\therefore AB = \begin{bmatrix} \frac{1}{6} + \frac{4}{15} & \frac{1}{6} + \frac{2}{6} \\ \frac{1}{8} + \frac{6}{20} & \frac{1}{8} + \frac{9}{20} \end{bmatrix} = \begin{matrix} X \\ Y \end{matrix} \begin{bmatrix} \frac{13}{30} & \frac{17}{30} \\ \frac{17}{40} & \frac{23}{40} \end{bmatrix}$$

The probabilities in AB represent the probabilities of the flow between Stage 1 and Stage 3. For example, the flow between Y and T are YLT and YMT for which the probabilities are $(\frac{1}{4} \times \frac{1}{2}) + (\frac{3}{4} \times \frac{3}{5}) = \frac{23}{40}$ which is the value of the Y, T element in Matrix $\times$ AB.

b. Share price movements.

The probability transition matrix is given and the initial condition is also supplied in that we are told that the price goes up today.

$\therefore$ Initial condition vector is [1 0]
The multiplication can now be done for each of the three days thus:-

$$\text{Probabilities tomorrow} = \begin{bmatrix} 1 & 0 \end{bmatrix} \begin{bmatrix} \frac{1}{2} & \frac{1}{2} \\ \frac{2}{3} & \frac{2}{3} \end{bmatrix} = \begin{bmatrix} \frac{1}{2} & \frac{1}{2} \end{bmatrix}$$

$\therefore$ P (price going up) = $\underline{\underline{\frac{1}{2}}}$

$$\text{Probabilities in two days} \begin{bmatrix} \frac{1}{2} & \frac{1}{2} \end{bmatrix} \begin{bmatrix} \frac{1}{2} & \frac{1}{2} \\ \frac{2}{3} & \frac{1}{3} \end{bmatrix} = \begin{bmatrix} \frac{7}{12} & \frac{5}{12} \end{bmatrix}$$

$\therefore$ P (price going up) = $\frac{7}{12}$

$$\text{Probabilties in three days} \begin{bmatrix} \frac{7}{12} & \frac{5}{12} \end{bmatrix} \begin{bmatrix} \frac{1}{2} & \frac{1}{2} \\ \frac{2}{3} & \frac{1}{3} \end{bmatrix} = \begin{bmatrix} \frac{41}{72} & \frac{31}{72} \end{bmatrix}$$

$\therefore$ P (price going up) = $\frac{41}{72}$

ii. To find the equilibrium position

Let μ = P (price going up) at equilibrium

d = P (price going down) at equilibrium

$\therefore$ d = 1 - μ

$\therefore$ at equilibrium

$$\text{i.e. as} \begin{bmatrix} \mu & d \end{bmatrix} \begin{bmatrix} \frac{1}{2} & \frac{1}{2} \\ \frac{2}{3} & \frac{1}{3} \end{bmatrix} = \begin{bmatrix} \mu & d \end{bmatrix}$$

$\therefore$ $\frac{1}{2}\mu + 2/3\, d = \mu$ and substituting for d, 1 - μ, we obtain
$\frac{1}{2}\mu + \frac{2}{3}(1-\mu) = \mu$
$\frac{1}{2}\mu + \frac{2}{3} - \frac{2}{3}\mu = \mu$
$\therefore$ $\mu = \frac{4}{7}$ and $d = \frac{3}{7}$
$\therefore$ P (price going up at equilibrium) = $\underline{\frac{4}{7}}$

SOLUTION A6

a. i. Matrix W

ie. the four products' (A, B, C, D) material requirements (P, Q, R) thus.

$$W = \begin{array}{c} \\ A \\ B \\ C \\ D \end{array} \begin{array}{c} \begin{array}{ccc} P & Q & R \end{array} \\ \begin{bmatrix} 2 & 1 & 4 \\ 5 & 0 & 3 \\ 4 & 3 & 2 \\ 4 & 1 & 2 \end{bmatrix} \end{array}$$

ii. Matrix X (ie. vector)

ie. the weekly demands for each product.

$$X = \begin{array}{cccc} [400 & 500 & 600 & 200] \\ A & B & C & D \end{array}$$

iii. Matrix Y (ie. a vector)

Unit raw material costs in £ 's

$$Y = \begin{array}{c} P \\ Q \\ R \end{array} \begin{bmatrix} 2 \\ 3 \\ 6 \end{bmatrix}$$

iv. Matrix Z (ie a vector
Direct production cost per unit in £ 's

$$Z = \begin{bmatrix} 4 \\ 2 \\ 3 \\ 5 \end{bmatrix}$$

b. Raw material costs per product. Required matrices are WY, thus

$$WY = \begin{bmatrix} 2 & 1 & 4 \\ 5 & 0 & 3 \\ 4 & 3 & 2 \\ 4 & 1 & 2 \end{bmatrix} \begin{bmatrix} 2 \\ 3 \\ 6 \end{bmatrix} = \begin{bmatrix} 31 \\ 28 \\ 29 \\ 23 \end{bmatrix}$$

∴ Raw material cost per product

A = £ 31, B = £ 28, C = £ 29 and D = £ 23

c. Matrices required for total weekly contribution.
Contribution per unit = Selling Price - (Unit Material Cost + direct production Cost).

$$= \begin{bmatrix} 40 \\ 40 \\ 36 \\ 32 \end{bmatrix} - \left[\begin{bmatrix} 31 \\ 28 \\ 29 \\ 23 \end{bmatrix} + \begin{bmatrix} 4 \\ 2 \\ 3 \\ 5 \end{bmatrix} \right]$$

$$= \begin{bmatrix} 5 \\ 10 \\ 4 \\ 4 \end{bmatrix}$$

∴ Total weekly contribution

$$= \begin{bmatrix} 400 & 500 & 600 & 200 \end{bmatrix} \begin{bmatrix} 5 \\ 10 \\ 4 \\ 4 \end{bmatrix} = \underline{£\ 10{,}200}$$

d. Interpretation of T = XWY
X is weekly demand W is unit material requirement. Y is unit material cost
∴ T = Total weekly raw material cost.

SOLUTION A7

a. i.

$$\begin{aligned} M &= 56{,}000 + 0.05M + 0.05L + 0.10C \\ L &= 250{,}000 + 0.25M + 0.15C \\ C &= 35{,}000 + 0.10M + 0.10L + 0.05C \end{aligned}$$

where M = Maintenance, L = Laundry and C = Cleaning
Transposing gives

$$\begin{aligned} 0.95M - 0.05L \quad -0.05C &= 56{,}000 \\ -0.25M + L \quad -0.15C &= 250{,}000 \\ -0.10M - 0.10L \quad -0.95L &= 35{,}000 \end{aligned}$$

The LHS values are the matrix coefficients.

Let X = the matrix coefficients in (1)

ii. S = the service department vector

T = total cost

Thus T = XS

$\therefore$ S = X^{-1}T

Algebraically the matrix of coefficients can be found using the row by row operation method thus:

$$\begin{bmatrix} 0.95 & -0.05 & -0.10 \\ -0.25 & 1 & -0.15 \\ -0.10 & -0.10 & 0.95 \end{bmatrix} \begin{bmatrix} 1 & 0 & 0 \\ 0 & 1 & 0 \\ 0 & 0 & 1 \end{bmatrix}$$

Working on each row will transform the identity matrix on the right into the required matrix inversion.

b.

$$\begin{bmatrix} 1.083 & 0.067 & 0.125 \\ 0.293 & 1.034 & 0.194 \\ 0.145 & 0.116 & 1.086 \end{bmatrix} \times \begin{bmatrix} 56,000 \\ 250,000 \\ 35,000 \end{bmatrix} = \begin{bmatrix} M \\ L \\ C \end{bmatrix}$$

Giving:

$$\begin{aligned} M &= (1.083 \times 56,000 + 1.034 \times 250,000 + 0.125 \times 35,000) \\ &= \underline{\underline{£81,773}} \end{aligned}$$

$$\begin{aligned} L &= (0.293 \times 56,000 + 1.034 \times 250,000 + 0.194 \times 35,000) \\ &= \underline{\underline{£281,698}} \end{aligned}$$

$$\begin{aligned} C &= (0.145 \times 56,000 + 0.116 \times 250,000 + 1.086 \times 35,000) \\ &= \underline{\underline{£75,130}} \end{aligned}$$

SOLUTION A8

a. Can be answered from the manual

b.

$$A = \begin{bmatrix} 1 & 5 & 0 \\ 4 & 10 & 2 \\ 3 & 15 & 1 \end{bmatrix}$$

c.

$$B = \begin{bmatrix} 36 & 104 \\ 18 & 75 \\ 25 & 30 \end{bmatrix}$$

d.

$$AB = \begin{bmatrix} 36+90+0 & 104+375+0 \\ 144+180+50 & 416+750+60 \\ 108+270+25 & 312+1125+30 \end{bmatrix}$$

$$AB = \begin{bmatrix} 126 & 479 \\ 374 & 1226 \\ 403 & 1467 \end{bmatrix}$$

AB shows the numbers employed at each grade in the two regions as follows:-

GRADE	MIDLAND	OTHER AREAS
Supervisors	126	479
Cashiers	374	1226
Storekeepers	403	1467

CHAPTER 32

SOLUTION A1

a. Average component life

$$= (1 \times 0.3) + (2 \times 0.45) + (3 \times 0.25) = \underline{\underline{1.95}}$$

b. Average number of replacements per week

$$= \frac{1000}{1.95} = \underline{\underline{513}}$$

c. Cost of individual replacement

$$= 513 \times £30 = \underline{\underline{£15,390}}$$

SOLUTION A2

FAILURE TABLE

	WEEK 1	WEEK 2	WEEK 3
ORIGINAL BATCH (1000)	300	450	250
300 WEEK 1 BATCH		90	135
450 WEEK 2 BATCH			135
90 WEEK 2 BATCH			27
TOTAL FAILURES	300	540	547

TOTAL COST OF MASS REPLACEMENT

	TOTAL COST	AVERAGE COST/WEEK
WEEK 1		
£ 5,000 + 300 × 30	£ 14,000	£ 14,000
WEEK 2		
£ 5000 + 840 × 30	£ 30,200	£ 15,100
WEEK 3		
£ 5,000 + 1387 × 30	£ 46,610	£ 15,537

∴ best replacement strategy is replace en masse each week.

SOLUTION A3

(A) Proportion of tools failing each month

Month	Proportion of failures
1	10%
2	15%
3	25%
4	30%
5	20%
	100%

∴ Average life is

$$(1 \times 0.1) + (2 \times 0.15) + (3 \times 0.25) + (4 \times 0.3) + (5 \times 0.2)$$

$$= \underline{3.35 \text{months}}$$

Given that 1000 toools are in use the average replacements per month is

$$\frac{1000}{3.35} = \underline{298.5}$$

$$\therefore \text{ INDIVIDUAL REPLACEMENT COST} = 298.5 \times £4 = \underline{\underline{£1,194 \text{per month}}}$$

GROUP REPLACEMENT

It is necessary to calculate the number of failures each month given that the failures are replaced and thus commence a new life cycle.

Failures Month 1

$$0.1 \times 1000 = \underline{100}$$

Failures Month 2

$$0.15 \times 1000 + 0.1 \times 100 = \underline{160}$$

Failures Month 3

$$0.25 \times 1000 + 0.15 \times 100 + 0.1 \times 160 = \underline{281}$$

Failures Month 4

$$0.3 \times 1000 + 0.25 \times 100 + 0.15 \times 160 + 0.1 \times 281 = \underline{377}$$

Failures Month 5

$$0.2 \times 1000 + 0.3 \times 100 + 0.25 \times 160 + 0.15 \times 281 + 0.1 \times 377 = \underline{350}$$

Thus the cost of group replacement plus individual replacement is as follows:

Month	Individual Replacement Cost	Cumulative Individual Replacement Cost	Cumulative Total Cost (incl £ 1000 group replacement	Average Monthly Cost
	£	£		
1	£ 4 × 100 = 400	400	1400	1400
2	£ 4 × 160 = 640	1040	2040	1020*
3	£ 4 × 281 = 1124	2164	3164	1055
4	£ 4 × 377 = 1508	3672	4672	1168
5	£ 4 × 350 = 1400	5072	6072	1214

*Group replacement at end of month 2 seems to be the most economical being cheaper than the £ 1194 'replace on failure' cost previously calculated.

(B)

$$\text{Contribution} = £\ 0.50 - 0.45 = £\ 0.05 \text{ per ton mile}$$

a.

$$\therefore \text{Break even} = \frac{£6500}{£0.05} = \underline{130{,}000 \text{ ton miles}}$$

b. Expected annual profit
$= £\ (180,000 \times 0.05) - 6500$
$= \underline{£\ 2500}$

c. i.

$$\text{P(Breakeven)} = \frac{180,000 - 130,000}{60,000} = 0.833 \text{ and from Table I}$$

$$\text{P(Breakeven)} = 0.8 \text{ ie } 80\%$$

ii. P(Profit $\geq$ £ 2000 p.a.)

Ton miles required $= \dfrac{6500 + 2000}{0.05} = 170{,}000$

$z = \left| \dfrac{170,000 - 180,000}{60,000} \right| = 0.167 \therefore$ P ($\geq$ £ 2000 profit) = 57%

iii. P ($\geq$ £ 5000 profit)

Ton miles required $= \dfrac{6500 + 5000}{0.05} = 230,000$

$z = \left| \dfrac{230,000 - 180,000}{60,000} \right| = 0.833$

$\therefore$ P ($\geq$ £ 500 profit) = 20%

iv. The value to management is dealt with in Chapter 2 on probability.

SOLUTION A4

Because the 600 hour period is common to all valves it can be ignored and the lives (100 - 400) in the table used.

a. i. Replacement on individual basis.
Average life.

$$= (100 \times 0.15 + 200 \times 0.45 + 300 \times 30 + 400 \times 0.10)$$

$$= \underline{235\text{hrs}}$$

Replacement at failure

$$= £400 \times \frac{100}{235} = \underline{£17.02 \text{ per hour}}$$

ii. Group Replacement
at 100 hours:

$$\text{Cost} = \frac{£2300 + 0.15 \times £40}{100} = \underline{£29 \text{ per hour}}$$

For longer periods the cumulative failures ie the failures of failures, need to be calculated.

LIFE	FAILURES	TOTAL FOR PERIOD	CUMULATIVE
100	15	15	15
200	45 + 2.25	47	62
300	30 + 6.75 + 7.05	44	106
400	10 + 4.5 + 21.05 + 6.6	42	148

Group Replacement
at 200 hours

$$\frac{£2300 + 62 \times 40}{200} = \underline{£23.90\text{hour}}$$

at 300 hours

$$\frac{£2300 + 106 \times 40}{300} = \underline{£21.80\text{hour}}$$

at 400 hours

$$\frac{£2300 + 148 \times 40}{300} = \underline{£20.55\text{hour}}$$

b. Thus the overall results are

		Cost per hour
Replacement at failure		£ 17.02
Group replacement	100 hours	29.00
	200 hours	23.90
	300 hours	21.80
	400 hours	20.55

∴ Replacement at failure is cheapest.

c. A simple form of sensitivity analysis could be used whereby the number of failures &/or costs could be altered to test the effect on the solution.
Alternatively a simulation of the problem could be undertaken.

Appendix

Application of Computers in Quantitative Techniques

INTRODUCTION

For examination purposes to gain real understanding of basic techniques there is no substitute for carrying out the data manipulation and calculations with only the aid of pencil, paper and a calculator. In these circumstances with a limited number of data items, manual calculation is useful and feasible. However, in many practical situations computer assistance is invaluable particularly where there is a large amount of data or where a series of tests have to be carried out on the data.

All computer systems above the 'hobby' level have a comprehensive statistical and quantitative techniques packages available. These packages provide facilities for manipulating, arranging and storing data and can perform a range of standard statistical tests such as significance testing, time series analysis, regression analysis and so on. Other packages are available which deal with various quantitative techniques, examples include, linear programming, network analysis, inventory control, investment appraisal and so on. An important facility which is invariably included is that of sensitivity analysis whereby the program shows the variations in results caused by altering input values or shows the range of values over which the original result would stand.

The only real way to learn how to handle a given package is sit at a computer terminal with the package operating instructions and attempt to solve a particular problem. Some prior instruction on the particular package is invaluable but as each package is different it is impossible in a manual such as this to give detailed operating instructions for any package that might be encountered. Students are strongly advised to take every opportunity to gain practice in using computers and computer packages whether at work or college.

Some examples follow of statistical or quantitative problems which have been solved using typical packages. As the problems are merely to demonstrate computer usage, the number of data items and variables has deliberately been kept low. Each problem is outlined and the results produced by the computer are reproduced together with the input data.

In addition to the summaries of package examples, which are given without details of the way the program deals with data or of the operating instructions, a more detailed example (No.5) is given of the use of a widely available teaching program; the PERT package available on Acorn (BBC) micros. The operating instructions and explanations for this latter example have been prepared by Mr. D W Bale of the Dorset Institute of Higher Education.

SUMMARY OF APPENDIX CONTENTS

EXAMPLE 1

CHI-SQUARE TEST

PROBLEM

A random sample of 1000 householders is classified by income level (A to D) and by whether they own a video recorder. The results of the sample are given below:

	INCOME LEVEL				
	A	B	C	D	TOTAL
VIDEO	85	283	114	58	540
NO VIDEO	147	203	93	17	460
	232	486	207	75	1,000

It is required to test for independence at the 5% and 1% levels.

EXAMPLE 1

PACKAGE OUTPUT (5% LEVEL)

Chi-Squared – Test of Association

A random sample of householders is classified by income level and whether they own a video recorder.

Observed (0)

Video	85	283	114	58 =	540
Non Video	147	203	93	17 =	460
	232	486	207	75 =	1,000

Expected (E)

125.280	262.440	111.780	40.500
106.720	223.560	95.220	34.500

Note: $E = \dfrac{\text{Row Total} \times \text{Column total}}{\text{Total observed}}$

(O – E)

40.280	20.560	2.220	17.500
40.280	20.560	2.220	17.500

$\dfrac{\mathbf{(O - E \times O - E)}}{\mathbf{E}}$

12.951	1.611	0.044	7.562
15.203	1.891	0.052	8.877

Chi-Squared = sum of all $\dfrac{(O - E \times O - E)}{E}$

= 48.190

From the tables for a 2-tailed test with a significance level of .05 and 3 degrees of freedom, we read a value of 7.815.

Our value of 48.190 exceeds 7.815 therefore the results ARE significant. We can reject the Null Hypothesis.

State the conclusion!

EXAMPLE 1

PACKAGE OUTPUT (1% LEVEL)

Chi-Squared – Test of Association

A random sample of householders is classified by income level and whether they own a video recorder.

Observed (0)

Video	85	283	114	58 =	540
Non Video	147	203	93	17 =	460
	232	486	207	75 =	1,000

Expected (E)

125.280	262.440	111.780	40.500
106.720	223.560	95.220	34.500

Note: $E = \dfrac{\text{Row Total} \times \text{Column total}}{\text{Total observed}}$

(O – E)

40.280	20.560	2.220	17.500
40.280	20.560	2.220	17.500

$$\frac{(O - E \times O - E)}{E}$$

12.951	1.611	0.044	7.562
15.203	1.891	0.052	8.877

Chi-Squared = sum of all $\frac{(O - E \times O - E)}{E}$
= 48.190

From the tables for a 2-tailed test with a significance level of .01 and 3 degrees of freedom, we read a value of 11.345.

Our value of 48.190 exceeds 11.345 therefore the results ARE significant. We can reject the Null Hypothesis.

State the Conclusion!

EXAMPLE 2

t tests

A baker wishes to test the effectiveness of a new raising additive and sub-divides the batches of dough putting additive into half the sub-batches. The time taken to rise is then noted.

BATCH	1	2	3	4	5	6	7	8
	Mins	Mins	Mins	Mins	Mins	Mins	Mins	Mins
DOUGH WITH ADDITIVE	17.2	16.8	17.9	18.1	22.1	18.6	19.4	20.8
DOUGH WITHOUT ADDITIVE	18.3	17.9	17.1	22.3	21.6	19.2	18.4	19.9

Do the results support the contention that the additive reduces the rising time, at the 95% confidence level? at the 99% level?

EXAMPLE 2

PACKAGE OUTPUT (95% LEVEL)
't' Test for Independent Samples

The hypothesis is that dough with additive reduces the rising time

List 1		4a
Subject	Score (Xa)	Squared Score (Xa2)
1	17.20	295.84
2	16.80	282.24
3	17.90	320.41
4	18.10	327.61
5	22.10	488.41
6	18.60	345.96
7	19.40	376.36
8	20.80	432.64
8 = Na 1a	150.90 5a	2869.47

2a = 1a x 1a	= 150.9 x 150.9	= 22770.81
3a = 2a / Na	= 22770.81 / 8	= 2846.351
6a = 5a - 3a	= 2869.47 - 2846.351	= 23.1189
7a = 1a / Na	= 150.9 / 8	= 18.8625

List 2		4b
Subject	Score (Xb)	Squared Score (Xb2)
1	18.30	334.89
2	17.90	320.41
3	17.10	292.41
4	22.30	497.29
5	21.60	466.56
6	19.20	368.64
7	18.40	338.56
8	19.90	396.01
8 = Nb 1b	154.70 5b	3014.77

2b = 1b x 1b	= 154.7 x 154.7	= 23932.09
3b = 2b / Nb	= 23932.09 / 8	= 2991.511
6b = 5b - 3b	= 3014.77 - 2991.511	= 23.25977
7b = 1b / Nb	= 154.7 / 8	= 19.3375

8 = 6a + 6b	= 23.1189 + 23.25977	= 46.37866
9 = Na + Nb - 2	= 8 + 8 - 2	= 14
10 = 8 / 9	= 46.37866 / 14	= 3.312762
11 = (1/Na) + (1/Nb)	= (1/8) + (1 / 8))	= .25
12 = 10 x 11	= 3.312762 x .25	= .8281904
13 = sqrt (12)	= sqrt (.8281904)	= .9100497
14 = 7a - 7b	= 18.8625 - 19.3375	= .4749985
t = 14 / 13	= .4749985 / .9100497	= .5219479

From the tables for a 1-tailed test with a significance level of .05 and 14 degrees of freedom, we read a value of 1.761.

Our value of .5219479 is less than 1.761 therefore the results are NOT significant and we cannot reject the Null Hypotehsis.

State the conclusion!

EXAMPLE 2

PACKAGE OUTPUT (99% LEVEL)

't' Test for Independent Samples

The hypothesis is that dough with additive reduces the rising time

List 1		4a
Subject	Score (Xa)	Squared Score (Xa2)
1	17.20	295.84
2	16.80	282.24
3	17.90	320.41
4	18.10	327.61
5	22.10	488.41
6	18.60	345.96
7	19.40	376.36
8	20.80	432.64
8 = Na 1a	150.90 5a	2869.47

2a = 1a x 1a	= 150.9 x 150.9	= 22770.81
3a = 2a / Na	= 22770.81 / 8	= 2846.351
6a = 5a - 3a	= 2869.47 - 2846.351	= 23.1189
7a = 1a / Na	= 150.9 / 8	= 18.8625

List 2		4b
Subject	Score (Xb)	Squared Score (Xb2)
1	18.30	334.89
2	17.90	320.41
3	17.10	292.41
4	22.30	497.29
5	21.60	466.56
6	19.20	368.64
7	18.40	338.56
8	19.90	396.01
8 = Nb 1b	154.70 5b	3014.77

2b = 1b x 1b	= 154.7 x 154.7	= 23932.09
3b = 2b / Nb	= 23932.09 / 8	= 2991.511
6b = 5b - 3b	= 3014.77 - 2991.511	= 23.25977
7b = 1b / Nb	= 154.7 / 8	= 19.3375

8 = 6a + 6b	= 23.1189 + 23.25977	= 46.37866
9 = Na + Nb - 2	= 8 + 8 - 2	= 14
10 = 8 / 9	= 46.37866 / 14	= 3.312762
11 = (1/Na) + (1/Nb)	= (1/8) + (1 / 8))	= .25
12 = 10 x 11	= 3.312762 x .25	= .8281904
13 = sqrt (12)	= sqrt (.8281904)	= .9100497
14 = 7a - 7b	= 18.8625 - 19.3375	= .4749985
t = 14 / 13	= .4749985 / .9100497	= .5219479

From the tables for a 1 tailed test with a significance level of .01 and 14 degrees of freedom, we read a value of 2.624

Our value of .5219479 is less than 2.624 therefore the results are NOT significant and we cannot reject the Null Hypothesis.

State the conclusion.

EXAMPLE 3

LINEAR PROGRAMMING

(Note: The following example is the problem used in Chapter 19 to explain the Simplex method. The results produced by the LP package can be compared with the chapter).

A company can produce three products, A, B and C. The products yield a contribution of £8, £5 and £10 respectively.

The products use a machine which has 400 hours capacity in the next period. Each unit of the products uses 2, 3 and 1 hour respectively of the machine's capacity.

There are only 150 units available in the period of a special component which is used singly in products A and C.

200 kgs only of a special alloy is available in the period. Product A uses 2 kgs per unit and Product C uses 4 kgs per unit.

There is an agreement with a trade association to produce no more than 50 units of Product B in the period.

The company wishes to find out the production plant which maximises contribution.

EXAMPLE 3

PACKAGE OUTPUT

LP OPTIMUM FOUND AT STEP 2

OBJECTIVE FUNCTION VALUE

1) 1050,00000

VARIABLE	VALUE	REDUCED COST
X1	100,000000	0,000000
X2	50,000000	0,000000
X3	0,000000	6,000000

ROW	SLACK OR SURPLUS	DUAL PRICES
2)	50,000000	0,000000
3)	50,000000	0,000000
4)	0,000000	4,000000
5)	0,000000	5,000000

NO. ITERATIONS = 2

RANGES IN WHICH THE BASIS IS UNCHANGED

OBJ COEFFICIENT RANGES

VARIABLE	CURRENT COEF	ALLOWABLE INCREASE	ALLOWABLE DECREASE
X1	8,000000	INFINITY	3,000000
X2	5,000000	INFINITY	5,000000
X3	10,000000	6,000000	INFINITY

RIGHTHAND SIDE RANGES

ROW	CURRENT RHS	ALLOWABLE INCREASE	ALLOWABLE DECREASE
2	400,000000	INFINITY	50,000000
3	150,000000	INFINITY	50,000000
4	200,000000	50,000000	200,000000
5	50,000000	16,666666	50,000000

EXAMPLE 4

INVESTMENT APPRAISAL

Acompany is considering a project with the following cash flows which arise at year ends.

YEAR	COSTS £'000	INCOME £'000
1	150	300
2	200	400
3	300	600
4	400	600
5	500	600
6	350	500
7	400	500
8	300	400

a. Assuming a £500,000 initial outlay and no scrap value calculate; the payback period, profitability index, accounting rate of return, internal rate of return and net present value at 15% and 20% cost of capital.

b. Recalculate the above assuming a £750,000 initial outlay and 20% cost of capital.

EXAMPLE 4(a) PACKAGE OUTPUT AT 15%

INVESTMENT Machine 1 – CASH FLOWS

PERIOD	COST	INCOME
0	500	0
1	150	300
2	200	400
3	300	600
4	400	600
5	500	600
6	350	500
7	400	500
8	300	400

CURRENT DISCOUNT RATE 15%

INVESTMENT Machine 1 – RESULTS

PERIOD	NET CASH FLOW	PV	
0	-500	-500	
1	150	130.43	
2	200	151.23	
3	300	197.25	
4	200	114.35	
5	100	49.72	
6	150	64.85	
7	100	37.59	
8	100	32.69	
TOTAL	800	278.12	AT 15%

PAYBACK PERIOD IS 7

PROFITABILITY INDEX IS 1.15

ACC. RATE OF RETURN IS 15.73%

INT. RATE OF RETURN IS 32.29%

EXAMPLE 4(a) PACKAGE OUTPUT AT 20%

INVESTMENT Machine 1 CASH FLOWS

PERIOD	COST	INCOME
0	500	0
1	150	300
2	200	400
3	300	600
4	400	600
5	500	600
6	350	500
7	400	500
8	300	400

CURRENT DISCOUNT RATE 20%

INVESTMENT Machine 1 - RESULTS

PERIOD	NET CASH FLOW	PV	
0	-500	-500	
1	150	125	
2	200	138.89	
3	300	173.61	
4	200	96.45	
5	100	40.19	
6	150	50.23	
7	100	27.91	
8	100	23.26	
TOTAL	800	175.54	AT 20%

PAYBACK PERIOD IS 7

PROFITABILITY INDEX IS 1.11%

ACC. RATE OF RETURN IS 15.73%

INT. RATE OF RETURN IS 32.29%

EXAMPLE 4(b) PACKAGE OUTPUT

INVESTMENT Machine 1 CASH FLOWS

PERIOD	COST	INCOME
0	750	0
1	150	300
2	200	400
3	300	600
4	400	600
5	500	600
6	350	500
7	400	500
8	300	400

CURRENT DISCOUNT RATE 20%

INVESTMENT Machine 1 - RESULTS

PERIOD	NET CASH FLOW	PV	
0	-750	-750	
1	150	125	
2	200	138.89	
3	300	173.61	
4	200	96.45	
5	100	40.19	
6	150	50.23	
7	100	27.91	
8	100	23.26	
TOTAL	550	-74.46	AT 20%

PAYBACK PERIOD IS 7
PROFITABILITY INDEX IS .96
ACC. RATE OF RETURN IS 14.55%
INT. RATE OF RETURN IS 16.26%

EXAMPLE 5 (Prepared by D.W. Bale)

Critical Path Analysis (CPA) Program

Outline

The CPA network programme 'PERT' is a learning program which uses extensive screen graphics. In order to contain the graphics within the normal screen size it is necessary to restrict the range of nework problems to those with a maximum of 26 activities and 27 events. It is also necessary to constrain the numbering system for events. The START event must be number 1 and the remaining events must be numbered sequentially. Activity durations and resource requirements are restricted to integer values less than 100.

The program enables the user to:

1. Check the logic of the network and view a full event analysis based on known or uncertain activity durations.
2. Determine the Critical Path sequence.
3. View a detailed Planning Chart based on earliest or latest start times.
4. Adjust the starting time of non critical activities and to observe the instant change in dependent activity start times and planning chart positions.
5. Obtain a Resource Histogram based on the Earliest, Latest, or Planned Start sequence.
6. See the full probability distribution of the completion times of critical and non critical sequences.
7. Alter any initial data to see "What if...?"

The program 'PERT' is available for Acorn 'B' (BBC) and Electron microcomputers, and is supplied with an example file called 'EXAMPLE' to enable the user to explore the full range of options and to provide a teaching example if needed. The data file 'EXAMPLE' is stored on the reverse side of the cassette (side 2) together with details of other programs available, which can be loaded by typing CH. "HAMA".

WALKING THROUGH THE PROGRAM 'PERT'

1. Load from the tape. The usual command for Acorn type micros is CH. "PERT". After the logo appears you are asked to specify whether an old problem is to be loaded from file or whether a new

problem is to be examined. Enter (1) since an existing data file is to be used. Now specify the system type by entering (1) for tape and press (RETURN). Now enter the filename (EXAMPLE) and press (RETURN). Reverse the tape and make sure it is fully rewound. Press (RETURN).

2. The example problem is a 26 activity network with uncertain activity durations given by the most optimistic, pessimistic, and most likely estimates. The logic network is shown below.

3. Select Option 'Display Activity Table' by typing (3). The resultant Activity and Event Analysis Table shows the Earliest and Latest Start and Finish times for all the activities and also the Total and Free Floats. The Critical Paths (there are two) are indicated by a '*'.

4. Press (RETURN) to see the option menu again. Type (4) to see the Planning or Gantt Chart. Initially, text is presented describing the options available i.e. Earliest, Latest, or Planned Start. Press (RETURN).

5. Press (P) for a typical planned sequence. The cursor '>' is adjacent to the first activity A. Press the cursor direction key (⇒) to try to shunt activity A one time unit to the left. An audible alarm is given since this is not possible, A cannot be moved. Press the cursor key (↓) until the cursor is adjacent to activity C. Press the cursor key (⇒) 3 times. Watch the movement of C and the subsequent alterations to depended activities. This is an irreversible operation, since pressing (⇐) once will return C one time unit, but will not 'pull back' the dependent activities.

6. Press (RETURN) to see option menu. Press (5) for Resource Histogram. The Histogram is empty until E,P, or L is pressed. Press (P) to show the histogram for resources according to the latest planned starts. Press (L) and then (E) to see the other histograms.

7. Press (RETURN) and then type (6) to 'Investigate Risks'. Type the following letters (A), (C), (F), (I), finishing with (*). The logical sequence of activities A+C+F+I has been entered. This is a logical sequence (see Network). Illogical sequences are not accepted. The presentation on the screen now shows the probability distribution for the completion of the sequence defined.

   Expected duration = 13

   95% confidence, duration will not exceed 14.8

   Since these activities are not part of the critical sequence, these values are solely the summation of the individual durations. The graph shows that there is a 20% probability that the actual overall time for this sequence is 17 days or less if all activities started as early as possible, and a 20% probability that the overall time would be 19 days or less if the activities started as late as possible. Although this risk analysis can be used for sub-paths the important use is for evaluating the risk that a non critical sequence (based on expected values) may in fact have a reasonable probability in dictating the duration of the project.

8. Press (SPACE BAR) for another path sequence. Type in the letters (A), (D), (J), (O), (T), (Y), (*) for the Critical Path sequence. The single curve indicates that there is no difference between the earliest and latest start times probabilities.

9. Press (RETURN). Type in (2) to 'Modify Risks'. The screen presentation gives the initial data for the 'EXAMPLE' file. Any of the values can be altered by pressing the (RETURN) key to position the cursor in a column and by over-typing the new value and pressing (RETURN). The (SPACE BAR) moves the cursor from column to column after a check question is answered by typing (Y) or (N). On completion of the latest modification the main option menu returns.

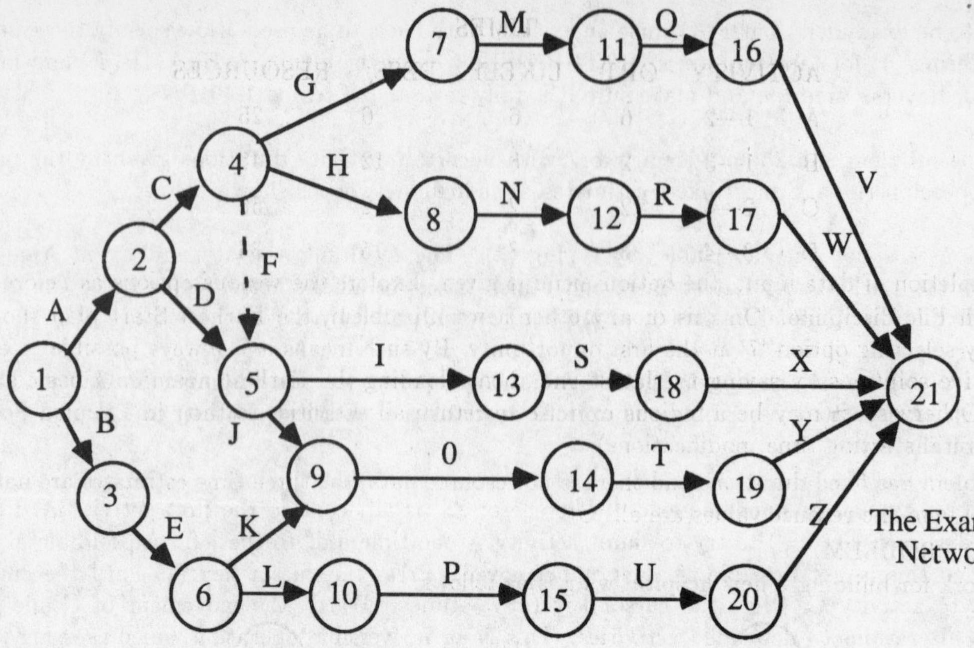

The Example Network

WALKTHROUGH WITH A NEW PROJECT

Assume a small nework shown as follows:

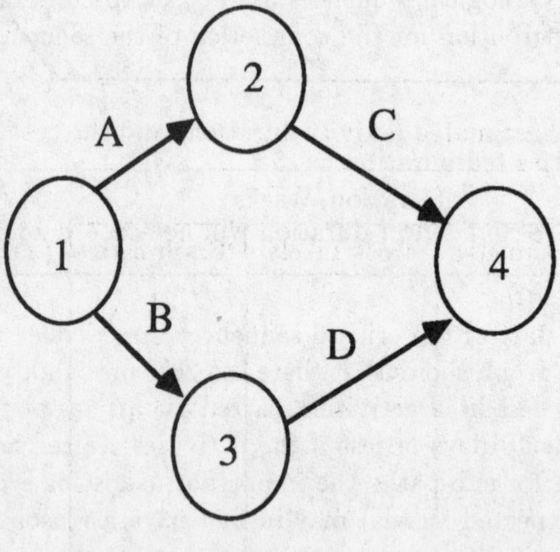

1. Load program PERT as before. After logo type (2) since a new problem is to be examined. A warning bell will be heard since a mistake at this point will lead to the loss of any previous data. Type (Y) in response to the check question.

2. There are 4 activities. Type (4) and (RETURN). There are 4 events. Type (4) and (RETURN). Type (Y) in response to check question.

3. Input the following data as instructed. If a mistake is made respond (N) at the end of each column to repeat column entries, otherwise type (Y).

ACTIVITY		TIMES OPT.	LIKELY	PESS¿	RESOURCES
A	1—2	6	6	6	25
B	1—3	2	8	12	45
C	2—4	2	2	2	56
D	3—4	3	8	15	34

4. On completion of data input, the option menu is given. Explore the various options as before. (Note on File discipline. On this or any other nework problem, the Earliest Start plan should be saved by selecting option '7' at the first opportunity. By such means it is always possible to explore alternative solutions by saving the latest and then reloading the Earliest again as a basic starting point. Otherwise, it may be a tedious exercise to return all activities to their initial plan positions after several starting time modifications).
5. If a problem has fixed durations and there is no resource data, the three time estimates are naturally identical, and the resouce values are all 'O'.

SUGGESTED PROBLEM

The Network for building a new hospital wing is as follows:

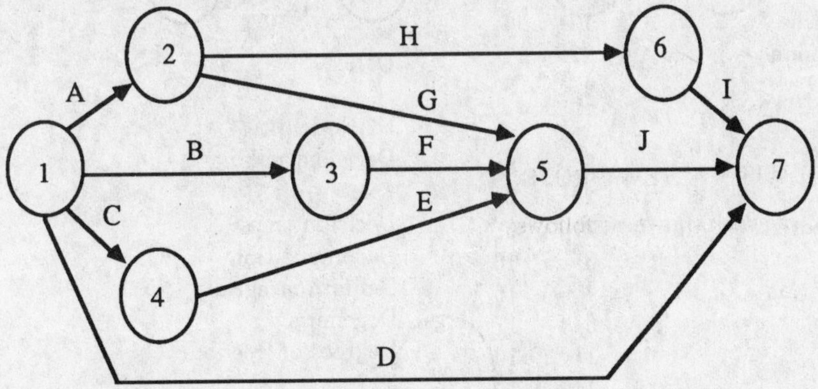

The following table shows the estimated activity durations and the cash flow (out) for each activity per week.

Activity ref.	Duration/Weeks Optimistic	Most Likely	Pessimistic	Cash flow (£000) per week
A	10	12	15	4
B	6	8	14	8
C	4	4	4	3
D	24	30	40	7
E	10	16	24	4
F	4	6	8	2
G	18	24	30	5
H	6	6	6	2
I	10	14	18	4
J	12	15	18	1

1. What is the 95% probable project completion time?
2. If expected cash flows each week are required to be as balanced as possible, what are planned starts for each activity?

Index